About This Book

This book starts where you are likely to start: at the point when you turn on your system and something new shows up. You might be in a state of panic, shock, or total excitement.

This book provides hands-on, task-oriented projects, useful tips, and technical information to get you started using your UNIX system. This book takes you from elementary operating system tasks, such as logging on and creating files, to advanced techniques, such as programming in C on a UNIX system and surfing the Internet. Everything in this book, by orientation and example, has the goal of assisting you in accomplishing everyday tasks.

Who Should Read This Book

Whether you need help with a specific UNIX task or you want a step-by-step tutorial on every aspect of the operating system, you will find what you need in this book. For beginners, there's coverage of basic concepts of working in an operating system and the basic techniques of using UNIX. For readers who are more technically advanced, there's reference information about various aspects of using UNIX. For people who need just to "dip into" the book and learn about a specific topic, the clear, task-oriented organization makes doing so fast and easy.

Conventions

Comment: These boxes will highlight interesting information to make your UNIX experience more enjoyable.

Don't Skip This: These boxes focus your attention on necessary information, problems, or side effects that can occur in specific situations.

Shortcut: These boxes show you how to streamline your approach to a task.

Each task has three parts—Description, Action, and Summary—to clarify your understanding of the topic. To help you review what you have learned, each chapter ends with a chapter summary, key terms, and questions (with answers provided in an appendix).

In this book, lines of output (what the computer shows you) are shown in a distinctive monospace type, the prompt % for example. What you enter, a command for example, is represented in monospace bold, `% ls -CF /`. Words or letters in monospace italic are placeholders; you should replace, for example, the words *command-number* in `!command-number` with the real command number.

The use of the Control key (sometimes labeled Ctrl on your keyboard) is represented in several ways. For example, Control-C, Ctrl-c, and ^c each mean you should press the Control key and, while holding it down, press the C key.

In several chapters, the examples show a part of a computer screen display. When the full screen is required to explain something, it will be shown. A smooth edge will indicate the edge of the display, and a jagged edge will indicate that the rest of the display has been omitted.

Teach
Yourself
UNIX®
in a Week

Teach Yourself
UNIX®
in a Week

Dave Taylor

SAMS
PUBLISHING

A Division of Prentice Hall Computer Publishing
201 West 103rd Street, Indianapolis, Indiana 46290

To my Ipo.

Copyright © 1994 by Sams Publishing

FIRST EDITION

International Standard Book Number: 0-672-30464-3

Library of Congress Catalog Card Number: 93-86988

97 96 95 94   4 3 2

Interpretation of the printing code: the rightmost double-digit number is the year of the book's printing; the rightmost single digit, the number of the book's printing. For example, a printing code of 94-1 shows that the first printing of the book occurred in 1994.

Composed in AGaramond and MCPdigital by Prentice Hall Computer Publishing

Printed in the United States of America

Trademarks

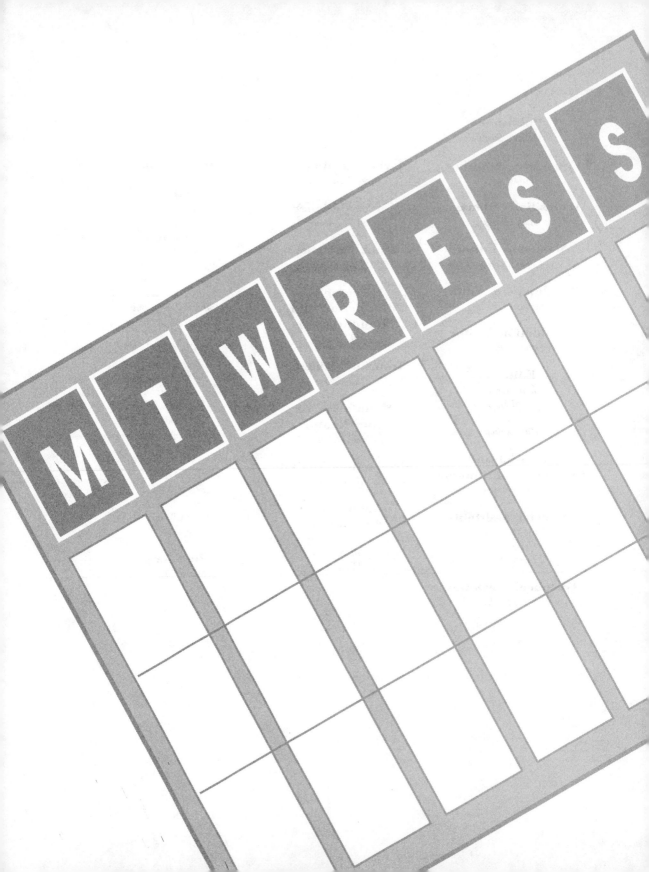

Overview

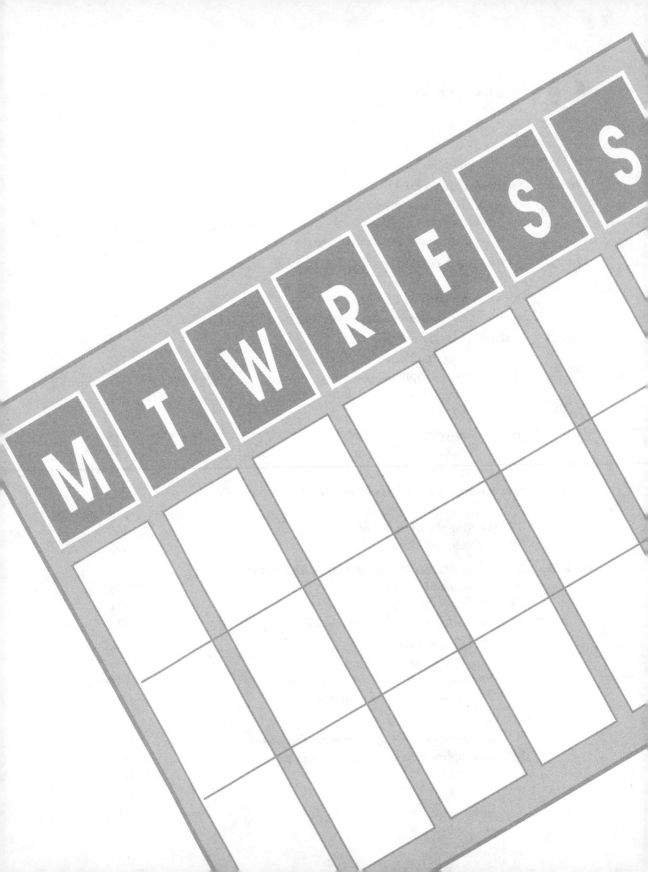

Contents

Acknowledgments

Even after lots of writing in the last few years, a project like *Teach Yourself UNIX in a Week* isn't done without many hours of individual labor. To my surprise, though, this book was a lot of fun to write, significantly due to the unflagging support of Linda Dunlap, without whom I would have stayed up even later each night, toiling over my Macintosh and gradually sinking into incoherence.

Tai Jin, Marvin Raab, and James Armstrong were a great help as I encountered information needing confirmation, further elucidation, or just another way to look at things. All of these guys answer e-mail incredibly quickly.

The team at Sams Publishing also helped make this an enjoyable, if rather fast-paced project. Particularly, I'd like to acknowledge the support of Jordan Gold, Scott Palmer, and Rosemarie Graham, who allowed my jokes through the editing process without more than a token protest or two. Marc Nehl was also invaluable as technical editor on this project, catching the errors in the nick of time.

Finally, any intense project requires a break now and then, and I'd like to graciously thank the injections of humor supplied by Crow, Tom Servo, Gypsy, Joel, and Mike (the new guy), trapped on the Satellite of Love.

About the Author

Dave Taylor has been working with UNIX since 1980, when he first logged in to a Berkeley-based DEC VAX computer while an undergraduate at the University of California, San Diego. Since then, he's used dozens of different UNIX systems and has contributed commands incorporated into HP's HP-UX UNIX operating system and UC Berkeley's BSD 4.4 UNIX release. His professional experience includes positions as research scientist at Hewlett-Packard Laboratories in Palo Alto, California; software and hardware reviews editor for *SunWorld Magazine;* interface design consultant for XALT Software; and president of Intuitive Systems. He has published more than 300 articles on UNIX, Macintosh, and technical computing topics, and also the book *Global Software*, addressing the challenges and opportunities for software internationalization from a marketing and programming viewpoint. He is well-known as the author of the Elm Mail System, the most popular screen-based electronic mail package in the UNIX community.

Currently he is working as a consultant for Intuitive Systems in West Lafayette, Indiana, while pursuing a graduate degree in Educational Computing at Purdue University and working on a new interface to the FTP program.

Introduction

If you're reading this introduction, you are either someone who knows very little about UNIX and wants to learn, or someone who knows something about the system and desires to expand your knowledge and perhaps pick up a trick or two along the way. Either way, you've found the right book!

I'll be frank. There are an incredible number of introductory UNIX books, each purporting to teach you UNIX. Usually these proceed either by reproducing the confusing UNIX electronic documentation within (even some UNIX experts don't know *all* the options to *all* the commands in the system) or by presenting such a small piece of the overall UNIX system that they don't really teach much at all.

This book falls into neither category. In *Teach Yourself UNIX in a Week*, you'll find 21 chapters that explain—and demonstrate—hundreds of UNIX commands, teaching and explaining the most valuable options of each command. There are lots of tips, historical notes, and even a sprinkling of pronunciation tips to make sure that when you talk with your UNIX friends, you'll sound like an expert too. If that doesn't whet your appetite, you also learn about how to use the various programming tools on UNIX, how to interact with friends and associates through the Internet, and even how to use some of the Information Highway vehicles, including Usenet, Gopher, Archie, the World-Wide Web, and WAIS.

To get the most out of this book, you will want to have a UNIX computer at your disposal. In particular, the examples will be considerably more meaningful if you can type along, comparing your output with that shown, and reading the explanation of what's on your computer screen. To reinforce the most important ideas, there are some questions ending each lesson; you won't get very far without a computer to explore the possible answers.

If you don't have a UNIX computer and are just interested in learning about the operating system, you can still pick up a great deal of information in this book. In particular, that's when the extensive examples will prove valuable: without touching your own keyboard, you will be able to see exactly what would be typed at the command prompt, what the results of each command are, and even catch some mistakes that I make along the way to show what happens when things go wrong with UNIX.

Before You Start

Before you begin your journey towards becoming a UNIX expert, read and keep in mind this advice:

1. **Don't be intimidated!** UNIX isn't really hard if you learn the underlying reasoning behind the system design and command design as you go along.

2. **Write in this book!** If you see a sample command that strikes you as particularly helpful, snap a paper clip on the page, circle the command, and show your colleagues or friends. Better yet, keep a pad next to your computer and scribble down these commands as a reference.

3. **Personalize your computer!** It never fails to amaze me how people talk about personal computers and completely miss that the most valuable aspect of *personal* computers is being able to make them do what *you* want, to personalize them. UNIX is like an eager puppy dog in this regard. Keep thinking about how you would like to personalize the interface, and, by the end of this book, you will know how to create new commands, rename existing commands, and even save yourself considerable typing by creating shortcuts and abbreviations.

4. **Have fun!** That learning has to be difficult is a myth perpetuated by a school system locked in bureaucracy. It doesn't have to be difficult, and an important goal I had while writing this book was to create an enjoyable tutorial that would give you the chance to chuckle, smile wryly, and along the way occasionally say, "Really? That's weird."

I have used UNIX for 15 years now, and I have used each and every command in this book more times than I want to consider. Even with that experience, however, I learned some slick new tricks as I went along. If you're already a UNIX expert, you'll learn some new stuff too.

If you're just learning, you're in the best position of all. You're ready to learn how to work productively within the UNIX environment, and you've put a week aside to *Teach Yourself UNIX in a Week!*

Introduction to UNIX

What Is This UNIX Stuff?

Welcome to *Teach Yourself UNIX in a Week!* This chapter starts you toward becoming a UNIX expert. Today the aim is to complete three lessons.

Goals for This Lesson

In the first lesson, you will learn

- ☐ The history of UNIX

- ☐ Why it's called UNIX

- ☐ What multiuser systems are all about

- ☐ The difference between UNIX and other operating systems

- ☐ Command-line interpreters and how users interact with UNIX

What Is UNIX?

UNIX is a computer operating system, a control program that works with users to run programs, manage resources, and communicate with other computer systems. Several people can use a UNIX computer at the same time; hence UNIX is called a multiuser system. Any of these users can also run multiple programs at the same time; hence UNIX is called multitasking. Because UNIX is such a pastiche—a patchwork of development—it's a lot more than just an operating system. UNIX has more than 250 individual commands. These range from simple commands—for copying a file, for example—to the quite complex, those used in high-speed networking, file revision management, and software development.

Most notably, UNIX is a multichoice system. As an example, UNIX has three different primary command-line-based user interfaces (in UNIX, the command-line user interface is called a *shell*). The three choices are the Bourne shell, C shell, and Korn shell. Often, soon after you learn to accomplish a task with a particular command, you discover there's a second or third way to do that task. This is simultaneously the greatest strength of UNIX and a source of frustration for both new and current users.

Why is having all this choice such a big deal? Think about why Microsoft MS-DOS and the Apple Macintosh interfaces are considered so easy to use. Both are designed to give the user less power. Both have dramatically fewer commands and precious little overlap in commands: you can't use copy to list your files in DOS, and you can't drag a Mac file icon around to duplicate it in its own directory. The advantage to these interfaces is that, in either system, you can learn the one-and-only way to do a task and be confident that you're as sophisticated in doing that task as is the next person. It's easy. It's quick to learn. It's exactly how the experts do it, too.

UNIX, by contrast, is much more like a spoken language, with commands acting as verbs, command options (which you learn about later in this lesson) acting as adjectives, and the more complex commands acting akin to sentences. How you do a specific task can, therefore, be completely different from how your UNIX-expert friend does the same task. Worse, some specific commands in UNIX have many different versions, partly because of the variations from different UNIX vendors. (You've heard of these variations and vendors, I'll bet. UNIXWare from Novell, Solaris from Sun, SCO from Santa Cruz, System V Release 4—pronounce that "system five release four" or, to sound like an ace, "ess-vee-are-four"—and BSD UNIX—pronounced "bee-ess-dee"—from University of California at Berkeley are the primary players. Each is a little different from the other.) Another contributor to the sprawl of modern UNIX is the energy of the UNIX programming community; plenty of UNIX users decide to write a new version of a command in order to solve slightly different problems, thus spawning many versions of a command.

Comment: I must admit that I too am guilty of rewriting a variety of UNIX commands, including those for an electronic mail system, a simple line-oriented editor, a text formatter, a programming language interpreter, calendar manager, and even slightly different versions of the file-listing command 1s and the remove files command rm. As a programmer, I found that trying to duplicate the functionality of a particular command or utility was a wonderful way to learn more about UNIX and programming.

Given the multichoice nature of UNIX, I promise to teach you the most popular UNIX commands, and, if there are alternatives, I will teach you about those, too. The goal of this book is for you to learn UNIX and to be able to work alongside long-time UNIX folk as a peer, sharing your expertise with them and continuing to learn about the system and its commands from them and other sources.

A Brief History of UNIX

To understand why the UNIX operating system has so many commands and why it's not only the premier multiuser, multitasking operating system, but also the most successful and the most powerful multichoice system for computers, you'll have to travel back in time. You'll need to learn where UNIX was designed, what were the goals of the original programmers, and what's happened to UNIX in the subsequent decades.

Unlike DOS, MS-Windows, OS/2, the Macintosh, VMS, MVS, and just about any other operating system, UNIX was designed by a few programmers as a fun project, and it evolved through the efforts of hundreds of programmers, each of whom was exploring his or her own ideas of particular aspects of operating system design and user interaction. In this regard, UNIX is not like other operating systems.

It all started back in the late 1960s in a dark and stormy laboratory deep in the recesses of the American Telephone and Telegraph (AT&T) corporate facility in New Jersey. Working with the Massachusetts Institute of Technology, AT&T Bell Labs was codeveloping a massive, monolithic operating system called Multics. On the Bell Labs team were Ken Thompson, Dennis Ritchie, Brian Kernighan, and other people in the Computer Science Research Group who would prove to be key contributors to the new UNIX operating system.

When 1969 rolled around, Bell Labs was becoming increasingly disillusioned with Multics, an overly slow and expensive system that ran on General Electric mainframe computers which themselves were expensive to run and rapidly becoming obsolete. The problem was that Thompson and the group really liked the capabilities Multics offered, particularly the individual-user environment and multiple-user aspects.

In that same year, Thompson wrote a computer game called Space Travel, first on Multics, then on the GECOS (GE computer operating system). The game was a simulation of the movement of the major bodies of the solar system, with the player guiding a ship, observing the scenery, and attempting to land on the planets and moons. The game wasn't much fun on the GE computer, however, because performance was jerky and irregular, and, more importantly, it cost almost $100 in computing time for each game.

In his quest to improve the game, Thompson found a little-used Digital Equipment Corporation PDP-7, and with some help from Ritchie, he rewrote the game for the PDP-7. Development was done on the GE mainframe and hand-carried on paper tape to the PDP-7.

Once he'd explored some of the capabilities of the PDP-7, Thompson couldn't resist building on the game, starting with an implementation of an earlier file system he'd designed, then adding processes, simple file utilities (cp, mv), and a command interpreter that he called a "shell." It wasn't until the following year that the newly created system acquired its name, UNIX, which Brian Kernighan suggested as a pun on Multics.

The Thompson file system was built around the low-level concept of *i-nodes* (linked blocks of information that together comprise the contents of a file or program)kept in a big list called the i-list, subdirectories, and special types of files that described devices and acted as the actual device driver for user interaction. What was missing in this earliest form of UNIX was *pathnames*. No slash (/) was present, and subdirectories were referenced through a combination of file links that proved too complex, causing users to stop using subdirectories. Another limitation in this early version was that directories couldn't be added while the system was running and had to be added to the preload configuration.

In 1970, Thompson's group requested and received a Digital PDP-11 system for the purpose of creating a system for editing and formatting text. It was such an early unit that the first disk did not arrive at Bell Labs until four months after the CPU showed up. The first important program on UNIX was the text-formatting program roff, which—keep with me now—was inspired by M.D. McIlroy's BCPL program on Multics, which in turn had been inspired by an earlier program called runoff on the CTSS operating system.

The initial customer was the Patent Department inside the Labs, a group that needed a system for preparing patent applications. There UNIX was a dramatic success, and it didn't take long for others inside Bell Labs to begin clamoring for their own UNIX computer systems.

The C Programming Language

That's where UNIX came from. What about C, the programming language that is integral to the system?

In 1969, the original UNIX had a very-low-level assembly language compiler available for writing programs; all the PDP-7 work was done in this primitive language. Just before the PDP-11 arrived, McIlroy ported a language called TMG to the PDP-7, which Thompson then tried to use to write a FORTRAN compiler. That didn't work, and instead he produced a language called B. Two years later, in 1971, Ritchie created the first version of a new programming language based on B, a language he called C. By 1973, the entire UNIX system had been rewritten in C for portability and speed.

UNIX Becomes Popular

In the 1970s, AT&T hadn't yet been split up into the many regional operating companies known today, and the company was prohibited from selling the new UNIX system. Hoping for the best, Bell Labs distributed UNIX to colleges and universities for a nominal charge. These institutions also were happily buying the inexpensive and powerful PDP-11 computer systems, a perfect match. Before long, UNIX was the research and software development operating system of choice.

The UNIX of today is not, however, the product of a couple of inspired programmers at Bell Labs. Many other organizations and institutions contributed significant additions to the system as it evolved from its early beginnings and grew into the monster it is today. Most important were the C shell, TCP/IP networking, vi editor, Berkeley Fast File System, and sendmail electronic-mail-routing software from the Computer Science Research Group of the University of California at Berkeley. Also most important were the early versions of UUCP and Usenet from the University of Maryland, Delaware and from Duke University. After dropping Multics development completely, MIT didn't come into the UNIX picture until the early 1980s, when it developed the X Window System as part of its successful Athena project. Ten years and four releases later, X is the predominant windowing system standard on all UNIX systems, and it is the basis of Motif, OpenWindows, and Open Desktop.

Gradually, big corporations have become directly involved with the evolutionary process, notably Hewlett-Packard, Sun Microsystems, and Digital Equipment Corporation. Little companies have started to get into the action too, with UNIX available from Apple for the Macintosh; from IBM for both PCs, RISC-based workstations, and new PowerPC computers; and even from Commodore for its worthy Amiga system.

Today UNIX runs on all sizes of computers, from humble PC laptops, to powerful desktop-visualization workstations, and even to supercomputers that require special cooling fluids to prevent them from burning up while working. It's a long way from Space Travel, a game that, ironically, isn't part of UNIX anymore.

What's All This About Multiuser Systems?

Among the many *multi-* words you learned earlier was one that directly concerns how you interact with the computer, *multiuser*. The goal of a multiuser system is for all users to feel as though they've each been given their own personal computer, their own individual UNIX system, though they are actually working within a large system. To accomplish this, each user is given an *account*—usually based on the person's last name, initials, or similar—and a *home directory*, the default place where his or her files are saved. This leads to a bit of a puzzle: when you're working on the system, how does the system know that you're you? What's to stop someone else from masquerading as you, going into your files, prying into private letters, altering memos, or worse?

On a Macintosh or PC, anyone can walk up to your computer when you're not around, flip the power switch, and pry, and you can't do much about it. You can add some security software, but security isn't a fundamental part of the system, which results in an awkward fit between system and software. For a computer sitting on your desk in your office, though, that's okay; the system is not a shared multiuser system, so verifying who you are when you turn on the computer isn't critical.

But UNIX *is* a system designed for multiple users, so it is very important that the system can confirm your identity in a manner that precludes others from masquerading as you. As a result, all accounts have passwords associated with them—like a PIN for a bank card, keep it a secret!—and, when you use your password in combination with your account, the computer can be pretty sure that you are who you're claiming to be. For obvious reasons, when you're done using the computer, you should always remember to end your session, or, in effect, to turn off your virtual personal computer when you're done.

In the next lesson, you learn your first UNIX commands. At the top of the list are commands to log in to the system, enter your password, and change your password to be memorable and highly secure.

Cracking Open the Shell

Another unusual feature of UNIX systems, especially for those of you who come from either the Macintosh or the Windows environments, is that UNIX is designed to be a command-line-based system, rather than a more graphically based (picture-oriented) system. That's a mixed blessing. It makes UNIX harder to learn, but the system is considerably more powerful than fiddling with a mouse to drag little pictures about on the screen.

There are graphical interfaces to UNIX, built within the X Window System environment. Notable are Motif, Open Windows, and Open Desktop. Even with the best of these, however, the command-line heart of UNIX still shines through, and in my experience, it's impossible really to use all the power that UNIX offers without turning to a shell.

If you're used to writing letters to your friends and family or even mere shopping lists, you won't have any problem with a command-line interface: it's a command program that you tell what to do. When you type in specific instructions and press the Return key, the computer leaps into action and immediately performs whatever command you've specified.

 Comment: Throughout this book, I refer to pressing the Return key, but your keyboard may have this key labeled as "Enter" or marked with a left-pointing, specially shaped arrow. These all mean the same thing.

In Windows you might move a file from one folder to another by opening the folder, opening the destination folder, fiddling around for a while to be sure that you can see both of them on the screen at the same time, then clicking and dragging the specific file from one place to the other. In UNIX it's much easier. Typing in the simple command

```
cp folder1/file folder2
```

does the trick, automatically ensuring the file has the same name in the destination directory too.

This might not seem much of a boon, but imagine the situation where you want to move all files with names that start with the word project or end with the suffix .c (C program files). This could be quite tricky and could take a lot of patience with a graphical interface. UNIX, however, makes it easy:

```
cp project* *.c folder2
```

Before today is over, you will not only understand this command, but also be able to compose your own examples!

Lesson Summary

In this first lesson, the goal was for you to learn a bit about what UNIX is, where it came from, and how it differs from other operating systems that you might have used in the past. You also learned about the need for security on a multiuser system and how a password helps maintain that security, so that your files are never read, altered, or removed by anyone but yourself.

Finally, you learned what a command shell, or command-line interpreter, is all about, how it differs from graphically oriented interface systems like the Macintosh and Windows, and how it's not only easy to use, but considerably more powerful than dragging-and-dropping little pictures.

Workshop
Key Terms

account This is the official one-word name by which the UNIX system knows you. Mine is `taylor`.

home directory This is your private directory. It is also where you start out when you log in to the system.

i-list See *i-node*.

i-node The UNIX file system is like a huge notebook full of sheets of information. Each file is like an index tab, indicating where the file starts in the notebook and how many sheets are used. The tabs are called i-nodes and the list of tabs (the index to the notebook) is the i-list.

multitasking A multitasking computer is one that actually can run more than one program, or task, at a time. By contrast, most personal computers lock you into a single program that you must exit before you launch another.

multiuser Computers intended to have more than a single person working on them simultaneously are designed to support multiple users, hence "multiuser." By contrast, personal computers are almost always single-user, because someone else can't be running a program or editing a file while you are using the computer for your own work.

pathname UNIX is split into a wide variety of different directories and subdirectories, often across multiple hard disks and even multiple computers. So that the system needn't search laboriously through the entire mess each time you request a program, the set of directories you reference are stored as your search path, and the location of any specific command is known as its pathname.

shell   To interact with UNIX, you type in commands to the command-line interpreter, which is known in UNIX as the shell, or command shell. It's the underlying environment within which you work with the UNIX system.

Questions

Each lesson concludes with a set of questions for you to contemplate. Here's a warning up front: not all of the questions have a definitive answer. After all, you are learning about a multichoice operating system!

1. Name the three *multi-s* that are at the heart of UNIX's power.

2. Is UNIX more like a grid of streets, letting you pick your route from point A to point B, or more like a directed highway with only one option? How does this compare with other systems you've used?

3. Systems that support multiple users always ask you to say who you are when you begin using the system. What's the most important thing to remember when you're done using the system?

4. If you're used to graphical interfaces, try to think of a few tasks that you feel are more easily accomplished by moving icons than by typing commands. Write those tasks on a separate paper, and in a few days, pull that paper out and see if you still feel that way.

5. Think of a few instances in which you needed to give a person written instructions. Was that easier than giving spoken instructions or drawing a picture? Was it harder?

Preview of the Next Chapter

In the next chapter, you learn how to log in to the system at the login prompt (`login:`), how to log out of the system, how to use `passwd` to change your password, how to use the `id` command to find out who the computer thinks you are, and lots more!

Getting onto the System and Using the Command Line

M

2

Lesson 2 marks the midpoint of your first day of UNIX lessons, so it's time you logged in to the system and tried some commands. This lesson focuses on teaching you the basics of interacting with your UNIX machine.

Goals for This Lesson

In this lesson, you learn how to

☐ Log in and log out of the system

☐ Change passwords with `passwd`

☐ Choose a memorable and secure password

☐ Find out who the computer thinks you are

☐ Find out who else is on the system

☐ Find out what everyone is doing on the system

☐ Check the current date and time

☐ Look at a month and year calendar

☐ Perform some simple calculations with UNIX

This lesson introduces a lot of commands, so it's very important that you have a UNIX system available on which you can work through all examples. Most examples have been taken from a Sun workstation running Solaris, a variant of System V Release 4 UNIX, and have been double-checked on a BSD-based system. Any variance between the two is noted, and if you have a UNIX system available, odds are good that it's based on either AT&T System V or Berkeley UNIX.

Task 2.1: Logging In and Out of the System
Step 1. Description

Because UNIX is a multiuser system, you need to start by finding a terminal, computer, or other way to access the system. I use a Macintosh and a modem to dial up various systems by telephone. You might have a similar approach, or you might have a terminal directly connected to the UNIX computer, or you might have the UNIX system itself on your desk. Regardless of how you connect to your UNIX system, the first thing you'll see on the screen is something like this:

```
4.3BSD DYNIX (mentor.utech.edu) 5:38pm on Fri, 1 Oct 1993
login:
```

The first line indicates what variant of UNIX the system is running (DYNIX is UNIX on Sequent computers), the actual name of the computer system, and the current date and time. The second line is asking for your *login*, your account name.

Step 2. Action

1. Connect your terminal or PC to the UNIX system until the point where you see a login prompt (`login:`) on your screen similar to that in the preceding example, using the phone and modem to dial up the computer if need be.

   It would be nice if computers could keep track of us users by simply using our full names, so I'd be able to enter Dave Taylor at the login prompt. Alas, like the Internal Revenue Service, Department of Motor Vehicles, and many other agencies, UNIX—rather than using names—assigns each user a unique identifier. This identifier is called an *account name*, has eight characters or fewer, and is usually based on the first or last name, though it can be any combination of letters and numbers. I have two account names, or logins, on the systems I use: taylor and, on another machine where someone already had that account name, dataylor.

2. You should know your account name on the UNIX system. Perhaps your account name is on a paper with your initial password, both assigned by the system administrator. If you do not have this information, you need to track it down before you can go further. Some accounts might not have an initial password; that means that you won't have to enter one the first time you log in to the system. In a few minutes, you will learn how you can give yourself the password of your choice by using a UNIX command called passwd.

3. At the login prompt, enter your account name. Be particularly careful to use all lowercase letters unless specified otherwise by your administrator.

   ```
   login: taylor
   Password:
   ```

   Once you've entered your account name, the system moves the cursor to the next line and prompts you for your password. When you enter your password, the system won't echo it (that is, won't display it) on the screen. That's okay. Lack of an echo doesn't mean anything is broken; instead, this is a security measure to ensure that even if people are looking over your shoulder, they can't learn your secret password by watching your screen.

4. If you enter either your login or your password incorrectly, the system complains with an error message:

2

```
login: taylor
Password:
Login incorrect
login:
```

Don't Skip This: Most systems give you three or four attempts to get both your login and password correct, so try again. Don't forget to enter your account name at the login prompt each time.

5. Once you've successfully entered your account name and password, you are shown some information about the system, some news for users, and an indication of whether you have electronic mail. The specifics will vary, but here's an example of what I see when I log in to my account:

```
login: taylor
Password:
Last login: Fri Oct 15 17:00:23 on ttyAe
You have mail.
%
```

Comment: The percent sign is UNIX's way of telling you that it's ready for you to enter some commands. The percent sign is the equivalent of an enlisted soldier saluting and saying, "Ready for duty!" or an employee saying, "What shall I do now, boss?"

Your system might be configured so that you have some slightly different prompt here. The possibilities include a $ for the Korn or Bourne shells, your current location in the file system, the current time, the command-index number (which you'll learn about when you learn how to teach the UNIX command-line interpreter to adapt to your work style, rather than vice versa), and the name of the computer system itself. Here are some examples:

```
[/users/taylor] :
(mentor) 33 :
taylor@mentor %
```

Your prompt might not look exactly like any of these, but it has one unique characteristic: it is at the beginning of the line that your cursor sits on, and it reappears each time you've completed working with any UNIX program.

6. At this point, you're ready to enter your first UNIX command—exit—to sign off from the computer system. Try it. On my system, entering exit shuts down all my programs and hangs up the telephone connection. On other systems, it returns the login prompt. Many UNIX systems offer a pithy quote as you leave, too.

```
% exit
He who hesitates is lost.
4.3BSD DYNIX (mentor.utech.edu) 5:38pm on Fri, 1 Oct 1993
login:
```

Don't Skip This: UNIX is *case-sensitive*, so the exit command is not the same as EXIT. If you enter a command all in uppercase, the system won't find it and instead will respond with the complaint command not found.

7. If you have a direct connection to the computer, odds are very good that logging out causes the system to prompt for another account name, allowing the next person to use the system. If you dialed up the system with a modem, you'll probably see something more like the following example. After being disconnected, you'll be able to shut down your computer.

```
% exit
Did you lose your keys again?

DISCONNECTED
```

Step 3. Summary

At this point, you've overcome the toughest part of UNIX. You have an account, know the password, logged in to the system, and entered a simple command telling the computer what you want to do, and the computer has done it!

2

Task 2.2: Changing Passwords with *passwd*
Step 1. Description

Having logged in to a UNIX system, you can clearly see that there are many differences between UNIX and a PC or Macintosh personal computer. Certainly the style of interaction is different. With UNIX, the keyboard becomes the exclusive method of instructing the computer what to do, and the mouse sits idle, waiting for something to happen.

One of the greatest differences is that UNIX is a multiuser system, as you learned in the previous lesson. As you learn more about UNIX, you'll find that this characteristic has an impact on a variety of tasks and commands. The next UNIX command you'll learn is one that exists because of the multiuser nature of UNIX: `passwd`.

With the `passwd` command, you can change the password associated with your individual account name. As with the personal identification number (PIN) for your automated-teller machine, the value of your password is directly related to how secret it remains.

> **Don't Skip This:** UNIX is careful about the whole process of changing passwords. It requires that you enter your current password to prove you're really you. Imagine that you are at a computer center and have to leave the room to make a quick phone call. Without much effort, a prankster could lean over and quickly change your password to something you wouldn't know. That's why you should log out if you're not going to be near your system, and that's also why passwords are never echoed in UNIX.

Step 2. Action

1. Consider what happens when I use the `passwd` command to change the password associated with my account:

```
% passwd
Changing password for taylor.
Old password:
```

```
New passwd:
Retype new passwd:
%
```

2. Notice that I never received any visual confirmation that the password I actually entered was the same as the password I thought I entered. This is not as dangerous as it seems, though, because if I had made any typographical errors, the password I entered the second time (when the system said `Retype new passwd:`) wouldn't have matched the first. In a no-match situation, the system would have warned me that the information I supplied was inconsistent:

```
% passwd
Changing password for taylor.
Old password:
New passwd:
Retype new passwd:
Mismatch - password unchanged.
%
```

Step 3. Summary

Once you change the password, don't forget it. To reset it to a known value if you don't know the current password requires the assistance of a system administrator or other operator. Remembering your password can be a catch-22, though: you don't want to write down the password because that reduces its secrecy, but you don't want to forget it either. You want to be sure that you pick a good password too.

Task 2.3: Picking a Secure Password
Step 1. Description

If you're an aficionado of old movies, you'll be familiar with the thrillers in which the hoods break into an office and spin the dial on the safe a few times, snigger a bit about how the boss shouldn't have chosen his daughter's birthday as the combination, and crank open the safe. (If you're really familiar with the genre, you'll remember films in which the criminals rifle the desk drawers and find the combination of the safe taped to the underside of a drawer as a fail-safe—or a failed safe, as the case may be.) The moral is that you should always choose good secret passwords or combinations and keep them secure.

For computers, security is tougher, because, in less than an hour, a fast computer system can test all the words in an English dictionary against your account password.

If your password is `kitten` or, worse yet, your account name, any semicompetent bad guy could be in your account and messing with your files in no time.

Many of the more modern UNIX systems have some *heuristics*, or smarts, built in to the `passwd` command; the heuristics check to determine whether what you've entered is reasonably secure.

The tests performed typically answer these questions:

☐ Is the proposed password at least six characters long? (A longer password is more secure.)

☐ Does it have both digits and letters? (A mix of both is better.)

☐ Does it mix upper- and lowercase letters? (A mix is better.)

☐ Is it in the online dictionary? (You should avoid common words.)

☐ Is it a name or word associated with the account? (`Dave` would be a bad password for my account `taylor` because my full name on the system is `Dave Taylor`.)

Some versions of the `passwd` program are more sophisticated, and some less, but generally these questions offer a good guideline for picking a secure password.

Step 2. Action

1. An easy way to choose memorable and secure passwords is to think of them as small sentences rather than as a single word with some characters surrounding it. If you're a fan of Alexander Dumas and *The Three Musketeers*, then "All for one and one for all!" is a familiar cry, but it's also the basis for a couple of great passwords. Easily remembered derivations might be `all4one` or `one4all`.

2. If you've been in the service, you might have the U.S. Army jingle stuck in your head: "Be All That You Can Be" would make a great password, `ballucanb`. You might have a self-referential password: `account4me` or `MySekrit` would work. If you're ex-Vice President Dan Quayle, `1Potatoe` could be a memorable choice (`potatoe` by itself wouldn't be particularly secure, because it lacks digits and lacks uppercase letters, and because it's a simple variation on a word in the online dictionary).

3. Another way to choose passwords is to find acronyms that have special meaning to you. Don't choose simple ones—remember, short ones aren't going to be secure—but, if you have always heard that "Real programmers

don't each quiche!" then Rpdeq! could be a complex password that you'll easily remember.

4. Many systems that you use every day require numeric passwords to verify your identity, including the automated-teller machine (with its PIN number), government agencies (with the social security number), and the Department of Motor Vehicles (your driver's license number or vehicle license). Each of these actually is a poor UNIX password: it's too easy for someone to find out your license number or social security number.

 Comment: The important thing is that you come up with a strategy of your own for choosing a password that is both memorable and secure. Then keep the password in your head rather than write it down.

Step 3. Summary

Why be so paranoid? For a small UNIX system that will sit on your desk in your office and won't have any other users, a high level of concern for security is, to be honest, unnecessary. As with driving a car, though, it's never too early to learn good habits. Any system that has dial-up access or direct computer-network access—you may need to use such a system—is a likely target for delinquents who relish the intellectual challenge of breaking into an account, altering and destroying files and programs purely for amusement.

The best way to avoid trouble is to develop good security habits now, when you're first learning about UNIX—learn how to recognize what makes a good, secure password; pick one for your account; and keep it a secret.

If you ever need to let someone else use your account for a short time, remember that you can use the passwd command to change your secure password to something less secure. Then you can let that person use the account, and, when he or she is done, you can change the password back to your original password.

With that in mind, log in again to your UNIX system now and try changing your password. First change it to easy and see if the program warns you that easy is too short or otherwise a poor choice, then try entering two different secret passwords to see if the program notices the difference. Finally, pick a good password, using the preceding guidelines and suggestions, and change your account password to be more secure.

Task 2.4: Who Are You?

Step 1. Description

While you're logged in to the system, you can learn a a few more UNIX commands, including a couple that can answer a philosophical conundrum that has bothered men and women of thought for thousands of years: Who am I?

Step 2. Action

1. The easiest way to find out "who you are" is to enter the `whoami` command:

```
% whoami
taylor
%
```

Try it on your system. The command lists the account name associated with the current login.

2. Ninety-nine percent of the commands you type with UNIX don't change if you modify the punctuation and spacing. With `whoami`, however, adding spaces to transform the statement into proper English—that is, entering `who am i`—dramatically changes the result. On my system I get the following results:

```
% who am i
mentor.utech.edu!taylor     ttyp4    Oct 5 14:34
%
```

This tells me quite a bit about my identity on the computer, including the name of the computer itself, my account name, and where and when I logged in. Try the command on your system and see what results you get.

In this example, mentor is a hostname—the name of the computer I am logged in to—and utech.edu is the full domain name, the address of mentor. The exclamation mark (!) separates the domain name from my account name, taylor. The ttyp4 (pronounced "tee-tee-why-pea-four") is the current communication line I'm using to access mentor, and October 5 at 2:34 p.m. is when I logged in to mentor today.

Comment: UNIX is full of oddities that are based on historical precedent. One is "tty" to describe a computer or terminal line. This comes from the earliest UNIX systems, in which Digital Equipment

Corporation teletypewriters would be hooked up as interactive devices. The teletypewriters quickly received the nickname "tty," and all these years later, when people wouldn't dream of hooking up a teletypewriter, the line is still known as a tty line.

3. One of the most dramatic influences UNIX systems have had on the computing community is the propensity for users to work together on a network, hooked up by telephone lines and modems (the predominant method until the middle to late 1980s) or high-speed network connections to the Internet (a more common type of connection today). Regardless of the connection, however, you can see that each computer needs a unique identifier to distinguish it from others on the network. In the early days of UNIX, systems had unique hostnames, but as hundreds of systems have grown into the tens-of-thousands, that proved to be an unworkable solution.

4. The alternative was what's called a "domain-based naming scheme," where systems are assigned unique names within specific subsets of the overall network. Consider the output that was shown in instruction 2, for example:

```
mentor.utech.edu!taylor      ttyp4   Oct 5 14:34
```

The computer I use is within the `.edu` domain (read the hostname and domain—`mentor.utech.edu`—from left to right), meaning that the computer's at an educational institute. Then, within the educational institute subset of the network, `utech` is a unique descriptor; and therefore, if other UTech universities existed, they couldn't use the same top-level domain name. Finally, `mentor` is the name of the computer itself.

5. Like learning to read addresses on envelopes, learning how to read domain names can unlock a lot of information about a computer and its location. For example, `lib.stanford.edu` is the library computer at Stanford University, and `ccgate.infoworld.com` tells you that the computer is at InfoWorld, a commercial computer site, and that its hostname is `ccgate`. You'll learn more about this a few lessons down the road, when you learn how to use electronic mail to communicate with people throughout the Internet.

6. Another way to find out who you are in UNIX is the `id` command. The purpose of this command is to tell you what group or groups you're in and the numeric identifier for your account name (known as your "user ID

2

number" or "userid"). Enter id and see what you get. I get the following result:

```
% id
uid=211(taylor)  gid=50(users0) groups=50(users0)
%
```

Comment: If you enter id and the computer returns a different result or indicates that you need to specify a filename, don't panic. On many Berkeley-derived systems, the id command is used to obtain low-level information about files.

7. In this example, you can see that my account name is taylor and that the numeric equivalent, the user ID, is 211. (Here it's abbreviated as uid. Pronounce it "you-eye-dee" to sound like a UNIX expert.) Just as the account name is unique on a system, the user ID is also unique. Fortunately, you rarely, if ever, need to know these numbers, so focus on the account name and group name.

8. Next you can see that my group ID (or gid) is 50, and that group number 50 is known as the users0 group. Finally, users0 is the only group to which I belong.

   On another system, I am a member of two different groups:

```
% id
uid=103(taylor) gid=10(staff) groups=10(staff),44(ftp)
%
```

   Though I have the same account name on this system (taylor), you can see that my user ID and group ID are both different from the earlier example. Note also that I'm a member of two groups: the staff group, with a group ID of 10, and the ftp group, with a group ID of 44.

Step 3. Summary

Later, you will learn how to set protection modes on your files so that people in your group can read your files, but those not in your group are barred from access. Now you have learned a couple of different ways to have UNIX give you some information about your account.

Task 2.5: Finding Out What Other Users Are on the System

Step 1. Description

The next philosophical puzzle that you can solve with UNIX is "Who else is there?" The answer, however, is rather restricted, limited to only those people currently logged into the computer at the same time. Three commands are available to get you this information, based on how much you'd like to learn about the other users: users, who, and w.

Step 2. Action

1. The simplest of the commands is the users command, which lists the account names of all people using the system:

```
% users
david mark taylor
%
```

2. In this example, david and mark are also logged in to the system with me. Try this on your computer and see what other users—if any—are logged in to your computer system.

3. A command that you've encountered earlier in this chapter can be used to find out who is logged on to the system, what line they're on, and how long they've been logged in. That command is who:

```
% who
taylor    ttyp0    Oct  8 14:10    (limbo)
david     ttyp2    Oct  4 09:08    (calliope)
mark      ttyp4    Oct  8 12:09    (dent)
%
```

Here you can see that three people are logged in, taylor (me), david, and mark. Further, you can now see that david is logged in by connection ttyp2 and has been connected since October 4 at 9:08 a.m. He is connected from a system called calliope. You can see that mark has been connected since just after noon on October 8 on line ttyp4 and is coming from a computer called dent. Note that I have been logged in since 14:10, which is 24-hour time for 2:10 p.m. UNIX rarely indicates a.m. or p.m.

Step 3. Summary

The commands user or who can inform you who is using the system at any particular moment in time, but how do you find out *what* they're doing?

Task 2.6: What Is Everyone Doing on the Computer?
Step 1. Description

To find out what everyone else is doing, there's a third command, w, that serves as a combination of "Who are they?" and "What are they doing?"

Step 2. Action

1. Consider the following output from the w command:

```
% w
2:12pm  up 7 days,  5:28,  3 users, load average: 0.33, 0.33, 0.02
User    tty       login@ idle   JCPU   PCPU  what
taylor  ttyp0     2:10pm                2           w
david   ttyp2     Mon 9am 2:11  2:04   1:13  xfax
mark    ttyp4     12:09pm 2:03               -csh
%
```

This is a much more complex command, offering more information than either users or who. Notice that the output is broken into different areas. The first line summarizes the status of the system and, rather cryptically, the number of programs that the computer is running at one time. Finally, for each user, the output indicates the user name, the tty, when the user logged in to the system, how long it's been since the user has done anything (in minutes and seconds), the combined CPU time of all jobs the user has run, and the amount of CPU time taken by the current job. The last field tells you what you wanted to know in the first place: what are the users doing?

In this example, the current time is 2:12 p.m. and the system has been up for seven days, five hours, and 28 minutes. Currently three users are logged in, and the system is very quiet, with an average of 0.33 jobs submitted (or programs started) in the last minute; 0.33, on average, in the last five minutes; and 0.02 jobs in the last fifteen minutes.

User taylor is the only user actively using the computer (that is, who has no idle time) and is using the w command. User david is running a program called xfax, which has gone for quite a while without any input from the user (two hours and 11 minutes of idle time). The program already has used one minute and 13 seconds of CPU time, and overall, david has used over two minutes of CPU time. User mark has a C shell running, -csh. (The leading dash indicates that this is the program that the computer launched automatically when mark logged in. This is akin to how the system automatically launches the Finder on a Macintosh on startup.) User mark hasn't actually done anything yet; notice there is *no* accumulated computer time for that account.

2. Now it's your turn. Try the w command on your system and see what kind of output you get. Try to interpret all the information based on the explanation here. One thing is certain: your account should have the w command listed as what you're doing.

Step 3. Summary

On a multiuser UNIX system, the w command gives you a quick and easy way to see what's going on.

Task 2.7: Checking the Current Date and Time
Step 1. Description

You've learned how to orient yourself on a UNIX system, and you are able now to figure out who you are, who else is on the system, and what everyone is doing. What about the current time and date?

Step 2. Action

1. Logic suggests that time shows the current time, and date the current date; but this is UNIX, and logic doesn't always apply. In fact, consider what happens when I enter time on my system:

```
% time
14.5u 17.0s 29:13 1% 172+217io 160pf+1w
%
```

The output is cryptic to the extreme and definitely *not* what you're interested in finding out. Instead, the program is showing how much user time, system time, and CPU time has been used by the command interpreter itself, broken down by input/output operations and more. This is not something I've ever used in 15 years of working with UNIX.

2. Well, time didn't work, so what about date?

```
% date
Tue  Oct 5 15:03:41 EST 1993
%
```

That's more like it!

3. Try the date command on your computer and see if the output agrees with your watch.

Step 3. Summary

How do you think date keeps track of the time and date when you've turned the computer off? Does the computer know the correct time if you unplug it for a few hours? (I hope so. Almost all computers today have little batteries inside for just this purpose.)

Task 2.8: Looking at a Calendar
Step 1. Description

Another useful utility in UNIX is the cal command, which shows a simple calendar for the month or year specified.

Step 2. Action

1. To confirm that 5 October 1993 is a Tuesday, turn to your computer and enter cal 10 93. You should see the following:

```
% cal 10 93
   October 93
 S  M Tu  W Th  F  S
          1  2  3  4  5
 6  7  8  9 10 11 12
13 14 15 16 17 18 19
20 21 22 23 24 25 26
27 28 29 30 31
%
```

2. If you look closely, you'll find that there's a bit of a problem here. October 5 is shown as a Saturday, rather than a Tuesday as expected.

   The reason is that cal can list any year from A.D. 0. In fact, what you have on your screen is how the month of October would have looked in A.D. 93, 1900 years ago.

Comment: This is a bit misleading, because Western society uses the Julian calendar, adopted in 1752. Before that, the program should really list Gregorian-format monthly calendars, but it cannot, so don't use this as a historical reference for ascertaining what day of the week the Emperor Hadrian was born.

3. To find out the information that you want, you'll need to specify to the `cal` program both the month and full year:

```
% cal 10 1993
     October 1993
 S  M Tu  W Th  F  S
                1  2
 3  4  5  6  7  8  9
10 11 12 13 14 15 16
17 18 19 20 21 22 23
24 25 26 27 28 29 30
31
%
```

This is correct. The 5th of October in 1993 is indeed a Tuesday. On some systems, `cal` has no intelligent default action, so entering `cal` doesn't simply list the monthly calendar for the current month. Later you'll learn how to write a simple shell script to do just that. For now, turn to your system and enter `cal` to see what happens.

4. My favorite example of the `cal` program is to ask for the year 1752, the year when the Western calendar switched from Gregorian to Julian. Note particularly the month of September, during which the switch actually occurred.

```
% cal 1752
                                1752
          Jan                    Feb                    Mar
 S  M Tu  W Th  F  S    S  M Tu  W Th  F  S    S  M Tu  W Th  F  S
             1  2  3  4                      1     1  2  3  4  5  6  7
 5  6  7  8  9 10 11    2  3  4  5  6  7  8    8  9 10 11 12 13 14
12 13 14 15 16 17 18    9 10 11 12 13 14 15   15 16 17 18 19 20 21
19 20 21 22 23 24 25   16 17 18 19 20 21 22   22 23 24 25 26 27 28
26 27 28 29 30 31      23 24 25 26 27 28 29   29 30 31
          Apr                    May                    Jun
 S  M Tu  W Th  F  S    S  M Tu  W Th  F  S    S  M Tu  W Th  F  S
             1  2  3  4                   1  2     1  2  3  4  5  6
 5  6  7  8  9 10 11    3  4  5  6  7  8  9    7  8  9 10 11 12 13
12 13 14 15 16 17 18   10 11 12 13 14 15 16   14 15 16 17 18 19 20
19 20 21 22 23 24 25   17 18 19 20 21 22 23   21 22 23 24 25 26 27
26 27 28 29 30         24 25 26 27 28 29 30   28 29 30
                       31
```

```
         Jul                    Aug                    Sep
  S  M Tu  W Th  F  S     S  M Tu  W Th  F  S     S  M Tu  W Th  F  S
           1  2  3  4                    1                 1  2 14 15 16
  5  6  7  8  9 10 11     2  3  4  5  6  7  8    17 18 19 20 21 22 23
 12 13 14 15 16 17 18     9 10 11 12 13 14 15    24 25 26 27 28 29 30
 19 20 21 22 23 24 25    16 17 18 19 20 21 22
 26 27 28 29 30 31       23 24 25 26 27 28 29
                         30 31

         Oct                    Nov                    Dec
  S  M Tu  W Th  F  S     S  M Tu  W Th  F  S     S  M Tu  W Th  F  S
  1  2  3  4  5  6  7              1  2  3  4                    1  2
  8  9 10 11 12 13 14     5  6  7  8  9 10 11     3  4  5  6  7  8  9
 15 16 17 18 19 20 21    12 13 14 15 16 17 18    10 11 12 13 14 15 16
 22 23 24 25 26 27 28    19 20 21 22 23 24 25    17 18 19 20 21 22 23
 29 30 31                26 27 28 29 30          24 25 26 27 28 29 30
                                                 31
%
```

Step 3. Summary

You can experiment with cal and easily find out fun information, for example, what day of the week you were born or your parents were born. Curious about whether Christmas 1999 is on a weekend? cal can answer that question too.

When you used cal, you entered the name of the command and then some additional information to indicate the exact action you desired. You tried both cal 10 93 and cal 10 1993. In UNIX parlance, the first word is the *command,* and the subsequent words are *arguments* or *options* to the command. A special class of options are those that begin with a single dash, called *flags,* and you'll learn about those starting in the next lesson.

Simple Math with UNIX

Having both an internal wall clock and an internal calendar, UNIX seems to have much of what you need in an office. One piece that's missing now, however, is a simple desktop calculator. UNIX offers two different types of calculators, though neither rightly can be called simple.

Mathematicians talk about "infix" and "postfix" notation as two different ways to write an expression, the former having the operation embedded in the operators and the latter having all the operators listed, followed by the operation required. Table 2.1 lists some examples of a mathematical expression in both formats.

Table 2.1. Comparing infix and postfix notation.

Infix	Postfix
75*0.85	75 0.85 *
(37*1.334)+44	37 1.334 * 44 +
cos(3.45)/4	3.45 cos 4 /

You're probably familiar with the infix notation, which is the form used in math textbooks throughout the world. Lots of calculators can work this way too; you'd press [1] [+] [1] [=] to find out that one plus one equals two.

Some calculators offer the postfix alternative, also known as (reverse) Polish notation, invented by Polish mathematician and logician Jan Lukasiewicz. Notably, for many years Hewlett-Packard has been making calculators that work with RPN notation. On an HP calculator, you'd press [1] [enter] [1] [+] to find out that one plus one equals two.

Notice that, though parentheses were required in the second equation in the table when using infix notation, parentheses weren't necessary to force a specific order of evaluation with postfix. Remember that in math you always work from the inside of the parenthesis outward, so (3*4) + 8 is solved by multiplying three by four, then adding eight, and that process is exactly what RPN mimics.

UNIX offers two calculator programs, one with infix notation and one with postfix notation.

Task 2.9: Using the *bc* Infix Calculator
Step 1. Description

The first calculator to learn is bc, the UNIX infix-notation calculator.

Step 2. Action

1. To use the infix calculator, enter the following command:

    ```
    % bc
    ```

Nothing happens, no prompt, nothing. The reason is that bc, like its RPN cousin dc, waits for you to enter commands. The quit command lets you leave the program. You can see how it works by seeing how I solve the first and second mathematical equation of Table 2.1:

```
% bc
75 * 0.85
63.75
(37*1.334)+44
93.358
quit
%
```

2. Unfortunately, bc is, in many ways, a typical UNIX command. Consider what happens when I enter help, hoping for some clue on how to use the bc program:

```
% bc
help
syntax error on line 1, teletype
```

3. This is not very helpful. If you get stuck in a command, there are two surefire ways to escape. Control-D (holding down the Control—also called Ctrl—key on your keyboard and simultaneously pressing the D key) indicates that you have no further input, which often causes programs to quit. If that fails, Control-C kills the program, that is, forces it to quit immediately.

Comment: On some keyboards, the Control key is called Ctrl.

The bc command has a number of powerful and useful options, as shown in Table 2.2.

Table 2.2. Helpful bc commands.

Notation	Description of Function
sqrt(n)	square root of n
%	remainder
^	to the power of (3^5 is three to the power of five)

Notation	Description of Function
s(*n*)	sine(*n*)
c(*n*)	cosine(*n*)
e(*n*)	exponential
l(*n*)	log(*n*)

4. If you wanted to calculate the sine of 4.5243 to the third power, you could do it with bc. You need to be sure, however, that the system knows you're working with higher math functions by specifying the *command flag* -l math (or, in some cases, just -l):

```
% bc -l math
s ( 4.5243 ^ 3 )
-.99770433540886100879
quit
%
```

Step 3. Summary

If you try this on your calculator, you probably won't get a result quite as precise as this. The bc and dc commands both work with extended precision, allowing for highly accurate results.

Task 2.10: Using the *dc* Postfix Calculator

Step 1. Description

By contrast, the dc command works with the postfix notation, and each number or operation must be on its own line. Further, the result of an operation isn't automatically shown; you have to enter p to see the most recently calculated result.

Step 2. Action

1. To use dc for the calculations shown previously, enter the following characters shown in bold. The result follows each completed entry.

```
% dc
75
0.85
*
p
```

```
63.75
37
1.334
*
44
+
p
93.358
quit
%
```

2. The set of commands available in dc are different because dc addresses a different set of mathematical equations. The dc command is particularly useful if you need to work in a nondecimal base. (For example, some older computer systems worked in octal, a base-eight numbering system. The number '210' in octal, therefore, represents 2*8*8 + 1*8 + 0, or 136 in decimal.) Table 2.3 summarizes some of the most useful commands available in dc.

Table 2.3. Helpful commands in dc.

Notation	Description of Function
v	square root
i	set radix (numeric base) for input
o	set radix for output
p	print top of stack
f	all values in the stack are printed

3. For example, I used dc to verify that 210 (octal) is indeed equal to 136 (decimal):

```
% dc
8
i
210
p
136
```

Step 3. Summary

With a little work, you can use different numeric bases within the bc program, so unless you're really used to the RPN notation, it's probably best to remember the bc command when you think of doing some quick calculations in UNIX.

> **Comment:** I find both bc and dc ridiculously difficult to use, so I keep a small hand-held calculator by my computer. For just about any task, simply using the calculator is faster than remembering the notational oddities of either UNIX calculator program. Your mileage may vary, of course.

If you're old enough, you'll remember the early 1980s as the time when IBM had introduced the PC and the industry was going wild, predicting that within a few years every home would have a PC and that everyone would use PCs for balancing checkbooks and keeping track of recipes. Fifteen years later, few people in fact use computers as part of their cooking ritual, though checkbook-balancing programs *are* amazingly popular. The point is that some tasks can be done by computer but are sometimes best accomplished through more traditional means. If you have a calculator and are comfortable using it, then the calculator is probably a better solution than learning how to work with bc to add a few numbers.

There are definitely situations where having the computer add the numbers for you is quite beneficial—particularly when there are a lot of them—but if you're like me, you rarely encounter that situation.

Lesson Summary

This lesson has focused on giving you the skills required to log in to a UNIX system, figure out who you are and what groups you're in, change your password, and log out again. You've also learned how to list the other users of the system, find out what UNIX commands they're using, check the date and time, and even show a calendar view of almost any month or year in history. Finally, you've learned some of the power of two similar UNIX utilities, bc and dc, the two UNIX desktop calculators.

2

Workshop
Key Terms

account name   This is the official one-word name by which the UNIX system knows you. Mine is `taylor`.

arguments   Not any type of domestic dispute, arguments are the set of options and filenames specified to UNIX commands. When you use a command like `vi test.c`, all words other than the command name itself (`vi`) are arguments, or parameters to the program.

case-insensitive   See *case-sensitive*.

case-sensitive   As you might know from working with other computer systems or typewriters, English has UPPERCASE and lowercase letters, meaning that in everyday language CAT and cat are two different words in appearance. They become the same word, however, if you're ignoring the case of each letter, which is when you're *case-insensitive*. The opposite of this is *case-sensitive*, when CAT and cat are considered two different words, not the same word.

command   Each program in UNIX is also known as a command; the two words are interchangeable.

domain name   UNIX systems on the Internet, or any other network, are assigned a domain within which they exist. This is typically the company (for example, `sun.com` for Sun Microsystems) or institution (for example, `lsu.edu` for Louisiana State University). The domain name is always the entire host address, except the hostname itself.

flags   Arguments given to a UNIX command that are intended to alter its behavior are called flags. They're always prefaced by a single dash. As an example, the command `ls -l /tmp` has `ls` as the command itself, `-l` as the flag to the command, and `/tmp` as the argument.

heuristic   A set of well-defined steps or a procedure for accomplishing a specific task.

hostname	UNIX computers all have unique names assigned by the local administration team. The computers I use are `limbo`, `well`, `netcom`, and `mentor`, for example. Type `hostname` to see what your system is called.
login	A synonym for *account name*, this also can refer to the actual process of connecting to the UNIX system and entering your account name and password to your account.

Questions

1. Why can't you have the same account name as another user? How about user ID? Can you have the same "uid" as someone else on the system?

2. Which of the following are good passwords, based on the guidelines you've learned in this chapter?

   ```
   foobar        4myMUM       Blk&Blu

   234334        Laurie       Hi!

   2cool.        rolyat       j j kim
   ```

3. Are the results of the two commands `who am i` and `whoami` different? Describe the difference. Which do you think you'd rather use when you're on a new computer?

4. List the three different UNIX commands to find out who is logged on to the system. Think about the differences between the commands.

5. One of these commands indicates how long the system has been running (in the example, it'd been running for seven days). What value do you think there is for keeping track of this information?

6. If you can figure out what other people are doing on the computer, they can figure out what you're doing, too. Does that bother you?

7. What day of the week were you born? What day of the week is July 4, 1997? For that matter, what day of the week was July 4, 1776?

2

8. Solve the following mathematical equations using both dc and bc, and then explain which command you prefer.

```
454 * 3.84          sin(3.1415)

log(2.45)+log(3)    2^16
```

Preview of the Next Chapter

The next lesson focuses on the UNIX hierarchical file system. You will learn about how the system is organized, how it differs from Macintosh and DOS hierarchical file systems, the difference between "relative" and "absolute" filenames, and what the mysterious "." and ".." directories are. Then you learn about the env, pwd, and cd commands, and the HOME and PATH environment variables.

Moving About
in the File
System

3

This final lesson of Day 1 focuses on the UNIX hierarchical file system. You learn about how the system is organized, how it differs from the Macintosh and DOS hierarchical file systems, the difference between "relative" and "absolute" filenames, and what the mysterious "." and ".." directories are. Then you learn about the env, pwd, and cd commands and the HOME and PATH environment variables.

Goals for This Lesson

In this lesson, you'll learn

- ☐ What a hierarchical file system is all about
- ☐ The UNIX file system organization
- ☐ How Mac and PC file systems differ from UNIX
- ☐ The difference between relative and absolute filenames
- ☐ Hidden files in UNIX
- ☐ The special directories "." and ".."
- ☐ The env command
- ☐ User environments, PATH and HOME
- ☐ Find where you are with pwd
- ☐ Move to another location with cd

The last lesson introduced a plethora of UNIX commands, but this chapter takes a more theoretical approach, focusing on the UNIX file system, how it's organized, and how you can navigate about. This lesson focuses on the environment that tags along with you as you move about, particularly the HOME and PATH variables. After that is explained, you learn about the env command as an easy way to show environment variables, and you learn the pwd and cd pair of commands for moving about directly.

What a Hierarchical File System Is All About

In a nutshell, a hierarchy is a system organized by graded categorization. A familiar example is the organizational structure of a company, where workers report to supervisors and supervisors report to middle managers. Middle managers, in turn, report to senior managers, and senior managers report to vice-presidents, who report to the president of the company. Graphically, this hierarachy looks like Figure 3.1.

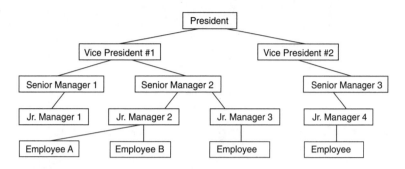

Figure 3.1. *A typical organizational hierarchy.*

You've doubtless seen this type of illustration before, and you know that a higher position indicates more control. Each position is controlled by the next highest position or row. The President is top dog of the organization, but each subsequent manager is also in control of his or her own small fiefdom.

To understand how a file system can have a similar organization, simply imagine each of the managers in the illustration as a "file folder" and each of the employees as a piece of paper, filed in a particular folder. Open any file cabinet, and you probably see things organized this way: filed papers are placed in labeled folders, and often these folders are filed in groups under specific topics. The drawer might then have specific labels to distinguish them from other drawers in the cabinet, and so on.

That's exactly what a hierarchical file system is all about. You want to have your files located in the most appropriate place in the file system, whether at the very top, in a folder, or in a nested series of folders. With careful usage, a hierarchical file system can contain hundreds or thousands of files and still allow users to find any individual file quickly.

On my computer, the chapters of this book are organized in a hierarchical fashion, as shown in Figure 3.2.

3

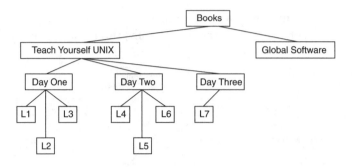

Figure 3.2. *"Teach Yourself UNIX in a Week" file organization.*

Task 3.1: The UNIX File System Organization
Step 1. Description

A key concept allowing the UNIX hierarchical file system to be so effective is that anything that is not a folder is a file. Programs are files in UNIX, device drivers are files, documents and spreadsheets are files, your keyboard is represented as a file, your display is a file, and even your tty line and mouse are files.

What this means is that as UNIX has developed, it has avoided becoming an ungainly mess. UNIX does not have hundreds of cryptic files stuck at the top (this is still a problem in DOS) or tucked away in confusing folders within the System Folder (as with the Macintosh).

The top level of the UNIX file structure (/) is known as the *root* or *slash* directory and always has a certain set of subdirectories, including bin, dev, etc, lib, mnt, tmp and usr. There can be a lot more, however. Listing 3.1 shows files found at the top level of the Limbo file system. Typical UNIX directories are shown in boldface in the listing.

Listing 3.1. Top-level directory listing from limbo.

AA	boot	flags/	rf/	userb/	var/
OLD/	core	gendynix	stand/	userc/	
archive/	**dev**/	**lib**/	sys/	userd/	
ats/	diag/	lost+found/	tftpboot/	usere/	
backup/	dynix	**mnt**/	**tmp**/	users/	
bin/	**etc**/	net/	usera/	**usr**/	

You can obtain a listing of the files and directories in your own top-level directory by using the `ls -CF /` command. (You'll learn all about the `ls` command in the next lesson. For now, just be sure that you enter exactly what's shown in the example.)

On a different computer system, here's what I see when I enter that command:

```
% ls -CF /
Mail/          export/        public/
News/          home/          reviews/
add_swap/      kadb*          sbin/
apps/          layout         sys@
archives/      lib@           tftpboot/
bin@           lost+found/    tmp/
boot           mnt/           usr/
cdrom/         net/           utilities/
chess/         news/          var/
dev/           nntpserver     vmunix*
etc/           pcfs/
```

In the listing, any filename that ends with a slash (/) is a folder (UNIX calls these directories). Any filename that ends with an asterisk (*) is a program. Anything ending with an @ is a symbolic *link*, and everything else is a normal, plain file.

As you can see from these two listings, and as you'll immediately find when you try the command yourself, there is much variation in how different UNIX systems organize the top-level directory. There are some directories and files in common— I've highlighted them in bold—and once you start examining the contents of specific directories, you'll find that hundreds of programs and files always show up in the same place from UNIX to UNIX.

It's as if you were working as a file clerk at a new law firm. Though this firm might have a specific approach to filing information, the approach may be similar to the filing system of other firms where you have worked in the past. If you know the underlying organization, you can quickly pick up the specifics of a particular organization.

Step 2. Action

1. Try the command `ls -CF /` on your computer system, and identify, as previously explained, each of the directories in your resultant listing.

Step 3. Summary

The output of the `ls` command shows the files and directories in the top level of your system. Next, you will learn what they are.

The *bin* Directory

In UNIX parlance, programs are considered *executables*, because users can execute them. (In this case, *execute* is a synonym for *run*, not an indication that you get to wander about murdering innocent applications!) When the program has been compiled (usually from a C listing), it is translated into what's called a *binary* format. Add the two together and you have a common UNIX description for an application— an *executable binary*.

It's no surprise that the original UNIX developers decided to have a directory labeled `binaries` to store all the executable programs on the system. Remember the primitive teletypewriter discussed in the last lesson? Having a slow system to talk with the computer had many ramifications that you might not expect. The single most obvious one was that everything became quite concise. There were no lengthy words like *binaries* or *listfiles*, but rather succinct abbreviations; `bin` and `ls` are, respectively, the UNIX equivalents.

The `bin` directory is where all the executable binaries were kept in early UNIX. Over time, as more and more executables were added to UNIX, having all of the executables in one place proved unmanageable, and the `bin` directory was split into multiple parts (`/bin`, `/1bin`, `/usr/bin`).

The *dev* Directory

Among the most important portions of any computer are its *device drivers*. Without them, you wouldn't have any information on your screen (the infomation arrives courtesy of the display device driver). You wouldn't be able to enter information (the information is read and given to the system by the keyboard device driver), and you wouldn't be able to use your floppy disk drive (managed by the floppy device driver).

Earlier, you learned how almost anything in UNIX is considered a file in the file system, and the `dev` directory is an example. All device drivers—often numbering into the hundreds—are stored as separate files in the standard UNIX `dev` (devices) directory.

Pronounce this directory name "dev," not "dee-ee-vee."

The *etc* Directory

UNIX administration can be quite complex, involving management of user accounts, the file system, security, device drivers, hardware configurations, and more. To help,

UNIX designates the etc directory as the storage place for all administrative files and information.

Pronounce the directory name either "ee-tea-sea", "et-sea," or "etcetera." All three pronunciations are common.

The *lib* Directory

Like your neighborhood community, UNIX has a central storage place for function and procedural libraries. These specific executables are included with specific programs, allowing programs to offer features and capabilities otherwise unavailable. The idea is that if programs want to include certain features, they can just reference the shared copy of that utility in the UNIX library, rather than having a new, unique copy.

In the last lesson, when you were exploring the dc calculator, you used the command dc -l math to access trigonometric functions. The -l math was to let dc know that you wanted to include the functions available through the math library, stored in the lib directory.

Many of the more recent UNIX systems also support what's called *dynamic linking*, where the library of functions is included on-the-fly as you start up the program, too. The wrinkle is that instead of the library reference being when the program is created, it's only resolved when you actually run the program itself.

Pronounce the directory name "libe" or "lib" (to rhyme with the word *bib*).

The *lost+found* Directory

With multiple users running many different programs simultaneously, it's been a challenge over the years to develop a file system that can remain synchronized with the activity of the computer. Various parts of the UNIX *kernel*—the brains of the system—help with this problem. When files are recovered after any sort of problem or failure, they are placed here, in the lost+found directory, if the kernel cannot ascertain the proper location in the file system. This directory should be empty almost all of the time.

This directory is commonly pronounced "lost and found," rather than "lost plus found."

3

The *mnt* and *sys* Directories

The mnt (pronounced "em-en-tea") and sys (pronounced "sis") directories also are safely ignored by UNIX users. The mnt directory is intended to be a common place to mount external media—hard disks, removable cartridge drives, and so on—in UNIX, and on many systems, though not all, sys contains files indicating the system configuration.

The *tmp* Directory

A directory that you can't ignore, the tmp directory—say "temp"—is used by many of the programs in UNIX as a temporary file storage space. If you're editing a file, for example, the program makes a copy of the file and saves it in tmp, and you work directly with that, saving the new file back to your original file only when you've completed your work.

On most systems, tmp ends up littered with various files and executables left by programs that don't remove their own temporary files. On one system I use, it's not uncommon to find here 10–30 megabytes of files wasting space.

Even so, if you're manipulating files or working with copies of files, tmp is the best place to keep the temporary copies of files. Indeed, on some UNIX workstations, tmp can actually be the fastest device on the computer, allowing for dramatic performance improvements over working with files directly in your home directory.

The *usr* Directory

Finally, the last of the standard directories at the top level of the UNIX file system hierarchy is the usr—pronounced "user"— directory. Originally, this directory was intended to be the central storage place for all user-related commands. Today, however, many companies have their own interpretation, and there's no telling what you'll find in this directory.

Comment: A growing trend is that /usr is reserved for UNIX operating system binaries.

Other Miscellaneous Stuff at the Top Level

Besides all the directories previously listed, a number of other directories and files commonly occur in UNIX systems. Some files might have slight variations in filename on your computer, so when you compare your listing to the following files and directories, be alert for possible alternative spellings.

A file you *must* have to bring up UNIX at all is one usually called `unix` or `vmunix`, or specifically named after the version of UNIX on the computer. The file contains the actual UNIX operating system. The file must have a specific name and must be found at the top level of the file system. Hand-in-hand with the operating system is another file called `boot`, which helps during initial startup of the hardware.

Notice on one of the previous listings that the files `boot` and `dynix` appear. (DYNIX is the name of the particular variant of UNIX used on Sequent computers.) By comparison, the listing from the Sun Microsystems workstation shows `boot` and `vmunix` as the two files.

Another directory that you might find in your own top-level listing is `diag`— pronounced "dye-ag"—which acts as a storehouse for diagnostic and maintenance programs. If you have any programs within this directory, it's best not to try them out without proper training!

The `home` directory, also sometimes called `users`, is a central place for organizing all files unique to a specific user. Listing this directory is usually an easy way to find out what accounts are on the system, too, because by convention each individual account directory is named after the user's account name. On one system I use, my account is `taylor`, and my individual account directory is also called `taylor`. Home directories are always created by the system administrator.

The `net` directory, if set up correctly, is a handy shortcut for accessing other computers on your network.

The `tftpboot` is a relatively new feature of UNIX. The letters stand for "trivial file transfer protocol boot." Don't let the name confuse you, though; this directory contains versions of the kernel suitable for X Window-based terminals and diskless workstations to run UNIX.

Some UNIX systems have directories named for specific types of peripherals that can be attached. On the Sun workstation, you can see examples with the directories `cdrom` and `pcfs`. The former is for a CD-ROM drive and the latter for DOS-format floppy disks.

There are many more directories in UNIX, but this will give you a sense of how things are organized.

3

How Mac and PC File Systems Differ from the UNIX File System

Though the specific information is certainly different, some parallels do exist between the hierarchical file system structure of the UNIX and the Macintosh systems.

For example, on the Macintosh, folders are distinguished by their icons. The common folders you'll find on all Macs include System Folder and Trash. Within the system folder, all Macs have a variety of system-related files, including Finder, System, and Clipboard. Folders include Extensions, Preferences, and Control Panels.

By comparison, DOS requires few files be present for the system to be usable: command.com *must* be present, and autoexec.bat and config.sys are usually present. Most DOS systems have all the commands neatly tucked into the \DOS directory on the system, but sometimes these commands appear at the very top level.

Directory Separator Characters

If you look at the organizational chart presented earlier in this lesson, you can see that employees are identified simply as "employee" where possible. Because each has a unique path upward to the president, each has a unique identifier if all components of the path upward are specified.

For example, the rightmost of the four employees could be described as "Employee managed by Jr. Manager 4, managed by Senior Manager 3, managed by Vice President #2, managed by the President." Using a single character, instead of "managed by," can considerably shorten the description: Employee/Jr. Manager 4/ Senior Manager 3/Vice President #2/President. Now consider the same path specified from the very top of the organization downward: President/Vice President #2/Senior Manager 3/Jr. Manager 4/Employee.

Because only one person is at the top, that person can be safely dropped from the path without losing the uniqueness of the descriptor: "/Vice President #2/Senior Manager 3/Jr. Manager 4/Employee."

In this example, the / (pronounce it "slash") is serving as a *directory separator character*, a convenient shorthand to indicate different directories in a path.

The idea of using a single character isn't unique to UNIX, but using the / is unusual. On the Macintosh, the system uses a colon to separate directories in a pathname.

(Next time you're on a Mac, try saving a file called test:file and see what happens.) DOS also uses a slash, but that slash character faces the other direction: \DOS indicates the DOS directory at the top level of DOS. The characters /tmp indicate the tmp directory at the top level of the UNIX file system, and :Apps is a folder called Apps at the top of the Macintosh file system.

On the Macintosh, you encounter the directory delineator rarely, because the system has a completely graphical interface. Windows also offers a similar level of freedom from having to worry about much of this complexity, though you'll still need to remember whether "A:" is your floppy disk or hard disk drive.

The Difference Between Relative and Absolute Filenames

Specifying the location of a file in a hierarchy to ensure that the filename is unique is known in UNIX parlance as specifying its *absolute filename*. That is, regardless of where you are within the file system, the absolute filename always specifies a particular file. By contrast, *relative filenames* are *not* unique descriptors.

To understand, consider the files shown in Figure 3.3.

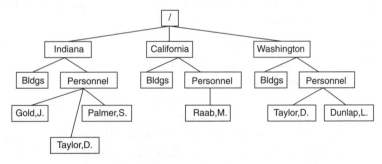

Figure 3.3. *A simple hierarchy of files.*

If you are currently looking at the information in the Indiana directory, then Bldgs uniquely describes one file: the Bldgs file in the Indiana directory. That same name, however, refers to a different file if you are in the California or Washington directories. Similarly, the directory Personnel leaves you with three possible choices until you also specify which state you're interested in.

As a possible scenario, imagine you're reading through the Bldgs file for Washington and some people come into your office, interrupting your work. After a few minutes of talk, they comment about an entry in the Bldgs file in California. You turn to your UNIX system and bring up the Bldgs file and it's the *wrong* file. Why? You're still in the Washington directory.

These problems arise because of the lack of specificity of relative filenames. Relative filenames describe files that are referenced relative to an assumed position in the file system. In Figure 3.3, even Personnel/Taylor,D. isn't unique, because that can be found in both Indiana and Washington.

To avoid these problems, you can apply the technique you learned earlier, specifying all elements of the directory path from the top down. To look at the Bldgs file for California, you could simply specify /California/Bldgs. To check the Taylor,D. employee in Indiana, you'd use /Indiana/Personnel/Taylor,D., which is different, you'll notice, from /Washington/Personnel/Taylor,D.

Learning the difference between these two notations is crucial to surviving the complexity of a hierarchical file system used with UNIX. Without it, you'll spend half your time verifying that you're where you think you are, or, worse, not moving about at all, not taking advantage of the organizational capabilities.

If you're ever in doubt as to where you are or what file you're working with in UNIX, simply specify its absolute filename. You can always differentiate between the two by looking at the very first character: if it's a slash, you've got an absolute filename (because the filename is *rooted* to the very top level of the file system). If you don't have a slash as the first character, the filename's a relative filename.

Earlier I told you that in the home directory at the top level of UNIX I have a private directory called taylor. In absolute filename terms, I'd properly say that I have /home/taylor as a unique directory.

Comment: To add to the confusion, most UNIX people don't pronounce the slashes, particularly if the first component of the filename is a well-known directory. I would pronounce /home/taylor as "home taylor," but I would usually pronounce /newt/awk/test as "slash newt awk test." When in doubt, pronounce the slash.

As you learn more about UNIX, particularly about how to navigate in the file system, you'll find that a clear understanding of the difference between a relative and absolute filename proves invaluable. The rule of thumb is that if a filename begins with /, it's absolute.

Task 3.2: Hidden Files in UNIX
Step 1. Description

One of the best aspects of living in an area for a long time, frequenting the same shops and visiting the same restaurants, is that the people who work at each place learn your name and preferences. Many UNIX applications can perform the same trick, remembering your preferred style of interaction, what files you last worked with, which lines you've edited, and more, through *preference files*.

On the Macintosh, because it's a single-user system, there's a folder within the System Folder called Preferences, which is a central storage place for preference files, organized by application. On my Macintosh, for example, I have about 30 different preference files in this directory, enabling me to teach programs *once* the defaults I prefer.

UNIX needs to support many users at once, so UNIX preference files can't be stored in a central spot in the file system. Otherwise, how would the system distinguish between your preferences and those of your colleagues? To avoid this problem, all UNIX applications store their preference files in your private, personal directory.

Programs want to be able to keep their own internal preferences and status stored in your directory, but these aren't for you to work with or alter. If you use DOS, you're probably familiar with how the DOS operating system solves this problem: certain files are hidden and do not show up when you use DIR to list files in a directory.

Macintosh people don't realize it, but the Macintosh also has lots of hidden files. On the topmost level of the Macintosh file system, for example, the following files are present, albeit hidden from normal display: AppleShare PDS, Deleted File Record, Desktop, Desktop DB, and Desktop DF. Displaying hidden files on the Macintosh is very difficult, as it is with DOS.

Fortunately, the UNIX rule for hiding files is much easier than that for either the Mac or PC. No secret status flag reminds the system not to display the file when printing listings. Instead, the rule is simple. Any filename starting with a dot is hidden.

Don't Skip This: A *hidden file* is any file with a dot as the first character of the filename.

If the filename or directory name begins with a dot, it won't show up in normal listings of that directory. If the filename or directory name has any other character as the first character of the name, it lists normally.

Step 2. Action

1. Knowing that, turn to your computer and enter the `ls` command to list all the files and directories in your private directory.

```
% ls -CF
Archives/     Mail/          RUMORS.18Sept  mailing.lists
InfoWorld/    News/          bin/           newlists
LISTS         OWL/           iecc.list      src/
%
```

2. You can see that I have 12 items in my own directory, seven directories (the directory names have a slash as the last character, remember) and five files. Files have minimal rules for naming, too. Avoid slashes, spaces, and tabs, and you'll be fine.

3. Without an explicit direction to the contrary, UNIX is going to let the hidden files remain hidden. To add the hidden files to the listing, you need merely add a `-a` flag to the command. Turn to your computer and try this command to see what hidden files are present in your directory. These are my results:

```
% ls -a
./             .gopherrc      .oldnewsrc     .sig          RUMORS.18Sep
../            .history*      .plan          Archives/     bin/
.Agenda        .info          .pnewsexpert   InfoWorld/    iecc.list
.aconfigrc     .letter        .report        LISTS         mail.lists
.article       .login         .rm-timestamp  Mail/         newlists
.cshrc         .mailrc        .rnlast        News/         src/
.elm/          .newsrc        .rnsoft        OWL/
%
```

Many dot files tend to follow the format of a dot, followed by the name of the program that owns the file, with "rc" as the suffix. In my directory, you can see six dot files that follow this convention: .aconfigrc, .cshrc, .gopherrc, .mailrc, .newsrc, and .oldnewsrc.

Step 3. Summary

Because of the particular rules of hidden files in UNIX, they are often called *dot files*, and you can see that I have 23 dot files and directories in my directory.

> **Comment:** The rc suffix tells you that this file is a configuration file for that particular utility. For instance, .cshrc is the configuration file for the C shell and is executed every time the C shell (/bin/csh) is executed.

> **Comment:** Because it's important to convey the specific filename of a dot file, pronunciation is a little different than elsewhere in UNIX. The name .gopherrc would be spoken as "dot gopher are-sea" and .mailrc would be "dot mail are-sea." If you can't pronounce the program name, odds are good that no one else can either, so .cshrc is "dot sea-ess-aitch are-sea."

Other programs create a bunch of different dot files and try to retain a consistent naming scheme. You can see that .rnlast and .rnsoft are both from the rn program, but it's difficult to know simply from the filenames that .article, .letter, .newsrc, .oldnewsrc, and .pnewsexpert are all also referenced by the rn program. Recognizing this problem, some application authors designed their applications to create a dot directory, with all preference files neatly tucked into that one spot. The elm program does that with its .elm hidden directory.

Some files are directly named after the programs that use them: the .Agenda file is used by the agenda program, and .info is used by the info program. Those almost have a rule of their own, but it's impossible to distinguish them from .login, from the sh program; .plan for the finger program; .rm-timestamp from a custom program of my own; and I frankly have no idea what program created the .report file!

This should give you an idea of the various ways that UNIX programs name and use hidden files. As an exercise, list all the dot files in your private directory and try to extract the name of the program that probably created the file. Check by looking in

3

the index of this book to see if a program by that name exists. If you can't figure out which programs created which files, you're not alone. Keep the list handy, refer to it as you learn more about UNIX while exploring *Teach Yourself UNIX in a Week*, and by the time you're done, you'll know exactly how to find out which programs created which dot files.

Task 3.3: The Special Directories "." and ".."

Step 1. Description

There are two dot directories I haven't mentioned, though they show up in my listing and most certainly also show up in your listing, too. They are *dot* and *dot dot* ("." and ".."), and they're shorthand directory names that can be terrifically convenient.

The dot directory is shorthand for the current location in the directory hierarchy; and the dot-dot directory moves you up one level, to the parent directory.

Consider again the list of files shown in Figure 3.3. If you were looking at the files in the California Personnel directory (best specified as /California/Personnel) and wanted to check quickly an entry in the Bldgs file for California, either you'd have to use the absolute filename and enter the lengthy /California/Bldgs, or, with the new shorthand directories, you could enter ../Bldgs.

As directories move ever deeper into the directory hierarchy, the dot-dot notation can save you much typing time. For example, what if the different states and related files were all located in my private directory /home/taylor in a new directory called business? In that case, the absolute filename for employee "Raab,M." in California would be /home/taylor/business/California/Personnel/Raab,M., which is unwieldy and an awful lot to type if you want to hop up one level and check on the buildings database in Indiana!

You can use more than one dot-dot notation in a filename too, so if you're looking at the Raab,M. file and want to check on Dunlap,L., you could save typing in the full filename by instead using ../../../Washington/Personnel/Dunlap,L. Look at Figure 3.3 to see how that would work, tracing back one level for each dot-dot in the filename.

This explains why the dot-dot shorthand is helpful, but what about the single dot notation that simply specifies the current directory?

I haven't stated it explicitly yet, but you've probably figured out that one ramification of the UNIX file system organization, combined with its ability to place applications anywhere in the file system, is that the system needs some way to know where to look for particular applications. Just as a person walks into a huge library, in UNIX an organization and strategy for searching is imperative for success and speed.

UNIX uses an ordered list of directories called a *search path* for this purpose. The search path typically lists five or six different directories on the system where the computer checks for any application you request.

The question that arises is, What happens if your own personal copy of an application has the same name as a standard system application? The answer is that the system always finds the standard application first if its directory is listed earlier in the search path.

To avoid this pitfall, you need to use the dot notation, forcing the system to look in the current directory rather than search for the application. If you wanted your own version of the `ls` command, for example, you'd need to enter `./ls` to ensure that UNIX uses your version rather than the standard version.

Step 2. Action

1. Enter `./ls` on your computer and watch what happens. Then enter `/ls` without the dot notation and notice how the computer searches through various directories in the search path, finds the `ls` program, and executes it, automatically.

Step 3. Summary

You'll learn other uses of the dot-dot directory, but the greatest value of the dot directory is that you can use it to force the system to look in the current directory and nowhere else for any file specified.

Task 3.4: The *env* Command
Step 1. Description

You've learned a lot of the foundations of the UNIX file system and how applications remember your preferences through hidden dot files. There's another way, however, that the system remembers specifics about you, and that's through your user environment. The user environment is a collection of specially named variables that have specific values.

3

Step 2. Action

1. To view your environment, you can use the env command. Here's what I see when I enter the env command on my system:

```
% env
HOME=/users/taylor
SHELL=/bin/csh
TERM=vt100
PATH=/users/taylor/bin:/bin:/usr/bin:/usr/ucb:/usr/local/bin:/usr/unsup/bin:.
MAIL=/usr/spool/mail/taylor
LOGNAME=taylor
TZ=EST5
```

Step 3. Summary

Try it yourself and compare your values with mine. You might find that you have more defined in your environment than I do because your UNIX system uses your environment to keep track of more information.

> **Don't Skip This:** Many UNIX systems offer the printenv command instead of env. If you enter env and the system complains that it can't find the env command, try using printenv instead. All examples here work with either env or printenv.

Task 3.5: *PATH* and *HOME*
Step 1. Description

The two most important values in your environment are the name of your private directory (HOME) and your search path (PATH). Your home directory (as it's known) is the name of the directory that you always begin your UNIX session within.

The PATH environment variable lists the set of directories, in left-to-right order, that the system searches to find commands and applications you request. You can see from the example that my search path tells the computer to start looking in the /users/taylor/bin directory then sequentially try /bin, /usr/bin, /usr/ucb, /usr/local/bin, /usr/unsup/bin, and . before concluding it can't find the requested command.

Without a PATH, the shell wouldn't be able to find any of the many, many UNIX commands. As a minimum, you should always have /bin and /usr/bin.

Step 2. Action

1. You can use the env command to list specific environment variables too. Enter env PATH and env HOME. When I do so, I get the following results:

```
% env PATH
/users/taylor/bin:/bin:/usr/bin:/usr/ucb:/usr/local/bin:/usr/unsup/bin:.
% env HOME
/users/taylor
%
```

Step 3. Action

Your PATH value is probably similar, though certainly not identical, to mine, and your HOME is /home/*account name* or something similar (*account name* is your account name).

Task 3.6: Find Where You Are with *pwd*
Step 1. Description

So far you've learned a lot about how the file system works but not much about how to move around in the file system. With any trip, the first and most important step is to find out your current location. In UNIX, the command pwd tells you the present working directory.

Step 2. Action

1. Enter pwd. The output should be identical to the output you saw when you entered env HOME because you're still in your home directory.

```
% env HOME
/users/taylor
% pwd
/users/taylor
%
```

Step 3. Summary

Think of pwd as a compass, always capable of telling you where you are. It also tells you the names of all directories above you, because it always lists your current location as an absolute directory name.

3

Task 3.7: Move to Another Location with *cd*

Step 1. Description

The other half of the dynamic duo is the cd command, used to change directory. The format of this command is simple, too: cd *new-directory* (where *new-directory* is the name of the new directory you want).

Step 2. Action

1. Try moving to the very top level of the file system and entering pwd to see if the computer agrees that you've moved.

   ```
   % cd /
   % pwd
   /
   %
   ```

2. Notice that cd doesn't produce any output. Many UNIX commands operate silently like this, unless an error is encountered. The system then indicates the problem. You can see what an error looks like by trying to change your location to a nonexistent directory. Try the /taylor directory to see what happens!

   ```
   % cd /taylor
   /taylor: No such file or directory
   %
   ```

3. Enter cd without specifying a directory. What happens? I get the following result:

   ```
   % cd
   % pwd
   /users/taylor
   %
   ```

4. Here's where the HOME environment variable comes into play. Without any directory specified, cd moves you back to your home directory automatically. If you get lost, it's a fast shorthand way to move to a known location without fuss.

   Remember the dot-dot notation for moving up a level in the directory hierarchy? Here's where it also proves exceptionally useful. Use the cd command without any arguments to move to your home directory, then use pwd to ensure that's where you've ended up.

5. Now, move up one level by using cd .. and check the results with pwd:

```
% cd
% pwd
/users/taylor
% cd ..
% pwd
/users
```

6. Use the ls -CF command to list all the directories contained at this point in the file system. Beware, though; on large systems this directory could easily have hundreds of different directories. On one system I use, there are almost 550 different directories one level above my home directory in the file system!

```
% ls -CF
armstrong/   christine/   guest/     laura/    patrickb/   shane/
bruce/       david/       higgins/   mac/      rank/       taylor/
cedric/      green/       kane/      mark/     shalini/    vicki/
%
```

Step 3. Summary

Try using a combination of cd and pwd to move about your file system, and remember that without any arguments cd always zips you right back to your home directory.

Lesson Summary

This lesson has focused on the UNIX hierarchical file system. You've learned the organization of a hierarchical file system, how UNIX differs from Macintosh and DOS systems, and how UNIX remembers preferences with its hidden dot files. This lesson has also explained the difference between relative and absolute filenames, and you've learned about the "." and ".." directories. You've learned three new commands too: env to list your current environment, cd to change directories, and pwd to find out your present working directory location.

Workshop
Key Terms

absolute filename	Any filename that begins with a leading slash (/), these always uniquely describe a single file in the file system.
binary	A file format that is intended for the computer to work with directly rather than for humans for peruse. See also *executable*.
device driver	All peripherals attached to the computer are called *devices* in UNIX, and each has a control program always associated, called a device driver. Examples are the device drivers for the display, keyboard, mouse, and all hard disks.
directory separator character	On a hierarchical file system, there must be some way to specify which items are directories and which is the actual filename itself. This becomes particularly true when you're working with *absolute filenames*. In UNIX, the directory separator character is the slash (/), so a filename like /tmp/testme is easily interpreted as a file called testme in a directory called tmp.
dot	A shorthand notation for the current directory.
dot dot	A shorthand notation for the directory, one level higher up the hierarchical file system from the current location.
dot file	A configuration file used by one or more programs, these are called dot files because the first letter of the filename is a dot, as in .profile or .login. Because they're dot files, the ls command doesn't list them by default, making them also *hidden files* in UNIX.

dynamic linking	Though most UNIX systems require all necessary utilities and library routines (like the routines for reading information from the keyboard and displaying it to the screen) to be plugged into a program when it's built (known in UNIX parlance as *static linking*), some of the more sophisticated systems can delay this inclusion until you actually need to run the program. In this case, the utilities and libraries are linked when you start the program, and this is called *dynamic linking*.
executable	A file that has been set up so that UNIX can run it as a program. This is also shorthand for a binary file. You also sometimes see the phrase *binary executable*, which is the same thing!
hidden file	By default, the UNIX file listing command ls only shows files whose first letter isn't a dot (those files that aren't *dot files*). All dot files, therefore, are hidden files and you can safely ignore them without any problems. Later you learn how to view these hidden files.
home directory	This is your private directory and is also where you start out when you log in to the system.
kernel	The underlying core of the UNIX operating system itself, this is akin to the concrete foundation under a modern skyscraper.
preference file	These are what *dot files* (*hidden files*) really are: they contain your individual preferences for many of the UNIX commands you use.
relative filename	Any filename that does not begin with a slash (/) is a filename whose exact meaning depends on where you are in the file system. For example, test might exist in both your

3

home directory and in the root directory: /test is an absolute filename and leaves no question which version is being used, but test could refer to either copy, depending on your current directory.

root directory
The directory at the very top of the file system hierarchy, also known as *slash*.

slash
The root directory.

symbolic link
A file that contains a pointer to another file rather than contents of its own. This can also be a directory that points to another directory rather than having files of its own too, a useful way to have multiple names for a single program or allow multiple people to share a single copy of a file.

Questions

1. Can you think of information you work with daily that's organized in a hierarchical fashion? Is a public library organized hierarchically?

2. Which of the following files are hidden files and directories according to UNIX?

```
.test   hide-me   ,test   .cshrc
../      .dot.     dot     .HiMom
```

3. What programs most likely created the following dot files and dot directories?

```
.cshrc    .rnsoft    .exrc     .print
.tmp334   .excel/    .letter   .vi-expert
```

4. In the following list, circle the items that are absolute filenames:

```
./Personnel/Taylor,D.
/home/taylor/business/California
../..
Recipe:Gazpacho
```

5. Which of the new commands accept arguments and which do not? What differentiates them?

6. Using the list of directories found on all UNIX systems (`/bia`, `/dev`, `/etc`, `/lib`, `/lost+found`, `/mnt`, `/sys`, `/tmp`, `/usr`), use `cd` and `pwd` to double check that they are all present on your own UNIX machine.

Preview of the Next Chapter

The next chapter begins Day 2 of *Teach Yourself UNIX in a Week*. In the next lesson, you learn about the `ls` command that you've been using, including a further discussion of command flags. The command `touch` allows you to create your own files, and `df` and `du` help you learn how much disk space is used and how much is available. You also learn how to use two valuable if somewhat esoteric UNIX commands, `compress` and `crypt`, which help you minimize your disk-space usage and ensure absolute security for special files.

3

Creating Your Own UNIX Space

Listing Files
and Disks

T

4

Welcome to the second day of learning UNIX. This lesson introduces you to the ls command, one of the most commonly used commands in UNIX. The discussion includes over a dozen different command options, or flags. You will also learn how to use the touch command to create files, how to use the du command to see how much disk space you're using, and how to use the df command to see how much disk space is available. Finally, the compress command can help you minimize your disk space usage, particularly on files you're not using very often, and the crypt command can ensure the security of files you want to keep private.

Goals for This Lesson

In this lesson, you'll learn

- ☐ All about the ls command

- ☐ Special ls command flags

- ☐ How to create files with touch

- ☐ How to check disk space usage with du

- ☐ How to check available disk space with df

- ☐ How to shrink big files with compress

- ☐ How to scramble secret files with crypt

Comment: The availability of the crypt command varies by vendors. If you find that you don't have the crypt command available now, you should read through this chapter anyway to learn about this capability in UNIX.

Your first day focused on some of the basic UNIX commands, particularly those for interacting with the system to accomplish common tasks. Today you will expand that knowledge by analyzing characteristics of the system you're using, and you'll learn a raft of commands that let you create your own UNIX workspace. You'll learn more about the UNIX file system and how UNIX interprets command lines. In addition to the cd and pwd commands you learned in the preceding lesson, you'll learn how to use ls to wander in the file system and see what files are kept where.

Unlike the DOS and Macintosh operating systems, information about the UNIX system is often difficult to obtain. In this lesson, you will learn easy ways to ascertain how much disk space you're using, with the du command. You will also learn how to interpret the oft-confusing output of the df command, which enables you to see instantly how much total disk space is available on your UNIX system.

This lesson concludes with a discussion of the compress command, which enables you to shrink the size of any file or set of files, and crypt, which scrambles the contents of files based on a secret key that you supply. When you're ready to unscramble the file, you simply provide the same secret key, and the file is restored to its original state.

Task 4.1: All About the *ls* Command

Step 1. Description

From the examples in the last lesson, you've already figured out that the command used to list files and directories in UNIX is the ls command.

All operating systems have a similar command, a way to see what's in the current location. In DOS, for example, you're doubtless familiar with the DIR command. DOS also has command flags, which are denoted by a leading slash before the specific option. For example, DIR /W produces a directory listing in wide-display format. The DIR command has quite a few other options and capabilities.

Listing the files in a directory is a pretty simple task, so why all the different options? You've already seen some examples, including ls -a, which lists hidden dot files. The answer is that there are many different ways to look at files and directories, as you will learn.

Step 2. Action

1. The best way to learn what ls can do is to go ahead and use it. Turn to your computer, log in to your account, and try each command as it's explained.

2. The most basic use of ls is to list files. The command ls lists all the files and directories in the present working directory (remember, you can check what directory you're in with the pwd command at any time).

```
% ls
Archives        Mail            RUMORS.18Sept   mailing.lists
InfoWorld       News            bin             newels
LISTS           OWL             iecc.list       src
```

Notice that the files are sorted alphabetically from top to bottom, left to right. This is the default, known as *column-first order*, because it sorts downward, then across. You should also note how things are sorted in UNIX. The system differentiates between upper- and lowercase letters, unlike DOS. (The Macintosh remembers whether you use upper- or lowercase letters for naming files, but it can't distinguish between them internally. Try it. Name a file TEST and a second file test the next time you're using a Macintosh.)

Comment: Some of the UNIX versions available for the PC—notably SCO and INTERACTIVE UNIX—have an ls that behaves slightly differently and may list all files in a single column rather than in multiple columns. If your PC does this, you can use the -C flag to ls to force multiple columns.

Step 3. Summary

It's important that you always remember to type UNIX commands in lowercase letters, unless you know that the particular command is actually uppercase; remember that UNIX treats Archives and archives as different filenames. Also, avoid entering your account name in uppercase when you log in. UNIX has some old compatibility features that make using the system much more difficult if you use an all-uppercase login. If you ever accidentally log in with all uppercase, log out and try again in lowercase.

Task 4.2: Having *ls* Tell You More
Step 1. Description

Without options, the ls command offers relatively little information. Questions you might still have about your directory include: How big are the files? Which are files and which are directories? How old are they? What hidden files do you have?

Step 2. Action

1. Start by entering ls -s to indicate file sizes:

```
% ls -s
total 403
    1 Archives      1 Mail      5 RUMORS.18Sept  280 mailing.lists
    1 InfoWorld     1 News      1 bin              2 newels
  108 LISTS         1 OWL       4 iecc.list        1 src
```

2. To ascertain the size of each file or directory listed, you can use the -s flag to ls. The size indicated is the number of kilobytes, rounded upward, for each file. The first line of the listing also indicates the total amount of disk space used, in kilobytes, for the contents of this directory. The summary number does not, however, include the contents of any subdirectories, so it's deceptively small.

Comment: A kilobyte is 1024 bytes of information, a byte being a single character. The preceding paragraph, for example, contains slightly more than 400 characters. UNIX works in units of a *block* of information, which, depending on which version of UNIX you're using, is either 1 kilobyte or 512 bytes. Most UNIX systems now work with a 1 kilobyte block.

3. Here is a further definition of what occurs when you use the -s flag: ls indicates the number of blocks each file or directory occupies. You can then use simple calculations to convert blocks into bytes. For example, the ls command indicates that the LISTS file in my home directory occupies 108 blocks. A quick calculation of block size × number of blocks reveals the actual file size, in bytes, of LISTS.

```
% bc
1024 * 108
110592
quit
%
```

Based on these results of the bc command, you can see that the file is 110,592 bytes in size. You can estimate size by multiplying the number of blocks by 1000. Be aware, however, that in large files, the difference between 1000 and 1024 is significant enough to introduce error into your calculation. As an example, I have a file that's more than 3 megabytes in size (a megabyte is 1024 kilobytes, which is 1024 bytes, so a megabyte is 1024×1024, or 1,048,576 bytes):

```
% ls -s bigfile
3648 bigfile
```

4. The file actually occupies 3,727,360 bytes. If I estimated its size by multiplying the number of blocks by 1000 (which equals 3,648,000 bytes), I'd have underestimated its size by 79,360 bytes. (Remember, blocks × 1000 is an easy estimate!)

Comment: The last example reveals something else about the `ls` command. You can specify individual files or directories you're interested in viewing and avoid having to see all files and directories in your current location.

5. You can specify as many files or directories as you'd like, and separate them by spaces:

```
% ls -s LISTS iecc.list newels
  108 LISTS        4 iecc.list     2 newels
```

In the last lesson, you learned that UNIX identifies each file that begins with a dot (.) as a hidden file. Your home directory is probably littered with dot files, which retain preferences, status information, and other data. To list these hidden files, use the `-a` flag to `ls`:

```
% ls -a
.                .gopherrc       .oldnewsrc      .sig           RUMORS.18Sept
..               .history        .plan           Archives       bin
.Agenda          .info           .pnewsexpert    InfoWorld      iecc.list
.aconfigrc       .letter         .report         LISTS          mailing.lists
.article         .login          .rm-timestamp   Mail           newels
.cshrc           .mailrc         .rnlast         News           src
.elm             .newsrc         .rnsoft         OWL
```

You can see that this directory contains more dot files than regular files and directories. That's not uncommon in a UNIX home directory. However, it's rare to find any dot files other than the standard dot and dot-dot directories (those are in *every* directory in the entire file system) in directories other than your home directory.

6. You used another flag to the `ls` command—the `-F` flag—in the previous lesson. Do you remember what it does?

```
% ls -F
Archives/      Mail/           RUMORS.18Sept  mailing.lists
InfoWorld/     News/           bin/           newels
LISTS          OWL/            iecc.list      src/
```

Adding the `-F` flag to `ls` appends suffixes to certain filenames, so you can more easily ascertain what types of files they are. Three different suffixes can be added, as shown in Table 4.1.

Table 4.1. Filename suffixes appended by `ls -F`.

Suffix	Example	Meaning
/	`Mail/`	`Mail` is a directory.
*	`prog*`	`prog` is an executable program.
@	`bin@`	`bin` is a symbolic link to another file or directory.

7. If you're familiar with the Macintosh and have used either System 7.0 or 7.1, you may recall the new feature that enables the user to create and use an *alias*. An alias is a file that does not contain information, but acts, instead, as a pointer to the actual information files. Aliases can exist either for specific files or for folders.

   UNIX has offered a similar feature for many years, which in UNIX jargon is called a symbolic link. A symbolic link, such as `bin` in Table 4.1, contains the name of another file or directory rather than any contents of its own. If you could peek inside, it might look like `bin = @/usr/bin`; every time someone tries to look at `bin`, the system shows the contents of `/usr/bin` instead.

   You'll learn more about symbolic links and how they help you organize your files a bit later. For now, just remember that if you see an @ after a filename, it's a link to another spot in the file system.

8. A useful flag for `ls` (one that might not be available in your version of UNIX) is the `-m` flag. This flag outputs the files as a comma-separated list. If there are many files, `-m` can be a quick and easy way to see what's available.

```
% ls -m
Archives, InfoWorld, LISTS, Mail, News, OWL, RUMORS.18Sept,
bin, iecc.list, mailing.lists, newels, src
```

Step 3. Summary

Sometime you might want to list each of your files on a separate line, perhaps for a printout you want to annotate. You've seen that the -C flag forces recalcitrant versions of ls to output in multiple columns. Unfortunately, the opposite behavior isn't obtained using a lowercase c. (UNIX should be so consistent!) Instead, use the -1 flag to indicate that you want one column of output. Try it.

Task 4.3: Combining Flags
Step 1. Description

The different flags you've learned so far are summarized in Table 4.2.

Table 4.2. Some useful flags to ls.

Flag	Meaning
-a	List all files, including any dot files.
-F	Indicate file types; / = directory, * = executable.
-m	Show files as a comma-separated list.
-s	Show size of files, in blocks (typically 1 block = 1024 bytes).
-C	Force multiple-column output on listings.
-1	Force single-column output on listings.

What if you want a list, generated with the -F conventions, that simultaneously shows you all files and indicates their types?

Step 2. Action

1. Combining flags in UNIX is easy. All you have to do is run them together in a sequence of characters, and prefix the whole thing with a dash:

```
% ls -aF
./          .gopherrc   .oldnewsrc   .sig        RUMORS.18Sept
../         .history*   .plan        Archives/   bin/
```

```
.Agenda        .info         .pnewsexpert    InfoWorld/    iecc.list
.aconfigrc     .letter       .report         LISTS         mailing.lists
.article       .login        .rm-timestamp   Mail/         newels
.cshrc         .mailrc       .rnlast         News/         src/
.elm/          .newsrc       .rnsoft         OWL/
```

2. Sometimes it's more convenient to keep all the flags separate. This is fine, as long as each flag is prefixed by its own dash:

```
% ls -s -F
total 403
    1 Archives/      1 Mail/        5 RUMORS.18Sept   280 mailing.lists
    1 InfoWorld/     1 News/        1 bin/              2 newels
  108 LISTS          1 OWL/         4 iecc.list         1 src/
```

3. Try some of these combinations on your own computer. Also try to list a flag more than once (for example, ls -sss -s), or list flags in different orders.

Step 3. Summary

Very few UNIX commands care about the order in which flags are listed. Because it's the presence or absence of a flag that's important, having listed a flag more than once doesn't make any difference.

Task 4.4: Listing Directories Without Changing Location
Step 1. Description

Every time I try to do any research in the library, I find myself spending hours and hours there, but it seems to me that I do less research than I think I should. That's because most of my time is spent on the tasks between the specifics of my research: finding the location of the next book and finding the book itself.

If ls constrained you to only listing the directory that you were in, it would hobble you in a similar way. Using only ls would slow you down dramatically and force you to use cd to move around each time.

Instead, just as you can specify certain files by using ls, you can specify certain directories you're interested in viewing.

Step 2. Action

1. Try this yourself. List /usr on your system:

```
% ls -F /usr
5bin/           diag/           lddrv/          share/          ucbinclude@
5include/       dict/           lib/            source/         ucblib@
5lib/           etc/            local/          spool@          xpg2bin/
acc/            export/         lost+found/     src@            xpg2include/
acctlog*        games/          man@            stand@          xpg2lib/
adm@            hack/           mdec@           sys@
bin/            hosts/          old/            system/
boot@           include/        pub@            tmp@
demo/           kvm/            sccs/           ucb/
```

You probably have different files and directories listed in your own /usr directory. Remember, @ files are symbolic links in the listing, too.

2. You can also specify more than one directory:

```
% ls /usr/local /home/taylor
/home/taylor:
Global.Software    Mail/              Src/                    history.usenet.Z
Interactive.Unix   News/              bin/
/usr/local/:
T/                 emacs/          ftp/            lists/          motd~
admin/             emacs-18.59/    gnubin/         lost+found/     netcom/
bin/               etc/            include/        man/            policy/
cat/               faq/            info/           menu/           src/
doc/               forms/          lib/            motd            tmp/
```

In this example, the ls command also sorted the directories before listing them. I specified that I wanted to see /usr/local and then /home/taylor, but it presented the directories in opposite order.

Comment: I've never been able to figure out how ls sorts directories when you ask for more than one to be listed—it's not an alphabetical listing. Consider it a mystery. Remember that if you must have the output in a specific order, you can use the ls command twice in a row.

3. Here's where the dot-dot shorthand can come in handy. Try it yourself:

```
% ls -m ..
armstrong, bruce, cedric, christine, david, green,
guest, higgins, james, kane, laura, mac, mark,
patrickb, rank, shalini, shane, taylor, vicki
```

If you were down one branch of the file system and wanted to look at some files down another branch, you could easily find yourself by using the commands `ls ../Indiana/Personnel` or `ls -s ../../source`.

4. There's a problem here, however. You've seen that you can specify filenames to look at those files, and directory names to look at the contents of those directories, but what if you're interested in the directory itself, not in its contents? Here I might want to list just two directories—not the contents, just the files themselves.

```
% ls -F
Archives/       Mail/           RUMORS.18Sept  mailing.lists
InfoWorld/      News/           bin/           newlists
LISTS           OWL/            iecc.list      src/
% ls -s LISTS Mail newlists
  108 LISTS             2 newlists
Mail:
total 705
  8 cennamo    27 ean_houts    4 kcs      21 mark     7 sartin
 28 dan_sommer  2 gordon_haight 34 lehman  5 raf      3 shelf
 14 decc       48 harrism      64 mac      7 rock    20 steve
  3 druby      14 james        92 mailbox  5 rustle  18 tai
```

5. The problem is that `ls` doesn't know that you want to look at `Mail` unless you tell it *not* to look inside the directories specified. The command flag needed is `-d`, which forces `ls` to list directories rather than their contents. The same `ls` command, but with the `-d` flag, has dramatically different output:

```
% ls -ds LISTS Mail newlists
  108 LISTS           1 Mail/       2 newlists
```

Try some of these flags on your own system, and watch how they work together.

Step 3. Summary

To list a file or directory, you can specify it to ls. Directories, however, reveal their contents, unless you also include the -d flag.

Special *ls* Command Flags

It should be becoming clear to you that UNIX is the ultimate toolbox. Even some of the simplest commands have dozens of different options. On one system I use, ls has more than 20 different flags.

Task 4.5: Changing the Sort Order in *ls*
Step 1. Description

What if you wanted to look at files, but wanted them to show up in a directory sorting order different from the default (that is, column-first) order? How could you change the sort order in ls?

Step 2. Action

1. The -x flag sorts across, listing the output in columns, or row-first order (entries are sorted across, then down):

```
% ls -a
.                   .elm            .plan           Global.Software
..                  .forward        .pnewsexpert    Interactive.Unix
.Pnews.header       .ircmotd        .rnlast         Mail
.accinfo            .login          .rnlock         News
.article            .logout         .rnsoft         Src
.cshrc              .newsrc         .sig            bin
.delgroups          .oldnewsrc      .tin            history.usenet.Z
% ls -x -a
.                   ..              .Pnews.header   .accinfo
.article            .cshrc          .delgroups      .elm
.forward            .ircmotd        .login          .logout
.newsrc             .oldnewsrc      .plan           .pnewsexpert
.rnlast             .rnlock         .rnsoft         .sig
.tin                Global.Software Interactive.Unix Mail
News                Src             bin             history.usenet.Z
```

2. There are even more ways to sort files in `ls`. If you want to sort by most-recently-accessed to least-recently-accessed, you use the `-t` flag:

```
% ls -a -t
./                   ../              .rnlock          .cshrc
.newsrc              News/            .rnlast          .sig
.oldnewsrc           .tin/            .rnsoft          .plan
.article             .ircmotd         Interactive.Unix Mail/
.elm/                .delgroups       .accinfo*        .Pnews.header*
.forward             .login           Src/             .pnewsexpert
history.usenet.Z     bin/             Global.Software  .logout
```

From this output, you can see that the most-recently-accessed files are `.newsrc` and `.oldnewsrc`, and that it's been quite a while since `.logout` was touched. Try using the `-t` flag on your system to see which files you've been accessing and which you haven't.

3. So far you know three different approaches to sorting files within the `ls` command: column-first order, row-first order, and most-recently-accessed-first order. But there are more options in `ls` than just these three; the `-r` flag *reverses* any sorting order.

```
% ls
Global.Software    Mail/      Src/        history.usenet.Z
Interactive.Unix   News/      bin/
% ls -r
history.usenet.Z   Src/       Mail/       Global.Software
bin/               News/      Interactive.Unix
```

4. Things may become confusing when you combine some of these flags. Try to list the contents of the directory that is one above the current directory, sorted so the most-recently-accessed file is last in the list. At the same time, indicate which items are directories and the size of each file.

```
% ls -r -t -F -s ..
total 150
    2 bruce/     2 rank/        2 kane/      14 higgins/
    2 laura/     2 christine/   2 shane/      6 mac/
    2 cedric     2 peggy/       4 patrickb/  10 mark/
    2 james@     4 taylor/      4 green/      6 armstrong/
    2 vicki/     2 guest/       6 shalini/    4 david/
```

Step 3. Summary

A better, easier way to type the previous command would be to bundle flags into the single argument, `ls -rtFs ..`, which would work just as well and make you look like an expert!

Task 4.6: Listing Directory Trees Recursively in *ls*
Step 1. Description

In case things aren't yet complicated enough with `ls`, two more important, valuable flags are available. One is the `-R` flag, which causes `ls` to list recursively directories below the current or specified directory. If you think of listing files as a numbered set of steps, then recursion is simply adding a step—the rule *if this file is a directory, list it too*—to the list.

Step 2. Action

1. When I use the `-R` flag, here's what I see:

```
% ls -R
Global.Software    Mail/      Src/       history.usenet.Z
Interactive.Unix   News/      bin/
Mail:
Folders/   Netnews/
Mail/Folders:
mail.sent  mailbox    steinman    tucker
Mail/Netnews:
postings
News:
uptodate   volts
Src:
sum-up.c
bin:
Pnews*    punt*     submit*
```

Try it yourself.

Notice that `ls` lists the current directory, then alphabetically lists the contents of all subdirectories. Notice also that the `Mail` directory has two directories within it and that those are also listed here.

Step 3. Summary

Viewing all files and directories below a certain point in the file system can be a valuable way to look for files (though you'll soon learn better tools for finding files). If you aren't careful, though, you may have hundreds or thousands of lines of information streaming across your screen. Do not enter a command like ls -R / unless you have time to sit and watch information fly past.

If you try to list the contents of a directory when you don't have permission to access the information, ls warns you with an error message:

```
% ls ../marv
../marv unreadable
```

Now ask for a recursive listing, with indications of file type and size, of the directory /etc, and see what's there. The listing will include many files and subdirectories, but they should be easy to wade through due to all the notations ls uses to indicate files and directories.

Task 4.7: Long Listing Format in ls
Step 1. Description

You've seen how to estimate the size of a file by using the -s flag to find the number of blocks it occupies. To find the exact size of a file in bytes, you need to use the -l flag. (Use a lowercase letter *L*. The numeral 1 produces single-column output, as you've already learned).

Step 2. Action

1. The first long listing shows information for the LISTS file.

   ```
   % ls -l LISTS
   -rw-------  1 taylor     106020 Oct  8 15:17 LISTS
   ```

   The output is explained in Figure 4.1.

Step 3. Summary

For each file and directory in the UNIX file system, the owner, size, name, number of other files pointing to it (links), and access permissions are recorded. The creation, modification, and access times and dates are also recorded for each file. The modification time is the default time used for the -t sorting option and listed by the ls long format.

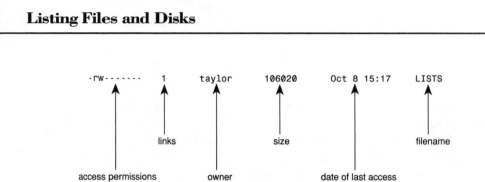

Figure 4.1. *The meaning of the* -l *output for a file.*

Interpreting permissions strings is a complex issue, because UNIX has a sophisticated security model for individual files. Security revolves around three different types of user: the *owner* of the file, the *group* that the file is a part of, and *everyone else*.

The first character of the permissions string, identified in Figure 4.1 as *access permissions*, indicates the kind of file. The two most common values are d for directories and - for regular files. Be aware that there are many other file types that you'll rarely, if ever, see.

The following nine characters in the permissions string indicate what type of access is allowed for different users. From left to right, these characters show what access is allowed for the *owner* of the file, the *group* that owns the file, and *everyone else*.

Figure 4.2. shows how to break down the permissions string for the LISTS file into individual components.

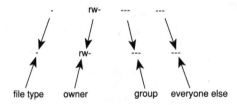

Figure 4.2. *Reading access permissions for* LISTS.

Each permissions string is identically composed of three components—permission for reading, writing, and execution—as shown in Figure 4.3.

Armed with this information—specifically, knowing that a - character means that the specific permission is denied—you can see that ls shows that the owner of the file, taylor, as illustrated in Figure 4.1, has read and write permission. Nobody else either in taylor's group or in any other group has permission to view, edit, or run the file.

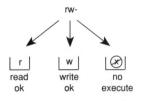

Figure 4.3. *Elements of a permissions string.*

Earlier you learned that just about everything in UNIX ends up as a file in the file system, whether it's an application, a device driver, or a directory. The system keeps track of whether a file is executable because that's one way it knows whether LISTS is the name of a file or the name of an application.

Task 4.8: Long Listing Format for Directories in *ls*
Step 1. Description

The long form of a directory listing is almost identical to a file listing, but the permissions string is interpreted in a very different manner.

Step 2. Action

1. Here is an example of a long directory listing:

```
% ls -l -d Example
drwxr-x---  2 taylor      1024 Sep 30 10:50 Example/
```

Remember that you must have *both* read and execute permission for a directory. If you have either read or execute permission but not both, the directory will not be usable (as though you had neither permission). Write permission, of course, enables the user to alter the contents of the directory or add new files to the directory.

2. The Example directory breaks down for interpretation as shown in Figure 4.4.

Comment: I've never understood the nuances of a directory with read but not execute permission, or vice versa, and explanations from other people have never proven to be correct. It's okay, though, because I've never seen a directory on a UNIX system that was anything other than ---, r-x, or rwx.

83

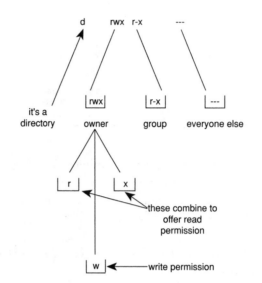

Figure 4.4. *Elements of directory permissions.*

3. Now try using the -1 flag yourself. Move to your home directory, and enter
ls -1:

```
% ls -l
total 403
drwx------   2 taylor        512 Sep 30 10:38 Archives/
drwx------   3 taylor        512 Oct  1 08:23 InfoWorld/
-rw-------   1 taylor     106020 Oct  8 15:17 LISTS
drwx------   2 taylor       1024 Sep 30 10:50 Mail/
drwx------   2 taylor        512 Oct  6 09:36 News/
drwx------   2 taylor        512 Sep 30 10:51 OWL/
-rw-------   1 taylor       4643 Sep 20 10:49 RUMORS.18Sept
drwx------   2 taylor        512 Oct  1 09:53 bin/
-rw-------   1 taylor       3843 Oct  6 18:02 iecc.list
-rw-rw----   1 taylor     280232 Oct  6 09:57 mailing.lists
-rw-rw----   1 taylor       1031 Oct  7 15:44 newlists
drwx------   2 taylor        512 Sep 14 22:14 src/
```

The size of a directory is usually in increments of 512 bytes. The second field, the "link," is an interesting and little-known value when a directory is being listed. Instead of counting up the number of other files that point to the file, (that is, the number of files that have a link to the current file) the second field instead indicates the number of directories that are contained in that specific directory. Remember, all directories have dot and dot-dot, so the minimum value is always 2.

4. Consider the following example:

```
% ls -Fa
./              .gopherrc      .oldnewsrc     .sig            OWL/
../             .history*      .plan          Archives/       RUMORS.18Sept
.Agenda         .info          .pnewsexpert   Cancelled.mail  bin/
.aconfigrc      .letter        .report        InfoWorld/      iecc.list
.article        .login         .rm-timestamp  LISTS           mailing.lists
.cshrc          .mailrc        .rnlast        Mail/           newlists
.elm/           .newsrc        .rnsoft        News/           src/
% ls -ld .
drwx------  10 taylor        1024 Oct 10 16:00 ./
```

5. Try entering ls -ld . and see if it correctly identifies the number of directories in your home directory. Move to other directories and see if the listing agrees with your own count of directories.

Step 3. Summary

The output from the ls -l command is unquestionably complex and packed with information. Interpretation of permissions strings is an important part of understanding and being able to use UNIX, and more explanation is offered in subsequent lessons.

Table 4.3 summarizes the many different command flags for ls that you have learned in this lesson.

Table 4.3. Summary of command flags for ls.

Flag	Meaning
-1	Force single-column output on listings.
-a	List all files, including any dot files.
-C	Force multiple-column output on listings.
-d	List directories rather than their contents.

continues

Table 4.3. continued

Flag	Meaning
-F	Indicate file types; / = directory, * = executable.
-l	Generate a long listing of files and directories.
-m	Show files as a comma-separated list.
-r	Reverse the order of any file sorting.
-R	Recursively show directories and their contents.
-s	Show size of files, in blocks (typically 1 block = 1024 bytes).
-t	Sort output in most-recently-modified order.
-x	Sort output in row-first order.

Without doubt, ls is one of the most powerful, and therefore also one of the most confusing, commands in UNIX. The best way for you to learn how all the flags work together is to experiment with different combinations.

Task 4.9: Creating Files with the *touch* Command
Step 1. Description

At this point, you have a variety of different UNIX tools that help you move through the file system and learn about specific files. The touch command is the first command that helps you create new files on the system, independent of any program other than the shell itself. This can prove very helpful for organizing a new collection of files, for example.

The main reason that touch is used in UNIX is to force the last-modified time of a file to be updated, as the following example demonstrates.

```
% ls -l iecc.list
-rw------- 1 taylor        3843 Oct  6 18:02 iecc.list
% touch iecc.list
% ls -l iecc.list
-rw------- 1 taylor        3843 Oct 10 16:22 iecc.list
```

Because the touch command changes modification times of files, anything that sorts files based on modification time will, of course, alter when the file is altered by touch.

Step 2. Action

1. Consider the following output:

```
% ls -t
mailing.lists    LISTS         News/         OWL/          src/
Cancelled.mail   newlists      bin/          Mail/
RUMORS.18Sept    iecc.list     InfoWorld/    Archives/
% touch iecc.list
% ls -t
iecc.list        RUMORS.18Sept News/         OWL/          src/
mailing.lists    LISTS         bin/          Mail/
Cancelled.mail   newlists      InfoWorld/    Archives/
```

You will probably not use touch for this purpose very often.

2. If you try to use the touch command on a file that doesn't exist, the program creates the file:

```
% ls
Archives/        LISTS         OWL/          iecc.list     src/
Cancelled.mail   Mail/         RUMORS.18Sept mailing.lists
InfoWorld/       News/         bin/          newlists
% touch new.file
% ls
Archives/        LISTS         OWL/          iecc.list     newlists
Cancelled.mail   Mail/         RUMORS.18Sept mailing:lists src/
InfoWorld/       News/         bin/          new.file
% ls -l new.file
-rw-rw---- 1 taylor           0 Oct 10 16:28 new.file
```

The new file has zero bytes, as can be seen by the ls -l output listing. Notice that by default the files are created with read and write permission for the user and anyone in the user's group. You will soon learn in another lesson how to determine, by using the umask command, your own default permission for files.

Step 3. Summary

You won't need touch very often, but it's valuable to know.

Task 4.10: Check Disk Space Usage with *du*
Step 1. Description

One advantage the DOS and Macintosh systems have over UNIX is that they make it easy to find out how much disk space you're using and how much remains available.

On a Macintosh, viewing folders by size shows disk space used, and the top-right corner of any Finder window shows available space. In DOS it's even easier; both items are listed at the end of the output from a DIR command:

```
C> DIR .BAT
 Volume in drive C is MS-DOS_5
 Volume Serial Number is 197A-A8D7
 Directory of C:\
AUTOEXEC BAT       142 02-28-93    8:19p
CSH      BAT        36 12-22-92    3:01p
       2 file(s)            178 bytes
                    5120000 bytes free
```

In this DOS example, you can see that the files listed take up 178 bytes, and that there are 5,120,000 bytes (about 5 megabytes, or 5M) available on the hard drive.

Like a close-mouthed police informant, UNIX never volunteers any information, so you need to learn two new commands. The du, *disk usage*, command is used to find out how much disk space is used; the df, *disk free*, command is used to find out how much space is available.

Step 2. Action

1. The du command lists the size, in kilobytes, of all directories at or below the current point in the file system.

```
% du
11         ./OWL
38         ./.elm
20         ./Archives
14         ./InfoWorld/PIMS
28         ./InfoWorld
710        ./Mail
191        ./News
25         ./bin
35         ./src
1627       .
```

Notice that du went two levels deep to find the InfoWorld/PIMS subdirectory, adding its size to the size indicated for the InfoWorld directory. At the very end, it lists 1627 kilobytes as the size of the dot directory—the current directory. As you know, 1024 kilobytes is a megabyte. Through division, you'll find that the `InfoWorld` directory is taking up 1.5M of disk space.

2. If you are interested in only the grand total, you can use the `-s` flag to output just a *summary* of the information.

```
% du -s
1627    .
```

Of course, you can look anywhere on the file system, but the more subdirectories there are, the longer it takes.

3. There are possible `du` error messages:

```
% du -s /etc
/etc/shadow: Permission denied
4417    /etc
```

In this example, one of the directories within the `/etc` directory has a permissions set denying access:

```
% ls -ld /etc/shadow
drwx------  2 root         512 Oct 10 16:34 /etc/shadow/
```

The `du` command summarizes disk usage only for the files it can read, so regardless of the size of the `shadow` directory, I'd still have the 4417 kilobytes size indicated.

4. Although by default `du` lists only the sizes of directories, it also computes the size of all files. If you're interested in that information, you can, by adding the `-a` flag, have the program list it for all files.

```
% cd InfoWorld
% du -a
9       ./PIM.review.Z
5       ./Expert.opinion.Z
4       ./PIMS/proposal.txt.Z
1       ./PIMS/task1.txt.Z
2       ./PIMS/task2.txt.Z
2       ./PIMS/task3.txt.Z
2       ./PIMS/task4.txt.Z
```

```
2        ./PIMS/task5.txt.Z
2        ./PIMS/task6.txt.Z
1        ./PIMS/contact.info.Z
14       ./PIMS
28       .
```

The problems of the -a flag for du are similar to those for the -R flag for ls. There may be more files in a directory than you care to view.

5. The -a flag for listing all files overrides the -s flag for summarizing, but without telling you it's doing so. A preferable way would be for the program to note that the two flags are incompatible, as many UNIX programs indicate, but that isn't how du works.

```
% du -s -a
9        ./PIM.review.Z
5        ./Expert.opinion.Z
4        ./PIMS/proposal.txt.Z
1        ./PIMS/task1.txt.Z
2        ./PIMS/task2.txt.Z
2        ./PIMS/task3.txt.Z
2        ./PIMS/task4.txt.Z
2        ./PIMS/task5.txt.Z
2        ./PIMS/task6.txt.Z
1        ./PIMS/contact.info.Z
28       .
```

6. The du command is an exception to the rule that multiple flags can be more succinctly stated as a single multiletter flag. With ls, you'll recall, -a -F -l could be more easily typed as -aFl. The command du fails to allow similar shorthand.

Comment: UNIX is nothing if not varied. Some systems will accept du -as, and others will *not* accept du -a -s. Try yours and see what does and doesn't work.

```
% du -sa
-sa: No such file or directory
```

> **Don't Skip This:** It isn't a problem that du does not allow multiletter flags, however, because you do not use the -s and -a flags to du at the same time.

Task 4.11: Check Available Disk Space with *df*

Step 1. Description

Figuring out how much disk space is available on the overall UNIX system is difficult for everyone except experts. The df command is used for this task, but it doesn't summarize its results—the user must add the column of numbers.

Step 2. Action

1. This is the system's response to the df command:

```
% df
Filesystem           kbytes      used    avail capacity  Mounted
/dev/zd0a             17259     14514     1019      93%   /
/dev/zd8d            185379    143995    22846      86%   /userf
/dev/zd7d            185379     12984   153857       8%   /tmp
/dev/zd3f            385689    307148    39971      88%   /users
/dev/zd3g            367635    232468    98403      70%   /userc
/dev/zd2f            385689    306189    40931      88%   /usere
/dev/zd2g            367635    207234   123637      63%   /userb
/dev/zd1g            301823    223027    48613      82%   /usera
/dev/zd5c            371507    314532    19824      94%   /usr
/dev/zd0h            236820    159641    53497      75%   /usr/src
/dev/zd0g            254987     36844   192644      16%   /var
```

You end up with lots of information, but it's not easily added quickly to find the total space available. Nonetheless, the output offers quite a bit of information.

2. Because I know that my home directory is on the disk /users, I can simply look for that directory in the rightmost column to find out that I'm using the hard disk /dev/zd3f. I can see that there are 385,689 kilobytes on the disk, and 88 percent of the disk is used, which means that 307,148 kilobytes are used and 39,971 kilobytes, or only about 38M, are unused.

3. Some UNIX systems have relatively few separate computer disks hooked up, making the df output more readable. The df output is explained in Figure 4.5.

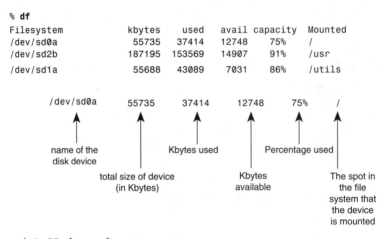

```
% df
Filesystem          kbytes      used    avail capacity  Mounted
/dev/sd0a            55735     37414    12748     75%    /
/dev/sd2b           187195    153569    14907     91%    /usr
/dev/sd1a            55688     43089     7031     86%    /utils
```

Figure 4.5. *Understanding df output.*

You can easily add the columns to find that the system has a total of about 300M of disk space (55,735 + 187,195 + 55,688), of which 230M are used. The remaining space is therefore 33M, or 16 percent of the total disk size.

Step 3. Summary

Try using the du and df commands on your system to figure out how much disk space is available on both the overall system and the disk you're using for your home directory. Then use du to identify how much space your files and directories are occupying.

Task 4.12: Shrink Big Files with the *compress* Program
Step 1. Description

Now that you can figure out how much space you're using with the files in your directory, you're ready to learn how to save space without removing any files. UNIX has a built-in program—the compress program—that offers this capability.

Step 2. Action

1. In this simple example, the compress program is given a list of filenames and then compresses each of the files, renaming them with a .Z suffix, which indicates that they are compressed.

```
% ls -l LISTS
-rw------- 1 taylor      106020 Oct 10 13:47 LISTS
% compress LISTS
% ls -l LISTS.Z
-rw------- 1 taylor       44103 Oct 10 13:47 LISTS.Z
```

Compressing the LISTS file has reduced its size from 106 kilobytes to a little more than 44 kilobytes (a savings of almost 60 percent in disk space). If you expect to have large files on your system that you won't access very often, using the compress program can save lots of disk space.

2. Using the compress program on bigger files can show even greater savings:

```
% ls -l huge.file
-rwxrwxrwx 1 root     3727360 Sep 27 14:03 huge.file
% compress huge.file
% ls -l huge.file.Z
-rwxrwxrwx 1 taylor   2121950 Sep 27 14:03 huge.file.Z
```

In this example, it took a powerful Sun computer with no other users exactly 20 seconds to compress huge.file. This single command was able to free over 1.5M of disk space. If you're using a PC to run UNIX, or if you are on a system with many users (which you can easily ascertain by using the w command), it might take a significant amount of time to compress files.

3. To reverse the operation, use the companion command uncompress, and specify either the current name of the file (that is, with the .Z suffix) or the name of the file before it was compressed (that is, without the .Z suffix).

Comment: Why would you compress files? You would do so to save disk space. Before you use any of the compressed files, though, you must uncompress them, so the compress utility is best used with large files you won't need for a while.

```
% uncompress LISTS
% ls -l LISTS
-rw------- 1 taylor       106020 Oct 10 13:47 LISTS
```

4. For information on how well the `compress` program shrunk your files, you
   can add a `-v` flag to the program for verbose output:

```
% compress -v huge.file
huge.file: Compression: 43.15% -- replaced with huge.file.Z
```

Step 3. Summary

Try using the `compress` program on some of the files in your directory, being careful
not to compress any files (particularly preference or dot files) that might be required
to run programs.

Task 4.13: Scramble Secret Files with *crypt*
Step 1. Description

For hundreds of years, people have found it valuable to create secret languages, codes,
and ciphers that enable them to communicate with those who know the code, leaving
others baffled and unable to glean a single snippet of information from the message.
Ian Flemings's James Bond would find secret messages hidden in the oddest places,
and his knowledge of codes enabled him to read them. Some spies use a cipher method
based on a certain book's page number, line number, and word number. Without
knowing to which book the cipher refers, you'll never be able to figure out the message.

Around World War II, this ciphering technique became more sophisticated. Machines were used to translate information into seemingly meaningless codes. The
German Army used enciphered text to communicate with spies throughout Europe,
but it didn't know that England had broken its code through the brilliant work of Alan
Turing and his Enigma Machine.

After the war, the United States Army and the National Security Agency (NSA)
recognized the need for computer systems to be able to communicate in a secure
fashion across lines that might not be secure. The Army and NSA, in cooperation with
various computer scientists, developed the Defense Encryption Standard (DES).

Almost from the beginning, UNIX included a version of the DES encryption
software. Today, all versions of UNIX include pieces of the UNIX DES-based `crypt`
software. Not all exported versions of UNIX have the actual `crypt` program, because
it is an export-restricted software item, but every UNIX system has at least the ability
to encrypt your password so others can't find out how to log on to your account.

The UNIX crypt program can make your files more secure than if you put your files on a floppy disk and locked the disk in your desk. The crypt program essentially enables the UNIX user to use the DES encryption machine to secure files.

Step 2. Action

1. crypt is your first example of what I call a *pure UNIX filter*, or a program that has no knowledge of files or filenames, but instead reads text from input, translates it, and lists the transformed text on the screen.

```
% crypt
Enter key:
this is a test
BQaJN    {J3;~>
```

A pure filter translates each line of text as it's entered into the program. In the preceding example, you can see that I entered the line this is a test and the program encrypted the information, printing what seems to be gibberish, BQaJN   {J3;~>. Before I typed any information, however, crypt prompted me for a key—a word that is my secret password for the file in question. Be sure to choose a password you can remember without writing it down; like written account passwords, written keys are potential security problems.

2. Learning how to use the crypt command enables you to encipher a file so that it remains secure. The crypt command translates your text into meaningless words, which can be restored to readable text with the key that only you hold.

Don't Skip This: You need to learn some new UNIX command line notation: the special character < means that the program should take input from the file named immediately afterwards, and > indicates that the output of the program should be saved to the file specified.

```
% translator < inputfile > outputfile
```

This command would cause UNIX to feed each line of the file inputfile to the translator program, saving each line of output from the program in a new file called outputfile. You can also use either of the file redirection commands, as they're called, without the other. The command

95

> `translator < inputfile` would list the translated lines on the screen, and the command `translator > outputfile` would enable you to enter information into the computer and automatically save all output in the file `outputfile`.

3. In the following example, `crypt < in > out` would encrypt the information in the input file `in` and save the new, encrypted information into the new file `out`.

```
% crypt < in > out
```

4. To encrypt a file, you use a notation similar to that in the preceding example, and press the encryption key when the `crypt` program prompts for it:

```
% crypt < LISTS > LISTS.locked
Enter key:
%
```

This command would encrypt the file `LISTS`, saving the encrypted text in the file `LISTS.locked`. Deleting the original file would ensure that no one else on the system could read the original, yet I could restore the file at any time using `crypt` and my secret key. It would look like the output of the `crypt` program. My line `this is a test` would display on the screen of other users as `BQaJN    {J3;~>`.

5. To decrypt, or restore, the file, use the following command:

```
% crypt < LISTS.locked > LISTS
Enter key:
%
```

If you entered the wrong encryption key, a key different from the one you used to encrypt the file, you would produce a new, unreadable, file.

Don't Skip This: It is very important that you use this command with caution before entrusting vital information. If you forget your key password, there's no way to restore the file. It's gone.

With the correct key, however, the file `LISTS` is restored to its original form and content.

Step 3. Summary

You can experiment with the crypt command yourself. You'll learn more about how to use crypt in a few lessons. Meanwhile, be aware that if you try to view the contents of an encrypted file, you'll find it looks like a lot of gibberish.

Lesson Summary

Most of this lesson was spent learning about the powerful and complex ls command and its many ways of listing files and directories. You also learned how to combine command flags to reduce typing. You learned how to use the touch command to create new files and update the modification time on older files, if needed. The lesson continued with a discussion of how to ascertain the amount of disk space you're using and how much space is left, using the du and df commands, respectively. Finally, you learned how the compress command can keep you from running out of space by ensuring that infrequently used files are stored in the minimum space needed, and how crypt can help you ensure the security of special private files.

Workshop
Key Terms

access permission   The set of accesses (read, write, and execute) allowed for each of the three classes of users (owner, group, and everyone else) for each file or directory on the system.

block   At its most fundamental, a block is like a sheet of information in the virtual notebook that represents the disk: A disk is typically composed of many tens, or hundreds, of thousands of blocks of information, each 512 bytes in size. You might also read the explanation of *i-node* in the glossary to learn more about how disks are structured in UNIX.

column-first order   When you have a list of items that are listed in columns and span multiple lines, column-first order is a sorting strategy in which items are sorted so that the items are in alphabetical order down the first column, then resume at the top of the second column, going down, then the third column, and so on. The alternate strategy is *row-first order.*

row-first order   In contrast to *column-first order*, this is when items are sorted across so that the first item of each column is in alphabetical order, then the second line contains the next set of items, and so on.

Questions

1. Try using the du command on different directories to see how much disk space each requires. If you encounter errors with file permissions, use ls -ld to list the permissions of the directory in question.

2. Why would you want all the different types of sorting alternatives available with ls? Can you think of situations in which each would be useful?

3. Use a combination of the ls -t and touch commands to create a few new files. Then update their modification times so that in a most-recently-modified listing of files, the first file you created shows up ahead of the second file you created.

4. Try using the du -s .. command from your home directory. Before you try it, however, what do you think will happen?

5. Use df and bc or dc to figure out the amounts of disk space used and available on your system.

6. Use the compress command to shrink a file in /tmp or your home directory. Use the -v flag to learn how much the file was compressed, and then restore the file to its original condition.

Preview of the Next Chapter

The next chapter is a bit easier. It offers further explanation of the various information given by the ls command and a discussion of file ownership, including an explanation of how to change the owner and group of any file or directory. You will learn about the chmod command, which can change the specific set of permissions associated with any file or directory, and the umask command, which can control the modes that new files are given upon creation.

Ownership and Permissions

This chapter, the middle of your second day of learning UNIX, focuses on teaching the basics of UNIX file permissions. Subjects in this area include setting and modifying file permissions with chmod, analyzing file permissions as shown by the ls -l command, and setting up default file permissions with the umask command. Permission is only half the puzzle, however, and you will also learn about file ownership and group ownership, and how to change either for any file or directory.

Goals for This Lesson

In this lesson, you will learn how to

☐ Understand file permissions settings

☐ Understand directory permissions settings

☐ Modify file and directory permissions with chmod

☐ Set new file permissions with chmod

☐ Establish default file and directory permissions with the umask command

☐ Identify owner and group for any file or directory

☐ Change the owner of a file or directory

☐ Change the group of a file or directory

The preceding lesson contained the first tutorial dealing with the permissions of a file or directory using the -l option with ls. If you haven't read that lesson recently, it would help to review the material. In this lesson, you will learn about another option to ls that tells UNIX to show the group and owner of files or directories. Four more commands are introduced and discussed in detail: chmod for changing the permissions of a file, umask for defining default permissions, chown for changing ownership, and chgrp for changing the group of a file or directory.

As you have seen in examples throughout the book, UNIX treats all directories as files; they have their own size (independent of the contents), their own permissions strings, and more. As a result, unless it's an important difference, from here on I talk about files with the intention of referring to files and directories both. Logic will confirm whether commands can apply to both, or to files only, or to directories only. (For example, you can't edit a directory and you can't store files inside other files.)

Task 5.1: Understand File Permissions Settings

Step 1. Description

In the last lesson you learned a bit about how to interpret the information ls offers on file permissions when ls is used with the -l flag. Consider the following example.

```
% ls -l
total 403
drwx------   2 taylor         512 Sep 30 10:38 Archives/
drwx------   3 taylor         512 Oct  1 08:23 InfoWorld/
-rw-------   1 taylor      106020 Oct 10 13:47 LISTS
drwx------   2 taylor        1024 Sep 30 10:50 Mail/
drwx------   2 taylor         512 Oct  6 09:36 News/
drwx------   2 taylor         512 Sep 30 10:51 OWL/
-rw-------   1 taylor        4643 Oct 10 14:01 RUMORS.18Sept
drwx------   2 taylor         512 Oct 10 19:09 bin/
-rw-------   1 taylor        3843 Oct 10 16:22 iecc.list
-rw-rw-r--   1 taylor      280232 Oct 10 16:22 mailing.lists
-rw-rw----   1 taylor        1031 Oct  7 15:44 newlists
drwx------   2 taylor         512 Oct 10 19:09 src/
```

The first item of information on each line is what is key here. You learned in the last chapter that the first item is called the *permissions string* or, more succinctly, *permissions*. It also is sometimes referred to as the *mode* or *permissions mode* of the file, a mnemonic that can be valuable for remembering how to change permissions.

The permissions can be broken into four parts: type, owner, group, and other permissions. The first character indicates the file type: d is a directory and - is a regular file. There are a number of other types of files in UNIX, each indicated by the first letter of its permissions string, as summarized in Table 5.1. You can safely ignore, however, any file that isn't either a regular file or directory.

Table 5.1. The ls file type indicators.

Letter	Indicated File Type
d	directory
b	block-type special file
c	character-type special file
l	symbolic link
p	pipe
s	socket
-	regular file

The next nine letters in the permissions string are broken into three groups of three each—representing the owner, group, and everyone else—as shown in Figure 5.1.

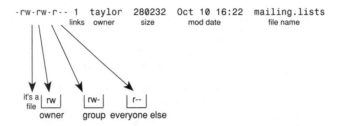

Figure 5.1. *Interpreting file permissions.*

To understand what the permissions actually mean to the computer system, remember that UNIX treats everything as a file. If you install an application, it's just like everything else, with one exception: the system knows that an application is executable. A letter to your Mum is a regular file, but if you were to tell UNIX that it was executable, the system would merrily try to run it as a program (and fail).

There are three primary types of permission for files: read, write, and execute. Read permission enables users to examine the contents of the file with a variety of different programs, but they cannot alter, modify, or delete any information. They can copy the file and then edit the new version, however.

Write permission is the next step up. Users with write access to a file can add information to the file. If you have write permission *and* read permission for a file, you can edit the file, because the read permission enables you to view the contents and the write permission lets you alter them. With write permission only, you'd be able to add information to the file, but you wouldn't be able to view the contents of the file at any time. Admittedly, write-only permission is unusual in UNIX, but you might see it for log files, which are files that track activity on the system. Imagine if each time anyone logged in to your UNIX system the computer recorded the fact, noting who logged in, where they logged in from, and the current time and date. Armed with that information, you could ascertain who last logged in, who uses dial-up phone lines, and who uses the computer the most. (In fact, there's a UNIX command that does just that. It's called `last`.)

So far you've learned that you can have files with read-only permission, read-write permission, and write-only permission. The third type of access permission is execute, noted by `ls` with an x in the third slot of the permissions string.

```
% ls -l bin
total 57
-rwx------  1 taylor      1507 Aug 17 13:27 bounce.msg
-rwxrwx---  1 taylor     32916 Oct 10 19:09 calc
-rwx------  1 taylor     18567 Sep 14 22:14 fixit
-rw-------  1 taylor       334 Oct  1 09:53 punt
-rwx------  1 taylor      3424 Sep 10 22:27 rumor.mill.sh
```

Step 2. Action

1. Try listing the files in the directory /etc on your system and see if you can identify which are executable files or programs, which are directories, which are symbolic links (denoted with an l as the first character of the permissions string; they're files that point to other files or directories that point to other directories), and which are regular files.

2. Execute permission is slightly different from either read or write permission. If the directory containing the file is in your search path (the value of the environment variable PATH), then any file that has execute permission is automatically started each time that filename is entered, *regardless* of where you are in the file system.

```
% pwd
/users/taylor
% env PATH
/users/taylor/bin:/bin:/usr/bin:/usr/ucb:/usr/local:/usr/local/bin:
% ls -l bin/say.hi
-rw-rw----  1 taylor          9 Oct 11 13:32 bin/say.hi
% say.hi
hi
```

You can now see the importance of your search path. Without a search path, the system wouldn't be able to find any commands, and you'd be left with a barely functional system. You can also see the purpose of checking the executable permission status. I'm going to jump ahead a bit to show you one use of the chmod function, so you can see what happens if I remove the execute permission from the say.hi program:

```
% chmod -x bin/say.hi
% ls -l bin/say.hi
-rw-rw----  1 taylor          9 Oct 11 13:32 bin/say.hi
% say.hi
/users/taylor/bin/say.hi: Permission denied.
```

This time UNIX searched through my search path, found a file that matched the name of the program I requested, then ascertained that it wasn't executable. The resultant error message: `Permission denied`.

3. Now try entering say.hi on your computer system. You'll get a different error message, `Command not found`, which tells you that UNIX searched all the directories in your search path but couldn't find a match anywhere.

4. Check your PATH and find a directory that you can add files within. You'll probably have a bin directory in your home on the list, as I have /users/ taylor/bin in my search path. That's a good place to add a file using the touch command:

```
% env PATH
/users/taylor/bin:/bin:/usr/bin:/usr/ucb:/usr/local:/usr/local/bin:
% touch bin/my.new.cmd
% ls -l bin
-rw-rw----  1 taylor          0 Oct 11 15:07 my.new.cmd
```

5. Now try to execute the command by entering its name directly:

```
% my.new.cmd
/users/taylor/bin/my.new.cmd: Permission denied.
```

Comment: If you're using the C shell as your command interpreter, it probably won't find the new command you just created. This is because to speed things up it keeps an internal table of where different commands are found in your search path. You need to force the program to rebuild its table, and you can do that with the simple command `rehash`. If, when you enter the filename, you don't get `permission denied` but instead see `Command not found`, then enter `rehash` and try again.

6. Finally, use chmod to add execute permission to the file and try executing it one more time.

```
% chmod +x bin/my.new.cmd
% ls -l bin/my.new.cmd
-rwxrw----  1 taylor          0 Oct 11 15:07 bin/my.new.cmd
% my.new.cmd
%
```

Voilà! You've created your first UNIX command, an achievement even though it doesn't do much. You can now see how the search path and the UNIX philosophy of having applications be identical to regular files except for the permission can be invaluable as you learn how to customize your environment.

Step 3. Summary

Execute permission enables the user to run the file as if it were a program. Execute permission is independent of other permissions granted—or denied—so it's perfectly feasible to have a program with read and execute permission, but no write permission. (After all, you wouldn't want others altering the program itself.) You can also have programs with execute permission only. This means that users could run the application, but they couldn't examine it to see how it works or copy it. (Copying requires the ability to read the file.)

Comment: Although actual programs with execute-only permission work fine, a special class of programs called *shell scripts* fail. Shell scripts act like a UNIX command-line macro facility, which enables you to save easily a series of commands in a file and then run them as a single program. To work, however, the shell must be able to read the file and execute it, too, so shell scripts always require both read and execute permission.

There are clearly quite a few permutations on the three different permissions: read, write, and execute. In practice, there are a few that occur most commonly, as listed in Table 5.2.

Table 5.2. The most common file permissions.

Permission	Meaning
- - -	No access is allowed.
r - -	Read-only access.
r - x	Read and execute access, for programs and shell scripts.
rw -	Read and write access, for files.
rwx	All access allowed, for programs.

These permissions have different meanings when applied to directories, but ···
always indicates that no one can access the file in question.

Interpretation of the following few examples should help.

```
-rw-------  1 taylor      3843 Oct 10 16:22 iecc.list
-rw-rw-r--  1 taylor    280232 Oct 10 16:22 mailing.lists
-rw-rw----  1 taylor      1031 Oct  7 15:44 newlists
-rwxr-x---  1 taylor        64 Oct  9 09:31 the.script
```

The first file, iecc.list, has read and write permission for the owner (taylor) and is
off-limits to all other users. The file mailing.lists offers similar access to the file
owner (taylor) and to the group, but read-only access to everyone else on the system.
The third file, newlists, has read and write access to both the file owner and group,
but no access to anyone not in the group.

The fourth file on the list, the.script, is a program that can be run by both the owner
and group members, read (or copied) by both the owner and group, and written
(altered) by the owner. In practice, this would probably be a shell script, as described
earlier, and these permissions would enable the owner (taylor) to use an editor to
modify the commands therein. Other members of the group could read and use the
shell script, but would be denied access to change it.

Task 5.2: Directory Permissions Settings
Step 1. Description

Directories are similar to files in how you interpret the permission strings. The
differences occur because of the unique purpose of directories, namely to store other
files or directories. I always think of directories as bins or boxes. You can examine the
box itself, or you can look at what's inside.

In many ways, UNIX treats directories simply as files in the file system, where the
contents of the file is a list of the files and directories stored within, rather than a letter,
program, or shopping list.

The difference, of course, is that when you operate with directories, you're operating
both with the directory itself, and, implicitly, with its contents. By analogy, when you
fiddle with a box full of toys, you're not altering just the state of the box itself, but also
potentially the toys within.

There are three permissions possible for a directory, just as for a file: read, write, and
execute. The easiest is write permission. If a directory has write permission enabled,
you can add new items and remove items from the directory. It's like owning the box;
you can do what you'd like with the toys inside.

The interaction between read and execute permission with a directory is confusing. There are two types of operations you perform on a directory: listing the contents of the directory (usually with `ls`) and examining specific, known files within the directory.

Step 2. Action

1. Start by listing a directory, using the `-d` flag:

```
% ls -ld testme
dr-x------   2 taylor          512 Oct 11 17:03 testme/
% ls -l testme
total 0
-rw-rw----  1 taylor            0 Oct 11 17:03 file
% ls -l testme/file
-rw-rw----  1 taylor            0 Oct 11 17:03 testme/file
```

   For a directory with both read and execute permission, you can see that it's easy to list the directory, find out the files therein, and list specific files within the directory.

2. Read permission on a directory enables you to read the "table of contents" of the directory, but by itself it does not allow you to examine any of the files therein. By itself, read permission is rather bizarre:

```
% ls -ld testme
dr--------   2 taylor          512 Oct 11 17:03 testme/
% ls -l testme
testme/file not found
total 0
% ls -l testme/file
testme/file not found
```

   Notice that the system indicated the name of the file contained in the `testme` directory. When I tried to list the file explicitly, however, the system couldn't find the file.

3. Compare this with the situation when you have execute permission—which enables you to examine the files within the directory—but you don't have read permission, and you are prevented from viewing the table of contents of the directory itself:

```
% ls -ld testme
d--x------   2 taylor          512 Oct 11 17:03 testme/
% ls -l testme
```

```
testme unreadable
% ls -l testme/file
-rw-rw----  1 taylor           0 Oct 11 17:03 testme/file
```

With execute-only permission, you can set up directories so that people who know the names of files contained in the directories can access those files, but people without that knowledge cannot list the directory to learn the filenames.

4. I've actually never seen anyone have a directory in UNIX with execute-only permission, and certainly you would never expect to see one set to read-only. It would be nice if UNIX would warn you if you set a directory to have one permission and not the other. However, UNIX won't do that. For directories, always be sure that you have both read and execute permission set. Table 5.3 summarizes the most common directory permissions.

Table 5.3. The most common directory permissions.

Permission	Meaning
- - -	No access allowed to directory.
r-x	Read-only access, no modification allowed.
rwx	All access allowed.

5. One interesting permutation of directory permissions is for a directory that's write-only. Unfortunately, the write-only permission doesn't do what you'd hope, that is, enable people to add files to the directory without being able to see what the directory already contains. Instead it's functionally identical to having it set for no access permission at all.

At the beginning of this lesson, I used ls to list various files and directories in my home directory:

```
% ls -l
total 403
drwx------  2 taylor         512 Sep 30 10:38 Archives/
drwx------  3 taylor         512 Oct  1 08:23 InfoWorld/
```

```
-rw-------      1 taylor      106020 Oct 10 13:47 LISTS
drwx------      2 taylor        1024 Sep 30 10:50 Mail/
drwx------      2 taylor         512 Oct  6 09:36 News/
drwx------      2 taylor         512 Sep 30 10:51 OWL/
-rw-------      1 taylor        4643 Oct 10 14:01 RUMORS.18Sept
drwx------      2 taylor         512 Oct 10 19:09 bin/
-rw-------      1 taylor        3843 Oct 10 16:22 iecc.list
-rw-rw-r--      1 taylor      280232 Oct 10 16:22 mailing.lists
-rw-rw----      1 taylor        1031 Oct  7 15:44 newlists
drwx------      2 taylor         512 Oct 10 19:09 src/
```

Now you can see that all my directories are set so that I have list, examine, and modify (read, execute, and write, respectively) capability for myself, and no access is allowed for anyone else.

6. The very top-level directory is more interesting, with a variety of different directory owners and permissions.

```
% ls -l /
-rw-r--r--      1 root         61440 Nov 29  1991 boot
drwxr-xr-x      4 root         23552 Sep 27 11:31 dev
-r--r--r--      1 root        686753 Aug 27 21:58 dynix
drwxr-xr-x      6 root          3072 Oct 11 16:30 etc
drwxr-xr-x      2 root          8192 Apr 12  1991 lost+found
lrwxr-xr-x      1 root             7 Jul 28  1988 sys -> usr/sys
drwxrwxrwx     65 root         12800 Oct 11 17:33 tmp
drwxr-xr-x    753 root         14848 Oct  5 10:07 usera
drwxr-xr-x    317 root         13312 Oct  5 10:17 userb
drwxr-xr-x    626 root         13312 Oct  8 13:02 userc
drwxr-xr-x    534 root         10752 Sep 30 13:06 users
drwxr-xr-x     34 root          1024 Oct  1 09:10 usr
drwxr-xr-x      5 root          1024 Oct  1 09:20 var
```

Clearly, this machine has a lot of users. Notice that the link counts for usera, userb, userc, and users are each in the hundreds. The dev directory has read and execute permission for everyone and write permission for the owner (root). Indeed, all the directories at this level are identical except for tmp, which has read, write, and execute permission for all users on the system.

7. Did you notice the listing for the sys directory buried in that output?

```
lrwxr-xr-x  1 root             7 Jul 28  1988 sys -> usr/sys
```

From the information in Table 5.1, you know that the first letter of the permissions string being an l means that the directory is a symbolic link. The filename shows just the specifics of the link, indicating that sys points to the directory usr/sys. In fact, if you count the number of letters in the name usr/sys, you'll find that it exactly matches the size of the sys link entry too.

8. Try using ls -l / yourself. You should be able to understand the permissions of any file or directory that you encounter.

Step 3. Summary

Permissions of files and directories will prove easier as your work with UNIX more.

Task 5.3: Modify File and Directory Permissions with *chmod*
Step 1. Description

Now that you can list directory permissions and understand what they mean, how about learning a UNIX command that lets you change them to meet your needs? You've already had a sneak preview of the command: chmod. The mnemonic is *change mode*, and it derives from early UNIX folk talking about permission modes of files. You can remember it by thinking of it as a shortened form of *change permission modes*.

Comment: To sound like a UNIX expert, pronounce chmod as "ch-mod," "ch" like the beginning of *child*, and "mod" to rhyme with *cod*.

The chmod command enables you to specify permissions in two different ways: symbolically or numerically. Symbolic notation is most commonly used to modify existing permissions, while numeric format always replaces any existing permission with the new value specified. In this section you learn about symbolic notation, and the next section focuses on the powerful numeric format.

Symbolic notation for chmod is a bit like having a menu of different choices, enabling you to pick the combination that best fits your requirements. Figure 5.2 shows the menus.

The command chmod is like a smorgasbord where you can choose any combination of items from either the first or last boxes, and stick your choice from the center box between them.

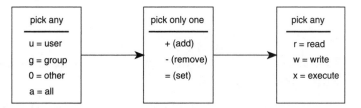

pick any	pick only one	pick any
u = user	+ (add)	r = read
g = group	- (remove)	w = write
0 = other	= (set)	x = execute
a = all		

Figure 5.2. *The menu of symbolic* chmod *values.*

For example, if you wanted to add write permission to the file test for everyone in your group, you would, working backwards from that description, choose g for group, + for add, and w for write. The finished UNIX command would be chmod g+w test.

If you decided to take away read and execute permission for everyone not in your group, you could use chmod o-rx test to accomplish the task.

Step 2. Action

1. Turn to your computer and, using touch and ls, try changing permissions and see what happens. I'll do the same:

```
% touch test
% ls -l test
-rw-rw----  1 taylor         0 Oct 11 18:29 test
```

2. The first modification I want to make is that people in my group should be able to read the file. Because I don't really want them altering it, I'll rescind write permission for group members:

```
% chmod g-w test
% ls -l test
-rw-r-----  1 taylor         0 Oct 11 18:29 test
```

3. But then my boss reminds me that everyone in the group should have *all* access permissions for everyone in that group. Okay, I'll do so.

```
% chmod g+wx test
% ls -l test
-rw-rwx---  1 taylor         0 Oct 11 18:29 test
```

I could also have done that with chmod g=rwx, of course.

4. Wait a second. This test file is just for my own use, and nobody in my group should be looking at it anyway. I'll change it back.

```
% chmod g-rwx test
% ls -l test
-rw------- 1 taylor          0 Oct 11 18:29 test
```

Great. Now the file is set so that I can read and write it, but nobody else can touch it, read it, modify it, or anything else.

5. If I relented a bit, I could easily add, with one last chmod command, read-only permission for everyone:

```
% chmod a+r test
% ls -l test
-rw-r--r-- 1 taylor          0 Oct 11 18:29 test
```

Step 3. Summary

Permissions in UNIX are based on a concentric access model from Multics. (In Chapter 1, "What Is This UNIX Stuff?," you learned that the name UNIX is also a pun on Multics.) Figure 5.3 illustrates this concept.

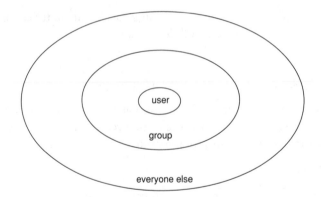

Figure 5.3. *The concentric circles of access.*

As a result, it's incredibly rare to see a file where the owner doesn't have the most access to a file. It'd be like buying a car and letting everyone but yourself drive it—rather silly. Similarly, members of the group are given better or equal permission to everyone else on the machine. You would never see r--r--rwx as a permissions string.

Experiment a bit more with the various combinations possible with the chmod symbolic notation. How would you change permission on a directory to enable all users to use ls to examine it, but deny them the ability to add or remove files? How about adding write access for the owner, but removing it for everyone else?

Task 5.4: Set New File Permissions with *chmod*
Step 1. Description

The second form of input that chmod accepts is absolute numeric values for permissions. Before you can learn how to use this notation, you have to learn a bit about different numbering systems.

The numbering system you're familiar with, the one you use to balance your checkbook and check the receipt from the market, is decimal, or base 10. This means that each digit—from right to left—has the value of the digit raised by a power of 10, based on the digit's location in the number. Figure 5.4 shows how you understand what the number 5,783 is in decimal.

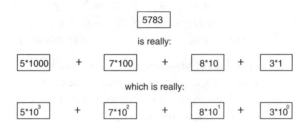

Figure 5.4. *Interpreting decimal numbers.*

You can see that in a base-10 numbering system, the value of a number is the sum of the value of each digit multiplied by the numeric base raised to the *Nth* power. The *N* is the number of spaces the digit is away from the right. That is, in the number 5,783, you know that the 7 is worth more than just seven, because it's two spaces away from the rightmost digit (the 3). Therefore, its value is the numeric base (10) raised to the *Nth* power, where *N* is 2 (it's two spaces away). Ten to the second power equals 100 ($10^2 = 100$), and when you multiply that by seven, sure enough, you find that the 7 is worth 700 in this number.

What does all this have to do with the chmod command? At their most fundamental, UNIX permissions are a series of on-off switches. Does the group have write permission? One equals yes, zero equals no. Each digit in a decimal system can have 10 different values (hence the name decimal). A binary system is one in which each digit can only have two values: on or off, yes or no. Therefore, you can easily and uniquely describe any permissions string as a series of zeroes and ones, as a binary number. Figure 5.5 demonstrates.

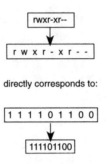

directly corresponds to:

Figure 5.5. *Permissions as binary numbers.*

The convention is that if a letter is present, the binary digit is a 1—that permission is permitted—and if no letter is present, the digit is a zero. Thus, r-xr----- can be described as 101100000, and r--r--r-- can be described in binary as 100100100.

You've already learned that the nine-character permission string is really just a three-character permission string duplicated thrice for the three different types of user (the owner, the group, and everyone else). That means that you can focus on learning how to translate a single tri-character permissions substring into binary and extrapolate for more than one permission. Table 5.4 lists all possible permissions and the binary equivalents.

Table 5.4. Permissions and binary equivalents.

Permissions String	Binary Equivalent
- - -	000
- - x	001
- w -	010
- wx	011
r - -	100
r - x	101
rw -	110
rwx	111

Knowing how to interpret decimal numbers using the rather complex formula presented earlier, you should not be surprised that the decimal equivalent of any binary number can be obtained by the same technique. Figure 5.6 shows how, with the binary equivalent of the r-x permission.

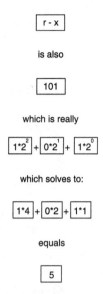

Figure 5.6. *Expressing* r-x *as a single digit.*

If r-x is equal to five, then it stands to reason that each of the possible three-character permissions has a single-digit equivalent, and Table 5.5 expands Table 5.4 to include the single-digit equivalents.

Table 5.5. Permissions and numeric equivalents.

Permissions String	Binary Equivalent	Decimal Equivalent
- - -	000	0
- - x	001	1
- w -	010	2
- wx	011	3
r - -	100	4
r - x	101	5
rw -	110	6
rwx	111	7

The value of having a single digit to describe any of the seven different permissions states should be obvious. Using only three digits, you can now fully express any possible combination of permissions for any file or directory in UNIX—one digit for owner permission, one for group, and a third for everyone else. Figure 5.7 shows how to take a full permissions string and translate it into its three-digit numeric equivalent.

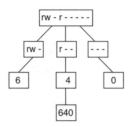

Figure 5.7. *Translating a full permissions string into its numeric equivalent.*

From that illustration, you can see how the permissions string rw-r----- (read and write permission for the owner, read permission for the group, and no access allowed for everyone else) is exactly equivalent to the numeric string 640.

Step 2. Action

1. Now try to create numeric strings on your own, using Table 5.5 to help. Turn to your computer and use ls to bring up some listings. Break each permissions string into three groups of three letters, and figure out the numeric equivalents.

   ```
   drwx------   2 taylor        512 Sep 30 10:38 Archives/
   ```

   For Archives/, the equivalent numeric permission is 700.

   ```
   -rw-------   1 taylor     106020 Oct 10 13:47 LISTS
   ```

   For LISTS, the equivalent numeric permission is 600.

   ```
   -rw-rw-r--   1 taylor     280232 Oct 10 16:22 mailing.lists
   ```

   For mailing.lists, the equivalent numeric permission is 664.

   ```
   -rw-rw----   1 taylor       1031 Oct  7 15:44 newlists
   ```

   For newlists, the equivalent numeric permission is 660.

Step 3. Summary

There's one last step required before you can try using the numeric permission strings with chmod. You need to be able to work backwards to determine a permission that you'd like to set and figure out the numeric equivalent for that permission.

Task 5.5: Calculating Numeric Permissions Strings
Step 1. Description

For example, if you wanted to have a directory set so that you have all access, and people in your group can look at the contents but not modify anything, and everyone else is shut out, how would you do it?

All permissions for yourself means you want read+write+execute for owner (or numeric permission 7); read and listing permission for others in the group means read+execute for group (numeric permission 5); and no permission for everyone else, numeric permission 0. Put the three together and you have the answer, 750.

That's the trick of working with chmod in numeric mode. You specify the absolute permissions you want as a three-digit number, and the system sets the permissions on the file or directory appropriately.

The *absolute* concept is important with this form of chmod. You cannot use the chmod numeric form to add or remove permissions from a file or directory. It is usable only for reassigning the permissions string of a file or directory.

The good news is that, as you learned earlier in this lesson, there is a relatively small number of commonly used file permissions, summarized in Table 5.6.

Table 5.6. Common permissions and their numeric equivalents.

Permissions	Numeric	Used With
---------	000	all types
r--------	400	files
r--r--r--	444	files
rw-------	600	files
rw-r--r--	644	files
rw-rw-r--	664	files

continues

Table 5.6. continued

Permissions	Numeric	Used With
rw-rw-rw-	666	files
rwx------	700	programs and directories
rwxr-x---	750	programs and directories
rwxr-xr-x	755	programs and directories

Step 2. Action

1. Turn to your computer and try using the numeric mode of chmod, coupled with ls, to display the actual permissions to learn for yourself how this works.

```
% touch example
% ls -l example
-rw-rw----  1 taylor          0 Oct 12 10:16 example
```

By default, files are created in my directory with mode 660.

2. To take away read and write permission for people in my group, I'd replace the 660 permission with what numeric permission string? I'd use 600:

```
% chmod 600 example
% ls -l example
-rw-------  1 taylor          0 Oct 12 10:16 example
```

3. What about if I change my mind and want to open the file up for everyone to read or write? I'd use 666:

```
% chmod 666 example
% ls -l example
-rw-rw-rw-  1 taylor          0 Oct 12 10:16 example
```

4. Finally, pretend that example is actually a directory. What numeric mode would I specify to enable everyone to use ls in the directory and enable only the owner to add or delete files? I'd use 755:

```
% chmod 755 example
% ls -l example
-rwxr-xr-x  1 taylor          0 Oct 12 10:16 example
```

Step 3. Summary

Try working through these examples, and see whether you prefer the numeric mode, which can take a bit of getting used to, or the symbolic mode, which is a bit easier.

> **Comment:** Somehow I've never gotten the hang of symbolic mode, so I almost always use the numeric mode for chmod. The only exception is when I want to add or delete simple permissions. Then I'll use something like chmod +r test to add read permission. Part of the problem is that I don't think of the *user* of the file but the *owner*, and specifying o+r causes chmod to change permission for others. It's important, therefore, that you remember that files have *users*, so you'll remember u as user, and that everyone not in the group is *other*, so you'll remember o. Otherwise, learn the numeric shortcut!

File permissions and modes are one of the most complex aspects of UNIX. You can tell—it's taken two lessons to explain it fully—and almost half of Day 2 in *Teach Yourself UNIX in a Week* is focused on this topic. It's very important that you spend the time really to understand how the permissions strings relate to directory permissions, how to read the output of ls, and how to change modes using both styles of the chmod command. It'll be time well spent.

Task 5.6: Establish Default File and Directory Permissions with the *umask* Command

Step 1. Description

When I've created files, they've had read+write permission for the owner and group, but no allowed access for anyone else. When you create files on your system, you might find that the default permissions are different.

The controlling variable behind the default permissions is the *file creation mask*, or umask for short.

Inexplicably, umask doesn't always list its value as a three-digit number, but you can find its value in the same way that you figured out the numeric permission strings for chmod. For example, when I enter umask, the system indicates that my umask setting is 07. A leading zero has been dropped, so the actual value is 007, a value that British MI6 could no doubt appreciate!

But 007 doesn't mean that the default file is created with read+write+execute for everyone else and no permissions for the owner or group. It means quite the opposite, literally.

The umask command is a screen through which permissions are pushed to ascertain what remains. Figure 5.8 demonstrates how this works.

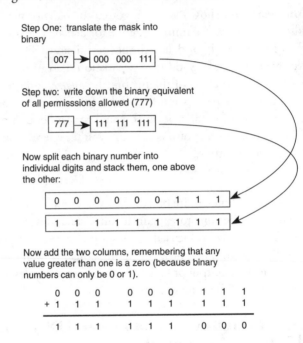

Step One: translate the mask into binary

    007 → 000 000 111

Step two: write down the binary equivalent of all permisssions allowed (777)

    777 → 111 111 111

Now split each binary number into individual digits and stack them, one above the other:

    0 0 0 0 0 0 1 1 1

    1 1 1 1 1 1 1 1 1

Now add the two columns, remembering that any value greater than one is a zero (because binary numbers can only be 0 or 1).

      0   0   0   0   0   0   1   1   1
    + 1   1   1   1   1   1   1   1   1
    ───
      1   1   1   1   1   1   0   0   0

And translate that back to a decimal value:

    7 7 0

default creation permission

Figure 5.8. *Interpreting the* umask *value.*

Think of your mask as a series of boxes: if the value is true, then the information can't exude through the box. If the value is false, it can. Your mask is therefore the direct opposite to how you want your permissions to be set. In the example, I want to have 770 as the default permission for any new file or directory I create, so I want to specify the exact opposite of that, 007. Sure enough, with this umask value, when I create new files, the default permission allows read and write access to the owner and group, but no access to anyone else.

Things are a bit trickier than that. You've probably already asked yourself, Why, if I have 007 as my mask (which results in 770 as the default permissions), do my files have 660 as the actual default permission?

The reason is that UNIX tries to be smart about the execute permission setting. If I create a directory, UNIX knows that execute permission is important, so it grants it. However, for some files (particularly text files), execute permission doesn't make sense, so UNIX actually masks it out internally.

Another way to look at this is that any time you create a file containing information, the original mask the system uses to compare against your umask is not 777 (not rwxrwxrwx, to put it another way) but rather 666 (rw-rw-rw-), in recognition of the unlikelihood that you'll want to execute the new file.

The good news is that you now know an easy way to set the execute permission for a file if the system gets it wrong: chmod +x *file* does the trick.

Step 2. Action

1. Turn to your computer and check your umask setting, then alternate between changing its values and creating new files with touch.

```
% umask
07
% touch test.07
% ls -l test.07
-rw-rw----  1 taylor          0 Oct 12 14:38 test.07
```

2. To change the value of your umask, add the numeric value of the desired mask to the command line:

```
% umask 077
```

This changes my umask value from 007 (------rwx) to 077 (---rwxrwx). Before you look at the following listing, what would you expect this modification to mean? Remember, you should read it as the exact *opposite* of how you want the default permissions.

```
% touch test.077
% ls -l test.077
-rw-------  1 taylor          0 Oct 12 14:38 test.077
```

Is that what you expected?

3. What would you do if you wanted to have the default permission keep files private to just the owner *and* make them read-only?

You can work through this problem in reverse. If you want r-x------ as the default permission (because the system takes care of whether execute permission is needed, based on file type), write down the opposite permission, which is -w-rwxrwx. Translate that to a binary number, 010 111 111, and then to a three digit value, 277 (010 = 2, 111 = 7, 111 = 7). That's the answer. The value 277 is the correct umask value to ensure that files you create are read-only for yourself and off-limits to everyone else.

```
% umask 277
% touch test.277
% ls -l test.277
-r-------- 1 taylor          0 Oct 12 14:39 test.277
```

4. What if you wanted to have files created with the default permissions being read-only for everyone, read-write for the group, but read-only for the owner? Again, work backwards. The desired permission is r-xrwxr-x, so create the opposite value (-w-----w-), translate it into binary (010 000 010) and then translate that into a three-digit value: 202 (010 = 2, 000 = 0, 010 = 2).

Comment: As a rule of thumb, it's best to leave the execute permission enabled when building umask values so the system doesn't err when creating directories.

Step 3. Summary

The umask is something set once and left alone. If you've tried various experiments on your computer, remember to restore your umask back to a sensible value to avoid future problems (though each time you log in to the system it's reset to your default value).

In the next lesson you will learn how to use the mkdir command to create new directories, and you'll be able to see how the umask value affects default directory access permissions.

Task 5.7: Identify Owner and Group for Any File or Directory

Step 1. Description

One of the many items of information that the ls command displays when used with the -l flag is the owner of the file or directory. So far all the files and directories in your home directory have been owned by you, with the probable exception of the ".." directory, which is owned by whomever owns the directory above your home.

In other words, when you enter ls -l, you should see your account name as the owner for every file in the listing.

If you're collaborating with another user, however, there might well be times when you'll want to change the owner of a file or directory once you've created and modified it. The first step in accomplishing this is to identify the owner and group.

Identifying the owner is easy; ls lists that by default. But how do you identify the group of which the file or directory is a part?

Step 2. Action

1. The ls command can show the group membership of any file or directory by addition of a new command flag, -g. By itself -g doesn't alter the output of ls, but when used with the -l flag, it adds a column of information to the listing. Try it on your system. Here is an example:

```
% ls -lg /tmp
-rw-r--r--  1 root     root          0 Oct 12 14:52 sh145
drwxr-xr-x  2 shakes   root        512 Oct 12 07:23 shakes/
-rw-------  1 meademd  com435        0 Oct 12 14:46 snd.12
-rw-------  1 dessy    stuprsac   1191 Oct 12 14:57 snd.15
-rw-------  1 steen    utech         1 Oct 12 10:28 snd.17
-rw-r-----  1 jsmith   utech    258908 Oct 12 12:37 sol2
```

Comment: On many System V-based systems, the output of ls -l always shows user and group. The -g flag actually turns off this display!

Both owners and groups vary for each of the files and directories in this small listing. Notice that files can have different owners while having the same group. (There are two examples here: sh145 and the shakes directory, and snd.17 and sol2.)

2. Directories where there are often a wide variety of different owners for directories are the directories above your own home directory and the `tmp` directory, as you can see in the preceding example. Examine both on your system and identify both the owner and group of all files. For files in the same group you're in (with the `id` command, you can find which group or groups you are in) but not owned by you, you'll need to check which of the three permissions values to identify your own access privileges.

Step 3. Summary

Files and directories have both owners and groups, although the latter is ultimately less important than the owner, particularly where permissions and access are involved.

Task 5.8: Change the Owner of a File or Directory
Step 1. Description

Now that you can ascertain the ownership of a file or directory, it's time to learn about the `chown` command. This command lets you change the ownership of whatever you specify.

> **Don't Skip This:** Before you go any further, however, a stern warning: Once you've changed the ownership of a file, you *cannot* restore it to yourself. Only the owner of a file can give away its ownership, so don't use the `chown` command unless you're absolutely positive you want to!

Step 2. Action

1. The format for changing the ownership of a file is to specify the new owner, then list the files or directory you are giving away.

```
% ls -l test
-rwxrwxrwx  1 taylor           0 Oct 12 15:17 mytest
% chown root test
% ls -l test
-rwxrwxrwx  1 root             0 Oct 12 15:17 mytest
```

This would change the ownership of the file `test` from me to the user `root` on the system.

2. If I now try to change the ownership back, it fails:

```
% chown taylor test
chown: test: Not owner
```

Most modern UNIX systems prevent users from changing the ownership of a file due to the inherent dangers. If you try chown and it returns Command not found or Permission denied, that means you're barred from making any file ownership changes.

3. On one of the systems I use, chown always reports Not owner when I try to change a file, regardless of whether I really am the owner or not.

```
% ls -l mytest
-rwxrwxrwx  1 taylor            0 Oct 12 15:17 mytest
% chown root mytest
chown: mytest: Not owner
```

This is needlessly confusing—a message like you're not allowed to change file ownership would be better—but like so much of UNIX, it's up to the user to figure out what's going on, alas.

Step 3. Summary

To change the ownership of a file or directory, you can use the chown command, if you have the appropriate access on your system. It's like a huge supertanker, though; you can't change course once underway, so be cautious!

Task 5.9: Change the Group of a File or Directory
Step 1. Description

Changing the group membership of a file or directory is quite analogous to the steps required for changing file ownership. Almost all UNIX systems enable users to use the chgrp command to accomplish this task.

Step 2. Action

1. Usage of chgrp is almost identical to that of chown, too: specify the name of the group, followed by the list of files or directories to reassign.

```
% ls -lg
-rwxrwxrwx  1 taylor    ci        0 Oct 12 15:17 mytest
% chgrp ftp mytest
% ls -lg
-rwxrwxrwx  1 taylor    ftp       0 Oct 12 15:17 mytest
```

The caveat on this command, however, is that you must be a member of the group you're assigning for the file, or it fails.

```
% ls -lg
-rwxrwxrwx 1 taylor    ftp            0 Oct 12 15:17 mytest
% chgrp root mytest
chgrp: You are not a member of the root group
```

Step 3. Summary

Portions of UNIX are well thought out and offer innovative approaches to common computer problems. File groups and file ownership aren't examples of this, unfortunately. The majority of UNIX users tend to be members of only one group, so they cannot change the group membership *or* ownership of any file or directory on the system. Instead, users seem to just use chmod to allow full access to files; then they encourage colleagues to copy the files desired, or they simply allow everyone access.

Unlike the other commands you've learned in this book, chown may be one you will not use. It's entirely possible that you'll never have need to change the ownership or group membership of any file or directory.

Lesson Summary

In this lesson you have learned the basics of UNIX file permissions, including how to set and modify file permissions with chmod, and how to analyze file permissions as shown by the ls -l command. You've learned about translating between numeric bases (binary and decimal) and how to convert permissions strings into numeric values. Both are foundations for the umask command, which you've learned to interpret and alter as desired. Permission is only half the puzzle, however. You've also learned about file ownership, group ownership, and how to change either for any file or directory.

Workshop
Key Terms

file creation mask   When files are created in UNIX, they inherit a default set of access permissions. These defaults are under the control of the user and are known as the file creation mask.

mode	A shorthand way of saying *permissions mode*.
permissions mode	The set of accesses (read, write, and execute) allowed for each of the three classes of users (owner, group, and everyone else) for each file or directory on the system. This is a synonym for *access permission*.
shell script	A collection of shell commands in a file.

Questions

1. In what situations can you imagine the following file permissions might be useful?

   ```
   r--rw-r--      r--r--rw-
   rw--w--w-      -w--w--w-
   rwxr-xr-x      r-x--x--x
   ```

2. Translate these six file permission strings into their binary and numeric equivalents.

3. Explain what the following umask values would make the default permissions for newly created files:

007	077	777
111	222	733
272	544	754

4. Count the number of groups that are represented by group membership of files in the tmp directory on your system. Use id to see if you're a member of any of them.

5. Which of the following directories could you modify, if the id command listed the following information? Which could you view using the ls command?

   ```
   % id
   uid=19(smith) gid=50(users) groups=50(users)
   % ls -lgF
   drw-r--r--  2 root     users      512 Oct 12 14:52 sh/
   drwxr-xr-x  2 shakes   root       512 Oct 12 07:23 shakes/
   drw-------  2 meademd  com435    1024 Oct 12 14:46 tmp/
   drwxr-x---  3 smith    users      512 Oct 12 12:37 viewer/
   drwx------  3 jin      users      512 Oct 12 12:37 Zot!/
   ```

5

Preview of the Next Chapter

The next lesson wraps up your second day of learning UNIX. In it you learn the various UNIX file-manipulation commands, including how to copy files, how to move them to new directories, and how to create new directories. You will also read about how to remove files and directories, including a discussion of the dangers of file removal on UNIX.

Creating, Moving, and Destroying

This is the last lesson of your second day of learning UNIX in a week. In this lesson you'll learn the basic UNIX file manipulation commands. These commands will explain how to create directories with `mkdir`, remove directories with `rmdir`, use `cp` and `mv` to move files about in the file system, and use `rm` to remove files. The `rm` command has its dangers. You'll learn that there isn't an "unremove" command in UNIX and how to circumvent the possible dangers that lurk in the program.

Goals for This Lesson

In this lesson, you will learn how to

☐ Create new directories using `mkdir`

☐ Copy files to new locations using `cp`

☐ Move files to new locations using `mv`

☐ Rename files using `mv`

☐ Remove directories using `rmdir`

☐ Remove files using `rm`

☐ Minimize the danger of the `rm` command

This lesson introduces a number of tremendously powerful commands that enable you to create a custom file system hierarchy (or wreak unintentional havoc on your files). As you learn these commands, you'll also learn hints and ideas on how to best use the UNIX file system to keep your files neat and organized. These simple UNIX commands, all new in this lesson, not only are found in all variants of UNIX, both BSD-based and System V-based, but also can be brought onto DOS through utilities like the MKS Toolkit from Mortice-Kern Systems.

Task 6.1: Creating New Directories Using *mkdir*
Step 1. Description

One important aspect of UNIX that has been emphasized continually in *Teach Yourself UNIX in a Week* is that the UNIX file system is hierarchical in nature. The UNIX file system includes directories containing files and directories, each of which can contain both files and directories. Your own home directory, however, probably doesn't contain any directories (except "." and ".." of course), which prevents you from exploiting what I call the virtual file cabinet of the file system.

The command for creating directories is actually one of the least complex and most mnemonic (for UNIX, at least) in this book: `mkdir`, called *make directory*.

> **Comment:** Pronounce the `mkdir` command as "make-dir."

Step 2. Action

1. Turn to your computer, move to your home directory, and examine the files and directories there. Here's an example:

```
% cd
% ls
Archives/               OWL/                    rumors.26Oct.Z
InfoWorld/              PubAccessLists.Z        rumors.5Nov.Z
LISTS                   bin/                    src/
Mail/                   educ
News/                   mailing.lists.bitnet.Z
```

2. To create a directory, you need to specify what you'd like to name the directory and where you'd like to locate it in the file system (the default location is your current working directory):

```
% mkdir NEWDIR
% ls
Archives/               News/                   mailing.lists.bitnet.Z
InfoWorld/              OWL/                    rumors.26Oct.Z
LISTS                   PubAccessLists.Z        rumors.5Nov.Z
Mail/                   bin/                    src/
NEWDIR/                 educ
```

3. That's all there is to it. You've created your first UNIX directory, and you can now list it with `ls` to see what it looks like.

```
% ls -ld NEWDIR
drwxrwx---  2 taylor          24 Nov  5 10:48 NEWDIR/
% ls -la NEWDIR
total 2
drwxrwx---  2 taylor          24 Nov  5 10:48 ./
drwx------ 11 taylor        1024 Nov  5 10:48 ../
```

6

Not surprisingly, the directory is empty other than the two default entries of "." (the directory itself) and ".." (the parent directory, your home directory).

4. Look closely at the permissions of the directory. Remember, the permissions is a result of your umask setting. As you learned in the last chapter, changing the umask setting changes the default directory permissions. Then when you create a new directory, the new permissions will be in place:

```
% umask
07
% umask 0
% mkdir NEWDIR2
% ls -ld NEWDIR2
drwxrwxrwx  2 taylor          24 Nov  5 10:53 NEWDIR2/
% umask 222
% mkdir NEWDIR3
% ls -ld NEWDIR3
dr-xr-xr-x  2 taylor          24 Nov  5 10:54 NEWDIR3/
```

5. What happens if you try to create a directory with a name that has already been used?

```
% mkdir NEWDIR
mkdir: NEWDIR: File exists
```

6. To create a directory other than your current location, prefix the new directory name with a location:

```
% mkdir /tmp/testme
% ls -l /tmp
-rwx------  1 zhongqi     22724 Nov  4 21:33 /tmp/a.out*
-rw-------  1 xujia       95594 Nov  4 23:10 /tmp/active.10122
-rw-r--r--  1 beast         572 Nov  5 05:59 /tmp/anon1
-rw-rw----  1 root            0 Nov  5 10:30 /tmp/bar.report
-rw-------  1 qsc             0 Nov  5 00:18 /tmp/lh013813
-rwx------  1 steen       24953 Nov  5 10:40 /tmp/mbox.steen*
-rwx------  1 techman      3711 Nov  5 10:45 /tmp/mbox.techman*
-rw-r--r--  1 root       997536 Nov  5 10:58 /tmp/quotas
-rw-------  1 zhongqi    163579 Nov  4 20:16 /tmp/sp500.1
drwxrwx---  2 taylor         24 Nov  5 10:56 /tmp/testme/
-rw-r--r--  1 aru            90 Nov  5 02:55 /tmp/trouble21972
```

Step 3. Summary

Like other basic UNIX utilities, mkdir has no command arguments, so it is quite easy to use. There are two things to keep in mind. You must have write permission to the current directory if you're creating a new directory, and you should ensure that the name of the directory is not the same as (or, to avoid confusion, similar to) a directory name that already exists.

Task 6.2: Copy Files to New Locations Using *cp*
Step 1. Description

One of the most basic operations in any system is moving files, the modern-office computer equivalent of paper shuffling. On a computer, moving files is a simple matter of using one or two commands: you can move a file to a different location, or you can create a copy of the file and move the copy to a different location.

The Macintosh has an interesting strategy for differentiating between *move* and *copy*. If you drag a file to another location that's on the same device (a hard disk, for example), then by default the computer moves the file to that location. If you drag the file to a location on a different device (from a floppy to a hard disk, for instance), then the computer automatically copies the file, placing the new, identically named, copy on the device.

UNIX lacks this subtlety. Instead, UNIX lets you choose which of the two operations you'd like to perform. The two commands are typically succinct UNIX mnemonics: mv to move, and cp to copy files. The mv command also serves the dual duty of enabling you to rename files.

> **Comment:** Pronounce cp as "see-pea." When you talk about copying a file, however, say "copy." Similarly, pronounce mv as "em-vee," but when you speak of moving a file, say "move."

I find myself using cp more than mv, because it offers a slightly safer way to organize files. If I get confused and rename it such that it steps on another file (you'll see what I mean in a moment), I still have original copies of all the files.

Step 2. Action

1. The format of a cp command is to specify first the name of the file you want to copy, then the new filename. Both names must be either *relative* filenames

(that is, without a leading slash or other indication of the directory) or *absolute* filenames. Start out by making a copy of your `.login` file, naming the new copy `login.copy`:

```
% cp .login login.copy
% ls -ld .login login.copy
-rw-------   1 taylor        1858 Oct 12 21:20 .login
-rw-------   1 taylor        1858 Nov  5 12:08 login.copy
```

You can see that the new file is identical in size and permissions, but that it has a more recent creation date, which certainly makes sense.

Don't Skip This: If you don't have a `.cshrc` file (you won't if you're using the Bourne or Korn shells), use the `touch` command to create one so that you can do the examples in this and subsequent chapters: `touch .cshrc`.

2. What happens if you try to copy a directory?

```
% cp . newdir
cp: .: Is a directory (not copied).
```

Generally, UNIX will not enable you to use the `cp` command to copy directories.

Comment: I found that this command worked—sort of—on one machine I have used. The system's response to the cp command indicated that something peculiar was happening with the message cp: .: Is a directory (copying as plain file), but the system also created newdir as a regular, executable file. You may find that your system reacts in this manner, but you probably do not have any use for it.

3. The cp command is quite powerful, and it can copy many files at once if you specify a directory as the destination rather than specifying a new filename. Further, if you specify a directory destination, the program will automatically create new files and assign them the same names as the original files.

First, you need to create a second file to work with:

```
% cp .cshrc cshrc.copy
```

Now try it yourself. Here is my result:

```
% cp login.copy cshrc.copy NEWDIR
% ls -l NEWDIR
total 4
-rw-------  1 taylor         1178 Nov  5 12:18 cshrc.copy
-rw-------  1 taylor         1858 Nov  5 12:18 login.copy
```

Don't Skip This: If you don't have a .login file (you won't if you're using the Bourne or Korn shells), use the touch command to create one so that you can do the examples in this and subsequent chapters: touch .login.

Step 3. Summary

You can use the cp command to copy an original file as a new file or to a specific directory (the format being cp *original-file new-file-or-directory*), and you can copy a bunch of files to a directory (cp *list-of-files new-directory*). Experiment with creating new directories using mkdir and copying the files into the new locations. Use ls to confirm that the originals aren't removed as you go along.

Task 6.3: Moving Files to New Locations Using *mv*
Step 1. Description

Whereas cp leaves the original file intact, making a sort of electronic equivalent of a photocopy of a paper I may pick up at my desk, mv functions like a more traditional desk; pages are *moved* from one location to another. Rather than creating multiple copies of the files you're copying, mv physically relocates them from the old directory to the new.

Step 2. Action

1. You use mv almost the same way that you use cp:

```
% ls -l login.copy
-rw-------  1 taylor         1858 Nov  5 12:08 login.copy
% mv login.copy new.login
% ls -l login.copy new.login
login.copy not found
-rw-------  1 taylor         1858 Nov  5 12:08 new.login
```

2. Also, you move a group of files together using mv almost the same way you do it using cp:

```
% cd NEWDIR
% ls
cshrc.copy   login.copy
% mv cshrc.copy login.copy ..
% ls -l
total 0
% ls ..
Archives/              OWL/                  mailing.lists.bitnet.Z
InfoWorld/             PubAccessLists.Z      new.login
LISTS                  bin/                  rumors.26Oct.Z
Mail/                  cshrc.copy            rumors.5Nov.Z
NEWDIR/                educ                  src/
News/                  login.copy
```

3. Because you can use mv to rename files or directories, you can relocate the new directory NEWDIR. However, you cannot use mv to relocate the dot directory because you're inside it:

```
% mv . new.dot
mv: .: rename: Invalid argument
```

4. Both mv and cp can be dangerous. Carefully consider the following example before trying either mv or cp on your own computer:

```
% ls -l login.copy cshrc.copy
-rw-------  1 taylor        1178 Nov  5 12:38 cshrc.copy
-rw-------  1 taylor        1858 Nov  5 12:37 login.copy
% cp cshrc.copy login.copy
% ls -l .login login.copy cshrc.copy
-rw-------  1 taylor        1178 Nov  5 12:38 cshrc.copy
-rw-------  1 taylor        1178 Nov  5 12:38 login.copy
```

Without bothering to warn me, UNIX copied the file cshrc.copy over the existing file login.copy. Notice that after the cp operation occurred, both files had the same size and modification dates.

The mv command will cause the same problem:

```
% ls -l cshrc.copy login.copy
-rw-------  1 taylor        1178 Nov  5 12:42 cshrc.copy
-rw-------  1 taylor        1858 Nov  5 12:42 login.copy
% mv cshrc.copy login.copy
% ls -l cshrc.copy login.copy
cshrc.copy not found
-rw-------  1 taylor        1178 Nov  5 12:42 login.copy
```

> **Comment:** The good news is that you can set up UNIX so it won't overwrite files. The bad news is that for some reason many systems don't default to this behavior. If your system is configured reasonably, when you try either of the two preceding danger examples, the system's response is `remove login.copy?` You can press the Y key to replace the old file, or press Enter to change your mind. If your system cannot be set up to respond this way, you can use the `-i` flag to both `cp` and `mv` to avoid this problem. Later you will learn how to permanently fix this problem with a *shell alias.*

Step 3. Summary

Together `mv` and `cp` are the dynamic duo of UNIX file organization. These commands enable you to put the information you want where you want it, leaving duplicates behind if desired.

Task 6.4: Renaming Files with *mv*
Step 1. Description

Both the DOS and Macintosh systems have easy ways to rename files. In DOS, you can use `RENAME` to accomplish the task. On the Mac, you can select the name under the file icon and enter a new filename.

UNIX has neither option. To rename files you use the `mv` command, which, in essence, moves the old name to the new name. It's a bit confusing, but it works.

Step 2. Action

1. Rename the file `cshrc.copy` with your own first name. Here's an example:

```
% ls -l cshrc.copy
-rw-------  1 taylor      1178 Nov  5 13:00 cshrc.copy
% mv cshrc.copy dave
% ls -l dave
-rw-------  1 taylor      1178 Nov  5 13:00 dave
```

2. Rename a directory, too:

```
% ls -ld NEWDIR
drwxrwx---  2 taylor       512 Nov  5 12:32 NEWDIR/
% mv NEWDIR New.Sample.Directory
% ls -ld New.Sample.Directory
drwxrwx---  2 taylor       512 Nov  5 12:32 New.Sample.Directory/
```

3. Be careful! Just as moving files with `cp` and `mv` can carelessly overwrite existing files, renaming files using `mv` can overwrite existing files:

```
% mv dave login.copy
%
```

If you try to use `mv` to rename a directory with a name that has already been assigned to a file, the command fails:

```
% mv New.Sample.Directory dave
mv: New.Sample.Directory: rename: Not a directory
```

The reverse situation works fine, because the file is moved *into* the directory as expected. It's the subtlety of using the `mv` command to rename files.

4. If you assign a new directory a name that belongs to an existing directory, some versions of `mv` will happily overwrite the existing directory and name the new one as requested:

```
% mkdir testdir
% mv New.Sample.Directory testdir
%
```

Step 3. Summary

Being able to rename files is another important part of building a useful UNIX virtual file cabinet for yourself. There are some major dangers involved, however, so tread carefully and always use `ls` in conjunction with `cp` and `mv` to ensure that in the process you don't overwrite or replace an existing file.

Task 6.5: Removing Directories with *rmdir*
Step 1. Description

Now that you can create directories with the `mkdir` command, it's time to learn how to remove directories using the `rmdir` command.

Step 2. Action

1. With `rmdir`, you can remove any directory for which you have appropriate permissions:

```
% mkdir test
% ls -l test
total 0
% rmdir test
%
```

Note that the output of ls shows there are no files in the test directory.

2. The rmdir command removes only directories that are empty:

```
% mkdir test
% touch test/sample.file
% ls -l test
total 0
-rw-rw----  1 taylor          0 Nov  5 14:00 sample.file
% rmdir test
rmdir: test: Directory not empty
```

To remove a directory, you must first remove all files therein using the rm command. In this example, test still has files within it.

3. Permissions are important, too. Consider what happens when I try to remove a directory that I don't have permission to touch:

```
% rmdir /tmp
rmdir: /tmp: Permission denied
% ls -l /tmp
drwxrwxrwt 81 root         15872 Nov  5 14:07 /tmp/
```

The permissions of the parent directory, rather than the directory you're trying to remove, are the important consideration.

Step 3. Summary

There's no way to restore a directory you've removed, so be careful and think through what you're doing. The good news is that, because with rmdir you can't remove a directory having anything in it (a second reason the attempt in the preceding example to remove /tmp would have failed), you're reasonably safe from major gaffes. You are not safe, however, with the next command—rm—because it will remove anything.

Task 6.6: Removing Files Using *rm*
Step 1. Description

The rm command is the most dangerous command in UNIX. Lacking any sort of archival or restoration feature, the rm command removes files permanently. It's like throwing a document into a shredder instead of into a dustbin.

Step 2. Action

1. Removing a file using rm is easy. Here's an example:

```
% ls -l login.copy
-rw-------  1 taylor      1178 Nov  5 13:00 login.copy
% rm login.copy
% ls -l login.copy
login.copy not found
```

If you decide that you removed the wrong file and actually wanted to keep the login.copy file, it's too late. You're out of luck.

2. You can remove more than one file at a time by specifying each of the files to the rm command:

```
% ls
Archives/            PubAccessLists.Z          new.login
InfoWorld/           bin/                      rumors.26Oct.Z
LISTS                cshrc.copy                rumors.5Nov.Z
Mail/                educ                      src/
News/                login.copy                test/
OWL/                 mailing.lists.bitnet.Z    testdir/
% rm cshrc.copy login.copy new.login
% ls
Archives/            OWL/                      rumors.26Oct.Z
InfoWorld/           PubAccessLists.Z          rumors.5Nov.Z
LISTS                bin/                      src/
Mail/                educ                      test/
News/                mailing.lists.bitnet.Z    testdir/
```

3. Fortunately, rm does have a command flag that to some degree helps avoid accidental file removal. When you use the -i flag to rm (the *i* stands for interactive in this case), the system will ask you if you're sure you want to remove the file:

```
% touch testme
% rm -i testme
rm: remove testme? n
% ls testme
testme
% rm -i testme
rm: remove testme? y
% ls testme
testme not found
```

Note that n is *no*, and y is *yes, delete the file*.

4. Another flag that is often useful for rm, but is very dangerous, is the -r flag for *recursive* deletion of files. When the -r flag to rm is used, UNIX will remove any specified directory along with all its contents:

```
% ls -ld test ; ls -lR test
drwxrwxrwx  3 taylor          512 Nov  5 15:32 test/
total 1
-rw-rw----  1 taylor            0 Nov  5 15:32 alpha
drwxrwx---  2 taylor          512 Nov  5 15:32 test2/

test/test2:
total 0
-rw-rw----  1 taylor            0 Nov  5 15:32 file1
% rm -r test
% ls -ld test
test not found
%
```

Without any warning or indication that it was going to do something so drastic, entering rm -r test caused not just the test directory, but all files and directories inside it as well, to be removed.

Comment: This latest example demonstrates that you can give several commands in a single UNIX command line. To do this, separate the commands with a semicolon. Instead of giving the commands ls -ld test and ls -lR test on separate lines, I opted for the more efficient ls -ld test; ls -lR test, which sends both commands at once.

Step 3. Summary

The UNIX equivalent of the paper shredder, the rm command allows easy removal of files. With the -r flag, you can even clean out an entire directory. Nothing can be retrieved after the fact, however, so use great caution.

Task 6.7: Minimizing the Danger of the *rm* Command
Step 1. Description

At this point, you might be wondering why I am making such a big deal of the rm command and the fact that it does what it is advertised to do, that is, remove files.

6

The answer is that learning a bit of paranoia now can save you immense grief in the future. It can prevent you from destroying a file full of information you really needed to save.

For DOS, there are commercial programs (Norton Utilities, for instance) that can retrieve accidentally removed files. The trash can on the Macintosh can be clicked open and the files retrieved with ease. If the trash can is emptied after a file is accidentally discarded, a program such as Symantec Utilities for the Macintosh can be used to restore files.

UNIX just doesn't have that capability, though, and files that are removed are gone forever.

The only exception is if you work on a UNIX system that has an automatic, reliable backup schedule. In this case, you may be able to retrieve from a storage tape an older version of your file (maybe).

That said, there are a few things you can do to lessen the danger of using rm and yet give yourself the ability to remove unwanted files.

Step 2. Action

1. You can use a shorthand, a shell alias, to attach the -i flag automatically to each use of rm. To do this, you need to ascertain what type of login shell you're running. This can most easily be done by using the following command. (Don't worry about what it all does right now. You'll learn about the grep command a few chapters from now.)

```
% grep taylor /etc/passwd
taylor:?:19989:1412:Dave Taylor/users/taylor:/bin/csh
```

The last word on the line is what's important. The /etc/passwd file is one of the database files UNIX uses to track accounts. Each line in the file is called a *password entry* or *password file entry*. On my password entry, you can see that the login shell specified is /bin/csh. If you try this and you don't have an identical entry, you should have /bin/sh or /bin/ksh.

2. If your entry is /bin/csh, enter *exactly* what is shown here (note the tilde):

```
% echo "alias rm /bin/rm -i" >> ~/.cshrc
% source ~/.cshrc
```

Now rm includes the -i flag each time it's used:

```
% touch testme
% rm testme
```

```
rm: remove testme? n
%
```

3. If your entry is /bin/ksh, enter exactly what is shown here, paying particular attention to the two different quotation mark characters and the tilde used in the example:

```
$ echo 'alias rm="/bin/rm -i"' >> ~/.profile
$ . ~/.profile
```

Now rm includes the -i flag each time it's used.

Don't Skip This: One thing to pay special attention to is the difference between the single quote ('), the double quote ("), and the backquote (`). UNIX interprets each differently, though single and double quotes are often interchangeable.

4. If your entry is /bin/sh, you cannot program your system to include the -i flag each time rm is used. The Bourne shell, as sh is known, is the original command shell of UNIX. The Bourne shell lacks an alias feature, a feature that both the Korn shell (ksh) and the C shell (csh) include. As a result, I recommend that you change your login shell to one of these alternatives, if available.

To see what's available, look in the /bin directory on your machine for the specific shells:

```
% ls -l /bin/sh /bin/ksh /bin/csh
-rwxr-xr-x  1 root        102400 Apr  8  1991 /bin/csh*
-rwxr-xr-x  1 root        139264 Jul 26 14:35 /bin/ksh*
-rwxr-xr-x  1 root         28672 Oct 10  1991 /bin/sh*
```

Most of the examples in this book focus on the C shell, because I think it's the easiest of the three shells to use. To change your login shell to csh, you can use the chsh—*change login shell*—command:

```
% chsh
Changing login shell for taylor.
Old shell: /bin/sh
New shell: /bin/csh
%
```

Now you can go back to instruction 2 and set up a C shell alias. This will help you avoid mischief with the `rm` command.

Step 3. Summary

The best way to avoid trouble with any of these commands is to learn to be just a bit paranoid about them. Before you remove a file, make sure it's the one you want. Before you remove a directory, make doubly sure that it doesn't contain any files you might want. Before you rename a file or directory, double-check to see if renaming it is going to cause any trouble.

Take your time with the commands you learned in this lesson and you should be fine. Even in the worst case, you might have the safety net of a system backup performed by a system administrator, but don't rely on it.

Lesson Summary

You have now completed your second day of UNIX instruction. You are now armed with enough commands to cause trouble and make UNIX do what *you* want it to do. From this lesson, you have learned the differences between `cp` and `mv` for moving files and how to use `mv` to rename both files and directories. This lesson also showed you how to create directories with the `mkdir` command and how to remove them with the `rmdir` command. You also learned about the `rm` command for removing files and directories, and how to avoid getting into too much trouble with it.

Finally, if you were really paying attention, you learned how to identify which login shell you're using (`csh`, `ksh`, or `sh`) and how to change from one to another through use of the `chsh` command.

Workshop
Key Terms

absolute filename	Any filename that begins with a leading slash (/), these always uniquely describe a single file in the file system.
password entry	For each account on the UNIX system, there is an entry in the account database known as the password file. This also contains an encrypted copy of the

account password. This set of information for an individual account is known as the password entry.

relative filename

Any filename that does not begin with a slash (/) is a filename whose exact meaning depends on where you are in the file system. For example, `test` might exist in both your home directory and in the root directory: `/test` is an absolute filename and leaves no question which version is being used, but `test` could refer to either copy, depending on your current directory.

shell alias

Most UNIX shells have a convenient way for you to create abbreviations for commonly used commands or series of commands, known as shell aliases. For example, if I always found myself typing `ls -CF`, an alias can let me type just `ls` and have the shell automatically add the `-CF` flags each time.

Questions

1. What's the difference between `cp` and `mv`?

2. If you were installing a program from a floppy disk onto a hard disk, would you use `cp` or `mv`?

3. If you know DOS, this question is for you. Although DOS has a RENAME command, it doesn't have both COPY and MOVE. Which of these two do you think DOS includes? Why?

4. Try using `mkdir` to create a directory. What happens and why?

5. You've noticed that both `rmdir` and `rm -r` can be used to remove directories. Which is safer to use?

6. The `rm` command has another flag that wasn't discussed in this lesson. The `-f` flag forces removal of files regardless of permission (assuming you're the owner, that is). In combination with the `-r` flag, this can be amazingly destructive. Why?

6

Preview of the Next Chapter

The first lesson of your third day introduces the useful `file` command, which indicates the contents of any file in the UNIX file system. With `file`, you will explore various directories in the UNIX file system to see what it reveals about different system and personal files. Then, when you've found some files worth reading, you will learn about `cat`, `more`, and `pg`, which are different ways of looking at the contents of a file.

day

3

Looking Inside Files

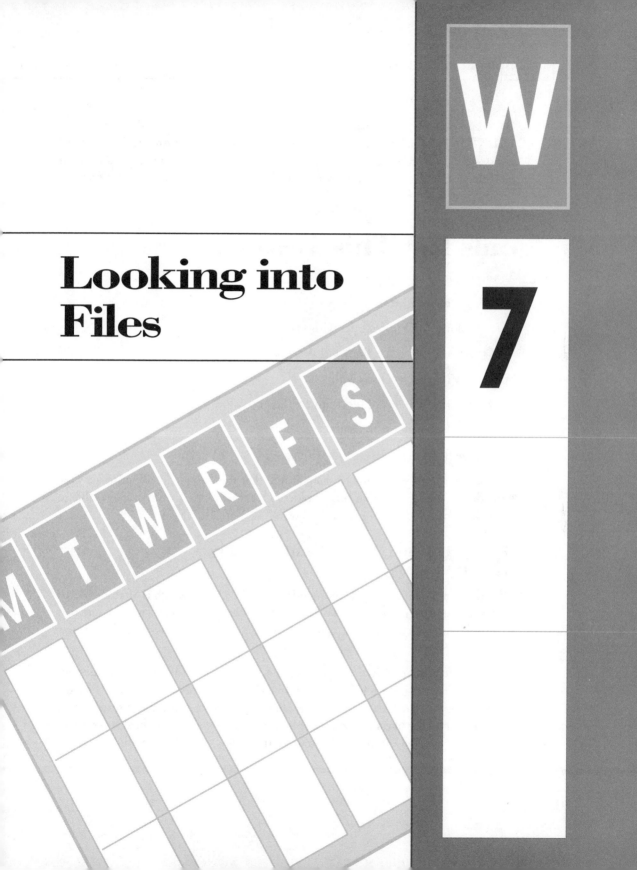

Looking into Files

W

7

By this point in *Teach Yourself UNIX in a Week* you've learned a considerable number of UNIX commands and a lot about the operating and file systems. This chapter focuses on UNIX tools to help you ascertain what type of files you've been seeing in all the different directories, then introduces five different, powerful tools for examining the content of files.

Goals for This Lesson

In this lesson, you learn how to

- ☐ Use `file` to identify file types

- ☐ Explore UNIX directories with `file`

- ☐ Peek at the first few lines with `head`

- ☐ View the last few lines with `tail`

- ☐ View the contents of files with `cat`

- ☐ View larger files with `more`

- ☐ Page through yet larger files with `pg`

This lesson begins with a tool to help ensure that the files you're about to view are intended for human perusal, then explores a number of the commands available to view the contents of the file in various ways.

Task 7.1: Using *file* to Identify File Types
Step 1. Description

One of the most undervalued commands in UNIX is `file`, which is often neglected and collecting dust is some corner of the system. The `file` command is a program that can easily offer you a good hint as to the contents of a file by looking at the first few lines.

Unfortunately, there is a problem with the `file` command: it isn't 100 percent accurate. The program relies on a combination of the permissions of a file, the filename, and an analysis of the first few lines of the text. If you had a text file that started out looking like a C program or had execute permission enabled, `file` might well identify it as an executable program, rather than an English text file.

Comment: You can determine how accurate your version of `file` is by checking the size of its database of file types. You can do this with the UNIX command `wc -l /etc/magic`. The number of entries in the database should be around 100. If you have many less than this number, you're probably going to have trouble. If you have considerably more, you might have a very accurate version of `file` at your fingertips! Remember, however, even if it's relatively small, `file` can still offer invaluable suggestions regarding file content anyway.

Step 2. Action

1. Start by logging in to your account and using the `ls` command to find a file or two to check.

```
% ls -F
Archives/              OWL/                  rumors.26Oct.Z
InfoWorld/             PubAccessLists.Z      rumors.5Nov.Z
LISTS                  bin/                  src/
Mail/                  educ                  temp/
News/                  mailing.lists.bitnet.Z
```

Next, simply enter the `file` command, listing each of the files you'd like the program to analyze:

```
% file LISTS educ rumors.26Oct.Z src
LISTS:   ascii text
educ:    ascii text
rumors.26Oct.Z: block compressed 16 bit code data
src:     directory
```

From this example, you can see that `file` correctly identified `src` as a directory, offers considerable information on the compressed file `rumors.26Oct.Z`, and tags both `LISTS` and `educ` as plain ASCII text files.

Comment: ASCII is the American Standard Code for Information Interchange and means that the file contains the letters of the English alphabet, punctuation, numbers, but not much else. There are no multiple typefaces, italics, or underlined passages, and there are no graphics. It's the lowest common denominator of text in UNIX.

2. Now try using the asterisk (*), a UNIX *wildcard*, to have the program analyze all files in your home directory:

```
% file *
Global.Software:        English text
Interactive.Unix:       mail folder
Mail:           directory
News:           directory
Src:            directory
bin:            directory
history.usenet.Z:       compressed data block compressed 16 bits
```

The asterisk (*) is a special character in UNIX. It tells the system to replace it with the names of all the files in the current directory.

This time you can begin to see how file can help differentiate files: using this command, I am now reminded that the file Global.Software is English text, but Interactive.Unix is actually an old electronic mail message (file can't differentiate between a single mail message and a multiple message folder, so it always errs on the side of saying that the file is a mail folder).

3. Mail folders are actually problematical for the file command. On one of the systems I use, the file command doesn't know what mail messages are, so asking it to analyze mail folders results in a demonstration of how accuracy is related to the size of the file database.

On a Sun system, I asked file to analyze two mail folders, with the following results:

```
% file Mail/mailbox Mail/sent
Mail/mailbox:   mail folder
Mail/sent: mail folder
```

Those same files on a Berkeley UNIX system, however, have very different results when analyzed:

```
% file Mail/mailbox Mail/sent Mail/netnews
Mail/mailbox:           ascii text
Mail/sent:      shell commands
Mail/netnews:           English text
```

Not only does the Berkeley version of UNIX not identify the files correctly, it doesn't even mis-identify them consistently.

4. Another example of the `file` command's limitations is how it interacts with file permissions. Use `cp` to create a new file and work through this example to see how your `file` command interprets the various changes.

```
% cp .cshrc test
% file test
test: shell commands
% chmod +x test
% file test
test: shell script
```

Adding execute permission to this file caused `file` to identify it as a `shell script` rather than `shell commands`.

Step 3. Summary

Don't misinterpret the results of these examples as proof that the `file` command is useless and that you shouldn't use it. Quite the opposite is true. UNIX has neither a specific file-naming convention (DOS has three-letter filename suffixes) nor indication of file ownership by icon (Macintosh does this with *creator* information added by each program). As a result, it's vital that you have a tool for helping ascertain file types without actually opening the file.

Why not just look at the contents? The best way to figure out the answer to this question is to display accidentally the contents of an executable file on the screen. You'll see it's quite a mess, loaded with special control characters that can be best described as making your screen go berserk.

Task 7.2: Exploring UNIX Directories with *file*
Step 1. Description

Now that you know how to work with the `file` command, it's time to look through the UNIX file system, learning more about types of files that tend to be found in specific directories. Your system might vary slightly—it'll certainly have more files in some directories than what I'm showing here in the examples—but you'll quickly see that `file` can offer some valuable insight into the contents of files.

Step 2. Action

1. First things first. Take a look at the files found in the very top level of the file system, in `/` (slash):

```
% cd /
% ls -CF
-No _rm_ star    boot         flags/         rhf@         userb/
OLD/             core         gendynix       stand/       userc/
archive/         dev/         lib@           sys@         userd/
ats/             diag@        lost+found/    tftpboot@    usere/
backup/          dynix        mnt/           tmp/         users/
bin@             etc/         net/           usera/       usr/
% file boot core gendynix tftpboot
boot:    SYMMETRY i386 stand alone executable version 1
core:    core from getty
gendynix:        SYMMETRY i386 stand alone executable not stripped version 1
tftpboot:        symbolic link to /usr/tftpboot
```

This example is from a Sequent computer running DYNIX, the Sequents'
version of Unix, based on Berkeley 4.3 BSD with some AT&T System V
extensions. It's the same machine that has such problems identifying mail
folders.

Executable binaries are explained in detail by the file command on this
computer: boot is listed as SYMMETRY i386 stand alone executable version
1. The specifics aren't vital to understand: the most important word to see in
this output is executable, indicating that the file is the result of compiling a
program. The format is SYMMETRY i386, version 1, and the file requires no
libraries or other files to execute—it's stand alone.

For gendynix, the format is similar, but one snippet of information is added
that isn't indicated for boot: the executable file hasn't been *stripped*.

Comment: Stripping a file doesn't mean that you peel its clothes off, but
rather that a variety of information included in most executables to help
identify and isolate problems has been removed to save space.

When a program dies unexpectedly in UNIX, the operating system tries to
leave a snapshot of the memory that the program was using, to aid in
debugging. Wading through these core files can be quite difficult—it's
usually reserved for a few experts at each site—but there is still some useful

information inside. The best, and simplest, way to check it is with the `file` command. You can see in the preceding listing that `file` recognized the file `core` as a crashed program memory image and further extracted the name of the program, `getty`, that originally failed, causing the *core dump*.

The fourth of the listings offers an easy way to understand symbolic links, indicated in the `ls -CF` output with the suffix @, as shown in the preceding example with `tftpboot@`. Using `file`, you can see that the file `tftpboot` in the slash directory is actually a symbolic link to a file with the same name elsewhere in the file system, `/usr/tftpboot`.

2. There are differences in output formats on different machines. The next example shows what the same command would generate on a Sun Microsystems workstation, examining analogous files:

```
% file boot core kadb tmp
boot:           sparc executable
core:           core file from 'popper'
kadb:           sparc executable not stripped
tmp:            symbolic link to /var/tmp
```

The Sun computer offers the same information, but less specifics about executable binaries. In this case, Sun workstations are built around SPARC chips (just like PCs are built around Intel chips), so the executables are identified as `sparc executable`.

3. Are you ready for another directory of weird files? It's time to move into the `/lib` directory to see what devices are present on your system and what type of files they are.

Entering `ls` will quickly demonstrate that there are a lot of files in this directory! The `file` command can tell you about any of them. On my Sun computer, I asked for information on a few select files, many of which you might also have on yours:

```
% file lib.b lib300.a diffh sendmail
lib.b:          c program text
lib300.a:       archive random library
diffh:          sparc pure dynamically linked executable not stripped
sendmail:       sparc demand paged dynamically linked set-uid executable
```

The first file, lib.b, demonstrates that the file command works regardless of the name of a file. Standard naming for C program files specifies that they end with the characters .c, as in test.c, so without file you might never have suspected that lib.b is a C program. The second file is an actual program library and is identified here as an archive random library, meaning that it's an archive and that the information within can be accessed in random order (by appropriate programs).

The third file is an executable, demonstrating another way that file can indicate programs on a Sun workstation. The sendmail program is an interesting program: it's an executable, but it has some new information that you haven't seen before. The set-uid indicates that the program is set up so that when anyone runs it, sendmail runs as the user who owns the file, *not* the user who launched the program. A quick ls can reveal a bit more about this:

```
% ls -l /lib/sendmail
-r-sr-x--x1 root        155648 Sep 14 09:11 /lib/sendmail*
```

Notice here that the fourth character of the permissions string is an *s*, rather than the expected *x* for an executable. Also check the owner of the file in this listing. Combined, the two mean that when anyone runs this program, sendmail will actually set itself to a different user id (root in this case) and have that set of access permissions. Having sendmail run with root permissions is how you can send electronic mail to someone else without fuss, but you can't view his or her mailbox.

4. Consider now one more directory full of weird files before you start the next section. This time, move into the /dev directory and see what's inside. Again, it's a directory with a lot of files, so don't be surprised if the output scrolls off the screen!

   Try to identify a few files that are similar in name to the ones I examine here and see what file says about them:

```
% cd /dev
% file MAKEDEV audio spx sr0 tty
MAKEDEV:        executable shell script
audio:          character special (69/0)
spx:            character special (37/35)
sr0:            block special (18/0)
tty:            character special (2/0)
```

UNIX has two different types of devices, or peripherals, that can be attached: those that expect information in chunks and those that are happier working on a byte-by-byte basis. The former are called *block special devices* and the latter *character special devices*. You don't have to worry about the differences, but notice that `file` can differentiate between them: `audio`, `spx`, and `tty` are all character-special-device files, whereas `sr0` is a block-special-device file.

The pair of numbers in parentheses following the description of each file are known as the *major number* and *minor number* of the file. The first indicates the type of device, and the second the physical location of the plug, wire, card, or other hardware that is controlled by the specific peripheral.

Step 3. Summary

The good news is that you don't have to worry a bit about what files are in the `/lib`, `/etc`, or any other directory other than your own home directory. There are thousands of happy UNIX folk working busily away each day without ever realizing that these other directories exist, let alone knowing what's in them.

What's important here is that you have learned that the `file` command is quite sophisticated at identifying special UNIX system files of various types. It can be a very helpful tool when you are looking around in the file system and even just when you are trying to remember which files are which in your own directory.

Task 7.3: Peeking at the First Few Lines with *head*
Step 1. Description

Now that you have the tools needed to move about in the file system, to double check where you are, and to identify the types of different files, it's time to learn about some of the many tools UNIX offers for viewing the contents of files. The first on the list is `head`, a simple program for viewing the first ten lines of any file on the system.

The `head` program is more versatile than it sounds: you can use it to view up to the first few hundred lines of a very long file, actually. To specify the number of lines you want to see, you need simply indicate how many as a starting argument, prefixing the number of lines desired with a dash.

> **Comment:** This command, head, is the first of a number of UNIX commands that tend to work with their own variant on the regular rules of starting arguments. Instead of a typical UNIX command argument of -l33 to specify 33 lines, head uses -33 to specify the same information.

Step 2. Action

1. Start by moving back into your home directory and viewing the first few lines of your .cshrc file:

```
% cd
% head .cshrc
#
# Default user .cshrc file (/bin/csh initialization).

set host=limbo

set path=(. ~/bin /bin /usr/bin /usr/ucb /usr/local /etc
/usr/etc/usr/local/bin /usr/unsup/bin)

# Set up C shell environment:

alias  diff      '/usr/bin/diff -c -w'
%
```

The contents of your own .cshrc file will doubtless be different, but notice that the program lists only the first few lines of the file.

2. To specify a different number of lines, use the -N format (where N is the number of lines). I'll look at just the first four lines of the .login file:

```
% head -4 .login
#
# @(#) $Revision: 62.2 $

setenv TERM vt100
%
```

3. You can also easily check multiple files by specifying them to the program:

```
% head -3 .newsrc /etc/passwd
==> .newsrc <==
misc.forsale.computers.mac: 1-14536
utech.student-orgs! 1
general! 1-546
```

```
==> /etc/passwd <==
root:?:0:0: root,,,,:/:/bin/csh
news:?:6:11:USENET News,,,,:/usr/spool/news:/bin/ksh
ingres:*?:7:519:INGRES Manager,,,,:/usr/ingres:/bin/csh
%
```

4. More importantly, head, and other UNIX commands, can also work as part of a *pipeline*, where the output of one program is the input of the next. The special symbol for creating UNIX pipelines is the pipe (¦) character. Pipes are read left-to-right, so you can easily have the output of who, for example, feed into head, offering powerful new possibilities. Perhaps you want to see just the first five people logged into the computer right now. Try this:

```
% who ¦ head -5
root      console Nov  9 07:31
mccool    ttyaO   Nov 10 14:25
millekl2 ttyaP   Nov 10 14:58
paulwhit ttyaR   Nov 10 14:50
bobweir   ttyaS   Nov 10 14:49
Broken pipe
%
```

Pipes are one of the most powerful features of UNIX, and there are many examples of how to use them to best effect throughout the remainder of this book.

5. Here is one last thing. Find an executable, /boot will do fine, and enter head -1 /boot. Watch what happens, or, if you'd like to preserve your sanity, take it from me that the random junk thrown on your screen is plenty to cause your program to get quite confused and possibly even quit or crash.

The point isn't to have that happen to your screen, but rather to remind you that using file to confirm file type for unfamiliar files can save you lots of grief and frustration!

Step 3. Summary

The simplest of programs for viewing the content of a file, head is easy to use, efficient, and works as part of a pipeline, too. The remainder of this lesson focuses on other tools in UNIX that offer other ways to view the contents of text and ASCII files.

Task 7.4: Viewing the Last Few Lines with *tail*
Step 1. Description

The head program shows you the first ten lines of the file you specify. What would you expect tail would do, therefore? I hope you guessed the right answer: it shows the last ten lines of a file. Like head, tail also understands the same format for specifying the number of lines to view.

Step 2. Action

1. Start out viewing the last 12 lines of your .cshrc file:

```
% tail -12 .cshrc

  set noclobber history=100 system=filec
  umask 007

  setprompt
endif

# special aliases:

alias info      ssinfo
alias ssinfo    'echo "connecting..." ; rlogin oasis'
%
```

2. Next, the last four lines of the file LISTS in my home directory can be shown with the following command line:

```
% tail -5 LISTS
        College of Education
        Arizona State University
        Tempe, AZ 85287-2411
        602-965-2692

%
```

Don't get too hung up trying to figure out what's inside my files. I'm not even sure myself sometimes.

3. Here's one to think about. You can use head to view the first *n* lines of a file, and tail to view the last *n* lines of a file. Can you figure out a way to

combine the two so you can see just the tenth, eleventh, and twelfth lines of a file?

```
% head -12 .cshrc | tail -3
alias   diff      '/usr/bin/diff -c -w'
alias   from      'frm -n'
alias   ll        'ls -l'
%
```

It's easy with UNIX command pipelines!

Step 3. Summary

Combining the two commands head and tail can give you considerable power in viewing specific slices of a file on the UNIX system. Try combining them in different ways for different effects.

Task 7.5: Viewing the Contents of Files with *cat*
Step 1. Description

Both head and tail offer the ability to view a piece of a file, either the top or bottom, but neither lets you see the entire file, regardless of length. For this job, the cat program is the right choice.

> **Comment:** The cat program got its name from its function in the early versions of UNIX; its function was to *concatenate* (or join together) multiple files. It isn't, unfortunately, an homage to feline pets or anything else so exotic!

The cat program also has a valuable secret capability too: through use of the -v flag, you can use cat to display any file on the system, executable or otherwise, with all characters that would normally not be printed (or would drive your screen bonkers) displayed in a special format I call *control key notation*. In control key notation, each character is represented as ^*n* where *n* is a specific printable letter or symbol. A character with the value of zero (also referred to as a *null* or *null character*) is displayed as ^@, character 1 is ^A, 2 is ^B, and so on.

Another cat flag that can be useful for certain files is -s, which suppresses multiple blank lines from a file. It isn't immediately obvious how that could help, but there are some files that can have a screenful (or more) of blank lines. To avoid having to watch them all fly past, you can use cat -s to chop 'em all down to a single blank line.

Step 2. Action

1. Move back to your home directory again, and use cat to display the complete contents of your .cshrc file:

```
% cd
% cat .cshrc
#
# Default user .cshrc file (/bin/csh initialization).

set path=(. ~/bin /bin /usr/bin /usr/ucb /usr/local /etc
/usr/etc/usr/local/bin /usr/unsup/bin )

# Set up C shell environment:

alias   diff      '/usr/bin/diff -c -w'
alias   from      'frm -n'
alias   ll        'ls -l'
alias   ls        '/bin/ls -F'
alias   mail      Mail
alias   mailq     '/usr/lib/sendmail -bp'

alias   newaliases 'echo you mean newalias...'

alias   rd        'readmsg $ ¦ page'
alias   rn        '/usr/local/bin/rn -d$HOME -L -M -m -e -S -/'

# and some special stuff if we're in an interactive shell

if ( $?prompt ) then             # shell is interactive.

  alias   cd                'chdir \!* ; setprompt'
  alias   env               'printenv'
  alias   setprompt         'set prompt="$system ($cwd:t) \! : "'

  set noclobber history=100 system=limbo filec
  umask 007

  setprompt
endif
```

```
# special aliases:

alias info     ssinfo
alias ssinfo   'echo "connecting..." ; rlogin oasis'
%
```

Don't be too concerned if the contents of your `.cshrc` file (or mine) makes any sense to you. You are slated to learn about the contents of this file within a few lessons, and, yes, it is complex.

You can see that `cat` is pretty simple to use. If you specify more than one filename to the program, it lists them in the order you specify. You can even list the contents of a file multiple times by specifying the same filename on the command line multiple times.

2. The cat program can also be used as part of a pipeline. Compare the following command with my earlier usage of `head` and `tail`:

```
% cat LISTS ¦ tail -5
          College of Education
          Arizona State University
          Tempe, AZ 85287-2411
          602-965-2692

%
```

3. Now find an executable file and try `cat -v` in combination with `head` to get a glimpse of the contents therein:

```
% cat -v /bin/ls ¦ head -1
M-k"^@^@^@M-^@^@^@^@^P^@^@M-45^@^@^@^@^@^@M-l^P^@^@

^@^@^@^@^@^@^@^@^@^@^@^@^@^@^@^@^@^@^@^@^@^@^@^@^@^@^@^@^@^@^@^@^@^@^@^

@^@^@^@^@^@^@^@^@^@^@^@^@^@^@^@^@^@^@^@^@^@^@^@^@^@^@^@^@^@^@^@^@^@^@^

@^@^@^@^@^@^@^@^@^@^@^@^@^@^@^@^@^@^A^@^@^@$Header: crt0.c 1.4 87/04/23

$^@^@@(#)Copyright (C) 1984 XXX Computer Systems, Inc. All rights

reserved.^@M-^KM-NM-^KM-tM-^MF^DM-^KM-XM-^K^F@M-^M^DM-^E^@^@^@^@M-^KM-S^AM-

BM-^I^U^@M-^@^@^@SM-^?6M-hw^T^@^@M-^CM-D^HM-^?5^@M-^@^@^@SM-^?6M-h&^@^@^@M-

^CM-D^LPM-h)[^@^@YM-tM-^PM-^PM-^PM-k^BM-IM-CUM-^KM-lM-kM-yM-^PM-^PM-^PM-k^BM-

IM-CUM-^KM-lM-kM-yM-^PM-^PM-^PUM-^KM-lM-^CM-l^XWVSM-^Ku^LM-^K]^HKM-^CM-F^DM-
```

163

```
hM-X^V^@^@M-^EM-@u^FM-^?^EM-1M-^L^@^@h^DM-^M^@^@M-hM-P7^@^@YM-^K^E^DM-^M^@^@-
^@NM-m^@M-^I^E^HM-^M^@^@M-^K^E^DM-^M^@^@^E^P^N^@^@M-^I^E^LM-^M^@^@M-^C^E^DM-
^M^@^@<M-G^E^PM-^M^@^@P^@^@^@j^AM-hM-%[^@^@YM-^EM-@tNh^TM-^M^@^@hM-HM-^J^@^
@M-h12^@^@M-^CM-D^HM-G^EM-pM-^L^@^@^A^@^@^@M-8^A^@^@^@M-^I^EM-hM-^L^@^@M-ht^
S^@^@M-^MEM-nPj^AM-h]^V^@^@M-^CM-D^H^OM-?EM-r%^@^L^@^@=^@Broken pipe%
```

This is complex and confusing, indeed! What's worse, this isn't the entire first line of the executable. You can see that, because this block of data ends with Broken pipe, indicating that a lot more was being fed to head than it could process due to the constraint of having only the first line listed, a line that head defines as no more than 512 characters long.

Step 3. Summary

The cat is useful for viewing files and is quite easy to use, too. The problem with it is that if the file you choose to view has more than the number of lines on your screen, the file will just fly past you without you having any way to slow it down. That's where the next two commands come in handy: more for stepping through files, and page for paging through files. Both solve this problem, albeit in slightly different ways.

Task 7.6: Viewing Larger Files with *more*
Step 1. Description

You can now wander about the file system, find files that might be of interest, check their type with file, and even view them with the cat command, but what if they're longer than the size of your screen? That's the job of the more program, a program that knows how big your screen is and displays the information page-by-page.

The pg command also displays files page-by-page, but there are two important differences: pg rewrites the screen for each page (whereas more simply scrolls through the file), and pg can search backwards and otherwise offer more sophistication on browsing.

There are three primary flags in more: -s to suppress multiple blank lines, just like the -s flag to cat; -d, which forces more to display friendlier prompts at the bottom of each page; and -c, which causes the program to clear the screen before displaying each

screenful of text. The program also allows you to start at a specific line in the file by using the curious *+n* notation, where *n* is a specific number. Finally, you can also start at the first occurrence of a specific pattern by specifying that pattern to the program in a format similar to *+/pattern*.

Step 2. Action

1. View the .cshrc file using more:

```
% more ~/.cshrc
#
# Default user .cshrc file (/bin/csh initialization).

set host=limbo

set path=(. ~/bin /bin /usr/bin /usr/ucb /usr/local /etc
/usr/etc /usr/local/bin /usr/unsup/bin)

# Set up C shell environment:

alias  diff      '/usr/bin/diff -c -w'
alias  from      'frm -n'
alias  ll        'ls -l'
alias  ls        '/bin/ls -F'
alias  mail      Mail
alias  mailq     '/usr/lib/sendmail -bp'

alias  newaliases 'echo you mean newalias...'


alias  rd        'readmsg $ ¦ page'
--More--(51%)
```

Unlike previous examples, where the program runs until completed, leaving you back on the command line, more is the first *interactive* program you've learned. When you see the --More--(51%) prompt, the cursor sits at the end of that line, waiting for you to tell it what to do. The more program lets you know how far into the file you've viewed, too; in the example, you've seen about half of the file (51 percent).

At this point there are quite a variety of different commands available. Press the spacebar to see the next screen of information, until you have seen the entire file.

2. Try starting up the program with the twelfth line of the file:

```
% more +12 ~/.cshrc
alias  mailq    '/usr/lib/sendmail -bp'

alias  newaliases 'echo you mean newalias...'

alias  rd        'readmsg $ ¦ page'
alias  rn        '/usr/local/bin/rn -d$HOME -L -M -m -e -S -/'

# and some special stuff if we're in an interactive shell

if ( $?prompt ) then            # shell is interactive.

  alias  cd              'chdir \!* ; setprompt'
  alias  env            'printenv'
  alias  setprompt      'set prompt="$system ($cwd:t) \! : "'

  set noclobber history=100 filec
  umask 007

  setprompt
endif
--More--(82%)
```

3. You can see that about halfway through the .cshrc file is a line that contains the word newaliases. I can start up more so that the line with this pattern is displayed on the top of the first screenful.

```
% more +/newaliases ~/.cshrc

...skipping
alias  mailq    '/usr/lib/sendmail -bp'

alias  newaliases 'echo you mean newalias...'

alias  rd        'readmsg $ ¦ page'
alias  rn        '/usr/local/bin/rn -d$HOME -L -M -m -e -S -/'

# and some special stuff if we're in an interactive shell

if ( $?prompt ) then            # shell is interactive.

  alias  cd              'chdir \!* ; setprompt'
  alias  env            'printenv'
  alias  setprompt      'set prompt="$system ($cwd:t) \! : "'
```

```
    set noclobber history=100 filec
    umask 007

    setprompt
endif

# special aliases:

alias info        ssinfo
--More--(86%)
```

Actually, you'll notice that the line containing the pattern newaliases shows up as the third line of the first screen, not the first line. That's so you have a bit of context to the matched line, but it can take some getting used to. Also note that more tells us—with the message ...skipping as the very first line—that it's skipping some lines to find the pattern.

4. The range of commands available at the --More-- prompt is quite extensive, as shown in Table 7.1.

Table 7.1. Commands available within the more program.

Command	Function
[space]	Display next screenful of text.
N [return]	Display next *N* lines (default is the next line only of text).
h	Help (display a list of commands).
d	Scroll down a half-page.
q	Quit.
N s	Skip forward *N* lines (default is 1).
N f	Skip forward *N* screenfuls (default is 1).
b or ctrl-B	Skip backwards a screen of text.

continues

Table 7.1. continued

Command	Function
=	Display current line number.
/pattern	Search for an occurrence of a *pattern*.
n	Search for next occurrence of the current pattern.
v	Start the vi editor at current line.
ctrl-L	Redraw screen.
:f	Display current filename and line number.

In this table and in the following text, the word *space* enclosed in brackets and set in a distinctive typeface [space] refers to pressing the spacebar as a command. Likewise, [return] means you should press the Return key as part of the command. As in the earlier part of this book, a hyphen in a command—for example ctrl-B—means that you should press the first indicated key while you press the second key. The lowercase-letter commands in the table indicate that you should press the corresponding key, the A key for the a command, for example. Two characters together, but without a hyphen (:f), mean that you should press the appropriate keys in sequence, as you would when typing text. Finally, entries that have an *N* before the command mean that you can prefix the command with a number, which will let it use that value to modify its action. For example, 3[return] displays the next three lines of the file and 250s skips the next 250 lines. Typically, pressing Return after typing a command within more is not necessary.

Try some commands on a file of your own. A good file that will have enough lines to make this interesting is /etc/passwd:

```
% more /etc/passwd
root:?:0:0: root:/:/bin/csh
news:?:6:11:USENET News:/usr/spool/news:/bin/ksh
```

```
ingres:*?:7:519:INGRES Manager:/usr/ingres:/bin/csh
usrlimit:?:8:800:(1000 user system):/mnt:/bin/false
vanilla:*?:20:805:Vanilla Account:/mnt:/bin/sh
charon:*?:21:807:The Ferryman:/users/tomb:
actmaint:?:23:809: Maintenance:/usr/adm/actmaint:/bin/ksh
pop:*?:26:819:,,,,:/usr/spool/pop:/bin/csh
lp:*?:70:10:System V Lp Admin:/usr/spool/lp:
trouble:*?:97:501:Trouble Report Facility:/usr/trouble:/usr/msh
postmaster:?:98:504:Mail:/usr/local/adm:/bin/csh
aab:?:513:1233:Robert Townsend:/users/aab:/bin/ksh
billing:?:516:1233:Accounting:/users/billing:/bin/csh
aai:?:520:1233:Pete Cheeseman:/users/aai:/bin/csh

--More--(1%) 60s


...skipping 60 lines

cq:?:843:1233:Rob Tillot:/users/cq:/usr/local/bin/tcsh
robb:?:969:1233:Robb:/users/robb:/usr/local/lib/msh
aok:?:970:1233:B Jacobs:/users/aok:/usr/local/lib/msh
went:?:1040:1233:David Math:/users/went:/bin/csh
aru:?:1076:1233:Raffie:/users/aru:/bin/ksh
varney:?:1094:1233:/users/varney:/bin/csh
brandt:?:1096:1233:Eric Brand:/users/brand:/usr/local/bin/tcsh
ask:?:1098:1233:/users/ask:/bin/csh
asn:?:1101:1233:Ketter Wesley:/users/asn:/usr/local/lib/msh

--More--(2%)
```

This example isn't exactly what you'll see on your screen because each time you type a command to more it erases its own prompt and replaces the prompt with the appropriate line of the file. Try pressing [return] to move down one line and you'll see what I mean.

Quit more in the middle of viewing this file by typing q.

Step 3. Summary

The more program is one of the best general purpose programs in UNIX, offering an easy and powerful tool for perusing files. The biggest limitation, however, is that you can't go backwards in the file: if you realize what you are looking for is on the previous page, you have to quit and start the program again.

By contrast, pg offers all of these capabilities and can go backwards in the file, allowing you to wander around to your heart's content.

Task 7.7: Paging Through Yet Larger Files with *pg*
Step 1. Description

Looking at simple files, it's easy to see how more can do a great job, helping with pattern searching and ensuring that information doesn't flow past without you being able to read it, something that cat has no compunction about. What if you're looking at a really big file, however, one that has so much information that you would prefer to be able to move around in the file, backing up as easily as moving forward?

If that's what you're looking for, then pg is the program for you. A program that you might not find on Berkeley-based systems, unfortunately, the pg program is the most powerful tool (other than an actual text editor) for viewing files.

Functionally, pg is very similar to more, sharing even many of the starting arguments, including -c to clear the screen before each new screenful of text is displayed, +N to start on the *Nth* line of the file, +/*pat* to start a line or two above the specified pattern, and -s to suppress multiple blank lines. The pg program does not support the -d flag for more understandable prompts but instead has its own, quite complex mechanism that I won't detail herein.

Once within pg, many of the commands available from within more, as listed in Table 7.1, also work. One notable change is that the [space] command no longer works as you would like; use [return] to display the next page of information. Some other commands are also added, as you might expect, shown in Table 7.2:

Table 7.2. Commands available within the pg program.

Command	Function
[return]	Display next screenful
N	Skip N screenfuls of text
N l	Move down N lines of text
ctrl-D	Scroll down a half-page
h	Help (displays a list of commands)

Command	Function
q	Quit
/pattern	Search forward for a *pattern*
?pattern	Search backward for a *pattern*
/	Search for next occurrence of pattern
?	Search for an earlier occurrence of pattern
v	Start up the vi editor at current line
.	Redraw current screenful
$	Display last screenful of the file

One notable difference between pg and more is that, within pg, any command taking a numeric modifier can move you in either direction. So whereas 15l moves you forward fifteen lines, -15l will move you *back* fifteen lines in the file. Similarly, -3[return] will move you *back* three screens.

Step 2. Action

1. Start out by looking at the same file, but using pg instead of more:

```
% pg -c ~/.cshrc
#
# Default user .cshrc file (/bin/csh initialization).

set host=limbo

set path=(. ~/bin /bin /usr/bin /usr/ucb /usr/local /etc
/usr/etc /usr/local/bin /usr/unsup/bin )

# Set up C shell environment:

alias  diff     '/usr/bin/diff -c -w'
alias  from     'frm -n'
alias  ll       'ls -l'
alias  ls       '/bin/ls -F'
```

```
alias  mail     Mail
alias  mailq    '/usr/lib/sendmail -bp'

alias  newaliases 'echo you mean newalias...'

alias  rd       'readmsg $ ¦ page'
:
```

The prompt here is a bit less friendly, being just a colon without any further suggestions on what to do. Type q to quit, so you can look at a different file.

2. Now look at the /etc/passwd file, and try moving down sixty lines:

```
% pg -c /etc/passwd
root:?:0:0:/:/bin/csh
news:?:6:11:USENET News:/usr/spool/news:/bin/ksh
ingres:*?:7:519:INGRES Manager:/usr/ingres:/bin/csh
usrlimit:?:8:800:(1000 user system):/mnt:/bin/false
vanilla:*?:20:805:Vanilla Account:/mnt:/bin/sh
charon:*?:21:807:The Ferryman:/userb/tomb:
actmaint:?:23:809: Maintenance:/usr/adm/actmaint:/bin/ksh
pop:*?:26:819:,,,,:/usr/spool/pop:/bin/csh
lp:*?:70:10:System V Lp Admin:/usr/spool/lp:
trouble:*?:97:501:Trouble Report:/usr/mrg/trouble:/usr/msh
postmaster:?:98:504:Mail:/usr/local/adm:/bin/csh
aab:?:513:1233:Robert Townsend:/users/aab:/bin/ksh
billing:?:516:1233:Accounting:/users/billing:/bin/csh
aai:?:520:1233:Pete Cheese:/users/aai:/bin/csh
:601
```

When you type this command, your screen will be *replaced* with the contents of the file at the new point:

```
cq:?:843:1233:Rob Tillot:/users/cq:/usr/local/bin/tcsh
robb:?:969:1233:Robb:/users/robb:/usr/local/lib/msh
aok:?:970:1233:B Jacobs:/users/aok:/usr/local/lib/msh
went:?:1040:1233:David Math:/users/went:/bin/csh
aru:?:1076:1233:Raffie:/users/aru:/bin/ksh
varney:?:1094:1233:/users/varney:/bin/csh
brandt:?:1096:1233:Eric Brand:/users/brand:/usr/local/bin/tcsh
ask:?:1098:1233::/users/ask:/bin/csh
asn:?:1101:1233:Ketter Wesley:/users/asn:/usr/local/lib/msh
:
```

3. I'll use this opportunity to search for my own account by specifying /Dave Taylor at the colon prompt:

```
:/Dave Taylor
...skipping forward
dataylor:?:3755:518:Dave Taylor:/users/dataylor:/usr/msh
kreppert:?:10315:1412:Karl Reppert:/users/kreppert:/bin/csh
jmark:?:10314:1412:John Mark:/users/jmark:/bin/csh
rvw:?:3780:1046:Rich Will:/users/rvw:/bin/csh
shirt:?:3576:1375:Sh Fu:/users/shirt:/bin/csh
ashvan:?:3794:1324:UD:/users/ashvan:/bin/csh
skwood:?:3800:1545:Steve:/users/skwood:/bin/csh
lucas:?:3801:1233:Jo Lucas:/users/lucas:/bin/csh
mwittrig:?:3824:1324:Mal Wittriger:/users/mwittrig:/bin/csh
dnuy:?:3822:1318:Duy Nuy:/users/dnuy:/bin/csh
nurad:?:3823:1409:Work:/users/nurad:/bin/csh
nard:?:3827:1545:Cheryl ard,,,,:/users/nard:/bin/csh
balt:?:3625:1526:Karl Balt,,,,:/users/balt:/bin/csh
:
```

That's good, but it isn't the entry I want. I can search for a subsequent occurrence by simply typing the slash:

```
:/
...skipping forward
taylor:?:198:1412:Dave Taylor:/users/taylor:/bin/csh
kiraj:?:1991:1297:Kent Johns:/users/kiraj:/bin/csh
larry:?:19992:1297:Lawrence:/users/larry:/bin/csh
avery:?:20204:1508:Al Avery,,,,:/users/avery:/bin/csh
jlhist:?:20165:1140:Joe Larson:/users/jlhist:/bin/csh
anders:?:9929:1067:Mike Anders:/users/anders:/bin/csh
evan:?:17097:1137:Joe Evens,,,,:/users/evans:/bin/csh
nuspl:?:5731:1042:Joe Naspl,,,,:/users/nuspljj:/bin/csh
slager:?:2716:1233:Steve Lager:/users/slager:/usr/local/bin/tcsh
may:?:2725:1233: Mary May:/users/may:/usr/local/bin/tcsh
tchin:?:5925:1233:Ted Chin:/users/tchen:/usr/local/bin/tcsh
mds:?:5983:1233:Mark D. Sund:/users/mds:/bin/ksh
animal:?:6056:1376:Animal Advocates:/users/animal:/bin/csh
:
```

If I wanted to step back to the previous match, I could easily use ?Dave Taylor to move backwards in the file too.

Step 3. Summary

You now have a number of different programs that you can use to view the contents of different files. Stop for a moment and consider the differences between cat, more, and pg, and suggest where you might find each most helpful.

Lesson Summary

Now that you can add this set of commands to your retinue of UNIX expertise, you are most certainly ready to wander about your own computer system, understanding what files are what, where they are, and how to peer inside. You learned about `file` to ascertain type; `head` and `tail` for seeing snippets of files; and `cat`, `more`, and `pg` to help easily view files of any size on your screen.

Workshop
Key Terms

block special device

A device driver that controls block-oriented peripherals. A hard disk, for example, is a peripheral that works by reading and writing blocks of information (as distinguished from a *character special device*).

character special device

A device driver that controls a character-oriented peripheral. Your keyboard and display are both character-oriented devices, sending and displaying information on a character-by-character basis.

control key notation

A notational convention in UNIX that denotes the use of a *control key*. There are three common conventions: Ctrl-C, ^c and C-C all denote the Control-C character, produced by pressing the Control key (labeled Control or Ctrl on your keyboard) and, while holding it down, pressing the C key.

file creator

On the Apple Macintosh, any application that creates a file (for example, a word processing document) records its own name as the file creator. This is then used by the Macintosh operating system to ascertain which program to launch if the file is opened by the user.

interactive program	An interactive UNIX application is one that expects the user to enter information and then responds as appropriate. The ls command is not interactive, but the more program, which displays text a screenful at a time, is interactive.
major number	For device drivers, the major number identifies the specific type of device in use to the operating system. This is easier remembered as the device id number.
minor number	Once the device driver is identified to the operating system by its *major number*, the address of the device in the computer itself (that is, which card slot a peripheral card is plugged in) is indicated by its minor number.
null character	Each character in UNIX has a specific value, and any character with a numeric value of zero is known as a null or null character.
pipeline	A series of UNIX commands chained by ¦, the *pipe* symbol.

Questions

1. Many people who use UNIX systems tend to stick with file-naming conventions. Indeed, UNIX has many of its own, including .c for C source files, .z for compressed files, and a single dot prefix for dot files. Yet file ignores filenames (test it yourself). Why?

2. Use more to check some of the possible file types that can be recognized with the file command by peeking in the configuration file /etc/magic.

3. Do you remember the television game show *Name that Tune*? If you do, you'll recall how contestants had to identify a popular song by hearing just the first few notes. The file command is similar; the program must guess at the type of the file by checking only the first few characters. Do you think it

would be more accurate by checking more of the file, or less accurate? (Think about this one.)

4. How did the `cat` command get its name? Do you find that a helpful mnemonic?

5. Here's an oddity: what will this command do?
   ```
   cat LISTS ¦ more
   ```
   How about this one?
   ```
   more LISTS ¦ pg
   ```

6. If you were looking at an absolutely huge file, and you were pretty sure that what you wanted was near the bottom, what command would you use, and why?

7. What about if the information was near the top?

Preview of the Next Chapter

There are lots of special characters in UNIX, as you have doubtless learned by accidentally typing a slash, asterisk, question mark, quote, or just about any other punctuation character. What may surprise you is that they all have different, specific meanings. The next lesson explains considerably more about how pipes work and how programs are used as *filters*. Among the new commands you will learn are `sort`, `wc`, `nl`, `uniq`, and `spell`. You also will learn a new, immensely helpful flag to `cat` that makes `cat` produce line numbers. You will also learn one of the secret UNIX commands for those really in the know, the secret-society pattern-matching program `grep`. Better yet, you will learn how it got its weird and confusing name!

Filters and Piping

W

8

If you've ever learned a foreign language, you know that the most common approach is to start by building your vocabulary (almost always including the names of the months, for some reason) and then learn about sentence construction rules. The UNIX command line is a lot like a language. Now you've learned a lot of UNIX words, so it's time to learn how to put them together as sentences using file redirection, filters, and pipes.

Commands to be added to your vocabulary this lesson include wc, sort, nl, spell, uniq, and grep (grep for searching within files). You will also learn about the -n flag to the cat command, which forces cat to add line numbers, and how you can use that to help find information within files.

Goals for This Lesson

In this lesson you will learn

- ☐ The secrets of file redirection

- ☐ How to count words and lines using wc

- ☐ How to remove extraneous lines using uniq

- ☐ How to sort information in a file using sort

- ☐ How to check spelling of a file's text using spell

- ☐ How to add line numbers to files with cat -n and nl

- ☐ Cool nl tricks and capabilities

- ☐ How to search files using grep

- ☐ About filename wildcards

This lesson begins by focusing on one aspect of constructing powerful custom commands in UNIX by using file redirection. The introduction of some *filters*, programs that are intended to be used as part of command pipes, will follow. Next you will learn another aspect of creating your own UNIX commands using pipelines. A foray into looking for lines within files using the grep command wraps up this lesson.

Task 8.1: The Secrets of File Redirection
Step 1. Description

So far, all the commands you've learned while teaching yourself UNIX have required you to enter information at the command line, and all have produced output on the screen. But, as Gershwin wrote in *Porgy and Bess,* "it ain't necessarily so." In fact, one of the most powerful features of UNIX is that the input can come from a file as easily as it can come from the keyboard, and the output can be saved to a file as easily as it can be displayed on your screen.

The secret is *file redirection,* the special commands in UNIX that instruct the computer to read from a file, write to a file, or even append information to an existing file. Each of these acts can be accomplished by placing a *file redirection command* in a regular command line: < redirects input, > redirects output, and >> redirects output and appends the information to the existing file. A mnemonic for remembering which is which is to remember that, just as in English, UNIX works from left to right, so a character that points to the left (<) changes the input, whereas a character that points right (>) changes the output.

Step 2. Action

1. Log in to your account and create an empty file using the `touch` command:

```
% touch testme
%
```

2. First, use this empty file to learn how to redirect output. Use `ls` to list the files in your directory, saving them all to the newly created file:

```
% ls -l testme
-rw-rw-r--  1 taylor        0 Nov 15 09:11 testme
% ls -l > testme
% ls -l testme
-rw-rw-r--  1 taylor      120 Nov 15 09:12 testme
```

Notice that when you redirected the output, nothing was displayed on the screen; there was no visual confirmation that it worked. But it did, as you can see by the increased size of the new file.

3. Instead of using `cat` or `more` to view this file, try using file redirection:

```
% cat < testme
total 127
drwx------  2 taylor       512 Nov  6 14:20 Archives/
drwx------  3 taylor       512 Nov 16 21:55 InfoWorld/
drwx------  2 taylor      1024 Nov 19 14:14 Mail/
drwx------  2 taylor       512 Oct  6 09:36 News/
drwx------  3 taylor       512 Nov 11 10:48 OWL/
drwx------  2 taylor       512 Oct 13 10:45 bin/
```

```
-rw-rw----  1 taylor       57683 Nov 20 20:10 bitnet.lists.Z
-rw-rw----  1 taylor       46195 Nov 20 06:19 drop.text.hqx
-rw-rw----  1 taylor       12556 Nov 16 09:49 keylime.pie
drwx------  2 taylor         512 Oct 13 10:45 src/
drwxrwx---  2 taylor         512 Nov  8 22:20 temp/
-rw-rw----  1 taylor           0 Nov 20 20:21 testme
```

The results are the same as if you had used the 1s command, but the output
file is saved, as well. You can now easily print the file or go back to it later to
compare the way it looks with the way your files look in the future.

4. Use the 1s command to add some further information at the bottom of the
testme file, by using >>, the append double arrow notation:

```
% ls -FC >> testme
%
```

Recall that the -C flag to 1s forces the system to list output in multicolumn
mode. Try redirecting the output of 1s -F to a file to see what happens
without the -C flag.

5. It's time for a real-life example. You've finished learning UNIX and your
colleagues now consider you an expert. One afternoon, Shala tells you she
has a file in her directory, but she isn't sure what it is. She wants to know
what it is, but she can't figure out how to get to it. You try the file command, and UNIX tells you the file is data. You are a bit puzzled. But then
you remember file redirection:

```
% cat -v < mystery.file > visible.mystery.file
```

This command has cat -v take its input from the file mystery.file and save
its output in visible.mystery.file. All the nonprinting characters are
transformed, and Shala can poke through the file at her leisure.

Find a file on your system that file reports as a data file, and try using the
redirection commands to create a version with all characters printable
through the use of cat -v.

Step 3. Summary

There is an infinite number of ways that you can combine the various forms of file
redirection to create custom commands and to process files in various ways. This
lesson has really just scratched the surface. Now you will learn about some popular
UNIX filters and how they can be combined with file redirection to create new
versions of existing files. Also study the example about Shala's file, which shows the

basic steps in all UNIX file redirection operations: specify the input to the command, specify the command, and specify where the output should go.

Task 8.2: Counting Words and Lines Using *wc*
Step 1. Description

Writers generally talk about the length of their work in terms of number of words, rather than number of pages. In fact, most magazines and newspapers are laid out according to formulas based on multiplying an average-length word by the number of words in an article.

These people are obsessed with counting the words in their articles, but how do they do it? You can bet they don't count each word themselves. If they're using UNIX, they simply use the UNIX program wc, which computes a *word count* for the file. It can also indicate the number of characters (which ls -l indicates, too) and number of lines in the file.

Step 2. Action

1. Start by counting the lines, words, and characters in the testme file you created earlier in this lesson:

```
% wc testme
      4      12     121
% wc < testme
      4      12     121
% cat testme ¦ wc
      4      12     121
```

All three of these commands offer the same result (which probably seems a bit cryptic now). Why do you need to have three ways of doing the same thing? Later you'll learn why this is so helpful. For now, stick to using the first form of the command.

The output is three numbers, which reveal how many lines, words, and characters, respectively, are in the file. You can see that there are 4 lines, 12 words, and 121 characters in testme.

2. You can have wc list any one of these counts, or a combination of two, by using different command flags: -w counts *words*, -c counts *characters*, and -l counts *lines*:

```
% wc -w testme
   12 testme
```

```
% wc -l testme
    4 testme
% wc -wl testme
       12       4 testme
% wc -lw testme
        4      12 testme
```

3. Now the fun begins. Here's an easy way to find out how many files you have in your home directory:

```
% ls ¦ wc -l
37
```

The ls command lists each file, one per line (because you didn't use the -c flag). The output of that command is fed to wc, which counts the number of lines it's fed. The result is that you can find out how many files you have (37) in your home directory.

4. How about a quick gauge of how many users are on the system?

```
% who ¦ wc -l
   12
```

5. How many accounts are on your computer?

```
% cat /etc/passwd ¦ wc -l
   3877
```

Step 3. Summary

The wc command is a great example of how the simplest of commands, when combined in a sophisticated pipeline, can be very powerful.

Task 8.3: Removing Extraneous Lines Using *uniq*
Step 1. Description

Sometimes when you're looking at a file, you'll notice that there are many duplicate entries, either blank lines or, perhaps, lines of repeated information. To clean up these files and shrink their size at the same time, you can use the uniq command, which lists each *unique* line in the file.

Well, it sort of lists each unique line in the file. What uniq really does is compare each line it reads with the previous line. If the lines are the same, uniq does not list the second line. You can use flags with uniq to get more specific results: -u lists only lines that are not repeated, -d lists only lines that are repeated (the exact opposite of -u), and -c adds a count of how many times each line occurred.

Step 2. Action

1. If you use `uniq` on a file that doesn't have any common lines, `uniq` has no effect.

```
% uniq testme
Archives/           OWL/                    keylime.pie
InfoWorld/          bin/                    src/
Mail/               bitnet.mailing-lists.Z  temp/
News/               drop.text.hqx           testme
```

2. A trick using the `cat` command is that `cat` lists the contents of each file sequentially, even if you specify the same file over and over again, so you can easily build a file with lots of lines:

```
% cat testme testme testme > newtest
```

Examine `newtest` to verify that it contains three copies of `testme`, one after the other. (Try using `wc`.)

3. Now you have a file with duplicate lines. Will `uniq` realize these files have duplicate lines? Use `wc` to find out:

```
% wc newtest
   12   36   363
% uniq newtest ¦ wc
   12   36   363
```

They're the same. Remember, the `uniq` command only removes duplicate lines if they're adjacent.

4. Now create a file that has duplicate lines:

```
% tail -1 testme > lastline
% cat lastline lastline lastline lastline > newtest2
% cat newtest2
News/               drop.text.hqx           testme
News/               drop.text.hqx           testme
News/               drop.text.hqx           testme
News/               drop.text.hqx           testme
```

Now you can see what `uniq` does:

```
% uniq newtest2
News/               drop.text.hqx           testme
```

8

5. Now obtain a count of the number of occurrences of each line in the file. The -c flag does that job:

```
% uniq -c newtest2
    4 News/                    drop.text.hqx          testme
```

This shows that this line occurs four times in the file. Lines that are unique have no number preface.

6. You can also see what the -d and -u flags do, and how they have exactly opposite actions:

```
% uniq -d newtest2
News/                    drop.text.hqx          testme
% uniq -u newtest2
%
```

Why did the -u flag list no output? The answer is that the -u flag tells uniq to list only those lines that are not repeated in the file. Because the only line in the file is repeated four times, there's nothing to display.

Step 3. Summary

Given this example, you probably think uniq is of marginal value, but you will find that it's not uncommon for files to have many blank lines scattered willy-nilly throughout the text. The uniq command is a fast, easy, and powerful way to clean up such files.

Task 8.4: Sorting Information in a File Using *sort*
Step 1. Description

Whereas wc is useful at the end of a pipeline of commands, uniq is a *filter*, a program that is really designed to be tucked in the middle of a pipeline. Filters, of course, can be placed anywhere in a line, anywhere that enables them to help direct UNIX to do what you want it to do. The common characteristic of all UNIX filters is that they can read input from *standard input*, process it in some manner, and list the results in *standard output*. With file redirection, standard input and output can also be files. To do this, you can either specify the filenames to the command (usually input only) or use the file redirection symbols you learned earlier in this chapter (<, >, and >>).

One of the most useful filters is `sort`, a program that reads information and sorts it alphabetically. You can customize the behavior of this program to ignore the case of words (for example, to sort *Big* **between** *apple* and *cat*, rather than **before**—most sorts put all uppercase letters before the lowercase letters), and to reverse the order of a sort (*z* to *a*). The program `sort` also enables you to sort lists of numbers.

Few flags are available for `sort`, but they are powerful, as shown in Table 8.1.

Table 8.1. Flags for the sort command.

Flag	Function
-b	Ignore leading blanks.
-d	Sort in dictionary order (only letters, digits, and blanks are significant).
-f	Fold uppercase into lowercase.
-n	Sort numerically.
-r	Reverse order of the sort.

Step 2. Action

1. By default, the `ls` command sorts the files in a directory in a case-sensitive manner. It first lists those files that begin with uppercase letters, then those that begin with lowercase letters:

```
% ls -1F
Archives/
InfoWorld/
Mail/
News/
OWL/
bin/
bitnet.mailing-lists.Z
drop.text.hqx
keylime.pie
src/
temp/
testme
```

Comment: To force ls to list output one file per line, you can use the -1 flag (that's the number *one*, not a lowercase *L*).

To sort filenames alphabetically regardless of case, you can use sort -f:

```
% ls -1 ¦ sort -f
Archives/
bin/
bitnet.mailing-lists.Z
drop.text.hqx
InfoWorld/
keylime.pie
Mail/
News/
OWL/
src/
temp/
testme
```

2. How about sorting the lines of a file? You can use the testme file you created earlier:

```
% sort < testme
Archives/         OWL/                     keylime.pie
InfoWorld/        bin/                     src/
Mail/             bitnet.mailing-lists.Z   temp/
News/             drop.text.hqx            testme
```

3. Here's a real-life UNIX example. Of the files in your home directory, which are the largest? The ls -s command indicates the size of each file, in blocks, and sort -n sorts numerically:

```
% ls -s ¦ sort -n
total 127
    1 Archives/
    1 InfoWorld/
    1 Mail/
    1 News/
    1 OWL/
  · 1 bin/
    1 src/
    1 temp/
```

```
   1 testme
  13 keylime.pie
  46 drop.text.hqx
  64 bitnet.mailing-lists.Z
```

It would be more convenient if the largest files were listed first in the output.
That's where the -r flag to *reverse* the sort order can be useful:

```
% ls -s ¦ sort -nr
  64 bitnet.mailing-lists.Z
  46 drop.text.hqx
  13 keylime.pie
   1 testme
   1 temp/
   1 src/
   1 bin/
   1 OWL/
   1 News/
   1 Mail/
   1 InfoWorld/
   1 Archives/
total 127
```

4. One more refinement is available to you. Instead of listing all the files, use
   the head command, and specify that you only want to see the top five
   entries:

```
% ls -s ¦ sort -nr ¦ head -5
  64 bitnet.mailing-lists.Z
  46 drop.text.hqx
  13 keylime.pie
   1 testme
   1 temp/
```

That's a powerful and complex UNIX command, yet it is composed of
simple and easy-to-understand components.

Step 3. Summary

Like many of the filters, sort isn't too exciting by itself. As you explore UNIX further
and learn more about how to combine these simple commands to build sophisticated
instructions, you will begin to see their true value.

8

Task 8.5: Checking Spelling of a File Using *spell*
Step 1. Description

As you can see, filters are quite useful additions to your vocabulary of UNIX commands. Most are designed for a specific purpose. Like a good set of tools, however, UNIX filters can be combined to allow a multitude of more sophisticated commands.

If you plan to use UNIX for writing letters, memos, or even a novel or two, you'll want to know about the `spell` utility. Although it is a simple program in some regards (the `spell` utility simply spits out a list of words it detects as misspelled in the input file) `spell` is terrific for that quick lookup. The `spell` command requires a number of large data files to work correctly. As a result, many smaller UNIX systems skip installation of the program, and some do not have the program at all. If your system is like that, please skip to the next task.

To use `spell`, you need to specify the file you want it to check, or use file redirection (or a pipe) to feed it input. As a last resort, you can enter words directly into the program to be checked. If you do, you'll need to know that the sequence of Ctrl-D is how you signal the end of your input.

Step 2. Action

1. Check the spelling of a few tough words:

```
% spell
pernicous
balerina
loquacious
Ctrl-D
balerina
pernicous
%
```

Learning to read the output of `spell` can be a bit tricky. Any word it lists is one the utility thinks is spelled incorrectly. Therefore, you can see in the example that `spell` thinks—rightly so—that `pernicous` and `balerina` are spelled incorrectly. The correct spellings are "pernicious" and "ballerina." Run these spellings through `spell`:

```
% spell
pernicious
ballerina
Ctrl-D
%
```

2. There are a couple of flags to spell, but they're not incredibly helpful. The spell utility is not nearly as sophisticated as the in-line spell-checking utilities available in most word processing software.

The flag -b checks British spelling:

```
% spell -b
I wish I knew what the colour of the lorry had been,
that day back in March when my Mum bid adieu.
Ctrl-D
%
```

Compare this to the same message checked with spell when I don't indicate that I'm using British spelling:

```
% spell
I wish I knew what the colour of the lorry had been,
that day back in March when my Mum bid adieu.
Ctrl-D
colour
lorry
%
```

Another flag is -v, which makes spell more picky. With this option, spell lists any word that isn't in the utility's dictionary *exactly as written* and indicates what rules could be applied to check its spelling.

Compare the output of the following two uses of spell:

```
% spell
She checked her gun and turned the hall, following the
bad guy into the den...
Ctrl-D
%
% spell -v
She checked her gun and turned the hall, following the
bad guy into the den...
Ctrl-D
+ed     checked
+ing    following
+ed     turned
%
```

8

Here you can see that spell doesn't have the words *checked, following,* or *turned* in its dictionary, but it can verify spelling by applying the "+*ed*" or "+*ing*" suffix rules to words it does know.

If you've ever wondered how spell-checking software works, a bit of experimentation reveals quite a bit about word modification rules, as you can see with the -v flag.

Step 3. Summary

Once you learn how to create files with the vi and emacs editors later in this book, you will be able to check spelling quickly. Some versions of EMACS have a rudimentary spell-checking facility built-in. In these versions, the program uses the spell program but processes the output and offers a more interactive environment for correcting spelling problems. Unfortunately, after more than 25 years, UNIX still fails to offer a general-purpose spelling correction program.

Task 8.6: Number Lines in Files Using *cat*, *-n*, and *nl*
Step 1. Description

It can often be helpful to have a line number listed next to each line of a file. It's quite simple to do with the cat program, by simply specifying the -n flag to number lines in the file displayed.

On many UNIX systems, there's a considerably better command for numbering lines in a file and for many other tasks. The command nl, for *number lines,* is an AT&T System V command. A system that doesn't have the nl command will complain nl: command not found. If you have this result, experiment with cat -n instead.

Step 2. Action

1. Because one of my own systems did not have the nl command, I moved to one that had the nl command for this example. I quickly rebuilt the testme file:

```
% ls -l > testme
%
```

Now to see line numbers, `cat -n` will work fine:

```
% cat -n testme
     1  total 60
     2  -rw-r--r--  1 taylor   1861 Jun  2  1992 Global.Software
     3  -rw-------  1 taylor  22194 Oct  1  1992 Interactive.Unix
     4  drwx------  4 taylor   4096 Nov 13 11:09 Mail/
     5  drwxr-xr-x  2 taylor   4096 Nov 13 11:09 News/
     6  drwxr-xr-x  2 taylor   4096 Nov 13 11:09 Src/
     7  drwxr-xr-x  2 taylor   4096 Nov 13 11:09 bin/
     8  -rw-r--r--  1 taylor  12445 Sep 17 14:56 history.usenet.Z
     9  -rw-r--r--  1 taylor      0 Nov 20 18:16 testme
```

2. The alternative, which does exactly the same thing here, is to try `nl` without any flags:

```
% nl testme
     1  total 60
     2  -rw-r--r--  1 taylor   1861 Jun  2  1992 Global.Software
     3  -rw-------  1 taylor  22194 Oct  1  1992 Interactive.Unix
     4  drwx------  4 taylor   4096 Nov 13 11:09 Mail/
     5  drwxr-xr-x  2 taylor   4096 Nov 13 11:09 News/
     6  drwxr-xr-x  2 taylor   4096 Nov 13 11:09 Src/
     7  drwxr-xr-x  2 taylor   4096 Nov 13 11:09 bin/
     8  -rw-r--r--  1 taylor  12445 Sep 17 14:56 history.usenet.Z
     9  -rw-r--r--  1 taylor      0 Nov 20 18:16 testme
```

3. Notice that both commands can also number lines fed to them by a command pipe:

```
% ls -CF | cat -n
     1  Global.Software    News/        history.usenet.Z
     2  Interactive.Unix   Src/         testme
     3  Mail/              bin/
% ls -CF | nl
     1  Global.Software    News/        history.usenet.Z
     2  Interactive.Unix   Src/         testme
     3  Mail/              bin/
```

Step 3. Summary

Like many other UNIX tools, `nl` and its doppelganger `cat -n` aren't very thrilling by themselves. As additional members in the set of powerful UNIX tools, however, they can prove tremendously helpful in certain situations. As you will soon see, `nl` also has some powerful options that can make it a bit more fun.

8

Task 8.7: Cool *nl* Tricks and Capabilities

Step 1. Description

A program that prefaces each line with a line number isn't much of an addition to the UNIX command toolbox, so the person who wrote the nl program added some further capabilities. With different command flags, nl can number all lines (by default it numbers only lines that are not blank) or skip line numbering (which means it's an additional way to display the contents of a file). The best option, though, is that nl can selectively number just those lines that contain a specified pattern.

> **Comment:** If you don't have the nl command on your system, I'm afraid you're out of luck in this section. Later in the book you learn other ways to accomplish these tasks, but for now, if you don't have nl, skip to the next task and start learning about the grep command.

The command flag format for nl is a bit more esoteric than you've seen up to this point. The different approaches to numbering lines with nl are all modifications of the -b flag (for *body* numbering options). The four flags are -ba, which numbers all lines; -bt, which numbers printable text only; -bn, which results in no numbering; and -bp *pattern*, for numbering lines that contain the specified pattern.

One final option is to insert a different separator between the line number and the line by telling nl to use -s, the separator flag.

Step 2. Action

1. To begin, I'll use a command that you haven't seen before to add a few blank lines to the testme file. The echo command simply writes back to the screen anything specified. Try echo hello.

```
% rm testme
% ls -CF > testme
% echo "" >> testme
% echo "" >> testme
% ls -CF >> testme
% cat testme
Global.Software      News/              history.usenet.Z
Interactive.Unix     Src/               testme
Mail/                bin/
```

```
Global.Software       News/              history.usenet.Z
Interactive.Unix      Src/               testme
Mail/                 bin/
%
```

> **Comment:** Parts of UNIX are rather poorly designed, as you have already
> learned. For example, if you use the echo command without arguments,
> you will get no output. However, if you add an empty argument (a set of
> quotation marks with nothing between them), echo will output a blank
> line. It doesn't make much sense, but it works.

2. Now watch what happens when nl uses its default settings to number the
   lines in testme:

```
% nl testme
     1  Global.Software       News/              history.usenet.Z
     2  Interactive.Unix      Src/               testme
     3  Mail/                 bin/

     4  Global.Software       News/              history.usenet.Z
     5  Interactive.Unix      Src/               testme
     6  Mail/                 bin/
```

   You can accomplish the same thing by specifying nl -bt testme. Try this to
   verify that your system gives the same results.

3. It's time to use one of the new two-letter command options to number the
   lines, including the blank lines:

```
% nl -ba testme
     1  Global.Software       News/              history.usenet.Z
     2  Interactive.Unix      Src/               testme
     3  Mail/                 bin/
     4
     5
     6  Global.Software       News/              history.usenet.Z
     7  Interactive.Unix      Src/               testme
     8  Mail/                 bin/
```

8

4. If you glance at the contents of my `testme` file, you can see that two lines contain the word *history*. To have `nl` number just those lines, try the `-bp` pattern-matching option:

```
% nl -bphistory testme
     1  Global.Software    News/                history.usenet.Z
        Interactive.Unix Src/                testme
        Mail/             bin/


     2  Global.Software    News/                history.usenet.Z
        Interactive.Unix Src/                testme
        Mail/             bin/
```

   Notice that numbering the two lines has caused the rest of the lines to fall out of alignment on the display.

5. This is when the `-s`, or separator, option comes in handy:

```
% nl -bphistory -s: testme
     1:Global.Software    News/                history.usenet.Z
        Interactive.Unix Src/                testme
        Mail/             bin/


     2:Global.Software    News/                history.usenet.Z
        Interactive.Unix Src/                testme
        Mail/             bin/
```

   In this case, I specified that instead of using a tab, which is the default separator between the number and line, `nl` should use a colon. As you can see, the output now lines up again.

   Just about anything can be specified as the separator, as sensible or weird as it might be:

```
% nl -s', line is: ' testme
     1, line is: Global.Software              News/                 history.
usenet.Z
     2, line is: Interactive.Unix    Src/                  testme
     3, line is: Mail/               bin/


     4, line is: Global.Software              News/                 history.
```

```
usenet.Z
    5, line is: Interactive.Unix    Src/                testme
    6, line is: Mail/               bin/
```

Notice the use of single quotation marks (') in this example. I want to include spaces as part of my pattern, so I need to ensure that the program knows. If I didn't use the quotation marks, nl would use a comma as the separator and then tell me that it couldn't open a file called line or is:.

Step 3. Summary

The nl command demonstrates that there are plenty of variations on simple commands. When you read earlier that you would learn how to number lines in a file, did you think that this many subtleties were involved?

Task 8.8: Searching Files Using *grep*
Step 1. Description

A couple key commands are most commonly used in UNIX. These commands are the key to you becoming a power user and becoming comfortable with the capabilities of the system. The ls command is one example, and the grep command is another. The oddly-named grep command makes it easy to find lost files or to find files that contain specific text.

Comment: After laborious research and countless hours debating with UNIX developers, I am reasonably certain that the derivation of the name grep is as follows. Before this command existed, UNIX users would utilize a crude line-based editor called ed to find matching text. Search patterns in UNIX are called *regular expressions*. To search throughout a file, the user prefixed the command with *global*. Once a match was made, the user wanted to have it listed to the screen, or *print*. To put it all together, the operation was global/regular expression/print. That phrase was pretty long, however, so users shortened it to g/re/p. Thereafter, when a command was written, grep seemed to be a natural, if odd and confusing, name.

The grep command not only has a ton of different command options, but it has two variations in UNIX systems, too. These variations are egrep, for specifying more complex patterns (regular expressions), and fgrep, for using file-based lists of words as search patterns.

You could spend the next 100 pages learning all the obscure and weird options to the grep family of commands. When you boil it down, however, you're probably only going to use the simplest patterns and maybe a useful flag or two. Think of it this way: just because there are more than 500,000 words in the English language (according to the *Oxford English Dictionary*) doesn't mean that you must learn them all to communicate effectively!

With this in mind, you'll learn the basics of grep today, but you'll pick up more insight into the program's capabilities and options during the next few days.

A few of the most important grep command flags are listed in Table 8.2.

Table 8.2. The most helpful grep flags.

Flag	Function
-c	List a count of matching lines only.
-i	Ignore the case of the letters in the pattern.
-l	List filenames of files that match pattern only.
-n	Include line numbers.

Step 2. Action

1. Begin by making sure you have a test file to work with. The example shows the testme file from the previous uniq examples:

```
% cat testme
Archives/           OWL/                keylime.pie
InfoWorld/          bin/                src/
Mail/               bitnet.mailing-lists.Z  temp/
News/               drop.text.hqx       testme
```

2. The general form of grep is to specify the command, any flags you want to add, the pattern, and a filename:

```
% grep bitnet testme
Mail/               bitnet.mailing-lists.Z  temp/
```

As you can see, grep easily pulled out the line in the testme file that contained the pattern bitnet.

3. Be aware that grep finds patterns in a case-sensitive manner:

```
% grep owl testme
%
```

Note that OWL was not found because the pattern specified with the grep command was all lowercase, owl.

But that's where the -i flag can be helpful, so grep ignores case:

```
% grep -i owl testme
Archives/                    OWL/                   keylime.pie
```

4. For the next few examples, I'll move into the /etc directory because some files therein there have lots of lines. The wc command shows that the file /etc/passwd has almost 4,000 lines:

```
% cd /etc
% wc -l /etc/passwd
   3877
```

My account is taylor. I'll use grep to see my account entry in the password file:

```
% grep taylor /etc/passwd
taylorj:?:1048:1375:James Taylor:/users/taylorj:/bin/csh
mtaylor:?:760:1375:Mary Taylor:/users/mtaylor:/usr/local/bin/tcsh
dataylor:?:375:518:Dave Taylor:/users/dataylor:/usr/local/lib/msh
taylorjr:?:203:1022:James Taylor:/users/taylorjr:/bin/csh
taylorrj:?:668:1042:Robert Taylor:/users/taylorrj:/bin/csh
taylorm:?:862:1508:Melanie Taylor:/users/taylormx:/bin/csh
taylor:?:1989:1412:Dave Taylor:/users/taylor:/bin/csh
%
```

Try this on your system too.

5. As you can see, many accounts contain the pattern taylor.

A smarter way to see how often the taylor pattern appears is to use the -c flag to grep, which will indicate how many case-sensitive matches are in the file before any of them are displayed on the screen:

```
% grep -c taylor /etc/passwd
7
%
```

The command located seven matches. Count the preceding listing to confirm this.

6. With 3,877 lines in the password file, it could be interesting to see if all the Taylors started their accounts at about the same time. (This would presumably mean they would all appear in the file at about the same point.) To do this, I'll use the -n flag to number the output lines:

```
% grep -n taylor /etc/passwd
319:taylorj:?:1048:1375:James Taylor:/users/taylorj:/bin/csh
1314:mtaylor:?:760:1375:Mary Taylor:/users/mtaylor:/usr/local/bin/tcsh
1419:dataylor:?:375:518:Dave Taylor:/users/dataylor:/usr/local/lib/msh
1547:taylorjr:?:203:1022:James Taylor:/users/taylorjr:/bin/csh
1988:taylorrj:?:668:1042:Robert Taylor:/users/taylorrj:/bin/csh
2133:taylorm:?:8692:1508:Melanie Taylor:/users/taylorm:/bin/csh
3405:taylor:?:1989:1412:Dave Taylor:/users/taylor:/bin/csh
%
```

This is a great example of a default separator adding incredible confusion to the output of a command. Normally, a line number followed by a colon would be no problem, but in the passwd file (which is already littered with colons), it's confusing. Compare this output with the output obtained earlier with the grep command alone to see what's changed.

You can see that my theory about when the Taylors started their accounts was wrong. If proximity in the passwd file is an indicator that accounts are assigned at similar times, then no Taylors started their accounts even within the same week.

Step 3. Summary

These examples of how to use grep barely scratch the surface of how this powerful and sophisticated command can be used. Explore your own file system using grep to search files for specific patterns.

Task 8.9: Filename Wildcards
Step 1. Description

By now you are doubtless tired of typing every letter of each filename into your system for each example. There is a better and easier way! Just like the special card in poker can have any value, UNIX has special characters that the various shells (the command line interpreter programs) all interpret as *wildcards*. This allows for much easier typing of patterns.

There are two wildcards to learn here: * acts as a match for any number and sequence of characters, and ? acts as a match for any single character. In the broadest sense, a lone * acts as a match for all files in the current directory (in other words, ls * is identical to ls), whereas a single ? acts as a match for all one-character-long filenames in a directory (for instance, ls ?, which will list only those filenames that are only one character long). The following examples will make this clear.

Step 2. Action

1. Start by using ls to list your home directory.

    ```
    % ls -CF
    Archives/            OWL/                    keylime.pie
    InfoWorld/           bin/                    src/
    Mail/                bitnet.mailing-lists.Z  temp/
    News/                drop.text.hqx           testme
    %
    ```

2. To experiment with wildcards, it's easiest to use the echo command. If you recall, echo repeats anything given to it, but—and here's the secret to its value—the shell interprets anything that is entered before the shell lets echo see it. That is, the * is expanded before the shell hands the arguments over to the command.

    ```
    % echo *
    Archives InfoWorld Mail News OWL bin bitnet.mailing-lists.Z
    drop.text.hqx keylime.pie src temp testme
    ```

    Using the * wildcard enables me to reference easily all files in the directory. This is quite helpful.

3. A wildcard is even more helpful than the example suggests, because it can be embedded in the middle of a word or otherwise used to limit the number of matches. To see all files that began with the letter *t*, use the *:

    ```
    % echo t*
    temp testme
    ```

    Try echo b* to see all your files that start with the letter *b*.

8

4. Variations are possible, too. I could use wildcards to list all files or directories that end with the letter *s*:

```
% echo *s
Archives News
```

Watch what happens if I try the same command using the ls command rather than the echo command:

```
% ls -CF *s
Archives:
Interleaf.story    Tartan.story.Z       nextstep.txt.Z
Opus.story         interactive.txt.Z    rae.assist.infoworld.Z

News:
mailing.lists.usenet  usenet.1            usenet.alt
```

Using the ls command here makes UNIX think I want it to list two directories, not just the names of the two files. This is where the -d flag to ls could prove helpful to force a listing of the directories rather than of their contents.

5. Notice that in the News directory I have three files with the word usenet somewhere in their names. The wildcard pattern usenet* would match two of them, and *usenet would match one. A valuable aspect of the * wildcard is that it can match *zero or more characters*, so the pattern *usenet* will match all three.

```
% echo News/*usenet*
News/mailing.lists.usenet News/usenet.1 News/usenet.alt
```

You can also see that wildcards can be embedded in a filename or pathname. In this example, I specified that I was interested in files in the News directory.

6. Could you match a single character? To see how this can be helpful, it's time to move into a different directory, OWL on my system.

```
% cd OWL
% ls -CF
Student.config   owl.c      owl.o
WordMap/         owl.data   simple.editor.c
owl*             owl.h      simple.editor.o
```

If I request `owl*`, which files will be listed?

```
% echo owl*
owl owl.c owl.data owl.h owl.o
```

What do I do if I am only interested in the source, header, and object files, which are here indicated by a *.c*, *.h*, or *.o* suffix. Using a wildcard that matches zero or more letters won't work; I don't want to see `owl` or `owl.data`. One possibility would be to use the pattern `owl.*` (by adding the period I can eliminate the `owl` file itself). What I really want, however, is to be able to specify all files that start with the four characters *owl.* and have exactly one more character. This is a situation in which the `?` wildcard works:

```
% echo owl.?
owl.c owl.h owl.o
```

Because no files have exactly one letter following the three letters `owl`, watch what happens when I specify `owl?` as the pattern:

```
% echo owl?
echo: No match.
```

This leads to a general observation. If you want to have `echo` return a question to you, you have to do it carefully, because the shell interprets the question mark as a wildcard:

```
% echo are you listening?
echo: No match.
```

To accomplish this, you simply need to surround the entire question with quotation marks:

```
% echo 'are you listening?'
are you listening?
```

Step 3. Summary

It won't surprise you that there are more complex ways of using wildcards to build filename patterns. What will likely surprise you is that the vast majority of UNIX users don't even know about the `*` and `?` wildcards! This knowledge gives you a definite advantage.

X **Comment:** Armed with wildcards, you can now try the `-l` flag to `grep`, which, as you recall, indicates the names of the files that contain a specified pattern, rather than printing the lines that match the pattern. If I go into my electronic mail archive directory—Mail—I can easily, using the command `grep -l -i chicago Mail/*`, search for all files that contain `Chicago`. Try using `grep -l` to search across all files in your home directory for words or patterns.

Lesson Summary

You have learned quite a bit in this lesson and are continuing down the road to UNIX expertise. You learned about file redirection, the `grep` command, and the wildcard filename formats. You can't go wrong by spending time studying these closely. The concept of using filters and building complex commands by combining simple commands with pipes has been more fully demonstrated here. This higher level of the UNIX command language is what makes UNIX so powerful and easy to mold.

This lesson hasn't skimped on commands either. This lesson introduced `wc` for counting lines, words, and characters in a file (or more than one file: try `wc *` in your home directory). You also learned to use the `uniq`, `sort`, and `spell` commands. You learned about `nl` for numbering lines in a file—in a variety of ways—and `cat -n` as an alternative "poor person's" line numbering strategy. You were also introduced to the `echo` command.

By the way, the `echo` command can also tell you about specific environment variables, just like `env` or `printenv` does. Try `echo $HOME` or `echo $PATH` to see what happens, and compare the output with `env HOME` and `env PATH`.

Workshop
Key Terms

file redirection   Most UNIX programs expect to read their input from the user (that is, *standard input*) and write their output to the screen (*standard output*). By use of file redirection, however, input can come from a previously created file, and output can be saved to a file instead of being displayed on the screen.

filter	Filters are a particular type of UNIX program that expects to work either with *file redirection* or as part of a *pipeline*. These programs read input from *standard input*, write output to *standard output*, and often don't have any starting arguments.
regular expressions	A convenient notation for specifying complex patterns. Notable special characters are ^ to match the beginning of the line and $ to match the end of the line.
standard input	UNIX programs always default to reading information from the user by reading the keyboard and watching what's typed. With *file redirection*, input can come from a file, and with *pipelines*, input can be the result of a previous UNIX command.
standard output	When processing information, UNIX programs default to displaying the output on the screen itself, also known as standard output. With *file redirection*, output can easily be saved to a file, and with *pipelines*, output can be sent to other programs.
wildcards	Special characters that are interpreted by the UNIX shell or other programs to have meaning other than the letter itself. For example, * is a shell wildcard and creates a pattern that matches zero or more characters. Prefaced with a particular letter X (x*) this shell pattern will match all files beginning with x.

Questions

1. The placement of file redirection characters is important to ensure that the command works correctly. Which of the following do you think will work, and why?

```
< file wc          wc file <          wc < file
cat file ¦ wc      cat < file ¦ wc    wc ¦ cat
```

Now try them and see if you're correct.

2. The wc command can be used for lots of different tasks. Try to imagine a few that would be interesting and helpful to learn (for example, how many users are on the system right now?). Try them on your system.

3. Does the file size listed by wc -c always agree with the file size listed by the ls command? With the size indicated by ls -s? If there is any difference, why?

4. What do you think would happen if you tried to sort a list of words by pretending they're all numbers? Try it with the command ls -1 ¦ sort -n to see what happens. Experiment with the variations.

5. Do you spell your filenames correctly? Use spell to find out.

6. Use a combination of ls -1, cat -n, and grep to find out the name of the eleventh or twenty-fourth file in the /etc directory on your system.

7. What wildcard expression would you use to find the following:

☐ All files in the /tmp directory?

☐ All files that contain a w in that directory?

☐ All files that start with a b, contain an e, and end with .c?

☐ All files that either start with test or contain the pattern hi? (Notice that it can be more than one pattern.)

Preview of the Next Chapter

The final lesson for Day 3 of *Teach Yourself UNIX in a Week* introduces two powerful and complex commands, awk and sed (even the names are weird). You'll learn how the names were chosen, and, more importantly, how these commands can help you extract data from even the most unwieldy files. You will also learn more about filename wildcards, the useful tee command, and the curious but helpful << file redirection command.

Power Filters
and File
Redirection

In this lesson, you get to put on your programming hat and learn about two powerful commands that can be customized infinitely and can be used for a wide variety of tasks. The first of them is sed, a program for modifying information traveling through a UNIX pipeline. The other is the awk program, a program that can let you grab specific columns of information, modify text as it flows past, and even swap the order of columns of information in a file.

Before you learn these two commands, you learn about the fourth of what I call the Big Four file redirection commands. Last lesson you learned about >, >>, and < to redirect output, replacing or appending to the existing file, or redirect input. In this lesson, you learn about << for redirecting input from the screen as if it were a file. The << redirection command is a trick of UNIX experts, and it's very helpful.

You conclude your third day of UNIX with tee and some new additions to the UNIX wildcards, allowing even more flexibility in naming files and specifying groups of files to UNIX commands.

Goals for This Lesson

In this lesson, you learn

- ☐ File redirection with <<
- ☐ Changing things en route with sed
- ☐ The wild and weird awk command
- ☐ Rerouting the pipeline with tee
- ☐ More filename wildcards

Beginning with the last lesson, in which you learned the grep command, you are learning about commands that can take months of study to master. Two of the commands treated in this chapter, awk and sed, have books written just about them, if you can imagine such a thing. I say this to set the scene; these are complex and very powerful commands. By necessity, you learn only some of the easier capabilities of these commands, but don't worry.

This lesson also continues to explore two other aspects of UNIX interaction: file redirection and filename wildcards. You learn some of the more esoteric notation and how it can help you work quicker and smarter with the system. Finally, what's a plumbing metaphor without a plumbing-related command or two? UNIX is just the system to have odd command names. The command in question is tee.

Task 9.1: File Redirection with <<

Step 1. Description

There are four ways to redirect the flow of information in a UNIX command line, and you have already learned about the three most common: < causes UNIX to read the input from the specified file rather than standard input, > writes the output to the specified file rather than standard output, and >> appends the output to the specified file. From a purely objective viewpoint, if you can have > change behavior by adding a second character (>>), then what happens when you try the same with the left angle bracket (<<)?

The double left angle bracket (<<) enables you to create what UNIX folk call *here documents*, a multiline stream of text that is treated exactly as if it were read from a file directly, rather than entered.

There are two reasons why this is worth learning: << offers a simple way to simulate keyboard input to commands that might require it, and << also allows you to have text with variables that are expanded automatically by the shell. This will be clearer with some examples.

To use here documents, you simply need to enter the double angle bracket followed by a one-word pattern that will be used to delineate the last line of the input. For example, cat << EOF will read all lines you type in until it sees a line containing just the letters EOF, which the shell will take to mean that it's the end of the file.

Step 2. Action

1. Try this on your system:

```
% cat -n << end
This is an example of what you can do with the
double << redirection character in UNIX.
end
     1 This is an example of what you can do with the
     2 double << redirection character in UNIX.
%
```

As you can see, the shell allowed me to enter as many lines of text as desired without any interruption, and once I typed in the word specified to end the file (end), the shell fed the entire virtual file to the cat command, which cheerfully wrote it back to the screen, with each line numbered accordingly. Note that the end line wasn't included in the output.

9

2. How about the following example?

```
% cat -n << endit
As I was telling you, my HOME directory, currently
set to $HOME, is just in the wrong place!
endit
     1  As I was telling you, my HOME directory, currently
     2  set to /users/taylor, is just in the wrong place!
%
```

The $HOME variable has been expanded to its value. Fortunately, the shell doesn't interpret wildcards, however, because they are meaningful only on the command line itself:

```
% cat -n << end-of-input
This is a weird test? You can *bet* it is!
end-of-input
     1  This is a weird test? You can *bet* it is!
%
```

3. Here documents can also be quite helpful for simulating keyboard input, as I mentioned earlier. Let's say that I wanted to change my login shell using the chsh command, but I didn't want to fiddle with waiting for the prompt. The usual interaction of the command is this:

```
% chsh
Changing login shell for taylor.
Old shell: /bin/csh
New shell: /bin/csh
Login shell unchanged.
```

But with a here document, I can instead automate the chsh:

```
% chsh << endit
/bin/csh
endit
Changing login shell for taylor.
Old shell: /bin/csh
New shell: Login shell unchanged.
%
```

In this example, because there's only one line of input, the echo command could work too, actually:

```
% echo /bin/csh | chsh
Changing login shell for taylor.
Old shell: /bin/csh
New shell: Login shell unchanged.
%
```

4. You cannot use echo to feed a command that requires multiple lines of input, but, again, here documents can prove invaluable. To demonstrate this, I'm going to jump about a day ahead and use the ftp—*file transfer protocol program*—utility to list what files are available through the Internet at a machine called ftp.uu.net in Falls Church, Virginia.

First, here's what ftp looks like when used interactively, with the -n flag to prevent automatic logging in to the remote file server:

```
% ftp -n ftp.uu.net
Connected to ftp.uu.net.
220 ftp.UU.NET FTP server (Version 2.0WU(13) Fri Apr 9 20:44:32 EDT 1993)
ready.
ftp> user ftp taylor@utech.edu
331 Guest login ok, send your complete e-mail address as password.
230-
230-                    Welcome to the UUNET archive.
230-    A service of UUNET Technologies Inc, Falls Church, Virginia
230 Guest login ok, access restrictions apply.
ftp> ls -CF
200 PORT command successful.
150 Opening ASCII mode data connection for /bin/ls.
ClariNet@      doc/         info/         news@         unix-today@
admin/         etc/         languages/    opinions/     unix-world@
applix@        faces@       library/      packages/     usenet/
archive@       ftp/         lost+found/   private/      usr/
bin/           government/  ls-1R.Z@      pub/          uumap@
by-name.gz@    graphics/    ls-1R.gz@     published/    uumap.tar.Z
by-time.gz@    gzip.tar     ls-ltR.Z@     receive/      uunet-info/
clarinet@      help@        ls-ltR.gz@    sco-archive@  uunet-sites@
compress.tar   index/       mail@         systems/      vendor/
dev/           inet/        networking/   tmp/
226 Transfer complete.
remote: -CF
547 bytes received in 0.08 seconds (6.7 Kbytes/s)
ftp> quit
221 Goodbye.
%
```

Using the double angle bracket redirection, I can considerably simplify this command:

```
% ftp -n ftp.uu.net << ENDIT
user ftp taylor@utech.edu
ls -CF
ENDIT
ClariNet@      doc/         info/         news@         unix-today@
admin/         etc/         languages/    opinions/     unix-world@
applix@        faces@       library/      packages/     usenet/
archive@       ftp/         lost+found/   private/      usr/
bin/           government/  ls-1R.Z@      pub/          uumap@
by-name.gz@    graphics/    ls-1R.gz@     published/    uumap.tar.Z
by-time.gz@    gzip.tar     ls-ltR.Z@     receive/      uunet-info/
clarinet@      help@        ls-ltR.gz@    sco-archive@  uunet-sites@
compress.tar   index/       mail@         systems/      vendor/
dev/           inet/        networking/   tmp/
%
```

In this case, using the here document also made the output vastly easier to read!

5. This is starting to look helpful, right? Armed with this new redirection command, you can also easily create files without having to use an editor. Do you want to have a post-it-like facility for jotting notes?

```
% cat << DONE > reminders
Call Mum at 4pm today, lest I get into trouble!
DONE
% cat reminders
Call Mum at 4pm today, lest I get into trouble!
%
```

With this trick for creating files in mind, I'm going to create a file that contains the ftp commands shown above:

```
% cat << ENDIT > ftpscript
user ftp taylor@utech.edu
ls -CF
ENDIT
% cat -n ftpscript
     1  user ftp taylor@utech.edu
     2  ls -CF
%
```

6. Now I'm ready to wander about, listing the contents of various FTP archive sites with ease:

```
% ftp -n ftp.uu.net < ftpscript
ClariNet@    doc/       info/        news@        unix-today@
admin/       etc/       languages/   opinions/    unix-world@
applix@      faces@     library/     packages/    usenet/
archive@     ftp/       lost+found/  private/     usr/
bin/         government/ ls-1R.Z@    pub/         uumap@
by-name.gz@  graphics/  ls-1R.gz@    published/   uumap.tar.Z
by-time.gz@  gzip.tar   ls-1tR.Z@    receive/     uunet-info/
clarinet@    help@      ls-1tR.gz@   sco-archive@ uunet-sites@
compress.tar index/     mail@        systems/     vendor/
dev/         inet/      networking/  tmp/
%
% cat ftpscript | ftp -n net-dist.mit.edu
README       etc/       lost+found/  private/     tytso/
bin/         for_mike/  netusers/    pub/         unix/
cao/         hosts/     oldol/       safety/      user/
cat-ietf/    installkits/ ols/       stash/       vms/
dev/         jis/       oval/        test/
%
```

The second example is looking at a different system, the network software distribution machine at MIT, the Massachusetts Institute of Technology, in Cambridge, Massachusetts.

7. Backing up a bit, what happens if you want to have $HOME as part of the message, rather than having it automatically expanded as read? To do this,

you need place quote marks around the end-of-file word. It's curious, but watch what happens:

```
% cat -n << 'endit'
As I was telling you, my HOME directory, currently
set to $HOME, is just in the wrong place!
'endit'
     1  As I was telling you, my HOME directory, currently
     2  set to $HOME, is just in the wrong place!
%
```

By putting the word in quotes, you tell the shell not to expand any of the variables encountered in the input. Both single and double quotes accomplish the same action: try it on your system to confirm.

Step 3. Summary

This is an important milestone. You now know how to create files with whatever contents you'd like, without any fuss and without having to learn an editor or other command. As you can see with the ftp example, here documents are useful for more than just creating files, too. Being able to feed multiple lines of input to a command without having to create a command input file proves quite helpful.

Task 9.2: Changing Things En Route with *sed*
Step 1. Description

I'm willing to bet that when you read about learning some UNIX programming tools in this lesson, you got anxious, your palms started to get sweaty, maybe your fingers shook, and the little voice in your head started to say, "It's too late! We can use a pad and paper! We don't need computers at all!"

Don't panic.

If you think about it, you've been programming all along in UNIX. When you enter a command to the shell, you're programming the shell to perform immediately the task specified. When you specify file redirection or build a pipe, you're really writing a small UNIX program that the shell interprets and acts upon. Frankly, when you consider how many different commands you now know and how many different flags there are for each of the commands, you've got quite a set of programming tools under your belt already, so onward!

With the | symbol, called a *pipe*, and commands tied together called *pipelines*, is it any wonder that the information flowing down a pipeline is called a *stream*? For example, the command cat test | wc means that the cat command opens the file test and streams it to the wc program, which counts the number of lines, words, and characters therein.

To edit or modify the information in a pipeline, then, it seems reasonable to use a *stream editor*, and that's exactly what the sed command is! Its name comes from its function: **st**ream **ed**itor.

Here's the bad news. The sed command is built on an old editor called ed, the same editor that's responsible for the grep command. Remember? The global/regular expression/print eventually became grep. A microcosm of UNIX itself, commands to sed are separated by a semicolon.

There are many different sed commands, but, in keeping with my promise not to overwhelm you with options and variations that aren't going to be helpful, I'll focus on using sed to substitute one pattern for another and for extracting ranges of lines from a file. The general format of the substitution command is: s/*old*/*new*/*flags*, where old and *new* are the patterns you're working with, s is the abbreviation for the substitute command, and the two most helpful flags are g (to replace all occurrences *globally* on each line) and n (to tell sed to only replace the first *n* occurrences of the pattern). By default, lines are listed to the screen, so a *sed expression* like 10q will cause the program to list the first 10 lines then quit (making it an alternative to the command head -10). Deletion is similar: the command is prefaced by one or two *addresses* in the file, reflecting a request to delete either all lines that match the specified address or all in the range of the first to last.

The format of the sed command is sed, followed by the expression in quotes, then, optionally, the name of the file to read for input.

Here are some examples.

Step 2. Action

1. I'll start with an easy example. I'll use grep to extract some lines from the /etc/passwd file, then replace all colons with a single space. The format of this command is to *substitute* each occurrence of : with a space, or s/:/ /:

```
% grep taylor /etc/passwd ¦ sed -e 's/:/ /'
taylorj ?:1048:1375:James Taylor:/users/taylorj:/bin/csh
mtaylor ?:769:1375:Mary Taylor:/users/mtaylor:/usr/local/bin/tcsh
dataylor ?:375:518:Dave Taylor,,,,:/users/dataylor:/usr/local/lib/msh
taylorjr ?:203:1022:James Taylor:/users/taylorjr:/bin/csh
taylorrj ?:662:1042:Robert Taylor:/users/taylorrj:/bin/csh
taylorm ?:869:1508:Melanie Taylor:/users/taylorm:/bin/csh
taylor ?:1989:1412:Dave Taylor:/users/taylor:/bin/csh
```

This doesn't quite do what I want, because I neglected to append the global instruction to the sed command to ensure that it would replace all occurrences of the pattern on each line. I'll try it again, this time adding a g to the instruction.

```
% grep taylor /etc/passwd ¦ sed -e 's/:/ /g'
taylorj ? 1048 1375 James Taylor /users/taylorj /bin/csh
mtaylor ? 769 1375 Mary Taylor /users/mtaylor /usr/local/bin/tcsh
dataylor ? 375 518 Dave Taylor /users/dataylor /usr/local/lib/msh
taylorjr ? 203 1022 James Taylor /users/taylorjr /bin/csh
taylorrj ? 662 1042 Robert Taylor /users/taylorrj /bin/csh
taylorm ? 869 1508 Melanie Taylor /users/taylorm /bin/csh
taylor ? 1989 1412 Dave Taylor /users/taylor /bin/csh
```

2. A more sophisticated example of substitution with sed would be to modify names, replacing all occurrences of Taylor with Tailor:

```
% grep taylor /etc/passwd ¦ sed -e 's/Taylor/Tailor/g'
taylorj:?:1048:1375:James Tailor:/users/taylorj:/bin/csh
mtaylor:?:769:1375:Mary Tailor:/users/mtaylor:/usr/local/bin/tcsh
dataylor:?:375:518:Dave Tailor:/users/dataylor:/usr/local/lib/msh
taylorjr:?:203:1022:James Tailor:/users/taylorjr:/bin/csh
taylorrj:?:662:1042:Robert Tailor:/users/taylorrj:/bin/csh
taylorm:?:869:1508:Melanie Tailor:/users/taylorm:/bin/csh
taylor:?:1989:1412:Dave Tailor:/users/taylor:/bin/csh
```

The colons have returned, which is annoying, so I'll use the fact that a semicolon can separate multiple sed commands on the same line and try it one more time:

```
% grep taylor /etc/passwd ¦ sed -e 's/Taylor/Tailor/g;s/:/ /g'
taylorj ? 1048 1375 James Tailor /users/taylorj /bin/csh
mtaylor ? 769 1375 Mary Tailor /users/mtaylor /usr/local/bin/tcsh
dataylor ? 375 518 Dave Tailor /users/dataylor /usr/local/lib/msh
taylorjr ? 203 1022 James Tailor /users/taylorjr /bin/csh
taylorrj ? 662 1042 Robert Tailor /users/taylorrj /bin/csh
taylorm ? 8692 1508 Melanie Tailor /users/taylorm /bin/csh
taylor ? 1989 1412 Dave Tailor /users/taylor /bin/csh
```

This last sed command can be read as "each time you encounter the pattern Taylor replace it with Tailor, even if it occurs multiple times on each line. Then each time you encounter a colon, replace it with a space."

3. Another example of using sed might be to rewrite the output of the who command to be a bit more readable. Consider the results of entering who on your system:

```
% who
strawmye ttyAc   Nov 21 19:01
eiyo     ttyAd   Nov 21 17:40
tzhen    ttyAg   Nov 21 19:13
kmkernek ttyAh   Nov 17 23:22
macedot  ttyAj   Nov 21 20:41
rpm      ttyAk   Nov 21 20:40
ypchen   ttyAl   Nov 21 18:20
kodak    ttyAm   Nov 21 20:43
```

The output is a bit confusing; sed can help:

```
% who ¦ sed 's/tty/On Device /;s/Nov/Logged in November/'
strawmye On Device Ac   Logged in November 21 19:01
eiyo     On Device Ad   Logged in November 21 17:40
tzhen    On Device Ag   Logged in November 21 19:13
kmkernek On Device Ah   Logged in November 17 23:22
macedot  On Device Aj   Logged in November 21 20:41
rpm      On Device Ak   Logged in November 21 20:40
ypchen   On Device Al   Logged in November 21 18:20
kodak    On Device Am   Logged in November 21 20:43
```

This time, each occurrence of the letters tty is replaced with the phrase On Device and, similarly, Nov is replaced with Logged in November.

4. The sed command can also be used to delete lines in the stream as it passes. The simplest version is to specify only the command:

```
% who ¦ sed 'd'
%
```

There's no output because the command matches all lines and deletes them. Instead, to delete just the first line, simply preface the d command with that line number:

```
% who ¦ sed '1d'
eiyo     ttyAd   Nov 21 17:40
tzhen    ttyAg   Nov 21 19:13
kmkernek ttyAh   Nov 17 23:22
macedot  ttyAj   Nov 21 20:41
rpm      ttyAk   Nov 21 20:40
ypchen   ttyAl   Nov 21 18:20
kodak    ttyAm   Nov 21 20:43
```

To delete more than just the one line, specify the first and last lines to delete, separating them with a comma. The following is to delete the first three lines:

```
% who ¦ sed '1,3d'
macedot  ttyAj   Nov 21 20:41
rpm      ttyAk   Nov 21 20:40
ypchen   ttyAl   Nov 21 18:20
kodak    ttyAm   Nov 21 20:43
```

5. There's more to deletion than that. You can also specify patterns by surrounding them with slashes, identically to the substitution pattern. To delete the entries in the who output between eiyo and rpm, the following would work:

```
% who ¦ head -15 ¦ sed '/eiyo/,/rpm/d'
root      console Nov  9 07:31
rick      ttyAa   Nov 21 20:58
brunnert  ttyAb   Nov 21 20:56
ypchen    ttyAl   Nov 21 18:20
kodak     ttyAm   Nov 21 20:43
wh        ttyAn   Nov 21 20:33
klingham  ttyAp   Nov 21 19:55
linet2    ttyAq   Nov 21 20:17
mdps      ttyAr   Nov 21 20:11
```

You can use patterns in combination with numbers too, so if you wanted to delete text from the first line to the line containing kmkernek, here's how you could do it:

```
% who ¦ sed '1,/kmkernek/d'
macedot  ttyAj   Nov 21 20:41
rpm      ttyAk   Nov 21 20:40
ypchen   ttyAl   Nov 21 18:20
kodak    ttyAm   Nov 21 20:43
```

6. Another aspect of sed is that the patterns are actually *regular expressions.* Don't be intimidated, though. If you understood the * and ? of filename wildcards, you've learned the key lesson of regular expressions: special characters can match zero or more letters in the pattern. Regular expressions are slightly different from *shell patterns,* because regular expressions are more powerful (though more confusing). Instead of using the ? to match a character, use the . character.

Within this context, it's rare that you need to look for patterns sufficiently complex to require a full regular expression, which is definitely good news. The only two characters you want to remember for regular expressions are ^, which is the imaginary character before the first character of each line, and $, which is the character after the end of each line.

Comment: Here are some pronunciation tips. UNIX folk tend to call the " *quote,* the ' *single quote,* and the ` *back quote.* The * is *star,* the . is *dot,* the ^ is *caret* or *circumflex,* the $ is *dollar,* and the - is *dash.*

What does this mean? It means that you can use sed to list everyone reported by who that doesn't have *s* as the first letter of his or her account. You can, perhaps a bit more interestingly, eliminate all blank lines from a file with sed too. I'll show you by returning to the testme file:

```
% cat testme
Archives/              OWL/                    keylime.pie
InfoWorld/             bin/                    src/
Mail/                  bitnet.mailing-lists.Z  temp/
News/                  drop.text.hqx           testme


Archives/              OWL/                    keylime.pie
InfoWorld/             bin/                    src/
Mail/                  bitnet.mailing-lists.Z  temp/
News/                  drop.text.hqx           testme


Archives/              OWL/                    keylime.pie
InfoWorld/             bin/                    src/
Mail/                  bitnet.mailing-lists.Z  temp/
News/                  drop.text.hqx           testme
```

Now I'll use sed and clean up this output.

```
% sed '/^$/d' < testme
Archives/              OWL/                    keylime.pie
InfoWorld/             bin/                    src/
Mail/                  bitnet.mailing-lists.Z  temp/
News/                  drop.text.hqx           testme
Archives/              OWL/                    keylime.pie
InfoWorld/             bin/                    src/
Mail/                  bitnet.mailing-lists.Z  temp/
News/                  drop.text.hqx           testme
Archives/              OWL/                    keylime.pie
InfoWorld/             bin/                    src/
Mail/                  bitnet.mailing-lists.Z  temp/
News/                  drop.text.hqx           testme
%
```

7. These commands can be used in combination, of course. To remove all blank lines and all lines that contain the word keylime, and substitute BinHex for each occurrence of hqx, one sed command can be used, albeit a complex one:

```
% cat testme | sed '/^$/d;/keylime/d;s/hqx/BinHex/g'
InfoWorld/             bin/                    src/
Mail/                  bitnet.mailing-lists.Z  temp/
News/                  drop.text.BinHex              testme
InfoWorld/             bin/                    src/
Mail/                  bitnet.mailing-lists.Z  temp/
News/                  drop.text.BinHex              testme
InfoWorld/             bin/                    src/
Mail/                  bitnet.mailing-lists.Z  temp/
News/                  drop.text.BinHex              testme
%
```

8. If you've ever spent any time on an electronic network, you've probably seen either electronic mail or articles wherein the author responds to a previous article. Most commonly, each line of the original message is included, each

prefixed by >. It turns out that sed is the appropriate tool either to add a prefix to a group of lines or to remove a prefix from lines in a file.

```
% cat << EOF > sample
Hey Tai! I've been looking for a music CD and none of
the shops around here have a clue about it. I was
wondering if you're going to have a chance to get into
Tower Records in the next week or so?
EOF
%
% sed 's/^/> /' < sample > sample2
% cat sample2
> Hey Tai! I've been looking for a music CD and none of
> the shops around here have a clue about it. I was
> wondering if you're going to have a chance to get into
> Tower Records in the next week or so?
%
% cat sample2 ¦ sed 's/^> //'
Hey Tai! I've been looking for a music CD and none of
the shops around here have a clue about it. I was
wondering if you're going to have a chance to get into
Tower Records in the next week or so?
%
```

Recall that the caret (^) signifies the beginning of the line, so the first invocation of sed searches for the beginning of each line and replaces it with "> ", saving the output to the file sample2. The second use of sed—wherein I remove the prefix—does the opposite search, finding all occurrences of "> " that are at the beginning of a line and replacing them with a null pattern (a null pattern is what you have when you have two slash delimiters without anything between them).

Step 3. Summary

I've only scratched the surface of the sed command here. It's one of those commands where the more you learn about it, the more powerful you realize it is. But, paradoxically, the more you learn about it, the more you'll really want a graphical interface to simplify your life, too.

Comment: The only sed command I use is substitution. I figure that matching patterns is best done with grep, and it's very rare that I need to delete specific lines from a file anyway. One helpful command I learned while researching this portion of the lesson is that sed can be used to delete from the first line of a file to a specified pattern, meaning that it can easily be used to strip headers from an electronic mail message by specifying the pattern 1,/^$/d. In a day or two, you will learn about e-mail and how this command can be so helpful.

9

Task 9.3: The Wild and Weird *awk* Command
Step 1. Description

Though the sed command can be helpful for simple editing tasks in a pipeline, for real power, you need to invoke the awk program. The awk program is a programming kit for analyzing and manipulating text files, with words. It's one of the most helpful general purpose filters in UNIX.

> **Comment:** Of course, you're wondering where awk got its name. The initial guess is that it refers to its awkward syntax, but that's not quite right. The name is derived from the last names of the authors: Aho, Weinberger, and Kernighan.

Similar to sed, awk can take its commands directly, as arguments. You can also write programs to a file and have awk read the file for its instructions. The general approach to using the program is awk '{ commands }'. There are two possible flags to awk: -f *file* specifies that the instructions should be read from the *file* file rather than the command line, and -F*c* indicates that the program should consider the letter *c* as the separator between fields of information, rather than the default of white space (for example, one or more space or tab characters).

Step 2. Action

1. The first awk command to learn is the most generally useful one, too. In my view, it's the print command. Without any arguments, it'll print the lines in the file, one by one:

```
% who | awk '{ print }'
root      console Nov  9 07:31
yuenca    ttyAo   Nov 27 17:39
limyx4    ttyAp   Nov 27 16:22
wifey     ttyAx   Nov 27 17:16
tobster   ttyAz   Nov 27 17:59
taylor    ttyqh   Nov 27 17:43   (vax1.umkc.edu)
```

A line of input is broken into specific fields of information, each field being assigned a unique identifier. Field one is $1, field two $2, and so on:

```
% who | awk '{ print $1 }'
root
yuenca
limyx4
wifey
tobster
taylor
```

The good news is that you can also specify any other information to print by surrounding it with double quotes:

```
% who ¦ awk '{ print "User " $1 " is on terminal line " $2 }'
User root is on terminal line console
User yuenca is on terminal line ttyAo
User limyx4 is on terminal line ttyAp
User hawk is on terminal line ttyAw
User wifey is on terminal line ttyAx
user taylor is on terminal line ttyqh
```

Don't Skip This: You couldn't use single quotes to surround parameters to the print command, because they would conflict with the single quotes surrounding the entire awk program!

2. You can see already that awk can be quite useful. Return now to the /etc/passwd file and see how awk can help you understand the contents:

```
% grep taylor /etc/passwd ¦ awk -F: '{ print $1 " has "$7" as a
login shell." }'
User taylorj has /bin/csh as their login shell.
User mtaylor has /usr/local/bin/tcsh as their login shell.
User dataylor has /usr/local/lib/msh as their login shell.
User taylorjr has /bin/csh as their login shell.
User taylorrj has /bin/csh as their login shell.
User taylormx has /bin/csh as their login shell.
User taylor has /bin/csh as their login shell.
```

3. An interesting question that came up while I was working with these examples is how many different login shells are used at my site and which one is most popular. On most systems, you'd be trapped, probably having to write a program to solve this question, but with awk and some other utilities, UNIX gives you all the tools you need:

```
% awk -F: '{print $7}' /etc/passwd ¦ sort ¦ uniq -c
   2
3365 /bin/csh
   1 /bin/false
  84 /bin/ksh
  21 /bin/sh
  11 /usr/local/bin/ksh
 353 /usr/local/bin/tcsh
  45 /usr/local/lib/msh
```

Here I'm using awk to extract just the seventh field of the password file, the home directory, handing them all to the sort program, then letting uniq figure out which ones occur how often and, with -c, report the count of occurrences to me. Try this on your system, too.

4. Sticking with the password file, notice that the names therein are all in first-name then last-name format. That is, my account is Dave Taylor,,,,. A common requirement that you might have is to generate a report of system users. You'd like to sort them by name, but by last name. You do it with awk, of course:

```
% grep taylor /etc/passwd ¦ awk -F: '{print $5}'
James Taylor,,,,
Mary Taylor,,,,
Dave Taylor,,,,
James Taylor,,,,
Robert Taylor,,,,
Melanie Taylor,,,,
Dave Taylor,,,,
```

That generates the list of users. Now I'll use sed to remove those annoying commas and awk again to reverse the order of names:

```
% grep taylor /etc/passwd ¦ awk -F: '{print $5}' ¦ sed 's/,//g'
¦ awk '{print $2", "$1}'
Taylor, James
Taylor, Mary
Taylor, Dave
Taylor, James
Taylor, Robert
Taylor, Melanie
Taylor, Dave
```

If I feed the output of this command to sort, the names will finally be listed in the order desired:

```
% grep taylor /etc/passwd ¦ awk -F: '{print $5}' ¦ sed 's/,//g'
¦ awk '{print $2", "$1}' ¦ sort
Taylor, Dave
Taylor, Dave
Taylor, James
Taylor, James
Taylor, Mary
Taylor, Melanie
Taylor, Robert
```

This is slick. You can also see how to use various UNIX commands incrementally to build up to your desired result.

5. The script earlier that looked for the login shell isn't quite correct. It turns out that if the user wants to have /bin/sh—the Bourne shell—as his or her default shell, the final field can be left blank:

```
joe:?:45:555:Joe-Bob Billiard,,,,:/home/joe:
```

This can be a problem, because the blank field will confuse the awk program; awk is just counting fields in the line. The good news is that each line has an associated *number of fields*, known as the NF variable. Used without a dollar sign, it indicates how many fields are on a line, and used with a dollar sign, it's always the value of the last field on the line itself:

```
% who ¦ head -3 ¦ awk '{ print NF }'
5
5
5
% who ¦ head -3 ¦ awk '{ print $NF }'
07:31
16:22
18:21
```

Because I'm interested in the last field in the /etc/passwd file, the best approach for the preceding command would be to use this $NF parameter explicitly:

```
% grep taylor /etc/passwd ¦ awk -F: '{print $NF}' ¦ sort ¦ uniq -c
3365 /bin/csh
   1 /bin/false
  84 /bin/ksh
  21 /bin/sh
  11 /usr/local/bin/ksh
 353 /usr/local/bin/tcsh
  45 /usr/local/lib/msh
```

6. Similar to NF is NR, which keeps track of the *number of records* (or lines) seen. Here's a quick way to number a file:

```
% ls -l ¦ awk '{ print NR": "$0 }'
1: total 29
2: drwx------   2 taylor      512 Nov 21 10:39 Archives/
3: drwx------   3 taylor      512 Nov 16 21:55 InfoWorld/
4: drwx------   2 taylor     1024 Nov 27 18:02 Mail/
5: drwx------   2 taylor      512 Oct  6 09:36 News/
6: drwx------   3 taylor      512 Nov 21 12:39 OWL/
7: drwx------   2 taylor      512 Oct 13 10:45 bin/
8: -rw-rw----   1 taylor    12556 Nov 16 09:49 keylime.pie
9: -rw-------   1 taylor    11503 Nov 27 18:05 randy
10: drwx------   2 taylor      512 Oct 13 10:45 src/
11: drwxrwx---  2 taylor      512 Nov  8 22:20 temp/
12: -rw-rw----   1 taylor        0 Nov 27 18:29 testme
```

Here you can see that the zero field of a line is the entire line. This can be useful, too:

```
% who ¦ awk '{ print $2": "$0 }'
ttyAp: limyx4   ttyAp   Nov 27 16:22
ttyAt: ltbei    ttyAt   Nov 27 18:21
ttyAu: woodson  ttyAu   Nov 27 18:19
ttyAv: morning  ttyAv   Nov 27 18:19
ttyAw: hawk     ttyAw   Nov 27 18:12
ttyAx: wifey    ttyAx   Nov 27 17:16
ttyAz: wiwatr   ttyAz   Nov 27 18:22
ttyAA: chong    ttyAA   Nov 27 13:56
ttyAB: ishidahx ttyAB   Nov 27 18:20
```

9

7. Here's another example of awk. I'll modify the output of the `ls -l` command so that I build a quick list of files and their sizes (which isn't what is shown with the `ls -s` command, remember):

```
% ls -1F ¦ awk '{ print $8 " " $4 }'
Archives/ 512
InfoWorld/ 512
Mail/ 1024
News/ 512
OWL/ 512
bin/ 512
keylime.pie 12556
randy 11503
src/ 512
temp/ 512
testme 582
```

The output is a bit messy, so you should learn about two special character sequences that can be embedded in the quoted arguments to `print`:

\n   generate a carriage return

\t   generate a tab character

In any case, the output is in the wrong order, anyway:

```
% ls -1F ¦ awk '{ print $4 "\t" $8 }'
512     Archives/
512     InfoWorld/
1024    Mail/
512     News/
512     OWL/
512     bin/
12556   keylime.pie
11503   randy
512     src/
512     temp/
582     testme
```

Piping the preceding results to `sort -rn` could easily be used to figure out your largest files:

```
% ls -l ¦ awk '{print $4"\t" $8 }' ¦ sort -rn ¦ head -5
12556   keylime.pie
11503   randy
1024    Mail/
582     testme
512     temp/
```

8. The awk program actually has three blocks of instructions that it works with: before the first line being scanned, once per line, and following the last line being scanned. These are delineated in the awk program by BEGIN and END, with the default being applied to each line scanned.

This can be very useful for computing the sum of a series of numbers. For example, I'd like to know the total number of bytes I'm using for all my files:

```
% ls -l ¦ awk '{print $4}'
512
512
1024
512
512
512
12556
11503
512
512
582
```

That generates the list of file sizes, but how do I sum them up? One way is to create a new variable `totalsize` and output its accumulated value each line:

```
% ls -l ¦ awk '{ totalsize = totalsize + $5; print totalsize }'
512
1024
2048
2560
3072
3584
16140
27643
28155
28667
29249
```

One easy cleanup is to learn that += is a shorthand notation for "add the following value to the variable":

```
% ls -l ¦ awk '{ totalsize += $5; print totalsize }'
512
1024
2048
2560
3072
3584
16140
27643
28155
28667
29249
```

I can use `tail` to get the last line only, of course, and figure out the total size that way:

```
% ls -l ¦ awk '{ totalsize += $5; print totalsize }' ¦ tail -1
29249
```

A better way, however, is to use the END programming block in the awk program:

```
% ls -l ¦ awk '{ totalsize += $4 } END { print totalsize }'
29249
```

One more slight modification and it's done:

```
% ls -l ¦ awk '{ totalsize += $4 } END { print "You have a
total of" totalsize " bytes used in files." }'
You have a total of 29249 bytes used in files.
```

9. Here's one further addition that can make this program even more fun:

```
% ls -l ¦ awk '{ totalsize += $5 } END { print "You have a
total of" totalsize " bytes used across "NR" files." }'
You have a total of 29249 bytes used across 11 files.
```

An easier way to see all this is to create an awk program file:

```
% cat << EOF > script
        { totalsize += $4 }
END     { print "You have a total of "totalsize     \
        " bytes used across "NR" files."
}
EOF
% ls -l ¦ awk -f script
You have a total of 29249 bytes used across 11 files.
```

10. Here's one last example before I leave awk. Scripts in awk are really programs, and they have all the flow control capabilities you'd want (and then some!). One thing you can do within an awk script is to have conditional execution of statements, the if-then condition. The length routine returns the number of characters in the given argument:

```
% awk -F: '{ if (length($1) == 2) print $0 }' /etc/passwd ¦ wc -l
    26
%
```

Can you tell what this does? First off, notice that it uses the /etc/passwd file for input and has a colon as the field delimiter (the -F:). For each line in the password file, this awk script tests to see if the length of the first field (the account name) is exactly two characters long or not. If it is, then the entire line from the password file is printed. All lines printed are then read by the wc program, which, because I used the -l flag, reports the total number of lines read.

What this command tells us is that on the machine there are exactly 26 accounts for which the account name is two characters long.

11. The next logical question is, How many account names have a length of each possible number of characters? To find out, I'll use an advanced feature

of awk just to tantalize you: I'll have the program build a table to keep track of count, with one entry per number of characters in the name:

```
% cat << EOF > awkscript
{
        count[length($1)]++
}
END {
        for (i=1; i < 9; i++)
          print "There are " count[i] " accounts with " i " letter names."
}
%
% awk -F: -f awkscript < /etc/passwd
There are 1 accounts with 1 letter names.
There are 26 accounts with 2 letter names.
There are 303 accounts with 3 letter names.
There are 168 accounts with 4 letter names.
There are 368 accounts with 5 letter names.
There are 611 accounts with 6 letter names.
There are 906 accounts with 7 letter names.
There are 1465 accounts with 8 letter names.
```

You can see that longer names are preferred at this site. How about that lone account with a single letter account name? That's easy to extract with the earlier script:

```
% awk -F: '{ if (length($1) = 1) print $0 }' < /etc/passwd
awk: syntax error near line 1
awk: illegal statement near line 1
```

Oops! I'll try it again with a double equal sign:

```
% awk -F: '{ if (length($1) == 1) print $0 }' < /etc/passwd
z:?:1325:1375:Chris Zed,,,,:/users/z:/bin/csh
```

Comment: The worst part of awk is its appalling error messages. Try deliberately introducing an error to one of these awk scripts, and you'll quickly learn just how weird it can be! The classic error is `syntax error on or near line 1: bailing out`.

Step 3. Summary

The awk program is incredibly powerful, but the good news is that you can easily use it and find it helpful and a great addition to your collection of UNIX tools without learning much at all about programming. I use awk almost daily, and 99 percent of those uses are simply to extract specific columns of information or to change the order of entries, as you saw when I reversed first name and last name from the /etc/passwd file.

I could easily fill the rest of this book with instructions on the awk program, teaching you how to write powerful and interesting scripts. Indeed, I could do the same with the sed program, though I think awk has an edge in power and capabilities. The point, though, isn't to learn exhaustively about thousands of command options and thousands of variations, but to have the key concepts and utilities at your fingertips, allowing you to build upon that knowledge as you grow more sophisticated with UNIX.

To this goal, I note that awk is a program that has more depth and capabilities than just about any other UNIX utility, short of actually writing programs in C. When you've mastered all seven days of this book, awk is a fruitful utility to explore further and expand your knowledge.

Task 9.4: Rerouting the Pipeline with *tee*
Step 1. Description

After the substantial sed and awk commands, this next command, tee, should be a nice reprieve. It's simple, can't be programmed, and has only one possible starting flag.

You'll recall that the ¦ symbol denotes a pipeline and that information traveling from one command to another is considered to be streaming down the pipe. For example, who ¦ sort has the output of the who command streaming down the pipe to the sort command. Imagine it all as some huge, albeit weird, plumbing construction.

With the plumbing metaphor in action, you can imagine that it is helpful at times to be able to split off the stream, making the steam travel down two different directions, rather than just one. If multiple pipelines were really allowed, neither you nor I could ever figure out what the heck was going on. The simpler goal, however, of saving a copy of the stream in a file as it whizzes past is more manageable, and that's exactly what the tee command can do.

The only option to tee is -a to have it append to the specified file, rather than replace the contents of the file each time.

Step 2. Action

1. At it's simplest, tee can grab a copy of the information being shown on the screen:

```
% who ¦ tee who.out
root      console Nov  9 07:31
jeffhtrt ttyAo   Nov 27 18:39
limyx4   ttyAp   Nov 27 16:22
cherlbud ttyAq   Nov 27 18:34
garrettj ttyAr   Nov 27 18:34
coyote   ttyAs   Nov 27 18:34
```

```
ltbei      ttyAt    Nov 27 18:21
woodson    ttyAu    Nov 27 18:19
morning    ttyAv    Nov 27 18:19
wifey      ttyAx    Nov 27 17:16
% cat who.out
root       console  Nov  9 07:31
jeffhtrt   ttyAo    Nov 27 18:39
limyx4     ttyAp    Nov 27 16:22
cherlbud   ttyAq    Nov 27 18:34
garrettj   ttyAr    Nov 27 18:34
coyote     ttyAs    Nov 27 18:34
ltbei      ttyAt    Nov 27 18:21
woodson    ttyAu    Nov 27 18:19
morning    ttyAv    Nov 27 18:19
wifey      ttyAx    Nov 27 17:16
```

This can be quite useful for saving output.

2. Better, though, is to grab a copy of the information going down a stream in the middle:

```
% ls -l ¦ awk '{ print $4 "\t" $8 }' ¦ sort -rn ¦ tee bigfiles ¦ head -5
12556    keylime.pie
8729     owl.c
1024     Mail/
582      tetme
512      temp/
```

This shows only the five largest files on the screen, but the bigfiles file actually has a list of *all* files, sorted by size:

```
% cat bigfiles
12556    keylime.pie
8729     owl.c
1024     Mail/
582      tetme
512      temp/
512      src/
512      bin/
512      OWL/
512      News/
512      InfoWorld/
512      Archives/
207      sample2
199      sample
126      awkscript
```

Step 3. Summary

The tee command is a classic little UNIX utility, where, as stated before, it seems useful but a bit limited in purpose. As you're learning through all the examples, however, from lots of little commands do big, powerful commands grow.

9

Task 9.5: More Filename Wildcards
Step 1. Description

Earlier, you learned about two special wildcard characters that can help you when specifying files for commands in UNIX. The first was the ?, which matches any single character, and the other was the *, which matches zero or more characters. There are more special wildcards for the shell when specifying filenames, and it's time to learn about another of them.

This new notation is known as a *character range*, serving as a wildcard less general than the question mark.

Step 2. Action

1. A pair of square brackets denotes a range of characters, which can be either explicitly listed or indicated as a range with a dash between them. I'll start with a list of files in my current directory:

```
% ls
Archives/    News/       bigfiles     owl.c       src/
InfoWorld/   OWL/        bin/         sample      temp/
Mail/        awkscript   keylime.pie  sample2     tetme
```

If I wanted to see both `bigfiles` and the `bin` directory, I could use b* as a file pattern:

```
% ls -ld b*
-rw-rw----   1 taylor        165 Dec  3 16:42 bigfiles
drwx------   2 taylor        512 Oct 13 10:45 bin/
```

If I want to see all entries that start with a lowercase letter, I can explicitly type each one:

```
% ls -ld a* b* k* o* s* t*
-rw-rw----   1 taylor        126 Dec  3 16:34 awkscript
-rw-rw----   1 taylor        165 Dec  3 16:42 bigfiles
drwx------   2 taylor        512 Oct 13 10:45 bin/
-rw-rw----   1 taylor      12556 Nov 16 09:49 keylime.pie
-rw-rw----   1 taylor       8729 Dec  2 21:19 owl.c
-rw-rw----   1 taylor        199 Dec  3 16:11 sample
-rw-rw----   1 taylor        207 Dec  3 16:11 sample2
drwx------   2 taylor        512 Oct 13 10:45 src/
drwxrwx---   2 taylor        512 Nov  8 22:20 temp/
-rw-rw----   1 taylor        582 Nov 27 18:29 tetme
```

That's clearly quite awkward. Instead, I can specify a range of characters to match. I specify the range by listing them all tucked neatly into a pair of square brackets:

```
% ls -ld [abkost]*
-rw-rw----  1 taylor      126 Dec  3 16:34 awkscript
-rw-rw----  1 taylor      165 Dec  3 16:42 bigfiles
drwx------  2 taylor      512 Oct 13 10:45 bin/
-rw-rw----  1 taylor    12556 Nov 16 09:49 keylime.pie
-rw-rw----  1 taylor     8729 Dec  2 21:19 owl.c
-rw-rw----  1 taylor      199 Dec  3 16:11 sample
-rw-rw----  1 taylor      207 Dec  3 16:11 sample2
drwx------  2 taylor      512 Oct 13 10:45 src/
drwxrwx---  2 taylor      512 Nov  8 22:20 temp/
-rw-rw----  1 taylor      582 Nov 27 18:29 tetme
```

In this case, the shell matches all files that start with an *a*, *b*, *k*, *o*, *s*, or *t*. This notation is still a bit clunky and would be more so, if there were more files involved.

2. The ideal is to specify a range of characters by using the hyphen character in the middle of a range:

```
% ls -ld [a-z]*
-rw-rw----  1 taylor      126 Dec  3 16:34 awkscript
-rw-rw----  1 taylor      165 Dec  3 16:42 bigfiles
drwx------  2 taylor      512 Oct 13 10:45 bin/
-rw-rw----  1 taylor    12556 Nov 16 09:49 keylime.pie
-rw-rw----  1 taylor     8729 Dec  2 21:19 owl.c
-rw-rw----  1 taylor      199 Dec  3 16:11 sample
-rw-rw----  1 taylor      207 Dec  3 16:11 sample2
drwx------  2 taylor      512 Oct 13 10:45 src/
drwxrwx---  2 taylor      512 Nov  8 22:20 temp/
-rw-rw----  1 taylor      582 Nov 27 18:29 tetme
```

In this example, the shell will match any file that begins with a lowercase letter, ranging from *a* to *z*, as specified.

3. Space is critical in all wildcard patterns, too. Watch what happens if I accidentally add a space between the closing bracket of the range specification and the asterisk following:

```
% ls -CFd [a-z] *
Archives/     News/       bigfiles      owl.c       src/
InfoWorld/    OWL/        bin/          sample      temp/
Mail/         awkscript   keylime.pie   sample2     tetme
```

This time, the shell tried to match all files whose names were one character long and lowercase, and then it tried to match all files that matched the asterisk wildcard, which, of course, is all regular files in the directory.

4. The combination of character ranges, single character wildcards, and multicharacter wildcards can be tremendously helpful. If I move to another directory, I can easily search for all files that contain a single digit, dot, or underscore in the name:

9

```
% cd Mail
% ls -CF
71075.446        emilyc          mailbox            sartin
72303.2166       gordon_hat      manley             sent
bmcinern         harrism         mark               shalini
bob_gull         j=taylor        marmi              siob_n
cennamo          james           marv               steve
dan_some         jeffv           matt_ruby          tai
dataylor         john_welch      mcwillia           taylor
decc             john_prage      netnews.postings   v892127
disserli         kcs             raf                wcenter
druby            lehman          rexb               windows
dunlaplm         lenz            rock               xd1f
ean_huts         mac             rustle
%
% ls *[0-9._]*
71075.446        ean_huts        matt_ruby      xd1f
72303.2166       gordon_hat      netnews.postings
bob_gull         john_welcher    siob_n
dan_some         john_prage      v892127
```

Step 3. Summary

I think that the best way to learn about pervasive features of UNIX like shell filename wildcards is just to use them. If you flip through this book, you immediately notice that the examples are building on earlier information. This will continue to be the case, and the filename range notation shown here will be used again, in combination with the asterisk and question mark, to specify groups of files or directories.

Remember that, if you want to experiment with filename wildcards, you can most easily use the echo command, because it'll dutifully print the expanded version of any pattern you specify.

Lesson Summary

In this lesson, you really have had a chance to build on the knowledge you're picking up about UNIX, with your introduction to two exciting and powerful UNIX utilities, sed and awk. Each could easily justify its own book, particularly awk, a favorite tool of my own for working with UNIX.

An interesting and useful notation you learned in this chapter is the << file redirection command, which allows you to create here documents, files that for all intents and purposes exist—particularly for pipelines—but never actually take up any space in the file system. If you progress to writing shell programs, here documents can prove invaluable additions to your UNIX tool belt.

Finally, what's a poker hand without some new wildcards? Because one-eyed jacks don't make much sense in UNIX, you instead learned about how to specify ranges of characters in filename patterns, further ensuring that you can type the minimum number of keys for maximum effect.

Workshop
Key Terms

here document The result of using the << redirection, it's a series of lines of input that appears as a file to the system, though it doesn't actually exist as a file.

end-of-file word The word used with here documents to specify the end of the series of lines. By default, variables in a here document are expanded, but if the end-of-file word is quoted, all characters remain untouched.

pipeline A series of UNIX commands chained by ¦, the *pipe* symbol.

addresses Used in sed notation to specify the range over which a command should be applied. The dot special character (.) represents the current line, and $ represents the last line.

regular expressions A convenient notation for specifying complex patterns. Notable special characters are ^ to match the beginning of the line and $ to match the end of the line.

Questions

1. What are the Big Four file redirection commands, and how do they differ?

2. Show how you could use file redirection to create a one-line command that will let you build a memo file, containing ideas and thoughts as you think of them. Make sure that additions don't overwrite previous entries!

3. Expand on the plumbing metaphor with UNIX. What program enables you to split the flow into multiple files? What lets you fit multiple commands into a pipeline? What lets you put something into the file? What lets you save the output when you're done?

4. What does the following do?

```
sed 's/:/ /;s/ /:/' /etc/passwd ¦ head
```

9

5. What does this one do?

```
sed 's/^/$ /' < testme
```

6. Will the following two commands do the same thing?

```
who ¦ awk '{print $1}' ¦ grep taylor
who ¦ grep taylor ¦ awk '{print $1}'
```

7. Will this command do the same as those in the sixth question?

```
who ¦ awk '{ if ($1 == "taylor") print }'
```

8. Create a simple awk script that will sort lines in a file by the number of words on the line. Pay attention to the NF record in awk itself.

Preview of the Next Chapter

Starting with the fourth day, you learn about another powerful and popular program in the entire UNIX system, a program so helpful that versions of it exist even on DOS and the Macintosh today. It fills in the missing piece of your UNIX knowledge; and, if what's been covered so far focuses on the plumbing analogy, this command finally moves you beyond considering UNIX as a typewriter (a tty). What's the program? Its the vi screen-oriented editor. It's another program that deserves a book or two, but in two chapters you learn the basics of vi and enough additional commands to let you work with the program easily and efficiently.

Editing Files

An
Introduction
to the *vi* Editor

If you like primitive tools, you've already figured out that you can use a combination of << and cat to add lines to a file, and you can use sed and file redirection to modify the contents of a file. These tools are rough and awkward, and when it's time either to create new files or to modify existing files, you need a screen-oriented editor. In UNIX, the screen editor of choice is called vi.

There are a number of editors that may be included with your UNIX system, including ed, ex, vi, and EMACS. The latter two use the entire screen, a big advantage, and both are powerful editors. You learn about both in today's lessons. I focus on vi, however, because I believe it's easier and, perhaps more importantly, it's guaranteed to be always part of UNIX, whereas most vendors omit EMACS, forcing you to find it yourself.

All three lessons in Day 4 of *Teach Yourself UNIX in a Week* focus on full-screen editing tools for UNIX. This is the first of two lessons in which you learn how to use vi to create and modify files. This lesson covers the basics, including how to move around in the file; how to insert and delete characters, words, and lines; and how to search for specific patterns in the text. The next lesson gives an introduction to key mapping, default files, and the ways to use the rest of UNIX while within vi. At the end of the fourth day, you will learn to use an alternate UNIX editor called EMACS.

Goals for This Lesson

In this lesson, you will learn

- ☐ How to start and quit vi
- ☐ Simple character motion in vi
- ☐ How to move by words and pages
- ☐ How to insert text into the file
- ☐ How to delete text
- ☐ How to search within a file
- ☐ How to have vi start properly
- ☐ The key colon commands in vi

In some ways, an editor is like another operating system living within UNIX; it is so complex that you will need two lessons to learn to use vi. If you're used to Windows or Macintosh editors, you'll be unhappy to find that vi doesn't know anything about your mouse. Once you spend some time working with vi, however, I promise it will grow on you. By the end of this lesson, you will be able to create and modify files on your UNIX system to your heart's content.

Task 10.1: How to Start and Quit *vi*
Step 1. Description

You may have noticed that many of the UNIX commands covered so far have one characteristic in common. They all do their work, display their results, and quit. Among the few exceptions are more and pg, where you work within the specific program environment until you have viewed the entire contents of the file being shown or until you quit. The vi editor is another program in this small category of *environments*, programs that you move in and use until you explicitly tell the program to quit.

Comment: Where did vi get its name? It's not quite as interesting as some of the earlier, more colorful command names. The vi command is so named because it's the **vi**sual **i**nterface to the ex editor. It was written by Bill Joy while he was at the University of California at Berkeley.

Before you start vi for the first time, you must learn about two aspects of its behavior. The first is that vi is a *modal* editor. A mode is like an environment. Different modes in vi interpret the same key differently. For example, if you're in *insert mode*, pressing the A key adds an *a* to the text, whereas in *command mode*, pressing the A key enters a, a single key abbreviation for the *append* command. If you ever get confused about what mode you're in, press the ESC key on your keyboard. Pressing ESC always returns you to the command mode (and if you're already in command mode, it simply beeps to remind you of that fact).

Comment: In vi, the Return key is a specific command (meaning move to the beginning of the next line). As a result, you never need to press Return to have vi process your command.

Comment: EMACS is a _modeless_ editor. In EMACS, the A key always adds the letter _a_ to the file. Commands in EMACS are all indicated by holding down the Control key while pressing the command key; for example, Control-C deletes a character.

The second important characteristic of vi is that it's a screen-oriented program. It _must_ know what kind of terminal, computer, or system you are using to work with UNIX. This probably won't be a problem for you because most systems are set up so that the default terminal type matches the terminal or communications program you're using. In this part of today's lesson, you will learn how to recognize when vi cannot figure out what terminal you're using, and what to do about it.

You can start vi in a number of different ways, and you will learn about lots of helpful alternatives later in this lesson. Right now you will learn the basics. The vi command by itself starts the editor, ready for you to create a new file. The vi command with a filename starts vi with the specified file, so you can modify that file immediately.

Let's get started!

Step 2. Action

1. To begin, enter vi at the prompt. If all is working well, the screen will clear, the first character on each line will become a tilde (~), and the cursor will be sitting at the top-left corner of the screen:

   ```
   % vi
   ```

Comment: I'm going to show you only the portion of the screen that is relevant to the command being discussed for vi, rather than show you the entire screen each time. When the full screen is required to explain something, it'll show up. A smooth edge will indicate the edge of the screen, and a jagged edge will indicate that the rest of the display has been omitted.

Type a colon character. Doing so moves the cursor to the bottom of the screen and replaces the last tilde with the colon:

```
~
~
~
~
~
~
~
~
:_
```

Press the q key and the Return key, and you should be back at the shell prompt:

```
~
~
~
~
~
~
~
~
:q
%
```

2. If that operation worked without a problem, skip to the next section, Action instruction 3. If the operation did not work, you received the unknown-terminal-type error message. You might see this on your screen:

```
% vi
"unknown": Unknown terminal type
I don't know what type of terminal you are on. All I have is "unknown"
[using open mode]
_
```

Alternatively, you might see this:

```
% vi
Visual needs addressible cursor or upline capability
:
```

Don't panic. You can fix this problem. The first step is to get back to the shell prompt. To do this, do exactly what you did in the first Action instruction. Type :q followed by the Return key. You should then see this:

```
% vi
"unknown": Unknown terminal type
I don't know what type of terminal you are on. All I have is "unknown"
[using open mode]
:q
%
```

The problem here is that vi needs to know the type of terminal you're using, but it can't figure that out on its own. Therefore, you need to tell the operating system by setting the TERM environment variable. If you know what kind of terminal you have, use that value; otherwise, try the default of vt100:

```
% setenv TERM vt100
```

If you have the $ prompt, which means you're using the Bourne shell (sh) or Korn shell (ksh) rather than the C shell (csh), try this:

```
$ TERM=vt100 ; export TERM
```

Either way, you can now try entering vi again, and it should work.

If it does work, append the command (whichever of these two commands was successful for you) to your .login file if you use csh or to .profile if you use sh or ksh:

```
% echo "setenv TERM vt100" >> .login
```

or

```
$ echo "TERM=vt100 ; export TERM" >> .profile
```

This way, the next time you log in, the system will remember what kind of terminal you're using.

If this didn't work, on the other hand, it's time to talk with your system administrator about the problem or to call your UNIX vendor to find out what the specific value should be. If you are connected through a modem or other line, and you are actually using a terminal emulator or communications package, then you might also try using ansi as a TERM setting. If that fails, call the company that makes your software and ask the company what terminal type the communications program is emulating.

3. Great! You have successfully launched vi, seen what it looks like, and even entered the most important command, the quit command. Now create a simple file and start vi so it shows you the contents of the file:

```
% ls -l > demo
% vi demo
```

```
total 29
drwx------    2 taylor         512 Nov 21 10:39 Archives/
drwx------    3 taylor         512 Dec  3 02:03 InfoWorld/
drwx------    2 taylor        1024 Dec  3 01:43 Mail/
drwx------    2 taylor         512 Oct  6 09:36 News/
drwx------    4 taylor         512 Dec  2 22:08 OWL/
-rw-rw----    1 taylor         126 Dec  3 16:34 awkscript
-rw-rw----    1 taylor         165 Dec  3 16:42 bigfiles
drwx------    2 taylor         512 Oct 13 10:45 bin/
-rw-rw----    1 taylor           0 Dec  3 22:26 demo
-rw-rw----    1 taylor       12556 Nov 16 09:49 keylime.pie
-rw-rw----    1 taylor        8729 Dec  2 21:19 owl.c
-rw-rw----    1 taylor         199 Dec  3 16:11 sample
-rw-rw----    1 taylor         207 Dec  3 16:11 sample2
drwx------    2 taylor         512 Oct 13 10:45 src/
drwxrwx---    2 taylor         512 Nov  8 22:20 temp/
-rw-rw----    1 taylor         582 Nov 27 18:29 tetme
~
~
~
~
~
~
~
"demo" 17 lines, 846 characters
```

You can see that vi reads the file specified on the command line. In this example, my file is 17 lines long, but my screen can hold 25 lines. To show that some lines lack any text, vi uses the tilde on a line by itself. Finally, note that, at the bottom, the program shows the name of the file, the number of lines it found in the file, and the total number of characters.

Type :q again to quit vi and return to the command line for now. When you type the colon, the cursor will flash down to the bottom line and wait for the q as it did before.

Step 3. Summary

You have learned the most basic command in vi—the :q command—and survived the experience. It's all downhill from here.

Task 10.2: Simple Character Motion in *vi*
Step 1. Description

Getting to a file isn't much good if you can't actually move around in it. Now you will learn how to use the cursor control keys in vi. To move left one character, press the h key. To move up, press the k key. To move down, press the j key; and to move right a single character, use the 1 key (lowercase *L*). You can move left one character by pressing the Backspace key, and you can move to the beginning of the next line with the Return key.

Step 2. Action

1. Launch vi again, specifying the demo file:

   ```
   % vi demo
   ```

   ```
   total 29
   drwx------  2 taylor       512 Nov 21 10:39 Archives/
   drwx------  3 taylor       512 Dec  3 02:03 InfoWorld/
   drwx------  2 taylor      1024 Dec  3 01:43 Mail/
   drwx------  2 taylor       512 Oct  6 09:36 News/
   drwx------  4 taylor       512 Dec  2 22:08 OWL/
   -rw-rw----  1 taylor       126 Dec  3 16:34 awkscript
   -rw-rw----  1 taylor       165 Dec  3 16:42 bigfiles
   drwx------  2 taylor       512 Oct 13 10:45 bin/
   -rw-rw----  1 taylor         0 Dec  3 22:26 demo
   -rw-rw----  1 taylor     12556 Nov 16 09:49 keylime.pie
   -rw-rw----  1 taylor      8729 Dec  2 21:19 owl.c
   -rw-rw----  1 taylor       199 Dec  3 16:11 sample
   -rw-rw----  1 taylor       207 Dec  3 16:11 sample2
   drwx------  2 taylor       512 Oct 13 10:45 src/
   ```

```
drwxrwx---   2 taylor          512 Nov  8 22:20 temp/
-rw-rw----   1 taylor          582 Nov 27 18:29 tetme
~
~
~
~
~
~
~
"demo" 17 lines, 846 characters
```

You should see the cursor sitting on top of the t in total on the first line or flashing underneath the t character. Perhaps you have a flashing box cursor or one that shows up in a different color. In any case, that's your starting spot in the file.

2. Press the h key once to try to move left. The cursor stays in the same spot, and vi beeps to remind you that you can't move left any farther on the line. Try the k key to move up; the same thing will happen.

Now try pressing the j key to move down a character:

```
total 29
drwx------   2 taylor          512 Nov 21 10:39 Archives/
drwx------   3 taylor          512 Dec  3 02:03 InfoWorld/
drwx------   2 taylor         1024 Dec  3 01:43 Mail/
```

Now the cursor is on the d directory indicator of the second line of the file.

Press the k key to move back up to the original starting spot.

3. Using the four cursor control keys—the h, j, k, and l keys—move around in the file for a little bit, until you are comfortable with what's happening on the screen. Now try using the Backspace and Return keys to see how they help you move around.

4. Move to the middle of a line:

```
total 29
drwx------   2 taylor          512 Nov 21 10:39 Archives/
drwx------   3 taylor          512 Dec  3 02:03 InfoWorld/
drwx------   2 taylor         1024 Dec  3 01:43 Mail/
```

Here I'm at the middle digit in the file size of the second file in the listing. Here are a couple new cursor motion keys: the 0 (zero) key moves the cursor to the beginning of the line, and $ moves it to the end of the line. First, I type 0:

```
total 29
drwx------  2 taylor        512 Nov 21 10:39 Archives/
drwx------  3 taylor        512 Dec  3 02:03 InfoWorld/
drwx------  2 taylor       1024 Dec  3 01:43 Mail/
```

Now I type $ to move to the end of the line:

```
total 29
drwx------  2 taylor        512 Nov 21 10:39 Archives/
drwx------  3 taylor        512 Dec  3 02:03 InfoWorld/
drwx------  2 taylor       1024 Dec  3 01:43 Mail/
```

5. If you have arrow keys on your keyboard, try using them to see if they work the same way the h, j, k, and 1 keys work. If the arrow keys don't move you about, they might have shifted you into insert mode. If you type characters and they're added to the file, you need to press the ESC key to return to command mode. Let's wrap this up by leaving this edit session. Because vi now knows that you have modified the file, it will try to ensure that you don't quit without saving the changes:

```
~
~
:q
No write since last change (:quit! overrides)
```

Use :q! (shorthand for :quit) to quit without saving the changes.

Comment: In general, if you try to use a colon command in vi and the program complains that it might do something bad, try the command again, followed by an exclamation point. I like to think of this as saying, "Do it anyway!"

Stay in this file for the next section if you'd like, or use :q to quit.

Step 3. Summary

Moving about a file using these six simple key commands is, on a small scale, much like using the entire process of using the vi editor when working with files. Stick with these simple commands until you're comfortable moving around, and you will be well on your way to becoming proficient using vi.

Task 10.3: Moving by Words and Pages
Step 1. Description

Earlier, in the description of the EMACS editor, I commented that because it's always in insert mode, all commands must include the Control key. Well, it turns out that vi has its share of *control-key commands*, commands that require you to hold down the Control key and press another key. In this section, you will learn about Control-F, Control-B, Control-U, and Control-D. These move you *forward* or *backward* a screen, and *up* or *down* half a screen of text, respectively.

I toss a few more commands into the pot, too: w moves you forward word by word, b moves you backward word by word, and the uppercase versions of these two commands have very similar, but not identical, functions.

Step 2. Action

1. To see how this works, you need to create a file that is longer than the size of your screen. An easy way to do this is to save the output of a common command to a file over and over until the file is long enough. The system I use has lots of users, so I needed to use the who command just once. You might have to append the output of who to the big.output file a couple times before the file is longer than 24 lines. (You can check using wc, of course.)

```
% who > big.output; wc -l big.output
    40
% vi big.output
```

```
leungtc   ttyrV   Dec  1 18:27   (magenta)
tuyinhwa  ttyrX   Dec  3 22:38   (expert)
hollenst  ttyrZ   Dec  3 22:14   (dov)
brandt    ttyrb   Nov 28 23:03   (age)
holmes    ttyrj   Dec  3 21:59   (age)
yuxi      ttyrn   Dec  1 14:19   (pc115)
frodo     ttyro   Dec  3 22:01   (mentor)
labeck    ttyrt   Dec  3 22:02   (dov)
```

```
chenlx2  ttyru   Dec  3 21:53   (mentor)
leungtc  ttys0   Nov 28 15:11   (gold)
chinese  ttys2   Dec  3 22:53   (excalibur)
cdemmert ttys5   Dec  3 23:00   (mentor)
yuenca   ttys6   Dec  3 23:00   (mentor)
janitor  ttys7   Dec  3 18:18   (age)
mathisbp ttys8   Dec  3 23:17   (dov)
janitor  ttys9   Dec  3 18:18   (age)
cs541    ttysC   Dec  2 15:16   (solaria)
yansong  ttysL   Dec  1 14:44   (math)
mdps     ttysO   Nov 30 19:39   (localhost)
md       ttysU   Dec  2 08:45   (muller)
jac      ttysa   Dec  3 18:18   (localhost)
eichsted ttysb   Dec  3 23:21   (pc1)
sweett   ttysc   Dec  3 22:40   (dov)
"big.output" 40 lines, 1659 characters
```

Because I have only a 25-line display and the output is 40 lines long (you can see that on the status line at the bottom), there is more information in this file than the screen can display at once.

2. To see the next screenful, hold down the Control key, press the F key, then let both go. In the future, when I indicate Control-F that's what I mean you should do.

   I press Control-F and get the following output:

```
eichsted ttysb   Dec  3 23:21   (pc1)
sweett   ttysc   Dec  3 22:40   (dov)
wellman  ttysd   Dec  3 23:01   (dov)
tuttleno ttyse   Dec  3 23:03   (indyvax)
wu       ttysf   Dec  3 23:10   (term01)
daurismj ttysg   Dec  3 23:10   (dov)
cs414    ttysh   Dec  3 23:12   (xds)
cq       ttysi   Dec  3 23:13   (expert)
cdemmert ttysk   Dec  3 22:37   (xsun22)
jrlee    ttysn   Dec  3 22:53   (mac1)
fitzgejs ttyso   Dec  3 23:18   (dov)
doerrhb  ttysp   Dec  3 23:20   (dov)
cdemmert ttysq   Dec  3 23:00   (xsun22)
frazierw ttysr   Dec  3 23:01   (dov)
buckeye  ttyss   Dec  3 23:20   (mac2)
mtaylor  ttyst   Dec  3 23:22   (dov)
look     ttysu   Dec  3 23:12   (age)
janitor  ttysw   Dec  3 18:29   (age)
ajones   ttysx   Dec  3 23:23   (rass)
~
~
~
~
```

Notice that the entire screen was rewritten, and that the familiar tilde characters have popped up again to let me know that I have reached the end of the file.

By default, vi has a two-line overlap when you move from screen to screen. If you look carefully, you can see that both eichsted and sweett show up on both screens of data. This doesn't mean that they appear twice in the file; rather, vi is trying to help me not get lost while I wander through the file.

3. Now, what do you think will happen if I press Control-U?

```
leungtc   ttys0   Nov 28 15:11   (gold)
chinese   ttys2   Dec  3 22:53   (excalibur)
cdemmert  ttys5   Dec  3 23:00   (mentor)
yuenca    ttys6   Dec  3 23:00   (mentor)
janitor   ttys7   Dec  3 18:18   (age)
mathisbp  ttys8   Dec  3 23:17   (dov)
janitor   ttys9   Dec  3 18:18   (age)
cs541     ttysC   Dec  2 15:16   (solaria)
yansong   ttysL   Dec  1 14:44   (math)
mdps      ttysO   Nov 30 19:39   (localhost)
md        ttysU   Dec  2 08:45   (muller)
jac       ttysa   Dec  3 18:18   (localhost)
eichsted  ttysb   Dec  3 23:21   (pc1)
sweett    ttysc   Dec  3 22:40   (dov)
wellman   ttysd   Dec  3 23:01   (dov)
tuttleno  ttyse   Dec  3 23:03   (indyvax)
wu        ttysf   Dec  3 23:10   (term01)
daurismj  ttysg   Dec  3 23:10   (dov)
cs414     ttysh   Dec  3 23:12   (xds)
cq        ttysi   Dec  3 23:13   (expert)
cdemmert  ttysk   Dec  3 22:37   (xsun22)
jrlee     ttysn   Dec  3 22:53   (mac1)
fitzgejs  ttyso   Dec  3 23:18   (dov)
```

The command has moved me *up* half a screen. Notice where eichsted and sweett are now. Instead of the text being replaced at once, as when I used Control-F, the text was scrolled downward a line at a time, each new line being added as the program went along. The Control-U command might work either way—one line or an entire screen at a time—for you.

4. Now it's time to try moving around in this file word by word. Find the W key on your keyboard, and press it *once* to see what happens.

```
leungtc  ttys0   Nov 28 15:11    (gold)
chinese  ttys2   Dec  3 22:53    (excalibur)
cdemmert ttys5   Dec  3 23:00    (mentor)
```

Now type w six times more, noting that the cursor stops three times in the field to indicate what time the user logged into the system (15:11 in this listing). Now your cursor should be sitting on the parenthesized field:

```
leungtc  ttys0   Nov 28 15:11    (gold)
chinese  ttys2   Dec  3 22:53    (excalibur)
cdemmert ttys5   Dec  3 23:00    (mentor)
```

5. It's time to move backward. Type b a few times; your cursor moves backward to the beginning of each word.

   What happens if you try to move backward, and you're already on the first word, or if you try to move forward with the w command, and you're already on the last word of the line? Let's find out.

6. Using the various keys you've learned, move back to the beginning of the line beginning with leungtc, which you used in the last exercise:

```
leungtc  ttys0   Nov 28 15:11    (gold)
chinese  ttys2   Dec  3 22:53    (excalibur)
cdemmert ttys5   Dec  3 23:00    (mentor)
```

This time, type W (the uppercase letter *W*), rather than the lowercase w, to move through this line. Can you see the difference? Notice what happens when you hit the time field and the parenthesized words. Instead of typing w seven times to move to the left parenthesis before gold, you can type W only five times.

7. Try moving backward using the B command. Notice that the B command differs from the b command the same way the W command differs from the w command.

Step 3. Summary

Moving about by words, both forward and backward, being able to zip through half screens or full screens at a time, and being able to zero in on specific spots with the h, j, k, and 1 cursor-motion keys give you quite a range of motion. Practice using these commands in various combinations to get your cursor to specific characters in your sample file.

Task 10.4: Inserting Text into the File Using *i, a, o,* and *O*
Step 1. Description

Being able to move around in a file is useful. The real function of an editor, however, is to enable you to easily add and remove—in editor parlance, insert and delete—information. The vi editor has a special *insert mode,* which you must use in order to add to the contents of the file. There are four different ways to shift into insert mode, and you will learn about all of them in this unit.

The first way to switch to insert mode is to enter the letter i, which, mnemonically enough, **i**nserts text into the file. The other commands that accomplish more or less the same thing are a, to append text to the file; o, to open up a line below the current line; and uppercase O, to open up a line above the current line.

Step 2. Action

1. This time you want to start with a clean file, so quit from the big.output editing session and start vi again, this time specifying a nonexistent file called buckaroo:

   ```
   % vi buckaroo
   ```

   ```
   ~
   ~
   ~
   ~
   ~
   ~
   ~
   ~
   ~
   ~
   ~
   ~
   ~
   ~
   ~
   ~
   ~
   ```

```
~
~
~
~
~
~
~
"buckaroo" [New file]
```

Notice that vi reminds you that this file doesn't exist; the bottom of the screen says New file, instead of indicating the number of lines and characters.

2. Now it's time to try using insert mode. Type k once:

```
~
~
~
~
```

The system beeps at you because you haven't moved into insert mode yet, and the k still has its command meaning of moving down a line (and of course, there isn't another line yet).

Press the i key to move into insert mode, then press the k key again:

```
k_
~
~
~
```

There you go! You've added a character to the file.

3. Press the Backspace key, which will move the cursor over the letter *k*:

```
k
~
~
~
```

Now see what happens when you press ESC to leave insert mode and return to the vi command mode:

```
~
~ ~
~ ~
~
```

Notice that the *k* vanished when you pressed ESC. That's because vi only saves text you've entered to the *left of or above* the cursor, not the letter the cursor is resting on.

4. Now move back into insert mode by pressing i, and enter a few sentences from a favorite book of mine:

Comment: Movie buffs will perhaps recognize that the text used in this chapter comes from the book *Buckaroo Banzai*. The film *The Adventures of Buckaroo Banzai Across the Eighth Dimension* is based on this very fun book.

```
"He's not even here," went the conservation.
"Banzai."
"Where is he?"
"At a hotpsial in El paso."
"What? Why werent' we informed? What's wrong with him?"_
~
~
```

I've deliberately left some typing errors in the text here. Fixing them will demonstrate some important features of the vi editor. If you fixed them as you went along, that's okay, and if you added errors of your own, that's okay, too!

Press ESC to leave insert mode. Press ESC a second time to ensure that it worked; remember that vi beeps to remind you that you're already in command mode.

5. Now use the cursor motion keys (h, j, k, and l) to move the cursor to any point on the first line:

```
"He's not even here," went the conservation.
"Banzai."
"Where is he?"
"At the hotpsial in El paso."
"What? Why werent' we informed? What's wrong with him?"
~
~
```

It turns out that I forgot a line of dialog between the line I'm on and the word *Banzai*. One way to enter the line would be to move to the beginning of the line "Banzai.", insert the new text, and press Return before pressing ESC to quit insert mode. But vi has a special command (o) to open a line immediately below the current line for inserting text. Press o on your keyboard and follow along:

```
"He's not even here," went the conservation.
_
"Banzai."
"Where is he?"
"At the hotpsial in El paso."
"What? Why werent' we informed? What's wrong with him?"
~
~
```

Now type the missing text:

```
"He's not even here," went the conservation.
"Who?"_
"Banzai."
"Where is he?"
"At the hotpsial in El paso."
"What? Why werent' we informed? What's wrong with him?"
~
~
```

That's it. Press ESC to return to command mode.

6. The problem with the snippet of dialog we're using is that there's no way to figure out who is talking. Adding a line above this dialog helps identify the speakers. Again, use cursor motion keys to place the cursor on the top line:

```
"He's not _even here," went the conservation.
"Banzai."
"Where is he?"
"At the hotpsial in El paso."
"What? Why werent' we informed? What's wrong with him?"
~
~
```

Now you face a dilemma. You want to open up a line for new text, but you want the line to be *above* the current line, not below it. It happens that vi can do that, too. Instead of using the o command, use its big brother O instead. When I press uppercase O, here's what I see:

```
_
"He's not even here," went the conservation.
"Banzai."
"Where is he?"
"At the hotpsial in El paso."
"What? Why werent' we informed? What's wrong with him?"
~
~
```

Type the new sentence, then press ESC.

```
I found myself stealing a peek at my own watch and overhead
General Catbird's
aide give him the latest._
"He's not even here," went the conservation.
"Banzai."
"Where is he?"
"At the hotpsial in El paso."
"What? Why werent' we informed? What's wrong with him?"
~
~
```

Now the dialog makes a bit more sense. The conversation, reported by the narrator, takes place between the general and his aide.

7. I missed a couple of words in one of the lines, so the next task is to insert them. Use the cursor keys to move the cursor to just after the word *Where*.

```
I found myself stealing a peek at my own watch and overhead
General Catbird's
aide give him the latest.
"He's not even here," went the conservation.
"Banzai."
"Where_is he?"
"At the hotpsial in El paso."
"What? Why werent' we informed? What's wrong with him?"
~
~
```

At this juncture, I need to add the words *the hell* to make the sentence a bit stronger (and correct). I can use i to insert the text, but then I end up with a trailing space. Instead, I can add text immediately *after* the current cursor location by using the a key to *append* the information. When I type a, the cursor moves one character to the right:

```
I found myself stealing a peek at my own watch and overhead
General Catbird's
aide give him the latest.
"He's not even here," went the conservation.
"Banzai."
"Where is he?"
"At the hotpsial in El paso."
"What? Why werent' we informed? What's wrong with him?"
~
~
```

Here's where vi can be difficult to use. I'm in insert mode, but there's no way for me to know that. When I type the letters I want to add, the screen shows that they are appended, but what if I thought I were in insert mode, when actually I was in command mode? One trick I could use to ensure I'm in insert mode is to press the command key a second time. If the letter *a* shows up in the text, I would simply backspace over it; now I would know that I'm in append mode. When I'm done entering the new characters, and I'm still in append mode, here's what my screen looks like:

```
I found myself stealing a peek at my own watch and overhead
General Catbird's
aide give him the latest.
"He's not even here," went the conservation.
"Banzai."
"Where the hell is he?"
```

```
"At the hotpsial in El paso."
"What? Why werent' we informed? What's wrong with him?"
~
~
```

Notice that the cursor always stayed on the *i* in *is* throughout this operation. Press ESC to return to command mode. Notice that the cursor finally hops off the i and moves left one character.

To differentiate between the i and a commands, remember that the *insert* command always adds the new information immediately before the character that the cursor is sitting upon, whereas *append* adds the information immediately to the right of the initial cursor position.

10

8. With this in mind, try to fix the apostrophe problem in the word *werent'* on the last line. Move the cursor to the n in that word:

```
"Where the hell is he?"
"At the hotpsial in El paso."
"What? Why werent' we informed? What's wrong with him?"
~
```

Now, to add the apostrophe immediately after the current character, do you want to use the insert command (i) or the append (a) command? If you said "append," give yourself a pat on the back! Type a to append the apostrophe:

```
"Where the hell is he?"
"At the hotpsial in El paso."
"What? Why werent' we informed? What's wrong with him?"
~
```

Press the ' key once, then press ESC.

9. Quit vi. Use :q, and the program reminds you that you haven't saved your changes to this new file:

```
~
~
No write since last change (:quit! overrides)
```

To write the changes, you need a new command, so I'll give you a preview of a set of colon commands you will learn later in this lesson. Type : (the colon character), which moves the cursor to the bottom of the screen.

```
~
~
:_
```

Now press w to *write out the file*, then press the Return key:

```
~
~
"buckaroo" 8 lines, 271 characters
```

It's okay to leave vi now. I'll use :q to quit and I'm safely back at the command prompt. A quick cat confirms that the tildes were not included in the file itself:

```
%
% cat buckaroo
I found myself stealing a peek at my own watch and overhead
General Catbird's
aide give him the latest.
"He's not even here," went the conservation.
"Banzai."
"Where the hell is he?"
"At the hotpsial in El paso."
"What? Why weren't' we informed? What's wrong with him?"
%
```

Step 3. Summary

As you can tell, the vi editor is quite powerful, and it has a plethora of commands. Just moving about and inserting text, you have learned 24 commands, as summarized in Table 10.1.

Table 10.1. Summary of **vi** motion and insertion commands.

Command	Meaning
0	Move to beginning of line.
$	Move to end of line.
a	Append text—move into insert mode after the current character.
^b	Back up one screen of text.
B	Back up one space-delimited word.
b	Back up one word.
Backspace	Move left one character.
^d	Move down half a page.
ESC	Leave insert mode, return to command mode.
^f	Move forward one screen of text.
h	Move left one character.
i	Insert text—move into insert mode before the current character.
j	Move down one line.
k	Move up one line.
l	Move right one character.
O	Open new line for insert above the current line.
o	Open new line for insert below the current line.
Return	Move to beginning of next line.
^u	Move up half a page.
W	Move forward one space-delimited word.
w	Move forward one word.
:w	Write the edit buffer to the system.
:q	Quit vi and return to the UNIX prompt.
:q!	Quit vi and return to the system, throwing away any changes made to the file.

> **Don't Skip This:** In this table, I've introduced a simple shorthand notation that's worth explaining. UNIX users often use a caret followed by a character instead of the awkward Control-*c* notation. Therefore, ^f has the same meaning as Control-F. Expressing this operation as ^f does not change the way it's performed: you'd still press and hold down the Control key, then press the lowercase F key. It's just a shorter notation.

You've already learned quite a few commands, but you have barely scratched the surface of the powerful *vi* command!

Task 10.5: Deleting Text
Step 1. Description

You now have many of the pieces you need to work efficiently with the *vi* editor, to zip to any point in the file, or to add text wherever you'd like. Now you need to learn how to delete characters, words, and lines.

The simplest form of the delete command is the x command, which functions as though you are writing an *X* over a letter you don't want on a printed page: it deletes the character under the cursor. Press x five times and you delete five characters. Deleting a line of text this way can be quite tedious, so *vi* has some alternate commands. (Are you surprised?) One command that many *vi* users don't know about is the D, or *delete through end of line*, command. Wherever you are on a line, if you type D, you will immediately delete everything after the cursor to the end of that line of text.

If there's an uppercase D command, you can just bet there's a lowercase d command, too. The d *delete* command is the first of a set of more sophisticated *vi* commands, which are followed by a second command that indicates what you'd like to do with the command. You already know that w and W move you forward a word in the file; they're known as *addressing commands* in *vi*. You can follow d with one of these addressing commands to specify what you would like to delete. For example, to delete a line, simply type dd.

Sometimes you might get a bit overzealous and delete more than you anticipated. That's not a problem—well, not too much of a problem—because *vi* remembers the state of the file prior to the most recent action taken. To *undo* a deletion (or insertion, for that matter), use the u command. To *undo a line of changes*, use the U command. Be aware that once you've moved off the line in question, the U command is unable to restore it!

Step 2. Action

1. Start vi again with the big.output file you used earlier:

```
leungtc  ttyrV   Dec  1 18:27   (magenta)
tuyinhwa ttyrX   Dec  3 22:38   (expert)
hollenst ttyrZ   Dec  3 22:14   (dov)
brandt   ttyrb   Nov 28 23:03   (age)
holmes   ttyrj   Dec  3 21:59   (age)
yuxi     ttyrn   Dec  1 14:19   (pc)
frodo    ttyro   Dec  3 22:01   (mentor)
labeck   ttyrt   Dec  3 22:02   (dov)
chenlx2  ttyru   Dec  3 21:53   (mentor)
leungtc  ttys0   Nov 28 15:11   (gold)
chinese  ttys2   Dec  3 22:53   (excalibur)
cdemmert ttys5   Dec  3 23:00   (mentor)
yuenca   ttys6   Dec  3 23:00   (mentor)
janitor  ttys7   Dec  3 18:18   (age)
mathisbp ttys8   Dec  3 23:17   (dov)
janitor  ttys9   Dec  3 18:18   (age)
cs541    ttysC   Dec  2 15:16   (solaria)
yansong  ttysL   Dec  1 14:44   (math)
mdps     ttysO   Nov 30 19:39   (localhost)
md       ttysU   Dec  2 08:45   (muller)
jac      ttysa   Dec  3 18:18   (localhost)
eichsted ttysb   Dec  3 23:21   (pc1)
sweett   ttysc   Dec  3 22:40   (dov)
"big.output" 40 lines, 1659 characters
```

Press the x key a few times to delete a few characters from the beginning of the file:

```
gtc  ttyrV   Dec  1 18:27   (magenta)
tuyinhwa ttyrX   Dec  3 22:38   (expert)
hollenst ttyrZ   Dec  3 22:14   (dov)
brandt   ttyrb   Nov 28 23:03   (age)
holmes   ttyrj   Dec  3 21:59   (age)
```

Now press u to undo the last deletion:

```
ngtc  ttyrV   Dec  1 18:27   (magenta)
tuyinhwa ttyrX   Dec  3 22:38   (expert)
hollenst ttyrZ   Dec  3 22:14   (dov)
brandt   ttyrb   Nov 28 23:03   (age)
holmes   ttyrj   Dec  3 21:59   (age)
```

If you press u again, what do you think will happen?

```
gtc ttyrV   Dec  1 18:27   (magenta)
tuyinhwa ttyrX   Dec  3 22:38   (expert)
hollenst ttyrZ   Dec  3 22:14   (dov)
brandt   ttyrb   Nov 28 23:03   (age)
holmes   ttyrj   Dec  3 21:59   (age)
```

The undo command alternates between the last command having happened or not having happened. To explain it a bit better, the undo command is an action unto itself, so the second time you type u, you're undoing the undo command that you just requested. Press the u key a few more times to convince yourself that this is the case.

2. It's time to make some bigger changes to the file. Type dw twice to delete the current word and the next word in the file. It should look something like this after using the first dw:

```
ttyrV   Dec  1 18:27   (magenta)
tuyinhwa ttyrX   Dec  3 22:38   (expert)
hollenst ttyrZ   Dec  3 22:14   (dov)
brandt   ttyrb   Nov 28 23:03   (age)
holmes   ttyrj   Dec  3 21:59   (age)
```

Then it should look like this after using the second dw:

```
Dec  1 18:27   (magenta)
tuyinhwa ttyrX   Dec  3 22:38   (expert)
hollenst ttyrZ   Dec  3 22:14   (dov)
brandt   ttyrb   Nov 28 23:03   (age)
holmes   ttyrj   Dec  3 21:59   (age)
```

Type u. You see that you can only undo the most recent command. At this point, though, because I haven't moved from the line I'm editing, the uppercase U, or *undo a line of changes*, command will restore the line:

```
leungtc ttyrV   Dec  1 18:27   (magenta)
tuyinhwa ttyrX   Dec  3 22:38   (expert)
hollenst ttyrZ   Dec  3 22:14   (dov)
brandt   ttyrb   Nov 28 23:03   (age)
holmes   ttyrj   Dec  3 21:59   (age)
```

3. Well, in the end, I really don't want to see some of these folks. Fortunately, I can change the contents of this file using the dd command to delete lines. What if I want to delete the entries for chinese and janitor, both of which are visible on this screen?

The first step is to use the cursor keys to move down to any place on the line for the chinese account, about halfway down the screen:

```
chenlx2  ttyru    Dec  3 21:53    (mentor)
leungtc  ttys0    Nov 28 15:11    (gold)
chinese  ttys2    Dec  3 22:53    (excalibur)
cdemmert ttys5    Dec  3 23:00    (mentor)
yuenca   ttys6    Dec  3 23:00    (mentor)
janitor  ttys7    Dec  3 18:18    (age)
mathisbp ttys8    Dec  3 23:17    (dov)
```

If your cursor isn't somewhere in the middle of this line, move it so that you too are not at an edge.

I had planned to remove this line completely, but perhaps I'd rather just remove the date, time, and name of the system (in parentheses) instead. To accomplish this, I don't need to type dw a bunch of times, or even x a lot of times, but rather just D to delete through the end of the line:

```
chenlx2  ttyru    Dec  3 21:53    (mentor)
leungtc  ttys0    Nov 28 15:11    (gold)
chinese  ttys2    _
cdemmert ttys5    Dec  3 23:00    (mentor)
yuenca   ttys6    Dec  3 23:00    (mentor)
janitor  ttys7    Dec  3 18:18    (age)
mathisbp ttys8    Dec  3 23:17    (dov)
```

Oh, that's not quite what I wanted to do. No problem, the undo command can fix it. Simply pressing the u key restores the text I deleted:

```
chenlx2  ttyru    Dec  3 21:53    (mentor)
leungtc  ttys0    Nov 28 15:11    (gold)
chinese  ttys2    Dec  3 22:53    (excalibur)
cdemmert ttys5    Dec  3 23:00    (mentor)
yuenca   ttys6    Dec  3 23:00    (mentor)
janitor  ttys7    Dec  3 18:18    (age)
mathisbp ttys8    Dec  3 23:17    (dov)
```

4. The problem is that I wanted to delete the two entries chinese and janitor from the file, but I used the wrong command. Instead of using the D command, I should use dd. Typing dd once has these results:

```
Dec  1 18:27     (magenta)
tuyinhwa ttyrX    Dec  3 22:38    (expert)
hollenst ttyrZ    Dec  3 22:14    (dov)
brandt   ttyrb    Nov 28 23:03    (age)
holmes   ttyrj    Dec  3 21:59    (age)
yuxi     ttyrn    Dec  1 14:19    (pc)
frodo    ttyro    Dec  3 22:01    (mentor)
labeck   ttyrt    Dec  3 22:02    (dov)
chenlx2  ttyru    Dec  3 21:53    (mentor)
leungtc  ttys0    Nov 28 15:11    (gold)
cdemmert ttys5    Dec  3 23:00    (mentor)
yuenca   ttys6    Dec  3 23:00    (mentor)
janitor  ttys7    Dec  3 18:18    (age)
mathisbp ttys8    Dec  3 23:17    (dov)
janitor  ttys9    Dec  3 18:18    (age)
cs541    ttysC    Dec  2 15:16    (solaria)
yansong  ttysL    Dec  1 14:44    (math)
mdps     ttysO    Nov 30 19:39    (localhost)
md       ttysU    Dec  2 08:45    (muller)
jac      ttysa    Dec  3 18:18    (localhost)
eichsted ttysb    Dec  3 23:21    (pc1)
sweett   ttysc    Dec  3 22:40    (dov)
wellman  ttysd    Dec  3 23:01    (dov)
```

Notice that a new line of information has been pulled onto the screen at the bottom, to replace the blank line that you removed.

If you try using the u command now, what happens?

I'm almost done. A few presses of the Return key and I'm down to the entry for the janitor account. Using dd removes that line too:

```
Dec  1 18:27     (magenta)
tuyinhwa ttyrX    Dec  3 22:38    (expert)
hollenst ttyrZ    Dec  3 22:14    (dov)
brandt   ttyrb    Nov 28 23:03    (age)
holmes   ttyrj    Dec  3 21:59    (age)
yuxi     ttyrn    Dec  1 14:19    (pc)
frodo    ttyro    Dec  3 22:01    (mentor)
labeck   ttyrt    Dec  3 22:02    (dov)
chenlx2  ttyru    Dec  3 21:53    (mentor)
leungtc  ttys0    Nov 28 15:11    (gold)
cdemmert ttys5    Dec  3 23:00    (mentor)
yuenca   ttys6    Dec  3 23:00    (mentor)
mathisbp ttys8    Dec  3 23:17    (dov)
janitor  ttys9    Dec  3 18:18    (age)
```

```
cs541      ttysC    Dec  2 15:16   (solaria)
yansong    ttysL    Dec  1 14:44   (math)
mdps       ttysO    Nov 30 19:39   (localhost)
md         ttysU    Dec  2 08:45   (muller)
jac        ttysa    Dec  3 18:18   (localhost)
eichsted   ttysb    Dec  3 23:21   (pc1)
sweett     ttysc    Dec  3 22:40   (dov)
wellman    ttysd    Dec  3 23:01   (dov)
tuttleno   ttyse    Dec  3 23:03   (indyvax)
```

Each line below the one deleted moves up a line to fill in the blank space, and a new line, for `tuttleno`, moves up from the following screen.

5. Now I want to return to the `buckaroo` file to remedy a few of the horrendous typographic errors! I don't care whether I save the changes I've just made to the file, so I'm going to use `:q!` to quit, discarding these edit changes to the `big.output` file. Entering `vi buckaroo` starts `vi` again:

```
I found myself stealing a peek at my own watch and overhead
General Catbird's
aide give him the latest.
"He's not even here," went the conservation.
"Banzai."
"Where the hell is he?"
"At the hotpsial in El paso."
"What? Why weren't' we informed? What's wrong with him?"
~
~
~
~
~
~
~
~
~
~
~
~
~
~
~
~
~
"buckaroo" 8 lines, 271 characters
```

There are a couple fixes you can make in short order. The first is to change *conservation* to *conversation* on the third line. To move there, press the Return key twice, then use `W` to zip forward until the cursor is at the first letter of the word you're editing:

```
I found myself stealing a peek at my own watch and overhead
General Catbird's
aide give him the latest.
"He's not even here," went the conservation.
"Banzai."
"Where the hell is he?"
```

Then use the dw command:

```
I found myself stealing a peek at my own watch and overhead
General Catbird's
aide give him the latest.
"He's not even here," went the .
"Banzai."
"Where the hell is he?"
```

Now enter insert mode by pressing i, and type in the correct spelling of the word *conversation*, then press ESC:

```
I found myself stealing a peek at my own watch and overhead
General Catbird's
aide give him the latest.
"He's not even here," went the conversation.
"Banzai."
"Where the hell is he?"
```

6. That's one fix. Now move down a couple lines to fix the atrocious mispelling of *hospital*:

```
"Banzai."
"Where the hell is he?"
"At the hotpsial in El paso."
"What? Why weren't' we informed? What's wrong with him?"
~
```

Again, use dw to delete the word, then i to enter insert mode. Type *hospital* and press ESC, and all is well on the line:

```
"Banzai."
"Where the hell is he?"
"At the hospital in El paso."
"What? Why weren't' we informed? What's wrong with him?"
~
```

Well, almost all is well. The first letter of *Paso* needs to be capitalized. Move to it by pressing w to move forward a few words:

```
"Banzai."
"Where the hell is he?"
"At the hospital in El paso."
"What? Why weren't' we informed? What's wrong with him?"
~
```

7. It's time for a secret vi expert command! Instead of typing x to delete the letter, then i to enter insert mode, then P as the correct letter, and ESC to return to command mode, there's a much faster way to *transpose case:* the ~ command. Type the ~ character once, and here's what happens:

```
"Banzai."
"Where the hell is he?"
"At the hospital in El Paso."
"What? Why weren't' we informed? What's wrong with him?"
~
```

Cool, isn't it? Back up to the beginning of the word again, using the h command, and press ~ a few times to see what happens. Notice that each time you type ~, the character's case switches—transposes—and the cursor moves to the next character. Type ~ four times and you should end up with this:

```
"Banzai."
"Where the hell is he?"
"At the hospital in El pASO."
"What? Why weren't' we informed? What's wrong with him?"
~
```

Back up to the beginning of the word, and press ~ four more times, until the word is correct.

8. Move to the last line of the file, to the extra apostrophe in the word *weren't*', and use the x key to delete the offending character. The screen should now look like this:

```
I found myself stealing a peek at my own watch and overhead
General Catbird's
aide give him the latest.
"He's not even here," went the conversation.
"Banzai."
"Where the hell is he?"
"At the hospital in El Paso."
"What? Why weren't we informed? What's wrong with him?"
~
~
~
~
~
~
~
~
~
~
~
~
~
~
```

It's time to save the file for posterity. Use `:wq`, a shortcut that has `vi` write out the changes, then immediately quit the program:

```
~
~
~
"buckaroo" 8 lines, 270 characters
%
```

Step 3. Summary

Not only have you learned about the variety of deletion options in `vi`, but you have also learned a few simple shortcut commands: `~` to transpose case; and `:wq` to write out the changes and quit the program all in one step.

You should feel pleased; you're now a productive and knowledgeable `vi` user, and you can modify files, making easy or tough changes. Go back to your system and experiment further, modifying some of the other files. Be careful, though, not to make changes in any of your dot files (for example, `.cshrc`) lest you cause trouble that would be difficult to fix!

Task 10.6: Searching Within a File
Step 1. Description

With the addition of two more capabilities, you'll be ready to face down any vi expert, demonstrating your skill and knowledge of the editor, and, much more importantly, you will be able to really fly through files, moving immediately to the information you desire.

The two new capabilities are for finding specific words or phrases in a file, and for moving to specific lines in a file. Similar to searching for patterns in more and page, the /*pattern* searches forward in the file for a specified pattern, and ?*pattern* searches backward for the specified pattern. To repeat the previous search, use the n command to tell vi to search again, in the same direction, for the same pattern.

You can easily move to any specific line in a file using the G, or *go to line*, command. If you type a number before you type G, the cursor will move to that line in the file. If you type G without a line number, the cursor will zip you to the very last line of the file (by default).

Step 2. Action

1. Start vi again with the big.output file:

```
leungtc   ttyrV   Dec  1 18:27   (magenta)
tuyinhwa  ttyrX   Dec  3 22:38   (expert)
hollenst  ttyrZ   Dec  3 22:14   (dov)
brandt    ttyrb   Nov 28 23:03   (age)
holmes    ttyrj   Dec  3 21:59   (age)
yuxi      ttyrn   Dec  1 14:19   (pc)
frodo     ttyro   Dec  3 22:01   (mentor)
labeck    ttyrt   Dec  3 22:02   (dov)
chenlx2   ttyru   Dec  3 21:53   (mentor)
leungtc   ttys0   Nov 28 15:11   (gold)
chinese   ttys2   Dec  3 22:53   (excalibur)
cdemmert  ttys5   Dec  3 23:00   (mentor)
yuenca    ttys6   Dec  3 23:00   (mentor)
janitor   ttys7   Dec  3 18:18   (age)
mathisbp  ttys8   Dec  3 23:17   (dov)
janitor   ttys9   Dec  3 18:18   (age)
cs541     ttysC   Dec  2 15:16   (solaria)
yansong   ttysL   Dec  1 14:44   (math)
mdps      ttysO   Nov 30 19:39   (localhost)
md        ttysU   Dec  2 08:45   (muller)
jac       ttysa   Dec  3 18:18   (localhost)
eichsted  ttysb   Dec  3 23:21   (pc1)
sweett    ttysc   Dec  3 22:40   (dov)
"big.output" 40 lines, 1659 characters
```

Remember that I used :q! to quit earlier, so my changes were not retained.

To move to the very last line of the file, I type G once, and see this:

```
cdemmert ttysk   Dec  3 22:37   (xsun)
jrlee    ttysn   Dec  3 22:53   (mac1)
fitzgejs ttyso   Dec  3 23:18   (dov)
doerrhb  ttysp   Dec  3 23:20   (dov)
cdemmert ttysq   Dec  3 23:00   (xsun)
frazierw ttysr   Dec  3 23:01   (dov)
buckeye  ttyss   Dec  3 23:20   (mac2)
mtaylor  ttyst   Dec  3 23:22   (dov)
look     ttysu   Dec  3 23:12   (age)
janitor  ttysw   Dec  3 18:29   (age)
ajones   ttysx   Dec  3 23:23   (rassilon)
~
~
~
~
~
~
~
~
~
~
~
```

To move to the third line of the file, I type 3 followed by G:

```
leungtc  ttyrV   Dec  1 18:27   (magenta)
tuyinhwa ttyrX   Dec  3 22:38   (expert)
hollenst ttyrZ   Dec  3 22:14   (dov)
brandt   ttyrb   Nov 28 23:03   (age)
holmes   ttyrj   Dec  3 21:59   (age)
yuxi     ttyrn   Dec  1 14:19   (pc)
frodo    ttyro   Dec  3 22:01   (mentor)
labeck   ttyrt   Dec  3 22:02   (dov)
chenlx2  ttyru   Dec  3 21:53   (mentor)
leungtc  ttys0   Nov 28 15:11   (gold)
chinese  ttys2   Dec  3 22:53   (excalibur)
cdemmert ttys5   Dec  3 23:00   (mentor)
yuenca   ttys6   Dec  3 23:00   (mentor)
janitor  ttys7   Dec  3 18:18   (age)
mathisbp ttys8   Dec  3 23:17   (dov)
janitor  ttys9   Dec  3 18:18   (age)
cs541    ttysC   Dec  2 15:16   (solaria)
yansong  ttysL   Dec  1 14:44   (math)
mdps     ttysO   Nov 30 19:39   (localhost)
md       ttysU   Dec  2 08:45   (muller)
jac      ttysa   Dec  3 18:18   (localhost)
eichsted ttysb   Dec  3 23:21   (pc1)
sweett   ttysc   Dec  3 22:40   (dov)
```

Notice that the cursor is on the third line of the file.

2. Now it's time to search. From my previous travels in this file, I know that the very last line is for the account ajones, but instead of using G to move there directly, I can *search* for the specified pattern by using the / search command.

Pressing the / immediately moves the cursor to the bottom of the screen:

```
md        ttysU   Dec  2 08:45   (mueller)
jac       ttysa   Dec  3 18:18   (localhost)
eichsted  ttysb   Dec  3 23:21   (pc1)
sweett    ttysc   Dec  3 22:40   (dov)
/_
```

Now I can type in the pattern *ajones*:

```
md        ttysU   Dec  2 08:45   (mueller)
jac       ttysa   Dec  3 18:18   (localhost)
eichsted  ttysb   Dec  3 23:21   (pc1)
sweett    ttysc   Dec  3 22:40   (dov)
/ajones_
```

When I press Return, vi spins through the file and moves me to the first line it finds that contains the specified pattern:

```
cdemmert  ttysk   Dec  3 22:37   (xsun)
jrlee     ttysn   Dec  3 22:53   (mac1)
fitzgejs  ttyso   Dec  3 23:18   (dov)
doerrhb   ttysp   Dec  3 23:20   (dov)
cdemmert  ttysq   Dec  3 23:00   (xsun)
frazierw  ttysr   Dec  3 23:01   (dov)
buckeye   ttyss   Dec  3 23:20   (mac2)
mtaylor   ttyst   Dec  3 23:22   (dov)
look      ttysu   Dec  3 23:12   (age)
janitor   ttysw   Dec  3 18:29   (age)
ajones    ttysx   Dec  3 23:23   (rassilon)
~
~
~
~
~
~
~
~
~
~
~
~
```

3. If I press n to search for this pattern again, a slash appears at the very bottom line to show that vi understood my request. But the cursor stays exactly where it is, which indicates that this is the only occurrence of the pattern in this file.

4. Looking at this file, I noticed that the account janitor has all sorts of sessions running. To search backward for occurrences of their account, I can use the ? command:

```
~
~
?janitor_
```

The first search moves the cursor up one line, which leaves the screen looking almost the same:

```
cdemmert ttysk   Dec  3 22:37   (xsun)
jrlee    ttysn   Dec  3 22:53   (mac1)
fitzgejs ttyso   Dec  3 23:18   (dov)
doerrhb  ttysp   Dec  3 23:20   (dov)
cdemmert ttysq   Dec  3 23:00   (xsun)
frazierw ttysr   Dec  3 23:01   (dov)
buckeye  ttyss   Dec  3 23:20   (mac2)
mtaylor  ttyst   Dec  3 23:22   (dov)
look     ttysu   Dec  3 23:12   (age)
janitor  ttysw   Dec  3 18:29   (age)
ajones   ttysx   Dec  3 23:23   (rassilon)
~
~
~
~
~
~
~
~
~
~
~
?janitor
```

Here's where the n, or *next search*, can come in handy. If I press n this time, and there is another occurrence of the pattern in the file, vi moves me directly to the match:

```
yuxi      ttyrn    Dec  1 14:19    (pc)
frodo     ttyro    Dec  3 22:01    (mentor)
labeck    ttyrt    Dec  3 22:02    (dov)
chenlx2   ttyru    Dec  3 21:53    (mentor)
leungtc   ttys0    Nov 28 15:11    (gold)
chinese   ttys2    Dec  3 22:53    (excalibur)
cdemmert  ttys5    Dec  3 23:00    (mentor)
yuenca    ttys6    Dec  3 23:00    (mentor)
janitor   ttys7    Dec  3 18:18    (age)
mathisbp  ttys8    Dec  3 23:17    (dov)
janitor   ttys9    Dec  3 18:18    (age)
cs541     ttysC    Dec  2 15:16    (solaria)
yansong   ttysL    Dec  1 14:44    (math)
mdps      ttysO    Nov 30 19:39    (localhost)
md        ttysU    Dec  2 08:45    (muller)
jac       ttysa    Dec  3 18:18    (localhost)
eichsted  ttysb    Dec  3 23:21    (pc1)
sweett    ttysc    Dec  3 22:40    (dov)
wellman   ttysd    Dec  3 23:01    (dov)
tuttleno  ttyse    Dec  3 23:03    (indyvax)
wu        ttysf    Dec  3 23:10    (term01)
daurismj  ttysg    Dec  3 23:10    (dov)
cs414     ttysh    Dec  3 23:12    (xds)
```

When you're done, quit vi by using :q.

Step 3. Summary

There are not dozens, but *hundreds* of commands in vi. Rather than overwhelm you with all of them, even in a table, I have opted instead to work with the most basic and important commands. By the time you're done with this lesson, your knowledge of vi commands will be substantial, and you will be able to use the editor with little difficulty. The next lesson will expand your knowledge with more shortcuts and efficiency commands.

This section focused on searching for patterns, which is a common requirement and helpful feature of any editor. In addition, you learned how to move to the top of the file (1G) and to the bottom of the file (G), as well as anywhere in between.

Task 10.7: How to Start *vi* Correctly
Step 1. Description

The vi command wouldn't be part of UNIX if it didn't have some startup options available, but there really are only two worth mentioning. The -R flag sets up vi as a read-only file, to ensure that you don't accidentally modify a file. The second option doesn't start with a dash, but with a plus sign: any command following the plus sign is used as an initial command to the program. This is more useful than it may sound. The command `vi +$ sample`, for example, starts the editor at the *bottom* of the file `sample`, and `vi +17 sample` starts the editor on the seventeenth line of `sample`.

Step 2. Action

1. First, this is the read-only format:

   ```
   % vi -R buckaroo
   ```

   ```
   I found myself stealing a peek at my own watch and overhead
   General Catbird's
   aide give him the latest.
   "He's not even here," went the conversation.
   "Banzai."
   "Where the hell is he?"
   "At the hospital in El Paso."
   "What? Why weren't we informed? What's wrong with him?"
   ~
   ~
   ~
   ~
   ~
   ~
   ~
   ~
   ~
   ~
   ~
   ~
   ~
   "buckaroo" [Read only] 8 lines, 270 characters
   ```

   Notice the addition of the `[Read only]` message on the status line. You can edit the file, but if you try to save the edits with `:w`, you will see this:

   ```
   ~
   ~
   "buckaroo" File is read only
   ```

   Quit `vi` with `:q!`.

2. Next, recall that `janitor` occurs in many places in the `big.output` file. I'll start `vi` on the file line that contains the pattern `janitor` in the file:

   ```
   % vi +/janitor big.output
   ```

```
brandt    ttyrb   Nov 28 23:03   (age)
holmes    ttyrj   Dec  3 21:59   (age)
yuxi      ttyrn   Dec  1 14:19   (pc)
frodo     ttyro   Dec  3 22:01   (mentor)
labeck    ttyrt   Dec  3 22:02   (dov)
chenlx2   ttyru   Dec  3 21:53   (mentor)
leungtc   ttys0   Nov 28 15:11   (gold)
chinese   ttys2   Dec  3 22:53   (excalibur)
cdemmert  ttys5   Dec  3 23:00   (mentor)
yuenca    ttys6   Dec  3 23:00   (mentor)
janitor   ttys7   Dec  3 18:18   (age)
mathisbp  ttys8   Dec  3 23:17   (dov)
janitor   ttys9   Dec  3 18:18   (age)
cs541     ttysC   Dec  2 15:16   (solaria)
yansong   ttysL   Dec  1 14:44   (math)
mdps      ttysO   Nov 30 19:39   (localhost)
md        ttysU   Dec  2 08:45   (muller)
jac       ttysa   Dec  3 18:18   (localhost)
eichsted  ttysb   Dec  3 23:21   (pc1)
sweett    ttysc   Dec  3 22:40   (dov)
wellman   ttysd   Dec  3 23:01   (dov)
tuttleno  ttyse   Dec  3 23:03   (indyvax)
wu        ttysf   Dec  3 23:10   (term01)
"big.output" 40 lines, 1659 characters
```

This time notice where the cursor is sitting.

3. Finally, launch vi with the cursor on the third line of the file buckaroo:

```
% vi +3 buckaroo
```

```
I found myself stealing a peek at my own watch and overhead
General Catbird's
aide give him the latest.
"He's not even here," went the conversation.
"Banzai."
"Where the hell is he?"
"At the hospital in El Paso."
"What? Why weren't we informed? What's wrong with him?"
~
~
~
~
~
~
~
~
~
~
~
```

```
~
~
~
~
"buckaroo" 8 lines, 270 characters
```

Again, notice where the cursor rests.

Step 3. Summary

At times it can be helpful to know these two starting options. In particular, I often use
+/*pattern* to start the editor at a specific pattern, but you can use vi for years without
ever knowing more than just the name of the command itself.

Task 10.8: The Key Colon Commands in *vi*
Step 1. Description

Without too much explanation, you have learned a couple of colon commands,
commands that have a colon as the first character. The colon immediately zooms the
cursor to the bottom of the screen for further input. These commands are actually a
subset of quite a large range of commands, all part of the ex editor that lives inside the
vi visual interface. (That's why vi is known an *interface* to an editor, rather than an
editor itself).

The colon commands that are most helpful are :w, to write the buffer back to the
system; :w *filename*, to write the buffer to the specified file; :q, to quit the editor; :q!,
to quit regardless of whether any changes have occurred; :r *filename*, to read another
file into the editor; :e *filename*, to switch to the specified file; and :n, to move to the
next file in a list of files.

Step 2. Action

1. Start vi again, this time specifying more than one file on the command line;
   vi quickly indicates that you want to edit more than one file:

   ```
   % vi buckaroo big.output
   2 files to edit.
   ```

   Then it clears the screen and shows you the first file:

```
I found myself stealing a peek at my own watch and overhead
General Catbird's
aide give him the latest.
"He's not even here," went the conversation.
```

```
"Banzai."
"Where the hell is he?"
"At the hospital in El Paso."
"What? Why weren't we informed? What's wrong with him?"
~
~
~
~
~
~
~
~
~
~
~
~
~
"buckaroo" 8 lines, 270 characters
```

Using :w results in this:

```
~
~
~
"buckaroo" 8 lines, 270 characters
```

2. Instead, try writing to a different file, using :w newfile:

```
~
~
:w newfile_
```

When you press Return, you see this:

```
~
~
"newfile" [New file] 8 lines, 270 characters
```

3. Now pay attention to where the cursor is in the file. The :r, or *read file*, command always includes the contents of the file *below* the current line. Just before I press Return, then, here's what my screen looks like:

```
I found myself stealing a peek at my own watch and overhead
General Catbird's
aide give him the latest.
"He's not even here," went the conversation.
"Banzai."
"Where the hell is he?"
"At the hospital in El Paso."
"What? Why weren't we informed? What's wrong with him?"
~
~
~
~
~
~
~
~
~
~
~
~
~
:r newfile_
```

Pressing Return yields this:

```
I found myself stealing a peek at my own watch and overhead
General Catbird's
I found myself stealing a peek at my own watch and overhead
General Catbird's
aide give him the latest.
"He's not even here," went the conversation.
"Banzai."
"Where the hell is he?"
"At the hospital in El Paso."
"What? Why weren't we informed? What's wrong with him?"

aide give him the latest.
"He's not even here," went the conversation.
"Banzai."
"Where the hell is he?"
"At the hospital in El Paso."
"What? Why weren't we informed? What's wrong with him?"
~
~
~
~
~
~
```

This can be a helpful way to include files within one another or to build a file that contains lots of other files.

4. Now that I've garbled the file, I want to save it to a new file, `buckaroo.confused`:

```
~
~
:w buckaroo.confused_
```

When I press Return, I see this:

```
~
~
"buckaroo.confused" [New file] 16 lines, 540 characters
```

Comment: Older UNIX systems have a 14-character filename limit. If yours does, you will see `buckaroo.confu` as the saved filename.

5. Now it's time to move to the second file in the list of files given to `vi` at startup. To do this, I use the `:n`, or *next file*, command:

```
~
~
:n_
```

Pressing Return results in the next file being brought into the editor to replace the text removed earlier:

```
leungtc    ttyrV    Dec  1 18:27    (magenta)
tuyinhwa   ttyrX    Dec  3 22:38    (expert)
hollenst   ttyrZ    Dec  3 22:14    (dov)
brandt     ttyrb    Nov 28 23:03    (age)
holmes     ttyrj    Dec  3 21:59    (age)
yuxi       ttyrn    Dec  1 14:19    (pc)
frodo      ttyro    Dec  3 22:01    (mentor)
labeck     ttyrt    Dec  3 22:02    (dov)
chenlx2    ttyru    Dec  3 21:53    (mentor)
leungtc    ttys0    Nov 28 15:11    (gold)
chinese    ttys2    Dec  3 22:53    (excalibur)
```

```
cdemmert ttys5   Dec  3 23:00   (mentor)
yuenca   ttys6   Dec  3 23:00   (mentor)
janitor  ttys7   Dec  3 18:18   (age)
mathisbp ttys8   Dec  3 23:17   (dov)
janitor  ttys9   Dec  3 18:18   (age)
cs541    ttysC   Dec  2 15:16   (solaria)
yansong  ttysL   Dec  1 14:44   (math)
mdps     ttysO   Nov 30 19:39   (localhost)
md       ttysU   Dec  2 08:45   (muller)
jac      ttysa   Dec  3 18:18   (localhost)
eichsted ttysb   Dec  3 23:21   (pc1)
sweett   ttysc   Dec  3 22:40   (dov)
"big.output" 40 lines, 1659 characters
```

6. In the middle of working on this, I suddenly realize that I need to make a slight change to the recently saved `buckaroo.confused` file. That's where the `:e` command comes in handy. Using it, I can switch to any other file:

```
~
~
:e buckaroo.confused_
```

I press Return and see this:

```
I found myself stealing a peek at my own watch and overhead
General Catbird's
I found myself stealing a peek at my own watch and overhead
General Catbird's
aide give him the latest.
"He's not even here," went the conversation.
"Banzai."
"Where the hell is he?"
"At the hospital in El Paso."
"What? Why weren't we informed? What's wrong with him?"

aide give him the latest.
"He's not even here," went the conversation.
"Banzai."
"Where the hell is he?"
"At the hospital in El Paso."
"What? Why weren't we informed? What's wrong with him?"
~
~
~
~
~
~
"buckaroo.confused" 16 lines, 540 characters
```

Step 3. Summary

That's it! You now know a considerable amount about one of the most important, and certainly most used, commands in UNIX. There's more to learn (isn't there always?), but you can now edit your files with aplomb!

Lesson Summary

Table 10.2 summarizes the basic vi commands you learned in this lesson.

Table 10.2. Basic vi commands.

Command	Meaning
0	Move to beginning of line.
$	Move to end of line.
/pattern	Search forward for the next line using a specified pattern.
?pattern	Search backward for the next line using a specified pattern.
a	Append text—move into insert mode after the current character.
^b	Back up one screen of text.
B	Back up one space-delimited word.
b	Back up one word.
Backspace	Move left one character.
^d	Move down half a page.
D	Delete through end of line.
d	Delete (dw = delete word, dd = delete line).
ESC	Leave insert mode, return to command mode.
^f	Move forward one screen of text.
G	Go to the last line of the file.
nG	Go to the *n*th line of the file.

continues

Table 10.2. continued

Command	Meaning
h	Move left one character.
i	Insert text—move into insert mode before the current character.
j	Move down one line.
k	Move up one line.
l	Move right one character.
n	Repeat last search.
O	Open new line for insert above the current line.
o	Open new line for insert below the current line.
Return	Move to beginning of next line.
^u	Move up half a page.
U	Undo—replace current line if changed.
u	Undo the last change made to the file.
W	Move forward one space-delimited word.
w	Move forward one word.
x	Delete a single character.
:e *file*	Edit a specified file without leaving *vi*.
:n	Move to the next file in the file list.
:q	Quit *vi* and return to the UNIX prompt.
:q!	Quit *vi* and return to the system, throwing away any changes made to the file.
:r *file*	Read the contents of a specified file, including it in the current edit buffer.
:w *file*	Write the contents of the buffer to a specified file.
:w	Write the edit buffer to the system.

Workshop

Key Terms

addressing commands	The set of vi commands that allow you to specify what type of object you want to work with. The d commands serve as an example: dw means *delete word*, and db means *delete the previous word*.
colon commands	The vi commands that begin with a colon, usually used for file manipulation.
command mode	The default mode of vi, to which you can return by pressing ESC at any time.
control keys	The term for various combinations of the Control key with another key for commands. You hold down the Control key while you press the other key. Control-U is the same as ^u.
insert mode	The vi mode that lets you enter text directly into a file. The i command starts the insert mode, and ESC exits it.
modal	A modal program has multiple environments, or modes, that offer different capabilities. In a modal program, the Return key, for example, might do different things, depending on which mode you were in.
modeless	A modeless program always interprets a key the same way, regardless of what the user is doing.
transpose case	Switch uppercase letters to lowercase or lowercase to uppercase.

Questions

1. What happens if you try to quit vi using :qw? Before you try it, do you expect it to work?

2. If you're familiar with word processing programs in the Mac or Windows environments, would you describe them as *modal* or *modeless*?

3. The d command is an example of a command that understands motion commands. You know of quite a few. Test them to see if they will all work following d. Make sure you see if you can figure out the command that has the opposite action to the D command.

4. Does using each of the following three commands give the same result?

   ```
   D      d$     dG
   ```

5. Imagine you're in command mode, in the middle of a line that's in the middle of the screen. Describe what would happen if you were to type the following:

   ```
   Badluck     Window     blad$
   ```

6. What would happen if you were to use the following startup flags?

   ```
   vi +0 test     vi +/joe/ names
   vi +hhjjhh     vi +:q testme
   ```

Preview of the Next Chapter

The next lesson will expand your knowledge of the vi editor. It will introduce the techniques of using numeric repeat prefixes for commands, changing characters (rather than deleting and inserting), searching and replacing, key mapping to enable arrow keys, and working with UNIX while in vi.

Advanced *vi* Tricks, Tools, and Techniques

In the last lesson you learned some 50 vi commands, which enable you to easily move about in files, insert text, delete other text, search for specific patterns, and move from file to file without leaving the program. This lesson expands your expertise by showing you some more powerful vi commands. Before this lesson, I strongly recommend you use vi to work with a few files. Make sure you're comfortable with the different modes of the program.

Goals for This Lesson

In this lesson, you learn

- [ ] The change and replace commands
- [ ] Numeric repeat prefixes
- [ ] Numbering lines in the file
- [ ] Search and replace
- [ ] Key mapping with the :map command
- [ ] Moving sentences and paragraphs
- [ ] Using the ! command to access UNIX commands

This may seem like a small list, but there's a lot packed into it. I'll be totally honest: you can do fine in vi without ever reading this chapter. You already know how to insert and delete text, save or quit without saving, and you can search for particular patterns too, even from the command line as you start vi for the first time! On the other hand, vi is like any other complex topic. The more you're willing to study and learn, the more the program will bow to your needs. This means you can accomplish a wider variety of different tasks on a daily basis.

Task 11.1: The Change and Replace Commands
Step 1. Description

In the last lesson, you saw me fix a variety of problems by deleting words then replacing them with new words. There is, in fact, a much smarter way to do this, and that is by using either the change or the replace commands.

Each command has a lowercase and uppercase version, and each is quite different from the other. The r command replaces the character that the cursor is sitting upon with the next character you type, whereas the R command puts you into *replace mode*, so that anything you type overwrites whatever is already on the line. By contrast, c replaces *everything* on the line with whatever you type. (It's a subtle difference, but I demonstrate it, so don't fear.) The c change command is the most powerful of them all. The change command c works just like the d command did, as described in the last chapter. You can use the c command with any address command, and it will allow you to change text through to that address, whether it's a word, line, or even the rest of the document.

Step 2. Action

1. Start vi with the buckaroo.confused file.

```
I found myself stealing a peek at my own watch and overhead
General Catbird's
I found myself stealing a peek at my own watch and overhead
General Catbird's
aide give him the latest.
"He's not even here," went the conversation.
"Banzai."
"Where the hell is he?"
"At the hospital in El Paso."
"What? Why weren't we informed? What's wrong with him?"

aide give him the latest.
"He's not even here," went the conversation.
"Banzai."
"Where the hell is he?"
"At the hospital in El Paso."
"What? Why weren't we informed? What's wrong with him?"


~
~
~
~
~
~
~
"buckaroo.confused" 16 lines, 540 characters
```

Without moving the cursor at all, type R. Nothing happens, or so it seems. Now type the words Excerpt from "Buckaroo Banzai" and watch what happens:

```
Excerpt from "Buckaroo Banzai"at my own watch and overhead
General Catbird's
I found myself stealing a peek at my own watch and overhead
General Catbird's
aide give him the latest.
"He's not even here," went the conversation.
```

Now press ESC and notice that what you see on the screen is *exactly* what's in the file.

2. This isn't, however, quite what I want. I could use either D or d$ to delete through the end of the line, but that's a bit awkward. Instead, I'll use 0 to move back to the beginning of the line. You do so also:

```
Excerpt from "Buckaroo Banzai" at my own watch and overhead
General Catbird's
I found myself stealing a peek at my own watch and overhead
General Catbird's
aide give him the latest.
"He's not even here," went the conversation.
```

This time, type C to change the contents of the line. Before you even type a single character of the new text, notice what the line now looks like:

```
Excerpt from "Buckaroo Banzai" at my own watch and overhead
General Catbird'$
I found myself stealing a peek at my own watch and overhead
General Catbird's
aide give him the latest.
"He's not even here," went the conversation.
```

Here's where a subtle difference comes into play! Where the *s* had been, when you pressed C, the program placed a $ instead to show the range of the text to be changed by the command. Press the Tab key once, and then type
`Excerpt from "Buckaroo Bansai" by Earl MacRauch.`

```
        Excerpt from "Buckaroo Bansai" by Earl MacRauchhead General Catbird'$
I found myself stealing a peek at my own watch and overhead
General Catbird's
aide give him the latest.
"He's not even here," went the conversation.
```

This time, watch what happens when I press ESC:

```
            Excerpt from "Buckaroo Bansai" by Earl MacRauch
I found myself stealing a peek at my own watch and overhead
General Catbird's
aide give him the latest.
"He's not even here," went the conversation.
```

3. I think I made another mistake. The actual title of the book is *Buckaroo Banzai* with a *z*, but I've spelled it with an *s* instead. This is a chance to try the new r command.

   Use cursor control keys to move the cursor to the offending letter. I'll use b to back up words, then h a few times to move into the middle of the word. My screen now looks like this:

```
            Excerpt from "Buckaroo Bansai" by Earl MacRauch
I found myself stealing a peek at my own watch and overhead
General Catbird's
aide give him the latest.
"He's not even here," went the conversation.
```

   Now press r. Again, nothing happens; the cursor doesn't move. Press r again to make sure it worked:

```
            Excerpt from "Buckaroo Banrai" by Earl MacRauch
I found myself stealing a peek at my own watch and overhead
General Catbird's
aide give him the latest.
"He's not even here," went the conversation.
```

   That's no good. It replaced the *s* with an *r*, which definitely isn't correct. Type rz, and you should have the following:

```
            Excerpt from "Buckaroo Banzai" by Earl MacRauch
I found myself stealing a peek at my own watch and overhead
General Catbird's
aide give him the latest.
"He's not even here," went the conversation.
```

4. Okay, those are the easy ones. Now it's time to see what the c command can do for you. In fact, it's incredibly powerful. You can change just about any range of information from the current point in the file in either direction!

To start, move to the middle of the file, where the second copy of the passage is found:

```
        Excerpt from "Buckaroo Banzai" by Earl MacRauch
I found myself stealing a peek at my own watch and overhead
General Catbird's
aide give him the latest.
"He's not even here," went the conversation.
"Banzai."
"Where the hell is he?"
"At the hospital in El Paso."
"What? Why weren't we informed? What's wrong with him?"

aide give him the latest.
"He's not even here," went the conversation.
"Banzai."
"Where the hell is he?"
"At the hospital in El Paso."
"What? Why weren't we informed? What's wrong with him?"


~
~
~
~
~
~
~
"buckaroo.confused" 16 lines, 540 characters
```

I think I'll just change the word *aide* that the cursor is sitting on to *The tall beige wall clock opted to* instead. First press c and note that, like many other commands in vi, nothing happens. Now I press w because I want to change just the first word. The screen should look like this:

```
"At the hospital in El Paso."
"What? Why weren't we informed? What's wrong with him?"

aid$ give him the latest.
"He's not even here," went the conversation.
"Banzai."
```

Again, the program has replaced the last character in the range of the change to a $ so I can eyeball the situation. Now I type The tall beige wall clock opted to. Once I reach the $, the editor stops overwriting characters and starts inserting them instead, so the screen now looks like this:

```
"At the hospital in El Paso."
"What? Why weren't we informed? What's wrong with him?"

The tall beige wall clock opted to_give him the latest.
"He's not even here," went the conversation.
"Banzai."
```

Press ESC and you're done (though you can undo the change with the u or U commands, of course).

5. Tall and beige or not, this section makes no sense now, so change this entire line, using the $ motion command you learned in the previous lesson. First, use 0 to move to the beginning of the line, then type c$:

```
"At the hospital in El Paso."
"What? Why weren't we informed? What's wrong with him?"

The tall beige wall clock opted to give him the latest$
"He's not even here," went the conversation.
"Banzai."
```

This is working. The last character changed to the dollar sign. Press ESC, and the entire line is deleted:

```
"At the hospital in El Paso."
"What? Why weren't we informed? What's wrong with him?"

_
"He's not even here," went the conversation.
"Banzai."
```

6. There are still five lines below the current line. I could delete them and then type in the information I want, but that's primitive. Instead, the c command comes to the rescue. Move down one line, then type c5 and press Return. Watch what happens:

```
"At the hospital in El Paso."
"What? Why weren't we informed? What's wrong with him?"



~
~
~
```

```
~
~
~
~
~
~
~
~
~
6 lines changed
```

In general, you can always change the current and next line by using c
followed by a Return (because the Return key is a motion key too, remember). By prefacing the command with a number, I changed the range from
two lines to five.

Comment: You might be asking, Why *two* lines? The answer is subtle. In
essence, anytime you use the c command, you change the current line
plus any additional lines that might be touched by the command. Pressing Return moves the cursor to the following line; therefore, the current
line (starting at the cursor location) through the following line are
changed. The command should probably just change to the beginning of
the following line, but that's beyond even my control!

Now press Tab four times, then type in the characters (page 8), followed by
the ESC key. The screen should look like this:

```
"Where the hell is he?"
"At the hospital in El Paso."
"What? Why weren't we informed? What's wrong with him?"



                          (page 8)

~
~
~
```

7. What if I change my mind? That's where the u command comes in handy. A
   single press of the key and the original copy is restored:

```
        Excerpt from "Buckaroo Banzai" by Earl MacRauch
I found myself stealing a peek at my own watch and overhead
General Catbird's
aide give him the latest.
"He's not even here," went the conversation.
"Banzai."
"Where the hell is he?"
"At the hospital in El Paso."
"What? Why weren't we informed? What's wrong with him?"


"He's not even here," went the conversation.
"Banzai."
"Where the hell is he?"
"At the hospital in El Paso."
"What? Why weren't we informed? What's wrong with him?"_


~
~
~
~
~
~
~
5 more lines
```

Step 3. Summary

The combination of replace and change commands adds a level of sophistication to an editor you might have suspected could only insert or delete. There's much more to cover in this lesson, so don't stop now!

Task 11.2: Numeric Repeat Prefixes
Step 1. Description

You have now seen two commands that were prefixed by a number to cause a specific action. The G command moves you to the very last line of the file, unless you type in a number first. If you type in a number, the G command moves to the specified line number. Similarly, in the previous section, you saw that typing a number before the Return key causes vi to repeat the key the specified number of times.

Numeric repeat prefixes are actually widely available in vi and is the missing piece of your navigational tool set.

Step 2. Action

1. I'll move back to the top of the buckaroo.confused file. This time, I use 1G to move there, rather than a bunch of k keys or other steps. The top of the screen now looks like this:

```
        Excerpt from "Buckaroo Banzai" by Earl MacRauch
I found myself stealing a peek at my own watch and overhead
General Catbird's
aide give him the latest.
"He's not even here," went the conversation.
```

Now I'll move forward fifteen words. Instead of pressing w fifteen times, I'll enter 15w.

```
        Excerpt from "Buckaroo Banzai" by Earl MacRauch
I found myself stealing a peek at my own watch and overhead
General Catbird's
aide give him the latest.
"He's not even here," went the conversation.
```

2. Now I'll move down seven lines by pressing the 7 key, followed by the Return key. I'll use o to give myself a blank line, then press ESC again:

```
"Where the hell is he?"
"At the hospital in El Paso."
"What? Why weren't we informed? What's wrong with him?"

-

"He's not even here," went the conversation.
"Banzai."
```

I'd like to have *Go Team Banzai!* on the bottom, and I want to repeat it three times. Can you guess how to do it? I simply type 3i to move into insert mode, then type Go Team Banzai! The screen looks like this:

```
"Where the hell is he?"
"At the hospital in El Paso."
"What? Why weren't we informed? What's wrong with him?"

Go Team Banzai! _

"He's not even here," went the conversation.
"Banzai."
```

Pressing ESC has a dramatic result:

```
"Where the hell is he?"
"At the hospital in El Paso."
"What? Why weren't we informed? What's wrong with him?"

Go Team Banzai! Go Team Banzai! Go Team Banzai!

"He's not even here," went the conversation.
"Banzai."
```

3. Now I'd like to get rid of all the lines below the current line. There are many different ways to do this, but I'm going to try to guess how many words are present and use a repeat count prefix to dw to delete that many words. (Actually, it's not critical I know the number of words, because vi will repeat the command only while it makes sense to do so.)

I type 75dw and the screen instantly looks like this:

```
         Excerpt from "Buckaroo Banzai" by Earl MacRauch
I found myself stealing a peek at my own watch and overhead
General Catbird's
aide give him the latest.
"He's not even here," went the conversation.
"Banzai."
"Where the hell is he?"
"At the hospital in El Paso."
"What? Why weren't we informed? What's wrong with him?"

Go Team Banzai! Go Team Banzai! Go Team Banzai!

~
~
~
~
~
~
~
~
~
~
7 lines deleted
```

Try the undo command here to see what happens!

Step 3. Summary

Almost all commands in vi can work with a numeric repeat prefix, even commands that you might not expect to work, such as the i insert command. Remember that a

11

request can be accomplished in many ways. To delete five words, for example, you could use 5dw or d5w. Experiment on your own, and you'll get the idea.

Task 11.3: Numbering Lines in the File
Step 1. Description

It's very helpful to have an editor that works with the entire screen, but sometimes you need only to know what line you're currently on. Further, sometimes it can be very helpful to have all the lines numbered on the screen. With vi, you can do both of these, the former by pressing ^g (remember, that's Control-G) while in command mode and the latter by using a complex colon command, :set number, followed by Return. To turn off the display of line numbers, simply type :set nonumber and press Return.

Step 2. Action

1. Much as I try to leave this file, I'm still looking at buckaroo.confused in vi. The screen looks like this:

```
        Excerpt from "Buckaroo Banzai" by Earl MacRauch
I found myself stealing a peek at my own watch and overhead
General Catbird's
aide give him the latest.
"He's not even here," went the conversation.
"Banzai."
"Where the hell is he?"
"At the hospital in El Paso."
"What? Why weren't we informed? What's wrong with him?"

Go Team Banzai! Go Team Banzai! Go Team Banzai!

~
~
~
~
~
~
~
~
~
~
7 lines deleted
```

Can you see where the cursor is? To find out what line number the cursor is on, press ^g and the information is listed on the status line at the bottom:

```
~
~
~
"buckaroo.confused" [Modified] line 10 of 11, column 1  --90%--
```

There's lots of information here. Included here is the name of the file
(buckaroo.confused), an indication that vi thinks I've changed it since I
started the program ([Modified]), the current line (10), total lines in the file
(11), what column I'm in, and, finally, an estimate of how far into the file
I am.

2. Eleven lines? Count the display again. There are 12 lines. What's going on?
The answer will become clear if I turn on line numbering for the entire file.
To do this, I type :, which zips the cursor to the bottom of the screen, where
I then enter the set number command:

```
~
~
~
:set number_
```

Pressing Return causes the screen to change, thus:

```
     1          Excerpt from "Buckaroo Banzai" by Earl MacRauch
     2  I found myself stealing a peek at my own watch and overhead General
Catbird's
     3  aide give him the latest.
     4  "He's not even here," went the conversation.
     5  "Banzai."
     6  "Where the hell is he?"
     7  "At the hospital in El Paso."
     8  "What? Why weren't we informed? What's wrong with him?"
     9
    10  Go Team Banzai! Go Team Banzai! Go Team Banzai!
    11
~
~
~
~
~
~
~
~
~
~
```

Now you can see how it only figures that there are 11 lines, even though it seems by the screens shown in the book that there are 12 lines.

3. To turn off the line numbering, use the opposite command `:set nonumber`, followed by Return, which restores the screen to how you're used to seeing it.

Step 3. Summary

There are definitely some times when being able to include the number of each line is helpful. One example is if you are using `awk`, and it's complaining about a specific line being in an inappropriate format (usually by saying `syntax error, bailing out!` or something similar).

Task 11.4: Search and Replace
Step 1. Description

Though most of `vi` is easy to learn and use, one command that always causes great trouble for users is the search and replace command. The key to understanding this command is to remember that there's a line editor (`ex`) hidden underneath `vi`. Instead of trying to figure out some arcane `vi` command, it's easiest to just drop to the line editor and use a simple colon command—one identical to the command used in `sed`—to replace an old pattern with a new one. To replace an existing word on the current line with a new word (the simplest case), use `:s/old/new/`. If you want to have all occurrences on the current line matched, you need to add the `g` suffix (just as with `sed`): `:s/old/new/g`.

To change all occurrences of one word or phrase to another across the entire file, the command is identical to the preceding command, except that you must prefix an indication of the range of lines affected. Recall that `$` is the last line in the file, and that ranges are specified (in this case, as in `sed`) by two numbers separated by a comma. It should be no surprise that the command is `:1,$ s/old/new/g`.

Step 2. Action

1. You won't be surprised to find I'm still working with the `buckaroo.confused` file, so your screen should look very similar to this:

```
        Excerpt from "Buckaroo Banzai" by Earl MacRauch
I found myself stealing a peek at my own watch and overhead
General Catbird's
aide give him the latest.
"He's not even here," went the conversation.
"Banzai."

"Where the hell is he?"
"At the hospital in El Paso."
"What? Why weren't we informed? What's wrong with him?"

Go Team Banzai! Go Team Banzai! Go Team Banzai!


~
~
~
~
~
~
~
~
~
~
~
~
~
```

11

The cursor is on the very first line. I'm going to rename Earl. I type `:`, the cursor immediately moves to the bottom, and then I type `s/Earl/Duke/`. Pressing Return produces this:

```
        Excerpt from "Buckaroo Banzai" by Duke MacRauch
I found myself stealing a peek at my own watch and overhead General Catbird's
aide give him the latest.
"He's not even here," went the conversation.
```

As you can see, this maneuver was simple and effective.

2. I've decided that development psychology is my bag. Now, instead of having this Banzai character, I want my fictional character to be called Bandura. I could use the previous command to change the occurrence on the current line, but I really want to change all occurrences within the file.

   This is no problem. I type `:1,$ s/Banzai/Bandura/` and press Return. Here's the result:

```
        Excerpt from "Buckaroo Bandura" by Duke MacRauch
I found myself stealing a peek at my own watch and overhead
General Catbird's
aide give him the latest.
"He's not even here," went the conversation.
"Bandura."
"Where the hell is he?"
"At the hospital in El Paso."
"What? Why weren't we informed? What's wrong with him?"

Go Team Bandura! Go Team Banzai! Go Team Banzai!

~
~
~
~
~
~
~
~
~
~
~
~
```

The result is not quite right. Because I forgot the trailing g, vi changed only the very first occurrence on each line, leaving the "go team" exhortation rather confusing.

To try again, I type :1,$ s/Banzai/Bandura/g, press Return, and the screen changes as desired:

```
        Excerpt from "Buckaroo Bandura" by Duke MacRauch
I found myself stealing a peek at my own watch and overhead
General Catbird's
aide give him the latest.
"He's not even here," went the conversation.
"Bandura."
"Where the hell is he?"
"At the hospital in El Paso."
"What? Why weren't we informed? What's wrong with him?"

Go Team Bandura! Go Team Bandura! Go Team Bandura!

~
~
~
~
~
```

```
~
~
~
~
~
7 substitutions
```

Notice that vi also indicates the total number of substitutions in this case.

3. I'll press u to undo the last change.

Step 3. Summary

Search and replace is one area where a windowing system like that of a Macintosh or PC running Windows comes in handy. A windowing system offers different boxes for the old and new patterns and shows each change and a dialog box asking, "Should I change this one?" Alas, this is UNIX and it's still designed to run on ASCII terminals.

Task 11.5: Key Mapping with the :*map* Command
Step 1. Description

As you have worked through the various examples, you might have tried pressing the arrow keys on your keyboard or perhaps a key labeled Ins or Del to insert or delete characters. Odds are likely that the keys not only didn't work, but instead caused all sorts of weird things to happen!

The good news is that within vi is a facility that enables you to map any key to a specific action. If these key mappings are saved in a file called .exrc in your home directory, the *mappings* will be understood by vi automatically each time you use the program. The format for using the map command is :map *key command-sequence*. (In a nutshell, mapping is a way of associating an action with another action or result. For example, by plugging your computer into the right wall socket, you could map your action of flipping the light switch on the wall with the result of having your computer turn on.)

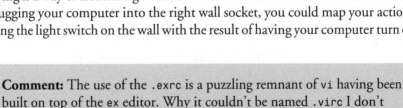

Comment: The use of the .exrc is a puzzling remnant of vi having been built on top of the ex editor. Why it couldn't be named .virc I don't know.

You can also save other things in your .exrc file, including the :set number option if you're a nut about seeing line numbers. More interestingly, vi can be taught abbreviations, so that each time you type the abbreviation, vi expands it. The format for defining abbreviations is :abbreviate *abbreviation expanded-value*. Finally, any line that begins with a double quote is considered a comment and is ignored.

Step 2. Action

1. It's finally time to leave the buckaroo.confused file, and restart vi, this time with the .exrc file in your home directory:

```
% cd
% vi .exrc
```

```
~
~
~
~
~
~
~
~
~
~
~
~
~
~
~
~
~
~
".exrc" [New file]
```

Before I actually add any information to this new file, I'm going to define a few abbreviations to make life a bit easier. To do this, I press :, which, as you know, moves the cursor to the bottom of the screen. Then I'm going to define tyu as a simple abbreviation for the lengthy phrase Teach Yourself UNIX in a Few Minutes:

```
~
~
~
:abbreviate tyu Teach Yourself UNIX in a Few Minutes_
```

Pressing Return moves the cursor back to the top.

2. Now I'll try the abbreviation. Recall that in the .exrc, lines beginning with a double quote are comments and are ignored when vi starts up. I press i to enter insert mode, then type " Sample .exrc file as shown in tyu. The screen looks like this:

```
" Sample .exrc file as shown in tyu_
~
~
```

As soon as I enter a space, punctuation character, or press Return, the abbreviation is expanded. In this case, I opt to move to the next line by pressing Return:

```
" Sample .exrc file as shown in Teach Yourself UNIX in a Few Minutes
_
~
~
```

Press ESC to leave the insert mode.

3. This feature can also be used to correct common typos you make. I know that I have a bad habit of typing *teh* instead of *the*. Because vi is smart about abbreviation expansion, I can "abbreviate" *the* as *teh* and not get into trouble:

```
~
~
:ab teh the_
```

Shortcut: You don't have to type the entire word abbreviation each time. The first two letters, ab, are sufficient for vi to figure out what's going on!

I press Return. Now I can use my typo whenever I want, and the editor will fix it. I can demonstrate this by adding a second comment to this file. Adding a comment is easy because I'm still at the beginning of the second line. When I type i, followed by " (subtly different from the example in teh, I get the following result:

```
" Sample .exrc file as shown in Teach Yourself UNIX in a Few Minutes
" (subtly different from the example in the_
~
~
```

If I enter another character, instead of pressing the spacebar, vi is smart enough *not* to expand the abbreviation. Try it yourself. After pressing the h key again, I'll see this:

```
" Sample .exrc file as shown in Teach Yourself UNIX in a Few Minutes
" (subtly different from the example in tehh_
~
~
```

Because I'm still in insert mode, however, I can backspace and replace the spare h with a space, which instantly fixes the spelling. Finally, I type book) and press ESC to return to command mode.

4. I have one more nifty abbreviation trick before moving to the map command. Type :ab by itself and press Return, and vi shows you a list of the abbreviations currently in effect:

```
~
~
:ab
tyu      tyu      Teach Yourself UNIX in a Few Minutes
teh      teh      the
[Hit any key to continue]  _
```

Okay, now you can move on to key mapping.

5. Key mapping is as easy as defining abbreviations, except you must remember one thing: any control character entered *must* be prefaced with a ^v so that vi doesn't interpret it immediately. The ESC key is included in this list, too.

To map the Clear key on my keyboard to the D function, which, as you recall, deletes text through the end of the current line, I type :map, followed by a single space:

```
~
~
:map
```

Comment: Your keyboard might not have a Clear key. If not, please read through the example anyway.

Don't Skip This: If you use many different terminals, you may have to remap the Clear (Clr) key.

Now I need to type the ^v; otherwise, when I press the Clear key, it will send an *escape sequence* that will confuse vi to no end. I press ^v and see this:

```
~
~
:map ^
```

The cursor is on the caret, which indicates the next character typed should be a control character. Instead of typing any specific character, however, I simply press the Clear key. The result is that it sends the escape sequence, and vi captures it without a problem:

```
~
~
:map ^[OP_
```

Now I type another space, because the *key* part of the key mapping has been defined, then type the command to which vi should map the Clear key:

```
~
~
:map ^[OP D_
```

Finally, I press Return, and it's done! To test the key mapping, I'll move back to the very first line, to the phrase Few Minutes:

```
" Sample .exrc file as shown in Teach Yourself UNIX in a Few Minutes
"  (subtly different from the example in the book)
~
~
```

To clear this line, I need only press Clear and it works.

6. To save this as a permanent key mapping in this .exrc file, I duplicate each keystroke, but this time while in insert mode, instead of at the bottom of the screen. The result is a file that now looks like this:

```
" Sample .exrc file as shown in Teach Yourself UNIX in a
"  (subtly different from the example in the book)
:map ^[OP D_
~
~
```

7. Mapping the arrow keys is done the same way, and in fact, just like typing :ab and then Return shows all abbreviations. Typing :map and then Return demonstrates that I already have my arrow keys mapped to the vi motion keys:

```
~
~
:map
up       ^[[A    k
down     ^[[B    j
left     ^[[D    h
right    ^[[C    l
^[OP     ^[OP    D
[Hit any key to continue] _
```

You can see that sometimes the system can be smart about defining specific keys by name rather than by value, but the end result is the same. I can now use the arrow keys and Clear key, and vi knows what they mean.

8. I will present a final demonstration of what you can do with keyboard mapping. Sometimes when I'm working, I find there's a simple, tedious activity I must do over and over. An example might be surrounding a specific word with quotes to meet a style guideline. This sounds more painful than it need be, because a simple key mapping can automate the entire process of quoting the current word.

I know that ^a isn't used by vi, so I can map that to the new quote-a-single-word command, making sure that I use ^v before each control character or ESC. I type the characters :map ^v^a i", and I see this:

```
~
~
:map ^A i"_
```

Now I again press ^v, then the ESC key. To insert a double quote, I need to have vi go into insert mode (the i), type the quote, then receive an ESC to leave insert mode. The e command moves to the end of the current word, so I then type that, followed by the commands needed to append the second double quote. The final map now looks like:

```
~
~
:map ^A i"^[ea"^[_
```

Press Return and it's done. Now move to the beginning of a word and try the new key mapping for ^a.

Step 3. Summary

There are a variety of customizations you can use with the vi editor, including teaching it about special keys on your keyboard, defining task-specific keys to save time. You can use it to abbreviate commonly used words or phrases to save time or avoid typographical errors. Be cautious when working with the .exrc file, however, because if you enter information that isn't valid, it can be a bit confusing to fix it. Always try the command directly before using it in a special key mapping, and you should stay out of trouble.

Task 11.6: Moving Sentences and Paragraphs
Step 1. Description

You have learned quite a variety of different commands for moving about in files, but there are two more vi movement commands for you to try before you learn about shell escapes in the next unit. So far, movement has been based on screen motion, but vi hasn't particularly known much about the information in the file itself: press k, and you move up a line, regardless of what kind of file you're viewing.

The vi editor is smarter than that, however. It has a couple of movement commands that are defined by the text you are currently editing. Each of these is simply a punctuation character on your keyboard, but each is quite helpful. The first is), which moves the cursor forward to the beginning of the next sentence in the file. Use the opposite, (, and you can move to the beginning of the current sentence in the file. Also worth experimenting with is }, which moves forward a *paragraph* in the file, or { to move backwards a paragraph.

Step 2. Action

1. To try this out, create a new file that has several sentences in a paragraph and a couple of paragraphs. Start vi and type the following text:

```
% cat dickens.note
                           A Tale of Two Cities
                               Preface

When I was acting, with my children and friends, in Mr Wilkie Collins's
drama of The Frozen Deep, I first conceived the main idea of this
story.  A strong desire was upon me then, to
embody it in my own person;
and I traced out in my fancy, the state of mind of which it would
necessitate the presentation
to an observant spectator, with particular
care and interest.

As the idea became familiar to me, it gradually shaped itself into its
present form.  Throughout its execution, it has had complete possession
of me; I have so far verified what
is done and suffered in these pages,
as that I have certainly done and suffered it all myself.

Whenever any reference (however slight) is made here to the condition
of the French people before or during the Revolution, it is truly made,
on the faith of the most trustworthy
witnesses.  It has been one of my hopes to add
something to the popular and picturesque means of
understanding that terrible time, though no one can hope
to add anything to the philosophy of Mr Carlyle's wonderful book.

Tavistock House
November 1859
```

When I start vi on this file, here's what my initial screen looks like:

```
                    A Tale of Two Cities
                         Preface

When I was acting, with my children and friends, in Mr Wilkie Collins's
drama of The Frozen Deep, I first conceived the main idea of this
story.  A strong desire was upon me then, to
embody it in my own person;
and I traced out in my fancy, the state of mind of which it would
necessitate the presentation
to an observant spectator, with particular
care and interest.

As the idea became familiar to me, it gradually shaped itself into its
present form.  Throughout its execution, it has had complete possession
of me; I have so far verified what
is done and suffered in these pages,
as that I have certainly done and suffered it all myself.

Whenever any reference (however slight) is made here to the condition
of the French people before or during the Revolution, it is truly made,
on the faith of the most trustworthy
witnesses.  It has been one of my hopes to add
something to the popular and picturesque means of
"dickens.note" 28 lines, 1122 characters
```

Now I'll move to the beginning of the first paragraph of text by typing
/When, followed by Return. Now the screen looks like this:

11

```
                    A Tale of Two Cities
                         Preface

When I was acting, with my children and friends, in Mr Wilkie Collins's
drama of The Frozen Deep, I first conceived the main idea of this
story.  A strong desire was upon me then, to
embody it in my own person;
```

2. Type) once. The cursor moves to the beginning of the next sentence:

```
When I was acting, with my children and friends, in Mr Wilkie Collins's
drama of The Frozen Deep, I first conceived the main idea of this
story.  A strong desire was upon me then, to
embody it in my own person;
and I traced out in my fancy, the state of mind of which it would
necessitate the presentation
```

Try the (to move back a sentence. I end up back on the W of When starting the sentence. Repeatedly typing the (and the) should let you fly back and forth through the file, sentence by sentence. Notice what occurs when you're at the top few lines of the title.

> **Don't Skip This:** A little experimentation will demonstrate that vi defines a sentence as anything that occurs either at the beginning of a block of text (for example, When I was...) or any word that follows a punctuation character followed by *two* spaces. This is a bit unfortunate, because modern typographic conventions have moved away from using two spaces after the end of a sentence. If you only use one space between sentences—as I have for this book—then moving by sentence is less helpful.

3. I can move back to the opening word of the first paragraph by pressing n to repeat the last search pattern. The screen now looks like this:

```
                        A Tale of Two Cities
                              Preface

When I was acting, with my children and friends, in Mr Wilkie Collins's
drama of The Frozen Deep, I first conceived the main idea of this
story.  A strong desire was upon me then, to
embody it in my own person;
and I traced out in my fancy, the state of mind of which it would
necessitate the presentation
to an observant spectator, with particular
care and interest.

As the idea became familiar to me, it gradually shaped itself into its
present form.  Throughout its execution, it has had complete possession
of me; I have so far verified what
is done and suffered in these pages,
as that I have certainly done and suffered it all myself.

of me; I have so far verified what
is done and suffered in these pages,
as that I have certainly done and suffered it all myself.
```

```
Whenever any reference (however slight) is made here to the condition
of the French people before or during the Revolution, it is truly made,
on the faith of the most trustworthy
witnesses.  It has been one of my hopes to add
something to the popular and picturesque means of
"dickens.note" 28 lines, 1122 characters
```

To move to the next paragraph, type } once:

```
                    A Tale of Two Cities
                         Preface

When I was acting, with my children and friends, in Mr Wilkie Collins's
drama of The Frozen Deep, I first conceived the main idea of this
story.  A strong desire was upon me then, to
embody it in my own person;
and I traced out in my fancy, the state of mind of which it would
necessitate the presentation
to an observant spectator, with particular
care and interest.

As the idea became familiar to me, it gradually shaped itself into its
present form.  Throughout its execution, it has had complete possession
of me; I have so far verified what
is done and suffered in these pages,
as that I have certainly done and suffered it all myself.

Whenever any reference (however slight) is made here to the condition
of the French people before or during the Revolution, it is truly made,
on the faith of the most trustworthy
witnesses.  It has been one of my hopes to add
something to the popular and picturesque means of
"dickens.note" 28 lines, 1122 characters
```

Press the { key, and you move right back to the beginning of the previous paragraph. In fact, you can easily fly back and forth in the file using sequences of the } character (or a numeric repeat prefix to get there faster).

Step 3. Summary

These two motion commands to move by sentence and to move by paragraph are helpful when working with stories, articles, or letters. Any time you're working with words rather than commands (as in the .exrc file), these commands are worth remembering.

By the way, try d) to delete a sentence, or c} to change an entire paragraph. Remember you can always undo the changes with u if you haven't done anything else between the two events.

Task 11.7: Access UNIX with *!*
Step 1. Description

This final section on vi introduces you to some of the most powerful, and least known, commands in the editor: the ! escape-to-UNIX command. When prefaced with a colon (:!, for example), it enables you to run UNIX commands without leaving the editor. More powerfully, the ! command in vi itself, just like d and c, accepts address specifications and feeds that portion of text to the command, and replaces that portion with the results of having run that command on the text.

Let's have a look.

Step 2. Action

1. You should still be in the dickens.intro file. I'll start by double-checking what files I have in my home directory. To do this, I type :!, which moves the cursor to the bottom line:

```
of the French people before or during the Revolution, it is truly made,
on the faith of the most trustworthy
witnesses.  It has been one of my hopes to add
something to the popular and picturesque means of
:!_
```

I simply type ls -CF and press Return, as if I were at the % prompt in the command line:

```
of the French people before or during the Revolution, it is truly made,
on the faith of the most trustworthy
witnesses.  It has been one of my hopes to add
something to the popular and picturesque means of
:!ls -CF
Archives/          big.output        dickens.note      src/
InfoWorld/         bigfiles          keylime.pie       temp/
Mail/              bin/              newfile           tetme
News/              buckaroo          owl.c
OWL/               buckaroo.confused sample
awkscript          demo              sample2
[Hit any key to continue] _
```

Press Return and I'm back in the editor, and I have quickly checked what files I have in my home directory.

2. Now for some real fun, move back to the beginning of the first paragraph and add the text `Chuck, here are my current files:`. Press Return *twice* before using the ESC key to return to command mode. My screen now looks like this:

```
                        A Tale of Two Cities
                             Preface

Chuck, here are my current files:
-

When I was acting, with my children and friends, in Mr Wilkie Collins's
drama of The Frozen Deep, I first conceived the main idea of this
story.  A strong desire was upon me then, to
```

Notice that the cursor was moved up a line. I'm now on a blank line, and the line following is also blank.

To feed the current line to the UNIX system and replace it with the output of the command, `vi` offers an easy shortcut: `!!`. As soon as I type the second `!` (or, more precisely, once `vi` figures out the desired range specified for this command), the cursor moves to the bottom of the screen and prompts with a single `!` character:

11

```
of the French people before or during the Revolution, it is truly made,
on the faith of the most trustworthy
witnesses. It has been one of my hopes to add
something to the popular and picturesque means of
!_
```

To list all the files in my directory, I can again type `ls -CF` and press Return. After a second, `vi` adds the output of that command to the file:

```
                        A Tale of Two Cities
                             Preface

Chuck, here are my current files:
Archives/              bigfiles             newfile
InfoWorld/             bin/                 owl.c
Mail/                  buckaroo             sample
News/                  buckaroo.confused    sample2
```

Advanced *vi* Tricks, Tools, and Techniques

```
OWL/                    demo                    src/
awkscript               dickens.note            temp/
big.output              keylime.pie             tetme

When I was acting, with my children and friends, in Mr Wilkie Collins's
drama of The Frozen Deep, I first conceived the main idea of this
story.  A strong desire was upon me then, to
embody it in my own person;
and I traced out in my fancy, the state of mind of which it would
necessitate the presentation
to an observant spectator, with particular
care and interest.

As the idea became familiar to me, it gradually shaped itself into its
present form.  Throughout its execution, it has had complete possession
6 more lines
```

Notice that this time that the status on the bottom indicates how many lines were added to the file.

Press u to undo this change. Notice that the vi status indicator on the bottom line says there are now six fewer lines.

3. Move back to the *W* in *When.* You are now ready to learn one of the commands that I like most in vi. This command gives you the ability to hand a paragraph of text to an arbitrary UNIX command.

   This time, I'm going to use a sed command that was first shown a few lessons ago: sed 's/^/> /', which prefaces each line with >. Ready? This is where the } command comes in handy, too. To accomplish this trick, I type !}, moving the cursor to the bottom of the screen, then type the sed command as you saw earlier: sed 's/^/> /'. Pressing Return feeds the lines to sed. The sed command makes the change indicated and replaces those lines with the output of the sed command. *Voilà!* The screen now looks like this:

```
                       A Tale of Two Cities
                            Preface

Chuck, here are my current files:


> When I was acting, with my children and friends, in Mr Wilkie Collins's
> drama of The Frozen Deep, I first conceived the main idea of this
> story.  A strong desire was upon me then, to
> embody it in my own person;
> and I traced out in my fancy, the state of mind of which it would
```

```
> necessitate the presentation
> to an observant spectator, with particular
> care and interest.

As the idea became familiar to me, it gradually shaped itself into its
present form.  Throughout its execution, it has had complete possession
of me; I have so far verified what
is done and suffered in these pages,
as that I have certainly done and suffered it all myself.

Whenever any reference (however slight) is made here to the condition
of the French people before or during the Revolution, it is truly made,
!sed 's/^/> /'
```

4. I hope you're excited to see this command in action! It's a powerful way to interact with UNIX while within vi.

I'll provide a few more examples of ways to interact with UNIX while within vi. First, I don't really want the prefix to each line, so I'm going to choose u to undo the change.

Instead, I would rather have the system actually tighten up the lines, ensuring that a reasonable number of words occur on each line, without any lines being too long. On the majority of systems, there is a command called either fmt or adjust to accomplish this. To figure out which works on your system, simply use the :! command, and feed a word or two to the fmt command to see what happens:

11

```
Whenever any reference (however slight) is made here to the condition
of the French people before or during the Revolution, it is truly made,
:!echo hi ¦ fmt
[No write since last change]
hi
[Hit any key to continue] _
```

In this case, fmt did what I hoped, so I am sure that the command exists on my system. If the response was command unknown, then adjust is a likely synonym. If neither exists, complain to your vendor!

Armed with this new command, you can try another variant of !}, this time by feeding the entire paragraph to the fmt command. I'm still at the beginning of the word *When* in the text. So when I type the command !}fmt, the paragraph is cleaned up, and the screen changes to this:

```
                        A Tale of Two Cities
                             Preface

Chuck, here are my current files:


When I was acting, with my children and friends, in Mr Wilkie Collins's
drama of The Frozen Deep, I first conceived the main idea of this
story.  A strong desire was upon me then, to embody it in my own
person; and I traced out in my fancy, the state of mind of which it
would necessitate the presentation to an observant spectator, with
particular care and interest.

As the idea became familiar to me, it gradually shaped itself into its
present form.  Throughout its execution, it has had complete possession
of me; I have so far verified what
is done and suffered in these pages,
as that I have certainly done and suffered it all myself.

Whenever any reference (however slight) is made here to the condition
of the French people before or during the Revolution, it is truly made,
on the faith of the most trustworthy
witnesses.  It has been one of my hopes to add
2 fewer lines
```

Again, vi tells us that the number of lines in the file have changed as a result of the command. In this situation, tightening up the paragraph actually reduced it by two display lines, too.

This command is so helpful that I often have it bound to a specific key with the keymap command. A typical way to do this in an .exrc might be this:

```
:map ^P !}fmt^M
```

The ^M is what vi uses to record a Return. (Remember that you need to use the ^v beforehand.) With this defined in my .exrc, I can press ^p to format the current paragraph.

5. I will provide one more example of the ! command before I wrap up this lesson. Remember the awk command? Remember how it can easily be used to extract specific fields of information? This can be tremendously helpful in vi. Rather than continue working with the dickens.intro file, however, I'll quit vi and create a new file containing some output from the ls command:

```
% ls -CF
Archives/        big.output       dickens.note     src/
InfoWorld/       bigfiles         keylime.pie      temp/
Mail/            bin/             newfile          tetme
```

```
News/              buckaroo          owl.c
OWL/               buckaroo.confused sample
awkscript          demo              sample2
% ls -l a* b* > listing
```

Now I can use vi listing to start the file with the output of the ls command:

```
-rw-rw----  1 taylor      126 Dec  3 16:34 awkscript
-rw-rw----  1 taylor     1659 Dec  3 23:26 big.output
-rw-rw----  1 taylor      165 Dec  3 16:42 bigfiles
-rw-rw----  1 taylor      270 Dec  4 15:09 buckaroo
-rw-rw----  1 taylor      458 Dec  4 23:22 buckaroo.confused
~
~
~
~
~
~
~
~
~
~
~
~
~
~
~
~
~
~
~
"listing" 5 lines, 282 characters
```

It would be nice to use this as the basis for creating a *shell script* (which is just a series of commands that you might type to the shell directly, all kept neatly in a single file). A shell script can show me both the first and last few lines of each file, with the middle chopped out.

The commands I'd like to have occur for each file entry are these:

```
echo ==== filename ====
head -5 filename; echo ...size bytes...; tail -5 filename
```

I'll do this with a combination of the ! command in vi and the awk program with the awk command:

```
awk '{ print "echo ==== "$8" ===="; print "head "$8"; echo
..."$4" bytes...; tail "$8}'
```

With the cursor on the very top line of this file, I can now type !G to pipe
the entire file through the command. The cursor drops to the bottom of the
screen, and I type in the awk script shown previously and press Return. The
result is this:

```
echo ==== awkscript ====
head -5 awkscript; echo ...126 bytes...; tail -5 awkscript
echo ==== big.output ====
head -5 big.output; echo ...1659 bytes...; tail -5 big.output
echo ==== bigfiles ====
head -5 bigfiles; echo ...165 bytes...; tail -5 bigfiles
echo ==== buckaroo ====
head -5 buckaroo; echo ...270 bytes...; tail -5 buckaroo
echo ==== buckaroo.confused ====
head -5 buckaroo.confused; echo ...458 bytes...; tail -5 buckaroo.confused~
~
~
~
~
~
~
~
~
~
!awk '{ print "echo ==== "$8" ===="; print "head "$8"; echo
...$4" bytes...; tail "$8}'
```

If I now quit vi and ask sh to interpret the contents, here's what happens:

```
% chmod +x listing
% sh listing
==== awkscript ====
{
        count[length($1)]++
}
END {
        for (i=1; i < 9; i++)
...126 bytes...
}
END {
        for (i=1; i < 9; i++)
           print "There are " count_i " accounts with " i " letter names."
}
```

```
==== big.output ====
leungtc  ttyrV   Dec  1 18:27   (magenta)
tuyinhwa ttyrX   Dec  3 22:38   (expert)
hollenst ttyrZ   Dec  3 22:14   (dov)
brandt   ttyrb   Nov 28 23:03   (age)
holmes   ttyrj   Dec  3 21:59   (age)
...1659 bytes...
buckeye  ttyss   Dec  3 23:20   (mac2)
mtaylor  ttyst   Dec  3 23:22   (dov)
look     ttysu   Dec  3 23:12   (age)
janitor  ttysw   Dec  3 18:29   (age)
ajones   ttysx   Dec  3 23:23   (rassilon)
==== bigfiles ====
12556   keylime.pie
8729    owl.c
1024    Mail/
582     tetme
512     temp/
...165 bytes...
512     Archives/
207     sample2
199     sample
126     awkscript

==== buckaroo ====
I found myself stealing a peek at my own watch and overhead
General Catbird's
aide give him the latest.
"He's not even here," went the conversation.
"Banzai."
"Where the hell is he?"
...270 bytes...
"Banzai."
"Where the hell is he?"
"At the hospital in El Paso."
"What? Why weren't we informed? What's wrong with him?"

==== buckaroo.confused ====
        Excerpt from "Buckaroo Bandura" by Duke MacRauch
I found myself stealing a peek at my own watch and overhead
General Catbird's
aide give him the latest.
"He's not even here," went the conversation.
"Bandura."
...458 bytes...
"At the hospital in El Paso."
"What? Why weren't we informed? What's wrong with him?"

Go Team Bandura! Go Team Bandura! Go Team Bandura!

%
```

11

Step 3. Summary

Clearly the ! command opens up vi to work with the rest of the UNIX system. There's almost nothing that you can't somehow manage to do within the editor, whether it's add or remove prefixes, clean up text, or even show what happens when you try to run a command or reformat a passage within the current file. Remember, you can also run spell without leaving vi, too. Be careful though, because spell will *replace* the entire contents of your file with the list of words it doesn't know. Fortunately, u can solve that problem.

A summary of the commands you have learned in this lesson is shown in Table 11.1.

Table 11.1. Advanced vi commands.

Command	Function
! !	Replace current line with output of UNIX command.
! }	Replace current paragraph with the results of piping it through the specified UNIX program or programs.
(	Move backward one sentence.
)	Move forward one sentence.
C	Change text through the end of line.
c	Change text in the specified range—cw changes the following word, whereas c} changes the next paragraph.
e	Move to the end of the current word.
^g	Show current line number and other information about the file.
R	Replace text until ESC.
r	Replace the current character with the next pressed.
^v	Prevent vi from interpreting the next character.
{	Move backward one paragraph.
}	Move forward one paragraph.

Command	Function
`:!`	Invoke specified UNIX command.
`:ab a bcd`	Define abbreviation *a* for phrase *bcd*.
`:ab`	Show current abbreviations, if any.
`:map a bcd`	Map key *a* to the `vi` commands *bcd*.
`:map`	Show current key mappings, if any.
`:s/old/new/`	Substitute *new* for *old* on the current line.
`:s/old/new/g`	Substitute *new* for all occurrences of *old* on the current line.
`:1,$s/old/new/g`	Substitute *new* for all occurrences of *old*. :set nonumber turn off line numbering.
`:set number`	Turn on line numbering.

Lesson Summary

Clearly, `vi` is a very complex and sophisticated tool, enabling you not only to modify your text files, but also to customize the editor for your keyboard. Just as important, you can access all the power of UNIX while within `vi`.

Workshop
Key Terms

replace mode   A mode of `vi` in which any characters typed replace those already in the file.

key mapping   A way of teaching `vi` what to do if you press a key that otherwise is unknown to the editor.

escape sequence   A sequence of characters where ESC is the first character. A typical result of pressing a special or function key on most keyboards.

shell script   A collection of shell commands in a file.

Questions

1. What does the following command do?

   ```
   :1,5 s/kitten/puppy
   ```

2. What do these commands do?

   ```
   15i?ESCh        i15?ESCh        i?ESC15h
   ```

3. Try ^g on the first and last lines of a file. Explain why the percentile indicator might not be what you expected.

4. What's the difference between:

   ```
   rrRrESC        cwrESC        CrESC
   ```

5. What key mappings do you have in your version of vi? Do you have labeled keys on your keyboard that could be helpful in vi but aren't defined? If so, define them in your .exrc file using the :map command.

6. Try the following command, but before you do, what do you think it will do?

   ```
   !}ls
   ```

Preview of the Next Chapter

With this chapter and the last, you now know more about vi than the vast majority of people using UNIX today. There's a second popular editor, however, one that is *modeless* and offers its own interesting possibilities for working with files and the UNIX system. It's called EMACS, and if you have it on your system, it's definitely worth a look. In the next lesson, you learn about this editor and some of the basics of using it.

An Overview of the EMACS Editor

The only screen-oriented editor that's guaranteed to be included with the UNIX system is vi, but that doesn't mean that it's the only good editor available in UNIX! An alternative editor that has become quite popular in the last decade (remember that UNIX is almost 25 years old) is called EMACS. This lesson teaches you the fundamentals of this very different and quite powerful editing environment.

Goals for This Lesson

In this lesson, you learn

☐ How to launch EMACS and insert text

☐ How to move around in a file

☐ How to delete characters and words

☐ Search and replace in EMACS

☐ Using the EMACS tutorial and help system

☐ Working with other files

Remember what I said in the last lesson, when I introduced the EMACS editor: EMACS is modeless, so be prepared for an editor that is quite unlike vi, and because it's modeless, there's no insert or command mode. The result is that you have ample opportunity to use the Control key.

Comment: Over the years, I have tried to become an EMACS enthusiast, once even forcing myself to use it for an entire month. I had crib sheets of commands taped up all over my office. At the end of the month, I had attained an editing speed that was about half of my speed in vi, an editor that I've used thousands of times in the past 14 years I've worked in UNIX. I think EMACS has a lot going for it, and generally I think that modeless software is better than modal software. The main obstacle I see for EMACS, however, is that it's begging for pull-down menus like a Mac or Windows program. Using Control, Meta, Shift-Meta, and other weird key combinations just isn't as easy to use for me. On the other hand, your approach to editing may be different, and you may not have years of vi experience affecting your choice of editing environments. I encourage you to give EMACS a fair shake by working through all the examples I have included. You may find it matches your working style better than vi.

Task 12.1: Launching EMACS and Inserting Text

Step 1. Description

Starting EMACS is as simple as starting any other UNIX program. Simply type the name of the program emacs, followed by any file or files you'd like to work with. The puzzle with EMACS is figuring out what it's actually called on your system, if you have it. There are a couple of ways to try to identify EMACS; I'll demonstrate these in the action section that follows.

Once in EMACS, it's important to take a look at your computer keyboard. EMACS requires you to use not just the Control key, but another key known as the *Meta key*, a sort of alternative Control key. If you have a key labeled Meta or Alt on your keyboard, that's the one. If, like me, you don't, then simply press ESC every time that a Meta key is indicated.

Because there are both Control and Meta keys in EMACS, the notation for indicating commands is slightly different. Throughout this book, a control key sequence has been shown either as Control-F or ^f. EMACS people write this differently, to allow the difference between Control and Meta keys. In EMACS notation, ^f is shown as C-f, where C- always means Control. Similarly, M-x is the Meta key plus x. If you lack a Meta key, the sequence is ESC, followed by x. Finally, some arcane commands involve both the Control and Meta keys being pressed (simultaneously with the other key involved). This notation is C-M-x and indicates that you need either to press and hold down both the Control and Meta keys while pressing x, or, if you don't have a Meta (or Alt) key, press ESC, followed by C-x.

With this notation in mind, you leave EMACS by pressing C-x C-c (Control-X, followed by Control-C).

Step 2. Action

1. First, see if your system has EMACS available. The easiest way to find out is to type emacs at the command line and see what happens.

   ```
   % emacs
   emacs: Command not found.
   %
   ```

   This is a good indication that EMACS isn't available. If your command worked, and you now are in the EMACS editor, move down to number 2 in this section.

   A popular version of EMACS is from the Free Software Foundation, and it's called GNU EMACS. To see if you have this version, type gnuemacs or gnumacs at the command line.

If this fails to work, you can try one more command before you accept that EMACS isn't part of your installation of UNIX. Online documentation for UNIX is accessible through the man command. You learn quite a bit about man in one of tomorrow's lessons. The actual database of documents also includes a primitive, but helpful, keyword search capability, accessible by specifying the -k option (for *keyword searches*) at the command line. To find out if you have EMACS, enter the following:

```
% man -k emacs
gnuemacs (11)    - GNU project Emacs
%
```

This indicates that GNU EMACS is on the system and can be started by entering gnuemacs at the command line.

2. Rather than start with a blank screen, quit the program (C-x C-c), and restart EMACS with one of the earlier test files, dickens.note:

```
% gnuemacs dickens.note
```

```
                        A Tale of Two Cities
 ▬                            Preface

When I was acting, with my children and friends, in Mr Wilkie Collins's
drama of The Frozen Deep, I first conceived the main idea of this
story. A strong desire was upon me then, to
embody it in my own person;
and I traced out in my fancy, the state of mind of which it would
necessitate the presentation
to an observant spectator, with particular
care and interest.

As the idea became familiar to me, it gradually shaped itself into its
present form. Throughout its execution, it has had complete possession
of me; I have so far verified what
is done and suffered in these pages,
as that I have certainly done and suffered it all myself.

Whenever any reference (however slight) is made here to the condition
of the French people before or during the Revolution, it is truly made,
on the faith of the most trustworthy
witnesses. It has been one of my hopes to add
----Emacs: dickens.note          (Fundamental)----Top------------------
```

As you can see, it's quite different from the display shown when vi starts up. The status line at the bottom of the display offers useful information as you edit the file at different points, also at all times reminding you of the name of the file, a feature that can be surprisingly helpful. EMACS can work with different kinds of files, and here you see by the word Fundamental in the status line that EMACS is prepared for a regular text file. If you're programming, EMACS can offer special features customized for your particular language.

3. Quit EMACS by using the C-x C-c sequence, but let a few seconds pass after you press C-x to watch what happens. When I press C-x, the bottom of the screen suddenly changes to this:

```
on the faith of the most trustworthy
witnesses. It has been one of my hopes to add
----Emacs: dickens.note          (Fundamental)----Top--------------------
C-x-
```

Confusingly, the cursor remains at the top of the file, but EMACS reminds me that I've pressed C-x and that I need to enter a second command once I've decided what to do. I now press C-c, and immediately exit EMACS.

Step 3. Summary

Already you can see there are some dramatic differences between EMACS and vi. If you're comfortable with multiple key sequences like C-x C-c to quit, then I think you're going to enjoy learning EMACS. If not, then stick with it anyway. Even if you never use EMACS, it's good to know a little bit about it.

Comment: Why learn about a tool you're not going to use? In this case, the answer is that UNIX people tend to be polarized around the question of which editor is better. Indeed, the debate between vi and EMACS is referred to as a "religious war" because of the high levels of heat and low levels of actual sensibility of the participants. My position is that different users will find different tools work best for them. If EMACS is closer to how you edit files, that's wonderful, and it's great that UNIX offers EMACS as an alternative to vi. Ultimately, the question isn't whether one is better than the other, but whether or not you can edit your files more quickly and easily in one or the other.

Task 12.2: How to Move Around in a File
Step 1. Description

Files are composed of characters, words, lines, sentences, and paragraphs, and in them EMACS has commands to help you move about. Most systems have the arrow keys enabled, which helps you avoid worrying about some of the key sequences, but it's best to know them all anyway.

The most basic motions are C-f and C-b, which are used to move the cursor forward and backward one character, respectively. Switch to the Meta command equivalents, and the cursor will move by words: M-f moves the cursor forward a word, and M-b moves it back a word. Pressing C-n moves the cursor to the next line, C-p to the previous line, C-a to the beginning of the line, and C-e to the end of the line. (The vi equivalents for all of these are l, h, w, and b for moving forward and backward a character or word; j and k for moving up or down a line; and 0 or $ to move to the beginning or end of the current line. Which makes more sense to you?)

To move forward a sentence, you can use M-e, which actually moves the cursor to the end of the sentence. Pressing M-a moves it to the beginning of a sentence. Notice the parallels between the Control and Meta commands: C-a moves the cursor to the beginning of the line, and M-a moves it to the beginning of the sentence.

Scrolling within the document is accomplished by using C-v to move forward a screen and M-v to move back a screen. To move forward an actual *page* (usually 60 lines of text, based on a printed page of information), you can use either C-x] or C-x [for forward or backward motion, respectively.

Finally, to move to the very top of the file, use M-<, and to move to the bottom, use the M-> command.

Step 2. Action

1. Go back into EMACS and locate the cursor. It should be at the very top of the screen:

```
_                    A Tale of Two Cities
                           Preface

When I was acting, with my children and friends, in Mr Wilkie Collins's
drama of The Frozen Deep, I first conceived the main idea of this
story. A strong desire was upon me then, to
```

```
embody it in my own person;
and I traced out in my fancy, the state of mind of which it would
necessitate the presentation
to an observant spectator, with particular
care and interest.

As the idea became familiar to me, it gradually shaped itself into its
present form. Throughout its execution, it has had complete possession
of me; I have so far verified what
is done and suffered in these pages,
as that I have certainly done and suffered it all myself.

Whenever any reference (however slight) is made here to the condition
of the French people before or during the Revolution, it is truly made,
on the faith of the most trustworthy
witnesses. It has been one of my hopes to add
----Emacs: dickens.note          (Fundamental)----Top------------------------
```

Move down four lines by using C-n four times. You should now be sitting on the *d* of *drama*:

```
                          Preface

When I was acting, with my children and friends, in Mr Wilkie Collins's
drama of The Frozen Deep, I first conceived the main idea of this
story. A strong desire was upon me then, to
embody it in my own person;
and I traced out in my fancy, the state of mind of which it would
```

2. Next, move to the end of this sentence by using the M-e command (just like vi, EMACS expects two spaces to separate sentences):

```
When I was acting, with my children and friends, in Mr Wilkie Collins's
drama of The Frozen Deep, I first conceived the main idea of this
story._ A strong desire was upon me then, to
embody it in my own person;
and I traced out in my fancy, the state of mind of which it would
```

Now type in the following text: I fought the impulse to write this novel vociferously, but, dear reader, I felt the injustice of the situation too strongly in my breast to deny. Don't press Return or ESC when you're done. The screen should now look similar to this:

```
drama of The Frozen Deep, I first conceived the main idea of this
story. I fought the impulse to write this novel vociferously, but, dear reader,\
 I felt
the injustice of the situation too strongly in my breast to deny_  A strong des\
ire was upon me then, to
embody it in my own person;
and I traced out in my fancy, the state of mind of which it would
necessitate the presentation
```

You can see that EMACS wrapped the line when the line became too long, and because the lines are still too long to display, a few of them end with a backslash. The backslash isn't actually a part of the file; with it, EMACS is telling me that those lines are longer than I might expect.

3. Now try to move back a few letters by pressing Backspace.

Uh oh! If your system is like mine, the Backspace key doesn't move the cursor back up a letter at all. Instead it starts the EMACS help system, where you're suddenly confronted with a screen that looks like this:

```
You have typed C-h, the help character. Type a Help option:

A  command-apropos.  Give a substring, and see a list of commands
            (functions interactively callable) that contain
            that substring. See also the  apropos  command.
B  describe-bindings. Display table of all key bindings.
C  describe-key-briefly. Type a command key sequence;
            it prints the function name that sequence runs.
F  describe-function. Type a function name and get documentation of it.
I  info. The  info  documentation reader.
K  describe-key. Type a command key sequence;
            it displays the full documentation.
L  view-lossage. Shows last 100 characters you typed.
M  describe-mode. Print documentation of current major mode,
            which describes the commands peculiar to it.
N  view-emacs-news. Shows emacs news file.
S  describe-syntax. Display contents of syntax table, plus explanations
T  help-with-tutorial. Select the Emacs learn-by-doing tutorial.
V  describe-variable. Type name of a variable;
            it displays the variable's documentation and value.
W  where-is. Type command name; it prints which keystrokes
            invoke that command.
--**-Emacs: *Help*            (Fundamental)----Top----------------------
A B C F I K L M N S T V W C-c C-d C-n C-w or Space to scroll: _
```

To escape the help screen (which you learn more about later in this lesson), press ESC and your screen should be restored. Notice that the filename has

been changed and is now shown as `*Help*` instead of the actual file. The status line also shows what file you're viewing, but you aren't always viewing the file you want to work with.

The correct key to move the cursor back a few characters is `C-b`. Use that to back up, then use `C-f` to move forward again to the original cursor location.

4. Check that the last few lines of the file haven't changed by using the EMACS move-to-end-of-file command `M->`. (Think of file redirection to remember the file motion commands.) Now the screen looks like this:

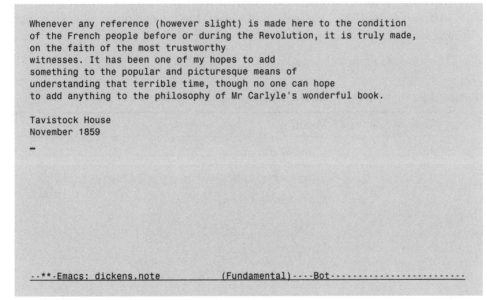

```
Whenever any reference (however slight) is made here to the condition
of the French people before or during the Revolution, it is truly made,
on the faith of the most trustworthy
witnesses. It has been one of my hopes to add
something to the popular and picturesque means of
understanding that terrible time, though no one can hope
to add anything to the philosophy of Mr Carlyle's wonderful book.


Tavistock House
November 1859

_




--**-Emacs: dickens.note          (Fundamental)----Bot----------------------
```

5. Changing the words of Charles Dickens was fun, so save these changes and quit. If you try to quit the program with `C-x C-c`, EMACS reminds you that there are unsaved changes:

```
--**-Emacs: dickens.note          (Fundamental)----Bot----------------------
Save file /users/taylor/dickens.note? (y or n) _
```

Typing y saves the changes; n quits without saving the changes; and if you instead decide to return to the edit session, ESC will cancel the action entirely. Pressing n reminds you a second time that the changes are going to be lost if you don't save them.

```
--**-Emacs: dickens.note          (Fundamental)----Bot----------------------
Modified buffers exist; exit anyway? (yes or no)  _
```

This time type yes and, finally, you're back on the command line.

Step 3. Summary

Entering text in EMACS is incredibly easy. It's as if the editor is always in insert mode. The price that you pay for this, however, is that just about anything else you do requires Control or Meta sequences: even the Backspace key did something other than what you wanted. (You could fix the problem with key mapping so that pressing that key results in a C-b command, but then you couldn't get to the help information.)

The motion commands are summarized in Table 12.1.

Table 12.1. EMACS motion commands.

Command	Meaning
M->	Move to end of file.
M-<	Move to beginning of file.
C-v	Move forward a screen.
M-v	Move backward a screen.
C-x]	Move forward a page.
C-x [	Move backward a page.
C-n	Move to the next line.
C-p	Move to the previous line.
C-a	Move to the beginning of the line.
C-e	Move to the end of the line.
M-e	Move to the end of the sentence.
M-a	Move to the beginning of the sentence.
C-f	Move forward a character.
C-b	Move backward a character.
M-f	Move forward a word.
M-b	Move backward a word.

Task 12.3: How to Delete Characters and Words
Step 1. Description

Inserting text into an EMACS buffer is quite simple, and once you get the hang of it, moving about in the file isn't too bad either. How about deleting text? The series of Control and Meta commands that enable you to insert text are a precursor to all commands in EMACS, and it should come as no surprise that C-d deletes the current character, M-d deletes the next word, M-k deletes the rest of the current sentence, and C-k deletes the rest of the current line. If you have a key on your keyboard labeled Del, Rubout or Delete, then you're in luck, because Del deletes the previous character, M-DEL deletes the previous word, and C-x DEL deletes the previous sentence.

Unfortunately, I have a Delete key, but it's tied to the Backspace function on my system, so every time I press it, it actually sends a C-h sequence to the system, not the Del sequence. The result is that I cannot use any of these backwards deletion commands.

Comment: Actually, VersaTerm Pro, the terminal emulation package I use on my Macintosh to connect to the various UNIX systems is smarter than that. I can tell it whether pressing the Delete key should send a C-h or a DEL function in the keyboard configuration screen. One flip of a toggle, and I'm fully functional in EMACS. Unfortunately, it's not always this easy to switch from Backspace to Del.

Step 2. Action

1. Restart EMACS with the dickens.note file, then move the cursor to the middle of the fifth line (remember, C-n moves to the next line, and C-f moves forward a character). It should look like this:

```
                            Preface

When I was acting, with my children and friends, in Mr Wilkie Collins's
drama of The Frozen Deep, I first conceived the main idea of this
story. A strong desire was upon me then, to
embody it in my own person;
and I traced out in my fancy, the state of mind of which it would
necessitate the presentation
to an observant spectator, with particular
```

Notice that my cursor is on the *w* in *was* here.

12

2. Press C-d C-d C-d to remove the word *was*. Now simply type came to revise the sentence slightly. The screen should now look like this:

```
                                  Preface

When I was acting, with my children and friends, in Mr Wilkie Collins's
drama of The Frozen Deep, I first conceived the main idea of this
story. A strong desire came_upon me then, to
embody it in my own person;
and I traced out in my fancy, the state of mind of which it would
necessitate the presentation
to an observant spectator, with particular
```

Now press Del once to remove the last letter of the new word, then press e to reinsert it. Instead of backing up a character at a time, I am instead going to use M-DEL to delete the word just added. The word is deleted, but the spaces on either side of the word are retained.

```
                                  Preface

When I was acting, with my children and friends, in Mr Wilkie Collins's
drama of The Frozen Deep, I first conceived the main idea of this
story. A strong desire _upon me then, to
embody it in my own person;
and I traced out in my fancy, the state of mind of which it would
necessitate the presentation
to an observant spectator, with particular
```

I'll try another word to see if I can get this sentence to sound the way I'd prefer. Type crept to see how it reads.

3. On the other hand, it's probably not good to revise classic stories like *A Tale of Two Cities*, so the best move is for me to delete this entire sentence. If I press C-x DEL, will it do the right thing? Remember, C-x DEL deletes the previous sentence. I press C-x DEL and the results are helpful, if not completely what I want to accomplish:

```
                                  Preface

When I was acting, with my children and friends, in Mr Wilkie Collins's
drama of The Frozen Deep, I first conceived the main idea of this
story. _upon me then, to
embody it in my own person;
and I traced out in my fancy, the state of mind of which it would
necessitate the presentation
to an observant spectator, with particular
```

That's okay. Now I can delete the second part of the sentence by using the
`M-k` command. Now the screen looks like what I want:

```
When I was acting, with my children and friends, in Mr Wilkie Collins's
drama of The Frozen Deep, I first conceived the main idea of this
story. _

As the idea became familiar to me, it gradually shaped itself into its
present form. Throughout its execution, it has had complete possession
of me; I have so far verified what
```

4. Here's a great feature of EMACS! I just realized that deleting sentences is
   just as wildly inappropriate as changing words, so I want to undo the last
   two changes. If I was using `vi`, I'd be stuck because `vi` remembers only the
   last change, but EMACS has that beat. With EMACS, you can back up as
   many changes as you'd like, usually until you restore the original file. To
   step backwards, use `C-x u`.

   The first time I press `C-x u`, the screen changes to this:

```
When I was acting, with my children and friends, in Mr Wilkie Collins's
drama of The Frozen Deep, I first conceived the main idea of this
story. _upon me then, to
embody it in my own person;
and I traced out in my fancy, the state of mind of which it would
necessitate the presentation
to an observant spectator, with particular
care and interest.

As the idea became familiar to me, it gradually shaped itself into its
present form. Throughout its execution, it has had complete possession
```

   The second time I press it, the screen goes even farther back in my revision
   history:

```
When I was acting, with my children and friends, in Mr Wilkie Collins's
drama of The Frozen Deep, I first conceived the main idea of this
story. A strong desire crept_upon me then, to
embody it in my own person;
and I traced out in my fancy, the state of mind of which it would
necessitate the presentation
to an observant spectator, with particular
care and interest.

As the idea became familiar to me, it gradually shaped itself into its
present form. Throughout its execution, it has had complete possession
```

12

Finally, pressing C-x u three more times causes the original text to be restored:

```
                          A Tale of Two Cities
                               Preface

When I was acting, with my children and friends, in Mr Wilkie Collins's
drama of The Frozen Deep, I first conceived the main idea of this
story. A strong desire came upon me then, to
embody it in my own person;
and I traced out in my fancy, the state of mind of which it would
necessitate the presentation
to an observant spectator, with particular
care and interest.

As the idea became familiar to me, it gradually shaped itself into its
present form. Throughout its execution, it has had complete possession
of me; I have so far verified what
is done and suffered in these pages,
as that I have certainly done and suffered it all myself.

Whenever any reference (however slight) is made here to the condition
of the French people before or during the Revolution, it is truly made,
on the faith of the most trustworthy
witnesses. It has been one of my hopes to add
--**-Emacs: dickens.note          (Fundamental)----Top-----------------------
Undo!
```

Step 3. Summary

If you don't have a Delete key, some of the deletion commands will be unavailable to you, regrettably. Generally, though, EMACS has as many way to delete text as vi has, if not more. The best feature, however, is that unlike vi, EMACS remembers edit changes from the beginning of your editing session. You can always back up as far as you want by using the C-x u undo request.

The delete keys are summarized in Table 12.2.

Table 12.2. Deletion commands in EMACS.

Command	Meaning
DEL	Delete the previous character.
C-d	Delete the current character.
M-DEL	Delete the previous word.

Command	Meaning
M-d	Delete the next word.
C-x DEL	Delete the previous sentence.
M-k	Delete the rest of the current sentence.
C-k	Delete the rest of the current line.
C-x u	Undo the last edit change.

Task 12.4: Search and Replace in EMACS

Step 1. Description

Because EMACS reserves the last line of the screen for its own system prompts, searching and replacing are easier than in vi. Moreover, the system prompts for the fields and asks, for each occurrence, whether to change it or not. On the other hand, this command isn't a simple key press or two, but rather it is an example of a *named EMACS command.*

Searching forward for a pattern is done by pressing C-s and searching backwards with C-r (the mnemonics are *search forward* or *reverse search*). To leave the search once you've found what you want, press ESC, and to cancel the search, returning to your starting point, use C-g.

Don't Skip This: Unfortunately, you might find that pressing C-s does very strange things to your system. In fact, ^s and ^q are often used as *flow control* on a terminal, and by pressing the C-s key, you're actually telling the terminal emulator to stop sending information until it sees a C-q. If this happens to you, then you need to try to turn off *XON/XOFF* flow control. Ask your system administrator for help.

12

Query and replace is really a whole new feature within EMACS. To start a query and replace, use M-x query-replace. EMACS will prompt for what to do next. Once a match is shown, you can type a variety of different commands to affect what happens: y makes the change; n means to leave it as is, but move to the next match; ESC or q quits replace mode; and ! automatically replaces all further occurrences of the pattern without further prompting.

Step 2. Action

1. I'm looking at the dickens.note file, and I have moved the cursor to the top left corner using M-<. Somewhere in the file is the word Revolution, but I'm not sure where. Worse, every time I press C-s, the terminal freezes up until I press C-q because of flow control problems. Instead of searching forward, I'll search backwards by first moving the cursor to the bottom of the file with M->, then pressing C-r.

```
----Emacs: dickens.note        (Fundamental)----Bot----------------------
I-search backward:
```

As I type each character of the pattern Revolution, the cursor goes backwards, matching the pattern as it grows longer and longer, until EMACS finds the word I seek:

```
Whenever any reference (however slight) is made here to the condition
of the French people before or during the Revolution, it is truly made,
on the faith of the most trustworthy
witnesses. It has been one of my hopes to add
something to the popular and picturesque means of
understanding that terrible time, though no one can hope
to add anything to the philosophy of Mr Carlyle's wonderful book.

Tavistock House
November 1859




----Emacs: dickens.note        (Fundamental)----Bot----------------------
I-search backward: Revol
```

2. Now I'll try the query-replace feature. To begin, I move to the top of the file with M-<, then type in M-x, which causes the notation to show up on the bottom status line:

```
of the French people before or during the Revolution, it is truly made,
on the faith of the most trustworthy
witnesses. It has been one of my hopes to add
--**-Emacs: dickens.note        (Fundamental)----Top----------------------
M-x _
```

I then type the words query-replace, followed by a Return. EMACS understands that I want to find all occurrences of a pattern and replace them with another. EMACS changes the prompt to this:

```
of the French people before or during the Revolution, it is truly made,
on the faith of the most trustworthy
witnesses. It has been one of my hopes to add
--**-Emacs: dickens.note        (Fundamental)----Top----------------------
Query replace: _
```

Now I type in the word that I want to replace. To cause confusion in the file, I think I'll change *French* to *Danish*, because maybe *A Tale of Two Cities* really takes place in London and Copenhagen! To do this, I type French, followed by Return. The prompt again changes to this:

```
of the French people before or during the Revolution, it is truly made,
on the faith of the most trustworthy
witnesses. It has been one of my hopes to add
--**-Emacs: dickens.note        (Fundamental)----Top----------------------
Query replace French with: _
```

I type Danish and again press Return.

```
as that I have certainly done and suffered it all myself.

Whenever any reference (however slight) is made here to the condition
of the French_people before or during the Revolution, it is truly made,
on the faith of the most trustworthy
witnesses. It has been one of my hopes to add
--**-Emacs: dickens.note        (Fundamental)----Top----------------------
Query replacing French with Danish:
```

It may not be completely obvious, but EMACS has found a match (immediately before the cursor) and is prompting me for what to do next. The choices here are summarized in Table 12.3.

12

Table 12.3. Options during query and replace.

Command	Meaning
y	Change this occurrence of the pattern.
n	Don't change this occurrence, but look for another.
q	Don't change. Leave query-replace completely (you can also use ESC for this function).
!	Change this occurrence and all others in the file.

I opt to make this, and all other possible changes in the file, by pressing !, and the screen changes to tell me that there were no more occurrences:

```
Whenever any reference (however slight) is made here to the condition
of the Danish_people before or during the Revolution, it is truly made,
on the faith of the most trustworthy
witnesses. It has been one of my hopes to add
--**-Emacs: dickens.note          (Fundamental)----Top--------------------
Done
```

Step 3. Summary

Searching in EMACS is awkward, particularly due to the flow control problems that you may incur because of your terminal. However, searching and replacing with the query-replace command is fantastic, much better and more powerful than the vi alternative. As I said earlier, your assessment of EMACS all depends on what features you prefer.

Task 12.5: Using the EMACS Tutorial and Help System
Step 1. Description

Unlike vi and, indeed, unlike most of UNIX, EMACS includes its own extensive built-in documentation and a tutorial to help you learn about how to use the package. As I noted earlier, the entire help system is accessed by pressing C-h. Pressing C-h three times brings up the general help menu screen. There is also an information browser called *info* (accessed by pressing C-h i) and a tutorial system you can start by pressing C-h t.

EMACS enthusiasts insist that the editor is modeless, but in fact it does have modes of its own. You used one just now, the query-replace mode. To obtain help on the current mode that you're working in, you can use C-h m.

Step 2. Action

1. Boldly, I opted to press C-h C-h C-h, and the entire screen is replaced with this:

```
You have typed C-h, the help character. Type a Help option:

A  command-apropos.  Give a substring, and see a list of commands
              (functions interactively callable) that contain
              that substring. See also the  apropos  command.
B  describe-bindings. Display table of all key bindings.
C  describe-key-briefly. Type a command key sequence;
              it prints the function name that sequence runs.
F  describe-function. Type a function name and get documentation of it.
I  info. The  info  documentation reader.
K  describe-key. Type a command key sequence;
              it displays the full documentation.
L  view-lossage. Shows last 100 characters you typed.
M  describe-mode. Print documentation of current major mode,
              which describes the commands peculiar to it.
N  view-emacs-news. Shows emacs news file.
S  describe-syntax. Display contents of syntax table, plus explanations
T  help-with-tutorial. Select the Emacs learn-by-doing tutorial.
V  describe-variable. Type name of a variable;
              it displays the variable's documentation and value.
W  where-is. Type command name; it prints which keystrokes
              invoke that command.
--**-Emacs: *Help*                (Fundamental)----Top--------------------
A B C F I K L M N S T V W C-c C-d C-n C-w or Space to scroll: _
```

What to do now? There are actually 17 different options from this point, as shown in Table 12.4.

Table 12.4. EMACS help system command options.

Command	Meaning
A	Lists all commands matching the specified word.
B	Lists all key mappings (EMACS calls them *key bindings*).
C	Describes any key sequence pressed, instead of doing it.
F	Describes the specified function.
I	Starts up the info browser.
K	Fully describes the result of a particular key sequence.

continues

12

Table 12.4. Continued

Command	Meaning
L	Shows the last 100 characters you typed.
M	Describes the current mode you're within.
S	Lists a command syntax table.
T	Starts the EMACS tutorial.
V	Defines and describes the specified variable.
W	Indicates what keystroke invokes a particular function.
C-c	EMACS copyright and distribution information.
C-d	EMACS ordering information.
C-n	Recent EMACS changes.
C-w	EMACS warranty.

2. I choose K and then press M-< to see what that command really does. The first thing that happens after entering K is that the table of help information vanishes, to be replaced by my original text, and then the prompt appears along the bottom:

```
of the Danish_people before or during the Revolution, it is truly made,
on the faith of the most trustworthy
witnesses. It has been one of my hopes to add
--**-Emacs: dickens.note          (Fundamental)----Top----------------------
Describe key:-
```

Pressing M-< brings up the desired information:

```
                        A Tale of Two Cities
                            Preface

When I was acting, with my children and friends, in Mr Wilkie Collins's
drama of The Frozen Deep, I first conceived the main idea of this
story. A strong desire came upon me then, to
embody it in my own person;
and I traced out in my fancy, the state of mind of which it would
necessitate the presentation
to an observant spectator, with particular
```

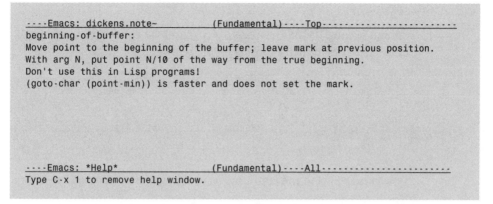

```
----Emacs: dickens.note~           (Fundamental)----Top----------------------
beginning-of-buffer:
Move point to the beginning of the buffer; leave mark at previous position.
With arg N, put point N/10 of the way from the true beginning.
Don't use this in Lisp programs!
(goto-char (point-min)) is faster and does not set the mark.




----Emacs: *Help*                  (Fundamental)----All----------------------
Type C-x 1 to remove help window.
```

A quick C-x 1 removes the help information when I'm done with it.

Step 3. Summary

There is a considerable amount of help available in the EMACS editor. If you're interested in learning more about this editor, the online tutorial is a great place to start. Try C-h t to start it, and go from there.

Task 12.6: Working with Other Files
Step 1. Description

By this point it should be no surprise that many commands are available within the EMACS editor, even though it can be a bit tricky to get to them. There are many file-related commands too, but I'm going to focus on just a few essential commands so you can get around in the program. The EMACS help system can offer lots more. (Try using C-h a file to find out what functions are offered in your version of the program.)

To add the contents of a file to the current edit buffer, use the command C-x i. It will prompt for a filename. Pressing C-x C-w prompts for a file to write the buffer into, rather than the default file. To save to the default file, use C-x C-s (that is, if you can; the C-s might again hang you up, just as it did when you tried to use it for searching). If that doesn't work, you can always use the alternative C-x s, which also works. To move to another file, use C-x C-f. (EMACS users never specify more than one filename on the command line. They use C-x C-f to move between files instead.) What's nice is that when you use the C-x C-f command, you load the contents of that file into another buffer, so you can zip quickly between files by using the C-x b command to switch buffers.

Step 2. Action

1. Without leaving EMACS, I press `C-x C-f` to read another file into the buffer. The system then prompts me as follows:

```
of the Danish people before or during the Revolution, it is truly made,
on the faith of the most trustworthy
witnesses. It has been one of my hopes to add
----Emacs: dickens.note          (Fundamental)----Top----------------------
Find file: ~/ _
```

I type buckaroo, and the editor opens up a new buffer, moving me to that file:

```
I found myself stealing a peek at my own watch and overhead
General Catbird's
aide give him the latest.
"He's not even here," went the conversation.
"Banzai."
"Where the hell is he?"
"At the hospital in El Paso."
"What? Why weren't we informed? What's wrong with him?"




----Emacs: buckaroo           (Fundamental)----All----------------------
```

2. Now I'll flip back to the other buffer with `C-x b`. When I enter that command, however, it doesn't automatically move me there. Instead it offers this prompt:

```
--**-Emacs: buckaroo           (Fundamental)----All----------------------
Switch to buffer: (default dickens.note) _
```

When I type ?, I receive a split screen indicating what the possible answers are here:

```
I found myself stealing a peek at my own watch and overhead
General Catbird's
aide give him the latest.
"He's not even here," went the conversation.
"Banzai."
"Where the hell is he?"
"At the hospital in El Paso."
"What? Why weren't we informed? What's wrong with him?"



--**-Emacs: buckaroo              (Fundamental)----All---------------------
Possible completions are:
*Buffer List*                     *Help*
*scratch*                         buckaroo
dickens.note




----Emacs:  *Completions*         (Fundamental)----All---------------------
Switch to buffer: (default dickens.note) _
```

The default is okay, so I press Return and voilà! I'm back in the Dickens file. I'll use one more C-x b; this time the default is buckaroo, so I again press Return to move back.

3. I'm in the buckaroo file, and I want to see what happens if I read the dickens.note into this file. This is done easily. I move the cursor to the end of the file with M->, then press C-x i, answering dickens.note to the prompt Insert file: ~/. Pressing Return yields the following screen display:

```
I found myself stealing a peek at my own watch and overhead
General Catbird's
aide give him the latest.
"He's not even here," went the conversation.
"Banzai."
"Where the hell is he?"
"At the hospital in El Paso."
```

12

```
"What? Why weren't we informed? What's wrong with him?"

                    A Tale of Two Cities
                         Preface

When I was acting, with my children and friends, in Mr Wilkie Collins's
drama of The Frozen Deep, I first conceived the main idea of this
story. A strong desire came upon me then, to
embody it in my own person;
and I traced out in my fancy, the state of mind of which it would
necessitate the presentation
to an observant spectator, with particular
care and interest.

As the idea became familiar to me, it gradually shaped itself into its
present form. Throughout its execution, it has had complete possession
--**-Emacs: buckaroo               (Fundamental)----Top----------------------
```

4. It's time to quit and split. To do this, I press C-x s and wait for an EMACS prompt or two. The first one displayed is this:

```
As the idea became familiar to me, it gradually shaped itself into its
present form. Throughout its execution, it has had complete possession
--**-Emacs: buckaroo               (Fundamental)----Top----------------------
Save file /users/taylor/buckaroo? (y or n) _
```

I answer y to save this muddled file. It returns me to the top of the file, and a quick C-x C-c drops me back to the system prompt.

Step 3. Summary

This has only scratched the surface of EMACS, a fantastically powerful editor. The best way to learn more is to work through the online tutorial in the editor or peruse the information available in the help system.

Lesson Summary

You have now learned quite a bit about the EMACS editor. Some capabilities exceed those of the vi editor, and some are considerably more confusing. Which one of these editors you choose is up to you, and your choice should be based on your own preferences for working on files. This is the end of this day's lessons. You should spend some time working with the editor you prefer, making sure you can create simple files and modify them without any problems.

Workshop

Key Terms

Meta key	Analogous to a Control key, this is labeled either Meta or Alt on your keyboard.
keyword search	A search through a database for a specific key concept or topic.
named EMACS command	A command in EMACS that requires you to type its name, like query-replace, rather than a command key or two.
key bindings	The EMACS term for key mapping.
flow control	The protocol used by your computer and terminal to make sure that neither outpaces the other during data transmission.
XON/XOFF	A particular type of *flow control*, the receiving end can send an XON (delay transmission) character until it's ready for more information, when it sends an XOFF (resume transmission).

Questions

1. How do you get to the EMACS help system?

2. Check your keyboard. If you don't have a Meta or Alt key, what alternative strategy can you use to enter commands like M-x?

3. What's the command sequence for leaving EMACS when you're done?

4. What was the problem I had with the Del key? How did I solve the problem? What's the alternative delete command if Del isn't available?

5. How do you do global search-and-replace in EMACS, and what key do you press to stop the global search-and-replace when you are prompted for confirmation at the very first match?

6. Use the EMACS help system to list the EMACS copyright information. What's your reaction?

Preview of the Next Chapter

Tomorrow's lesson is an in-depth look at the different shells available in UNIX, how to configure them, and how to choose which you'd like to use. You also learn about the contents of the default configuration files for both `csh` and `sh`, the two most common shells in UNIX.

Exploring Your Environment

Introduction to Command Shells

Welcome to your fifth day of learning UNIX. You should take a moment to pat yourself on the back. You've come a long way, and you're already quite a sophisticated user. In the past few days, I've occasionally touched on the differences between the shells, but I haven't really stopped to explain what shells are available, how they differ from one another, and which is the best for your style of interaction. That's what this lesson is all about.

Shells, you'll recall, are the command-line interface programs through which you tell the computer what to do. All UNIX systems include C shell (csh) and its predecessor the Bourne shell (su). Some also include a newer version of the Bourne shell, called the Korn shell (ksh).

Goals for This Lesson

In this lesson, you will learn

- ☐ What shells are available, and how they differ from one another

- ☐ How to identify which shell you're running

- ☐ How to choose a new shell

- ☐ More about the environment of your shell

- ☐ How to explore csh configuration files

A variety of different shells are available in UNIX, but two are quite common: the Bourne shell (sh) and the C shell (csh). You will learn about some of the other shells available, notably the Korn shell (ksh) and the terminal-based C shell (tcsh). Because the C shell is so popular, most of this book will focus on it.

Task 13.1: What Shells Are Available?
Step 1. Description

If I asked a PC expert how many command interpreters are available for DOS, the immediate answer would be "one, of course." After a few minutes of reflection, however, the answer might be expanded to include The Norton Desktop, DesqView, Windows, Windows for Workgroups, and others. This expanded answer reflects the reality that whenever there are different people using a computer, there will evolve different styles of interacting with the machine and different products to meet these needs. Similarly, the Macintosh has several command interpreters. If you decide that you don't like the standard interface, perhaps you will find that At Ease, DiskTop, or Square One works better.

From the very beginning, UNIX has been a programmer's operating system, designed to allow programmers to extend the system easily and gracefully. It should come as no surprise, then, that there are quite a few different shells available. Not only that, but *any* program can serve as a command shell, so you could even start right in EMACS if you wanted, then use escapes to UNIX for actual commands. (Don't laugh—I've heard it's done sometimes).

The original shell was written by Ken Thompson, back in the early UNIX's laboratory days, as part of his design of the UNIX file system. Somewhere along the way, Steven Bourne, also at AT&T, got hold of the shell and started expanding it. By the time UNIX began to be widely distributed, sh was known as the Bourne shell. Characterized by speed and simplicity, it is the default shell for writing shell scripts, but it is rarely used as a command shell for users today.

The next shell was designed by the productive Bill Joy, author of vi. Entranced by the design and features of the C programming language, Joy decided to create a command shell that shared much of the C language structure, and that would make it easier to write sophisticated shell scripts (the C shell, or csh). He also expanded the shell concept to add *command aliases, command history,* and *job control.* Command aliases allow users to rename and reconfigure commands easily. Command history ensures that users never have to enter commands a second time. Job control enables users to run multiple programs at once. The C shell is by far the most popular shell on all systems I've ever used, and it's the shell that I have been using myself for about 15 years now, since I first logged in to a BSD Unix system in 1980.

In the past few years, another AT&T Labs software wizard, David Korn, has begun distributing another shell on various UNIX platforms. The Korn shell, also known as ksh, is designed to be a superset of the Bourne shell, sharing its configuration files (.profile) and command syntax, but including many of the more powerful features of the C shell, too, including command aliases (albeit in a slightly different format), command history, and job control. This shell is slowly becoming more popular, but it isn't yet widely distributed. You might not have it on your version of UNIX.

Other shells exist in special niches. A modified version of the C shell, a version that incorporates the slick history editing features of the Korn shell, has appeared: it is called tcsh. Maintained by some engineers at Cornell University, it is 95 percent csh and 5 percent new features. The most important tcsh additions to the C shell are these:

☐ EMACS-style command line editing

☐ Visual perusal of the history list

☐ Interactive command, file, and user name completion

☐ Spelling correction of command, file, and user names

☐ Automatic logout after an extended idle period

☐ The capability to monitor logins, users, or terminals

☐ New preinitialized environment variables $HOST and $HOSTTYPE.

☐ Support for a meaningful and helpful system status line

Another shell that you might bump into is called the MH shell, or msh. It's designed around the MH electronic mail program, originally designed at the Rand Corporation. In essence, the MH shell lets you have instant access to any electronic mail that you might encounter. For sites that have security considerations, a restricted version of the Bourne shell is also available, called rsh (ingeniously, it's called the *restricted sh shell*). Persistent rumors of security problems with rsh suggest that you should double-check before you trust dubious users on your system with rsh as their login shell.

Two other variants of the Bourne shell are worth mentioning: jsh is a version of the Bourne shell that includes C shell-style job control features, and bash, also humorously called the Bourne Again shell, is a reimplementation of the original shell with many new features and no licensing restrictions.

Comment: Licensing restrictions and intellectual property laws have occasionally stymied the growth of UNIX. Although UNIX is unquestionably popular with programmers, these same programmers have a burning desire to see what's inside, to learn about how UNIX works by examining UNIX itself. UNIX is owned by AT&T. Few people are able to view the source legally. Those who do look into UNIX are "tainted": anything they write in the future might be inspired by proprietary code of AT&T. The situation is fuzzy in many ways, and that's where the Free Software Foundation comes in. The brainchild of Richard Stallman, the FSF is slowly rewriting all the major UNIX utilities and then distributing them with the source, as part of the ambitious GNU project. GNU EMACS is one example, and the Bourne Again shell is another.

Step 2. Action

1. In Chapter 9, "Power Filters and File Redirection," you learned how to use awk to extract the default login shell of each user on your system, then use

sort and uniq to collate the data and present an attractive output. Armed with the description of all the different shells, you can now take another look:

```
% awk -F: '{print $7}' /etc/passwd | sort | uniq -c
   2
3361 /bin/csh
   1 /bin/false
  85 /bin/ksh
  21 /bin/sh
  11 /usr/local/bin/ksh
 361 /usr/local/bin/tcsh
   7 /usr/local/lib/msh
```

2. You can see that the vast majority of the people on this system use the C shell. To look at it a different way, compute the number of entries in the password file:

```
% wc -l /etc/passwd
        3849
%
```

Now, what percentage of users have chosen each of these shells? This is a job for bc!

```
% bc
x=3849
scale=4
3361/x*100
87.3200
85/x*100
2.2000
361/x*100
9.3700
^d
%
```

It's a tad difficult to interpret, but this output says that 87.3 percent of the users have csh as their login shell, another 9.4 percent use the modified tcsh, and only 2.2 percent use ksh. The remaining 1.1 percent use either the Bourne shell or the MH shell, or they default to the Bourne shell (the two accounts in the preceding output, without *any* shell indicated).

Comment: The scale=4 command tells bc how many digits to display after the decimal point in numbers. By default, unfortunately, bc displays no digits after the decimal point.

Step 3. Summary

Quite a variety of different shells are available, but the most common one on sites I'm familiar with is the C shell. Clearly the system that I used for this particular set of examples has an overwhelming majority of C shell users: a combined total of 97 percent of the users are working within either the C shell or its descendent tcsh.

Task 13.2: Identifying Your Shell
Step 1. Description

There are many different approaches to identifying which shell you're using. The easiest, however, is just to swoop into the /etc/passwd file to see what your account lists. It's helpful to know some alternatives, because the /etc/passwd option isn't always available (some systems don't have an /etc/passwd file in the interest of security).

Step 2. Action

1. One simple technique to identify your shell is to check your prompt. If your prompt contains a %, you are probably using the C shell or tcsh. If your prompt contains $, you could be using the Bourne shell, the Korn shell, or a variant thereof.

2. A much more reliable way to ascertain which shell you're using is to actually ask the operating system what program you're currently running. If you recall, the notation $$ expands to the process identification number of the shell. You can use $$ as a search pattern to grep to check the processor status tables (which can be obtained by using the ps command, either with the -ef flags to SVR4, or with the -aux flags to BSD). Here's what happens when I try it:

```
% ps -ef ¦ grep $$
taylor   26905   0.0  0.2  256   144 Ai S        0:03 -csh (csh)
taylor   29751   0.0  0.1   52    28 Ai S        0:00 grep 26905
%
```

You can see that I'm running the C shell. Using ps in this fashion also matches the grep process (notice that the two dollar signs have expanded to the current shell process identification, 26905). There is a leading dash on the indication of what shell I'm running because that's how the system denotes whether it's my *login shell* or just a shell that I'm running.

3. Another way to find out what shell I'm running is to peek into the /etc/
   passwd file, which you can do with some sophistication now that awk is no
   longer a mystery:

```
% awk -F: '{ if ($1 == "taylor") print "your shell is: "$7}' < /etc/passwd
your shell is: /bin/csh
%
```

4. The best way to figure out what shell you're running, however, is to use
   chsh. You will learn how to use chsh in the following unit.

Step 3. Summary

Once you've identified your shell, you can contemplate choosing a different one.

Task 13.3: How to Choose a New Shell
Step 1. Description

In the past, the only way to switch login shells on many systems was to ask the system
administrator to edit the /etc/passwd file directly. This usually meant waiting until
the system administrator had time. The good news is that there's now a simple
program (on almost all UNIX systems) to change login shells—it's chsh, or *change
shell.* It has no starting flags or options, does not require that any files be specified, and
can be used regardless of your location in the file system. Simply type chsh and press
Enter.

Step 2. Action

1. The first step is to identify what shells are available for use. By convention,
   all shells have sh somewhere in their name, and they are located in /bin:

```
% ls -1F /bin/*sh*
-rwsr-xr-x  3 root          49152 Apr 23  1992 /bin/chsh*
-rwxr-xr-x  1 root         102400 Apr  8  1991 /bin/csh*
-rwxr-xr-x  1 root         139264 Jul 26 14:35 /bin/ksh*
-rwxr-xr-x  1 root          28672 Oct 10  1991 /bin/sh*
%
```

   The chsh command enables you to change your login shell, as you will learn.
   The most common shells are csh, ksh, and sh.

   On one of the machines I use, some shells are also stored in the /usr/local/
   bin directory:

```
% ls -1F /usr/local/bin/*sh*
lrwxr-xr-x  1 root              8 Jul 26 14:46 /usr/local/bin/ksh -> /bin/ksh*
-rwxr-xr-x  1 root         266240 Jan 19  1993 /usr/local/bin/tcsh*
%
```

You can see that there's an entry in /usr/local/bin for the ksh shell, but that it's actually just a link pointing to the file in the /bin directory.

2. You might find quite a few more matches to these simple ls commands. On another, very different system, I tried the same two commands and found the following:

```
% ls -CF /bin/*sh*
/bin/chsh*          /bin/ksh*           /bin/shelltool@     /bin/tcsh*
/bin/csh*           /bin/sh*            /bin/shift_lines@   /bin/ypchsh*
% ls -CF /usr/local/bin/*sh*
/usr/local/bin/bash*              /usr/local/bin/showpicture*
/usr/local/bin/bash112*           /usr/local/bin/sun-audio-file.csh*
/usr/local/bin/ircflush@          /usr/local/bin/sun-to-mime.csh*
/usr/local/bin/mush*              /usr/local/bin/tcsh*
/usr/local/bin/mush.old*          /usr/local/bin/tcsh603*
/usr/local/bin/mush725*           /usr/local/bin/unshar*
/usr/local/bin/ntcsh*             /usr/local/bin/unship*
/usr/local/bin/shar*              /usr/local/bin/uupath.sh*
/usr/local/bin/ship*              /usr/local/bin/vsh*
/usr/local/bin/showaudio*         /usr/local/bin/zsh*
/usr/local/bin/showexternal*      /usr/local/bin/zsh210*
/usr/local/bin/shownonascii*      /usr/local/bin/zsh231*
/usr/local/bin/showpartial*
%
```

Two more shells show up here: vsh and zsh. The visual shell, vsh, is an interface very like the Norton Desktop on DOS. Watch what happens to my screen when I launch it by entering vsh:

```
Directory: /u1/taylor  User: taylor                     Page 2 / 2

a    .tin/
b    Global.Software
c    Interactive.Unix
d    Mail/
e    News/
f    Src/
g    bin/
h    history.usenet.Z
i    testme




-
```

If you have vsh on your system, you might be interested in experimenting with this very different shell.

The zsh shell is another command shell, one written by Paul Falstad of Princeton University. The Bourne Again shell, bash, also appears in the listing, as does the mush program, which is an electronic mail package.

3. Needless to say, many different shells are available! To change my login shell to any of these alternate shells, or even just to verify what shell I'm running, I can use the change shell command:

```
% chsh
Changing login shell for taylor.
Old shell: /bin/csh
New shell: _
```

At this point, the program shows me that I currently have /bin/csh as my login shell and asks me to specify an alternative shell. I'll try to confuse it by requesting that EMACS become my login shell:

```
% chsh
Changing login shell for taylor.
Old shell: /bin/csh
New shell: /usr/local/bin/gnuemacs
/usr/local/bin/gnuemacs is unacceptable as a new shell.
%
```

4. The program has some knowledge of valid shell names, and it requires you to specify one. Unfortunately, it doesn't divulge that information, so typing ? to find what's available results in the program complaining that ? is unacceptable as a new shell.

You can, however, peek into the file that chsh uses to confirm which programs are valid shells. It's called /etc/shells and looks like this:

```
% cat /etc/shells
/bin/ksh
/bin/sh
/bin/csh
/usr/local/bin/ksh
/usr/local/bin/tcsh
%
```

I'll change my shell from /bin/csh to /usr/local/bin/tcsh:

```
% chsh
Changing login shell for taylor
Old shell: /bin/csh
New shell: /usr/local/bin/tcsh
%
```

Notice that, in typical UNIX style, there is no actual confirmation that anything was done. I conclude that because I did not get any error messages, the program worked. Fortunately, I can easily check by either using `chsh` again or redoing the `awk` program with a C shell history command:

```
% !awk
awk -F: '{ if ($1 == "taylor") print "your shell is: "$7}' < /etc/passwd
your shell is: /usr/local/bin/tcsh
%
```

In the next lesson you will learn more about the powerful C shell command history mechanism.

Comment: Because of the overwhelming popularity of the C shell, the next few chapters will focus on the C shell. To get the most out of the chapters, I strongly recommend that you use the C shell.

5. A quick reinvocation of the `chsh` command changes my shell back to `/bin/csh`:

```
% chsh
Changing login shell for taylor
Old shell: /usr/local/bin/tcsh
New shell: /bin/csh
%
```

Comment: If you can't change your login shell, perhaps because of not having `chsh`, you can always enter C shell upon login by typing `csh`.

Step 3. Summary

It's easy to change your login shell. You can try different ones until you find the one that best suits your style of interaction. For the most part, though, they all have the same basic syntax and use the same commands: `ls -l` does the same thing in any shell. The differences, then, really come into play when you use the more sophisticated capabilities, including programming the shell (with shell scripts), customizing its features through command aliases, and saving on keystrokes using a history mechanism. That's where the C shell has an edge, and why it's so popular. It's easy, straightforward, and has powerful aliasing, history, and job control capabilities, as you will learn in the next lesson.

Task 13.4: Learning the Shell Environment
Step 1. Description

Earlier in this book, you used the env or printenv command to find out the various characteristics of your working environment. Now it's time to use this command again to look more closely at the C shell environment and define each of the variables therein.

Step 2. Action

1. To start out, I enter env to list the various aspects of my working environment. Do the same on your system, and, although your environment will not be identical to mine, there should be considerable similarity between the two.

```
% env ¦ cat -n
1   HOME=/users/taylor
2   SHELL=/bin/csh
3   TERM=vt100
4   USER=taylor
5   PATH=.:/users/taylor/bin:/bin:/usr/bin:/usr/ucb:/usr/local:/etc:
/usr/etc:/usr/local/bin:/usr/unsup/bin:
6   MAIL=/usr/spool/mail/taylor
7   LOGNAME=taylor
8   EDITOR=/ucb/bin/vi
9   NAME=Dave Taylor
10  EXINIT=:set ignorecase
11  RNINIT=-hmessage -hreference -hdate-r -hsender -hsummary -hreply
 -hdistr -hlines -hline -hfollow -hnews -hkey -hresent -hreturn -hto
 -hx-original -hx-sun -hx-note -horiginator -hnntp
12  SUBJLINE=%t -- %s
13  ORGANIZATION=Educational Computing group, School of Education
%
```

This probably initially seems pretty overwhelming. What *are* all these things, and why on earth should they matter? They matter because it's important for you to learn exactly how your own environment is set up so that you can change things if you desire. As you will soon be able to recognize, I have modified much of my system's environment so that the C shell does what I want it to do, rather than what its default would tell it to do.

2. When I log in to the system, the system defines some environment variables, indicating where my home directory is located, what shell I'm running, and so on. These variables are listed in Table 13.1.

Table 13.1. Default variables set by UNIX upon login.

Variable	Explanation
HOME	This is my home directory, obtained from the fourth field of the password file. Try `grep $USER /etc/passwd ¦ awk -F: '{print $6}'` to see what your home directory is set to, or just use `env HOME` or `echo $HOME`. This is not only the directory that I start within, but it's also the directory that `cd` moves me back to when I don't specify a different directory. My HOME variable is `/users/taylor`.
SHELL	When UNIX programs, such as `vi`, process the `!` command to execute UNIX commands, they check this variable to see which shell I'm using. If I were to type `:!` followed by Return in `vi`, the program would create a new C shell for me. If I had `SHELL=/bin/sh`, `vi` would start up a Bourne shell. My SHELL variable is set to `/bin/csh`.
TERM	By default, your terminal is defined by the value of this environment variable, which starts out as `unknown`. (Remember that when you were first learning about `vi`, the program would complain `unknown: terminal not known`.) Many sites know what kind of terminals are using which lines, however, so this variable is often set to the correct value before you even see it. If not, you can define it to the appropriate value within your `.login` file. (You will learn to do this.) My TERM is set to `vt100`, for a Digital Equipment Corporation Visual Terminal model 100, which is probably the most commonly emulated terminal in communications packages.
USER	Programs can quickly look up your user identification number and match it with an account name. However, predefining your account name as an environment setting saves time. That's exactly what this, and its companion LOGNAME, are. My USER is set to `taylor`.

Variable	Explanation
PATH	A few days ago, you learned that the UNIX shell finds a command by searching from directory to directory until it finds a match. The environment variable that defines which directories to search *and the order in which to search them* is the PATH variable. Rather than keep the default settings, I've added a number of additional directories to my search path, which is now `.:/users/taylor/bin:/bin:/usr/bin: /usr/ucb:/usr/local:/etc:/usr/etc:/usr/local/bin:/usr/unsup/bin:`. I have told the shell always to look first for commands in the current directory (`.`), then in my bin directory (`/users/taylor/bin`), then in the standard system directories (`/bin`, `/usr/bin`, `/usr/ucb`, `/usr/local`). If the commands are not found in any of those areas, the shell should try looking in some unusual directories (`/etc`, `/usr/etc`, `/usr/local/bin`). If the shell still has not found my command, it should check in a weird directory specific to my site: `/usr/unsup/bin` for unsupported software.
MAIL	One of the most exciting and enjoyable aspects of UNIX is its powerful and incredibly well-connected electronic mail capability. A variety of programs can be used to check for new mail, to read mail, and to send mail messages. Most of these programs need to know where my default incoming mailbox is located, which is what the MAIL environment variable defines. My MAIL is set to `/usr/spool/mail/taylor`.
LOGNAME	The LOGNAME is a synonym for USER. My LOGNAME is set to `taylor`.
NAME	In addition to wanting to know the name of the current account, some programs, such as many electronic mail and printing programs, need to ascertain my full, human name. The NAME variable contains this information for the environment. It's obtained from the `/etc/passwd` file. You can check yours with the command `grep $USER /etc/passwd ¦ awk -F: '{print $5}'`. You can change your NAME variable, if desired, using the chfn, or *change full name*, command. My NAME is set to `Dave Taylor`.

Don't Skip This: I admit it, using . as the first entry in the PATH variable is a security hazard. Why? Imagine this: A devious chap has written a program that will do bad things to my directory when I invoke that bad program. But how will he make me invoke it? The easiest way is to give the bad program the same name as a standard UNIX utility, such as ls, and leave it in a commonly accessed directory, such as /tmp. So what happens? Imagine that the . (current directory) is the *first* entry in my PATH, and I change directories to /tmp to check something. While I'm in /tmp I enter ls without thinking, and voila! I've run the bad program without knowing it. Having the . at the end of the search path would avoid all this, because then the default ls command is the correct version. I have it because I often *do* want to override the std commands with new ones that I'm working on (an admittedly foolish practice).

Comment: Having both LOGNAME and USER defined in my environment demonstrates how far UNIX has progressed since the competition and jostling between the Berkeley and AT&T versions (BSD and SVR3, respectively) of UNIX. Back when I started working with UNIX, if I was on a BSD system, the account name would be defined as LOGNAME, and if I used an SVR3 system, the account name would be defined as USER. Programs had to check for both, which was frustrating. Over time, each system has begun to use both terms (instead of using the solution that you and I might think is most obvious, that is, to agree on a single word).

3. A glance back at the output of the env command reveals that there are more variables in my environment than are listed in Table 13.1. That's because you can define *anything* you want in the environment. Certain programs can read many environment variables that customize their behavior.

   Many UNIX programs allow you to enter text directly, then spin off into an editor, if needed. Others start your favorite editor for entering information. Both types of programs use the EDITOR environment variable to identify which editor to use. I have mine set to /usr/ucb/vi.

   You learned earlier that vi can have default information stored in the .exrc file, but the program can also read configuration information from the environment variable EXINIT. To make all my pattern searches "case insensitive" (that is, searching for *precision* will match *Precision*), I set the appropriate vi variable in the EXINIT. Mine is set to :set ignorecase. If you want line numbers to show up always, you could easily have your EXINIT set to :set number.

Another program that I use frequently is rn, or *read Netnews*. If electronic mail is the electronic equivalent of letters and magazines that you receive through the postal service, then *Netnews* is the electronic equivalent of a super bulletin board. The difference is that there are thousands of different boards, and any time a note is tacked onto any board, copies of the note shoot to other UNIX systems throughout the world. You will learn more about this exciting aspect of UNIX on the last day of *Teach Yourself UNIX in a Week*. For now, you can see that I have three environment variables all defined for the rn program: RNINIT, my personal rn configuration options; SUBJLINE, indicating the format for displaying summary subject lines of new messages; and ORGANIZATION, indicating exactly what organization I'm associated with on this system.

They are set as shown earlier.

Step 3. Summary

There are many different possible environment variables that you can define for yourself. Most large UNIX programs have environment variables of their own, allowing you to tailor the program's behavior to your needs and preferences. UNIX itself has quite a few environment variables, too. Until you're an expert, however, I recommend that you stick with viewing these variables and ensuring that they have reasonable values, rather than changing them. Particularly focus on the set of variables defined in Table 13.1. If they're wrong, it could be trouble, whereas if other environment variables are wrong, it's probably not going to be too much trouble.

Task 13.5: Exploring *csh* Configuration Files
Step 1. Description

The C shell uses two files to configure itself, and, though neither of them need be present, both can probably be found in your home directory: .login and .cshrc. The difference between them is subtle, but very important. The .login file is read *once only, when you log in,* and the .cshrc file is read *every time a C shell is started.* As a result, if you're working in vi, and you enter :!ls, vi carries out the command by starting up a new shell and then feeding the command to that shell. Therefore, new csh shells started from within programs such as vi won't see key shell configurations that are started in .login.

This split between two configuration files isn't too bad, actually, because many modifications to the environment are automatically included in all subshells invoked. To be specific, all environment variables are pervasive, but any C shell command aliases are lost, and therefore must be defined in the .cshrc file to be available upon all occurrences of csh. You will learn more about command aliases in the C shell in the next lesson.

Step 2. Action

1. To begin, I use cat to list the contents of my .login file. Remember that any line beginning with a # is a comment and is ignored.

```
% cat .login
#
# @(#) $Revision: 62.2 $

setenv TERM vt100

stty erase "^H" kill "^U" intr "^C" eof "^D"
stty crtbs crterase            # special DYNIX stuff for bs processing

# shell vars

set noclobber history=100 savehist=50 filec

# set up some global environment variables...

setenv EXINIT ":set ignorecase"

# Some RN related variables...

setenv RNINIT        "-hmessage -hreference -hdate-r -hsender -hsummary -
hreply
-hdistr -hlines -hline -hfollow -hnews -hkey -hresent -hreturn -hto
 -hx-original -hx-sun -hx-note -horiginator -hnntp"
setenv SUBJLINE      "%t -- %s"
setenv ORGANIZATION  "Educational Computing group, School of Education
"

setenv NAME "Dave Taylor"

newmail

mesg y
%
```

This is pretty straightforward, once you remove all the comments. Three different kinds of environmental configuration commands are shown: setenv, stty, and set. The setenv command defines environment variables; indeed, you can see that many of the variables shown in the previous unit are defined in my .login file.

I can use `stty` commands to set specific configuration options related to my terminal (`stty` stands for *set tty driver options*). I use this to ensure that `^h` is erase (backspace), `^u` is a convenient shortcut allowing me to kill an entire line, and `^c` sends an interrupt to a running program. I indicate the end of a file (`eof`) with `^d`. The second line of the preceding output example indicates that my `crt` is capable of backspacing and erasing characters on the display.

Comment: Here's more arcane UNIX nomenclature: `crt` (as used in `stty crtbs` or cathode-ray tube) is the technology used in the screen of a standard terminal. A terminal is not accurate anymore, however, because the command `stty crtbs` also will work on my `lcd` (liquid-crystal diode, if you must know) laptop.

Finally, the `set` commands are configuration options for the C shell. I have told the C shell to warn me before it overwrites existing files with file redirection (`noclobber`), to remember the last 100 commands (`history=100`), and to remember 50 of those even if I log out and log back in (`savehist=50`). I also want the C shell to try, if possible, to complete filenames for me, hence the `filec` addition. Notice that there are two different types of settings: on/off options (`noclobber`, `filec`), and options to which I must assign a specific numeric value (`history`, `savehist`).

The two commands at the very end of the login file are invoked as if I'd entered them on the command line. The `newmail` variable watches for new electronic mail (in the mailbox defined by the environment variable `MAIL`, in fact) and tells me when it arrives. The `mesg y` variable makes sure that I have my terminal configured so that other folks can beep me or say hello using `write` or `talk`. (You will learn about both of them later today.)

2. How about the other file, the one that's read by the C shell each time a shell is started?

```
% cat .cshrc
#
# Default user .cshrc file (/bin/csh initialization).

set path=(. ~/bin /bin /usr/bin /usr/ucb /usr/local /etc /usr/etc
/usr/local/bin /usr/unsup/bin /

# Define a bunch of C shell aliases
```

```
alias   diff     '/usr/bin/diff -c -w'
alias   env      'printenv'
alias   from     'frm -n'
alias   info     ssinfo
alias   library  'echo " "; echo " " ; echo "remember: ^J is ENTER";
tn3270 lib
alias   ll       'ls -l'
alias   ls       '/bin/ls -F'
alias   mail     Mail
alias   mailq    '/usr/lib/sendmail -bp'
alias   newaliases 'echo you mean newalias...'
alias   rd       'readmsg $ ¦ page'
alias   rn       '/usr/local/bin/rn -d$HOME -L -M -m -e -S -/'
alias   ssinfo   'echo "connecting..." ; rlogin oasis'

# and some special stuff if we're in an interactive shell

if ( $?prompt ) then              # shell is interactive.

  alias   cd               'chdir \!* ; setprompt'
  alias   setprompt        'set prompt="$system ($cwd:t) \! : "'

  set noclobber history=100 system=mentor filec
  umask 007

  setprompt
endif

%
```

Again, any line that begins with a # is considered a comment. There are, therefore, two primary types of commands in this script: the C shell environment modification (set) and the command alias (alias). The first defines the PATH I want to use, although in a format slightly different from the colon-separated list shown by env. The csh command always ensures that the environment variable and shell variable match, so although I opt to change the path here as a set, I could just as easily use setenv PATH.

You will learn all about aliases in the next lesson, but for now you should know that the format is alias *word command (or commands) to execute.* When I enter ls, for example, you can see that the shell has that aliased to /bin/ls -F, which saves me from having to type the -F flag each time.

The C shell also has conditional statements and a variety of other control flow options. Here I'm using the if *(expression)* then to define a set of commands that should be used only when the shell is interactive (that is, I'm going to be able to enter commands). An example of a noninteractive shell is the shell vi uses to create a listing when I enter !!ls within the editor. The $?prompt notation is true if there is a prompt defined for the shell (it's interactive). If not, then the condition is false, and the shell zips to the endif before resuming execution of the commands.

If it is an interactive shell, however, I create a few further aliases and again define some C shell configuration options, to ensure that the options are always set in *subshells*. The umask value is set, and I then invoke setprompt, which is a command alias that runs the command set prompt="$system ($cwd:t) \! : ".

Step 3. Summary

If you're thinking that there are a variety of ways to configure the shell, you are correct. You can have an incredibly diverse set of commands in both your .login and .cshrc files, allowing you to customize many aspects of the C shell and the UNIX environment. If you use either the Bourne shell or the Korn shell, the configuration information is kept in a similar file called .profile.

Lesson Summary

Armed with the information learned in this chapter about shells and shell environments, explore your own enviroment and examine your .login and .cshrc files, too.

Workshop
Key Terms

case insensitive	Something that treats upper- and lowercase letters identically, especially in searching.
command alias	A shorthand command mapping, with which you can define new command names that are *aliases* of other commands or sequences of commands. This is helpful for renaming commands so that you can remember them, or for having certain flags added by default.
command history	A mechanism for remembering what commands you have entered already, and for repeating them without having to enter them again.
job control	A mechanism for managing the various programs that are running. Job control enables you to push programs into the background and pull them back into the foreground as desired.
login shell	The shell you use, by default, when you log in to the system.
subshell	A shell other than the login shell.

Questions

1. Draw lines to connect the original shells with their newer variants:

   sh   ksh   tcsh   csh

2. What does chsh do? What about chfn?

3. What shell are you running? What shells are your friends on the system running?

4. What's the difference between the .login and the .cshrc files?

5. What's the sh equivalent of the csh .login file?

6. What aliases do you think could prove helpful for your daily UNIX interaction?

Preview of the Next Chapter

I hope this lesson has whetted your appetite for learning more about the C shell! In the next chapter, you will learn how to customize the shell and make your interaction with UNIX quite a bit easier. Topics include how to create command aliases, how to use the history mechanism, and how to create simple shell scripts when aliases just don't suffice.

Getting the Most out of C Shell

The last lesson gave you an overview of the different shells available in UNIX. There are quite a few, but the C shell, originally from Berkeley, California, is the most popular shell at most sites. In this lesson, you will learn all about the C shell and how to use it to your best advantage. The goal is for you to be able to customize your UNIX environment to fit your working style.

Goals for This Lesson

In this lesson, you will learn

☐ How to turn on the C shell and Korn shell history mechanism

☐ How to use csh history and ksh history to cut down on typing

☐ About command aliases in the C and Korn shells

☐ Some power aliases for csh

☐ How to set custom prompts

☐ How to create simple shell scripts

This lesson focuses on two key facets of the C and Korn shells: the history mechanism and the command alias capability. I guarantee that within a few minutes of learning about these two functions, it will be clear that you couldn't have survived as happily in UNIX without them. There are three ways to ensure that you don't enter commands more than once: csh history enables you to repeat previous commands without re-entering them, an alias enables you to name one command as another, and shell scripts enable you to toss a bunch of commands into a file to be used as a single command. You will learn the basics about building shell scripts in this lesson.

One of the fun parts of UNIX is that you can customize the prompt that greets you each time you use the system. There's no need to be trapped with a boring % prompt anymore!

Task 14.1: The C Shell and Korn Shell
History Mechanisms
Step 1. Description

If you went through school in the United States, you have doubtless heard the aphorism, "Those who do not study history are doomed to repeat it." UNIX stands this concept on its head. For UNIX, the aphorism is best stated, "Those who are aware of their history can easily repeat it."

Both the C shell and the Korn shell build a table of commands as you enter them and assigns them a command number. Each time you login, the first command you enter is command 1, and the command number is incremented for each subsequent command you enter. You can easily review or repeat any previous command with just a few keystrokes.

To review your history in the C shell, enter `history` at the `csh` prompt. Odds are that nothing will happen, though, because by default `csh` remembers only the very last command. To have it begin building a list of commands, you must turn on this feature through an environment setting `set history=`*n*, where *n* is the number of commands you'd like it to recall.

By contrast, `ksh` has a default history list size of 128 commands, plenty for anyone. To review your history in `ksh`, you also can use the `history` command. Actually, though, it's an alias, and the real command is the more cryptic `fc -l`.

Step 2. Action

1. Log in to your system so that you have a C shell prompt. If you're currently in the Bourne shell, this would be a great time to use `chsh` to change shells.

   ```
   % history
   %
   ```

   The shell indicates that it has no history. Sir Winston Churchill would doubtless shake his head and mutter under his breath, "To have become such a sophisticated operating system yet never to have studied history!"

2. I need to turn on the shell history mechanism, so I will enter the following command:

   ```
   % set history=100
   %
   ```

   Still there is no feedback, but I can check the status of all the shell parameters by entering `set` at the `csh` prompt:

   ```
   % set
   argv     ()
   cwd      /users/taylor
   filec
   history  100
   home     /users/taylor
   host     limbo
   noclobber
   path     (. /users/taylor/bin /bin /usr/bin /usr/ucb /usr/local /etc
   /usr/etc /usr/local/bin /usr/unsup/bin
   savehist       50
   shell    /bin/csh
   ```

```
status  0
system  limbo
term    unknown
user    taylor
%
```

3. To take a break, I use w to see who is logged on and what they're doing, then
   ls to check my files again, and date to see if my watch is working:

```
% w | head
  11:41am  up 17:59, 103 users,  load average: 0.54, 0.53, 0.49
User     tty      login@ idle   JCPU   PCPU  what
root     console  6:02pm 12:13     1      1  -csh
taylor   ttyAf    11:40am          5      2  w
bev      ttyAg    9:25am    14  1:09      3  -csh
rekunkel ttyAh    11:37am          4      3  rlogin ccn
gabh     ttyAi    10:41am    6    46     16  talk dorits
af5      ttyAj    8:27am     21   33      1  -ksh
techman  ttyAk    9:47am          25      7  gopher
tuccie   ttyAl    11:37am          1      1  mail
Broken pipe
% ls
Archives/        OWL/              buckaroo.confused  sample
InfoWorld/       awkscript         dickens.note       sample2
Mail/            bin/              keylime.pie        src/
News/            buckaroo          owl.c              temp/
% date
Tue Dec  7 11:41:29 EST 1993
%
```

Comment: Notice that at the end of the w command output the system
noted Broken pipe. This is nothing to be anxious about; it's just an
indication that there was lots more in the pipeline when the program
quit. You can see that head only read the first ten lines. The first line of
the w output shows that there are 103 users on the system, which means
that head ignored 94 lines of output. Unlike real plumbing, fortunately,
this broken pipe doesn't allow the spare data to spill onto the basement
floor!

4. Now if I enter history, the shell remembers the previous commands,
   presenting them all in a neat, numbered list:

```
% history
     1  set history=100
     2  w | head
     3  ls
     4  date
     5  history
%
```

5. To turn this on permanently, add the `set history` command to your
   `.cshrc`. If you want the shell to remember commands even if you log out
   and log back in, also specify the setting `savehist`. I choose to do this by
   entering `vi +$ .cshrc` and adding the following line:

```
    set noclobber system=limbo filec
    umask 007

    setprompt
endif

set history=100 savehist=50 _
~
~
```

If you glance back at the output of the `set` command, you can see that I
already have both of these parameters set: 100 commands will remain in the
history list while I'm working, and 50 commands will be remembered next
time I log in. What's particularly helpful is that any time I specify a number
n for either history list, the shell actually saves the most recent n commands,
so I have the most recent 100 commands for review while I'm using the
system, and the 50 most recent commands remembered when I log in later.

Make this change to your `.cshrc` file, log out, and log in again to ensure that
your history mechanism is set up correctly.

Step 3. Summary

Like much of UNIX, turning on the history mechanism of the C shell is quite easy
once you learn the trick. In this case, simply remember that you need to specify a `set`
`history` value to have the shell begin remembering what's going on with your
interaction. In Korn shell, you don't need to make *any* changes; it's ready to use
immediately.

Task 14.2: Using History to Cut Down on Typing
Step 1. Description

There are three main mechanisms for working with the history list. You can specify
a previous command by its *command number*, by the first word of the command, or,
if you're working with the most recently executed command, by a special notation
that easily fixes any mistakes you might have made as you typed it.

Every history command begins with an exclamation point. If the 33rd command you entered was the who command, for example, you can execute it by referring to its command number. Enter !33 at the command line. You can execute it also by entering one or more characters of the command: !w, !wh, or !who.

To edit a previous command, type a caret, the pattern you want to change, another caret, and the correct pattern. If you just entered awk -F, '{print $2}' and realized that you meant to type a colon, not a comma, as the field delimiter, then ^,^: will do the trick.

A very useful shorthand is !!, which repeats the most recently executed command. Two other history references are valuable to know: !$ expands to the last word of the previous line (which makes sense because $ always refers to the end of something, whether it be a line, the file, or, in this case, a command), and !* expands to all the words in the previous command except the very first.

Korn shell offers all of this and more. You can repeat commands by number by specifying rn, where n is the command number (for example, r33). You can also repeat by name with r name, as in r who to repeat the most recent who command. Much more useful is the ksh capability to edit directly a command with the familiar vi or EMACS command keys, without leaving the command line. Without any arguments, r will repeat the previous command.

Step 2. Action

1. First I need to spend a few minutes building up a history list by running various commands:

```
% w | head
  11:58am  up 18:15,  81 users,  load average: 0.54, 0.44, 0.38
  User     tty      login@ idle   JCPU   PCPU  what
  root     console  6:02pm 12:30     1      1  -csh
  hopkins  ttyAe    11:49am          4      4  telnet whip.isca.uiowa.edu
  taylor   ttyAf    11:40am          8      2  w
  bev      ttyAg    9:25am    31   1:09      3  -csh
  af5      ttyAj    8:27am    37     33      1  -ksh
  techman  ttyAk    9:47am     4   1:11      4  elm
  tuccie   ttyAl    11:37am           2      1  mail
  trice    ttyAm    8:16am  1:21      5      2  -csh
  Broken pipe
% date
Tue Dec  7 11:58:19 EST 1993
% ls
Archives/        OWL/              buckaroo.confused  sample
InfoWorld/       awkscript         dickens.note       sample2
Mail/            bin/              keylime.pie        src/
News/            buckaroo          owl.c              temp/
% cat buckaroo
```

```
I found myself stealing a peek at my own watch and overhead
General Catbird's
aide give him the latest.
"He's not even here," went the conversation.
"Banzai."
"Where the hell is he?"
"At the hospital in El Paso."
"What? Why weren't we informed? What's wrong with him?"
%
```

2. Now I will check my history list to see what commands are squirreled away for later:

```
% history
    51  set history=100
    52  history
    53  w ¦ head
    54  date
    55  ls
    56  cat buckaroo
    57  history
%
```

Comment: I already have my history mechanism turned on, so my commands begin numbering with 51 rather than with 1. Your system might be different. Regardless of what the command numbers are, they'll work!

14

3. To repeat the date command, I can specify its command number:

```
% !54
date
Tue Dec  7 12:04:08 EST 1993
%
```

Notice that the shell shows the command I've entered as command number 54. The ksh equivalent here would be r 54.

4. A second way to accomplish this repeat, a way that is much easier, is to specify the first letter of the command:

```
% !w
w ¦ head
 12:05pm  up 18:23,  87 users,  load average: 0.40, 0.39, 0.33
User     tty      login@ idle   JCPU   PCPU  what
root     console  6:02pm 12:37    1      1   -csh
lloyds   ttyAb    12:05pm         1      1   mail windberg
lusk     ttyAc    12:03pm         3      2   gopher
hopkins  ttyAe    11:49am         8      8   telnet whip.isca.uiowa.edu
taylor   ttyAf    11:40am    1   14      3   w
bev      ttyAg    9:25am    38  1:09     3   -csh
```

```
libphar  ttyAh    12:03pm        3      3   elm
dgrove   ttyAi    12:02pm        5      2   more inbox/16
Broken pipe
%
```

5. Now glance at the history list:

```
% history
    51   set history=100
    52   history
    53   w ¦ head
    54   date
    55   ls
    56   cat buckaroo
    57   history
    58   date
    59   w ¦ head
    60   history
%
```

Commands expanded by the history mechanism are stored as the expanded command, not as the history command that was actually entered. Thus, this is an exception to the earlier rule that the history mechanism always shows what was previously entered. It's an eminently helpful exception! History commands are quite helpful for people working on a software program. The most common cycle for programmers to repeat is edit-compile-run, over and over again. The commands UNIX programmers use most often will probably look something like vi test.c, cc -o test test.c, and test to edit, compile, and run the program. Using the C shell history mechanism, a programmer can easily enter !v to edit the file, !c to compile it, then !t to test it. As your commands become longer and more complex, this function proves more and more helpful.

6. It's time to experiment a bit with file wildcards.

```
% ls
Archives          awkscript           dickens.note       src
InfoWorld         bin                 keylime.pie        temp
Mail              buckaroo            owl.c
News              buckaroo.confused   sample
OWL               cshrc               sample2
%
```

Oops! I meant to specify the -F flag to ls. I can use !! to repeat the command, then I can add the flag:

```
% !! -F
ls -F
Archives/         awkscript           dickens.note       src/
InfoWorld/        bin/                keylime.pie        temp/
Mail/             buckaroo            owl.c
News/             buckaroo.confused   sample
OWL/              cshrc               sample2
%
```

> **Comment:** The general idea of all these history mechanisms is that you
> specify a pattern that is replaced by the appropriate command in the
> history list. So you could enter `echo !!` to have the system echo the last
> command, and it would end up echoing twice. Try it.

> **Comment:** Korn shell users will find that `echo !!` produces `!!` and that
> the `ksh` repeat last command of `r` will also fail. If your last command was
> `echo r`, the result will be `r`. Further, there is no analogous shorthand to
> the convenient `!!` `-F` in `csh`. Alternatively, if `FCEDIT` is set to `vi` or
> EMACS, you can go into the editor to alter the command by typing `fc`.

I want to figure out a pattern or two that will let me specify both `buckaroo`
files, the `dickens` file, and `sample2`, but not `sample`. This is a fine example of
where the `echo` command can be helpful:

```
% echo b* d* s*
bin buckaroo buckaroo.confused dickens.note sample sample2 src
```

That's not quite it. I'll try again:

```
% echo bu* d* sa*
buckaroo buckaroo.confused dickens.note sample sample2
```

That's closer. Now I just need to remove the `sample` file:

```
% echo bu* d* sa*2
buckaroo buckaroo.confused dickens.note sample2
```

That's it. Now I want to compute the number of lines in each of these files.
If I use the `csh` history mechanism, I can avoid having to enter the filenames
again:

```
% wc -l !*
wc -l bu* d* sa*2
     36 buckaroo
     11 buckaroo.confused
     28 dickens.note
      4 sample2
     79 total
%
```

Notice that the `!*` expanded to the entire previous command *except the very
first word.*

7. What happens if I use !$ instead?

```
% wc -l !$
wc -l sa*2
        4 sample2
%
```

8. In the middle of doing all this, I became curious about how many people on my system have first names four letters long. Is this impossible to compute? Not with UNIX!

The first step is to extract the full names from the /etc/passwd file:

```
% awk -F: '{ print $5 }'
```

The system does not respond. I forgot to specify the filename!

```
% !! < /etc/passwd
awk -F: '{print $5}' < /etc/passwd
limbo root,,,,
USENET News,,,,
INGRES Manager,,,,
(1000 user system) DO NOT,,,,
Vanilla Account,,,,
The Ferryman,,,,
```

I can use ^c to stop this output, because I've seen enough to know that it's what I want. Next I use awk again to pull just the first names out of this list:

```
% !! | awk '{print $1}'
awk -F: '{print $5}' < /etc/passwd | awk '{print $1}'
root
USENET
INGRES
(1000
Vanilla
The
Account
^c
%
```

It looks okay. Now the final step: I need to revise this awk script to look at the length of each name, and only output the name if it's four letters long:

```
% !-2 | awk '{ if (lng($1) == 4) print $0 }'
awk -F: '{print $5}' < /etc/passwd | awk '{ if (lng($1) == 4) print $0 }'
%
```

I got no output at all! The reason is that I mistyped length as lng. Fortunately, to fix this is simplicity itself with C shell history commands. Remember, the format is ^old^new:

```
% ^lng^length
awk -F: '{print $5}' < /etc/passwd ¦ awk '{ if (length($1) == 4) print $0 }'
,,,,
Paul Town,,,,
Pete Cheese,,,,
John Smith,,,,
Dana Tott,,,,
Dick Ply,,,,
Mike Moliak,,,,
Bill Born,,,,
Dale Tott,,,,
Bill Rison,,,,
Gary Flint,,,,
Doug Sherwood,,,,
Ruth Raffy,,,,
Dave Sean,,,,
^c
%
```

That's very close. I just need to pipe the output of this command to wc:

```
% !! ¦ wc -l
awk -F: '{print $5}' < /etc/passwd ¦ awk '{ if (length($1) == 4) print
$0 }' ¦ wc -l
     723
%
```

9. If you are using Korn shell, here's where it shines! Make sure that the environment variable EDITOR is set to your preferred editor:

```
$ echo $EDITOR
vi
$
```

14

Now any time you're entering a command, you can press the ESC key and be in ksh history-edit command mode. The usual vi commands work, including h and l to move back and forth; i and ESC to enter and leave insert mode; w, W, b, and B to zip about by words; and 0 and $ to move to the beginning or end of the line.

Much more useful are k and j, which replace the current command with the previous or next, enabling you to zip through the history list.

If I'd just entered who and then ls, to append ¦ wc -l to the who command, I could press the ESC key:

```
$_.
```

Now each time I press k, I will see the previous command. Pressing k once reveals this:

```
$ls
```

Pressing k a second time reveals this:

```
$who
```

That's the right command, so $ moves the cursor to the end of the line:

```
$who
```

Pressing a appends, at which point I can add ¦ wc -1 like this:

```
$who ¦ wc -1
```

Pressing Return results in ksh actually executing the command:

```
$ who ¦ wc -1
    130
$_
```

Step 3. Summary

The history mechanisms of the shells are wonderful timesavers when you're working with files. I find myself using the csh !! and !*word* mechanisms daily either to build up complex commands (such as the previous example, in which I built up a very complex command, step by step), or to repeat the most recently used edit commands. Table 14.1 summarizes the different csh history mechanisms available. I encourage you to learn and use them. They will soon become second nature and will save you lots of typing.

Table 14.1. C shell history commands.

Command	Function
!!	Repeat previous command.
!$	Repeat last word of previous command.
!*	Repeat all but the first word of previous command.
^a^b	Replace *a* with *b* in previous command.
!*n*	Repeat command *n* from the history list.

Task 14.3: Command Aliases
Step 1. Description

If you think the history mechanism has the potential to save you typing, you just haven't learned about the command alias mechanism in the Korn and C shells. Using aliases, you can define new commands that do whatever you'd like, or redefine existing commands to work differently, have different default flags, and more!

The general format for using the alias mechanism in csh is alias *word command-sequence* and alias *word=commands* in ksh. If you enter alias without any specified words, the output will show a list of aliases you have defined. If you enter alias *word* in csh, the output will list the current alias, if there is one, for the specified word.

Step 2. Action

1. One of the most helpful aliases you can create specifies certain flags to ls so that each time you enter ls, the output will look as though you used the flags with the command. I like to have the -FC flags set.

```
% ls
Archives            awkscript            dickens.note        src
InfoWorld           bin                 keylime.pie         temp
Mail                buckaroo            owl.c
News                buckaroo.confused   sample
OWL                 cshrc               sample2
%
```

   Now I'll try to create a C shell alias and try it again:

```
% alias ls 'ls -CF'
% ls
Archives/           awkscript           dickens.note        src/
InfoWorld/          bin/                keylime.pie         temp/
Mail/               buckaroo            owl.c
News/               buckaroo.confused   sample
OWL/                cshrc               sample2
```

   This is very helpful!

   The ksh equivalent would be alias ls = 'ls -CF'.

2. If you're coming from the DOS world, you might have found some of the UNIX file commands confusing. In DOS, for example, you use DIR to list directories, REN to rename files, COPY to copy them, and so on. With aliases, you can re-create all those commands, mapping them to specific UNIX equivalents:

```
% alias DIR 'ls -lF'
% alias REN 'mv'
% alias COPY 'cp -i'
% alias DEL 'rm -i'
% DIR
total 33
drwx------    2 taylor          512 Nov 21 10:39 Archives/
drwx------    3 taylor          512 Dec  3 02:03 InfoWorld/
drwx------    2 taylor         1024 Dec  3 01:43 Mail/
drwx------    2 taylor          512 Oct  6 09:36 News/
drwx------    4 taylor          532 Dec  6 18:31 OWL/
-rw-rw----    1 taylor          126 Dec  3 16:34 awkscript
drwx------    2 taylor          512 Oct 13 10:45 bin/
-rw-rw----    1 taylor         1393 Dec  5 18:48 buckaroo
```

14

```
-rw-rw----  1 taylor      458 Dec   4 23:22 buckaroo.confused
-rw-------  1 taylor     1339 Dec   2 10:30 cshrc
-rw-rw----  1 taylor     1123 Dec   5 18:16 dickens.note
-rw-rw----  1 taylor    12556 Nov  16 09:49 keylime.pie
-rw-rw----  1 taylor     8729 Dec   2 21:19 owl.c
-rw-rw----  1 taylor      199 Dec   3 16:11 sample
-rw-rw----  1 taylor      207 Dec   3 16:11 sample2
drwx------  2 taylor      512 Oct  13 10:45 src/
drwxrwx---  2 taylor      512 Nov   8 22:20 temp/
% COPY sample newsample
%
```

3. To see what aliases have been defined, use the `alias` command:

```
% alias
COPY    cp -i
DEL     rm -i
DIR     ls -1F
REN     mv
ls      ls -CF
%
```

4. You could improve the alias for DIR by having the output of `ls` fed directly into the `more` program, so that a directory listing with a lot of output will automatically pause at the end of each page. To redefine an alias, just define it again:

```
% alias DIR 'ls -1F ¦ more'
%
```

To confirm that the alias is set as you desire, try this:

```
% alias DIR
DIR     ls -1F ¦ more
%
```

Comment: If you're just defining one command with an alias, you don't really need to use the quotation marks around the command argument. But what would happen if you entered `alias DIR ls -1F ¦ more`? The alias would be set to `ls -1F` and the output of the `alias` command would be fed to the `more` program, which is quite different from what you desired. Therefore, it's just good form to use the quotation marks and a good habit to get into.

Step 3. Summary

Aliases are a great addition to any command shell, and with the arcane UNIX commands, they can also be used to define full-word commands as synonyms. For example, if you decide you'd like the simplicity of remembering only the command move to move a file somewhere else, you could add the new alias `alias move mv` to your .cshrc file if you're using C shell or `alias move=mv` to your .profile if you prefer Korn shell, and the shell would include a new command.

Task 14.4: Some Power Aliases

Step 1. Description

Because I have used the C shell for many years, I have created a variety of different aliases to help me work efficiently. A few of the best are shown in this section.

Step 2. Action

1. To see what aliases I have defined, I can use the same command I used earlier:

```
% alias
cd       chdir !* ; setprompt
diff     /usr/bin/diff -c -w
env      printenv
from     frm -n
info     ssinfo
library echo " "; echo " " ; echo "remember: ^J is ENTER"; tn3270 lib
ll       ls -l
ls       /bin/ls -F
mail     Mail
mailq    /usr/lib/sendmail -bp
netcom   echo Netcom login: taylor;rlogin netcom.com
newaliases       echo you mean newalias...
rd       readmsg $ ¦ page
rn       /usr/local/bin/rn -d$HOME -L -M -m -e -S -/
setprompt        set prompt="$system ($cwd:t) ! : "
ssinfo  echo "connecting..." ; rlogin oasis
sunworld         echo SunWorld login: taylor;rlogin sunworld.com
%
```

Remember that each of these aliases started out in my .cshrc file surrounded by single quote marks:

```
% grep alias .cshrc
alias  diff      '/usr/bin/diff -c -w'
alias  from      'frm -n'
alias  ll        'ls -l'
alias  ls        '/bin/ls -F'
alias  mail      Mail
alias  mailq     '/usr/lib/sendmail -bp'
alias  netcom    'echo Netcom login: taylor;rlogin netcom.com'
alias  sunworld 'echo SunWorld login: taylor;rlogin sunworld.com'
alias  newaliases 'echo you mean newalias...'
alias  rd        'readmsg $ ¦ page'
alias  rn        '/usr/local/bin/rn -d$HOME -L -M -m -e -S -/'
alias  cd                'chdir \!* ; setprompt'
```

14

```
alias   env              'printenv'
alias   setprompt        'set prompt="$system ($cwd:t) \! : "'
# special aliases:
alias info      ssinfo
alias ssinfo    'echo "connecting..." ; rlogin oasis'
alias library   'echo " "; echo " " ; echo "remember: ^J is ENTER";
tn3270 lib'
%
```

Also notice that the shell always keeps an alphabetically sorted list of aliases, regardless of the order in which they were defined.

2. Most of these aliases are easy to understand. For example, the first alias, `diff`, ensures that the command `diff` always has the default flags `-c` and `-w`. If I enter `from`, I want the system to invoke `frm -n`; if I enter `ll`, I want the system to invoke `ls -l`, and so on.

   Some commands can cause trouble if entered, so creating an alias for each of those commands is a good way to stay out of trouble. For example, I have an alias for `newaliases`; if I accidentally enter that command, the system gently reminds me that I probably meant to use the `newalias` command:

```
% newaliases
you mean newalias...
%
```

3. I have created aliases for connecting to accounts on other systems. I like to name each alias after the system to which I'm connecting (for example, `netcom, sunworld`):

```
% alias netcom
echo Netcom login: taylor;rlogin netcom.com
% alias sunworld
echo SunWorld login: taylor;rlogin sunworld.com
%
```

Don't Skip This: You can't enter `alias netcom sunworld` to list the netcom and sunworld aliases, because that command means to replace the alias for `netcom` with the command `sunworld`.

Separating commands with a semicolon is the UNIX way of having multiple commands on a single line, so when I enter the alias `netcom`, for example, it's as if I'd entered all these commands one after another:

```
echo Netcom login: taylor
rlogin netcom.com
```

4. Two aliases worth examining more closely are those for the `cd` and `setprompt` commands. As you will learn in a few moments, you can set your shell prompt to be just about any characters you'd like. (Hang on just a paragraph or two and you will learn all about what's occurring in the next example!) I like to have my prompt indicate where in the file system I'm currently working. To ensure that the prompt is always up to date, I simply alias the `cd` command so that each time I change directories, the prompt is recalculated.

```
% alias cd
chdir !* ; setprompt
% alias setprompt
set prompt="$system ($cwd:t) ! : "
%
```

 Comment: The `chdir` command does the same thing as `cd` and is intended for use within aliases as shown. So if you find `chdir` easier to remember than `cd`, you can use it instead.

Step 3. Summary

Aliases are what makes both the C shell and Korn shell such great command interfaces. I can, and do, easily customize the set of commands and the default flags (look at all the options I set as default values for the `rn` command). I even turn off some commands that I don't want to enter accidentally. Let your imagination run wild with aliases. If you decide you really like one and you're using `csh`, add the alias to your `.cshrc` so it's permanent (`.profile` if you're using `ksh`). If you want to turn off an alias, you can use `unalias command`, and it's gone until you log in again.

Task 14.5: Setting Custom Prompts
Step 1. Description

Up to this point, the command prompt I've seen is a boring `%`. It turns out that the C shell enables you to set your prompt to just about any possible value, with `set prompt="value"`.

The Korn shell equivalent is even easier: `PS1="value"`. Note that `PS1` must be all uppercase for this to work.

Step 2. Action

1. I'm getting tired of UNIX being so inhospitable. Fortunately I can easily change how it responds to me:

```
% set prompt="Yes, master? "
Yes, master?
```

That's more fun!

The ksh equivalent is PS1="Yes, master? "

2. There are a lot of things you can tuck away in your prompt that can be of great help. The first useful variable is cwd, which holds the current working directory:

```
Yes, master? set prompt="In $cwd, oh master: "
In /users/taylor, oh master:
```

What happens if I change directories?

```
In /users/taylor, oh master: cd /
In /users/taylor, oh master: pwd
/
In /users/taylor, oh master:
```

This is not so good. Now you can see why it's necessary to alias cd to maintain the prompt.

3. Some special ! values can be added to the prompt definition, as shown in Table 14.2.

Table 14.2. Special values for the system prompt.

Value	Expands to
`cmd`	the results of executing *cmd*.
\!	the current command number.
$var	the value of *var*.
$var:t	the *tail* of the value of *var*.

Here are a few examples of other C shell prompts and what happens when you use them:

```
In /, oh master: set prompt="(\!) % "
(132) %
```

The ksh equivalent is PS1="(\!) $ ".

The number in parentheses is the command number, as used by the C shell history mechanism:

```
(132) % echo hi
hi
(133) % ls News
mailing.lists.usenet  usenet.1                usenet.alt
(134) % !132
echo hi
hi
(135) %
```

Every time I log in, I automatically set the variable system to the name of the current computer:

```
(135) % set prompt="$system (\!) % "
limbo (136) %
```

I like to include in my prompt the basename of the current directory as shown in the following example. Also, I replace the percent sign with a colon, which is a bit easier to read. There is a slight problem, however; having a : instead of % means that I have to remember I'm in C shell (or Korn shell, as the case may be).

```
limbo (136) % set prompt="$system ($cwd:t) \! : "
limbo (taylor) 137 :
```

4. Now I glance back at the alias for setprompt and cd, with all these things in mind:

```
limbo (taylor) 139 : alias cd
chdir !* ; setprompt
limbo (taylor) 140 : alias setprompt
set prompt="$system ($cwd:t) ! : "
limbo (taylor) 141 :
```

You can see that the setprompt alias defines the C shell prompt as $system ($cwd:t) ! : ", although the actual line in the .cshrc file includes the backslash (as expected):

```
limbo (taylor) 141 : grep prompt= .cshrc
  alias  setprompt       'set prompt="$system ($cwd:t) \! : "'
limbo (taylor) 142 :
```

Each time I change directories, I use the combined commands of the cd alias (chdir !*) to change the current directory, then I use setprompt to compute the new prompt.

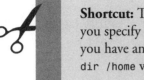

Shortcut: The !* notation in a shell alias expands to all the words you specify *after the alias word* on the command line. For example, if you have an alias for dir that is "echo !* ; ls !*", then entering dir /home will actually execute echo /home followed by ls /home.

Step 3. Summary

Experiment and find a set of variables to help you customize your UNIX prompt. I strongly recommend that you use command numbers to familiarize yourself with the history mechanism.

Task 14.6: Creating Simple Shell Scripts
Step 1. Description

The command alias capability is one helpful way to cut down on entering short commands time and again, but what if you have a series of five or ten commands that you often enter in sequence? That's where shell scripts help. At their simplest, shell scripts are a series of shell commands that appear in a file in exactly the order in which they'll be entered. If you change the permissions of the file to add execute permission, you can enter the name of the file as if it were just another UNIX command.

Step 2. Action

1. It's amazing how pervasive shell scripts are in UNIX. A listing of /bin and /usr/ucb on one system reveals that 13 and 17 commands in these files, respectively, are actually shell scripts:

```
limbo (taylor) 33: cd /bin
limbo (bin) 34 : file * ¦ grep script
68k:    executable shell script
false:  executable shell script
i386:   executable shell script
ns32000:        executable shell script
pblock: executable shell script
pdp11:  executable shell script
true:   executable shell script
u370:   executable shell script
u3b:    executable shell script
u3b10:  executable shell script
u3b2:   executable shell script
u3b5:   executable shell script
vax:    executable shell script
limbo (bin) 38 : cd /usr/ucb
limbo (ucb) 39 : file * ¦ grep script
msgs:   executable shell script
print:  executable c-shell script
script: SYMMETRY i386 executable (0 @ 0) version 1
```

```
tarmail:         shell script
trman:  executable shell script
uncompressdir:  shell script
untarmail:       shell script
vgrind: executable c-shell script
vpq:    executable c-shell script
vpr:    executable c-shell script
vprint: executable c-shell script
vprm:   executable c-shell script
vtroff: executable c-shell script
which:  executable c-shell script
zcmp:   shell script
zdiff:  shell script
zmore:  shell script
```

Shell scripts can be quite short. The script `/bin/true` is only one line:
`exit 0`. The script `/bin/false` contains the opposite command, and it, also,
contains only one line: `exit 1`. The helpful script `print` is also just one line:
`lpr -p $*`. Most of the others, however, are too complex to explain here.

2. Instead of examining these confusing scripts, I'll move to my own `bin`
   directory and consider a script or two that I have there:

```
limbo (ucb) 42 : cd
limbo (taylor) 43 : cd bin
limbo (bin) 44 : file *
bounce.msg:      executable shell script
calc:   SYMMETRY i386 executable (0 @ 0) not stripped version 1
fixit:  SYMMETRY i386 executable (0 @ 0) not stripped version 1
massage:         SYMMETRY i386 executable (0 @ 0) not stripped version 1
punt:   shell script
rumor.mill.sh:  shell script
say.hi: ascii text
limbo (bin) 45 : cat -n punt
     1  : Use /bin/sh
     2
     3  # Punt: punt a news article from within "rn" to yourself.
     4
     5  trap "/bin/rm -f /tmp/punt.$$" 0 1 9 15
     6
     7  SENDTO=taylor@netcom.com
     8
     9  cat - > /tmp/punt.$$
    10
    11  if [ "$1" != "" ] ; then
    12    ADDRESS=$1
    13  else
    14    ADDRESS=$SENDTO
    15  fi
    16
    17  /usr/lib/sendmail $ADDRESS < /tmp/punt.$$
    18
    19  echo Punted a `wc -l </tmp/punt.$$` line news article to $ADDRESS
    20
    21  exit 0
    22
```

14

This script is intended to be part of a pipeline, and it will send a copy of the stream of information either to the default address (SENDTO) or to a specified person ($1 is the first argument given to the script in this case). As shown earlier in the discussion of system prompts, any text that appears in backquotes is interpreted as a command, and executed. The results of that command are added in its place in the subsequent command. In this case, the echo command on line 19 computes the number of lines in the specified file, and that number is then included in the output, which typically looks like this: Punted a 17 line news article.

Comment: Notice that the very first character of this file is a colon. It turns out that the C shell only interprets scripts if the very first character of the script is a #. Otherwise it lets the Bourne shell (sh) run the commands, as in this case.

3. That's all well and interesting, but I want to create a new shell script. The first step is to make sure that I'm creating the script in a directory that is included in my search path (otherwise I won't be able to use the script as a command):

```
limbo (bin) 46 : pwd
/users/taylor/bin
limbo (bin) 47 : echo $PATH
.:/users/taylor/bin:/bin:/usr/bin:/usr/ucb:/usr/local:/etc:/usr/etc:
/usr/local/bin:/usr/unsup/bin (bin) 48 :
```

Here's a very simple shell script that shows how shell scripts can be of assistance:

```
limbo (bin) 86 : cat new.script
# sample shell script

echo searching for shell scripts
pwd
echo " "

file * ¦ grep script ¦ sed 's/:/ /' ¦ awk '{print $1}'

exit 0
```

This script lists the names of all files in the current directory which it identifies as shell scripts:

```
limbo (bin) 88 : chmod +x new.script
limbo (bin) 89 : new.script
searching for shell scripts
/users/taylor/bin

bounce.msg
locate
new.script
punt
rumor.mill.sh
```

To confirm that the new command works, look at what file reports about this same directory:

```
limbo (bin) 90 : file *
bounce.msg:      executable shell script
calc:   SYMMETRY i386 executable (0 @ 0) not stripped version 1
fixit:  SYMMETRY i386 executable (0 @ 0) not stripped version 1
locate: shell script
massage:         SYMMETRY i386 executable (0 @ 0) not stripped version 1
new.script:      commands text
punt:   shell script
rumor.mill.sh:   shell script
say.hi: ascii text
limbo (bin) 91 :
```

4. A more interesting script is one that can search through all the directories in my PATH, looking for any occurrences of a specified filename:

```
limbo (bin) 92 : cat locate
# locate - find copies of a file
#
# this should be run by the C shell

set name=$1

foreach directory (`echo $PATH | sed 's/:/ /g'`)
  if ( -f $directory/$name) then
    ls -l $directory/$name
  endif
end
```

The foreach loop is evaluated from the inside out. Because of the backquotes, my PATH is echoed to sed, which removes the colons separating the directories. Then the C shell goes through the foreach loop once for each directory in my PATH, setting the variable directory to the subsequent value. Each time through the loop, the -f test checks for the existence of the file: if the file exists in that directory, then ls -l lists some information about it.

14

> X **Comment:** Pay careful attention to the backquotes and single quotes in this script.

Here is `locate` at work:

```
limbo (bin) 93 : locate ls
-rwxr-xr-x  1 root        32768 May 29  1990 /bin/ls*
limbo (bin) 94 : locate vi
-rwxr-xr-t  7 root       163840 Nov 29  1990 /usr/ucb/vi*
limbo (bin) 95 :
```

Step 3. Summary

It would really take an entire book (or two!) to describe fully all the ins and outs of shell scripts. The main idea here, however, is that if you use a lot of commands repetitively, then you should make them into a command alias (if they're short) or drop them all into a shell script. In shell scripts, as in `awk`, `$1` is always the first argument, `$2` the second, and so on.

Lesson Summary

This lesson introduced you to many of the most powerful aspects of UNIX command shells. Practice creating aliases and working with the history list to minimize your typing. Also, you can now find a prompt you like and set it in your `.cshrc` or `.profile` (for `csh` and `ksh`, repsectively) so it will be the default.

Workshop
Key Terms

command number
The unique number by which the shell indexes all commands. You can place this number in your prompt using `\!` and use it with the history mechanism as `!command-number`.

Questions

1. How do you tell the C shell that you want it to remember the last 30 commands during a session and to remember the last 10 commands across login sessions?

2. Assume that you get the following output from entering `history`:

```
1 ls -CF
2 who ¦ grep dunlaplm
3 wc -l < test
4 cat test
5 history
```

What would be the result of entering each of the following history commands?

```
!2     !w    !wh     echo !1
```

3. Some UNIX systems won't enable you to do the following. What danger do you see lurking in this alias?

```
alias who    who -a
```

4. Which of the following aliases do you think would be useful?

```
alias alias who
alias ls cp
alias copy cp -i
alias logout vi
alias vi logout
alias bye logout
```

5. Set your prompt to the following value. Remember that 33 should be replaced with the appropriate command number each time.

```
#33 - I know lots about UNIX. For example:
```

6. Find and examine two shell scripts that are found in either the /bin or /usr/ bin directories on your system. Remember, any line beginning with a # is a comment.

Preview of the Next Chapter

In the next chapter, you will learn some of the most exciting and enjoyable commands in UNIX. You will learn how to interact with other users on the computer. This includes directly trading lines of information using `write`, and sending electronic memos and notes to someone using `mail` or the `elm` package. You will also learn how to use `mesg` to allow users to interact with you or to force them to leave you alone.

Talking to Others

F

15

Now that you're wrapping up your fifth day of working with UNIX and have most of the complexity well under control, it's time to learn about what's probably the single most exciting aspect of the operating system: the ability to communicate with other users on your computer, both interactively and through electronically transmitted mail, *e-mail.*

Goals for This Lesson

In this lesson, you will learn about

- ☐ Enabling messages using `mesg`
- ☐ Writing to other users with `write`
- ☐ Reading electronic mail with `mailx`
- ☐ Sending electronic mail with `mailx`
- ☐ The smarter alternative for sending mail, `elm`

Of all the places in UNIX where there is variety, surely most of it is found in electronic mail. At least 15 different programs are available from various vendors to accomplish one task: to read mail from and send mail to other folks. In this lesson you will learn about the standard electronic mail system, Berkeley Mail. I will also take a little time to whet your appetite by showing you the Elm Mail System, a full-screen alternative mail program that's widely distributed.

Comment: There's a much bigger world than the machine you're on; it's called the Internet. You learn lots about how to use this valuable resource on your last day of *Teach Yourself UNIX in a Week.*

Task 15.1: Enabling Messages Using *mesg*
Step 1. Description

Earlier you learned that all peripherals hooked up to UNIX are controlled by *device drivers*, and that each device driver has an associated /dev file. If you want to talk with other users on the system, you need to ensure that they can communicate with you, too. (This only pertains to `write`, however; e-mail works regardless of the `mesg` setting.)

Step 2. Action

1. To find out through what device I'm connected to the system, I can use the UNIX command tty:

```
% tty
/dev/ttyAo
```

The tty device is just another UNIX file, so I can look at it like I'd look at any other file:

```
% ls -l /dev/ttyAo
crw---x--- 1 taylor    21, 71 Dec  8 10:34 /dev/ttyAo*
```

Notice that I own the file and that I have write permission, but others do not.

2. To enable other users to communicate with me directly, I need to ensure that they can run programs that can write to my terminal. That is, I need to give them write permission to my tty device. Instead of using the chmod command, tracking down what line I'm on and all that, I can use a simple alternative, mesg. To turn messages on—allowing other users to communicate with me—I specify the y flag to mesg:

```
% mesg y
% ls -l `tty`
crw-rwx--- 1 taylor    21, 71 Dec  8 10:33 /dev/ttyAo*
```

To disable messages (perhaps if I'm busy and don't want to be bothered), I can use the n flag, which says that *no, I don't want messages*:

```
% mesg n
% ls -l `tty`
crw---x--- 1 taylor    21, 71 Dec  8 10:34 /dev/ttyAo*
```

3. At any point, you can double-check your current terminal write permission by entering mesg without any flags. The output is succinct, but it tells you what you want to know:

```
% mesg
is n
%
```

15

Shortcut: To see the settings of your tty, use the backquotes with the `tty` command as shown in the preceding examples.

Step 3. Summary

Don't tell anyone this secret. Once you have write permission to someone else's terminal, you can redirect the output of commands to their tty device as easily as to any other file in UNIX. In fact, that's how the `write` command works. It opens the other person's tty device for writing, and each line you enter is also written to the other person's screen. I note this simply so you can see why the permissions of your `/dev/tty` line is so important, not so you can go wild and start tormenting your fellow UNIX users!

Task 15.2: Writing to Other Users with *write*
Step 1. Description

Now that you can allow and prevent others writing to your terminal, it's time to find out how to write to theirs, and what you can do with that capability. The command for interacting directly with other users is the `write` command. It's a relatively simple command. When you start `write`, you specify the other user with whom you want to communicate and `write` starts up *for you only*, while it pages the other user to let him or her know that you're interested in communicating.

Once you're in the program, each line that you type will be sent to the other person as soon as you press Return. Until they respond by using `write` on their system to respond, however, they can't send any messages to you. Electronic etiquette suggests that you connect, then wait without typing until the other user connects with you. Then you can have a conversation!

To connect with someone, you need merely specify the person's account name to `write`. If the user is logged in more than once, `write` will try to choose the most recently used line, but it isn't always successful. Using `w` is a good strategy. You need merely look at the idle time on each connection to identify which line the person is actually using. Once you identify the connection, you can invoke `write` with the user's account name and the tty line you desire.

Step 2. Action

1. I always start out by ensuring that I've turned on `mesg`. Otherwise, the chap at the other end is going to be pretty darn frustrated trying to talk with me:

```
% mesg
is y
```

2. The best way to find out if your friend is on the system is to use who, piping the output into the grep program.

```
% who ¦ grep marv
marv    ttyAx   Dec  8 10:30
```

He's logged in on tty line /dev/ttyAx (simply add /dev/ before the line indicated by who). I can use ls to see if he has his messages turned on:

```
% ls -l /dev/ttyAx
crw-rwx--- 1 marv      21,  71 Dec  8 10:33 /dev/ttyAx*
```

3. To ask him to join a write session, I simply enter the following:

```
% write marv
```

What he sees on his screen is the following:

```
Message from taylor@netcom.com on ttyAo at 10:38 ...
—
```

4. Now I must wait until he responds, which should take only a few seconds.

```
Message from marv@netcom.com on ttyAx at 10:40 ...
```

We're both connected. Etiquette suggests I wait until his initial hello, which appears on my screen without preamble:

```
Hi Dave! -o
—
```

I can enter lines to him, and he can enter lines to me. When I'm done with my communication, I press ^d to end it, and he does the same:

```
Okay, I'll talk with you tomorrow. -oo
See ya! -oo
^d
EOF
```

A single press of Return gets me back to the system prompt, %.

15

> **Comment:** Because it's so easy for people to step all over each other's communication in `write`, a simple protocol is borrowed from radio communication. When you're done with a transmission (one or more lines of text, in this case) you should indicate "over," or `-o`. Then the other person types and sends you information, ending with an `-o`. When you're done with the conversation, end with an "over and out," or `-oo`. It makes life a lot more pleasant!

Step 3. Summary

Like many things in life, the `write` command is simple—it has almost no options and precious little sophistication—yet it is valuable and enjoyable. If you have a quick question for someone who is logged in, or if you just want to ask your buddy if he's ready to have lunch, this is the best way to do it.

Task 15.3: Reading Electronic Mail with *mailx*
Step 1. Description

The `write` command is helpful for those situations when your friend or colleague is logged in to the computer at the same time you are, but what do you do if the person is not logged in and you want to leave a note? What if you want a friend to receive a copy of a note you're sending to, say, your boss?

That's where electronic mail moves into the spotlight. Of all the capabilities of UNIX, one of the most popular is undoubtedly this capability to send electronic mail to another user—even on another computer system—with a few keystrokes. In this lesson you will learn how to work with other users on your own computer, and later you will learn how to send mail to folks who are on different computers, even in different countries.

A variety of different programs for reading mail can be used on UNIX systems, but the two most common are `mail` and `Mail`. (The latter is also often called `mailx` on SVR4 systems.) Because of the similarity of the names, the former is known as `mail` and the latter as either *cap mail* or *Berkeley Mail*. I refer to the latter either as Berkeley Mail or as its AT&T name, `mailx`. You should never use `mail` to read or write mail if Berkeley Mail is available to you, because Berkeley Mail is much easier to use. I will focus on using Berkeley Mail.

To envision electronic mail, imagine that you have a butler who is friendly with the local post office. You can hand him mail with only the name of the recipient written on the envelope, and the butler will make sure it's delivered. If new mail arrives, the butler discreetly lets you know about it, so you can then display the messages, one by one, and read them. Furthermore, your butler organizes your old mail in a big filing cabinet, filing each message by any criteria you request.

That's almost exactly how Berkeley Mail works. To send mail, you simply state on the command line the account name of the recipient, indicate a subject, enter the message itself, and poof! Your message is sent through the system and arrives at the recipient's terminal posthaste. When mail arrives for you, the C shell or one of a variety of utilities, such as `biff` or `newmail`, can notify you. Each time you log in, the system checks for electronic mail, and if you have any, the system will say `You have mail` or `You have new mail`. You can save mail in files called *mail folders*.

Berkeley Mail has many command options, both starting flags and commands used within the program. Fortunately you can always enter `help` while you're in the program to review these options. The most noteworthy flags are `-s` *subject*, which enables you to specify the subject of the message on the command line, and `-f` *mail folder*, which enables you to specify a mail folder to read rather than the default (which is your incoming mailbox).

The most valuable commands to use within the program are summarized in Table 15.1.

Table 15.1. Berkeley Mail command summary.

Command	Meaning
delete *msgs*	Mark the specified messages for deletion.
headers	Display the current page of headers. Add a + to see the next page, or a - to see the previous page.
help	Display a summary of Berkeley Mail commands.
mail *address*	Send mail to the specified address.
print *msgs*	Show the specified message or messages.
quit	Leave the Berkeley Mail program.
reply	Respond to the current message.
save *folder*	Save the current message to the specified mail folder.
undelete *msgs*	Undelete the messages specified for deletion.

15

Step 2. Action

1. I have lots of electronic mail in my mailbox. When I logged into the system today, the shell indicated that I have new mail. To find out what the new messages are, I use `mailx`:

```
% mailx
Mail version 5.2 6/21/85.  Type ? for help.
"/usr/spool/mail/taylor": 9 messages 5 new
     1 disserli Mon Nov 22 19:40  54/2749 "Re: Are you out there somewhe"
>N   2 Laura.Ramsey Tue Nov 30 16:47  46/1705 "I've got an idea..."
 N   3 ljw      Fri Dec  3 22:57  130/2712 "Re: Attachments to XALT mail"
 N   4 sartin   Sun Dec  5 15:15  15/341 "I need your address"
 N   5 rustle   Tue Dec  7 15:43  29/955 "flash cards"
     6 harrism  Tue Dec  7 16:13  58/2756 "Re: Writing Lab OWL project ("
     7 CBUTCHER Tue Dec  7 17:00  19/575 "Computer Based GRE's"
     8 harrism  Tue Dec  7 21:46  210/10636 "Various writing environments"
 N   9 v892127  Wed Dec  8 07:09  38/1558 "Re: Have you picked up the co"
& _
```

I have lots of information here. On the very first line, the program identifies itself as Mail version 5.2, built June 21, 1985. Somewhat tucked away in that top corner is the reminder that I can enter ? at any point to get help on the commands.

The second line tells me what mailbox I'm reading. In this case, I'm looking at the default mailbox for my incoming mail, which is /usr/spool/mail/ taylor. On your system, you might find your mailbox in this directory or you might find it in a directory similarly named /usr/mail. Either way, you don't have to worry about where it's located, because Berkeley Mail can automatically find it.

The third through eleventh lines list mail messages that I have received from various people. The format is N in the first column if I haven't seen the piece of mail before, a unique index number (the first item in each listing is one), the account that sent the message, the date and time the message was sent, the number of lines and characters in the message, and the subject of the message, if known. Figure 15.1 illustrates this more clearly.

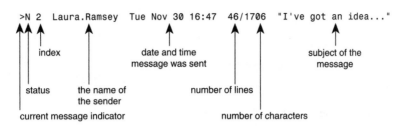

Figure 15.1. *Understanding the message display in* `mailx`.

2. To read a specific message, I need enter only the index number of that message:

```
& 7
Message  7:
From: CBUTCHER Tue Dec  7 17:00:28 1993
From: Cheryl <CBUTCHER>
Subject:     Computer Based GRE's
To: Dave Taylor <TAYLOR>

I've scheduled to take the computer based GRE's in Indy on Jan. 6th.
Call me crazy but someone's got to do it.  I'll let you know how it goes.

Do you know anyone else that has taken the GRE's this way?  I figure
there's a paper in it somewhere.......

If you have that handout from seminar in a file, could you please send it
to me?

Thanks.

& _
```

This message is from my friend Cheryl Butcher. Collectively, the first set of lines in the message—each a single word, a colon, and some information or other—is the *header* of the message, or the electronic equivalent of the postmark and envelope. The header will always include From:, Subject:, and To:, specifying the name and electronic address of the sender, the subject of the message, and the list of recipients.

15

3. To respond to this message, I enter reply:

```
& reply
To: CBUTCHER
Subject: RE: Computer Based GRE's

_
```

Anything I now enter will be sent back to Cheryl:

```
Hi. I am very interested in hearing about your reaction to the
computer-based GRE test. I'm sure you're correct that there is
a paper there, but wouldn't it be best to work with ETS on the
project?

I'll dig around and find those handouts soonest.

Happy holidays!

Dave
```

To end the message, I enter ^d on its own line or use the shorthand . by itself:

```
.
Cc: _
```

Berkeley Mail is now asking me to specify any other people I might like to have receive *carbon copies* of this message. Entering an account name or two here will allow the designated people to see a copy of this message to Cheryl. Because I don't want anyone else to read this message, I press Return, which sends the message and returns me to the & prompt:

```
& _
```

4. I can now use the headers command to see what is the current message (the one I just read). It's the message indicated by the >. (Look at Figure 15.1 if you're having trouble finding it.)

```
& headers
      1 disserli Mon Nov 22 19:40  54/2749 "Re: Are you out there somewhe"
      2 Laura.Ramsey Tue Nov 30 16:47  46/1705 "I've got an idea..."
  N   3 ljw      Fri Dec  3 22:57  130/2712 "Re: Attachments to XALT mail"
  N   4 sartin   Sun Dec  5 15:15  15/341 "I need your address"
  N   5 rustle   Tue Dec  7 15:43  29/955 "flash cards"
```

SAMS

Sams
Learning
Center

SAMS
PUBLISHING

```
    6 harrism  Tue Dec  7 16:13  58/2756 "Re: Writing Lab OWL project ("
>   7 CBUTCHER Tue Dec  7 17:00  19/575 "Computer Based GRE's"
    8 harrism  Tue Dec  7 21:46  210/10636 "Various writing environments"
N  9 v892127  Wed Dec  8 07:09  38/1558 "Re: Have you picked up the co"
&  _
```

To save Cheryl's message in a folder, I use the save command:

```
& save cheryl
"cheryl" [New file] 19/575
&  _
```

5. Now that I'm done with this message, I can mark it for deletion with the delete command:

```
& delete 7
&
```

Notice that after I enter headers, Cheryl's message vanishes from the list:

```
& headers
    1 disserli Mon Nov 22 19:40  54/2749 "Re: Are you out there somewhe"
    2 Laura.Ramsey Tue Nov 30 16:47  46/1705 "I've got an idea..."
N  3 ljw      Fri Dec  3 22:57  130/2712 "Re: Attachments to XALT mail"
N  4 sartin   Sun Dec  5 15:15  15/341 "I need your address"
N  5 rustle   Tue Dec  7 15:43  29/955 "flash cards"
    6 harrism  Tue Dec  7 16:13  58/2756 "Re: Writing Lab OWL project ("
>   8 harrism  Tue Dec  7 21:46  210/10636 "Various writing environments"
N  9 v892127  Wed Dec  8 07:09  38/1558 "Re: Have you picked up the co"
&
```

Look closely at the list and you will see that it hasn't completely forgotten the message; the program hides message 7 from this list. I could still read the message using print 7, and I could use undelete 7 to pull it off the deletion list.

Comment: Deleted messages in Berkeley Mail are actually marked for future deletion and aren't removed until you quit the program. Once you quit, however, there's no going back. A deleted message is gone. While you're within the program you can delete and undelete to your heart's content.

15

6. Now I want to delete both the messages from harrism (numbers 6 and 8):

```
& delete 6 8
&
```

Now the list of messages in my mailbox is starting to look pretty short:

```
& h
      1 disserli Mon Nov 22 19:40  54/2749 "Re: Are you out there somewhe"
      2 Laura.Ramsey Tue Nov 30 16:47  46/1705 "I've got an idea..."
  N   3 ljw      Fri Dec  3 22:57  130/2712 "Re: Attachments to XALT mail"
  N   4 sartin   Sun Dec  5 15:15  15/341 "I need your address"
  N   5 rustle   Tue Dec  7 15:43  29/955 "flash cards"
 >N   9 v892127  Wed Dec  8 07:09  38/1558 "Re: Have you picked up the co"
&
```

Shortcut: Most commands in Berkeley Mail can be abbreviated to just their first letter, which cuts down on typing.

7. You can save a group of messages to a file by specifying the numbers between the save command and the folder name:

```
& save 6 8 harris
6: Inappropriate message
&
```

Oops. I had deleted messages 6 and 8. I must *undelete* them before I can proceed:

```
& undelete 6 8
& save 6 8 harris
"harris" [New file] 268/13392
&
```

8. Use the quit command to get out of this program:

```
& quit
Saved 1 message in mbox
Held 6 messages in /usr/spool/mail/taylor
%
```

The messages that I viewed and didn't delete are moved out of my incoming mailbox to the file mbox. The messages that I saved *and* the messages I marked for deletion are silently removed, and all remaining messages are retained in /usr/spool/mail/taylor.

> **Comment:** The biggest complaint I have with Berkeley Mail is that it does all this activity silently. I don't like the fact that saved messages are automatically deleted from the incoming mailbox when I quit and that —more importantly—messages I've read are automatically tossed into another folder. To ensure that messages you've read aren't moved into mbox when you quit, you can use the preserve command, which you can use with a list of numbers, the same way you can use other Berkeley Mail commands. Any message with which you use preserve will remain in your incoming mailbox.

Step 3. Summary

Once you get the hang of it, Berkeley Mail offers quite a lot of power, allowing you to read through your electronic mail, save it, and respond as needed with ease. The program has considerably more commands than shown here, so further study is helpful.

Task 15.4: Sending Mail with *mailx*
Step 1. Description

Now you know how to read your electronic mail using Berkeley Mail (mailx), and you know how to send mail from within the program. How do you send messages and files to people from the command line? It's quite simple. You can even specify the message subject with the -s starting flag.

Step 2. Action

1. To send a message to someone, enter the name of the command followed by the recipient's account name:

```
% mail marv
Subject: Interested in lunch tomorrow?

_
```

I can now enter as many lines of information as desired, ending, as within the Berkeley Mail program itself, with either ^d or . :

```
I'm going to be in town tomorrow and would like to
rustle up some Chinese food. What's your schedule
look like?
```

15

```
Dave
.
Cc: _
```

Again, I'm offered the option of copying someone else, but, again, I opt not to do so. Pressing Return sends the message.

2. To send a file to someone, combine file redirection with use of the -s flag:

```
% mail -s "here's the contents of sample.file" marv < sample.file
%
```

The file was sent without any fuss.

3. Without any indication that any commands are available at all, a number of commands are available for use while entering the text of a message, and all can be listed with ~?:

```
% mail dunlaplm
Subject: Good morning!
~?
-----------------------------------------------------------
The following ~ escapes are defined:
~~              Quote a single tilde
~b users        Add users to "blind" cc list
~c users        Add users to cc list
~d              Read in dead.letter
~e              Edit the message buffer
~h              Prompt for to list, subject and cc list
~m messages     Read in messages, right shifted by a tab
~p              Print the message buffer
~r file         Read a file into the message buffer
~s subject      Set subject
~t users        Add users to to list
~v              Invoke display editor on message
~w file         Write message onto file.
~?              Print this message
~!command       Invoke the shell
~|command       Pipe the message through the command
-----------------------------------------------------------

_
```

The ones most important to remember are ~v, to start up vi in the message; ~r, to read in a file; ~h, to edit the message headers; ~!, to invoke a shell command; and ~p, to show the message that's been entered so far:

```
    I wanted to wish you a cheery good morning!  You asked about
the contents of that one file, so here it is:
~!ls
Archives/       bin/            deleteme        sample
InfoWorld/      buckaroo        dickens.note    sample2
```

```
Mail/          buckaroo.confused  keylime.pie   src/
News/          cheryl             mbox          temp/
OWL/           csh.man            newsample
awkscript      dead.letter        owl.c
!
```

The output of the command isn't included in the message, as is shown if you use the ~p command:

~p
```
------
Message contains:
To: taylor
Subject: Good morning!


Linda,

    I wanted to wish you a cheery good morning!  You asked about
the contents of that one file, so here it is:
(continue)
_
```

4. To read in a file, use the ~r command:

~r dickens.note
```
"dickens.note" 28/1123
```

Here, the contents of the file are included in the note, but `mailx` didn't list the contents to the screen. Again using ~p will list the current message:

~p
```
------
Message contains:
To: taylor
Subject: Good morning!


Linda,

    I wanted to wish you a cheery good morning!  You asked about
the contents of that one file, so here it is:

                         A Tale of Two Cities
                              Preface

When I was acting, with my children and friends, in Mr Wilkie Collins's
drama of The Frozen Deep, I first conceived the main idea of this
story.  A strong desire came upon me then, to
embody it in my own person;
and I traced out in my fancy, the state of mind of which it would
necessitate the presentation
to an observant spectator, with particular
care and interest.
```

15

```
As the idea became familiar to me, it gradually shaped itself into its
present form.  Throughout its execution, it has had complete possession
of me; I have so far verified what
is done and suffered in these pages,
as that I have certainly done and suffered it all myself.

Whenever any reference (however slight) is made here to the condition
of the Danish people before or during the Revolution, it is truly made,
on the faith of the most trustworthy
witnesses.  It has been one of my hopes to add
something to the popular and picturesque means of
understanding that terrible time, though no one can hope
to add anything to the philosophy of Mr Carlyle's wonderful book.

Tavistock House
November 1859
(continue)
```

5. I can fine-tune the headers using the ~h command:

```
~h
To: dunlaplm_
```

Pressing Return leaves it as is, and pressing Backspace lets me change it as desired. A Return moves to the next header in the list:

```
Subject: Good morning!
```

Pressing Return a few more times gives me the opportunity to change other headers in the message:

```
Cc:
Bcc:
(continue)
```

The `Cc:` header allows me to specify other people to receive this message. The `Bcc:` is what's known as a *blind carbon copy*, an invisible copy of the message. If I send a message to `dunlaplm` and a carbon copy to `cbutcher`, then each can see that the other received a copy, because the message will have `To: dunlaplm` as a header and will also list the other's name after `Cc:`. If I want to send a copy to someone without any of the other parties knowing about it, that's where a blind carbon copy can be helpful. Specifying someone on the `Bcc:` list means that that person receives a copy of the message, but his or her name doesn't show up on any header in the message itself.

6. Finally, I use ^d to end the message.

```
^d
Cc:
%
```

Step 3. Summary

All so-called *tilde commands* (so named because they all begin with the ~, or *tilde*, character) are available when you send mail from the command line, also when you send mail while within the Berkeley Mail program.

Task 15.5: The Smarter Electronic Mail Alternative, *elm*
Step 1. Description

Just as line editors pale compared to screen editors like vi, so does Berkeley Mail when compared to the Elm Mail System, or elm. Although it's not available on all UNIX systems, the Elm Mail System is widely distributed, and if you don't have it on your system, your system's vendor should be able to help out.

The basic premise of elm is that the user should be able to focus on the message, not the medium. Emphasis is placed on showing human information. The best way to show how it works is to go straight into it!

> **Comment:** I'm probably just a bit biased about elm, as I am the author of the program. The widespread acceptance of the design, however, suggests that I'm not alone in having sought a friendlier alternative to Berkeley Mail.

Step 2. Action

1. To start up the Elm Mail System, enter elm:

```
% elm
```

The screen clears and is replaced with this:

15

```
Mailbox is '/usr/spool/mail/taylor' with 15 messages [ELM 2.3 PL11]


--> 1    Dec 8  v892127@nooteboom. (52)   Re: Have you picked up the computer?
     2    Dec 7  Mickey Harris      (214)  Various writing environments
     3    Dec 7  Cheryl             (24)   Computer Based GRE's
     4    Dec 7  Mickey Harris      (69)   Re: Writing Lab OWL project (fwd)
     5    Dec 7  Russell Holt       (37)   flash cards
     6    Dec 7  Bill McInerney     (121)  New Additions to U.S. Dept. of Educa
     7    Dec 5  Mickey Harris      (29)   Re: OWL non-stuff
     8    Dec 5  Rob Sartin         (31)   I need your address
     9    Dec 4  J=TAYLOR@MA@168ARG (28)   Note to say HI!
OU  10    Dec 3  Linda Wei          (143)  Re: Attachments to XALT mail


   You can use any of the following commands by pressing the first character;
 d)elete or u)ndelete mail,  m)ail a message,  r)eply or f)orward mail,  q)uit
   To read a message, press <return>.  j = move down, k = move up, ? = help

Command: _
```

The current message is indicated by the arrow (or, on some screens, the entire message line appears in inverse video). Whenever possible, elm shows the name of the person who sent the message (for example, Mickey Harris rather than mharris as in Berkeley Mail), indicates the number of lines in the message (in parenthesis), and shows the subject of the message.

The last few lines on the screen indicate the options available at this point. Notice that j and k move the cursor up and down the list, just as they move up and down lines in vi.

2. To read a message, use the j key to zip down to the appropriate message and press Return. You will then see this:

```
Message 3/15  From Cheryl                          Dec 7 '93 at 4:57 pm
est
                         Computer Based GRE's


I've scheduled to take the computer based GRE's in Indy on Jan. 6th.
Call me crazy but someone's got to do it.  I'll let you know how it goes.

Do you know anyone else that has taken the GRE's this way?  I figure there's
a paper in it somewhere.......
```

```
If you have that handout from seminar in a file, could you please send it
to me?

Thanks.
Command ('i' to return to index): _
```

At this point, you can use j to read the next message directly, r to reply, or i to return to the table of contents.

3. I realized that I said something in my message to Cheryl that was incorrect. I can press r here to reply to her message. Pressing r causes the last few lines of the screen to be replaced with this:

```
- - - - - - - - - - - - - - - - - - - - - - - - - - - - - - - - - - - - - - - - - - - -
Command: Reply to message                    Copy message? (y/n) n
```

To include the text of the message in your response, press y. I don't want to, so I press Return:

```
- - - - - - - - - - - - - - - - - - - - - - - - - - - - - - - - - - - - - - - - - - - -
Command: Reply to message     To: CBUTCHER (Cheryl)
Subject of message: Re: Computer Based GRE's_
```

Now you can see the address the response will be sent to, the name of the recipient (in parentheses), and the subject of the message. (The elm command automatically adds the Re prefix to the subject.) The cursor sits at the end of the subject line so you can change the subject if you wish. It's fine, so I again press return:

```
- - - - - - - - - - - - - - - - - - - - - - - - - - - - - - - - - - - - - - - - - - - -
Command: Reply to message     To: CBUTCHER(Cheryl)
Subject of message: Re: Computer Based GRE's
Copies To: _
```

15

No copies are needed, so I again press Return. The bottom of the screen now looks like this:

```
- - - - - - - - - - - - - - - - - - - - - - - - - - - - - - - - - - - - - - - - - - - - - - - - -
Command: Reply to message      To: CBUTCHER(Cheryl)
Subject of message: Re: Computer Based GRE's
Copies to:

Enter message.  Type Elm commands on lines by themselves.
Commands include:  ^D or '.' to end, ~p to list, ~? for help.


_
```

Notice that ~p and ~? are available. In fact, all the tilde commands available in Berkeley Mail are also available in the Elm Mail System.

I enter the message, and end with a .:

Just a reminder that we have that seminar tomorrow
afternoon too. See ya there?   -- Dave
.

Ending the message calls up this:

```
Please choose one of the following options by parenthesized letter: s
               e)dit message, edit h)eaders, s)end it, or f)orget it.
```

I press Return once more, and the message is sent.

4. I press i to return to the index page and q to quit.

Step 3. Summary

There's a lot more that the Elm Mail System can do to simplify your electronic mail interaction. If elm is available on your system, I encourage you to check it out further, and if you don't, try calling your vendor or a user group to see if someone else can arrange for you to have a copy. Like the Free Software Foundation applications, elm is free. With it you even get the source so you can see how things are done internally if you're so inclined.

Lesson Summary

For a while you've known that there are other users on your computer system, and you've even learned how to find out what they're doing (with the w command). Now you know how to communicate with them, too!

Here's a word of advice. It can be frustrating and annoying to be pestered by unknown folk, so I recommend that you begin by sending mail to yourself and then to just your friends on the system. After some practice, you'll learn how net etiquette works and what is or isn't appropriate from `write` or mail.

Workshop

Key Terms

blind carbon copy	An exact copy of a message, sent without the awareness of the original recipient.
carbon copy	An exact copy of a message sent to other people. Each recipient can see the names of all other recipients on the distribution list.
device driver	A special program that manages peripherals.
e-mail	Electronically transmitted and received mail or messages.
mail folder	A file containing one or more e-mail messages.
mail header	The `To:`, `From:`, `Subject:`, and other lines at the very beginning of an e-mail message. All lines up to the first blank line are considered headers.
mailbox	A synonym for *mail folder*.
preserve	Ensure that a message doesn't move out of your incoming mailbox even though you've read it.
tilde command	A command beginning with ~ in Berkeley Mail or the Elm Mail System.
undelete	Restore a deleted message to its original state.

Questions

1. Use `tty` to identify your terminal device name, then use `ls` to look at its current permissions. Do you have messages enabled or disabled? Confirm with the `mesg` command.

2. Try using the `write` command by writing to yourself; or, if you have a friend on the system, try using `write` to say hi and see if the person knows how to respond. If he or she doesn't respond in about 30 seconds, you might want to enter `To respond to me, type "write joe" at the command line!` (filling in your account name in place of *joe*).

3. Send yourself a message using `mailx`.

4. Now use Berkeley Mail to read your new message, then save it to a file, delete it, undelete it, and save it to a mail folder.

5. Start Berkeley Mail so that it reads in the newly created mail folder rather than in your default mailbox. What's different?

6. If `elm` is available to you, try using it to read your mail. Do you like this mail program or Berkeley Mail better? Why?

Preview of the Next Chapter

In the next lesson you will learn to use the online documentation that's included with UNIX, and you will learn how UNIX works with processes. Commands you will learn include `jobs` and `ps`, to see what processes are running; `fg` and `bg`, to move jobs back and forth; and `kill`, to kill jobs that you no longer want around.

For now, you have finished five of the seven days, and you should congratulate yourself. You're doing a good job and cruising on, building your UNIX knowledge. At this point you have quite a bit of UNIX expertise, given your knowledge of `vi`, `mailx`, customizing the C shell, and the myriad of other UNIX utilities you've learned.

T W R F S S

day

6

Jobs, Printing, Searching, and More

Job Control
and Finding
Help for
Commands

S

16

If you started this book on Monday and are working through a day at a time, it's now Saturday morning. Welcome back. When I was a kid, I used to watch cartoons on Saturday morning, but now they're so violent that I surmise UNIX is a safe and less anxiety-provoking alternative. In any case, today you will learn a number of important functions, including basic UNIX online documentation, C shell job control, printing, and using `find` to dig up files lost in the system.

This lesson focuses on using the online documentation that's included with UNIX, and how UNIX works with processes. Commands you will learn include `man` and `apropos`, for documentation; `jobs` and `ps`, to see what processes are running; `fg` and `bg`, to move jobs back and forth between the foreground and background; and `kill`, to kill jobs that you no longer want around.

Goals for This Lesson

In this lesson, you will learn about

☐ Using `man` pages, UNIX online reference material

☐ Other ways to find help in UNIX

☐ Job control in the shell, stopping jobs

☐ Putting jobs in the background and bringing them into the foreground

☐ Finding out what tasks are running with `jobs` and `ps`

☐ Killing errant processes with `kill`

Throughout this book, I've indicated that my focus is on the most important and valuable flags and options for the commands covered. That's all well and good, but how do you find out about the other alternatives that might actually work better for your use? That's where the UNIX man pages come in. You will learn to browse them to find the information desired. Also in this lesson is an explanation of a UNIX philosophical puzzle: What *is* a running program? To learn the answer, you will be introduced to `ps` and `jobs`, for controlling processes; `fg` and `bg`, to move your own processes back and forth between the foreground and background; and the quasi-omnipotent `kill` command, for stopping programs in their proverbial tracks.

Task 16.1: Man Pages, UNIX Online Reference
Step 1. Description

It's not news to you that UNIX is a very complex operating system, with hundreds of commands that can be combined to execute thousands of possible actions. Most commands have a considerable number of options, and all seem to have some subtlety or other that is important to know. But how do you figure all this out? You need to look up commands in the UNIX online documentation set. Containing purely reference materials, the UNIX *man pages* ("man" for "manual") cover every command available.

To search for a man page, enter man followed by the name of the command to search. Many sites also have a table of contents of the man pages. (It's called a whatis database, for obscure historical reasons.) You can use the all-important -k flag for keyword searches to find the name of a command if you know what it should do but you just can't remember what it's called.

Comment: The command apropos is available on most UNIX systems and is often just an alias to man -k. If it's not on your system, you can create it by adding the line alias apropos 'man -k \!' to your .cshrc file.

The UNIX man pages are organized into nine sections, as shown in Table 16.1. This table is organized for System V, but it generally holds true for Berkeley systems, too, with these few changes. BSD has I/O and special files in Section 4, administrative files in Section 5, and miscellaneous files in Section 7. Some BSD systems also split user commands into further categories, Section 1C for intersystem communications and Section 1G for commands used primarily for graphics and computer-aided design.

Table 16.1. System V UNIX man page organization.

Section	Category
1	User commands
1M	System maintenance commands
2	System calls
3	Library routines
4	Administrative files
5	Miscellaneous
6	Games

continues

Table 16.1. continued

Section	Category
7	I/O and special files
8	Administrative commands

Step 2. Action

1. The mkdir man page is succinct and exemplary:

```
% man mkdir

MKDIR(1)          DYNIX Programmer's Manual      MKDIR(1)

NAME
     mkdir - make a directory

SYNOPSIS
     mkdir dirname ...

DESCRIPTION
     Mkdir creates specified directories in mode 777. Standard
     entries, `.', for the directory itself, and `..' for its
     parent, are made automatically.

     Mkdir requires write permission in the parent directory.

SEE ALSO
     rmdir(1)

Revision 1.4.2.2 88/08/13                                      1
%
```

The very first line of the output tells me that it's found the mkdir command
in Section 1 (user commands) of the man pages, with the middle phrase,
DYNIX Programmer's Manual, indicating that I'm running on a version of
UNIX called DYNIX. The NAME section always details the name of the
command and a one-line summary of what it does. SYNOPSIS lists how to use
the command, including all possible command flags and options.

DESCRIPTION is where all the meaningful information is, and it can run on
for dozens of pages, explaining how complex commands like csh or vi work.
SEE ALSO suggests other commands that are related in some way. The
Revision line at the bottom is different on each version of man, and it
indicates the last time, presumably, that this document was revised.

2. The same man page from a Sun workstation is quite different:

```
% man mkdir
MKDIR(1)                  USER COMMANDS                  MKDIR(1)

NAME
     mkdir - make a directory

SYNOPSIS
     mkdir [ -p ] dirname...

DESCRIPTION
     mkdir creates directories.  Standard entries, `.', for  the
     directory itself, and `..' for its parent, are made automat-
     ically.

     The -p flag allows missing parent directories to be  created
     as needed.

     With the exception of the set-gid bit, the current umask(2V)
     setting  determines  the  mode  in  which  directories  are
     created.  The new directory inherits the set-gid bit of  the
     parent  directory.   Modes may be modified after creation by
     using chmod(1V).

     mkdir requires write permission in the parent directory.

SEE ALSO
     chmod(1V), rm(1), mkdir(2V), umask(2V)

Sun Release 4.1    Last change: 22 August 1989               1
%
```

Notice that there's a new flag in this version of mkdir, the -p flag. More importantly, note that the flag is shown in square brackets within the SYNOPSIS section. By convention, square brackets in this section mean that the flag is optional. You can see that the engineers at Sun have a very different idea about what other commands might be worth viewing!

3. One thing I always forget on Sun systems is the command that lets me format a floppy disk. That's exactly where the apropos command comes in handy:

```
% apropos floppy
fd (4S)                  - disk driver for Floppy Disk Controllers
%
```

That's not quite what I want, unfortunately. Because it's in Section 4 (note that the item in parentheses is 4S, not 1), this document will describe the disk driver, rather than any command to work with floppy disks.

I can look up disk instead:

```
% man -k disk
acctdisk, acctdusg, accton, acctwtmp (8)    - overview of accounting and
miscellaneous accounting commands
add_client (8)           - create a diskless network bootable NFS client on
a server chargefee, ckpacct, dodisk, lastlogin, monacct, nulladm, prctmp,
prdaily,
prtacct, runacct, shutacct, startup, turnacct (8) - shell procedures for
accounting client (8)               - add or remove diskless Sun386i systems
df (1V)                  - report free disk space on file systems
diskusg (8)              - generate disk accounting data by user
dkctl (8)                - control special disk operations
dkinfo (8)               - report information about a disk's geometry and
                           partitioning
dkio (4S)                - generic disk control operations
du (1L)                  - summarize disk usage
du (1V)                  - display the number of disk blocks used per direc-
                           tory or file
fastboot, fasthalt (8)   - reboot/halt the system while disabling disk check-
                           ing
fd (4S)                  - disk driver for Floppy Disk Controllers
fdformat (1)             - format diskettes for use with SunOS
format (8S)              - disk partitioning and maintenance utility
fsync (2)                - synchronize a file's in-core state with that on
                           disk
fusage (8)               - RFS disk access profiler
id (4S)                  - disk driver for IPI disk controllers
installboot (8S)         - install bootblocks in a disk partition
pnpboot, pnp.s386 (8C)   - pnp diskless boot service
quota (1)                - display a user's disk quota and usage
quotactl (2)             - manipulate disk quotas
root (4S)                - pseudo-driver for Sun386i root disk
sd (4S)                  - driver for SCSI disk devices
sync (1)                 - update the super block; force changed blocks to
                           the disk
xd (4S)                  - Disk driver for Xylogics 7053 SMD Disk Controller
xy (4S)                  - Disk driver for Xylogics 450 and 451 SMD Disk
                           Controllers
%
```

This yields quite a few choices! To trim the list down to just those that are in Section 1 (user commands section) I use grep:

```
% man -k disk | grep '(1'
df (1V)                  - report free disk space on file systems
du (1L)                  - summarize disk usage
du (1V)                  - display the number of disk blocks used per direc-
                           tory or file
fdformat (1)             - format diskettes for use with SunOS
quota (1)                - display a user's disk quota and usage
sync (1)                 - update the super block; force changed blocks to the
                           disk
%
```

That's better! The command I was looking for is fdformat.

4. To learn a single snippet of information about a UNIX command, you can check to see if your system has the whatis utility. You can even ask it to describe itself (a bit of a philosophical conundrum):

```
% whatis whatis
whatis (1)              - display a one-line summary about a keyword
%
```

In fact, this is the line from the NAME field of the relevant man page. The whatis command is different from the apropos command because it only considers command names, rather than all words in the command description line:

```
% whatis cd
cd (1)                  - change working directory
%
```

Now see what apropos does:

```
% apropos cd
bcd, ppt (6)            - convert to antique media
cd (1)                  - change working directory
cdplayer (6)            - CD-ROM audio demo program
cdromio (4S)            - CDROM control operations
draw, bdraw, cdraw (6)  - interactive graphics drawing
fcdcmd, fcd (1)         - change client's current working directory in the
FSP database
getacinfo, getacdir, getacflg, getacmin, setac, endac (3)   - get audit
control
file information
ipallocd (8C)           - Ethernet-to-IP address allocator
mp, madd, msub, mult, mdiv, mcmp, min, mout, pow, gcd, rpow, itom, xtom,
mtox,
mfree (3X)    - multiple precision integer arithmetic
rexecd, in.rexecd (8C)  - remote execution server
sccs-cdc, cdc (1)       - change the delta commentary of an SCCS delta
sr (4S)                 - driver for CDROM SCSI controller
termios, tcgetattr, tcsetattr, tcsendbreak, tcdrain, tcflush, tcflow,
cfgetospeed, cfgetispeed, cfsetispeed,
cfsetospeed (3V) - get and set terminal attributes,
line control, get and set baud rate, get and set terminal
foreground process group ID
tin, rtin, cdtin, tind (1)  - A threaded Netnews reader
tin, rtin, cdtin, tind (1)  - A threaded Netnews reader
tin, rtin, cdtin, tind (1)  - A threaded Netnews reader
tin, rtin, cdtin, tind (1)  - A threaded Netnews reader
uid_allocd, gid_allocd (8C) - UID and GID allocator daemons
%
```

5. One problem with man is that it really isn't too sophisticated. As you can see

16

in the listing above, apropos (which, recall, is man -k) lists a line more than once if more than one man page matches the specified pattern. You can create your own apropos alias to improve the command:

```
% alias apropos 'man -k \!* | uniq'
%
% apropos cd
bcd, ppt (6)             - convert to antique media
cd (1)                   - change working directory
cdplayer (6)             - CD-ROM audio demo program
cdromio (4S)             - CDROM control operations
draw, bdraw, cdraw (6)   - interactive graphics drawing
fcdcmd, fcd (1)          - change client's current working directory in the
FSP database
getacinfo, getacdir, getacflg, getacmin, setac, endac (3)   -
get audit
control file information
ipallocd (8C)            - Ethernet-to-IP address allocator
mp, madd, msub, mult, mdiv, mcmp, min, mout, pow, gcd, rpow, itom, xtom,
mtox, mfree (3X)   - multiple precision integer arithmetic
rexecd, in.rexecd (8C)   - remote execution server
sccs-cdc, cdc (1)        - change the delta commentary of an SCCS delta
sr (4S)                  - driver for CDROM SCSI controller
termios, tcgetattr, tcsetattr, tcsendbreak, tcdrain, tcflush, tcflow,
cfgetospeed, cfgetispeed, cfsetispeed, cfsetospeed (3V) - get and set termi-
nal
attributes, line control, get and set baud rate, get and set
terminal
foreground process group ID
tin, rtin, cdtin, tind (1)  - A threaded Netnews reader
uid_allocd, gid_allocd (8C) - UID and GID allocator daemons
%
```

That's better, but I'd like to have the command tell me only about user commands, because I don't care much about file formats, games, or miscellaneous commands when I'm looking for a command. I'll try this:

```
% alias apropos 'man -k \!* | uniq | grep 1'
%
% apropos cd
cd (1)                   - change working directory
fcdcmd, fcd (1)          - change client's current working directory in the
FSP database
sccs-cdc, cdc (1)        - change the delta commentary of an SCCS delta
tin, rtin, cdtin, tind (1)  - A threaded Netnews reader
%
```

That's much better.

6. I'd like to look up one more command—sort—before I'm done here.

```
% man sort

SORT(1)                DYNIX Programmer's Manual              SORT(1)

NAME
     sort - sort or merge files

SYNOPSIS
     sort [ -mubdfinrtx ] [ +pos1 [ -pos2 ] ] ... [ -o name ]
[      -T directory ] [ name ] ...

DESCRIPTION
     Sort sorts lines of all the named files together and writes
     the result on the standard output.  The name `-' means the
     standard input.  If no input files are named, the standard
     input is sorted.

     The default sort key is an entire line.  Default ordering is
     lexicographic by bytes in machine collating sequence.  The
     ordering is affected globally by the following options, one
     or more of which may appear.

     b    Ignore leading blanks (spaces and tabs) in field com-
--More--  _
```

On almost every system, the man command feeds output through the more program so that information won't fly past. You also can save the output of a man command to a file if you'd like to study the information in detail. To save this particular manual entry to the file sort.manpage, you could use man sort > sort.manpage.

Notice in this man page that there are many options to the sort command (certainly more than are discussed in this book). As you learn UNIX, if you find areas you'd like more information about, or if you need a capability that doesn't seem to be available, check the man entry. There might just be a flag for what you seek.

Comment: You can obtain lots of valuable information by reading the introduction to each section of the man pages. Use man 1 intro to read the introduction to Section 1, for example.

If your version of man doesn't stop at the bottom of each page, you can remedy the situation using alias man 'man \!* ¦ more'.

Step 3. Summary

UNIX was one of the very first operating systems to include online documentation. The man pages are an invaluable reference. Most are poorly written, unfortunately, and precious few include examples of actual usage, but as a quick reminder of flags and options, or as an easy way to find out the capabilities of a command, man is great. I encourage you to explore the man pages, and perhaps even read the man page on the man command itself.

Task 16.2: Other Ways to Find Help in UNIX
Step 1. Description

The man pages are really the best way to learn about what's going on with UNIX commands, but some alternatives can also prove helpful. Some systems have a help command. Many UNIX utilities make information available with the -h or -? flag, too. Finally, one trick you can try is to feed some gibberish flags to a command, which sometimes generates an error and a helpful message reminding you what possible options the command accepts.

Step 2. Action

1. At the University Tech Computing Center, the support team has installed a help command:

```
% help
Look in a printed manual, if you can, for general help.  You should
have someone show you some things and then read one of the tutorial papers
(e.g. UNIX for Beginners or An Introduction to the C Shell) to get started.
Printed manuals covering all aspects of Unix are on sale at the bookstore.

Most of the material in the printed manuals is also available online
via "man" and similar commands; for instance:

    apropos keyword        lists commands relevant to keyword
    whatis filename        lists commands involving filename
    man command            prints out the manual entry for a command
    help command           prints out the pocket guide entry for a command
```

```
are helpful; other basic commands are:

        cat             - display a file on the screen
        date            - print the date and time
        du              - summarize disk space usage
        edit            - text editor (beginner)
        ex              - text editor (intermediate)
        finger          - user information lookup program
        learn           - interactive self-paced tutorial on Unix
--More(40%)-- _
```

Your system might have something similar.

2. Some commands offer helpful output if you specify the -h flag:

```
% ls -h
usage: ls [ -acdfgilqrstu1ACLFR ] name ...
%
```

Then again, others don't:

```
% ls -h
Global.Software   Mail/         Src/          history.usenet.Z
Interactive.Unix  News/         bin/          testme
%
```

A few commands offer *lots* of output when you use the -h flag:

```
% elm -h

Possible Starting Arguments for ELM program:

        arg                     Meaning
        -a              Arrow - use the arrow pointer regardless
        -c              Checkalias - check the given aliases only
        -dn             Debug - set debug level to 'n'
        -fx             Folder - read folder 'x' rather than incoming mailbox
        -h              Help - give this list of options
        -k              Keypad - enable HP 2622 terminal keyboard
        -K              Keypad&softkeys - enable use of softkeys + "-k"
        -m              Menu - Turn off menu, using more of the screen
        -sx             Subject 'x' - for batchmailing
        -V              Enable sendmail voyeur mode.
        -v              Print out ELM version information.
        -w              Supress warning messages...
        -z              Zero - don't enter ELM if no mail is pending

%
```

Unfortunately, there isn't a command flag common to all UNIX utilities that lists the possible command flags.

3. Sometimes you can obtain help from a program by incurring its wrath. You can do so by specifying a set of flags that are impossible, unavailable, or just plain puzzling. I always use -xyz because they're uncommon flags:

```
% man -xyz
man: unknown option `-x', use `-h' for help
```

Okay, I'll try it:

```
% man -h
man: usage [-S ¦ -t ¦ -w] [-ac] [-m path] [-M path] [section] pages
man: usage -k [-ac] [-m path] [-M path] [section] keywords
man: usage -f [-ac] [-m path] [-M path] [section] names
man: usage -h
man: usage -V
a        display all manpages for names
c        cat (rather than page) manual pages
f        find whatis entries for pages by these names
names    names to search for in whatis
h        print this help message
k        find whatis entries by keywords
keywords keywords to search for in whatis
m path   add to the standard man path directories
M path   override standard man path directories
S        display only SYNOPSIS section of pages
t        find the source (rather than the formatted page)
V        show version information
w        only output which pages we would display
section  section for the manual to search
pages    pages to locate
```

For every command that does something marginally helpful, there are a half-dozen commands that give useless, and amusingly different, output for these flags:

```
% bc -xyz
unrecognizable argument
% cal -xyz
Bad argument
% file -xyz
-xyz:   No such file or directory
% grep -xyz
grep: unknown flag
%
```

You can't rely on programs to be helpful about themselves, but you can rely on the man page being available for just about everything on the system.

Step 3. Summary

As much as I'd like to tell you that there is a wide variety of useful and interesting information available within UNIX on the commands therein, in reality UNIX has man pages but precious little else. Furthermore, some commands installed locally might not even have man page entries, which leaves you to puzzle out how they work. If you encounter commands that are undocumented, I recommend that you ask your system administrator or vendor what's going on and why there's no further information on the program.

Some vendors are addressing this problem in innovative, if somewhat limited, ways. Sun Microsystems, for example, offers its complete documentation set, including all tutorials, user guides, and man pages, on a single CD-ROM disk. AnswerBook, as it's called, is helpful, but has some limitations, not the least of which is that you must have a CD-ROM drive and keep the disk in the drive at all times.

Task 16.3: Job Control in the Shell: Stopping Jobs
Step 1. Description

Whether you're requesting a man page, listing files with ls, starting vi, or running just about any UNIX command, you're starting one or more *processes*. In UNIX, any program that's running is a process. You can have multiple processes running at once. The pipeline ls -l ¦ sort ¦ more invokes three processes: ls, sort, and more. Processes in both the C and Korn shells are also known as *jobs*, and the program that you're running is known as the *current job*.

Any job or process can have a variety of different states, with *running* being the most typical. In both shells you can stop a job by pressing ^z. To restart it, enter fg when you are ready.

Step 2. Action

1. Earlier I was perusing the man page entry for sort. I had reached the bottom of the first screen:

```
% man sort

SORT(1)              DYNIX Programmer's Manual              SORT(1)

NAME
     sort - sort or merge files

SYNOPSIS
     sort [ -mubdfinrtx ] [ +pos1 [ -pos2 ] ] ... [ -o name ] [
     -T directory ] [ name ] ...

DESCRIPTION
     Sort sorts lines of all the named files together and writes
     the result on the standard output.  The name `-' means the
     standard input.  If no input files are named, the standard
     input is sorted.
```

```
         The default sort key is an entire line.  Default ordering is
         lexicographic by bytes in machine collating sequence.  The
         ordering is affected globally by the following options, one
         or more of which may appear.
  b      Ignore leading blanks (spaces and tabs) in field com-
  --More--  _
```

I'd like to try using the -b flag mentioned at the bottom of this screen, but I want to read the rest of the man page, too. Instead of entering q to quit, then starting the man program again later, I can stop the program. I press ^z, and see this:

```
             ordering is affected globally by the following options, one
  or more of which may appear.

       b       Ignore leading blanks (spaces and tabs) in field com-
  --More--
  Stopped
  %
```

At this point I can do whatever I'd like:

```
% ls -s ¦ sort -b ¦ head -4
   1 Archives/
   1 InfoWorld/
   1 Mail/
   1 News/
   1 OWL/
%
```

2. I can resume at any time. I enter fg, then the program reminds me where I was, and man (which is actually the more program invoked by man) returns to its prompt:

```
% fg
man sort
--More--  _
```

3. Screen-oriented programs are even smarter about stopping and starting jobs. For example, -vi refreshes the entire screen when you return from it having been stopped. If I were in vi working on the dickens.note file, the screen would look like this:

```
                        A Tale of Two Cities
                              Preface

When I was acting, with my children and friends, in Mr Wilkie Collins's
drama of The Frozen Deep, I first conceived the main idea of this
story.  A strong desire came upon me then, to
embody it in my own person;
and I traced out in my fancy, the state of mind of which it would
necessitate the presentation
to an observant spectator, with particular
care and interest.

As the idea became familiar to me, it gradually shaped itself into its
present form.  Throughout its execution, it has had complete possession
of me; I have so far verified what
is done and suffered in these pages,
as that I have certainly done and suffered it all myself.

Whenever any reference (however slight) is made here to the condition
of the Danish people before or during the Revolution, it is truly made,
on the faith of the most trustworthy
witnesses.  It has been one of my hopes to add
something to the popular and picturesque means of
"dickens.note" 28 lines, 1123 characters
```

Pressing ^z would result in this:

```
witnesses.  It has been one of my hopes to add
something to the popular and picturesque means of
"dickens.note" 28 lines, 1123 characters

Stopped
% _
```

I can check to see if someone is logged in, then return to vi with the fg command.

```
% who ¦ grep marv
%
% fg
```

```
                        A Tale of Two Cities
                              Preface

When I was acting, with my children and friends, in Mr Wilkie Collins's
drama of The Frozen Deep, I first conceived the main idea of this
story.  A strong desire came upon me then, to
embody it in my own person;
```

```
and I traced out in my fancy, the state of mind of which it would
necessitate the presentation
to an observant spectator, with particular
care and interest.

As the idea became familiar to me, it gradually shaped itself into its
present form.  Throughout its execution, it has had complete possession
of me; I have so far verified what
is done and suffered in these pages,
as that I have certainly done and suffered it all myself.

Whenever any reference (however slight) is made here to the condition
of the Danish people before or during the Revolution, it is truly made,
on the faith of the most trustworthy
witnesses.  It has been one of my hopes to add
something to the popular and picturesque means of
"dickens.note" 28 lines, 1123 characters
```

Step 3. Summary

There are many aspects to processes and jobs in UNIX, particularly regarding the level of control offered by the shell. The rest of this lesson talks about how to exploit these capabilities to make your work easier and faster.

Task 16.4: Foreground/Background and UNIX Programs
Step 1. Description

Now that you know how to stop programs in their tracks, it's time to learn how to have them keep running in the background (by using the bg command) while you're doing something else, and how to have programs instantly go into the background (by using the & notation).

In the very first lesson, you learned that one of the distinguishing characteristics of UNIX is that it's a true multitasking operating system. It is capable of running hundreds of programs at the same time. The best part is that you're not limited to just one process! If you want to save a couple man pages to a file, for example, you can run those processes in the background while you are working on something else.

Once a job is stopped, you can enter fg to start it up again as the program you're working with. (The fg command takes its name from *foreground*, which refers to the program that your display and keyboard are working with.) If the process will continue without any output to the screen and without any requirement for input, you can use bg to move it into the background, where it runs until it is done. If the program needs to write to the screen or read from the keyboard, the system will automatically stop its execution and inform you. You can then use fg to bring the program into the foreground to continue running.

Comment: If you find that background jobs are just writing information to your screen, try the stty tostop command to fix the problem.

You can also use job control to start up a couple programs and then use fg to start the one you want to work with. If your system takes a long time to start up big applications (such as EMACS or vi), this could save you lots of time.

Comment: Although a job may be stopped, it still consumes resources, so you should be careful not to have too many stopped programs sitting, in deference to the other users of your machine.

A different strategy is to start a program in the background, letting UNIX manage it. If the program needs some input or output, it stops, just like processes you've put into the background with bg after they've already started running. To have a program (or pipeline!) automatically start in the background, simply stick an & at the end of the command line.

Step 2. Action

1. Here's an example of a command that processes files without needing any input or offering any output:

```
% awk -F: '{print $1" = "$5}' < /etc/passwd ¦ \
awk -F, '{print $1}' ¦ \
awk '{ if (NF > 2) print $0 }' ¦ \
sort > who.is.who
```

After about 20 seconds, the % prompt returns; it takes that long to feed the password file through the three-part awk filter, sort the entire output, and save it to the file who.is.who.

Don't Skip This: When you're working with long commands, it's useful to know that you can always move to the next line, even in the middle of entering something, by ending the current line with a single backslash. Note that the backslash must be the *very last character* on the line!

With this new file, I can easily look up an account to see the full name of that user:

```
% alias lookup 'grep -i \!* who.is.who'
%
% who ¦ head
root      console Dec  6 18:02
maritanj ttyAa   Dec  8 21:20
efb      ttyAb   Dec  8 12:12
wifey    ttyAc   Dec  8 19:41
phamtu   ttyAe   Dec  8 21:14
curts    ttyAf   Dec  8 21:14
seifert  ttyAg   Dec  8 21:11
taylor   ttyAh   Dec  8 21:09
halcyon  ttyAi   Dec  8 18:34
jamilrr  ttyAj   Dec  8 20:25
Broken pipe
% lookup maritanj
maritanj = Jorge Maritan
% lookup efb
efb = Edward F. Billiard
%
```

2. To have this process run in the background, I can stop the process immediately after I start it, using ^z:

```
% !awk
awk -F: '{print $1" = "$5}' < /etc/passwd ¦ awk -F, '{print $1}' ¦ awk '{ if
(NF > 2) print $0 }' ¦ sort > who.is.who
Stopped
%
```

Comment: Notice that the command I repeated using the history mechanism was listed as being all on a single line!

At this point, bg will continue the program, running it in the background:

```
% bg
[1]   awk -F: {print $1" = "$5} < /etc/passwd ¦ awk -F, {print $1} ¦ awk {
if (
NF > 2) print $0 } ¦ sort > who.is.who &
%
```

The number in square brackets is this job's *control number* in the shell. In a moment you will learn why this is a handy number to note.

On some systems, a completed background job will immediately notify you that it's done, but on most systems, after a completed background job has finished running, it waits until you press Return to get a new system prompt before it lets you know. After about 30 or 40 seconds, I press Return and see this:

```
%
[1]    Done                    awk -F:
{print $1" = "$5} < /etc/passwd ¦ awk -F,
{print $1} ¦ awk { if (NF > 2) print $0 } ¦ sort > who.is.who
%
```

3. Alternatively, a better strategy for moving a program into the background is to move the process to the background automatically by adding an & to the very end:

```
% !awk &
awk -F: '{print $1" = "$5}' < /etc/passwd ¦ awk -F, '{print $1}' ¦ awk '{ if
(NF > 2) print $0 }' ¦ sort > ! who.is.who &
[1] 27556 27557 27558 27559
%
```

This is more interesting. This command is shown with a control number of 1, but the four numbers listed after that are the actual process ID numbers of each piece of the pipeline: 27556 is the first awk process, 27557 is the second awk process, 27558 is the third awk process, and 27559 is the sort program.

Again, when complete, pressing Return lets me know:

```
%
[1]    Done                    awk -F: {print $1" = "$5} < /etc/passwd ¦ awk -F,
{print $1} ¦ awk { if (NF > 2) print $0 } ¦ sort > who.is.who
%
```

4. What happens if I try to automatically move a program that has input or output to the background?

```
% vi &
[1] 28258
%
```

This looks fine. Pressing Return indicates otherwise, though:

```
%
[1]  + Stopped (tty output) vi
%
```

You can see that this program has stopped because of some information (output) that it wants to display. If the program expected input, the message would be `Stopped (tty input)` *program name*.

437

I can use fg to bring this program into the foreground and work with it, or even just to quit vi.

Step 3. Summary

Because so much of the UNIX design focuses on running streams of data through filters and saving the output to a file, there are a number of commands that you could be running in the background, freeing you up to do other work in the meantime. Remember also that you can put in the background jobs that take a fair amount of processing time and then display information on the screen. When it's time to write something to the screen, the program will automatically stop until you enter fg to pull it back into the foreground.

Task 16.5: Finding Out What Tasks Are Running
Step 1. Description

There are two ways to keep tabs on what programs are flying around in the UNIX operating system. The easier way, jobs, shows what processes you've stopped and moved into the background in the shell. Enter jobs, and csh (or ksh) tells you what programs, if any, are stopped or running.

The alternative is a complex command called ps, which shows the *processor status* for the entire computer. The *processor* is another name for the computer itself. Fortunately, without any arguments, it shows the active or stopped programs associated with your terminal. The ps program actually has more flags than ls, I think. The vast majority of them, however, are never going to be of value to you or any normal UNIX user. The ones that are most helpful are summarized in Table 16.2.

Table 16.2. Useful flags to the ps command, BSD.

Flag	Meaning
-a	Shows all processes associated with terminals.
-g	Shows all *interesting* processes on the system (that is, all processes other than those required by the operating system).
-l	Gives long listing format for each line.
-t *tty*	Lists only processes associated with *tty*.
-u	Produces user-oriented output.
-w	Uses wide output format. If repeated (-ww) it will show as much of each command as possible.

Flag	Meaning
-x	Shows all processes in the system.

The -a, -g, and -x flags affect how much information is displayed by the program. To use either the -g or -x command, you must also use the -a command. On most machines, -ax yields considerably more output than -ag. The most commonly used flags (and flag combinations) are -u, to have only your processes listed in a friendly format; -aux, to see everything on the machine (you almost always want to pipe this to grep or more, lest you be overrun with hundreds of lines of information); and -wt*XX*, to show all the processes associated with tty*xx*, in wide format.

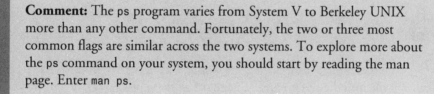

> **Comment:** The ps program varies from System V to Berkeley UNIX more than any other command. Fortunately, the two or three most common flags are similar across the two systems. To explore more about the ps command on your system, you should start by reading the man page. Enter man ps.

Step 2. Action

1. To begin, I'm going to start vi in the background:

```
% vi dickens.note &
[1] 4352
%
```

I'll start that awk job again, too:

```
% !awk
awk -F: '{print $1" = "$5}' < /etc/passwd ¦ awk -F, '{print $1}' ¦ awk '{ if
(NF > 2) print $0 }' ¦ sort > ! who.is.who &
[2] 4532 4534 4536 4537
%
```

The jobs command will now show what processes I have running:

```
% jobs
[1]  + Stopped (tty output) vi dickens.note
[2]  - Running                awk -F: {print $1" = "$5} < /etc/passwd ¦ awk -F,
{print $1} ¦ awk { if (NF > 2) print $0 } ¦ sort > who.is.who
%
```

2. Now that you know the job numbers (the numbers in square brackets here), you can easily move specific jobs into the foreground or the background by

specifying the job number prefixed by %. To show what I mean, I'll put a few
more vi jobs in the background:

```
% vi buckaroo.confused &
[2] 13056
% vi awkscript csh.man cheryl mbox &
[3] 13144
%
```

Now I'll use the jobs command to see what's running:

```
% jobs
[1]     Stopped (tty output) vi dickens.note
[2]   - Stopped (tty output) vi buckaroo.confused
[3]   + Stopped (tty output) vi awkscript csh.man cheryl mbox
%
```

Comment: Notice the awk job finished.

To edit the buckaroo.confused note, I need merely enter fg %2 to pull the
file into the foreground. To kill off all these processes (something you will
learn more about later in this lesson), I can use the kill command:

```
% kill %1 %2 %3
%
```

Nothing happened. Or did it? Pressing Return reveals what occurred in the
operating system:

```
%
[3]   - Done                    vi awkscript csh.man cheryl mbox
[2]   - Done                    vi buckaroo.confused
[1]   + Done                    vi dickens.note
%
```

3. Restart the awk command with !awk. Contrast the output of jobs with the
   output of the Berkeley (BSD) ps command:

```
% ps
  PID TT STAT   TIME COMMAND
 4352 Ah T     0:00 vi dickens.note
 4532 Ah R     0:03 awk - : {print $1"
 4534 Ah R     0:02 awk - , {print $1}
 4536 Ah S     0:01 - k { if (NF > 2) print $0 } (awk)
 4537 Ah S     0:00 sort
 4579 Ah R     0:00 ps
%
```

You can see here that there really are four unique processes running for that pipeline: three awk processes and one sort process. In addition, the vi program and ps are listed as running. Note that my login shell (csh) isn't in this listing.

Figure 16.1 explains each field, and Table 16.3 lists possible values for the STAT program status column.

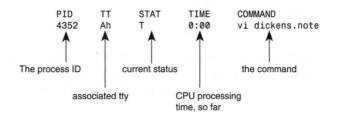

```
PID     TT    STAT    TIME    COMMAND
4352    Ah    T       0:00    vi dickens.note
```

The process ID — associated tty — current status — CPU processing time, so far — the command

Figure 16.1. *The* ps *default process output.*

Table 16.3. Possible process status values.

Value	Meaning
R	Running
S	Sleeping (20 seconds or less)
I	Idle (sleeping more than 20 seconds)
T	Stopped
Z	Zombie process

There are other process states, but they rarely show up for most users. A *zombie process* is one that has ended but hasn't freed up its resources. Usually it takes a second or two for the system to completely recover all memory used by a program. Sometimes zombies are stuck in the process table for one reason or other. UNIX folk refer to this as a *wedged process*, which stays around until the system is rebooted. Sometimes it's listed as <defunct> in process listings. Any process that is preceded by a sleep command is noted as sleeping.

4. Adding some flags can also change the output of ps quite dramatically:

```
% ps -x
  PID TT STAT  TIME COMMAND
 4352 Ah T     0:00 vi dickens.note
 6171 Ah R     0:02 awk - : {print $1"
 6172 Ah R     0:01 awk - , {print $1}
 6173 Ah S     0:01 - k { if (NF > 2) print $0 } (awk)
 6174 Ah S     0:00 sort
 6177 Ah R     0:00 ps -x
19189 Ah S     0:06 -csh (csh)
19649 Ah I     0:02 newmail
%
```

Two new processes show up here: -csh (csh), which is, finally, my login shell; and newmail, a program that automatically starts up in the background when I log in to the system (it's found at the end of my .login).

Comment: The shell process is shown with a leading dash to indicate that it's a *login shell*. Any other copies of csh that I run won't have that leading dash. That's one way that the C shell knows not to read through the .login file every time it's run.

5. To see more about what's happening, I add yet another flag, -u, to expand the output on the display:

```
% ps -xu
USER       PID %CPU %MEM  SZ  RSS TT STAT ENG   TIME COMMAND
taylor    7011 10.4  0.2 184 100 Ah R     6   0:02 awk - : {print $1"
taylor    7012  6.3  0.1 160  92 Ah S         0:01 awk - , {print $1}
taylor    7013  5.9  0.1 160  92 Ah R     3   0:01 - k { if (NF > 2)
print
taylor   19189  1.1  0.2 256 148 Ah S         0:07 -csh (csh)
taylor    7014  1.0  0.1 316  64 Ah S         0:00 sort
taylor    7022  0.1  0.2 180 116 Ah R     0   0:00 ps -xu
taylor    4352  0.0  0.3 452 168 Ah T         0:00 vi dickens.note
taylor   19649  0.0  0.1 124  60 Ah I         0:02 newmail
%
```

Figure 16.2 explains these fields.

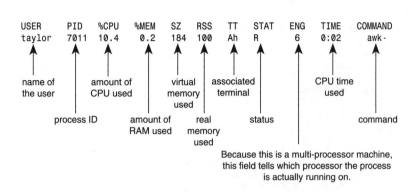

Figure 16.2. *The* -u *user-oriented output of* ps.

6. I won't show the output from the -aux flags, but you should look at the number of lines produced by both the -ag and -ax flags:

```
% ps -ag ¦ wc -l
    377
%
% ps -ag ¦ head
  PID TT STAT  TIME COMMAND
 1403 co IW   0:01 -csh (csh)
 2200 p3 IW   0:18 server
 6076 p6 I    0:13 rlogin sage -l hirschna
 6082 p6 I    0:11 rlogin sage -l hirschna
25341 p8 IW   0:06 -tcsh (tcsh)
  681 pa IW   0:05 -tcsh (tcsh)
10994 pa IW   2:10 ghostview pop5.ps
11794 pa IW   0:12 pwlookup
13861 pa I    0:56 gs
Broken pipe
%
```

You can see here that each process is owned by a specific terminal, but that these processes are all idle (that is, they've been sleeping for more than 20 seconds). This probably means that these users have turned away for a little while. Look back at the output generated by ps -xu, and you will see that newmail is also idle. That's because the program runs in a loop: it sleeps for five minutes, checks for new mail, goes back to sleep again, and so on. Those processes that have the W after the I in the status column are processes that have actually been moved out of main memory and are *swapped out* to disk. This is not a problem, and the users might not even realize anything has happened; the only symptom of this is that when the users wake up their programs, the programs will take an additional second or two to return.

What is the output from ps -ax?

```
% ps -ax ¦ wc -l
     765
%
% ps -ax ¦ head
  PID TT STAT  TIME COMMAND
    0 ?  D     8:58 swapper
    1 ?  S    14:45 (init)
    2 ?  D    20:43 pagedaemon
   27 ?  I     0:00 rpc.rquotad
   59 ?  S     6:36 /etc/syslogd -m480
   70 ?  I     0:02 /etc/portmap
   74 ?  IW    0:00 (biod)
   75 ?  IW    0:00 (biod)
   76 ?  IW    0:00 (biod)
Broken pipe
%
```

These are some of the "guts" of the UNIX operating system. Notice that none of these processes are actually associated with a terminal. Also notice that some of these processes have incredibly low process ID numbers! Any one-digit process ID is a program that is a part of the core UNIX system and must be running for UNIX to be alive. Any two-digit process is also started by the system itself, but is probably optional. The D status for some of these processes indicates that they're waiting for disk resources of some sort. Finally, note how much time these processes have taken. I venture that you will never have a process that takes 20 minutes of CPU time, ever!

7. On a Sun workstation, the output of the ps commands is a bit different:

```
% ps
  PID TT STAT  TIME COMMAND
 8172 qb S     0:00 -csh (csh)
 8182 qb T     0:00 vi
 8186 qb R     0:00 ps
%
```

In many ways though, these different workstations have very similar output from the ps commands. For example, compare this Sun output from ps -xu to the ps -xu output on the Sequent that I already showed:.

```
% ps -xu
USER       PID %CPU %MEM  SZ  RSS TT STAT START  TIME COMMAND
taylor    8191  7.7  0.4 284  536 qb R   19:16  0:00 ps -xu
taylor    8182  0.0  0.4 140  432 qb T   19:16  0:00 vi
taylor    8172  0.0  0.3  68  400 qb S   19:16  0:00 -csh (csh)
taylor    8180  0.0  0.1  52  144 qb S   19:16  0:00 newmail
%
```

The ENG column of the previous examples is replaced by a START column on the Sun workstation. The numbers in the ENG column indicate the exact time that the processes were started on the computer.

Step 3. Summary

UNIX works with processes. Your login shell, the edit session you run, and even the ls program listing your files are all processes in the operating system. This means that you can work with processes. You can stop programs to do something else, restart them as you choose, and even look at all the programs you're running at any time, including otherwise hidden processes such as your login shell itself.

16

Task 16.6: Killing Errant Processes with *kill*
Step 1. Description

Now that you know how to create multiple processes, tuck some into the background, and find stray processes, you need some way to stop them running, as needed. The command to accomplish this in UNIX is kill. For the most part, to use kill you specify the process ID numbers of those programs you want to terminate. Both the C shell and Korn shell have a convenient shorthand that you've already seen: the percent-job number notation.

There are a variety of different signals that the kill command can send to a process. In fact, you don't have to actually stop a process with kill at all! To control this, you need to specify to kill one of a variety of different signals. Table 16.4 lists signals you can use with kill.

Table 16.4. Some signals to use with kill.

Number	Name	Meaning
1	SIGHUP	hang up
2	SIGINT	interrupt
9	SIGKILL	kill (cannot be caught or ignored)
15	SIGTERM	software termination signal from kill

There are over 30 different signals that UNIX knows about, but Table 16.4 lists the ones that are most helpful. The SIGHUP signal is what's sent to every process you are running just before you hang up (log out of the system). SIGINT is the signal sent when you press ^c; many programs respond in specific ways when this signal is received.

SIGKILL is the "Terminator" of the UNIX signals. Programs cannot ignore it and cannot process it. The process is killed immediately, without even a chance to clean up after itself. SIGTERM is the more graceful alternative; it requests an immediate termination of the program, but allows the program an opportunity to remove temporary files it might have created.

By default, kill sends a SIGTERM to the processes specified. You can specify other signals, however, by using either the number or the name of the signal (minus the SIG prefix, that is). On many systems you can also specify the -1 flag to kill to see what signals are available.

Step 2. Action

1. The simplest way to use the kill command is with the shell notation. First, start a job in the background:

```
% vi &
[1] 6016
%
```

I can now kill this process with either kill %1 or kill 6016, but if I try both of them, the second will fail because the first will have already killed the process:

```
% kill %1
% kill 6016
6016: No such process
[1]    Done                  vi
%
```

Just as if I had dropped a process into the background and it instantly stopped because it needed to produce output, the kill process also had no feedback and took a second or two to occur. In the interim, I entered the second kill command, which then output the error message No such process. Following that, I get an indication that the job ended from the shell itself.

2. Using the ps command, I can find that pesky newmail program that's always running in the background:

```
% ps -ux | grep newmail
taylor    6899   0.1  0.1   52   28 Av S      0:00 grep newmail
taylor   25817   0.0  0.1  124   60 Av I      0:01 newmail
%
```

I want to send that process a hang-up signal (SIGHUP):

```
% kill -HUP 25817
%
```

There's no output at all. Another way I could have sent this request is by using the numeric value of SIGHUP, or kill -1 25817. To see if it worked, I'll have to use the ps command again:

```
% !ps
ps -ux ¦ grep newmail
taylor    7220   0.0  0.1   52    28 Av S           0:00 grep newmail
%
```

Because the newmail program isn't in this listing, I can't conclude that the SIGHUP signal stopped newmail.

Comment: Because kill tells you if a process cannot be found, the typical UNIX solution to finding out if the command worked is to enter !! immediately to repeat the kill command a second time. If kill worked, you see No such process.

3. Some processes are pesky and can resist the benign signals SIGTERM and SIGHUP. That's when you need to use what I call The Big Gun, or SIGKILL. You see this referred to sometimes as the *kill with extreme prejudice* command; the format is kill -9 *process ID*, and it's not for the faint of heart!

   I strongly recommend that you just let kill send the SIGTERM signal and see if that does the job. If it doesn't, try SIGHUP, and if that also fails, use SIGKILL as a last resort.

4. What happens if you try to use kill on jobs that aren't yours? Fortunately, it doesn't work:

```
% ps -aux ¦ head -5
USER        PID  %CPU %MEM    SZ  RSS TT STAT ENG    TIME COMMAND
news       7460  97.7  0.4   336  252 ?  R N    4    4:33 sort -u /tmp/
nnsubj6735a
phaedrus   8693  18.1  1.1  1260  720 rm S           0:03 nn
root       8741  14.4  0.4   416  252 ?  R      9    0:03 nntpd
root       8696  13.9  0.4   416  252 ?  S           0:03 nntpd
Broken pipe
%
% kill 7460
7460: Not owner
%
```

5. Finally, if you leave jobs that have stopped in the background and try to log out, here's what happens:

```
% logout
There are stopped jobs.
%
```

You must use either `fg` to bring each job into the foreground, or `kill` to kill each of the jobs, then quit.

Step 3. Summary

The `kill` command should be used with caution. It can get you into a lot of trouble. For example, do you want to log out rather suddenly? Find the process ID of your login shell and `kill` it. Learn to use `kill`, but learn to use it cautiously.

Lesson Summary

While the file is the underlying unit in the UNIX file system, including all directories, the most fundamental piece of UNIX is the process. In this lesson, you learned how to have background processes, how to stop and restart processes, and how to use `kill` to quit any errant program—running or not.

Another important part of UNIX is the online documentation, the man pages. The combination of `apropos` and `man` enables easy access to this online information.

Workshop
Key Terms

background job	A job that's running but not attached to the terminal or keyboard, or a running program that's not in the foreground.
control number	A unique number the C shell assigns to each background job for easy reference.
current job	The job that is currently attached to the terminal and keyboard (it's the program you're actually running and working within).
foreground job	A synonym for *current job*.
job	A synonym for *process*.

login shell	The shell process that started when you logged in to the system. This is usually where you're working when you're logged in to UNIX.
man pages	The set of online help documents in UNIX that is accessible through the man command.
process	A program running within the UNIX operating system.
signals	Special messages that can be sent to stopped or running processes.
stop a job	Stop the running program without killing it.
wedged process	A process that is stuck in memory and can't free up its resources, even though it's ceased running. This is rare, but annoying.

Questions

1. Look up the man page for the kill command. Does it make sense, given what you learned in this lesson? Would it have made sense before you read this lesson?

2. Use apropos to see if you can find the UNIX command that lets you print mail in a readable format.

3. Use whatis to find how UNIX describes vi, csh, and date. Do they make sense?

4. Start a program, such as vi, and use ^z to stop it. Now kill the process using kill.

5. Start vi again, stop it, and put it in the background. Work on something else, then bring vi back into the foreground.

6. Check ps status to see what processes you have running that aren't shown on jobs. Why might ps and jobs list different processes?

Preview of the Next Chapter

The next lesson focuses on the many facets of printing and generating hard copy on the UNIX system. It's not as easy as you might think, so stay tuned!

Printing in the UNIX Environment

One of the greatest shortcomings of UNIX is printing. Generating printouts is a common task that should be fairly easy to accomplish. However, in this one area of UNIX, there has been continual conflict between the System V and Berkeley groups to the detriment of all.

This lesson focuses on some of the most common UNIX commands for working with printers. It is a primer on how to find out what printers are hooked up to your system, how to send print requests, how to check that your print requests are in the queue for printing, and how to remove your print requests from the queue if you change your mind for any reason.

Goals for This Lesson

In this lesson, you will learn to

☐ Find local printers with `printers`

☐ Send a printout to a printer with `lpr` or `lp`

☐ Format printouts with `pr`

☐ Work with the printer queue, using `lpq`, `lprm`

Various techniques can minimize the complexity of printing in UNIX. The best is to create an alias called `print` that has all the default configuration information you want. If you define `PRINTER` as an environment variable, most of the UNIX print utilities will then default to the printer you specify as the value of the `PRINTER` environment variable, for example, when searching print queues for jobs.

Comment: The differing "philosophies" of BSD and System V have caused problems in the area of printing. In a nutshell, because UNIX systems are always networked (hooked together with high-speed data communications lines), the most valuable feature of a printing tool would be allowing the user to choose to print on any of the many printers attached. For this to work, each machine with an attached printer must be listening for requests from other machines. The root of the BSD versus System V problem is that the two listen for different requests. A System V machine can't send a printout to a printer attached to a BSD machine, and vice versa.

Task 17.1: Find Local Printers with *printers*
Step 1. Description

Of the many problems with printing in UNIX, none is more grievous than trying to figure out the names of all the different printers available, what kinds of printers they are, and where they're located. A complicated configuration file—`/etc/printcap`—contains all this information, but it's definitely not easy to read. So what do you do?

> **Comment:** Some systems have an `lpstat` command, which lists printers available on the system. I find the output of this command difficult to read, hence my inclusion of the `printers` script here. If you find the output acceptable (see the next unit in this lesson for a sample), then you can skip this first unit, although you still might want to spend a few minutes looking at the `printers` script anyway.

I will present a simple 20-line shell script, `printers`, that reads through the `/etc/printcap` file and creates an attractive and easily read listing of all printers configured on your system. This first lesson presents the script and shows it at work on a few different computer systems. I encourage you to enter this script and place it in your own `bin` directory (`$HOME/bin` should be in your `PATH` for this to work.)

Step 2. Action

1. To start, take a quick look at the contents of the `/etc/printcap` file:

```
% head -23 /etc/printcap
# $Header: /usr/msrc/usr/etc/printcap/RCS/printcap,v 1.235 93/11/04 10:55:21 mm
Exp Locker: mm $
aglw\ag\Iwag:\
        :dr=/usr/local/lib/lp/lpmq:\
        :gc=cc:\
        :lf=/usr/spool/lpr/aglw/logfile:\
        :lo=/usr/spool/lpr/aglw/lock:lp=/dev/null:\
        :mj#25:mx#3000:nd=/usr/local/lib/lp/lpnc:\
        :pf=gnpt:\
        :rm=server.utech.edu:rw:sd=/usr/spool/lpr/aglw:sh:\
        :gf=/usr/local/bin/psplot:\
```

```
            :nf=/usr/local/lib/devps/devps:\
            :qo=age:mq=aglw1,aglw2,aglw3,aglw4:mu:\
            :wi=AG 23:wk=multiple Apple LaserWriter IINT:
aglw1:\
            :dr=/usr/local/lib/lp/lwp.sh:\
            :gc=cc:\
            :lf=/usr/spool/lpr/aglw1/logfile:\
            :lo=/usr/spool/lpr/aglw1/lock:lp=/dev/null:\
            :mj#25:mx#3000:nd=/usr/local/lib/lp/lpnc:\
            :pf=gnpt:\
            :rm=server.utech.edu:rw:sd=/usr/spool/lpr/aglw1:sh:\
            :gf=/usr/local/bin/psplot:\
            :nf=/usr/local/lib/devps/devps:\
            :wi=AG 23:wk=Apple LaserWriter IINT:
```

I won't go into exhaustive detail about the meaning of each field in this
listing. It suffices to say that the first line in each entry lists the name of the
printer, a ¦ character, and any other possible names for the printer. Each
field following the printer name is surrounded by colons and has a two-letter
field name (for example, dr, nf), followed by the value of that particular field
or setting. The fields of interest are the printer name; the wi field, which
indicates the location of the printer; and the wk field, which indicates the
type of printer.

2. There are no UNIX utilities to keep you from having to slog through this
   configuration file. I have written a short, yet powerful, C shell script called
   printers to list the desired information in a readable format. Notice the use
   of a here document to create the awk script and the multiple-line pipeline at
   the end of the script that does all the actual work.

```
% cat bin/printers
# printers - create a simple list of printers from the /etc/printcap
#            file on the system.
#
# From
# Teach Yourself UNIX in a Week

set printcap=/etc/printcap
set awkscript=/tmp/awkscript.$$

/bin/rm -f $awkscript
```

```
cat << 'EOF' > $awkscript
NF == 2 { split($1, words, "|");
          prname=words[1]
        }
NF > 2  { printf("%-10s %s\n", prname, $0) }
'EOF'

egrep '(^[a-zA-Z]|:wi)' $printcap | \
  sed 's/:/ /g' | \
  awk -f $awkscript | \
  sed 's/wi=//;s/wk=/(/;s/ $/)/' | \
  more

/bin/rm -f $awkscript

  exit 0
%
```

Some of this script is beyond what you have learned in this book about commands and scripts. In particular, the awk script, although only four lines long, shows some of the more powerful features of the program. Enter this as shown, being careful to match the quotes and slash characters.

3. Once you've entered this script, enter the following:

```
% chmod +x bin/printers
%
```

That will ensure that it's an executable script. Next you need to inform the C shell, using the rehash command, that you have added a new command to the search path. Then you can try your new shell script:

```
% rehash
%
% printers | head -15
aglw        AG 23 (multiple Apple LaserWriter IINT)
aglw1       AG 23 (Apple LaserWriter IINT)
aglw2       AG 23 (Apple LaserWriter IINT)
aglw3       AG 23 (Apple LaserWriter IINT)
aglw4       AG 23 (Apple LaserWriter IINT)
alpslw      LIB 111 (Apple LaserWriter IINTX)
bio         COM B117 (DataPrinter (self-service))
cary        CQuad (NE-B7) (IBM 4019 Laser Printer)
```

17

```
cslw          CS 2249 (Apple LaserWriter IIg)
cs115lw       CS 115 (IBM 4019 LaserPrinter (for CS180))
cs115lw2      CS 115 (IBM 4019 LaserPrinter (for CS180))
csg40lw       CS G040 (IBM 4019 LaserPrinter )
csg50lw       CS G050 (IBM 4019 LaserPrinter )
cslp1         CS G73 (C.Itoh, white paper (self-service))
eng130ci      ENG 130 (C.Itoh, white paper (self-service))
Broken pipe
%
```

You can also use this script to find printers of a certain type or in a specific location, if the descriptions in your /etc/printcap file are configured in the correct manner:

```
% printers ¦ grep -i plotter
knoxhp       KNOX 316A (Hewlett Packard 7550+ Plotter)
ccp          MATH G109 (CALCOMP 1073 Plotter)
cvp          MATH G109 (VERSATEC V-80 Plotter)
%
% printers ¦ grep -i math
lwg186       MATH G186 (Apple LaserWriter IINT(private))
mathci       MATH B9 (C.Itoh, white paper (self-service))
mathlw       MATH 734 (multiple Apple LaserWriter IINT)
mathlw1      MATH 734 (Apple LaserWriter IINT)
mathlw2      MATH 734 (Apple LaserWriter IINT)
mathlw3      MATH 734 (Apple LaserWriter IINT)
cci          MATH G109 (C.Itoh, 3 hole white paper)
ccp          MATH G109 (CALCOMP 1073 Plotter)
cil          MATH G109 (IBM 4019 Laser Printer)
cvp          MATH G109 (VERSATEC V-80 Plotter)
%
```

4. You should now be able to choose a printer that's most convenient for your location. Set the environment variable PRINTER to that value. You might also want to tuck that into the last line of your .login file so that next time you log in, the system will remember your printer selection.

```
% setenv PRINTER mathlw
% vi .login
```

Comment: If your printer is not responding to what you set the PRINTER variable to, try using the LPDEST variable, especially on System V.

```
setenv NAME "Dave Taylor"
setenv BIN  "889"


newmail


mesg y
setenv PRINTER mathlw
~
~
```

Step 3. Summary

The first, and perhaps biggest, hurdle for printing on UNIX has been solved: figuring out what the system calls the printer you're interested in using. Not only do you now have a new command for your UNIX system—printers—but you can see how you can customize UNIX to meet your needs by creating aliases and shell scripts.

Task 17.2: Printing Files with *lpr* or *lp*
Step 1. Description

Now that you have identified the name of the printer to use, how about sending information to the printer? If your are on a BSD system, the command to do this is lpr. You can print the results of a pipe command by entering lpr at the end of the pipeline, or you can directly print files by specifying them to the program, or you can even use < to redirect input.

If you're using a System V version of UNIX, you will need to use the lp command instead. As you read through this lesson, you will see the differences between lpr and lp indicated. Note how the philosophies of the two vary.

The flags available for lpr and lp are numerous, and the most valuable ones are listed in Table 17.1 and Table 17.2.

Table 17.1. Useful flags for `lpr`.

Flag	Meaning
-h	Do not print the header page.
-i	Indent entire file eight spaces before printing.
-L	Print in landscape (sideways) mode, if printer is able to do so.
-P*pr*	Send printout to printer *pr*.
-R	Print pages in reverse order.

Table 17.2. Useful flags for `lp`.

Flag	Meaning
-d *ptr*	Send printout to printer *ptr*.
-P *n*	Print only page *n*.
-t *title*	Use *title* as the cover page title.

Step 2. Action

1. Here's a demonstration of what happens if you try to use `lp` or `lpr` without specifying a printer and without having the PRINTER environment variable set. First, use the unsetenv command to remove environment variable definitions:

```
% unsetenv PRINTER
% who ¦ lpr
lpr: No printer specified
Broken pipe
%
```

Some systems default to a printer named `lp` in this situation, so if you don't get an error message, that's what happened. If you have `lpstat`, the -d flag will result in `lpstat` listing your default printer.

To specify a printer, use the -P flag with lpr or the -d flag with lp, followed immediately by the name of the printer:

```
% who ¦ lpr -Pmathlw
%
```

Specifying a printer with the -P flag (or -d with lp) will always override the environment variable specified in PRINTER; therefore, you can specify the default printer with PRINTER and specify other printers as needed without any further work.

Notice that I printed the output of the who command but received absolutely no information from the lpr command regarding what printer it was sent to, the print job number, or any other information.

To make life easier, I'm going to redefine PRINTER:

```
% setenv PRINTER mathlw
%
```

2. To find out what's in the printer queue, I can use lpstat -p *printer* on SVR4 or the lpq -P*printer* command:

```
% lpq -Pmathlw

mathlw@server.utech.edu:   driver not active
        Printing is disabled.

Pos  User      Bin    Size  Jobname
--   ----      ----   ----  ------
  1  KOSHIHWE  0104   008   KOSHIHWE0104a
  2  KOSHIHWE  0104   008   KOSHIHWE0104b
  3  KOSHIHWE  0104   008   KOSHIHWE0104c
  4  kleimanj  0317   032   kleimanj0317a
  5  zeta      0042   008   zeta0042a
  6  jharger   0167   008   jharger0167a
  7  jharger   0167   008   jharger0167b
  8  ssinfo    0353   000   ssinfo0353a
  9  fuelling  0216   024   fuelling0216a
 10  zeta      0042   152   zeta0042b
 11  tkjared   0142   012   tkjared0142a
 12  SUJATHA   0043   016   SUJATHA0043a
 13  SUJATHA   0043   024   SUJATHA0043b
 14  SUJATHA   0043   044   SUJATHA0043c
 15  bee       0785   012   bee0785a
```

17

```
16  bee       0785   056   bee0785b
17  bee       0785   028   bee0785c
18  ssinfo    0353   004   ssinfo0353b
19  ssinfo    0353   000   ssinfo0353c
20  ssinfo    0353   000   ssinfo0353d
21  ssinfo    0353   004   ssinfo0353e
22  stacysm2  0321   000   stacysm20321a
23  ssinfo    0353   000   ssinfo0353f
24  taylor    0889   000   taylor0889a

mathlw: waiting to be transmitted to server.utech.edu

The queue is empty.
%
```

Quite a few print requests are waiting to be sent, but it's not obvious why the printer is disabled. The output of the lpq and lpstat commands are explained in detail later in this lesson.

3. To print the file dickens.note in landscape mode, without a header page, indented eight spaces, and in reverse order, I can use the following flags:

```
% lpr -hiLR < dickens.note
%
```

If I did this often, a C shell alias could be helpful:

```
% alias lpr...'lpr -hiLR'
%
```

On a System V machine, you could also create the alias alias lpr 'lp', though none of these particular options are available with lp.

If you find yourself printing to a couple different printers quite often, you can easily define a few shell aliases to create printer-specific print commands:

```
% alias mathprint   'lpr -Pmathlw'
% alias libprint     'lpr -Plibrary'
% alias edprint      'lpr -Pedlw'
%
```

On SVR4 machines, the name would be this:

```
% alias mathprint   'lp -dmathlw'
% alias libprint     'lp -dlibrary'
```

```
% alias edprint     'lp -dedlw'
%
```

4. Some systems have a command `lpinfo` that also offers information about printers:

```
% lpinfo mathlw
mathlw: server.utech.edu; MATH 734; multiple Apple LaserWriter IINT
%
```

To find out more information about the printer, you can specify the `-v` flag:

```
% lpinfo -v mathlw
mathlw description:
        driver: /usr/local/lib/lp/lpmq
        printer control group: cc
        graphic filter: /usr/local/bin/psplot
        log file: /usr/spool/lpr/mathlw/logfile
        lock file: /usr/spool/lpr/mathlw/lock
        hardware line: /dev/null
        maximum job count per user = 25
        subqueue list: mathlw1,mathlw2,mathlw3
        maximum print file blocks = 3000
        make unique via bin change
        network driver: /usr/local/lib/lp/lpnc
        ditroff filter: /usr/local/lib/devps/devps
        print formats: graphics, ditroff, use pr, troff
        queue ordering: age
        host attachment: server.utech.edu
        spooling directory: /usr/spool/lpr/mathlw
        location: MATH 734
        description: multiple Apple LaserWriter IINT
%
```

5. The `lpinfo` command can also show you a list of what printers are available, but I find the output format considerably more difficult to understand:

```
% lpinfo -a | head -15
aglw:   server.utech.edu; AG 23; multiple Apple LaserWriter IINT
aglw1:      server.utech.edu; AG 23; Apple LaserWriter IINT
aglw2:      server.utech.edu; AG 23; Apple LaserWriter IINT
aglw3:      server.utech.edu; AG 23; Apple LaserWriter IINT
aglw4:      server.utech.edu; AG 23; Apple LaserWriter IINT
alpslw: sentinel.utech.edu; LIB 111; Apple LaserWriter IINTX
```

17

```
bio:    ace.utech.edu; COM B117; DataPrinter (self-service)
cary:   franklin.utech.edu; CQuad (NE-B7); IBM 4019 Laser Printer
cslw: server.utech.edu; CS 2249; Apple LaserWriter IIg
cs115lw:    expert.utech.edu; CS 115; IBM 4019 LaserPrinter (for CS180)
cs115lw2:   expert.utech.edu; CS 115; IBM 4019 LaserPrinter (for CS180)
csg40lw:    franklin.utech.edu; CS G040; IBM 4019 LaserPrinter
csg50lw:    franklin.utech.edu; CS G050; IBM 4019 LaserPrinter
cslp1: expert.utech.edu; CS G73; C.Itoh, white paper (self-service)
eng130ci:   age.utech.edu; ENG 130; C.Itoh, white paper (self-service)
Broken pipe
%
```

If you find this output readable, then you're undoubtedly becoming a real UNIX expert!

Step 3. Summary

The output of the printers command specifies the location of the printer that printed the file. I need to go to another building to pick up my hard copy. (The location is specified in the output of the printers command.)

Task 17.3: Formatting Printouts with *pr*
Step 1. Description

The printout I generated looked good, but boring. I would like to have a running header on each page, specifying the name of the file and the page number. I'd also like to have a bit more control over some other formatting characteristics. This is exactly where the pr command comes in handy. Not intended just for printing, pr is a general text pagination and formatting command that can be used to display information on the screen. Even better, pr is on both BSD and SVR4 UNIX.

The pr program is loaded with options, most of which are quite useful at times. For example, -2 makes the output two columns, which is useful for printing the who command in landscape mode! The most useful options are shown in Table 17.3.

Table 17.3. Useful flags in pr.

Flag	Meaning
-n	Produce n-column output per page.
+n	Begin printing on the nth page.

Flag	Meaning
-f	Skip the page header and footer information.
-h*hdr*	Use *hdr* as the head of each page.
-w*n*	Set page width to *n* characters (for landscape mode).
-m	Print all files at once, one per column.

Comment: On some UNIX systems, the -f flag to pr causes the program to output form feeds at the bottom of each printed page. To suppress the header and footer, use -t.

Step 2. Action

1. My printout of the who command showed me that my choice of paper was poor. In a 128-character wide landscape printout, I was actually only using the first 30 characters or so of each line. Instead, I can use pr to print in two column mode:

```
% who ¦ pr -2 ¦ more


Dec  9 13:48 1993    Page 1


root     console Dec  6 18:02    ab       ttypk  Dec  9 07:57  (nova)
princess ttyaV   Dec  9 13:44    dutch    ttypl  Dec  8 13:36  (dov)
tempus   ttyaW   Dec  9 13:43    malman   ttypm  Dec  9 13:07  (dov)
enatsuex ttyaY   Dec  9 13:41    bakasmg  ttypq  Dec  9 13:09  (age)
coxt     ttyaZ   Dec  9 13:35    dodsondt ttyps  Dec  8 11:37  (age)
scfarley ttyAa   Dec  9 13:36    md       ttypv  Dec  8 08:23  (kraft)
nancy    ttyAb   Dec  9 13:12    rothenba ttypw  Dec  9 13:15  (trinetra)
rick     ttyAc   Dec  9 13:12    xuxiufan ttypy  Dec  9 13:16  (ector)
fitzte   ttyAd   Dec  9 13:47    nashrm   ttyq3  Dec  9 13:04  (pc115)
```

```
maluong   ttyAe   Dec  9 13:46      dls        ttyq5   Dec  9 13:06   (dialup01)
af5       ttyAg   Dec  9 09:12      myounce    ttyq8   Dec  9 02:14   (limbo)
zjin      ttyAh   Dec  9 13:44      liyan      ttyq9   Dec  9 13:11   (volt)
herbert1  ttyAi   Dec  9 13:29      daffnelr   ttyqA   Dec  9 13:36   (localhost)
ebranson  ttyAj   Dec  9 13:44      mm         ttyqB   Dec  9 10:32   (mm)
billiam   ttyAk   Dec  9 13:36      jlapham    ttyqC   Dec  9 12:46   (mac18)
linet2    ttyAm   Dec  9 11:04      chuicc     ttyqE   Dec  9 13:38   (icarus)
--More-- _
```

Notice that the pr program added a page header that indicates the current date and page number.

2. The header still doesn't contain any information about the command name, which is what would really be helpful. Fortunately, I can easily add the header information I want using pr:

```
% who ¦ pr -h "(output of the who command)" -2 ¦ more


Dec  9 13:50 1993   (output of the who command) Page 1


root      console Dec  6 18:02      ab         ttypk   Dec  9 07:57   (nova)
princess  ttyaV   Dec  9 13:44      dutch      ttypl   Dec  8 13:36   (dov)
tempus    ttyaW   Dec  9 13:43      malman     ttypm   Dec  9 13:07   (dov)
enatsuex  ttyaY   Dec  9 13:41      bakasmg    ttypq   Dec  9 13:09   (age)
coxt      ttyaZ   Dec  9 13:35      dodsondt   ttyps   Dec  8 11:37   (age)
scfarley  ttyAa   Dec  9 13:36      md         ttypv   Dec  8 08:23   (kraft)
nancy     ttyAb   Dec  9 13:12      rothenba   ttypw   Dec  9 13:15   (trinetra)
rick      ttyAc   Dec  9 13:12      xuxiufan   ttypy   Dec  9 13:16   (ector)
fitzte    ttyAd   Dec  9 13:47      dls        ttyq5   Dec  9 13:06   (dialup01)
maluong   ttyAe   Dec  9 13:46      myounce    ttyq8   Dec  9 02:14   (limbo)
maritanj  ttyAf   Dec  9 13:49      liyan      ttyq9   Dec  9 13:11   (volt)
af5       ttyAg   Dec  9 09:12      daffnelr   ttyqA   Dec  9 13:36   (localhost)
zjin      ttyAh   Dec  9 13:48      mm         ttyqB   Dec  9 10:32   (mm)
herbert1  ttyAi   Dec  9 13:29      jlapham    ttyqC   Dec  9 12:46   (mac18)
ebranson  ttyAj   Dec  9 13:44      chuicc     ttyqE   Dec  9 13:38   (icarus)
--More-- _
```

That's much better.

3. I might want to compare the contents of two different directories. Remember that the -1 flag to ls forces the ls program to list the output one filename per line, so I can easily create a couple of files in this format:

```
% ls -1 src > src.listing
% ls -1 /tmp > tmp.listing
%
```

These files look like this:

```
% head src.listing tmp.listing
==> src.listing <==
calc-help
calc.c
fixit.c
info.c
info.o


==> tmp.listing <==
Erik/
GIri/
Garry/
MmIsAlive
Re01759
Re13201
Sting/
VR001187
VR002540
VR002678
%
```

Now I will use pr to build a two-column output:

```
% pr -m src.listing tmp.listing ¦ head -15


Dec  9 13:53 1993    Page 1


calc-help                        Erik/
calc.c                           GIri/
fixit.c                          Garry/
info.c                           MmIsAlive
info.o                           Re01759
massage.c                        Re13201
                                 Sting/
                                 VR001187
                                 VR002540

Broken pipe
%
```

4. This would be more helpful if I could turn off the blank lines automatically included at the top of each listing page, which is a job for the -f flag (or -t if your version of pr was -f for form feeds):

```
% ^pr^pr -f
pr -f -m src.listing tmp.listing ¦ head -15
Dec  9 13:56 1993    Page 1


calc-help                      Erik/
calc.c                         GIri/
fixit.c                        Garry/
info.c                         MmIsAlive
info.o                         Re01759
massage.c                      Re13201
                               Sting/
                               VR001187
                               VR002540
                               VR002678
                               VR002982
                               VR004477
Broken pipe
%
```

5. It looks good. Now it's time to print by piping the output of the pr command to the 1pr command:

```
% !pr ¦ lpr
pr -f -m src.listing tmp.listing ¦ head -15 ¦ lpr
%
```

Step 3. Summary

The pr command can be used to ensure that your printouts are always clean and readable. Again, it's a perfect place to create an alias: alias print 'pr ¦ lpr' or alias print 'pr ¦ lp'. Without any flags, pr automatically adds page numbers to the top of each page.

Task 17.4: Working with the Printer Queue
Step 1. Description

On a personal computer, you might be used to having your printer directly connected to your system, so anything you send to PRT: (on DOS) or File/Print... (on the

Mac) instantly prints. Unfortunately, UNIX doesn't grant you the luxury of using your own personal printer. Instead, it handles print requests in a *printer queue*, a managed list of files to print. When you send a file to a printer with lpr or lp, the request is added to a queue of files waiting to print. Your request goes to the bottom of the list, and any subsequent print requests are added below yours. Your print request gradually moves up to the top of the list and prints, without interrupting the print requests of those folks ahead of you.

Sometimes it can be frustrating to wait for a printout. However, there are some advantages to using a queueing system over simply allowing users to share a single printer. The greatest is that you can use the lprm command to change your mind and remove print requests from the queue before they waste paper. The lprm command works with the *print job name*, which you can learn by checking the print queue, using lpq. Both lprm and lpq can use the default PRINTER setting, or can have printers specified with -Pprinter. The lpq command can also limit output to just your jobs by adding your account name to the command.

If your system doesn't have lprm, then use the cancel command to remove entries from the printer queue. The lpstat command is also the System V replacement for the lpq command, though many sites alias lpq = lpstat to make life a bit easier.

To use cancel, you need to specify the name of the printer and the job ID, as shown in the lpstat output. If I had print request ID 37 on printer hardcopy, then I could cancel the print request with the command cancel hardcopy -37.

Step 2. Action

1. A glance at the math1w queue shows that there are a lot of files waiting to print:

```
% lpq

math1w@server.utech.edu:   driver not active
        Printing is disabled.

Pos  User      Bin   Size  Jobname
--   ----      ----  ----  ------
  1  KOSHIHWE  0104  008   KOSHIHWE0104a
  2  KOSHIHWE  0104  008   KOSHIHWE0104b
```

```
 3   KOSHIHWE  0104   008   KOSHIHWE0104c
 4   kleimanj  0317   032   kleimanj0317a
 5   zeta      0042   008   zeta0042a
 6   jharger   0167   008   jharger0167a
 7   jharger   0167   008   jharger0167b
 8   ssinfo    0353   000   ssinfo0353a
 9   fuelling  0216   024   fuelling0216a
10   zeta      0042   152   zeta0042b
11   tkjared   0142   012   tkjared0142a
12   SUJATHA   0043   016   SUJATHA0043a
13   SUJATHA   0043   024   SUJATHA0043b
14   SUJATHA   0043   044   SUJATHA0043c
15   bee       0785   012   bee0785a
16   bee       0785   056   bee0785b
17   bee       0785   028   bee0785c
18   info      0353   004   info0353b
19   info      0353   000   info0353c
20   info      0353   000   info0353d
21   info      0353   004   info0353e
22   stacysm2  0321   000   stacysm20321a
23   info      0353   000   info0353f
24   taylor    0889   000   taylor0889a

mathlw: waiting to be transmitted to server.utech.edu

The queue is empty.
%
```

My printout is job number 24, with the print job name `taylor0889a`.
Figure 17.1 explains the different fields in the queue listing.

The printer is also turned off. You can see at the top of the `lpq` output the
telltale message `driver not active, printing is disabled`. Obviously, if
the printer is disabled, it's rather futile to wait for a printout.

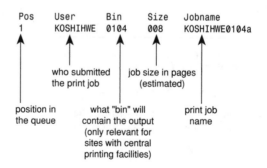

Figure 17.1. *The `lpq` output format explained.*

2. To limit the output to just those printouts that are mine, I specify my account name:

```
% lpq taylor
mathlw@server.utech.edu:   driver not active
       Printing is disabled.

Pos  User      Bin   Size  Jobname
--   ----      ----  ----  ------
  1  taylor    0889  004   taylor0889a

mathlw: waiting to be transmitted to server.utech.edu

The queue is empty.
%
```

3. To check the status of another printer, I can specify the printer with the -P flag:

```
% lpq -Pb280il

b280il@franklin.utech.edu:        driver not active

The queue is empty.

b280il:    waiting to be transmitted to franklin.utech.edu

The queue is empty.
%
```

That's better. The queue is empty.

4. To remove my printout from the mathlw printer queue, I simply specify the print job name from the lpq output:

```
% lprm taylor0889a
%
```

UNIX carries out my command without giving me confirmation that it has done so, but a quick check with lpq shows me what's up:

```
% lpq taylor
mathlw@server.utech.edu:   driver not active
       Printing is disabled.

The queue is empty.
```

```
mathlw: waiting to be transmitted to server.utech.edu

The queue is empty.
%
```

 **Comment:** I wish the default for the lpq command would show only printouts that I have in the queue, and I could use the -a flag to show all printouts queued. Furthermore, instead of incorrectly saying The queue is empty, the lpq should report something more useful, like there are 23 other print jobs in the queue.

5. Now I resubmit the printout request, this time to the b280il printer:

```
% !pr -Pb280il
pr -f -m src.listing tmp.listing ¦ head -15 ¦ lpr -Pb280il
%
```

Uh oh! I don't want that head -15 cutting off the information in the printout.

```
% lpq -Pb280il
b280il@franklin.utech.edu:       driver active; no job printing

Pos  User      Bin   Size  Jobname
--   ----      ---   ----  ------
  1  nfsuser   0058  268   nfsuser0058a
  2  nfsuser   0054  012   nfsuser0054a
  3  taylor    0889  000   taylor0889a

b280il:    waiting to be transmitted to franklin.utech.edu

The queue is empty.
%
```

To remove my print request, I use lprm:

```
% lprm taylor0889a
"taylor0889a" not located.
%
```

I've made a second mistake! I need to specify the printer.

```
% lprm -Pb280i1 taylor0889a
%
```

Now I can fix the original command and print the files correctly:

```
% pr -f -m src.listing tmp.listing ¦ lpr -Pb280i1
%
```

Step 3. Summary

UNIX offers some printing capabilities that you might not be used to working with, particularly the ability to change your mind and stop a print request before it touches paper. You can see that it's a good idea to set the PRINTER environment variable to your favorite printer, to save struggling to enter weird printer names each time you print a file.

Lesson Summary

A few judiciously defined aliases can save you a lot of frustration down the road. Choose your favorite printer, define the PRINTER environment variable to point to that printer, and give yourself an alias like print to include all the default options you like for your printouts. You might consider creating an alias pq to show your own print requests queued for your favorite printer. (This is easy to do. Use alias pq 'lpq $LOGNAME' or alias pq 'lpstat -u $LOGNAME'.) You could also show only your print requests, if any, by tucking a grep into the command: alias pq 'lpq ¦ grep $LOGNAME'.

Workshop
Key Terms

printer queue   The queue, or list, in which all printouts are placed for processing by the specific printer.

print job name   The unique name assigned to a printout by the lpr or lp command.

Questions

1. Use the `lpinfo -a` or `printers` command to find out what printers are available on your system. Which command is easier to use? How many are available?

2. Is your `PRINTER` variable already set to a printer? Is it the printer you would choose?

3. Use `man -k` to see what commands you have on your system that work with the printers and print queues. Use `man` to peruse them.

4. Show three ways to print the file `dickens.note` with `lpr`.

5. Add a printout to the queue, then remove it with `lprm`. What happened?

6. How would you use `pr` to add `A Tale of Two Cities` as a running title across each printout page of the file `dickens.note`? How would you start the printout on the second page of the file?

Preview of the Next Chapter

In the next lesson, you will revisit the `grep` command to learn how it can work for you. You have had a preview of that in this lesson in the use of `grep` in the `printers` script. Also in the next lesson, you will learn about the `find` command with its unique command flags and its partner `xargs`.

Searching for Information and Files

S

18

One of the greatest challenges in UNIX is to find the files you want, when you want them. Even the best organization in the world, with mnemonic subdirectories and carefully named files, can break down and leave you saying to yourself, "I know it's somewhere, and I remember that it contains a bid for Acme Acres Construction to get that contract, but for the life of me, I just can't remember where it is!"

Goals for This Lesson

In this lesson, you will learn about

☐ Creating sophisticated regular expressions

☐ Using egrep for complex expressions

☐ Searching for multiple patterns with fgrep

☐ The find command and its weird options

☐ Using find with xargs

In this lesson you will learn sophisticated ways to find specific information on the UNIX system. First you will revisit the grep command to learn more flags and more about regular expressions. The grep command has two sibling commands—egrep and fgrep—both of which you will also learn. The powerful find command and its partner, xargs, wrap up this lesson.

Task 18.1: Creating Sophisticated Regular Expressions
Step 1. Description

In Chapter 8, "Filters and Piping," back on the third day of your UNIX odyssey, you were introduced to the grep command. You learned how to use grep to find lines containing specified patterns. The four grep flags you learned were -c, to list a count of matches; -i, to ignore the case of the pattern; -l, to list only files containing the specified pattern; and -n, to add line numbers. There's a lot more to grep and particularly a lot more to the patterns that grep can work with. Even better, grep has two sibling search commands in UNIX, fgrep and egrep. If you look at the printers script in the last lesson, you can see that I used egrep with quite a complex pattern.

A valuable flag to grep and its cousins is the -v flag, which inverts the meaning of the command. That is, if grep hawaii travel.plans searches for the word hawaii in the file travel.plans, adding a -v will result in the program showing all lines that *don't* match the pattern specified: grep -v hawaii travel.plans will show all lines that don't contain the pattern hawaii.

The heart of the grep command is the regular expression language used to specify patterns. A regular expression can be as simple as a word to be matched letter for letter, such as acme, or as complex as the example in the printers script, '(^[a-zA-Z]¦:wi)', which matches all lines that begin with an upper- or lowercase letter *or* that contain :wi.

The language of regular expressions is full of punctuation characters and other letters used in unusual ways. It is important to remember that *regular expressions are different from shell wildcard patterns*. It's unfortunate, but it's true. In the C shell, for example, a* lists any file that starts with the letter *a*. Regular expressions aren't *left rooted*, which means that you need to specify ^a if you want to match only lines that begin with the letter *a*. The shell pattern a* only matches filenames that *start with* the letter *a*. The * has a different interpretation completely when used as part of a regular expression: a* is a pattern that matches zero or more occurrences of the letter *a*. The notation for regular expressions is shown in Table 18.1. The egrep command has additional notation that you will learn shortly.

Table 18.1. Summary of regular expression notation.

Notation	Meaning
c	Matches the character c.
\c	Forces c to be read as the letter c, not as another meaning the character might have.
^	Beginning of the line.
$	End of the line.
.	Any single character.
[xy]	Any single character in the set or range specified.
[^xy]	Any single character *not* in the range specified.
c*	Zero or more occurrences of character c.

The notation isn't as complex as it looks in this table. The most important things to remember about regular expressions with grep are that the * denotes zero or more occurrences of the previous character and . is any single character. Remember that shell patterns use * to match any set of zero or more characters *independent* of the previous character and ? to match a single character.

Step 2. Action

1. The easy searches with grep are those that search for specific words without any special regular expression notation:

```
% grep taylor /etc/passwd
taylorj:?:1048:1375:James Taylor:/users/taylorj:/bin/csh
mtaylor:?:769:1375:Mary Taylor:/users/mtaylor:/usr/local/bin/tcsh
dataylor:?:375:518:Dave Taylor:/users/dataylor:/usr/local/lib/msh
taylorjr:?:203:1022:James Taylor:/users/taylorjr:/bin/csh
taylorrj:?:662:1042:Robert Taylor:/users/taylorrj:/bin/csh
taylorm:?:869:1508:Melanie Taylor:/users/taylorm:/bin/csh
taylor:?:1989:1412:Dave Taylor:/users/taylor:/bin/csh
%
```

I searched for all entries in the passwd file that contain the pattern taylor.

2. I've found more matches than I wanted, though. If I'm looking for my own account, I don't want to see all these alternatives. Using the ^ character before the pattern left-roots the pattern:

```
% grep "^taylor" /etc/passwd
taylorj:?:1048:1375:James Taylor:/users/taylorj:/bin/csh
taylorjr:?:203:1022:James Taylor:/users/taylorjr:/bin/csh
taylorrj:?:662:1042:Robert Taylor:/users/taylorrj:/bin/csh
taylorm:?:869:1508:Melanie Taylor:/users/taylorm:/bin/csh
taylor:?:1989:1412:Dave Taylor:/users/taylor:/bin/csh
%
```

Now I want to narrow the search further. I want to specify a pattern that says show me all lines that start with taylor, followed by a character that is not a lowercase letter.

3. To accomplish this, I use the [^xy] notation, which indicates an *exclusion set*, or set of characters that cannot match the pattern:

```
% grep "^taylor[^a-z]" /etc/passwd
taylor:?:1989:1412:Dave Taylor:/users/taylor:/bin/csh
%
```

It worked! You can specify a set two ways. You can either list each character or use a hyphen to specify a range starting with the character to the left of the hyphen and ending with the character to the right of the hyphen. That is, a-z is the range beginning with *a* and ending with *z*, and 0-9 includes all digits.

4. To see which accounts were excluded, remove the ^ to search for an *inclusion range*, which is a set of characters of which one must match the pattern:

```
% grep '^taylor[a-z]' /etc/passwd
taylorj:?:1048:1375:James Taylor:/users/taylorj:/bin/csh
taylorjr:?:203:1022:James Taylor:/users/taylorjr:/bin/csh
```

```
taylorrj:?:668:1042:Robert Taylor:/users/taylorrj:/bin/csh
taylorm:?:869:1508:Melanie Taylor:/users/taylorm:/bin/csh
%
```

5. To see some other examples, I use head to view the first 10 lines of the password file:

```
% head /etc/passwd
root:?:0:0:root:/:/bin/csh
news:?:6:11:USENET News:/usr/spool/news:/bin/ksh
ingres:*?:7:519:INGRES Manager:/usr/ingres:/bin/csh
usrlimit:?:8:800:(1000 user system):/mnt:/bin/false
vanilla:*?:20:805:Vanilla Account:/mnt:/bin/sh
charon:*?:21:807:The Ferryman:/users/tomb:
actmaint:?:23:809:Maintenance:/usr/adm/actmaint:/bin/ksh
pop:*?:26:819::/usr/spool/pop:/bin/csh
lp:*?:70:10:Lp Admin:/usr/spool/lp:
trouble:*?:97:501:Report Facility:/usr/mrg/trouble:/usr/local/lib/msh
%
```

Now I'll specify a pattern that tells grep to search for all lines that contain zero or more occurrences of the letter *z*.

```
% grep 'z*' /etc/passwd ¦ head
root:?:0:0:root:/:/bin/csh
news:?:6:11:USENET News:/usr/spool/news:/bin/ksh
ingres:*?:7:519:INGRES Manager:/usr/ingres:/bin/csh
usrlimit:?:8:800:(1000 user system):/mnt:/bin/false
vanilla:*?:20:805:Vanilla Account:/mnt:/bin/sh
charon:*?:21:807:The Ferryman:/users/tomb:
actmaint:?:23:809:Maintenance:/usr/adm/actmaint:/bin/ksh
pop:*?:26:819::/usr/spool/pop:/bin/csh
lp:*?:70:10:Lp Adminuniverse(att):/usr/spool/lp:
trouble:*?:97:501:Report Facility:/usr/mrg/trouble:/usr/local/lib/msh
Broken pipe
%
```

The result is identical to the previous command, but it shouldn't be a surprise. Specifying a pattern that matches zero or more occurrences will match every line! Specifying only the lines that have one or more *z*'s produces output that is a bit more odd-looking:

```
% grep 'zz*' /etc/passwd ¦ head
marg:?:724:1233:Guyzee:/users/marg:/bin/ksh
axy:?:1272:1233:martinez:/users/axy:/bin/csh
wizard:?:1560:1375:Oz:/users/wizard:/bin/ksh
zhq:?:2377:1318:Zihong:/users/zhq:/bin/csh
mm:?:7152:1233:Michael Kenzie:/users/mm:/bin/ksh
tanzm:?:7368:1140:Zhen Tan:/users/tanzm:/bin/csh
mendozad:?:8176:1233:Don Mendoza:/users/mendozad:/bin/csh
pavz:?:8481:1175:Mary L. Pavzky:/users/pavz:/bin/csh
hurlz:?:9189:1375:Tom Hurley:/users/hurlz:/bin/csh
tulip:?:9222:1375:Liz Richards:/users/tulip:/bin/csh
Broken pipe
```

18

6. Earlier I found that a couple lines in the /etc/passwd file were for accounts that didn't specify a login shell. Each line in the password file must have a certain number of colons, and the very last character on the line for these accounts will be a colon, an easy grep pattern:

```
% grep ':$' /etc/passwd
charon:*?:21:807:The Ferryman:/users/tomb:
lp:*?:70:10:System V Lp Adminuniverse(att):/usr/spool/lp:
%
```

7. Consider this. I get a call from my accountant, and I need to find a file containing a message about a $100 outlay of cash to buy some software. I can use grep to search for all files that contain a dollar sign, followed by a 1, followed by one or more zeroes:

```
% grep '$100*' * */*
Mail/bob_gale:     Unfortunately, our fees are currently $100 per test drive,
budgets
Mail/dan_sommer:We also pay $100 for Test Drives, our very short "First
Looks" section. We often
Mail/james:has been dropped, so if I ask for $1000 is that way outta line
Mail/john_spragens:time testing things since it's a $100 test drive: I'm
willing to
Mail/john_spragens:     Finally, I'd like to request $200 rather than $100
for
Mail/mac:again: expected pricing will be $10,000 - $16,000 and the BriteLite
LX with
Mail/mark:I'm promised $1000 / month for a first
Mail/netnews.postings:  Win Lose or Die, John Gardner (hardback)        $10
Mail/netnews.postings:I'd be willing to pay, I dunno, $100 / year for the
space? I would
Mail/sent:to panic that they'd want their $10K advance back, but the good
news is
Mail/sent:That would be fine.  How about $100 USD for both, to include any
Mail/sent:     Amount: $100.00
%
```

That's quite a few matches. Notice that among the matches are $1000, $10K, and $10. To match the specific value $100, of course, I can use $100 as the search pattern.

Shortcut: You can use the shell to expand files not just in the current directory, but one level deeper into subdirectories, too: * expands your search beyond files in the current directory, and */* expands your search to all files contained one directory below the current point. If you have lots of files, you might instead see the error arg list too long; that's where the find command proves handy.

This pattern demonstrates the sophistication of UNIX with regular expressions. For example, the $ character is a special character that can be used to indicate the end of a line, but only if it is placed at the very end of the pattern. Because I did not place it at the end of the pattern, the grep program reads it as the $ character itself.

8. Here's one more example. In the old days, when people were tied to typewriters, an accepted convention for writing required that you put two spaces after the period at the end of a sentence, though only one space followed the period of an abbreviation like J. D. Salinger. Nowadays, with more text being produced through word processing and desktop publishing, the two-space convention is less accepted, and indeed, when submitting work for publication, I often have to be sure that I *don't* have two spaces after punctuation, lest I get yelled at! The grep command can help ferret out these inappropriate punctuation sequences, fortunately; but the pattern needed is tricky.

To start, I want to see if, anywhere in the file dickens.note, I have used a period followed by a single space:

```
% grep '. ' dickens.note
                          A Tale of Two Cities
                                 Preface
When I was acting, with my children and friends, in Mr Wilkie Collins's
drama of The Frozen Deep, I first conceived the main idea of this
story.  A strong desire came upon me then, to
embody it in my own person;
and I traced out in my fancy, the state of mind of which it would
necessitate the presentation
to an observant spectator, with particular
care and interest.
As the idea became familiar to me, it gradually shaped itself into its
present form.  Throughout its execution, it has had complete possession
of me; I have so far verified what
is done and suffered in these pages,
as that I have certainly done and suffered it all myself.
Whenever any reference (however slight) is made here to the condition
of the Danish people before or during the Revolution, it is truly made,
on the faith of the most trustworthy
witnesses.  It has been one of my hopes to add
something to the popular and picturesque means of
understanding that terrible time, though no one can hope
to add anything to the philosophy of Mr Carlyle's wonderful book.
Tavistock House
November 1859
%
```

What's happening here? The first line doesn't have a period in it, so why does grep say it matches the pattern? In grep, the period is a special character

18

that matches any single character, not specifically the period itself. Therefore, my pattern matches any line that contains a space preceded by any character.

To avoid this interpretation, I must preface the special character with a backslash if I want it to be read as the . character itself:

```
% grep '\. ' dickens.note
story.  A strong desire came upon me then, to
present form.  Throughout its execution, it has had complete possession
witnesses.  It has been one of my hopes to add
%
```

Ahhh, that's better. Notice that all three of these lines have two spaces after each period.

Step 3. Summary

With the relatively small number of notations available in regular expressions, you can create quite a variety of sophisticated patterns to find information in a file.

Task 18.2: For Complex Expressions, Try *egrep*
Step 1. Description

Sometimes a single regular expression can't accomplish what you seek. For example, maybe you're looking for lines that have either one pattern or a second pattern. That is where the egrep command proves helpful. The command gets its name from *expression grep*. It has a notational scheme more powerful than that of grep, as shown in Table 18.2.

Table 18.2. Regular expression notation for egrep.

Notation	Meaning
c	Matches the character c.
\c	Forces c to be read as the letter c, not as another meaning the character might have.
^	Beginning of the line.
$	End of the line.
.	Any single character.
[xy]	Any single character in the set or range specified.

Notation	Meaning
[^xy]	Any single character *not* in the range specified.
c*	Zero or more occurrences of character c.
c+	One or more occurrences of character c.
c?	Zero or one occurrences of character c.
a¦b	Either a or b.
(a)	Regular expression.

Step 2. Action

1. Now I'll search the password file to demonstrate egrep. A pattern that seemed a bit weird was the one used with grep to search for lines containing one or more occurrences of the letter z: 'zz*'. With egrep, this search is much easier:

```
% egrep 'z+' /etc/passwd ¦ head
marg:?:724:1233:Guyzee:/users/marg:/bin/ksh
axy:?:1272:1233:martinez:/users/axy:/bin/csh
wizard:?:1560:1375:Oz:/users/wizard:/bin/ksh
zhq:?:2377:1318:Zihong:/users/zhq:/bin/csh
mm:?:7152:1233:Michael Kenzie:/users/mm:/bin/ksh
tanzm:?:7368:1140:Zhen Tan:/users/tanzm:/bin/csh
mendozad:?:8176:1233:Don Mendoza:/users/mendozad:/bin/csh
pavz:?:8481:1175:Mary L. Pavzky:/users/pavz:/bin/csh
hurlz:?:9189:1375:Tom Hurley:/users/hurlz:/bin/csh
tulip:?:9222:1375:Liz Richards:/users/tulip:/bin/csh
Broken pipe
%
```

2. To search for lines that have either a z or a q, I can use the following:

```
% egrep '(z¦q)' /etc/passwd ¦ head
aaq:?:528:1233:Don Kid:/users/aaq:/bin/csh
abq:?:560:1233:K Laws:/users/abq:/bin/csh
marg:?:724:1233:Guyzee:/users/marg:/bin/ksh
ahq:?:752:1233:Andy Smith:/users/ahq:/bin/csh
cq:?:843:1233:Rob Till:/users/cq:/usr/local/bin/tcsh
axy:?:1272:1233:Alan Yeltzin:/users/axy:/bin/csh
helenq:?:1489:1297:Helen Schoy:/users/helenq:/bin/csh
wizard:?:1560:1375:Oz:/users/wizard:/bin/ksh
qsc:?:1609:1375:Enid Grim:/users/qsc:/usr/local/bin/tcsh
zhq:?:2377:1318:Zong Qi:/users/zhq:/bin/csh
Broken pipe
%
```

18

3. Now I can revisit the egrep pattern used in the last chapter, and it should make sense to you:

```
% egrep '(^[a-zA-Z]|:wi)' /etc/printcap | head
aglw:\
        :wi=AG 23:wk=multiple Apple LaserWriter IINT:
aglw1:\
        :wi=AG 23:wk=Apple LaserWriter IINT:
aglw2:\
        :wi=AG 23:wk=Apple LaserWriter IINT:
aglw3:\
        :wi=AG 23:wk=Apple LaserWriter IINT:
aglw4:\
        :wi=AG 23:wk=Apple LaserWriter IINT:
Broken pipe
%
```

Now you can see that the pattern specified looks either for lines that begin (^) with an upper- or lowercase letter ([a-zA-Z]) *or* for lines that contain the pattern :wi.

Step 3. Summary

Any time you want to look for lines that contain more than a single pattern, egrep is the best command to use.

Task 18.3: Searching for Multiple Patterns at Once with *fgrep*

Step 1. Description

Sometimes it's helpful to look for many patterns at once. For example, you might want to have a file of patterns and invoke a UNIX command that searches for lines that contain any of the patterns in that file. That's where the fgrep, or *file-based grep*, command comes into play. A file of patterns can contain any pattern that grep would understand (which means, unfortunately, that you can't use the additional notation available in egrep) and is specified with the -f *file* option.

Step 2. Action

1. I use fgrep with wrongwords, an alias and file that contains a list of words I commonly misuse. Here's how it works:

```
% alias wrongwords
fgrep -i -f .wrongwords
% cat .wrongwords
effect
affect
```

```
insure
ensure
idea
thought
%
```

Any time I want to check a file, for example `dickens.note`, to see if it has any of these commonly misused words, I simply enter the following:

```
% wrongwords dickens.note
drama of The Frozen Deep, I first conceived the main idea of this
As the idea became familiar to me, it gradually shaped itself into its
%
```

I need to determine whether to use *ideas* or *thoughts*. It's a subtle distinction I often forget in my writing.

2. Here's another sample file that contains a couple words from `wrongwords`:

```
% cat sample3
At the time I was hoping to insure that the cold weather
would avoid our home, so I, perhaps foolishly, stapled the
weatherstripping along the inside of the sliding glass
door in the back room. I was surprised how much affect it
had on our enjoyment of the room, actually.


%
```

Can you see the two incorrectly used words in this sentence? The `spell` program can't:

```
% spell sample3
%
```

The `wrongwords` alias, on the other hand, can detect lines with these words:

```
% wrongwords sample3
At the time I was hoping to insure that the cold weather
door in the back room. I was surprised how much affect it
%
```

3. This would be a bit more useful if it could show just the individual words matched, rather than the entire lines. That way I wouldn't have to figure out which words are incorrect. To do this, I can use the `awk` command. This time the command will use a *for loop*. That is, it will repeat the command starting from the initial state (`i=1`) and keep adding one to the counter (`i++`) until the end condition is met (`i>NF`): `'{for (i=1;i<=NF;i++) print $i}'`. Each line seen by `awk` will be printed one word at a time with this command. Remember that `NF` is the number of fields in the current line.

Here is a short example:

```
% echo 'this is a sample sentence' ¦ awk '{for (i=1;i<=NF;i++) print $i}'
this
is
a
sample
sentence
%
```

4. I could revise my alias, but trying to get the quotation marks correct is a nightmare. It would be much easier to make this a simple shell script instead:

```
% cat bin/wrongwords
# wrongwords - show a list of commonly misused words in the file

cat $* ¦ \
  awk '{for (i=1;i<=NF;i++) print $i}' ¦\
  fgrep -i -f .wrongwords

%
```

To make this work correctly, I need to remove the existing alias for wrongwords by using the C shell `unalias` command, add execute permission to the shell script, then use `rehash` to ensure that the C shell can find the command when requested:

```
% unalias wrongwords
% chmod +x bin/wrongwords
% rehash
```

Now it's ready to use:

```
% wrongwords sample3
insure
affect
%
```

5. The `fgrep` command can also *exclude* words from a list. If you have been using the `spell` command, it's quickly clear that the program doesn't know anything about acronyms or some other correctly spelled words that you might use in your writing. That's where `fgrep` can be a helpful compatriot. Build a list of words that you commonly use that aren't misspelled, but that `spell` reports as being misspelled:

```
% alias myspell 'spell \!* ¦ fgrep -v -i -f $HOME/.dictionary'
% cat $HOME/.dictionary
BBS
FAX
Taylor
Utech
Zygote
%
```

Now spell can be more helpful:

```
% spell newsample
FAX
illetterate
Letteracy
letteracy
letterate
Papert
pre
rithmetic
Rs
Taylor
Utech
Zygote
%
% myspell newsample
illetterate
Letteracy
letteracy
letterate
Papert
pre
rithmetic
Rs
%
```

Step 3. Summary

You have now met the entire family of grep commands. For the majority of your searches for information, you can use the grep command itself. Sometimes, though, it's nice to have options, particularly if you decide to customize your commands as shown in the scripts and aliases explored in this lesson.

Task 18.4: The *find* Command and Its Weird Options
Step 1. Description

The grep family can help you find files by their content. There are a lot of other ways to look for things in UNIX, and that's where the find command can help. This command has a notation that is completely different from all other UNIX commands. It has full-word options rather than single-letter options. Instead of -n *pattern* to match filenames, for example, find uses -name *pattern*.

The general format for this command is to specify the starting point for a search through the file system, followed by any actions desired. The list of possible options, or flags, is show in Table 18.3.

18

Table 18.3. Useful options for the `find` command.

Option	Meaning
`-atime` *n*	True if file was accessed *n* days ago.
`-ctime` *n*	True if the file was created *n* days ago.
`-exec` *cmd*	Execute command.
`-mtime` *n*	True if file was modified *n* days ago.
`-name` *pat*	True if filename matches pattern.
`-print`	Print name of files found.
`-type` *c*	True if file is of type *c* (as shown in Table 18.4).
`-user` *name*	True if file is owned by user *name*.

The `find` command checks the specified options, going from left to right, once for each file or directory encountered. Further, `find` with any of the time-oriented commands can search for files more recent than, older than, or exactly the same age as a specified date, with the specifications *-n*, *+n*, and *n*, respectively. Some examples will make this clear.

Step 2. Action

1. At its simplest, `find` can be used to create a list of all files and directories below the current directory:

```
% find . -print
.
./OWL
./OWL/owl.h
./OWL/owl
./OWL/owl.c
./OWL/simple.editor.c
./OWL/ask.c
./OWL/simple.editor.o
./OWL/owl.o
./OWL/Doc
./OWL/Doc/Student.config
./OWL/handout.c
./OWL/owl.question
./OWL/WordMap
./OWL/WordMap/a.out
./OWL/WordMap/lots_of_lines
./OWL/WordMap/msw_to_txt.c
```

```
lots and lots of output removed

./src/info.o
./src/massage.c
./keylime.pie
./csh.man
./sample
./sample2
./awkscript
./dickens.note
./newsample
././.sh_history
./mbox
./cheryl
./temp
./temp/zmail
./temp/attach.msg
././.profile
./buckaroo
./sample3
./buckaroo.confused
./deleteme
./dead.letter
./who.is.who
./src.listing
./tmp.listing
././.wrongwords
./papert.article
%
```

2. To limit the output to just those files that are C source files (those that have a .c suffix), I can use the -name option *before* the -print option:

```
% find . -name "*.c" -print
./OWL/owl.c
./OWL/simple.editor.c
./OWL/ask.c
./OWL/handout.c
./OWL/WordMap/msw_to_txt.c
./OWL/WordMap/newtest.c
./OWL/feedback.c
./OWL/define.c
./OWL/spell.c
./OWL/submit.c
./OWL/utils.c
./OWL/parse.c
./OWL/sendmail.c
./owl.c
./src/calc.c
./src/info.c
./src/fixit.c
./src/massage.c
%
```

Using the -name option before the -print option can be very handy.

18

3. To find just those files that have been modified in the last seven days, I can use -mtime with the argument -7 (include the hyphen):

```
% find . -mtime -7 -name "*.c" -print
./OWL/owl.c
./OWL/simple.editor.c
./OWL/ask.c
./OWL/utils.c
./OWL/sendmail.c
%
```

If I just use the number 7 (without a hyphen), then I will only match those files that were modified exactly seven days ago:

```
% find . -mtime 7 -name "*.c" -print
%
```

To find those C source files that I haven't touched for at least 30 days, I use +30:

```
% find . -mtime +30 -name "*.c" -print
./OWL/WordMap/msw_to_txt.c
./OWL/WordMap/newtest.c
./src/calc.c
./src/info.c
./src/fixit.c
./src/massage.c
%
```

4. With find, I now have a tool for looking across vast portions of the file system for specific file types, filenames, and so on.

To look across the /bin and /usr directory trees for filenames that contain the pattern cp, I can use the following command:

```
% find /bin /usr -name "*cp*" -print
/usr/diag/sysdcp
/usr/spool/news/alt/bbs/pcbuucp
/usr/spool/news/alt/sys/amiga/uucp
/usr/spool/news/comp/mail/uucp
/usr/spool/news/comp/os/cpm
/usr/spool/news/comp/protocols/tcp-ip
/usr/spool/uucp
find: cannot open <"/usr/spool/nqs">
/usr/spool/lpr/mathcp
/usr/spool/mail/cpotter
/usr/spool/mail/mcpherso
/usr/spool/erpcd/support/acp_config
/usr/spool/erpcd/support/acp_portinfo
/usr/local/bin/cnews/input/recpnews
/usr/local/bin/cppstdin
/usr/local/lib/libXdmcp.a
/usr/local/lib/gcc-lib/i386-sequent-bsd4.2/2.4.5/include/netinet/tcp.h
```

```
/usr/local/lib/gcc-lib/i386-sequent-bsd4.2/2.4.5/include/netinet/tcp_var.h
/usr/local/lib/gcc-lib/i386-sequent-bsd4.2/2.4.5/cpp
/usr/local/etc/tcpd
/usr/local/etc/acp_restrict
/usr/local/etc/acp_logfile
/usr/local/man/man1/cccp.1
/usr/man/man1/RCS/rcp.1c,v
/usr/man/man1/RCS/cpp.1,v
/usr/man/man1/RCS/cp.1,v
/usr/man/man1/RCS/uucp.1c,v
/usr/man/man1/cpplot.1l
/usr/man/man1/cpio.1u
/usr/man/man1/cp.1
/usr/man/man1/cpp.1
/usr/man/man1/rcp.1c
/usr/man/man1/macptopbm.1u
/usr/man/man1/pbmtomacp.1u
/usr/man/man3/RCS/p_cpus_online.3p,v
/usr/man/man3/RCS/cpus_online.3p,v
/usr/man/man3/RCS/getrpcport.3r,v
/usr/man/man3/cpus_online.3p
/usr/man/man3/getrpcport.3r
/usr/man/man3/p_cpus_online.3p
/usr/man/man3/unitcp.3f
/usr/man/man3/strcpy.3
/usr/man/man3/strncpy.3
/usr/man/man4/RCS/tcp.4p,v
/usr/man/man4/tcp.4p
/usr/man/man8/tcpd.8l
/usr/man/cat3f/%unitcp.3f.Z
/usr/man/cat3f/unitcp.3f.Z
/usr/unsup/bin/cpio
/usr/unsup/gnu/man/man1/cccp.1
/usr/news/cpulimits
/usr/doc/local/form/cp
/usr/doc/local/form/cpio
/usr/doc/local/form/rcp
/usr/doc/uucp
%
```

Comment: This type of search can take a long time on a busy system. When I ran this command on my system, it took almost an hour to complete!

18

5. To find a list of the directories I've created in my home directory, I can use the -type specifier with one of the values shown in Table 18.4:

```
% find . -type d -print
.
./OWL
./OWL/Doc
./OWL/WordMap
./.elm
./Archives
./InfoWorld
./InfoWorld/PIMS
./Mail
./News
./bin
./src
./temp
%
```

Table 18.4. Helpful find-type file types.

Letter	Meaning
d	Directory
f	File
l	Link

6. To find more information about each of these directories, I can use the
   -exec option to find. Unfortunately, I cannot simply enter the command.
   The exec option must be used with {}, which will be replaced by the
   matched filename, and \; at the end of the command. (If the \ is left out,
   the C shell will interpret the ; as the end of the find command.) You must
   also ensure that there is a space between the {} and the \; as shown:

```
% find . -type d -exec ls -ld {} \;
drwx------ 11 taylor      1024 Dec 10 14:13 .
drwx------  4 taylor       532 Dec  6 18:31 ./OWL
drwxrwx---  2 taylor       512 Dec  2 21:18 ./OWL/Doc
drwxrwx---  2 taylor       512 Nov  7 11:52 ./OWL/WordMap
drwx------  2 taylor       512 Dec 10 13:30 ./.elm
drwx------  2 taylor       512 Nov 21 10:39 ./Archives
drwx------  3 taylor       512 Dec  3 02:03 ./InfoWorld
drwx------  2 taylor       512 Sep 30 10:38 ./InfoWorld/PIMS
drwx------  2 taylor      1024 Dec  9 11:42 ./Mail
drwx------  2 taylor       512 Oct  6 09:36 ./News
drwx------  2 taylor       512 Dec 10 13:58 ./bin
drwx------  2 taylor       512 Oct 13 10:45 ./src
drwxrwx---  2 taylor       512 Nov  8 22:20 ./temp
%
```

7. The find command is commonly used to remove core files that are more
   than a few days old. These core files, as you recall, are copies of the actual

memory image of a running program when the program dies unexpectedly. They can be huge, so occasionally trimming them is wise:

```
% find . -name core -ctime +4 -exec /bin/rm -f {} \;
%
```

There's no output from this command because I didn't use the -print at the end of the command.

Step 3. Summary

The find command is a powerful command in UNIX. It helps you find files by owner, type, filename, and other attributes. The most awkward part of the command is the required elements of the -exec option, and that's where the xargs command helps immensely.

Task 18.5: Using *find* with *xargs*
Step 1. Description

You can use find to search for files, and you can use grep to search within files, but what if you want to search a combination? That's where xargs is helpful.

Step 2. Action

1. A few days ago, I was working on a file that was computing character mappings of files. I'd like to find it again, but I don't remember either the filename or where the file is located.

   First off, what happens if I use find and have the -exec argument call grep to find files containing a specific pattern?

```
% find . -type f -exec grep -i mapping {} \;
typedef struct mappings {
map_entry character_mapping[] = {
int        long_mappings = FALSE;
         case 'l': long_mappings = TRUE;
           if (long_mappings)
       /** do a short mapping **/
       /** do a long mapping **/
       /** Look up the specified character in the mapping database **/
       while ((character_mapping[pointer].key < ch) &&
             (character_mapping[pointer].key > 0))
       if (character_mapping[pointer].key == ch)
         return ( (map_entry *) &character_mapping[pointer]);
# map,uucp-map    = The UUCP Mapping Project = nca-maps@apple.com
grep -i "character*mapping" * */* */*/*
to print PostScript files produced by a mapping application that runs on the
bionet.genome.chromosomes        Mapping and sequencing of eucaryote chromo-
somes.
```

Searching for Information and Files

```
./bin/my.new.cmd: Permission denied
typedef struct mappings {
map_entry character_mapping[] = {
int         long_mappings = FALSE;
        case 'l': long_mappings = TRUE;
            if (long_mappings)
        /** do a short mapping **/
        /** do a long mapping **/
        /** Look up the specified character in the mapping database **/
        while ((character_mapping[pointer].key < ch) &&
                (character_mapping[pointer].key > 0))
        if (character_mapping[pointer].key == ch)
            return ( (map_entry *) &character_mapping[pointer]);
or lower case values. The table mapping upper to
%
```

The output is interesting, but it doesn't contain any filenames!

2. A second, smarter strategy would be to use the -l flag to grep so that grep only specifies the matched filename:

```
% find . -type f -exec grep -l -i mapping {} \;
./OWL/WordMap/msw_to_txt.c
./.elm/aliases.text
./Mail/mark
./News/usenet.alt
./bin/my.new.cmd: Permission denied
./src/fixit.c
./temp/attach.msg
%
```

3. That's a step in the right direction, but the problem with this approach is that each time find matches a file, it invokes grep, which is a very resource-intensive strategy. Instead, you use the xargs to read the output of find and build calls to grep (remember that each time a file is seen, the grep program will check through it) that specify a lot of files at once. This way, grep is only called four or five times even though it might check through 200 or 300 files. By default, xargs always tacks the list of filenames to the end of the specified command, so using it is as easy as can be:

```
% find . -type f -print ¦ xargs grep -l -i mapping
./OWL/WordMap/msw_to_txt.c
./.elm/aliases.text
./Mail/mark
./News/usenet.alt
./bin/my.new.cmd: Permission denied
./src/fixit.c
./temp/attach.msg
%
```

This gave the same output, but it was a lot faster.

4. What's nice about this approach to working with find is that because grep is getting multiple filenames, it will automatically include the filename of any file that contains a match when grep shows the matching line. Removing the -l flag results in exactly what I want:

```
% ^-1^
find . -type f -print ¦ xargs grep -i mapping
./OWL/WordMap/msw_to_txt.c:typedef struct mappings {
./OWL/WordMap/msw_to_txt.c:map_entry character_mapping[] = {
./OWL/WordMap/msw_to_txt.c:int          long_mappings = FALSE;
./OWL/WordMap/msw_to_txt.c:     case 'l': long_mappings = TRUE;
./OWL/WordMap/msw_to_txt.c:        if (long_mappings)
./OWL/WordMap/msw_to_txt.c:     /** do a short mapping **/
./OWL/WordMap/msw_to_txt.c:     /** do a long mapping **/
./OWL/WordMap/msw_to_txt.c:     /** Look up the specified character in the
mapping database **/
./OWL/WordMap/msw_to_txt.c:     while ((character_mapping[pointer].key < ch)
&&
./OWL/WordMap/msw_to_txt.c:                (character_mapping[pointer].key > 0))
./OWL/WordMap/msw_to_txt.c:     if (character_mapping[pointer].key == ch)
./OWL/WordMap/msw_to_txt.c:      return ( (map_entry *)
&character_mapping[pointer]);
./.elm/aliases.text:# map,uucp-map    = The UUCP Mapping Project = nca-
maps@apple.com
./.history:grep -i "character*mapping" * */* */*/*
./.history:find . -type f -exec grep -i mapping {} \;
./Mail/mark:to print PostScript files produced by a mapping application that
runs on the
./News/usenet.alt:bionet.genome.chromosomes     Mapping and sequencing of
eucaryote chromosomes.
./bin/my.new.cmd: Permission denied
./src/fixit.c:typedef struct mappings {
./src/fixit.c:map_entry character_mapping[] = {
./src/fixit.c:int          long_mappings = FALSE;
./src/fixit.c:    case 'l': long_mappings = TRUE;
./src/fixit.c:        if (long_mappings)
./src/fixit.c:    /** do a short mapping **/
./src/fixit.c:    /** do a long mapping **/
./src/fixit.c:    /** Look up the specified character in the mapping database
**/
./src/fixit.c:    while ((character_mapping[pointer].key < ch) &&
./src/fixit.c:            (character_mapping[pointer].key > 0))
./src/fixit.c:    if (character_mapping[pointer].key == ch)
./src/fixit.c:     return ( (map_entry *) &character_mapping[pointer]);
./temp/attach.msg:or lower case values. The table mapping upper to
%
```

Step 3. Summary

When used in combination, find, grep, and xargs are a potent team to help find files lost or misplaced anywhere in the UNIX file system.

Lesson Summary

I encourage you to experiment further with these important commands to find ways they can help you work with UNIX.

Workshop
Key Terms

exclusion set	A set of characters that the pattern must not contain.
for loop	A programming structure that iterates once for each specified value, or that increments a variable a specified number of times. For example, `for (i=0;i<10;i++) print i` will initialize the variable `i` to 0, then print the value of `i` (`print i`) and increment it by one (`i++`) until this has been done ten times (`i<10` becomes false). The output of this loop is the numbers 0, 1, 2, 3, 4, 5, 6, 7, 8, and 9.
inclusion range	A range of characters that a pattern must include.
left-rooted	Patterns that must occur at the beginning of a line.
right-rooted	Patterns that must occur at the end of a line.

Questions

1. Create regular expressions to match the following:

   ☐ lines that contain the words *hot* and *cold*

   ☐ lines that contain the word *cat* but not *cats*

   ☐ lines that begin with a numeral

2. There are two different ways you could have UNIX match all lines that contain the words *hot* and *cold*. One uses `grep`, and one uses pipes. Show both.

3. Use the -v flag with various grep commands and show the command and pattern needed to match lines that:

☐ begin with a numeral

☐ don't contain *cabana*

☐ don't contain either *jazz* or *funk*

☐ don't contain *jazz, funk, disco, blues,* or *ska.*

4. There are two ways to look for lines containing any one of the words *jazz, funk, disco, blues,* and *ska.* Show both of them.

5. Use find and wc -l to count how many files you have. Be sure to include the -type f option so that you don't include directories in the count.

6. Use the necessary commands to list

☐ all filenames that contain abc

☐ all files that contain abc

Preview of the Next Chapter

Tomorrow is your last day of learning UNIX. I will introduce you to the power UNIX tools that are available. The next lesson explores ways of interacting with computers and communicating with people on other computer systems, using telnet, rlogin, talk, and ftp. I will give you a brief lesson on the user@host notation for Internet e-mail. You will also learn about the many UNIX programming tools available. The book ends with a look at some of the fascinating and powerful information servers and systems available on the Internet, including Netnews, archie, and gopher. See you tomorrow!

Power UNIX
Tools

Connecting with Remote UNIX Systems

Today is your last day of learning about UNIX. You've come a long way in a short time and now have a considerable amount of knowledge. To wrap up *Teach Yourself UNIX in a Week*, these last lessons focus on specific advanced topics. This lesson looks at the myriad of different commands available for working with other computer systems. The next lesson introduces the various commands available for programming on UNIX, and the final lesson is a brief tour of some of the most exciting information sources available on the Internet and how to use them on UNIX systems.

Goals for This Lesson

In this lesson you will learn about:

- ☐ Connecting to modems and dialing remote computers
- ☐ Sending e-mail to UUCP users
- ☐ Copying files to other UUCP sites
- ☐ Connecting to remote Internet sites
- ☐ Sending e-mail to Internet users
- ☐ Copying files from other Internet sites
- ☐ Talking with remote Internet users

As you can see, this lesson really breaks down into two categories of commands—those used if you're connected to other UNIX systems through a telephone line and those used if you're connected directly via a network connection of some sort. If you're on a university or corporate UNIX system, there's an excellent chance that you're hooked into the Internet, a massive worldwide network of UNIX and other computer systems connected through very high-speed dedicated wires.

If you have a stand-alone UNIX system, then you still might want to read through this lesson to familiarize yourself with the various communication options available in UNIX. It's inevitable that sooner or later you will be hooked up to the network, and when that time comes you will have some familiarity with the range of UNIX options available.

Task 19.1: Connecting to Modems and Dialing Remote Computers
Step 1. Description

Connecting to remote UNIX sites, or to remote computers at all via modem and telephone lines in UNIX, has a long and honorable history. Indeed, before there was ever any concept of local area networks, TCP/IP, and all this high-speed jazz, UNIX systems were talking back and forth through modems and telephone lines. If you're familiar with PC communications, you know that there are various *protocols* for transmitting files, the most popular being *xmodem, zmodem,* and *kermit.* UNIX had all that first, and the UNIX protocol for transferring files is known as the *UUCP g Protocol.* The entire file transmission protocol for modem-based connections is called *UUCP,* or UNIX-to-UNIX Copy Program.

Unfortunately, once networks started to take off, companies stopped being interested in working with UUCP connectivity, so it's quite tricky to configure a system to work with the modem. It is difficult to both offer a `login:` prompt to those who dial in and be able to dial out with the same line.

> **Comment:** Try to imagine the problem. The tty line device driver for the modem line has to be a regular login line, but at the same time it has to be able to instantly transform into an outbound communications line. The UNIX solution is to have different device drivers share the single tty line, one dedicated to any incoming connection, one for outbound connections, and one to be the mediator. By convention, the incoming line is `ttyNN`, the outbound line is `cuaNN` and the mediator is `culNN`, where *NN* is the specific device line.
>
> For example, `tty0`, `cul0`, and `cua0` are a typical set of devices you might see on a UNIX machine configured to have a modem hooked up.

To work with modems on UNIX, therefore, the first, and often most difficult, step is to identify the exact name of the device driver that allows you to connect with your modem directly. For purposes of illustration, I use `cua0` herein, though yours may be different.

Once you know the name of your modem line, you can use a wide variety of commands for working with the modem line. The standard UNIX utility for calling remote sites is cu, or *call UNIX*, and it has a number of different flags: -b*n* sets the number of bits per byte, -e sets even *parity* (parity is a simple error-checking protocol), -o sets odd parity, -h specifies *half-duplex* lines (which are needed if the remote computer doesn't echo what you type), -l*line* specifies which line you want to use and -s*speed* indicates the desired speed. Following the set of flags you desire, specify the phone number, the system name, or the network address. A typical usage for cu might be to connect at 2400 baud, even parity, to a remote system at 555-1212 on line cua0, or cu -e -s2400 5551212.

Comment: It sounds quite convenient to enter only the name of a system and have the computer know the telephone number, but the reality is a bit more harsh. If the named system doesn't exist in a file called /usr/lib/uucp/Systems, then you can't specify it by name. Worse, you can't look at the Systems file because it's off-limits. To find out what computer systems your system knows in its UUCP database, use uuname -c (the -c flag specifies that it should show the cu names).

In the last few years, an alternate, much easier command has arisen, tip. In fact, this is so much easier that it doesn't have any flags: just enter tip *host* or tip *number* to connect to a remote system.

Step 2. Action

1. Typically, the first few times you use cu you dance about with the program trying to figure out the syntax:

```
% cu -s2400 att44
cu: warning: -s flag ignored when system name used
Connect failed: SYSTEM NOT IN Systems File
%
```

How about finding a list of what machines are known?

```
% uuname -c
att33
%
```

2. Let's try again to connect:

```
% cu att33
DIALING..._
```

At this point, the system has found the telephone number of the remote host called `att33`, it has connected to the modem, and it is dialing the remote computer.

```
% cu att33
DIALING...CONNECTED

_
```

When a connection with a remote system is established, it's usually required that you press Return a couple times so the other side knows you're there. After I do so, this is what I see:

```
% cu att3
DIALING...CONNECTED


Welcome to AT&T Research Facility #33. You must be an authorized user
to log in to this system. If you aren't, log out now.
Login: _
```

I'm not actually an authorized user, so I can drop the connection by using a tilde command, similar to those tilde commands you learned with `mailx`. Use ~? to obtain a list, and you can always log out with ~.:

```
Welcome to AT&T Research Facility #33. You must be an authorized user
to log in to this system. If you aren't, log out now.
Login: ~.
DISCONNECTED
%
```

3. To call a particular number, I simply specify the number at the end of the line. This time, though, I also have to specify a connection speed:

```
% cu -s2400 5551212
DIALING..._
```

The same sequence of events as shown in earlier examples occurs.

When specifying a phone number, some further capabilities can be used, though unfortunately they can be a bit confusing. Any time the cu program sees a dash, it adds a four-second pause on the dialog sequence, and any time it sees an equals sign it waits for a dial tone on the line. If you were in an inside PBX system, you could use 9= to request and wait for an outside line (or you could use 9- and assume that four seconds is always plenty long enough to get the second dial tone).

4. Once connected, using ~? results in this:

```
DIALING...CONNECTED
~?
Possible options:
~.    drop connection and exit
~!    escape to interactive shell on local system
~!cmd    execute cmd on local system
~$cmd    run cmd on local system, sending output to remote
~%cd    change directory on local system
~%take a b    copy file a on remote system to b on local system
~%put b a    copy local file b to remote system, calling it a on the remote
~%break    send a BREAK character
—
```

I use ~. to again drop the connection.

```
~.
DISCONNECTED
%
```

5. The tip command is quite similar:

```
% tip att33
connected
~?
  ~!      shell
  ~<      receive file from remote host
  ~>      send file to remote host
  ~t      take file from remote UNIX
  ~p      put file to remote UNIX
  ~¦      pipe remote file
  ~$      pipe local command to remote host
  ~c      change directory
  ~.      exit from tip
  ~^D     exit from tip
  ~^Y     suspend tip (local+remote)
  ~^Z     suspend tip (local only)
```

```
~s       set variable
~?       get this summary
~#       send break
~{       receive xmodem text file
~}       send xmodem text file
~(       receive xmodem binary file
~)       send xmodem binary file
```

I can use ~. to disconnect from the system and return to the shell:

```
~.
disconnected
%
```

Step 3. Summary

Working with modems has really fallen out of favor with the majority of UNIX vendors. The only companies still offering any support and training documents for these commands are those that target UNIX for PC environments, such as the Santa Cruz Operation and Univel, which offers the product UnixWare. Your computer system should include some documentation on how to work with cu, tip, or similar communications commands, and on how to configure the modem to work correctly. The best situation is when you have a system administrator who can work through all the complexities and supply you with a simple command or two. Once you've figured it all out and have the phone number for the system you are trying to reach, make an alias for it and forget about it!

Comment: It's been many years since anyone I know dialed out from a UNIX system. It seems like now everyone spends their time dialed *in* to UNIX systems instead. As time goes on, more and more systems will be connected via higher-speed networks, leaving phones and modems in the proverbial dust.

Task 19.2: Sending E-mail to UUCP Users
Step 1. Description

In the first few years of telephone-based computer connections, the UUCP network grew and blossomed to the point where there were thousands of computer systems calling each other hourly. One place I worked had a computer that could directly call

180 different systems! The strategy of this network design was pretty intriguing: Each machine would call other machines in its local calling area, and usually one or two long-distance hosts. To send mail to someone, you'd therefore need to work out the *path* of connections between your own computer and the other person's. Figure 19.1 shows a typical network layout.

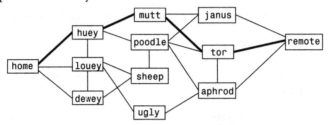

Figure 19.1. *A sample UUCP map.*

Imagine you're at the computer called home and your friend is at the computer called remote. There are a variety of different paths you could use to get your message across, but the most direct is the best: huey to mutt to tor to remote. In UUCP notation, each system is followed by an exclamation point, so you would write your path as huey!mutt!tor!remote, and at the end you would paste the account name of your pal. If she's on account sheri on that end, the full UUCP address would be huey!mutt!tor!remote!sheri.

Step 2. Action

1. Given the improvements in UUCP routing, the vast majority of UUCP mail will probably first be sent to a well-known site such as uunet, then branch directly from there. Instead of the long address huey!mutt!tor!remote!sheri, you could use uunet!remote!sheri to get the same results.

   To send mail to my friend Sheri in this situation, I can use Berkeley Mail very much like I did before, only this time instead of using just an account name, I specify the UUCP hosts involved in the routing:

```
% mail huey!mutt!tor!remote!sheri
huey!mutt!tor!remote!sheri: Event not found
%
```

What happened? The C shell saw the exclamation points and thought I was making a history request. It couldn't find any entries in my history list that match any of these possible sequences.

2. To avoid having the C shell interpret the exclamation points as history commands, I can surround the address with single quotes:

```
% mail 'huey!mutt!tor!remote!sheri'
Subject: _
```

Alternatively, I can use a backslash before each exclamation point:

```
% mail huey\!mutt\!tor\!remote\!sheri
Subject: _
```

19

Comment: UNIX folks don't say *exclamation point* when they talk about UUCP address routes; they say *bang*. Therefore, this route would be called *huey bang mutt bang tor bang remote bang sheri.*

3. As *domain naming* (a *domain name* is a unique name for an organization, which becomes part of the address) has come into vogue, so have UUCP names changed from being simple words like mutt and tor to being more complex names including domain specifiers (for example, mutt.princeton.edu and tor.rnd.mot.com). The up side is that each system name contains more information, but the down side is that you have to do more typing.

If you're connected to UUCP, you can most likely send mail to people on the Internet by sending mail in UUCP format until it gets to an Internet-savvy host, then simply specify the Internet address in UUCP notation. For example, say Sheri tells me that her e-mail address is sheri@remote.ai.mit.edu. I can't use that notation directly because I'm on a UUCP system, which doesn't know what the @ means. On the other hand, I find out that my neighboring system huey does know all about this stuff, so I can then use the following:

```
% mail 'huey!remote.ai.mit.edu!sheri'
Subject: _
```

The file will get to Sheri directly (that is, once it reaches huey, it will be sent via Internet rather than via e-mail) and with much less typing.

Once you identify an Internet host that you can access via UUCP, you can send mail to any Internet address by swapping the login name and host information and prefixing your route to that system. So, if I wanted to send mail to my friend marv@netcom.com via Internet, I could switch the elements that are on either side of the @ (netcom.com marv), add a ! between them (netcom.com!marv), and preface the whole thing with the name of my local Internet-savvy system (huey!netcom.com!marv).

Comment: Electronic mail addresses that contain an @ are called Internet addresses, and they're read as *user at host*, with all periods read as "dot." One of my accounts is taylor@well.sf.ca.us, which is read as *taylor at well dot sf dot ca dot us*.

An address that contains both the @ and ! notations (both UUCP and Internet notations) is called a *mixed mode address*, and it's usually a bad idea to use it. If I wanted to send mail to Marv, I could try the mixed mode address huey!marv@netcom.com. The problem is that the address could be interpreted as *huey!marv* @ netcom.com or as huey! *marv@netcom.com*. It's usually a lot safer to flip it all around into a pure UUCP notation.

Step 3. Summary

As the Internet has become more pervasive, fewer sites work with only UUCP notation. Even if you only have a telephone connection to other sites, your computer might still accept and understand the Internet addressing notation, which is definitely good news. If you're still using UUCP notation, remember that once you find a local site that understands Internet notation, you can forward all your messages there and that location will figure out the Internet addresses.

Task 19.3: Copying Files to Other UUCP Sites
Step 1. Description

The third part of working with modem-based connection using the UUCP protocol is file transfer. To do this, you need to use the uucp program itself. You can also remember the name of uucp as *UNIX to UNIX* cp. The notation is almost identical to that which you use to send electronic mail, with a few differences. There are a variety of flags available for uucp, the two most important being -m, to have the UUCP system send mail to you when the copy is complete, and -n*user*, to notify *user* on the remote system when the file transfer is complete. The format of the command is uucp *files destination.*

To copy files from the local system to a remote site, simply list the names of the files you want to copy followed by a UUCP notation indication of system, ending with a directory rather than an account. If you have an account with the same account name on the remote system, you can use ~ to indicate your home directory. To retrieve files from a remote site, specify files with a UUCP path prefix on each name. The final destination in this case should be a path on the local system, or . for the current directory.

Files are not retrieved immediately. Instead, a UUCP file transfer request is queued up for the next time the modem is used (you can check the status of your uucp requests with uustat). That's why it is so helpful to have the system send you e-mail notification once the transfer has been completed (remember that you use the -m flag to do this).

Step 2. Action

1. To send a copy of my .login file from my account at netcom.com to my similarly named account at Atari, I would use this:

```
% hostname
netcom.com
% uucp
Usage:  uucp [-c¦-C] [-d¦-f] [-gGRADE] [-j] [-m] [-nUSER]\
        [-r] [-sFILE] [-xDEBUG_LEVEL] source-files destination-file
uucp failed completely (2)
%
```

I've always liked the uucp failed completely error!

2. I'll try again to send the file, this time correctly:

```
% uucp login atari\!~
Illegal filename (/login).
uucp failed partially: 0 file(s) sent; 1 error(s)
%
```

It still didn't work. For some obscure reason, the uucp program assumes that all filenames are located in the slash directory unless otherwise indicated. I will try to send the file one more time:

```
% uucp ~/login atari\!~
%
```

It worked fine. To check, I use uustat:

```
% uustat
atariN7dd8    12/13-09:41  S  atari  taylor 1237 /u1/taylor/login
%
```

 Comment: Some smarter UUCP packages default to the current directory, which is a lot easier. Many systems are also configured to allow only transfers to or from the public directory /usr/spool/uucppublic.

3. To retrieve a file from the remote system, I would flip the two filenames around:

```
% uucp atari\!/etc/motd .
Illegal filename (/.).
uucp failed partially: 0 file(s) sent; 1 error(s)
%
```

Well, that is, flip the two words around and also be sure to specify a filename for the local copy:

```
% uucp atari\!/etc/motd ~/atari.motd
%
```

To check the queue, I use uustat:

```
% uustat
atariN7dd8    12/13-09:41  S  atari  taylor 1237 /u1/taylor/login
atariN7dd9    12/13-09:44  R  atari  taylor      /etc/motd
%
```

4. To cancel a UUCP request, use the uustat command, but specify -k to kill the job. In the list of jobs shown by the program's default output, the very first word in the line is the UUCP job ID. You can see that I have two jobs in the queue now, atariN7dd8 and atariN7dd9. To remove them both is easy:

```
% uustat -katariN7dd8
Job: atariN7dd8 successfully killed
% uustat -katariN7dd9
Job: atariN7dd9 successfully killed
%
```

Now uustat shows that nothing is queued:

```
% uustat
%
```

Step 3. Summary

As you can see, the uucp command allows you to copy files from one UUCP system to another, though the notation is awkward at best. There's no simple solution: UUCP by its very nature is a slow point-to-point relay protocol, so there's no easy way to have, for example, a listing of files available on the remote system without logging in and figuring it out for yourself. For simple tasks, however, uucp can work fine.

Task 19.4: Connecting to Remote Internet Sites
Step 1. Description

The really fun part of UNIX, and one reason that it's grown dramatically in the last few years, is that it's the most connected operating system in the world. The variety of different services available for users of a networked UNIX machine is staggering. Not only can you use all the commands explained in this lesson, but you can use some additional services, such as Gopher and Archie, that are on the cutting edge of information services and which will be explained in the final lesson.

At its simplest, the connectivity all relies on very high-speed wires coming out of the back of the computer you're on and connecting to other computers. Unlike the telephone-based connections of UUCP, this line is always alive and is much, much faster, able to stream literally megabytes of information in under a minute. The big network itself, the Internet, evolved from an earlier network called the ARPAnet, funded by the Advanced Research Projects Agency of the U.S. Government in the 1970s and into the 1980s. Somewhere along the way, it began to grow beyond the vision and capabilities of the original design, and began being known as the ARPA Internet. In the last few years the government (and particularly the National Science Foundation) has begun to withdraw from its overseer role, and as a result the system is now known as the Internet.

If you've heard of the Information Highway (which is now being called the Information Superhighway) then you've also heard about the Internet, which is the existing roadway that is growing to become this high-speed thoroughfare of information. In fact, next time a friend mentions the Information Highway, you can say that you've already experienced some of it by working on the Internet.

There are three main tasks that the Internet can help you with: using remote systems, sending mail to remote users, and working with remote file systems. In addition, you can find out who is logged on to any system on the Internet and use the `talk` program to talk with someone else.

If you know that the remote site is a UNIX system, the easiest way to log in to that site is to use the `rlogin` command, which has the awkward notation of `rlogin host -l account`. If you aren't sure about the system, use `telnet`, which is the universal program for connecting to remote computer systems. Unlike any of the other programs you've learned so far, `telnet` actually works either as a simple program you can invoke from the command line, or as a sophisticated environment for connecting to various systems.

Step 2. Action

1. First off, I'll use `rlogin` to connect to a remote system and see if I have a file there:

    ```
    % rlogin netcom.com
    Password:_
    ```

    By default, `rlogin` assumes that your account on the remote system has the same name as your account on your home system. If you forget to use the `-l account` option, press Return here and it prompts for an account name:

    ```
    % rlogin netcom.com
    Password:
    Login incorrect
    login: taylor
    Password:_
    ```

    Once I enter my password, I'm logged in to the remote system:

    ```
    Last login: Mon Dec 13 09:38:35 from utech

    SunOS Release 4.1.3 (NETCOM) #1: Wed Sep 23 05:06:55 PDT 1992
    ```

```
NETCOM On-line Communication Services, Inc.

  >>>>
  >>>>   Washington DC:  Additional modems have been added.
  >>>>   Santa Cruz:  Additional modems have been added.
  >>>>
  >>>>   Elm has been updated to version 2.4 (PL 21).  Users
  >>>>   using elm with aliases should run the
  >>>>   "/usr/local/bin/newalias" program.
  >>>>

%
```

Using ls tells me what I want to know:

```
netcom % ls
Global.Software   News/          history.usenet.Z
Interactive.Unix  Src/           login
Mail/             bin/           testme
netcom %
```

2. The rlogin command offers a shorthand notation for logging out of the remote system; instead of logout, you can simply enter ~.. To stop the rlogin session, use ~^z. No other tilde commands are available in rlogin.

I choose to log out the normal way:

```
netcom % logout
Connection closed
%
```

Now I'm back on the original computer system.

3. The alternate way to connect to a remote computer is to use telnet. The easiest way to use this command is the same way you use rlogin. At the command prompt, specify the name of the system to connect with:

```
% telnet netcom.com
Trying...
Connected to netcom.com.
Escape character is '^]'.

SunOS UNIX (netcom)

login: _
```

Notice that this way is much more like having a terminal connected to this system. I can log in, enter my password, and then have a new login session on the remote system as if I were sitting in that computer room working away.

4. Instead, though, I'm going to use the ^] control character to switch into the telnet program itself:

```
SunOS UNIX (netcom)
login: ^]
telnet > _
```

Now I enter help to see what the options are:

```
telnet> help
Commands may be abbreviated.  Commands are:

close           close current connection
display         display operating parameters
mode            try to enter line-by-line or character-at-a-time mode
open            connect to a site
quit            exit telnet
send            transmit special characters ('send ?' for more)
set             set operating parameters ('set ?' for more)
status          print status information
toggle          toggle operating parameters ('toggle ?' for more)
z               suspend telnet
?               print help information
telnet>  _
```

There are lots of possible commands. I choose to return to my connection to Netcom, however, so I just press Return and I'm back at the login prompt. If I don't enter anything quickly enough, the remote system automatically drops the connection:

```
login: Login timed out after 60 seconds
Connection closed by foreign host.
%
```

To log out of the remote system, the best strategy is simply to exit the telnet session, which will automatically drop the line. If that doesn't work, then the ^] sequence followed by either quit or close will do the trick.

5. To start out directly in the `telnet` command mode, simply enter the command without specifying a remote host:

```
% telnet
telnet> _
```

From here, connecting to the remote host is also quite simple:

```
telnet> open netcom.com
Trying...
Connected to netcom.com.
Escape character is '^]'.


SunOS UNIX (netcom)

login: _
```

Again, I use `^]` and `close` to close the connection.

Step 3. Summary

Both the `rlogin` and `telnet` commands are useful in different situations, but I find myself using the `rlogin` command more often because it sends much of the current environment along to the remote system. So if I have my system set for a specific type of terminal (that is, the TERM variable is set to a specific value), then that's automatically copied into the new environment of the remote system, which saves lots of hassle.

Task 19.5: Sending E-mail to Internet Users
Step 1. Description

The most common use of the Internet is probably to send electronic mail between individuals and to mailing lists. What's really a boon is that everyone, from New York to Los Angeles, Japan to Germany, South Africa to India, has an address that's very similar, and you've already seen it shown here! The notation is *user @ host.domain*, where *user* is the account name or full name, *host* is the name of the user's machine, and *domain* is the user's location in the world.

By reading the host and domain information from right to left (really from the outside in), you can decode information about someone simply by looking at the person's e-mail address. My address at a system called Netcom, for example, is `taylor@netcom2.netcom.com`, which, reading right to left, tells you that I'm at a commercial site (`com`), with a company by the name of Netcom (`netcom`), and the name of the computer I'm using is `netcom2`. My account on Netcom is `taylor`.

There are lots of top-level domains, and the most common are shown in Table 19.1.

Table 19.1. Common top-level Internet domains.

Domain	Type of Site or Network
edu	Educational sites
com	Commercial businesses
mil	Military or defense systems
net	Alternate networks accessible via Internet
org	Nonprofit organizations
ca	Canadian systems not otherwise classified
us	United States systems not otherwise classified

Step 2. Action

1. To send mail to someone on the Internet is easy, because the C shell doesn't view the @ as a special character. If you'd like to send me a message, for example, you could use this:

```
% mailx taylor@netcom.com
Subject: _
```

Enter the message and end with a ^d as you would in any e-mail message. It is immediately sent to me!

Comment: I encourage you to drop me a note if you're so inclined, letting me know how you're enjoying this book, any problems you might have encountered, and any commands you were puzzled by that might be easier with a bit more explanation. If nothing else, just say hi!

2. Although electronic mail addresses always follow the same format, they can vary quite a bit. To give you an idea of the variation, I used grep to extract the From: addresses of some mail I've recently received:

```
% grep '^From:' /usr/spool/mail/taylor
From: Steve Frampton <frampton@vicuna.ocunix.on.ca>
From: Joanna Tsang <tsang@futon.SFSU.EDU>
From: "Debra Isserlis" <disserli@us.oracle.com>
From: "Jay Munro [PC Mag]" <72241.554@CompuServe.COM>
From: ljw@ras.amdahl.com (Linda Wei)
From: Cheryl <CBUTCHER@VM.CC.PURDUE.EDU>
From: harrism@mace.utech.edu (Mickey Harris)
From: v892127@nooteboom.si.hhs.nl
From: "ean houts" <ean_houts@ccgate.infoworld.com>
From: harrism@mace.utech.edu (Mickey Harris)
From: "Barbara Maxwell" <maxwell@sales.synergy.com>
From: steve@xalt.com (Steve Mansour)
From: abhasin@itsmail1.hamilton.edu (Aditya Bhasin)
From: gopher@scorpio.kent.edu
From: marv@netcom.com (Marvin Raab)
%
```

The national convention for the From: line in electronic mail clearly varies. There are three basic notations you see in this line: just an address, such as the one from gopher@scorpio.kent.edu; an address with the name in parentheses, such as the message from Linda Wei about halfway down the list; and a line with the person's name followed by his or her e-mail address in angle brackets, such as the first listed line.

Note the sites from which I've received e-mail in the past few days: SFSU.EDU is San Francisco State University, oracle.com is Oracle Corporation in California, PURDUE.EDU is Purdue University, CompuServe.COM is the CompuServe network, ccgate.infoworld.com is InfoWorld magazine's Macintosh network running Cc:Mail, xalt.com is from XALT Corporation, and kent.edu is Kent State University. The v892127@nooteboom.si.hhs.nl message is from an educational institution in the Netherlands!

To be able to decode these addresses you need to have a lot of information, some excellent guesses, a glance at an Organization: line that might appear in the messages, or, if you're on a system with all the latest software, an invocation of the netinfo command to explain the site you're curious about.

Step 3. Summary

Sending electronic mail back and forth with users throughout the world is one of the most exciting and fun parts of learning UNIX. I often read magazine articles, for example, in which the author lists an electronic mail address. It's a simple task to zip out a message if I have questions or kudos on the piece. Many magazines, from the *Utne Reader* to *MacWorld* magazine, even list electronic mail addresses for the editorial staff. Even reporters from the *Wall Street Journal* and the *New York Times* are on the Internet now.

Task 19.6: Copying Files from Other Internet Sites
Step 1. Description

The main program used to copy files on the Internet is ftp, which is named after the protocol it implements, the *file transfer protocol*. Like much of UNIX, ftp can take a while to master, particularly because no effort has been made to make it at all user-friendly. Nonetheless, it functions very similarly to the telnet command; you either enter ftp to start the program then specify what system you'd like to connect with, or you specify the name of the system on the command line. Either way, you are then prompted for an account and password, then you are dropped into the ftp prompt with the connection open and waiting.

Many sites talk about having *anonymous ftp* capabilities. Systems allowing this connection indicate that you don't need your own computer account on that machine to be able to connect and copy files from their archives. To use these systems, enter ftp as the account name, then enter your own e-mail address as the password (that is, I'd enter ftp then taylor@netcom.com as the password). The most important commands available in ftp are summarized in Table 19.2. The most important one to remember is bye, which you use when you're done.

Table 19.2. Valuable ftp commands.

Command	Meaning
ascii	Set ftp to transfer a text (ASCII) file
binary	Set ftp to transfer a binary file, probably a program or database of information
bye	Quit the ftp program

Command	Meaning
cd *dir*	Change the remote directory to *dir*
close	Close the current connection
dir	Print a listing of files in the current remote directory
get	Get a file from the remote system
lcd *dir*	Change the current directory on the local system to *dir* or your home directory if no argument is given
ls	List the files in the current remote directory
mget	*Multiple get*—get files with a wildcard matching capability
mput	*Multiple put*—put files with a wildcard matching capability
open	Open a connection to the specified remote machine
prompt	Control whether or not to ask for confirmation of each file transferred if using mget or mput
put	Put a file onto the remote system from the local system
pwd	Show the present working directory on the remote

Step 2. Action

1. To start out, I want to pick up a file from netcom that I saw earlier, when I used rlogin to look at the remote system. To start ftp I use the short notation of specifying the host at the command line:

```
% ftp netcom.com
Connected to netcom.com.
220 netcom FTP server (Version 2.0WU(10) Fri Apr 9 13:43:51 PDT 1993) ready.
Name (netcom.com:taylor): _
```

By default ftp assumes that I want to use the same account name, which in this case I do, so I press Return, then enter my password:

```
Name (netcom.com:taylor):
331 Password required for taylor.
Password:
230 User taylor logged in.
ftp> _
```

2. Now I'm at the `ftp` program prompt, and any of the commands shown in Table 19.2 will work here. To start, I use `dir` and `ls` to list my files in different formats:

```
ftp> dir
200 PORT command successful.
150 Opening ASCII mode data connection for /bin/ls.
total 140
-rwxr-xr-x  1 taylor   users0      4941 Oct  4  1991 .Pnews.header
-rwx------  1 taylor   daemon       987 Sep 20  1992 .accinfo
-rw-r--r--  1 taylor   users0      2103 Sep 30 19:17 .article
-rw-r--r--  1 taylor   users0       752 Apr 17  1992 .cshrc
-rw-r--r--  1 taylor   users0      1749 Jun  8  1993 .delgroups
drwx------  2 taylor   daemon      4096 Dec  6 14:25 .elm
-rw-r--r--  1 taylor   users0        28 Nov  5 09:50 .forward
-rw-------  1 taylor   users0         0 Jun  9  1993 .ircmotd
-rw-r--r--  1 taylor   users0      1237 Dec 13 09:40 .login
-rw-r--r--  1 taylor   users0         6 Aug  6  1991 .logout
-rw-r--r--  1 taylor   users0       538 Dec  6 14:32 .newsrc
-rw-r--r--  1 taylor   users0       537 Dec  6 14:30 .oldnewsrc
-rw-r--r--  1 taylor   users0      1610 Feb 17  1992 .plan
-rw-r--r--  1 taylor   users0         0 Aug  6  1991 .pnewsexpert
-rw-r--r--  1 taylor   users0        45 Feb  2  1993 .rnlast
-rw-r--r--  1 taylor   users0         6 Feb  8  1993 .rnlock
-rw-r--r--  1 taylor   users0     16767 Jan 27  1993 .rnsoft
-rw-r--r--  1 taylor   users0       114 Apr  6  1992 .sig
drwxr-xr-x  4 taylor   users0      4096 Nov 13 11:09 .tin
-rw-r--r--  1 taylor   users0      1861 Jun  2  1992 Global.Software
-rw-------  1 taylor   users0     22194 Oct  1  1992 Interactive.Unix
drwx------  4 taylor   users0      4096 Nov 13 11:09 Mail
drwxr-xr-x  2 taylor   users0      4096 Nov 13 11:09 News
drwxr-xr-x  2 taylor   users0      4096 Nov 13 11:09 Src
drwxr-xr-x  2 taylor   users0      4096 Nov 13 11:09 bin
-rw-r--r--  1 taylor   users0     12445 Sep 17 14:56 history.usenet.Z
-rw-r--r--  1 taylor   users0      1237 Oct 18 20:55 login
-rw-r--r--  1 taylor   users0       174 Nov 20 19:21 testme
226 Transfer complete.
1792 bytes received in 3.1 seconds (0.56 Kbytes/s)
ftp> ls
200 PORT command successful.
150 Opening ASCII mode data connection for file list.
.cshrc
.login
.elm
Mail
News
.logout
.newsrc
.rnlast
.rnsoft
bin
.tin
Global.Software
.sig
```

```
.oldnewsrc
.pnewsexpert
.plan
.Pnews.header
history.usenet.Z
.rnlock
Src
.ircmotd
.article
.delgroups
.accinfo
.forward
Interactive.Unix
testme
login
226 Transfer complete.
269 bytes received in 0.02 seconds (13 Kbytes/s)
ftp>
```

As you can see, ftp can be long-winded.

Comment: One trick for using the ls command within ftp is that if you specify a set of command flags as a second word, it works fine. Specify a third argument, however, and it saves the output of the command into a local file by that name, so ls -l -C would create a file called -C on your system with the output of the ls -l command.

Since you can supply some flags to the ls command, I always use -CF to force the output to list in multiple columns and show directories, which makes the output readable:

```
ftp> ls -CF
200 PORT command successful.
150 Opening ASCII mode data connection for /bin/ls.
.Pnews.header*          .newsrc              Interactive.Unix
.accinfo*               .oldnewsrc           Mail/
.article                .plan                News/
.cshrc                  .pnewsexpert         Src/
.delgroups              .rnlast              bin/
.elm/                   .rnlock              history.usenet.Z
.forward                .rnsoft              login
.ircmotd                .sig                 testme
.login                  .tin/
.logout                 Global.Software
226 Transfer complete.
remote: -CF
287 bytes received in 0.05 seconds (5.6 Kbytes/s)
ftp>
```

3. To transfer the file login from the remote system, I can use the get command:

```
ftp> get
(remote-file) login
(local-file) login.netcom
200 PORT command successful.
150 Opening ASCII mode data connection for login (1237 bytes).
226 Transfer complete.
local: login.netcom remote: login
1281 bytes received in 0.22 seconds (5.7 Kbytes/s)
ftp>
```

4. Alternatively, I could use mget and specify a wildcard pattern similar to one I'd give the shell:

```
ftp> mget log*
mget login? y
200 PORT command successful.
150 Opening ASCII mode data connection for login (1237 bytes).
226 Transfer complete.
local: login remote: login
1281 bytes received in 0.03 seconds (42 Kbytes/s)
ftp>
```

There was only one match so the transfer was easy. Entering anything other than y at the mget login? prompt would have resulted in the file not being transferred.

That was easily accomplished. Now I will look on another system in the anonymous FTP directory to see what's available.

5. To disconnect, I enter close so that I don't leave the ftp program:

```
ftp> close
221 Goodbye
ftp>
```

There are hundreds of information servers on the Internet, offering an astounding variety of information, from weather service maps to the full text of the Bible and *Alice in Wonderland,* to the source listings of thousands of different programs.

In this example, I want to look at the anonymous FTP archive at the Massachusetts Institute of Technology's Artificial Intelligence Laboratory. The host is called ftp.ai.mit.edu:

```
ftp> open ftp.ai.mit.edu
Connected to mini-wheats.ai.mit.edu.
220 mini-wheats FTP server (Version wu-2.1b(4) Wed Aug 25 09:20:50 EDT 1993)
ready.
Name (ftp.ai.mit.edu:taylor): ftp
331 Guest login ok, send your complete e-mail address as password.
Password:
230-
230-
230-Welcome to the MIT Artificial Intelligence Laboratory. If you are
230-interested in Artificial Intelligence Laboratory publications please
230-ftp to publications.ai.mit.edu.
230-
230-
230-
230 Guest login ok, access restrictions apply.
ftp>
```

Now I can use ls -CF to look around:

```
ftp> ls -CF
200 PORT command successful.
150 Opening ASCII mode data connection for /bin/ls.
.message        bin/            etc/            pub/
ai-pubs/        dev/            incoming/       usr/
226 Transfer complete.
remote: -CF
58 bytes received in 0.39 seconds (0.15 Kbytes/s)
ftp>
```

It looks like there might be something of interest in the pub directory (a
directory by this name usually contains public information). I use cd to
change to that directory, then ls -CF to see what's available there:

```
ftp> cd pub
250 CWD command successful.
ftp> ls -CF
200 PORT command successful.
150 Opening ASCII mode data connection for /bin/ls.
6.824/                          medical-white-paper.ps.Z*
Address:                        memtr
BL.tar.Z                        minsky/
GA/                             misc/
ICv2.45.sit.hqx                 mit1345.tar
Iterate/                        mobile-dist-telecomp/
MC132p_structures.cif           mobot-survey.text
MSV_array.cif                   mr-sd-mapped.ps
MSV_structures.cif              mr-sd.ps
Peng_Wu_Thesis.ps.Z             mtm/
README                          ontic/
TS/                             patches.c
```

```
aal                              pdp8-lovers-archive
adage/                           pgs-th.ps.Z
ai3/                             pinouts/
aimr/                            poker/
akcl.Z                           psabalone.tar.Z
alan@                            pset32new.c
aop/                             publications/
ariel/                           qobi/
autoclass/                       ra.ps
bson/                            rbl-94.archive
cki/                             refer-to-bibtex/
clmath.tar                       sanger-figures/
cube-lovers/                     sanger-papers/
cva/                             sanger.mackey.tar.Z
cwitty/                          sanger.mackey.tar.gz
dam/                             scheme-libraries/
doc/                             screamer/
dssa/                            screamer.tar.Z
dssa.ps                          screamer3.04/
eel/                             screen/
ellens@                          series/
engine/                          square-dancing/
fax/                             squash-ladder
hebrew/                          surf-hippo/
incoming@                        swill
iter-man.ps                      swillcoxswillcoxswillcoxAddress:
iterate.lisp                     systems/
iterate.tar.Z                    tandems@
jupiter/                         tbs/
lemacs/                          texture.tiff
linalg.shar                      tgif.tar.Z
lisp3/                           transition-space.lisp
logtalk.uue.Z                    turing_option
loop-macro.tar                   turing_option.ps
lptrs/                           users/
ltalk*                           viola-fbr.ps.Z
lyskom-0.33.1.english.el.Z       vis/
maddog/                          who-line-gc-thermometer.lisp@
medical-white-paper.dvi          x3j13/
226 Transfer complete.
remote: -CF
1388 bytes received in 3.4 seconds (0.4 Kbytes/s)
ftp>
```

6. A README file is usually a good thing to start with. A handy ftp trick is that you can copy files directly to your screen by using /dev/tty as the local filename, or even pipe them to programs by using the pipe symbol as the first character:

```
ftp> get README |more
200 PORT command successful.
150 Opening ASCII mode data connection for README (186 bytes).
This file will be expanded eventually.
```

If you've been looking at directories of specific users, such as 'ian' or 'ellens', those directories have been moved into the users directory.

```
226 Transfer complete.
local: ¦more remote: README
193 bytes received in 0.55 seconds (0.34 Kbytes/s)
ftp>
```

In this case the README file is not incredibly helpful.

7. It's time to split and check another FTP archive, this time one at Apple Computer (ftp.apple.com):

```
ftp> close
221 Goodbye.
ftp> open ftp.apple.com
Connected to bric-a-brac.apple.com.
220 bric-a-brac.apple.com FTP server (IG Version 5.93 (from BU, from UUNET
5.51)
 Sun Nov 21 14:24:29 PST 1993) ready.
Name (ftp.apple.com:taylor): ftp
331 Guest login ok, send ident as password.
Password:
230 Guest login ok, access restrictions apply.
ftp>
```

Again, ls -CF shows what files are available:

```
ftp> ls -CF
200 PORT command successful.
150 Opening ASCII mode data connection for /bin/ls.
.cshrc          alug/           boot/           echt90/         public/
.login          apda/           cdrom/          etc/            shlib/
.logout         apple/          dev/            pie/            software/
README          bin/            dts/            pub/
226 Transfer complete.
remote: -CF
143 bytes received in 0.01 seconds (14 Kbytes/s)
ftp>
```

Use the ¦more trick to see what the README file has to say:

```
ftp> get README ¦more
200 PORT command successful.
150 Opening ASCII mode data connection for README (424 bytes).
This is the top level of our FTP server.

If you're an authorized person, and you want to have a directory on the
top level, please contact Erik Fair <ftp@apple.com>, (408) 974-1779,
and explain why you want one, and what you're going to use it for.
Otherwise, please make your stuff available in the "public" directory.
```

```
There are no writeable directories for anonymous FTP on this server; it
cannot be used as a drop box.
226 Transfer complete.
local: ¦more remote: README
433 bytes received in 0.21 seconds (2.01 Kbytes/s)
ftp>
```

8. There's a new Macintosh application that I've been interested in seeing available on this system in dts/mac/hacks. I can move directly there with cd, confirming that I'm where I think I am with pwd:

```
ftp> cd dts/mac/hacks
250 CWD command successful.
ftp> pwd
257 "/dts/mac/hacks" is current directory.
ftp> ls -CF
200 PORT command successful.
150 Opening ASCII mode data connection for /bin/ls.
aetracker-3-0.hqx*              mountalias-1-0.hqx*
applicon-2-1.hqx*              newswatcher.hqx*
appmenu-3-5.hqx*              okey-dokey-1-0-1.hqx*
bison-flex.hqx*              oscar.hqx*
colorfinder.hqx*              piston.hqx*
darkside-of-the-mac-4-1.hqx*     snake.hqx*
dropper.hqx*              switchapp-1-1.hqx*
escape-dammit-0-4.hqx*          system-picker-1-0.hqx*
extensions-manager-2-0-1.hqx*    thread-manager-exten-1-2.hqx*
flipper.hqx*              trashman-4-0-2.hqx*
folder-icon-maker-1-1.hqx*      understudy.hqx*
fsid.hqx*              unlockfolder.hqx*
im-mac-1-0b26w.hqx*          virtual-controllers.hqx*
lockdisk-1-0.hqx*          xferit-1-4.hqx*
226 Transfer complete.
remote: -CF
559 bytes received in 0.14 seconds (3.9 Kbytes/s)
ftp>
```

Notice that there's an asterisk following the names of these files. This indicates, as you know from the -F flag to ls, that it's a binary file. Therefore, I need to specify to ftp that it should transfer the file in *binary mode*, by entering binary:

```
ftp> binary
200 Type set to I.
ftp>
```

I check to see how big the file is, then I can use get to transfer it, and drop the connection with bye:

```
ftp> dir colorfinder.hqx
200 PORT command successful.
150 Opening ASCII mode data connection for /bin/ls.
```

```
-rw-r-xr-x  1 mjohnson archivis    43442 May 24  1991 colorfinder.hqx
226 Transfer complete.
remote: colorfinder.hqx
71 bytes received in 0 seconds (0.069 Kbytes/s)
ftp> get colorfinder.hqx
200 PORT command successful.
150 Opening BINARY mode data connection for colorfinder.hqx (43442 bytes).
226 Transfer complete.
local: colorfinder.hqx remote: colorfinder.hqx
43442 bytes received in 2.09 seconds (20 Kbytes/s)
ftp> bye
221 CUL8R.
%
```

Now that I'm back at the command prompt, I can use ls again to confirm that I've received both the colorfinder.hqx and login.netcom files:

```
% ls
Archives/        bin/                keylime.pie      sample3
InfoWorld/       buckaroo            login.netcom     src/
Mail/            buckaroo.confused   newsample        src.listing
News/            cheryl              papert.article   temp/
OWL/             colorfinder.hqx     sample           tmp.listing
awkscript        dickens.note        sample2          who.is.who
%
```

Step 3. Summary

The FTP system is a terrific way to obtain information from the Internet. Thousands of systems offer various services via anonymous FTP, too: Table 19.3 lists a few of the most interesting ones.

Table 19.3. Some interesting ftp archives.

Site	Institution and Available Information
aenas.mit.edu	Massachusetts Institute of Technology Free Software Foundation site. Files: GNU EMACS
aisun1.ai.uga.edu	University of Georgia. Files: LISP, PROLOG, natural language processing, MS-DOS utilities
archive.nevada.edu	University of Nevada. Files: U.S. Constitution and supporting documents, religious texts, the Bible
brownvm.brown.edu	Brown University. Files: Mac

continues

Table 19.3. continued

Site	Institution and Available Information
`cc.sfu.ca`	San Francisco University. Files: MS-DOS, Mac
`clvax1.cl.msu.edu`	Michigan State University. Files: MS Windows
`cs.rice.edu`	Rice University. Files: Sun-Spots, Amiga, `ispell`, `ofiles`
`cscihp.ecst.csuchico.edu`	California State University, Chico. Files: online chemistry manual
`cu.nih.gov`	U.S. National Institute of Health
`deja-vu.aiss.uiuc.edu`	University of Illinois Urbana-Champaign. Files: Rush Limbaugh transcripts, Monty Python, humor, song lyrics, movie scripts, urban legends
`f.ms.uky.edu`	University of Kentucky. Files: Mac, MS-DOS, UNIX, Mac, Amiga, NeXT, 386BSD, AppleII, GNU, RFCs, various usenet archives
`ftp.apple.com`	Apple Computer. Files: Apple (Mac, II, IIgs) product info, software, developer support
`ftp.cica.indiana.edu`	Indiana University. Files: UNIX, MS-DOS, NeXT updates, MS Windows 3.x archive
`ftp.csc.liv.ac.uk`	Liverpool University Computer Science Department. Files: Ports to HP-UX machines (especially Series 700), including X11R4 clients, GNU, recreational software, text editors, sysadmin tools
`ftp.eff.org`	Electronic Frontier Foundation.
`gatekeeper.dec.com`	Digital Equipment Corporation, Palo Alto, California. Files: X11, recipes, `cron`, `map`, Modula-3

Site	Institution and Available Information
`hobiecat.cs.caltech.edu`	California Institute of Technology. Files: GNU (Free Software Foundation)
`hpcvaaz.cv.hp.com`	Hewlett-Packard, Corvallis, Oregon. Files: Motif, archives
`info.umd.edu`	University of Maryland. Files: government-related, books, economics, MS-DOS, Novell, Mac
`midgard.ucsc.edu`	University of California, Santa Cruz. Files: amoeba, U.S. Constitution
`nnsc.nsf.net`	National Science Foundation Network. Files: Network Info, Internet Resource Guide
`nssdca.gsfc.nasa.gov`	NASA. Files: Hubble space telescope images
`sciences.sdsu.edu`	San Diego State University. Files: sounds
`sparkyfs.erg.sri.com`	SRI International. Files: Improving the Security of your UNIX system
`tesla.ee.cornell.edu`	Cornell University. Files: `tcsh`
`vax.ftp.com`	FTP Software. Files: FTP-related programs
`watsun.cc.columbia.edu`	Columbia University. Files: kermit
`wsmr-simtel20.army.mil`	U.S. Army—White Sands Missile Range. Files: MS-DOS, UNIX, CPM, Mac

There's no question that the interface to `ftp` is awkward, however, and there are a couple different programs that have tried to address this problem, as you will learn in the last lesson in this book.

There's no way here to fully cover all the information available on the Internet, so if you're excited by these possibilities, I strongly recommend that you obtain a copy of the book *Navigating the Internet* by Mark Gibbs and Richard Smith. It's a terrific introduction to the many services available on the Internet, including `gopher`, `archie`, the `WorldWideWeb`, `telnet`, and `ftp`. Those that aren't covered in this lesson are shown in the last lesson of this book, however, so you will have at least seen most of these important Internet information-related commands.

Task 19.7: Talking with Remote Internet Users
Step 1. Description

To see who is logged in to a remote system, you can use a command called `finger`, which by default will show you a summary of who is on the local machine. Add a user name to the command, and it will show information about the specified account. Specify a user on a remote system, and you can find out if that user is logged in. Specify just the remote site, and it shows you who is logged in at the current moment. To check on a local account, use `finger` *accountname*. To make it a remote system, append the hostname: `finger` *account@host.domain*. To check all users on a remote site, use `finger` *@host.domain*.

Once you've ascertained that a friend is logged in to a local or remote system, you can use the `talk` program to chat with the person *live* across the Internet. As opposed to the primitive line-oriented mode of `write`, `talk` is a full-screen program that enables you both to type at the same time. Your screen always shows the other person's typing on the bottom half of your screen.

Step 2. Action

1. A quick glance at the output of `finger` shows that there are a lot of people currently logged in to the local system:

```
% finger
Login       Name                    TTY Idle   When    Location
root        root                    *co 1:13 Mon 18:02
taylor      Dave Taylor             aV       Mon 16:49
kippje      Jeff Kip                Ab       Mon 16:41
adamr       Adam Coy                *Ae      Mon 18:36
daffnelr    Lawrence Daff           sK       Mon 12:45  (dov27)
tsa         Earl the Unctuous Aardva sL   42 Mon 12:48  (expert)
daffnelr    Lawrence Daff           *sM      Mon 12:49  (localhost)
ben         Ben Moon                sN  8:42 Mon 09:16  (corona)
ben         Ben Moon                sR  8:47 Mon 09:22  (corona)
marteldr    David Martel            *sY   7d Mon 18:41  (limbo)
gerlema     David Geman             sb       Mon 18:38  (mac19)
mk          Michael Kenzie          *sc 2:48 Mon 08:07  (mk)
mzabel      Mary Zabeliski          *sf      Mon 18:45  (sun1)
fritzg      Geoff Fritzen           sh     9 Mon 18:45  (pc43)
brynta      Bryan Ayerson           *si      Mon 18:46  (limbo)
deckersl    Sharon Deck             sk     3 Mon 18:51  (xds31)
```

2. To learn more about the account `mk`, I can specify that account name to the `finger` program:

```
% finger mk

Login name: mk          (messages off) Real name: Michael Kenzie
Office: Math 204                        Home phone:
```

```
Directory: /users/mk                    Shell: /bin/ksh
Universe: universe(ucb)
Member of groups: utech root actadmin source
On since Dec 13 08:07:12 on ttysc from mk
2 hours 50 minutes Idle Time
No unread mail on this host.
Plan:

%
```

You can see that this is full of information. Notice that Michael is currently logged into the system (the output says `On since Dec 13 08:07:12 on ttysc`).

3. To see who is logged in to the USENIX Association main computer in Berkeley, California, I can use this:

```
% finger @usenix.org
[usenix.org]
Login        Name               TTY Idle    When     Where
pmui         Peter Mui           co   2d Tue 10:10
ah           Alain Henon        Z5      Mon 15:58   remote # 5408955 Dia
toni         Toni Veglia         p1   3d Thu 17:09   exec
diane        Diane DeMartini     p3    9 Mon 08:41   mac2.usenix.ORG
mis          Mark Seiden         p4   3d Thu 21:46   seiden.com
mis          Mark Seiden         p5   2d Fri 15:18   msbnext.internex
scott        Scott Seebass       p6   3d Tue 14:54   biohazard
lilia        Lilia Carol Scott   p7 1:12 Mon 08:39   thing1
mis          Mark Seiden         p8   3d Thu 22:09   seiden.com
toni         Toni Veglia         pa   3d Mon 10:38   exec
ellie        Ellie Young         q1 1:00 Mon 10:33   boss:0.0
scott        Scott Seebass       q2  18: Wed 15:36   biohazard
ellie        Ellie Young         q3 1:01 Mon 10:33   boss:0.0
mis          Mark Seiden         q6   1d Fri 11:28   seiden.com
%
```

Here you can see that lots of folks are logged in, but that almost everyone has a lot of idle time. A d suffix indicates the number of days idle. So you can see that Peter Mui's account has been idle for two days.

Comment: To find out what the weather is like in the greater San Francisco area, try finger weather@rogue.llnl.gov, which will connect you to the Lawrence Livermore National Laboratories in Walnut Creek, California.

4. To learn more information about a specific user on a remote site, specify the name of the user and the name of the user's system:

```
% finger ellie@usenix.org
[usenix.org]
Login name: ellie                       In real life: Ellie Young
Directory: /staff/ellie                 Shell: /bin/csh
On since Dec 13 10:33:57 on ttyq1 from boss:0.0
1 hour 3 minutes Idle Time
Mail last read Mon Dec 13 15:05:08 1993
No Plan.

%
```

You can see that Ellie has been logged in since December 13, but has had over an hour of idle time.

5. To talk with someone on a remote system, use `finger` to verify that the person is logged in, not off doing something else (which is what a high idle time usually suggests), then use `talk`:

```
% finger marv@netcom.com
Login name: marv                        In real life: Marvin Raab
Directory: /u1/marv                     Shell: /bin/csh
Logged in since Mon Dec  6 15:22 on ttys8
5 seconds idle time
Mail last read Mon Dec 13 15:22:22 1993
No Plan.
%
% talk marv@netcom.com
```

```
[Waiting for your party to respond]




- - - - - - - - - - - - - - - - - - - - - - - - - - - - - - - - - - - - - - - - - - - - - - - - - - - -




%
```

On the remote system here's what Marvin sees:

```
Message for marv(ttyaV) from Talk_Daemon@limbo.utech.edu at 18:55 ...
talk: connection requested by taylor@limbo.utech.edu.
talk: respond with: "talk taylor@limbo.utech.edu"
```

Once he responds, the screen looks like this:

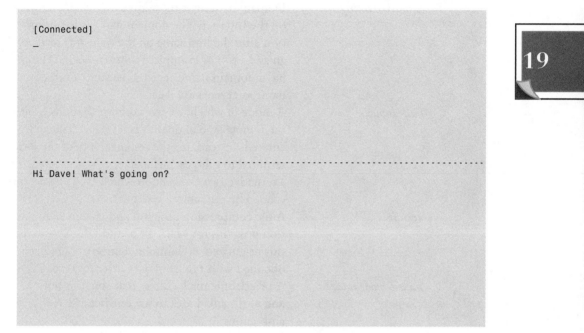

Notice that the cursor is in the top pane. Anything I enter will, character by character, be sent along to Marvin, so we can interactively chat and even type at the same time without our words getting jumbled.

Step 3. Summary

When I'm done, I simply press ^C to quit out of the program.

Lesson Summary

The finger program offers further information about users on your own and remote systems, and it is an essential first step in talking with your friends on the Internet via talk. Try entering taylor@netcom.com, and if I'm logged in, what the heck! Try using talk to say hi interactively!

Workshop
Key Terms

anonymous `ftp`	A system set up to respond to `ftp` queries that does not require you to have an account on the system.
domain naming	Domain naming is the addressing scheme for hosts on the Internet. The domain name is the information after the hostname on the right side of the @ in an address. For example, `joe@mutt.cornell.edu` has a domain name `cornell.edu` and a full domain name `mutt.cornell.edu`.
half-duplex	A mode in which, to save communications time, the remote system doesn't echo each character entered. Instead, it's the responsibility of the local terminal to echo each character as it is entered. The alternative is *full-duplex*, in which each character is echoed by the remote system.
kermit	A file compression program and terminal emulation program for Macs, PCs, and UNIX systems, this originated at Columbia University (and can be obtained with `ftp` from `watsun.cc.columbia.edu`).
mixed-mode address	An electronic mail address that contains both ! and @. It's a bad idea to use one because it's ambiguous.
parity	By checking parity, you can check the integrity of each character transmitted. Parity can be even, odd, or none. Each type affects how the high bit on each byte is interpreted.
protocol	An agreed-upon language for transfer of information between two computers.
UUCP g protocol	The standard protocol for UNIX systems communicating between themselves via telephone connections.
xmodem	A fairly old PC file transfer protocol for sending and receiving files from remote systems.
zmodem	A new PC file transfer protocol that includes built-in compression of information on most systems.

Questions

If you have a system that's connected via modem to other UNIX computer systems, do the following:

1. Use cu to connect to that system, then obtain the help information screen by entering ~?. Does it match what's in this book?

2. Use UUCP addressing and Figure 19.1 to figure out how to send mail messages to the following:

   ```
   joe@sheep          nancy@aphrod
   pookie@poodle      twoface@janus
   ```

3. List at least four different ways to get mail from home to remote, using the map in Figure 19.1.

4. Use uucp to send a file from your account on home to your new account on remote.

   If you have a system that's hooked up to the Internet, try the following:

5. Use telnet and rlogin to log in to one of the sites shown in Table 19.3. You don't have an account, so drop the connection once you see a login: prompt.

6. Use ftp to connect to ftp.eff.org and see what files the Electronic Frontier Foundation has made available to anonymous FTP users. Copy one to your system and read through it to see what you think about the organization itself.

7. Use finger to see if there's anyone logged in at one of the systems in the list, and then use it to find out more information about a person on that list of users.

8. If you have a friend on your system or another system, use talk to say hello.

Preview of the Next Chapter

The next lesson focuses on the many tools available on UNIX for C programmers and includes a valuable C utility that can help you work with the FTP program free of charge! If you're not interested in the C tools, you still might find it valuable to enter the program on your computer and see if it can help your FTP interaction.

Programming in C on a UNIX System

This lesson focuses on tools and techniques for creating your own programs written in the C programming language on your UNIX system. It covers the variety of different commands available, including some special features of vi that can be quite helpful for working on programs. Along the way, I list a short C program fget that proves a much easier way to work with anonymous FTP sites.

Goals for This Lesson

In this lesson, you will learn about

- ☐ Special commands in vi for programmers
- ☐ Using cc to compile programs
- ☐ Using make to avoid extra compilation
- ☐ Checking the quality of your code with lint
- ☐ Debugging your program with dbx
- ☐ Making it beautiful with cb
- ☐ Cross-reference lists with cxref

This lesson does not pretend to teach you anything about programming in the C language; that's the subject of a variety of other books, notably *Teach Yourself C in 21 Days* by Peter Aitken and Bradley Jones, and *The C Programming Language* by Brian Kernighan and Dennis Ritchie.

What is covered here are some of the basic tools available in your UNIX environment to help you build C programs, with a simple example program to demonstrate the various capabilities. If you don't understand how the program works, you should look into obtaining the aforementioned books.

Before beginning this chapter, please read through Listings 20.1, 20.2, and 20.3, which contain the source files for the fget routine: Listing 20.1 is fget.c, Listing 20.2 is utils.c, and Listing 20.3 contains all the header information in fget.h. The fget program offers an easy front end to the ftp program, enabling you to list files on a remote anonymous FTP archive and to get files with very little effort:

```
% fget
usage: fget host:file {localfile}

If you omit the ':file' portion, then fget will produce a listing of the
files on the remote system. To specify a particular directory on the
remote system, replace 'localfile' with that directory name. For example,
```

```
the command 'fget netcom.com /etc' will list the contents of the /etc
directory on that machine. To display a file use '-' as the localfile.
%
```

To list the files available on the remote FTP archive `ftp.uu.net`, for example, I need merely enter the following:

```
% fget ftp.uu.net
total 3960
    1 admin/          1 ftp/            1 ls-1R.Z@       1 sco-archive@
    1 applix@         1 government/     1 ls-1R.gz@      1 systems/
    1 archive@        1 graphics/       1 ls-1tR.Z@      3 tmp/
    1 bin/          792 gzip.tar        1 ls-1tR.gz@     1 unix-today@
    1 by-name.gz@     1 help@           1 mail@          1 unix-world@
    1 by-time.gz@     1 index/          1 networking/   13 usenet/
   88 compress.tar    1 inet/           1 news@          1 usr/
    1 dev/            1 info/           1 packages/      1 uumap@
    1 doc/            1 languages/      1 private/    3016 uumap.tar.Z
    1 etc/            1 library/        2 pub/           2 uunet-info/
    1 faces@          8 lost+found/     1 published/     1 vendor/
%
```

What's available on the Apple Computer FTP archive?

```
% fget ftp.apple.com
total 21
    1 .cshrc     1 alug/     1 boot/     1 echt90/    2 public/
    1 .login     1 apda/     1 cdrom/    1 etc/       1 shlib/
    1 .logout    1 apple/    1 dev/      1 pie/       1 software/
    1 README     1 bin/      1 dts/      2 pub/
%
```

To get the file README, I add it to the remote host name with a colon between the two words:

```
% fget ftp.apple.com:README
% ls -l README
-rw-rw----  1 taylor          424 Dec 14 12:35 README
%
```

This file was copied to my own system with the same filename. I could have easily specified a different filename, or, to read it directly on the screen, I could have used a dash:

```
% fget ftp.apple.com:README -
This is the top level of our FTP server.

If you're an authorized person, and you want to have a directory on the
top level, please contact Erik Fair <ftp@apple.com>, (408) 974-1779,
and explain why you want one, and what you're going to use it for.
Otherwise, please make your stuff available in the "public" directory.

There are no writeable directories for anonymous FTP on this server; it
cannot be used as a drop box.
%
```

Finally, you can also use fget to list a specific directory on the remote system by specifying the name of the remote directory as the second argument:

```
% fget ftp.apple.com apda
total 122
    1 APDA_Service_Announce.txt    33 Price_Lists.hqx*
   40 Current_Promotions.hqx*       7 Technical_Resources.txt*
    6 How_to_Order.txt*             2 What_is_APDA.txt*
   33 Ordering.hqx*                 0 Whats_New.hqx
%
```

Listing 20.1. The fget.c program listing.

```
/**                            fget.c                    **/

/** This is intended to be an easy way to copy files from a remote
    anonymous FTP archive site to your local system.  The format is

        fget host:filename {localfilename}

    "host" can be any Internet hostname, and "filename" must be a
    complete file specifier, including all path information as
    needed. If no "localfilename" is specified, then the file
    is saved under the same name in your own directory. If,
    instead, you use '-' as a filename, it sends the file to
    stdout instead.

    If no path information is specified, then the program invokes an
    "ls" on the remote machine instead: a second argument specifies
    the directory to examine, so "fget netcom.com /etc" will
    result in a listing of the "/etc" directory.

    This program is included in "Teach Yourself UNIX In A Week", a
    new introduction to UNIX from Prentice Hall / SAMS.

***/

#include "fget.h"

main(argc, argv)
int argc;
char **argv;
{
        FILE *fd;
        char buffer[SLEN], username[NLEN], hostname[NLEN];
        char remotehost[SLEN], remotefile[SLEN], localfname[SLEN];

        if (argc < 2) usage();  /* too few args: usage and quit */

        splitword(argv[1], remotehost, remotefile);    /* split host/file */

        if (argc == 2) strcpy(localfname, basename_of(remotefile));
        else           strcpy(localfname, argv[2]);

        initialize(username, hostname); /* get username and local host */
```

```
        if ((fd = fopen(TEMPFILE, "w")) == NULL) {
          fprintf(stderr,
             "Couldn't open tempfile '%s': move into your home directory?\n",
             TEMPFILE);
          exit(1);
        }

        /** now build the information to hand to ftp in the temp file **/

        fprintf(fd, "ascii\nuser %s %s@%s\n", ANONFTP, username, hostname);

        if (strlen(remotefile) == 0) {
          if (strlen(localfname) > 0)            /* directory specified? */
            fprintf(fd, "cd %s\n", localfname); /*    add 'cd' command */
          fprintf(fd, "ls -sCF\n");              /* always ls -sCF      */
        }
        else    /* get a file from the remote site */
          fprintf(fd, "get %s %s\n", remotefile, localfname);

        fprintf(fd, "bye\n");

        fclose(fd);

        /* the input file is built, now to hand it to 'ftp' */

        sprintf(buffer, "ftp -n %s < %s; rm %s", remotehost, TEMPFILE,TEMPFILE);

        exit(system(buffer));
}
```

Listing 20.2. The `utils.c` program listing.

```
/**                          utils.c                    **/

/** Utilities used in the FGET program. See "fget.c" for more info.**/



#include "fget.h"

initialize(username, hostname)
char *username, *hostname;
{
        /** figure out username and hostname for this system **/

        if (strcpy(username, getenv("USER")) == NULL)
          strcpy(username, getenv("LOGNAME"));

        gethostname(hostname, NLEN);
}

splitword(buffer, word1, word2)
char *buffer, *word1, *word2;
```

continues

Listing 20.2. continued

```
        {
                /** Given a buffer that's in the form of host.name:/file/path, break
                    it into two words around the colon, with the first word stored as
                    word1, and the second as word2. Initialize word2 to NULL if no
                    argument is present.  **/

                register int i, j = 0;

                for (i=0; buffer[i] != ':' && buffer[i] != 0; i++)    /* copy word1 */
                  word1[i] = buffer[i];
                word1[i] = 0;

                word2[0] = 0;                          /* initialize word2 to NULL */

                if (buffer[i] == 0) return;      /* no colon or nothing following it */

                i++;                             /* skip the colon */

                while (buffer[i] != 0)           /* copy word2 */
                  word2[j++] = buffer[i++];
                word2[j] = 0;
        }

        char *basename_of(filename)
        char *filename;
        {
                /** returns just the information to the right of all the directory
                    slashes in the given filename, or the filename if no slashes! **/

                register int i;

                for (i=strlen(filename)-1; i>0 && filename[i] != '/' &&
                    filename[i] != ':'; i--)
                  /** zoom backwards through the filename **/ ;

                if (i <= 0)      /* no directories specified, return NULL */
                  return( (char *) filename );

                return( (char *) filename + i + 1);
        }

        usage()
        {
                fprintf(stderr, "usage: fget host:file {localfile}\n\n");
                fprintf(stderr,
        "If you omit the ':file' portion, then fgets will produce a listing of the\n");
                fprintf(stderr,
        "files on the remote system. To specify a particular directory on the\n");
                fprintf(stderr,
        "remote system, replace 'localfile' with that directory name. For example,\n");
                fprintf(stderr,
        "the command 'fgets netcom.com /etc' will list the contents of the /etc\n");
                fprintf(stderr,
        "directory on that machine. To display a file use '-' as the localfile.\n\n");
                exit(1);
        }
```

Listing 20.3. The `fget.h` header file listing.

```
/**                          fget.h                **/

/** Headers file for the FGET program.  See "fget.c" for more info.


***/

#include <stdio.h>

#define FTP            "ftp -n"      /* how to invoke FTP in silent mode */
#define TEMPFILE       ".fget.tmp"   /* the temp file for building cmds */
#define ANONFTP        "ftp"         /* anonymous FTP user account */

#define SLEN           256           /* length of a typical string */
#define NLEN           40            /* length of a short string   */

char *basename_of();
```

Task 20.1: Special Commands in *vi* for Programmers
Step 1. Description

Although the vi editor was designed to work with text, many people who use the program work with C source programs. After all, C is the language of the operating system itself, as you learned in the very first lesson! As a result, there are some interesting and valuable commands available in vi that can greatly help you work with C programs.

Besides specific vi commands, there's something called a *tags file* that vi can work with, enabling you to create a set of indexes to routines that's file independent. With tags set up, you can specify the name of a routine, and vi will take you there, even if it means opening another file. Fortunately, there's a UNIX command for building C program tag files, called ctags. To use the program, specify on the command line the names of all C source files. Then ctags builds a file called tags that vi automatically reads. You can specify the -t *tag* option to vi, and vi figures out which file the specified routine is within and starts up the editor looking at that file, with the cursor pointing to the beginning of the specified routine or macro definition.

Within the editor, :tag *tagname* lets you move about, switching files as needed, to learn about routines in use. Also, within vi you might find the % command handy. It shows matching parentheses and curly braces. The]] command moves you to the beginning of the next function definition, and [[moves you to the beginning of the previous function definition.

Step 2. Action

1. To build a tags file for the fget program is simple:

```
% ctags *.c *.h
%
```

The file created is called tags and can be viewed by using head or cat:

```
% cat tags
ANONFTP  fget.h  /^#define ANONFTP             "ftp"              \/* anonymous FTP
user acco/
FTP      fget.h  /^#define FTP       "ftp -n"      \/* how to invoke FTP in
sile/
Mfget    fget.c  /^main(argc, argv)$/
NLEN     fget.h  /^#define NLEN      40          \/* length of a short string
*\//
SLEN     fget.h  /^#define SLEN      256         \/* length of a typicalstring
*/
TEMPFILE   fget.h  /^#define TEMPFILE    ".fget.tmp"   \/* the temp file for
/
basename_of   utils.c /^char *basename_of(filename)$/
initialize    utils.c /^initialize(username, hostname)$/
splitword     utils.c /^splitword(buffer, word1, word2)$/
usage   utils.c /^usage()$/
%
```

2. To start up vi looking at, say, splitword, use the -t option:

```
% vi -t splitword
```

```
char *username, *hostname;
{
        /** figure out username and hostname for this system **/


        if (strcpy(username, getenv("USER")) == NULL)
          strcpy(username, getenv("LOGNAME"));


        gethostname(hostname, NLEN);
}


splitword(buffer, word1, word2)
char *buffer, *word1, *word2;
{
        /** Given a buffer that's in the form of host.name:/file/path, break
            it into two words around the colon, with the first word stored as
```

```
              word1, and the second as word2. Initialize word2 to NULL if no
              argument is present.  **/

          register int i, j = 0;

          for (i=0; buffer[i] != ':' && buffer[i] != 0; i++)   /* copy word1 */
            word1[i] = buffer[i];
          word1[i] = 0;
"utils.c" 78 lines, 2142 characters
```

Notice that the cursor is positioned at the very first letter of the actual function definition, not at any invocation of the function in other files.

3. To switch to the definition of NLEN, a variable used to size arrays throughout the program, I can use :tag NLEN as a vi command:

```
          register int i, j = 0;

          for (i=0; buffer[i] != ':' && buffer[i] != 0; i++)   /* copy word1 */
            word1[i] = buffer[i];
          word1[i] = 0;
:tag NLEN
```

Entering Return results in this:

```
***/

#include <stdio.h>

#define FTP            "ftp -n"      /* how to invoke FTP in silent mode */
#define TEMPFILE       ".fget.tmp"   /* the temp file for building cmds */
#define ANONFTP        "ftp"         /* anonymous FTP user account */

#define SLEN           256           /* length of a typical string */
#define NLEN           40            /* length of a short string   */
```

20

```
char *basename_of();
~
~
~
~
~
~
~
~
~
~
"fget.h" 17 lines, 486 characters
```

Comment: For some odd reason, the one tag missing from the tags file is a definition for the main program itself. Try using :tag main and you'll find that that particular tag isn't defined. I have no explanation for this curious oversight.

4. One neat feature of vi is that if you're looking at a particular function call, you can enter ^] and the tags file will move you right to the definition of that function. For example, I used G to move to the bottom of the fget.h file shown in the last box, then moved forward until the cursor was on the b in basename_of():

```
#define SLEN        256             /* length of a typical string */
#define NLEN        40              /* length of a short string   */

char *basename_of();
~
~
~
```

in question:

```
        if (buffer[i] == 0) return;      /* no colon, or nothing following it */


        i++;                             /* skip the colon */


        while (buffer[i] != 0)           /* copy word2 */
          word2[j++] = buffer[i++];
        word2[j] = 0;
}


char *basename_of(filename)
char *filename;
{
        /** returns just the information to the right of all the directory
            slashes in the given filename, or the filename if no slashes! **/


        register int i;

        for (i=strlen(filename)-1; i>0 && filename[i] != '/' &&
            filename[i] != ':'; i--)
          /** zoom backwards through the filename **/ ;


        if (i <= 0)     /* no directories specified, return NULL */
"utils.c" 78 lines, 2142 characters
```

5. To move to the beginning of the actual listing for this routine, I use]] (that is, I press the] key twice):

```
        word2[j] = 0;
}


char *basename_of(filename)
char *filename;
{
```

```
/** returns just the information to the right of all the directory
        slashes in the given filename, or the filename if no slashes! **/
```

To move to the next routine, I enter]] again, and the screen looks like this:

```
        filename[i] != ':'; i--)
      /** zoom backwards through the filename **/ ;

    if (i <= 0)      /* no directories specified, return NULL */
      return( (char *) filename );

    return( (char *) filename + i + 1);
}

usage()
{
      fprintf(stderr, "usage: fget host:file {localfile}\n\n");
      fprintf(stderr,
"If you omit the ':file' portion, then fgets will produce a listing of the\n");
      fprintf(stderr,
"files on the remote system. To specify a particular directory on the\n");
      fprintf(stderr,
"remote system, replace 'localfile' with that directory name. For example,\n");
      fprintf(stderr,
"the command 'fgets netcom.com /etc' will list the contents of the /etc\n");
      fprintf(stderr,
"directory on that machine. To display a file use '-' as the localfile.\n\n");
      exit(1);
```

6. Now I'll move down one line, to the first `fprintf` system call:

```
usage()
{
      fprintf(stderr, "usage: fget host:file {localfile}\n\n");
      fprintf(stderr,
"If you omit the ':file' portion, then fgets will produce a listing of the\n");
```

```
        fprintf(stderr,
"files on the remote system. To specify a particular directory on the\n");
```

Using % zips the cursor to the closing parenthesis that matches the open parenthesis:

```
usage()
{
        fprintf(stderr, "usage: fget host:file {localfile}\n\n"];
        fprintf(stderr,
"If you omit the ':file' portion, then fgets will produce a listing of the\n");
        fprintf(stderr,
"files on the remote system. To specify a particular directory on the\n");
```

Try this command at blocks of programming instructions too, particularly at if and repeat loops.

Step 3. Summary

Surprisingly, the vi editor has a variety of different capabilities that make it quite helpful in carrying out programming tasks. The ctags command works quickly and easily to help create a useful file that enables you to move around in multiple-source-file programs quite simply.

Task 20.2: Using *cc* to Compile Programs

Step 1. Description

Unlike programming languages such as BASIC, the C language cannot be read and interpreted as you execute it. Instead, the UNIX system reads and translates the source program into an *executable binary*, through a process called *compilation*. You need to compile a program only once for each modification or change you make, so as soon as the program is working correctly, you never have to compile it again; and, better, the program, having been compiled into an executable, runs quite a bit faster than any interpreted version could run.

The command to compile a C program is cc, and it has quite a variety of options. The most important ones are -o *output*, to specify the name of the executable binary (the default is the puzzling name a.out); -O, to optimize the program, making it as fast and efficient as possible; and -c, to build an intermediate compiled version, but not actually produce an executable file. The -c option is vital for situations in which the program is split across multiple files.

Any errors in the C source program will cause the compiler to complain and produce a helpful error message that specifies which file contains the error, which line contains the error, and the nature of the problem. If all goes well, no messages are printed on the screen.

Step 2. Action

1. I added an error to the fget.c file so I can see if the cc program finds it:

```
% cc fget.c
"fget.c", line 39: remote undefined
"fget.c", line 39: syntax error
%
```

It did. To see the problem line and one on each side of it, use this trick:

```
% cat -n fget.c ¦ head -40 ¦ tail -3
    38
    39          splitword(argv[1], remote host, remotefile);    /* split
host/file */
    40
%
```

This would be a great alias, called showline perhaps. Anyway, you can see that I added an incorrect space between remote and host on line 39. A quick modification with vi and I can compile the program again:

```
% cc fget.c
Undefined:
_usage
_splitword
_basename_of
_initialize
%
```

This error makes sense, because the routines that aren't defined are included in the file utils.c, which isn't specified in this command line.

2. To compile a program without actually having the compiler try to generate an executable binary, the -c option stops the compilation process partway:

```
% cc -c fget.c
%
```

Although there was no output, I can tell that the command worked without a hitch. The intermediate file is called fget.o: The final c in the filename is

always replaced by an o for the output of the intermediate compilation. The file command shows what was produced:

```
% file fget.o
fget.o: SYMMETRY i386 .o not stripped version 1
%
```

3. One way to compile a group of source files into a single output is to specify them all at once to the compiler:

```
% cc fget.c utils.c
fget.c:
utils.c:
%
```

The output is a.out, and it's ready to examine and use:

```
% file a.out
a.out:  SYMMETRY i386 executable (0 @ 0) not stripped version 1
% a.out
usage: fget host:file {localfile}

If you omit the ':file' portion, then fgets will produce a listing of the
files on the remote system. To specify a particular directory on the
remote system, replace 'localfile' with that directory name. For example,
the command 'fgets netcom.com /etc' will list the contents of the /etc
directory on that machine. To display a file use '-' as the localfile.

%
```

4. A better move would be to specify the name of the output file with the -o option and also have the compiler try to optimize the code so it can run faster at the same time:

```
% cc -o fget -O fget.c utils.c
fget.c:
utils.c:
%
```

These are the results:

```
% file fget
fget:   SYMMETRY i386 executable (0 @ 0) not stripped version 1
%
```

Step 3. Summary

I am making the process of compilation look easy here. The cc command itself is easy to work with, as you can see, but the compiler is very picky about what are and aren't valid and proper C programs. You might find yourself making many frustrating attempts at getting cc to compile your program properly. If you have too many problems, then you might find it valuable to go back to your C programming language reference book and reread sections that are appropriate to the problem area.

Task 20.3: Using *make* to Avoid Extra Compilation

Step 1. Description

The cc program is easily used to create executable programs from a set of source files, but if you're like other programmers, you doubtless find the hassle of typing cc -o fget -O fget.c utils.c time after time quite laborious. You could use an alias to make it easier, or you could use the C shell history mechanism, in which case !cc is the entire command.

The problem with this is that each time you alter any of the files you must recompile all of them, which is incredibly inefficient and more trouble than necessary. The UNIX system has a powerful program called make that lets you specify a set of rules for building your program, then make figures out what, if anything, has changed, and what needs to be recompiled. If anything does need to be recompiled, make invokes cc for you.

All these rules are kept in a file called Makefile in the same directory. You can add some other helpful rules to the file for other tasks, such as a tags file for vi or for invoking lint to analyze the program. The default action of the make program is to follow the first rule specified in the Makefile, but you can specify any rule by adding its name to the command. For example, make tags would find the rule tags: in the Makefile and invoke the commands required to satisfy the rule.

There is one notable option for make; n causes the program to list the commands it would invoke without actually executing them. If you're not sure that your file is up-to-date, this option can be very helpful.

Step 2. Action

1. The Makefile for fget is short:

```
% cat Makefile
#
#  Makefile for the FGET ftp front-end program
#

SRC= fget.c utils.c
OBJ= fget.o utils.o
HDR= fget.h
TARGET=fget
cc=/bin/cc

$(TARGET): $(OBJ) $(HDR)
        $(CC) -o $(TARGET) $(OBJ)

lint:
        lint $(SRC) | tee Lint.Analysis
```

```
clean:
        rm -f $(OBJ)

strip: $(TARGET)
        strip $(TARGET)

tags: $(SRC) $(HDRS)
        ctags $(SRC) $(HDRS)

fget.o : fget.c fget.h
utils.o: utils.c fget.h
%
```

This is a typical Makefile, where the first few lines are a comment (any line in a Makefile beginning with # is a comment), then the SRC, OBJ, and HDRS are defined. The TARGET is the name of the final program to create.

The first rule in the file is the line that begins with $(TARGET): and specifies that the executable target depends on the OBJ and HDR files, and if not up-to-date (that is, if the executable hasn't been created more recently than all the source files) the program can be made up-to-date with cc -o *target obj*.

2. To build the entire program I simply enter make:

```
% make
        cc  -c fget.c
        cc  -c utils.c
        cc -o fget fget.o utils.o
%
```

The program deduced that both the fget.c and utils.c files had changed since the last compilation, and it rebuilt .o files for them. Then the program put them all together to create the fget program itself.

3. A second invocation of the make program shows where it's worth its weight in faster computing:

```
% make
`fget' is up to date.
%
```

No work needed to be done because the files hadn't changed since the previous compilation!

4. To create a tags file, I use make tags:

```
% make tags
        ctags fget.c utils.c
%
```

20

Step 3. Summary

If you are building programs that are spread across more than a single file (which is a good idea 99 percent of the time), then five minutes building a Makefile can pay back dividends in faster compilations, less typing, and confirmation that the executable binary reflects the latest version of all source and header files. I strongly recommend it for programming tasks!

Task 20.4: Checking the Quality of Your Code with *lint*
Step 1. Description

Now you have a program and it compiles, but it's not necessarily the best possible program. To check for matching function parameters, ensure that all variables are used and that they're used appropriately. To double-check that you're using the various system library routines correctly, you can use the lint program to pick through the source.

Step 2. Action

1. Because it's already one of the alternate targets in the Makefile presented in the previous section, using lint is a breeze:

```
% make lint
        lint fget.c utils.c ¦ tee Lint.Analysis
fget.c:
utils.c:
strcpy value declared inconsistently        llib-lc(421)  ::  fget.c(42)
strcpy, arg. 2 used inconsistently          llib-lc(421)  ::  utils.c(15)
strcpy value used inconsistently            llib-lc(421)  ::  utils.c(15)
getenv value used inconsistently            llib-lc(290)  ::  utils.c(15)
strcpy, arg. 2 used inconsistently          llib-lc(421)  ::  utils.c(16)
getenv value used inconsistently            llib-lc(290)  ::  utils.c(16)
strcpy value declared inconsistently        llib-lc(421)  ::  utils.c(16)
getenv value declared inconsistently        llib-lc(290)  ::  utils.c(16)
strcpy returns value which is sometimes ignored
fclose returns value which is always ignored
gethostname returns value which is always ignored
%
```

Did you notice that a copy of the output has also been saved to the file Lint.Analysis through use of the tee command?

This output shows that I have amazingly few problems with this program; lint output can often sprawl for pages. Here I can see that the official system definition of some of the functions I use, notably strcpy and getenv, differ from how they're used in the program itself. The last few lines remind me that strcpy, fclose, and gethostname all return values that I'm ignoring completely.

2. A typical step before distributing code is to spend some time working with lint to ensure that there are minimal problems and portability gotchas. Given enough effort, it *is* possible to receive no output from lint.

Step 3. Summary

If you're used to working in PC or Mac development environments, the wealth of different tools on UNIX should be starting to surprise you. There are a lot of utilities that help with the creation, modification, compilation, analysis, and execution of code. The lint program is a cornerstone of quality UNIX code.

Task 20.5: Debugging Your Program with *dbx*
Step 1. Description

Sometimes when you run a program it doesn't do what you want or it just outright crashes, resulting in the dreaded core dump message from the operating system. When that happens, it's time to call in a symbolic debugger to help track down the bugs in the program. There are a variety of different debuggers, including cdb, dbx, xdb, and cscope. I focus on dbx here because it's a common program. Check with your own documentation to see which debugger is included with your version of UNIX.

To work with any debugging software, you need to rebuild the original source program to include extra debugging options. The easiest way to do that is to specify the -g option to cc, which you can do while still using make by cheating a little and specifying make CFLAGS=-g. Once created, either run the program in the debugger or specify the program and core file to the program, letting it offer initial information on the cause of the problem.

For this example, I have gone into one of the utility routines and introduced a bug to track down.

Step 2. Action

1. To build a version of the program suitable for debugging, I need to use the -g option to the compiler:

```
% make CFLAGS=-g
        cc -g -c fget.c
        cc -g -c utils.c
        cc -o fget fget.o utils.o
%
```

Now I try the new version of the program:

```
% fget ftp.apple.com:/README -
Segmentation fault (core dumped)
%
```

2. It looks like there's trouble. To identify where the core dump occurred, I use dbx, specifying the name of the program:

```
% dbx fget
dbx version 5.13 of 3/10/89 13:23 (Sequent).
Type 'help' for help.
reading symbolic information ...
[using memory image in core]
(dbx)
```

The help information is illuminating:

```
(dbx) help
Refer to "DYNIX Pdbx Debugger User's Manual" for complete details
run                        - begin execution of the program
ps                         - print status of processes/core dumps
print <exp>                - print the value of the expression
where                      - print currently active procedures
%<number>                  - switch to context of process `number'
stop at <line>             - suspend execution at the line
stop in <proc>             - suspend execution when <proc> is called
cont                       - continue execution
step                       - single step one line
next                       - step to next line (skip over calls)
trace <line#>              - trace execution of the line
trace <proc>               - trace calls to the procedure
trace <var>                - trace changes to the variable
trace <exp> at <line#>     - print <exp> when <line> is reached
status                     - print trace/stop's in effect
delete <number>            - remove trace or stop of given number
call <proc>                - call a procedure in program
whatis <name>              - print the declaration of the name
list <line>, <line>        - list source lines
quit                       - exit dbx
(dbx)
```

To see where the core dump occurred, I use the ps command to dbx:

```
(dbx) ps
* %1  Core in "core" caused by Segmentation fault in splitword at line 35 in
fil
e "utils.c"
(dbx)
```

3. Ahhh...the culprit is in the splitword routine, on line 35 of file utils.c. I can check that without leaving the debugger. I want to run the program again to see if I can duplicate the problem. To run the code while within the debugger, I use the run command:

```
(dbx) run
usage: fget host:file {localfile}

If you omit the ':file' portion, then fgets will produce a listing of the
files on the remote system. To specify a particular directory on the
remote system, replace 'localfile' with that directory name. For example,
```

```
the command 'fgets netcom.com /etc' will list the contents of the /etc
directory on that machine. To display a file use '-' as the localfile.

  %2  Stopped by Exit in _exit at 0x1913
00001913  ret
(dbx)
```

Oops. I need to specify some starting options:

```
(dbx) run ftp.apple.com:/README
  %3  Stopped by Segmentation fault in splitword at line 35 in file "utils.c"
  35          word2[9999999] = 0;                      /* initialize word2
to
NULL */
(dbx)
```

This time it shows the problem line in the `utils.c` file, where I can see that
the line has been altered (from `word2[0] = 0;`) to `word2[9999999] = 0;`,
which is a problem. I quit `dbx` with `quit`, then make a quick visit to the file
with `vi` to fix the problem.

Step 3. Summary

Rarely are bugs found quite this quickly, but if you've been working with `printf`
statements as your approach to debugging programs, then you've got a wonderful
surprise coming when you start using a UNIX symbolic debugger! Just don't forget
to use the all-important `-g` option when you compile the program.

Task 20.6: Making It Beautiful with *cb*
Step 1. Description

Reversing transmogrification of source code is the job of the `cb` program, which, to
use smaller words, tries to ensure that there's a standard and consistent scheme for
indentation of statements and location of brackets beginning and ending blocks of
statements. The program itself is primitive, with input coming exclusively from a pipe
or file redirection, and output showing on the screen.

Step 2. Action

1. Recently I've been working on a program, written by another programmer,
   that can be typified by the sample file `sample.c`:

```
% cat sample.c
#include <include.h>

main()
{
        char buffer[80];
```

```
                    if (getenv("HOME") == NULL)
                        /* if my HOME is set this won't be true */
                    if (getenv("PATH") == NULL)
                      if (getenv("USER") == NULL) {
                        printf("where am I?\n"); }

                        printf("only print if PATH is null.\n");
            }
            %
```

The puzzle I have is this: What's executed when? Furthermore, the format of this program is pretty abysmal. Although the programmer attempted to have some indentation, she failed to have it make sense. For example, does the condition that checks PATH execute always, as suggested by the indentation level, or only if HOME is NULL?

2. To clean up code of any sort, I use the cb program, to *beautify the C*. The cb is a weird utility in that it reads only from standard input (some new versions let you specify the filename directly: cb sample.c), so I must redirect it:

```
% cb < sample.c
#include <include.h>

main()
{
        char buffer[80];

        if (getenv("HOME") == NULL)
                /* if my HOME is set this won't be true */
                if (getenv("PATH") == NULL)
                        if (getenv("USER") == NULL) {
                                printf("where am I?\n");
                        }

        printf("only print if PATH is null.\n");
}
%
```

Now the program is a bit more clear, and you can see that the comment doesn't actually affect the control flow. The test of PATH only occurs when HOME is NULL, and although the last printf is indented, in fact the command prints every time the program is run.

Step 3. Summary

If you're working on your own programs, the cb program is of limited value. Indeed, because it has its own approach to indentation, it might well mess up your format (cb uses one tab per level). On the other hand, if you are perusing software from another programmer and you're puzzled by what's executed and when, then the cb program can be very helpful, normalizing the program format to a common standard.

Task 20.7: Cross-Reference Lists with *cxref*

Step 1. Description

One useful item that can help you work through a large body of software is a cross-reference listing showing where things are defined and where they're referenced, on a file-by-file basis. Although you'd think it should be easy to produce something of this nature in UNIX, the tools available are primitive. The best of the batch is cxref, which, used with grep, offers some valuable information. If that's not on your system, then you have xref, which is barely useful, because it misses some variables and lists many words that are used in actual printable strings.

Step 2. Action

1. By default, cxref has a lot of output:

```
% cxref fget.c utils.c fget.h
fget.c:

SYMBOL          FILE                    FUNCTION   LINE

ANONFTP         ./fget.h                 --        *12
                fget.c                   --         55
BUFSIZ          /usr/ucbinclude/stdio.h --        *4
EOF             /usr/ucbinclude/stdio.h --        *27
FILE            /usr/ucbinclude/stdio.h --         3 *26   53   54   55   56   57
                fget.c                   --         33
FTP             ./fget.h                 --        *10
L_ctermid       /usr/ucbinclude/stdio.h --        *67
L_cuserid       /usr/ucbinclude/stdio.h --        *68
L_tmpnam        /usr/ucbinclude/stdio.h --        *70
NLEN            ./fget.h                 --        *15
                fget.c                   --         34
NULL            /usr/ucbinclude/stdio.h --        *25
                fget.c                   --         46
P_tmpdir        /usr/ucbinclude/stdio.h --        *69
SLEN            ./fget.h                 --        *14
                fget.c                   --         34   35
TEMPFILE        ./fget.h                 --        *11
                fget.c                   --         46   49   71
_IOEOF          /usr/ucbinclude/stdio.h --        *20
_IOERR          /usr/ucbinclude/stdio.h --        *21
_IOFBF          /usr/ucbinclude/stdio.h --        *15
_IOLBF          /usr/ucbinclude/stdio.h --        *23
_IOMYBUF        /usr/ucbinclude/stdio.h --        *19
_IONBF          /usr/ucbinclude/stdio.h --        *18
_IOREAD         /usr/ucbinclude/stdio.h --        *16
_IORW           /usr/ucbinclude/stdio.h --        *24
_IOSTRG         /usr/ucbinclude/stdio.h --        *22
_IOWRT          /usr/ucbinclude/stdio.h --        *17
_SBFSIZ         /usr/ucbinclude/stdio.h --        *5
_base           /usr/ucbinclude/stdio.h --        *9
_bufsiz         /usr/ucbinclude/stdio.h --        *10
```

20

_cnt	/usr/ucbinclude/stdio.h	--	*7					
_file	/usr/ucbinclude/stdio.h	--	*12					
_flag	/usr/ucbinclude/stdio.h	--	*11					
_iob	/usr/ucbinclude/stdio.h	--	*13					
	fget.c	main	47					
_iobuf	/usr/ucbinclude/stdio.h	--	*6	53	54	55	56	57
	fget.c	main	33					
_ptr	/usr/ucbinclude/stdio.h	--	*8					
argc	fget.c	--	29					
	fget.c	main	*30	37	41			
argv	fget.c	--	29					
	fget.c	main	*31	39	42			
basename_of()								
	./fget.h	--	*17					
	fget.c	main	41					
buffer	fget.c	main	*34	71	73			
clearerr()								
	/usr/ucbinclude/stdio.h	--	*51					
ctermid()								
	/usr/ucbinclude/stdio.h	--	*62					
cuserid()								
	/usr/ucbinclude/stdio.h	--	*63					
exit	fget.c	main	50	73				
fclose	fget.c	main	67					
fd	fget.c	main	*33	46	55	59	60	63
65								
67								
fdopen()								
	/usr/ucbinclude/stdio.h	--	*54					
feof()								
	/usr/ucbinclude/stdio.h	--	*48					
ferror()								
	/usr/ucbinclude/stdio.h	--	*49					
fgets()								
	/usr/ucbinclude/stdio.h	--	*59					
fileno()								
	/usr/ucbinclude/stdio.h	--	*50					
fopen()								
	/usr/ucbinclude/stdio.h	--	*53					
	fget.c	main	46					
fprintf	fget.c	main	47	55	59	60	63	65
freopen()								
	/usr/ucbinclude/stdio.h	--	*55					
ftell()								
	/usr/ucbinclude/stdio.h	--	*58					
getc()								
	/usr/ucbinclude/stdio.h	--	*37					
getchar()								
	/usr/ucbinclude/stdio.h	--	*46					
gets()								
	/usr/ucbinclude/stdio.h	--	*60					
hostname	fget.c	main	*34	44	55			
initialize	fget.c	main	44					
lint	/usr/ucbinclude/stdio.h	--	33					
localfname	fget.c	main	*35	41	42	58	59	63
main()								

```
                    fget.c                   --       *29
p                   /usr/ucbinclude/stdio.h --       37 *37  38 *38  39  40
41
42  43  44  48 *48  49 *49  50 *50  51       *51
popen()
                    /usr/ucbinclude/stdio.h --       *56
putc()
                    /usr/ucbinclude/stdio.h --       *38
putchar()
                    /usr/ucbinclude/stdio.h --       *47
remotefile          fget.c                   main    *35  39  41  57  63
remotehost          fget.c                   main    *35  39  71
splitword           fget.c                   main     39
sprintf()
                    /usr/ucbinclude/stdio.h --       *61
                    fget.c                   main     71
stderr              /usr/ucbinclude/stdio.h --       *31
                    fget.c                   --       47
stdin               /usr/ucbinclude/stdio.h --       *29
stdout              /usr/ucbinclude/stdio.h --       *30
strcpy              fget.c                   main     41  42
strlen              fget.c                   main     57  58
system              fget.c                   main     73
tempnam()
                    /usr/ucbinclude/stdio.h --       *64
tmpfile()
                    /usr/ucbinclude/stdio.h --       *57
tmpnam()
                    /usr/ucbinclude/stdio.h --       *65
usage               fget.c                   main     37
username            fget.c                   main    *34  44  55
x                   /usr/ucbinclude/stdio.h --       *38  39  41  44  47 *47
utils.c:

SYMBOL              FILE                     FUNCTION  LINE

ANONFTP             ./fget.h                 --       *12
BUFSIZ              /usr/ucbinclude/stdio.h --       *4
EOF                 /usr/ucbinclude/stdio.h --       *27
FILE                /usr/ucbinclude/stdio.h --       3 *26  53  54  55  56  57
FTP                 ./fget.h                 --       *10
L_ctermid           /usr/ucbinclude/stdio.h --       *67
L_cuserid           /usr/ucbinclude/stdio.h --       *68
L_tmpnam            /usr/ucbinclude/stdio.h --       *70
NLEN                ./fget.h                 --       *15
                    utils.c                  --        18
NULL                /usr/ucbinclude/stdio.h --       *25
                    utils.c                  --        15  59
P_tmpdir            /usr/ucbinclude/stdio.h --       *69
SLEN                ./fget.h                 --       *14
TEMPFILE            ./fget.h                 --       *11
_IOEOF              /usr/ucbinclude/stdio.h --       *20
_IOERR              /usr/ucbinclude/stdio.h --       *21
_IOFBF              /usr/ucbinclude/stdio.h --       *15
_IOLBF              /usr/ucbinclude/stdio.h --       *23
_IOMYBUF            /usr/ucbinclude/stdio.h --       *19
```

```
_IONBF           /usr/ucbinclude/stdio.h --       *18
_IOREAD          /usr/ucbinclude/stdio.h --       *16
_IORW            /usr/ucbinclude/stdio.h --       *24
_IOSTRG          /usr/ucbinclude/stdio.h --       *22
_IOWRT           /usr/ucbinclude/stdio.h --       *17
_SBFSIZ          /usr/ucbinclude/stdio.h --       *5
_base            /usr/ucbinclude/stdio.h --       *9
_bufsiz          /usr/ucbinclude/stdio.h --       *10
_cnt             /usr/ucbinclude/stdio.h --       *7
_file            /usr/ucbinclude/stdio.h --       *12
_flag            /usr/ucbinclude/stdio.h --       *11
_iob             /usr/ucbinclude/stdio.h --       *13
                 utils.c                 usage    66  67  69  71  73  75
_iobuf           /usr/ucbinclude/stdio.h --       *6  53  54  55  56  57
_ptr             /usr/ucbinclude/stdio.h --       *8
basename_of()
                 ./fget.h                --        *17
                 utils.c                 --        46
buffer           utils.c                 --        21
                 utils.c                 splitword *22  31  32  37  41  42
clearerr()
                 /usr/ucbinclude/stdio.h --       *51
ctermid()
                 /usr/ucbinclude/stdio.h --       *62
cuserid()
                 /usr/ucbinclude/stdio.h --       *63
exit             utils.c                 usage    77
fdopen()
                 /usr/ucbinclude/stdio.h --       *54
feof()
                 /usr/ucbinclude/stdio.h --       *48
ferror()
                 /usr/ucbinclude/stdio.h --       *49
fgets()
                 /usr/ucbinclude/stdio.h --       *59
filename         utils.c                 --        46
                 utils.c                 basename_of *47  54  55  61
fileno()
                 /usr/ucbinclude/stdio.h --       *50
fopen()
                 /usr/ucbinclude/stdio.h --       *53
fprintf          utils.c                 usage    66  67  69  71  73  75
freopen()
                 /usr/ucbinclude/stdio.h --       *55
ftell()
                 /usr/ucbinclude/stdio.h --       *58
getc()
                 /usr/ucbinclude/stdio.h --       *37
getchar()
                 /usr/ucbinclude/stdio.h --       *46
getenv           utils.c                 initialize  15  16
gethostname      utils.c                 initialize  18
gets()
                 /usr/ucbinclude/stdio.h --       *60
hostname         utils.c                 --        10
                 utils.c                 initialize  *11  18
```

```
i               utils.c                 basename_of  *52  54  55  58  61
                utils.c                 splitword    *29  31  32  33  37  39
41
42
initialize()
                utils.c                 --           *10
j               utils.c                 splitword    *29  42  43
lint            /usr/ucbinclude/stdio.h --           33
p               /usr/ucbinclude/stdio.h --           37 *37  38 *38  39  40
41
42  43  44  48 *48  49 *49  50 *50  51
                                                     *51
popen()
                /usr/ucbinclude/stdio.h --           *56
putc()
                /usr/ucbinclude/stdio.h --           *38
putchar()
                /usr/ucbinclude/stdio.h --           *47
splitword()
                utils.c                 --           *21
sprintf()
                /usr/ucbinclude/stdio.h --           *61
stderr          /usr/ucbinclude/stdio.h --           *31
                utils.c                 --           66  67  69  71  73  75
stdin           /usr/ucbinclude/stdio.h --           *29
stdout          /usr/ucbinclude/stdio.h --           *30
strcpy          utils.c                 initialize   15  16
strlen          utils.c                 basename_of  54
tempnam()
                /usr/ucbinclude/stdio.h --           *64
tmpfile()
                /usr/ucbinclude/stdio.h --           *57
tmpnam()
                /usr/ucbinclude/stdio.h --           *65
usage()
                utils.c                 --           *64
username        utils.c                 --           10
                utils.c                 initialize   *11  15  16
word1           utils.c                 --           21
                utils.c                 splitword    *22  32  33
word2           utils.c                 --           21
                utils.c                 splitword    *22  35  42  43
x               /usr/ucbinclude/stdio.h --           *38  39  41  44  47 *47
%
```

2. To trim the output down a bit, you can limit it to just those items that are defined in your file, and you can use the -c option to have the program combine the output of the different files it checks:

```
% cxref -c fget.c utils.c fget.h | egrep '(fget|utils)'
fget.c:
utils.c:
ANONFTP         ./fget.h                --           *12
                fget.c                  --           55
                fget.c                  --           33
```

FTP	./fget.h	--	*10						
NLEN	./fget.h	--	*15						
	fget.c	--	34						
	utils.c	--	18						
	fget.c	--	46						
	utils.c	--	15	59					
SLEN	./fget.h	--	*14						
	fget.c	--	34	35					
TEMPFILE	./fget.h	--	*11						
	fget.c	--	46	49	71				
	fget.c	main	47						
	utils.c	usage	66	67	69	71	73	75	
	fget.c	main	33						
argc	fget.c	--	29						
	fget.c	main	*30	37	41				
argv	fget.c	--	29						
	fget.c	main	*31	39	42				
	./fget.h	--	*17						
	fget.c	main	41						
	utils.c	--	46						
buffer	fget.c	main	*34	71	73				
	utils.c	--	21						
	utils.c	splitword	*22	31	32	37	41	42	
exit	fget.c	main	50	73					
	utils.c	usage	77						
fclose	fget.c	main	67						
fd	fget.c	main	*33	46	55	59	60	63	
65									
67									
fgets()									
filename	utils.c	--	46						
	utils.c	basename_of	*47	54	55	61			
	fget.c	main	46						
fprintf	fget.c	main	47	55	59	60	63	65	
	utils.c	usage	66	67	69	71	73	75	
getenv	utils.c	initialize	15	16					
gethostname	utils.c	initialize	18						
hostname	fget.c	main	*34	44	55				
	utils.c	--	10						
	utils.c	initialize	*11	18					
i	utils.c	basename_of	*52	54	55	58	61		
	utils.c	splitword	*29	31	32	33	37	39	
41									
42									
	fget.c	main	44						
	utils.c	--	*10						
j	utils.c	splitword	*29	42	43				
localfname	fget.c	main	*35	41	42	58	59	63	
	fget.c	--	*29						
remotefile	fget.c	main	*35	39	41	57	63		
remotehost	fget.c	main	*35	39	71				
	fget.c	main	39						
	utils.c	--	*21						
	fget.c	main	71						
	fget.c	--	47						
	utils.c	--	66	67	69	71	73	75	

```
strcpy          fget.c                  main            41  42
                utils.c                 initialize      15  16
strlen          fget.c                  main            57  58
                utils.c                 basename_of     54
system          fget.c                  main            73
                fget.c                  main            37
                utils.c                 --              *64
username        fget.c                  main            *34  44  55
                utils.c                 --              10
                utils.c                 initialize      *11  15  16
word1           utils.c                 --              21
                utils.c                 splitword       *22  32  33
word2           utils.c                 --              21
                utils.c                 splitword       *22  35  42  43
%
```

This is useful but still a bit awkward. It's the best UNIX can do to build a cross-reference of routines used in a program.

Comment: I don't know of any UNIX programmers who use this capability, but you might be a trailblazer. The information *can* be useful when perusing code.

3. There's also a less sophisticated cross-referencing tool that works with just about any file, rather than with only C language constructs, called xref. To use it, you must first use another program—stripcom—to strip comments. This is the result of using these programs on fget.c and utils.c:

```
% stripcom -b/\* -e\*/ -n fget.c utils.c ¦ xref -s
0                       57      58      103     105     105     107
109     109     111     115     117     128     132
1                       39      50      128     135     151
2                       37      41      42
ANONFTP                 55
Couldn                  48
FILE                    33
For                     146
If                      142
LOGNAME                 90
NLEN                    34      34      92
NULL                    46      89      133
SLEN                    34      35      35      35
TEMPFILE                46      49      71      71
To                      144     150
USER                    89
a                       142     144     150
argc                    29      30      37      41
argv                    29      31      39      42
as                      150
```

n	48	55	59	60	63	65	71
140	140	142	144	146	148	150	150
name	146						
netcom	148						
nuser	55						
of	142	148					
omit	142						
on	144	144	150				
open	48						
particular	144						
portion	142						
produce	142						
register	103	126					
remote	144	146					
remotefile	35	39	41	57	63		
remotehost	35	39	71				
replace	146						
return	111	133	135				
rm	71						
s	48	55	55	55	59	63	63
71	71	71					
sCF	60						
specify	144						
splitword	39	95					
sprintf	71						
stderr	47	140	141	143	145	147	149
strcpy	41	42	89	90			
strlen	57	58	128				
system	73	144	146				
t	48						
tempfile	48						
that	146	150					
the	142	142	144	144	148	148	148
150							
then	142						
usage	37	138	140				
use	150						
username	34	44	55	84	85	89	90
w	46						
while	115						
will	142	148					
with	146						
word1	95	96	106	107			
word2	95	96	109	116	117		
you	142						
your	48						
%							

Frankly, this is pretty useless. However, if you cobbled things together a bit, you could use the tags file to see what routines and defines are used in the program, save that output to a file, then use that file and fgrep to extract just the meaningful lines from the output of xref.

Step 3. Summary

I think it's safe to conclude that C programmers don't use cross-reference listings very often; otherwise better cross-referencing tools would be available.

Lesson Summary

There's a lot to learn if you want to program a UNIX system—a lot more than just the C programming language. You should be familiar with all information in Section 2 (system calls) and Section 3 (library calls) of the online manual. The more UNIX source code you read, the better. Two more programs you might want to check out are calls and indent. To see what other C-related programs are on your system, try the command man -k c ¦ grep C ¦ grep 1 ¦ more.

Workshop
Key Terms

tags file	A file created by the ctags program that contains a table of contents for multifile C-source programs, and is used directly by the vi program.
executable binary	A file in UNIX that is the result of a compilation process and that can be run directly.

Questions

1. What's the command in vi for moving to a specific tag? How about finding the actual definition of a routine that the cursor is sitting on?

2. What command in vi lets you match parentheses and curly braces?

3. What options to cc tell it not to assume that the file you've specified is a stand-alone program, but instead to create a .o file?

4. What option to cc is required for using any of the UNIX debugging tools?

5. What file does make use to store its rules about how to build your program?

6. What program can you use to check the quality and robustness of your code? To improve the indenting style? To create a cross-reference?

7. What debugger do you have on your system? What cross-referencing tools? What other UNIX tools for C programming?

Preview of the Next Chapter

The final lesson of *Teach Yourself UNIX in a Week* is a guided tour of some of the most exciting information services available on the Internet, including electronic mailing lists, the Usenet, Gopher servers, the Archie archive identification program, and the WorldWide Web, a central point for inspecting all these types of information.

The Great Beyond: The Internet

21

You've learned quite a bit in the last 20 lessons. You've made it to the final lesson in this book. Here I thought you might enjoy a guided tour of some of the more astounding resources on the *Internet*, a global network of UNIX and other computer systems—all connected by high-speed links. Most of these resources require you to have an account on a machine that's connected to the Internet, but a surprising number of them have electronic mail alternatives too, so you won't be completely in the cold even if you don't have an account. If you don't have access to the Internet, I encourage you to read this final lesson just to get a feel for the astounding amount and variety of information and services already available on the fastest-growing network in the world.

Goals for This Lesson

In this lesson, you will learn about

☐ Finding archives with `archie`

☐ Searching databases with WAIS

☐ Flying through the Net with the `WorldWide Web`

☐ Having the whole world with `gopher`

☐ A few interesting telnet sites

☐ Visiting libraries around the world

☐ All the news that's fit or otherwise

This lesson is intended to offer a quick and enjoyable overview of the many services available through the Internet. From finding that long-lost archive to looking for a book at a library overseas, the range of information available will undoubtedly astound you!

Task 21.1: Finding Archives with *archie*
Step 1. Description

If you spent any time at all looking at the list of FTP archive sites in Chapter 19, you already realize that just obtaining a list of files available in *one* system can be quite a chore. Yet computers are ideally suited to serve as their own navigational aides, as they easily work with large and complex databases.

The `archie` system was developed at McGill University in Canada. It is a huge database of all files and directories available on all registered FTP sites in the world.

That's quite a bit. Over 2.5 million different files are in the database!

Nonetheless, `archie` is a fairly simple-minded program, and there's only so much information you can glean by being able to analyze just file and directory names. For example, if I have a program called "Wallpaper Demo for the Mac" and save it in a file `wallpaper.demo.MAC`, then odds are pretty good that people who search for Macintosh demonstration programs could find it. What if I decided that was too many letters and instead named it `wp.mac`? Then it would be much less likely that folks would know what the file contains.

There are a few options worth knowing before using `archie`, most notably that the format of the program itself is `archie` *search-string*. By default the program only lists exact matches to the pattern, but `-c` forces it to match on either upper- or lowercase letters, depending on the pattern; `-e` forces exact matches (this is the system default, but some sites have other default actions—it's up to your local system administrator); `-s` considers the search pattern as a possible substring; `-r` searches for the specified regular expressions; and `-l` lists the results in a format suitable for use with other programs (such as `fget!`). The `-L` option lists all `archie` servers known to the program.

> **Don't Skip This:** If you don't have the `archie` program on your system, don't despair! You can use `telnet` to connect to `archie.rutgers.edu`, `archie.sura.net`, or `archie.unl.edu` to interact with the `archie` databases directly (although this isn't necessarily faster than using the `archie` program if you have it on your system). Finally, if you aren't on the Internet at all, you can send electronic mail to `archie` at any of the three systems listed. Use `prog` *search-string*, and ensure that the last line of your message is `quit` so it knows when to stop reading your mail for commands.

Step 2. Action

1. To start out, I want to check to see what `archie` servers are known by my version of `archie`:

```
% archie -L
Known archie servers:
        archie.ans.net (USA [NY])
        archie.rutgers.edu (USA [NJ])
        archie.sura.net (USA [MD])
```

21

```
          archie.unl.edu (USA [NE])
          archie.mcgill.ca (Canada)
          archie.funet.fi (Finland/Mainland Europe)
          archie.au (Australia)
          archie.doc.ic.ac.uk (Great Britain/Ireland)
          archie.wide.ad.jp (Japan)
          archie.ncu.edu.tw (Taiwan)
   * archie.sura.net is the default Archie server.
   * For the most up-to-date list, write to an Archie server and give it
     the command `servers'.
%
```

Notice the third line from the end. My default `archie` server is
`archie.sura.net`. The other servers listed can be accessed, but they aren't
checked directly. Usually it doesn't matter which server is used because the
information available through different servers is mostly identical. If you just
know something's out there but can't find it, check a few different servers
with `archie -h` *servername*.

2. To search for a specific program, I can simply enter the name of the program. I'm interested in finding a UNIX program called `newmail`:

```
% archie newmail

Host plaza.aarnet.edu.au

    Location: /usenet/comp.sources.unix/volume25
          FILE -r--r--r--      15049  Dec 20 1991  newmail

Host gum.isi.edu

    Location: /share/pub/vmh/bin
          FILE -rwxr-xr-x        104  Jul  9 18:26  newmail

Host venera.isi.edu

    Location: /pub/vmh/bin
          FILE -rwxr-xr-x        104  Jul  9 11:26  newmail

Host pith.uoregon.edu

    Location: /pub/Solaris2.x/bin
          FILE -rwxr-xr-x      46952  Oct 27 12:09  newmail
    Location: /pub/Sun4/bin
          FILE -rwxr-xr-x      65536  Oct 27 12:10  newmail

Host ee.utah.edu

    Location: /screen/bin
          FILE -rwxr-xr-x      57344  Oct 11 1992  newmail
%
```

You can see that plaza.aarnet.edu.au (an educational facility in Australia—you can tell because of the .au suffix), gum.isi.edu, venera.isi.edu, pith.uoregon.edu, and ee.utah.edu all have one or more programs called newmail. There's no way, however, to ascertain from this listing whether it's the program I'm seeking.

3. The same list can be produced in a more succinct format by using the -l command:

```
% archie -l newmail
19911220000000Z   15049 plaza.aarnet.edu.au /usenet/comp.sources.unix/
volume25/newmail
19930709182600Z     104 gum.isi.edu /share/pub/vmh/bin/newmail
19930709112600Z     104 venera.isi.edu /pub/vmh/bin/newmail
19931027120900Z   46952 pith.uoregon.edu /pub/Solaris2.x/bin/newmail
19931027121000Z   65536 pith.uoregon.edu /pub/Sun4/bin/newmail
19921011000000Z   57344 ee.utah.edu /screen/bin/newmail
%
```

4. To search for all files that have something, anything, to do with mail (which is going to generate a lot of output!), I can use the -s option:

```
% archie -s mail ¦ more

Host plaza.aarnet.edu.au

    Location: /usenet/comp.sources.unix/volume7
        DIRECTORY drwxr-xr-x        512  Jan 16 1993  smail

Host metro.ucc.su.oz.au

    Location: /pub/netinfo/sendmail
        FILE -rw-r--r--      12410  Jul  9 1992  sendmail.cf
    Location: /pub/netinfo/sendmail/sendmail.mu
        FILE -rw-r--r--      15745  Oct 10 1990  sendmail.cf

Host brolga.cc.uq.oz.au

    Location: /comp.sources.unix/volume7
        DIRECTORY drwxr-xr-x        512  Dec  1 1987  smail

Host cs.ubc.ca

    Location: /mirror3/386BSD/386bsd-0.1/filesystem/etc
        FILE -rw-r--r--      17933  Jul  8 1992  sendmail.cf
--More-- _
```

It turns out that there are 95 matches, mostly sendmail.cf, smail, or Rnmail.

5. The archie system also has a relatively limited database of descriptions called the *Software Description Database*, which you can check by directly connecting to a remote archie system with telnet:

```
% telnet archie.unl.edu
Trying...
Connected to crcnis2.unl.edu.
Escape character is '^]'.


SunOS UNIX (crcnis2)

login: archie
Last login: Wed Dec 15 10:47:17 from INS.INFONET.NET
SunOS Release 4.1.2 (CRCNIS2) #1: Wed Dec 16 12:10:12 EST 1992


too many archie users... try again later
Connection closed by foreign host.
%
```

As you can see, sometimes there are already too many people using the system for you log in.

6. I try an alternate site, archie.internic.net, the Internet Network Information Center, and I do connect:

```
% telnet archie.internic.net
Trying...
Connected to ds.internic.net.
Escape character is '^]'.
            InterNIC Directory and Database Services

Welcome to InterNIC Directory and Database Services provided by AT&T.
These services are partially supported through a cooperative agreement
with the National Science Foundation.

First time users may login as guest with no password to receive help.

Your comments and suggestions for improvement are welcome, and can be
mailed to admin@ds.internic.net.

AT&T MAKES NO WARRANTY OR GUARANTEE, OR PROMISE, EXPRESS OR IMPLIED,
CONCERNING THE  CONTENT OR  ACCURACY OF THE  DIRECTORY  ENTRIES AND
DATABASE  FILES  STORED  AND  MAINTAINED  BY  AT&T.  AT&T EXPRESSLY
DISCLAIMS AND EXCLUDES ALL EXPRESS WARANTIES AND IMPLIED WARRANTIES
OF MERCHANTABILITY AND FITNESS FOR A PARTICULAR PURPOSE.


SunOS UNIX (ds)
login: _
```

Any time you're logging into an archie system, using the archie login is a good bet:

```
login: archie

****************************************************************************

Welcome to the InterNIC Directory and Database Server.

****************************************************************************

# Message of the day from the localhost Prospero server:

        Welcome to Archie  server for the
        InterNIC Directory and Database Services.

# Bunyip Information Systems, 1993

# Terminal type set to `vt100 24 80'.
# `erase' character is `^?'.
# `search' (type string) has the value `sub'.
archie>
```

Now I'll try the whatis command to search the software description database for mail and generate a staggering number of matches:

> **Comment:** In fact, there were many more matches than shown here. About 80 matches were made to *Request for Comment* documents available through the Network Information Center.

```
archie> whatis mail
NMail                   Novice Mail
answer                  vacation(1) replacement. Answer mail while you're
away
batchmail               Convert batched news articles to a format
suitable for exchanging via electronic mail
bencode-bdecode         Binary-to-ASCII encoding scheme for mail
brkdig                  Break mailing list digest into USENET messages
bsmtp                   Batch SMTP (Simple Mail Transfer Protocol)
cfc                     "Compile" sendmail.cf files into EASE language
cheap-fax               El-cheapo E-mail to Fax for sendmail
ck                      Check mailboxes for new mail
ckmail                  Check a user's mail and report the "from" lines
clr-queue               Clean out the sendmail mail queue and send the
results to the system administrator
clr.queue               sendmail clean-up script
```

21

cms-unix	Transfer files (and files of mail data) between UNIX and CMS (or MVS) systems
cobwebs	Check for old or unusually large mailboxes
cryptmail	Send and receive encrypted mail
deliver	Mail delivery agent which uses shell scripts as its configuration files
distantbiff	Monitor distant mailboxes
dmail	Mail reading and sending program which supports folders and various methods of grouping messages by subject, address etc
dnamail	Send DECNET mail to/from a Sun running Sunlink/DNI
ease	Ease, a language for writing sendmail.cf files
elm	Elm (user agent) mail system
faces	Visual mail/print monitor
fido-usenet-gw	Implement a gateway between UUCP/Usenet/ Mail and Fidonet
from	Mail summary generator
gate	Simple mail->news->mail gateway suite
gatech	GaTech Sendmail files
ida-sendmail	Enable sendmail to have direct access to dbm(3) files and Sun Yellow Pages, separate envelope/header rewriting rulesets, and multi-token class matches
junkmail	Delete outdated mail automatically
labels	Program to make mailing labels
lmail	A local mail delivery program
m	The more/mail/make/man thing
mail-s	Mail transmission with subject and suppression
mail.fixes	Patches to BSD4.2 mail (SysV mailx?)
maildigest	Construct a ARPA-style digest from a file of mail messages
mailias	"decode" mail aliases from your .mailrc and tell you who things are going to
mailsplit	Send files and/or directories via electronic mail using "tar", "compress", etc
mailwatcher	A Simple Mailwatcher
malias	Expand .mailrc aliases
mep102b	Mail Extensions Package. Handles things like automatically tossing mail from people you don't want to hear from, logging incoming mail, and so on
mh-rn-interface	Method of interfacing the Rand MH mail handler with the "rn" USENET news reading program
ml	Sort mail by Subject into separate files
mn	Mail summary/tally utility
mp	Mail pretty printer (aka mail->postscript)
mp23	A PostScript pretty printer for mail etc
mq	Display mail queue and "from" output
mq-from	PD replacements for mailq(1) and from(1) commands
msg	Screen oriented mail User agent
mush	Mail user's shell
mverify	Mail alias/user verification
na-digest (argonne)	Archive of mailings to NA distribution list
netdata	Transfer data (and mail) between SysV and CMS
newsmail	Mail news articles to users automagically
nmail	Do UUCP mail routing using the output of the pathalias(1) program
pc-mail-nfs	pc-mail over nfs

```
pcmail                    Turn a PC into a (non-routing) UUCP node (DOS, PC
unix)
pmdc                      A "personal mail daemon" which filters mail much
like GNU Emacs does but without the overhead of Emacs and LISP
procmail                  Mail processing package
returnmail                PD vacation(1). Answer your mail while you're away
rmail-uucp                Domain Capable rmail for UUCP sites
round-robin               Mail round-robiner
savemap.nawk              A safe comp.mail.maps saver
sendmail-qref             A sendmail quick reference card
sendmail.ms               Sendmail reference card (troff -ms)
showhook.mh               MH Mail patch to allow actions when mail is read
sm-smtp                   Sendmail replacement for smail sites
smail                     A smart mailer and UUCP path router
smsmtp                    SMTP server/client implementation for System V and
the SMAIL program
smtp_send                 SMTP SEND command for Sendmail
soundmail                 Sound mail
sunmailwatch              A mail watcher for SUNwindows
tar-untar-mail            Sending tar(1) files through mail
uumail                    Routing program to use the pathalias(1) database
uumailclean               Clean-up backlogged UUCP mail
ux-maze                   UX-Maze Mail Based File Server
vacation                  PD vacation(1) replacement for Berkeley systems not
running sendmail
vmail                     Screen-based mail handler
watch                     A SysV program to display mail, time/date, and
users on/off
wrap                      Line wrapper for BIT/EARNnet mailings
xbiff                     Noification of new mail under X11
xmail                     Mail front end for X11
xmh                       X11 front end to the mh(1) mail agent
xwatch                    Replacement for xbiff and the mailbox widget(X11)
archie>
```

Now that the search is done, it's time to log out:

```
archie> quit
# Bye.
Connection closed by foreign host.
%
```

7. To find where one of these programs is located I can again use the local
   archie program:

   ```
   % archie mverify

   Host ftp.germany.eu.net

       Location: /pub/mail
          DIRECTORY drwxr-xr-x         512  Jul  7 15:15  mverify
   %
   ```

   It looks like the only host that has the program is in Germany!

Step 3. Summary

With the capability to search the software description database, archie is a powerful package for finding programs and information on the Internet. Remember that it's still limited by the ways that people might phrase or describe things and by file-naming conventions on each server.

Task 21.2: Searching Databases with WAIS
Step 1. Description

The next stop on your tour of Internet information resources is the *Wide Area Information Server,* or WAIS. The WAIS system is a collection of databases accessible through a single search or query. It was developed as a joint research project of Apple Computer, Dow Jones News Service, and Thinking Machines, Inc. You can access WAIS by using telnet to connect to a system called quake.think.com at Thinking Machines, Inc. in Boston.

WAIS is a database of databases. There are over 500 databases accessible for conducting searches and queries through the WAIS system. The range of information is astounding—from databases of acronyms to the CIA World Factbook, from White House press releases to cold fusion. The program is reasonably friendly to use, though it takes a bit of experience to be comfortable doing searches.

Step 2. Action

1. To connect to the WAIS system, use telnet to connect to quake.think.com and log in as wais:

Comment: You can find an alternative WAIS server at the address wais.com if quake.think.com is unavailable.

```
% telnet quake.think.com
Trying...
Connected to quake.think.com.
Escape character is '^]'.


SunOS UNIX (quake.think.com)

login: wais
Last login: Wed Dec 15 11:13:56 from alexia.lis.uiuc.
SunOS Release 4.1.3 (SUN4C-STANDARD) #9: Wed Oct 27 18:18:30 EDT 1993
Welcome to swais.
```

```
Please type user identifier (optional, i.e user@host): taylor@netcom.com
TERM = (vt100)
Starting swais (this may take a little while)...
```

After a few seconds, the screen clears, and is replaced by this:

```
SWAIS                              Source Selection              Sources: 510
  #            Server                        Source                     Cost
001: [            archie.au] aarnet-resource-guide                      Free
002: [ndadsb.gsfc.nasa.gov] AAS_jobs                                    Free
003: [ndadsb.gsfc.nasa.gov] AAS_meeting                                 Free
004: [       munin.ub2.lu.se] academic_email_conf                       Free
005: [wraith.cs.uow.edu.au] acronyms                                    Free
006: [     archive.orst.edu] aeronautics                                Free
007: [ ftp.cs.colorado.edu] aftp-cs-colorado-edu                        Free
008: [nostromo.oes.orst.ed] agricultural-market-news                    Free
009: [     archive.orst.edu] alt.drugs                                  Free
010: [      wais.oit.unc.edu] alt.gopher                                Free
011: [       sunsite.unc.edu] alt.sys.sun                               Free
012: [      wais.oit.unc.edu] alt.wais                                  Free
013: [alfred.ccs.carleton.] amiga-slip                                  Free
014: [       munin.ub2.lu.se] amiga_fish_contents                       Free
015: [     coombs.anu.edu.au] ANU-Aboriginal-EconPolicies      $0.00/minute
016: [     coombs.anu.edu.au] ANU-Aboriginal-Studies           $0.00/minute
017: [     coombs.anu.edu.au] ANU-Ancient-DNA-L                $0.00/minute
018: [     coombs.anu.edu.au] ANU-Ancient-DNA-Studies          $0.00/minute

Keywords:

<space> selects, w for keywords, arrows move, <return> searches, q quits, or ?  _
```

You can see here a table of contents of the different databases available for searching through WAIS. Although they're all free of charge at this point, it is entirely possible that at some point in the future some of these databases will have costs associated with them.

Use J and K to move up and down a screen at a time, respectively, and j and k to move up and down a single source. To add a database to a search, use . to select it. An asterisk will show up just before the name of the system that holds the database selected. Use q to quit.

2. To find out more about a particular database, use the v command for *version information*. When I choose that option for acronyms, here's what I find out:

```
Name:        acronyms.src
Directory:   /sources/
Maintainer:  steve@wraith.cs.uow.edu.au
Selected:    Yes
```

21

```
Cost:          Free
Server:        wraith.cs.uow.edu.au (Accessed)
Service:       210
Database:      acronyms
Description:
Server created with WAIS release 8 b5 on Oct 23 10:49:48 1992 by
steve@wraith.
cs
.uow.edu.au

     A public domain database of acronyms and abbreviations maintained
     by Dave Sill (de5@ornl.gov).

The files of type one_line used in the index were:
   /shr/lib/wais/wais-sources/acronyms
(END)
```

3. I'm interested in how many acronyms have the word `mail` in them, so I choose the acronym database by pressing the spacebar (an asterisk appears to show that the database has been selected), then use `w` to specify a key word, in this case `mail`. After a quick search, the screen now looks like this:

```
SWAIS                              Search Results                      Item
  #    Score    Source                    Title                       Lines
001:  [1000] (      acronyms) EMAIL  - Electronic MAIL, "E-MAIL"         1
002:  [ 333] (      acronyms) ECOM   - Electronic Computer Originated Ma 1
003:  [ 333] (      acronyms) EMA    - Electronic Mail Association       1
004:  [ 333] (      acronyms) IMAP   - Interactive Mail Access Protocol  1
005:  [ 333] (      acronyms) IMAP3  - Interactive Mail Access Protocol  1
006:  [ 333] (      acronyms) MIME   - Multipurpose Internet Mail Extens 1
007:  [ 333] (      acronyms) MO     - Mail Order                        1
008:  [ 333] (      acronyms) MTA    - Mail Transfer Agent               1
009:  [ 333] (      acronyms) MUA    - Mail User Agent                   1
010:  [ 333] (      acronyms) MX     - Mail eXchange                     1
011:  [ 333] (      acronyms) PBM    - Play By Mail game                 1
012:  [ 333] (      acronyms) PEM    - Privacy Enhanced Mail             1
013:  [ 333] (      acronyms) RMS    - Royal Mail Ship                   1
014:  [ 333] (      acronyms) SMTP   - Simple Mail Transfer Protocol     1
015:  [ 333] (      acronyms) USM    - United States Mail                1
016:  [ 333] (      acronyms) VMS    - Voice Mail System                 1




<space> selects, arrows move, w for keywords, s for sources, ? for help_
```

4. Here's another way this can be helpful: WAIS lists a database of recipes, and I've been looking for a good oatmeal cookie recipe for quite a while. I can search the `recipe` database by returning to the main WAIS screen, then entering `/rec` to move to that particular database:

```
SWAIS                          Source Selection              Sources: 510
   #           Server                    Source                    Cost
 397:   [    munin.ub2.lu.se]   rec.gardens                        Free
 398:   [ wais.wu-wien.ac.at]   rec.music.early                    Free
 399:   [    wais.oit.unc.edu]  rec.pets                           Free
 400:   [    wais.oit.unc.edu]  recipes                            Free
 401:   [bloch.informatik.uni]  reports-abstracts                  Free
 402:   [        gopher.uv.es]  Research-in-Surgery                Free
 403:   [       wais.cic.net]   rfc-index                          Free
 404:   [      ds.internic.net] rfcs                               Free
 405:   [         ns.ripe.net]  ripe-database                      Free
 406:   [         ns.ripe.net]  ripe-internet-drafts               Free
 407:   [         ns.ripe.net]  ripe-rfc                           Free
 408:   [ cmns-moon.think.com]  risks-digest                       Free
 409:   [        wais.cic.net]  roget-thesaurus                    Free
 410:   [    mpcc3.rpms.ac.uk]  RPMS-pathology                     Free
 411:   [ cmns-moon.think.com]  RSInetwork                         Free
 412:   [      uniwa.uwa.oz.au] s-archive                          Free


 413:   [athena3.cent.saitama]  saitama-jp                         Free
 414:   [RANGERSMITH.SDSC.EDU]  Salk_Genome_Center                 Free



<space> selects, w for keywords, arrows move, <return> searches, q quits, or ? _
```

Don't Skip This: One problem I consistently have with the WAIS programs is that I can't use my Backspace key to erase previous search words. The trick to getting around this is to use ^u to erase the entire line of keywords!

I choose the `recipes` database, again by pressing the spacebar, then search for keywords `cookie` and `oatmeal` to see what kind of oatmeal cookie recipes are available. It indicates 18 matches, sorted in order of the "quality" of the match—the more each keyword occurs, the better the hit. The first number in square brackets indicates the "quality" of the match, with 1,000 being the best possible score. This time, however, the recipe I'm looking for appears to be the lowest-rated in the list:

21

```
SWAIS                        Search Results                    Item
  #    Score    Source                 Title                   Lines
001:  [1000] (        recipes)  shafer@rig Re: COLLECTION BAKERY Pumpkin   186
002:  [ 957] (        recipes)  shafer@rig Re: COLLECTION BAKERY VEG Bis  1038
003:  [ 696] (        recipes)  Anne Louis Re: BREAD: Bread Recipes Coll  1101
004:  [ 522] (        recipes)  darsie@eec Re: Re: world-wide cookie rec   130
005:  [ 522] (        recipes)  kyoung@prs Re: Diabetic Cookie Recipes      91
006:  [ 522] (        recipes)  the1edr@ca Re: 3 Recipes for Oatmeal Pea   122
007:  [ 435] (        recipes)  WHITEJER@c Re: Re: REQUEST Cookie dough     53
008:  [ 391] (        recipes)  julie@eddi Re: Re: REQUEST Cookie dough     47
009:  [ 348] (        recipes)  anne@csrux Re: Re: REQUEST Cookie dough     53
010:  [ 348] (        recipes)  arielle@ta Re: Appetizers (Long)          1591
011:  [ 348] (        recipes)  kyoung@prs Re: Diabetic Cookie Recipes C    77
012:  [ 348] (        recipes)  arielle@ta Re: Muffins 5                   717
013:  [ 348] (        recipes)  arielle@ta Re: Appetizers                 1590
014:  [ 304] (        recipes)  springer@k Re: Re: REQUEST Cookie dough     44
015:  [ 304] (        recipes)  kyoung@prs Re: Diabetic Treats Cont'd.     109
016:  [ 261] (        recipes)  arielle@ta Re: RECIPE: Ice Cream Sandwic    63
017:  [ 261] (        recipes)  arielle@ta Re: REQUEST Cookie dough for     22
018:  [ 261] (        recipes)  laura@hobb Re: Oatmeal Rasin Cookies (ca    31


<space> selects, arrows move, w for keywords, s for sources, ? for help  _
```

To read recipe number 18, I can enter **18** to retrieve the recipe itself:

```
Getting "laura@hobb Re: Oatmeal Rasin Cookies (cake like)" from recipes.src...
Newsgroups: rec.food.recipes
From: laura@hobb.mystery.edu (Laura Smith)
Subject: Oatmeal Rasin Cookies (cake like)
Apparently-To: rec-food-recipes@uunet.uu.net
Organization: The Mystery University
Date: Tue, 22 Dec 1992 15:33:33 GMT
Approved: arielle@taronga.com
Lines: 18

Hi,

      My father was over helping me bake cookies this year for christmas.
He got to talking about an oatmeal cookie that his mother used to make.
These cookies were almost like little individual oatmeal rasin cakes
Unfortunately.. he never got the recipe written down.... I'd really like to
find a recipe and surprise him with them.

--More--  _
```

Voilà! I can sit at my UNIX system and dig up just about anything on the Internet, even cookie recipes!

Step 3. Summary

Of the different services on the Internet, the WAIS system is the one I find the most promising, yet least useful. There are many problems with the system, but it's evolving at such a fast pace that I encourage you to try it for yourself. By the time you read this, the program will doubtless have changed a fair bit.

Task 21.3: Flying Through the Net with the *WorldWide Web*

Step 1. Description

One of the most fascinating approaches to navigating the vast bodies of information on the Internet is through a project in Switzerland called the *WorldWide Web*, or "the Web" for short. It's on a computer called nxoc01.cern.ch, and you connect by using telnet.

The design is based on something called *hypertext*, a scheme first proposed by Ted Nelson quite a few years ago. In this book, each time a phrase is presented in italics, you can be confident that there's probably an entry for the phrase in the glossary. But why there? What if you imagined books as being three-dimensional, and you could touch a word so that information "behind" the word would pop up, in this case, the explanation of a term or phrase? Take that further and you could have each occurrence of any UNIX command linked to an entry about that command, and then in the information entries, more *hypertext links* (generally any connection between two items of information), and so on and so on. Nelson calls it "information space," and it's a sexy concept.

Step 2. Action

1. The telnet command, again, is the key to connecting to the rest of the Internet:

```
% telnet nxoc01.cern.ch
Trying...
Connected to nxoc01.cern.ch.
Escape character is '^]'.


CERN Information Service
(ttyq4 on nxoc01)
```

```
                                        Overview of the Web
                      GENERAL OVERVIEW OF THE WEB

    There is no "top" to the World-Wide Web. You can look at it from many
points
    of view. Here are some places to start.

    by Subject[1]          The Virtual Library organises information by
                           subject matter.

    List of servers[2]     All registered HTTP servers by country

    by Service Type[3]     The Web includes data accessible by many other
                           protocols. The lists by access protocol may help if
                           you know what kind of service you are looking for.

    If you find a useful starting point for you personally, you can configure
    your WWW browser to start there by default.

    See also: About the W3 project[4] .
       [End]



1-4, Up, Quit, or Help:_
```

Each hypertext link is indicated by a trailing number in square brackets, so to find information by subject I could press 1. I'd find a list of servers by pressing 2, and pressing 3 would produce service types. Pressing 4 would explain a bit about the Web itself.

2. I choose 1 to see, by subject, what's available:

```
           The World-Wide Web Virtual Library: Subject Catalogue (23/135)
                      THE WWW VIRTUAL LIBRARY

    This is a distributed subject catalogue. See also arrangement  by  service
    type[1] ., and other subject catalogues of network information[2] .

    Mail www-request@info.cern.ch to add pointers to this list, or if you would
    like to contribute to administration of a subject area.

    Aeronautics            Mailing list archive index[3] . See also NASA LaRC[4]

    Agriculture[5]         Separate list, see also Almanac mail servers[6] ; the
                           Agricultural Genome[7] (National Agricultural Library,
                           part of the U.S. Department of Agriculture)

    Archaeology            Classics and Mediterranean Archaeology[8]

    Astronomy and Astrophysics[9]
                           Separate list.
```

```
Bio Sciences[10]        Separate list .

   Chemistry                 Department of Chemistry[11] at the University of
1-108, Back, Up, <RETURN> for more, Quit, or Help:_
```

That's quite a variety. Notice the last line, where the system indicates that
there are 108 possible links from this document. I can only see 11, so there
must be more pages. (I also know there must be more pages because the
<RETURN> for more only shows up when there's more than a single page of
information.)

3. I'm interested in finding out about an early Hitchcock film, so I step
through a few pages, hoping to see something, and I have success!

```
                  The World-Wide Web Virtual Library: Subject Catalogue (89/135)
   History[48]          Separate list. See also Literature & Art[49] ,
                        Newsgroup , soc.history[50] .

   Languages            Some Esperanto information[51] ; Computational
                        Phonology[52]

   Law[53]              US Copyright law[54] ., Uniform Commercial Code[55],
                        etc, NASDAQ Finance Executive Journal[56] ; the
                        "English Server" Judiciary[57] ; Ananse International
                        Trade Law Server[58] ; University of Tromsoe Law
                        Faculty[59]

   Libraries[60]        Separate list etc.

   Literature & Art[61] separate list.

   Mathematics[62]      separate list.

   Meteorology          US weather[63] , state by state.  Satelite Images
                        [64]. Weather index[65] . ANU weather services[66]

   Movies               Movie database browser[67] , the "English Server"
1-108, Back, Up, <RETURN> for more, Quit, or Help:_
```

I enter 67 to get to the database:

```
                                        Cardiff's Movie Database Browser.
                   CARDIFF'S MOVIE DATABASE BROWSER.

   Can anyone draw a nice icon to replace the ET one ?
```

21

```
Search the rec.arts.movies databases[1]...

      Movie title substring searching.[2] (for non-forms browsers)

      Movie people substring searching.[3] (for non-forms browsers)

      Lookup titles by genre.[4] (uses plot summary info. 330 titles so far, many
      more on the way)

      List my votes[5]. If you've voted for movies, your votes are here.

      To get the most out of this database, use a fill-out forms browser such as
      Mosaic for X[6] 2.0. Without one, you can't see what you're missing !.

      [7][8]

                                                                   Rob.H[9]

      1-9, Back, Up, <RETURN> for more, Quit, or Help:_
```

4. I use 2 to check by title. I'm looking for some information on *The 39 Steps*, a film I'm pretty sure Hitchcock directed:

```
Movie Info
                          TITLE SUBSTRINGS.

Enter a movie title or substring.

  Example, to search for movies with the word ``alien'' in their title,  type
  ``alien''.

This will return details on several movies, including Aliens

Note: if the title begins with A or The, leave it out. If you're determined
to include it, then put  ', A' or ', The' at the end of the of the substring
e.g.

      Enforcer, The

      Gauntlet, The

  Searching is case insensitive.

  [1][2][3][4]
```

```
FIND <keywords>, 1-5, Back, Up, <RETURN> for more, or Help: 39 steps
                                                   Movie Info
                          TITLE SUBSTRINGS.

  Here are the results from the search for 39 steps
```

```
                    39 Steps, The (1935)[1]

                    I haven't found the item you wanted ?, why ?[2]

        [3][4][5][6]


                                                        Rob.H[7]

                                        Robert.Hartill@cm.cf.ac.uk



        [End]




    FIND <keywords>, 1-7, Back, Up, Quit, or Help:_
```

Comment: One downside of the Web is that if you're using it from a terminal, it can look pretty ugly and confusing, as is shown in this example. The good news is that, like many of the other services shown here, there are some excellent Mac, Windows, and X interfaces that offer easier browsing, more attractive information presentation, and a more efficient use of resources. If you have the capabilities to run any of these, check 'em out!

5. The listing with the correct title looks like it could be from about the right year, so I enter 1 to see what's available on the subject.

```
                                                    Movie Info
                    MOVIE DETAILS.

                    39 STEPS, THE (1935)

Also Known As Thirty-Nine Steps, The (1935)

1935

    Plot Summmary[1]

    Cast            Ashcroft, Peggy[2] ......Margaret
                    Carroll, Madeleine[3] ......Pamela
                    Cellier, Frank[4] ......Sheriff
```

21

```
                         Donat, Robert[5] ......Richard Hannay
                         Haye, Helen[6] ......Mrs. Jordan
                         Laurie, John[7] ......John
                         MacNaughton, Gus[8] ......Commercial Traveler
                         Mannheim, Lucie[9] ......Annabella Smith
                         Simpson, Peggy[10] ......Maid
                         Tearle, Godfrey[11] ......Professor Jordan
                         Verno, Jerry[12] ......Commercial Traveler
                         Watson, Wylie[13] ......Memory
    Directed by          Hitchcock, Alfred[14]

    Music by             Bath, Hubert[15]

    Written by           Reville, Alma[16]
                         Bennett, Charles[17]
                         Buchan, John[18] (novel)

    Cinematography by    Knowles, Bernard[19]

    Costume Design by    No match. Can you help ? [20]

    Production Design by No match. Can you help ? [21]

    Editing by           No match. Can you help ? [22]

    Trivia and/or Goofs[23]

    Ratings[24]

    Vote here for "39 Steps, The (1935)" (out of 10)

    Trivia and/or Goofs[23]

    Ratings[24]

    Vote here for "39 Steps, The (1935)" (out of 10)

  _ 1[25]  __ 2[26]  __ 3[27]  __ 4[28]  __ 5[29]  __ 6[30]  __ 7[31]  __ 8[32]
  __ 9[33]  __10[34]  _

    (this page was cached)

    [35][36][37][38]

                                                      Rob.H[39]
                                          Robert.Hartill@cm.cf.ac.uk

      [End]
    1-39, Back, Up, Quit, or Help:_
```

Ahhh…As I had recalled, the film was directed by Hitchcock, and it starred Robert Donat and Peggy Ashcroft.

To quit the Web, I enter `quit`.

Step 3. Summary

The Web is one of the most exciting and easy-to-use information services on the Internet. If you choose to learn only one or two services after reading this lesson, I strongly encourage you to make this one of them!

Task 21.4: Having the Whole World with *gopher*
Step 1. Description

At this point you're probably wondering how people are supposed to choose from and navigate all these different services—and rightfully so! A team of programmers at the University of Minnesota wondered just that. They realized that what they wanted was a "gofer," a program that would "go for things." Conveniently, the gopher is their school mascot, so the `gopher` program was born.

Of all the different systems on the Internet, `gopher` is undoubtedly the easiest to use. It has a simple, menu-based interface that enables you to step through information sources, seamlessly switching from machine to machine throughout the Internet. The program offers some helpful customization, too. As you travel through what's called *gopherspace*, you can mark interesting locations with a *bookmark* (simply press a at the item), then zoom straight to your list of bookmarks with the v key, to *view* your bookmarks. If you have bookmarks, `gopher -b` will start you up with your bookmark page; otherwise it will display the default `gopher` introductory page, which varies quite a bit from site to site.

> **Shortcut:** If you don't have the `gopher` program on your system, you can log in as `gopher` at `consultant.micro.umn.edu`, `gopher.uiuc.edu`, or `panda.uiowa.edu`. Use `telnet` to connect.

Step 2. Action

1. I enter `gopher` at the command line of my account at the UTech University, and the screen is rewritten:

The Great Beyond: The Internet

```
                Internet Gopher Information Client v1.12S

             Root gopher server: thorplus.utech.edu

 -->  1.  About UTech University.
      2.  About THOR+ the UTech University Libraries Gopher Site.
      3.  Other Information Servers at UTech University/
      4.  Other information Servers on the Internet/
      5.  Thor+ Suggestion Form <TEL>
      6.  Administrivia/
      7.  E-Mail & Telephone Directory for Utech & World Wide/
      8.  Library Catalogs and Gophers/
      9.  University Libraries/
     10.  Weather Reports and Maps/
     11.  Interesting items on the Net (12/7/93)/
     12.  Current Contents On Diskette/
     13.  Instructions for searching Directories of all UTech Gophers .
     14.  Search Directories of all UTech Gophers (experimental) <?>
     15.  *************Explore Internet Teleconference********/

Press ? for Help, q to Quit, u to go up a menu            Page: 1/1
```

2. By contrast, if I were logged in to the Whole Earth 'lectronic Link (well) computer in San Francisco, I'd get a completely different first screen:

```
                Internet Gopher Information Client v1.11

             Root gopher server: gopher2.tc.umn.edu

 -->  1.  Information About Gopher/
      2.  Computer Information/
      3.  Discussion Groups/
      4.  Fun & Games/
      5.  Internet file server (ftp) sites/
      6.  Libraries/
      7.  News/
      8.  Other Gopher and Information Servers/
      9.  Phone Books/
     10.  Search Gopher Titles at the University of Minnesota <?>
     11.  Search lots of places at the University of Minnesota  <?>
     12.  University of Minnesota Campus Information/



Press ? for Help, q to Quit, u to go up a menu            Page: 1/1
```

3. The sixth entry—Libraries/—sounds interesting, and because it ends with a slash, I can tell that it will move me to another set of menu choices in

gopher. The two lines that end with <?> will actually invoke a program (probably to connect me to the University of Minnesota), and lines that end with a dot are files and can be viewed by choosing them.

To move to a specific location, I can enter its number or use j and k to move up and down, just like in vi. Pressing Return chooses the specific item, so I press j five times to move down five items (the arrow moves so that it points to item 6). Then I press Return, which changes the screen:

```
                    Internet Gopher Information Client v1.11

                                   Libraries

  --> 1.  Electronic Books/
      2.  Electronic Journal collection from CICnet/
      3.  Information from the U.S. Federal Government/
      4.  Library Catalogs via Telnet/
      5.  Library of Congress Records/
      6.  Newspapers, Magazines, and Newsletters /
      7.  Reference Works/




Press ? for Help, q to Quit, u to go up a menu                   Page: 1/1
```

4. Electronic books sounds interesting, but reference works could be even more interesting, so I press 7, which instantly moves the arrow to the last item. Then I press Return:

```
                    Internet Gopher Information Client v1.11

                                Reference Works

  --> 1.  ACM SIGGRAPH Online Bibliography Project/
      2.  American English Dictionary (from the UK) <?>
      3.  CIA World Fact Book 1991/
      4.  Current Contents/
      5.  ERIC-archive.
      6.  ERIC-archive Search <?>
      7.  Periodic Table of Elements/
      8.  Roget's Thesaurus (Published 1911)/
      9.  The Hacker's Dictionary/
      10. U.S. Geographic Names Database/
```

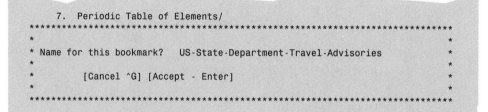

```
   11. U.S. Telephone Area Codes/
   12. US-State-Department-Travel-Advisories/
   13. Webster's Dictionary/


Press ? for Help, q to Quit, u to go up a menu          Page: 1/1
```

5. The entry for U.S. State Department travel advisories looks valuable, so I'll use a to add it to my bookmark collection:

```
   7.  Periodic Table of Elements/
***************************************************************************
*                                                                         *
* Name for this bookmark?    US-State-Department-Travel-Advisories         *
*                                                                         *
*          [Cancel ^G] [Accept - Enter]                                    *
*                                                                         *
***************************************************************************
```

The default name works fine, so I press Return to move into the choice. I see three choices: 1. Search US-State-Department-Travel-Advisories <?>, 2. Current-Advisories/, and 3. FTP-Archive/. I opt to see what's current, and I press 2:

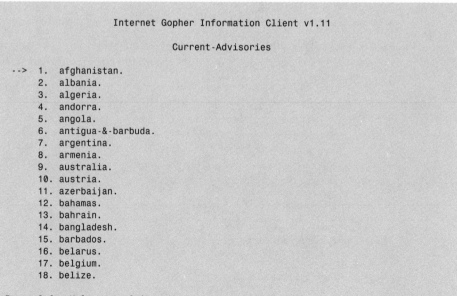

```
              Internet Gopher Information Client v1.11

                        Current-Advisories

  --> 1.  afghanistan.
      2.  albania.
      3.  algeria.
      4.  andorra.
      5.  angola.
      6.  antigua-&-barbuda.
      7.  argentina.
      8.  armenia.
      9.  australia.
     10.  austria.
     11.  azerbaijan.
     12.  bahamas.
     13.  bahrain.
     14.  bangladesh.
     15.  barbados.
     16.  belarus.
     17.  belgium.
     18.  belize.

Press ? for Help, q to Quit, u to go up a menu          Page: 1/13
```

Notice that this time the bottom-right corner indicates that this is page 1 of 13, so there's a lot more information. To move to the next page of information, use the + key; to move to the previous page, use -. I have visited Belize, so I'd be interested to see if there are any current travel advisories on the country. I choose 18, and the following information is displayed on my screen:

```
STATE DEPARTMENT TRAVEL INFORMATION - Belize
=================================================================
Belize - Consular Information Sheet
 May 27, 1993

Country Description:  Belize is a developing country.  Its tourism
facilities vary in quality.

Entry Requirements:  A passport, a return/onward ticket, and
sufficient funds are required for travel to Belize.  U. S. citizens
who stay less than three months do not need visas.  However, for
visits exceeding one month, travelers must obtain permits from
immigration authorities in Belize.  For further information,
travelers may contact the Embassy of Belize at 2535 Massachusetts
Avenue N.W., Washington, D.C. 20008, tel. (202) 332-9636, the Belize
Consulate in Miami, or the Belize Mission to the U.N. in New York.

Medical Facilities:  Medical care is limited.  Doctors and
hospitals often expect immediate cash payment for health services.
U.S. medical insurance is not always valid outside the United
States.  In some cases, supplemental medical insurance with specific
overseas coverage has proved useful.  For additional health
--More--(9%)[Hit space to continue, Del to abort] _
```

This is only nine percent of the information, so there's a lot more to view. Fortunately, I can electronically mail this file to myself when I've finished viewing it by selecting the m, or *mail file*, command at the end-of-listing prompt.

Comment: Gopher notation usually has a nested series of lines indicating the actual text that you'd find on a line of gopher output, so this search would be written much more succinctly as:

```
Libraries/
  Reference Works/
    US-State-Department-Travel-Advisories/
      Current Advisories
        belize.
```

21

I quit by entering q at any prompt in the gopher system.

6. Back at the U., I have heard that there are electronic books available through gopher. I am particularly interested in *Paradise Lost*, a poem I read years ago. After a bit of nosing about, I found it through the following gopherspace path:

```
Other Information Servers on the Internet/
  Academic Resources on the Internet (by Subject)/
    Electronic Journals & Texts/
      Project Gutenberg: National Clearinghouse for Machine Readable Texts/
        etext92/
          AAINDEX.NEW.
```

The AAINDEX.NEW file produced a list of what books are available through this clearinghouse for electronic books. Skipping the introductory matter, I find that the following books are currently online:

```
(Books from earlier years will available in 1992)
(but not yet:  to be announced, don't ask yet!!!)

    1971 Declaration-Independence  (whenxxxx.xxx)
    1972 Bill of Rights            (billxxxx.xxx)
    1973 U.S. Constitution         (constxxx.xxx)
    1974-1982 The Bible            (biblexxx.xxx)
    1983-1990 Complete Shakespeare (shakesxx.xxx)

(Watch for these entries to be moved below later.
The Bible mentioned above is a different edition
from the one we just post for Easter, 1992)


Books currently available on mrcnext (do a dir):

(These 1991 etexts are now in> cd /etext/etext91)

Jan 1991 Alice in Wonderland      (alice29x.xxx)
Feb 1991 Through the Looking Glass (lglass16.xxx)
Mar 1991 The Hunting of the Snark  (snark12x.xxx)
Apr 1991 1990 CIA World Factbook   (world11x.xxx)
May 1991 Moby Dick (From OBI)*     (mobyxxxx.xxx)
Jun 1991 Peter Pan (for US only)** (peter14a.xxx)
Jul 1991 The Book of Mormon        (mormon11.xxx)
Aug 1991 The Federalist Papers     (feder11x.xxx)
Sep 1991 The Song of Hiawatha      (hisong10.xxx)
Oct 1991 Paradise Lost             (plboss10.xxx)
Nov 1991 Aesop's Fables            (aesop10x.xxx)
Dec 1991 Roget's Thesaurus         (roget11x.xxx)
*Moby Dick is missing Chapter 72
**Please do not download Peter Pan outside the US
```

```
(These 1992 etext releases in> cd /etext/etext92)

Jan 1992 Frederick Douglass        (duglas10.xxx)
Jan 1992 O Pioneers!  Willa Cather (opion10x.xxx)
Feb 1992 1991 CIA World Factbook   (world91a.xxx)
Feb 1992 Paradise Lost (Raben)     (plrabn10.xxx)
Mar 1992 Far From the Madding Crowd(crowd13x.xxx)
Mar 1992 Aesop's Fables (Advantage)(aesopa10.xxx)
Apr 1992 Data From the 1990 Census (uscen901.xxx)
Apr 1992 New Etext of Bible (KJV)  (bible10x.xxx)
May 1992 Sophocles' Oedipus Trilogy(oedip10x.xxx)
May 1992*Herland (not yet in place (hrlnd10x.xxx)
```

There are more resources than this, but here you can see that if you're interested in obtaining a copy of *Paradise Lost*, you can use gopher to find it and have it sent via Internet to your home account—in a matter of a few steps!

Step 3. Summary

The gopher system offers a wide variety of capabilities, as you can see, and the connectivity is astounding. One aid to finding information in gopherspace is a search program called veronica, with which you can specify one or more words that you think might show up in the one-line menu listings. Overall, I find it enjoyable just to wander about and see what's available. At any point, you can enter u to return to a previous menu, so you can wander to your heart's content.

> **Comment:** I'm not making this up: veronica stands for *very easy rodent-oriented net-wise index to computerized archives.*

Task 21.5: A Few Interesting Telnet Sites
Step 1. Description

Two tasks on which I spend too much time are purchasing compact discs and books. With the Internet, I can do both without leaving the privacy of my own computer desk! Although these are commercial services, I illustrate them here to demonstrate the incredible breadth of services available on the Internet.

Step 2. Action

1. The first place to search is the *Compact Disk Connection,* an electronic record store available through a system called Holonet:

```
% telnet orac.holonet.net
Trying...
Connected to orac.holonet.net.
Escape character is '^]'.


HoloNet(SM) -- A service of IAT

HoloNet Member Name (Non-members type "guest"): _
```

To log in to the CD Connection, I enter cdc:

```
HoloNet Member Name (Non-members type "guest"): cdc
Last login: Wed Dec 15 13:04:18 from intrepid.ece.uc.

----------------------
HoloNet Services Gateway
----------------------

The HoloNet Services Gateway provides access to electronic services
through HoloNet.  Use of this service is subject to HoloNet Terms
and Conditions.

The Compact Disc Connection is an independent service not affiliated
with Information Access Technologies, Inc.

Control-C to abort connect
Waiting for the Compact Disc Connection.....................
Connected to CD Connection.
Escape character is '^]'.



                     Welcome to the

            **   Compact Disc Connection   **

         Dealing Exclusively in the Online Sale of

                  * Compact Discs *

                   and Featuring:

+=.=-.=-.=-.=-.=-.=-.=-.=-.=-.=-.=-.=-.=-.=-.=-.=-.=-.=-.=-.=-.=-.=+
| FREE access from the Internet & from 75 Cities, NOW!  |
+=.=-.=-.=-.=-.=-.=-.=-.=-.=-.=-.=-.=-.=-.=-.=-.=-.=-.=-.=-.=-.=-.=+
```

```
            - More Than 75,000 CDs Online -

                - Discount Prices -

          We accept VISA and MasterCard

   *** CDC News ***************************************************************

      Want to know the status of your latest order?  See the (C)heck order
      status feature just added to the CDC Database Menu...

      COMPACT DISC EUROPE, a Florida-based import company, is now online!
      Looking for imports that aren't in our catalog?  Dial into their
      online database of more than 100,000 imports from Europe and Japan
      at: 408 730-8138.  Any speed up to 9600, 8N1.  Voice: 305 481-8984.

      And speaking of imports, all

          PHANTOM IMPORTS
          ALEX IMPORTS

      in our catalog are on sale now!  See (S)ales at the Main Menu...

      *********************************************************************

   ** CDC Main Menu **

      (C)Ds            Enter CD database.
      (I)nformation    Display CDC policies and general information.
      (N)umbers        Display free modem access telephone numbers.
      (O)verseas       Display details of shipping to overseas destinations.
      (A)ll-Music      Display details of the All-Music Guide.
      (G)olden Ears    Display details of the Golden Ears Society.
      (S)ales          Display details of current sales.
      (F)ree CDs       Display details of the (almost) free Adventures-in-Music.
      (T)op Selling    Display Top Selling/Grammy Award Winning CDs.
      (D)irectory      Display the directory of CD labels and manufacturers.
      (P)ausing        Toggle automatic pausing/no pausing of scrolling displays.
      (B)rief          Toggle brief/full menu displays.
      (M)essage        Leave a message to the management.
      (R)etrieve       Retrieve messages from the management to you.
      (Q)uit           Sign off & hang up.

=> Your command: C
```

I want to search the CD database, so I enter C:

```
** CDC Database Menu **

   (S)earch          Search database and select CDs.
   (R)eview          Review CDs you've selected.
   (O)rder           Order CDs you've selected.
```

```
   (C)heck Status   Check the status of your recent orders.
   (P)assword       Change the password to your CDC account.
   (Q)uit           Return to the Main Menu.

=> Your command: S
```

I use the S key to request a search:

```
** CDC Search Menu **

   (A)rtist     Search by artist or composer's last name, e.g., Mozart, Dylan.
   (S)ong       Search by song or track title, e.g., Star Spangled Banner.
   (T)itle      Search by CD title, e.g., Woodstock.
   (P)erformer  Search for performers of classical music, e.g. Berlin Phil.
   (M)anuf'er   Search by manufacturer's label, e.g., CBS
   (N)umber     Search by manufacturer's catalog number, e.g., 422 493-2.
   (C)ategory   Search by category of music, e.g., classical, rock.
   (L)imits     Set limits for release date, music type, or Golden Ears ratings.
   (1)-line     Toggle 1 or 2-line CD displays.
   (E)xample    Display an example CD and an explanation of its components.
   (Q)uit       Return to the Database Menu.

=> Your command: A
```

Then I search by artist:

```
** CDC Search by Artist **

Enter the first few letters of the artist/composer's name (last name, first),
or enter =STRING to search all positions in the artist name for STRING,
or press ENTER to repeat the previous search:
or enter a Q to quit: coltrane,j

  MCA42001   +COLTRANE*JOHN            AFRICA/BRASS VOL.1 & 2         10/1
  $10.58       MCA  9/88  1:07

  PAB20101   COLTRANE*JOHN             AFRO BLUE IMPRESSIONS
  $18.99       PABLO  12/93

  CAP99175   +COLTRANE*JOHN            ART OF JOHN COLTRANE           9/1 ***
  $12.02       CAPITOL  8/92

  oRi415     COLTRANE*JOHN             BAHIA                             **
  $10.50     &ORIGINAL JAZZ CLASSICS  2/90  WILBUR HARDEN, RED GARLAND, PAUL CHAM

  MCA5885    +COLTRANE*JOHN            BALLADS                       8.7/3 **
  $10.79     &MCA  5/88  :32

  ATL1541    +COLTRANE*JOHN            BEST OF                          ***
  $10.74       ATLANTIC  9/90  :41
```

```
   PAB2405417+COLTRANE*JOHN              BEST OF                       **
   $10.59    &PABLO  9/92

=> Enter a CD selector, a Q, or a ? for help: mca42001

=> Selected:

*MCA42001  +COLTRANE*JOHN             AFRICA/BRASS VOL.1 & 2        10/1
 $10.58     MCA  9/88  1:07

=> 1 item(s) selected.  $10.58

=> Enter a CD selector, a Q, or a ? for help:_
```

That's the CD I want. I could easily choose to buy it here, enter my VISA or
MasterCard number when prompted, and the disc would be mailed to me
within a week or so. For some cryptic reason, I decide I don't need this disc,
and I quit the program.

2. Now that I've exercised such self-restraint in avoiding the purchase of the
   Coltrane disc, how about buying a book or two? To connect to Book Stacks
   Unlimited in Cleveland, Ohio, I use telnet books.com:

```
% telnet books.com
Trying...
Connected to books.com.
Escape character is '^]'.




Book Stacks Unlimited, Inc.
Cleveland, Ohio  USA


The On-Line Bookstore


Modem    : (216)861-0469
Internet : telnet books.com




Enter your FULL Name (e.g SALLY M. SMITH) :
```

I have an account, so follow me as I step through the book database, find a
book, and ensure that it's the correct choice.

```
Type P to Pause, S to Stop listing


                    BOOK STACKS UNLIMITED, INC.
                      >>>>  NEWS  <<<<


    1 - Internet Connection Is Now Available.

    2 - Biblio-Tech -- The December Book.

    3 - Helpful Information for Internet Callers.
        NOTE: TELNET must be in character mode to echo keystrokes.

    4 - Biblio-Tech. The Online Book Discussion Group.

   99 - Recent Enhancements (Updated 10/23/93).

    Press Enter to proceed to the Main Menu.

    Type File # to View
    <L>ist Files Again
    <ENTER> To Exit :
```

```
*****************************************
*       Book Stacks Unlimited, Inc.     *
*              MAIN MENU                 *
*****************************************




           <B>ook Store

           <M>essages

           <N>ews/Notes

           <S>uggestions/Comments

           <F>iles/Magazines


           <U>tilities

           <H>elp

           <G>oodBye

    Command: B
```

```
*******************************************************
*              The Book Store                         *
*              273,481 Titles                         *
*******************************************************

 <A>uthor Search          <R>eview Your Selections

 <T>itle Search           <O>rder (when done)

 <K>eyWord Title Search   <C>heck Order Status

 <I>SBN Search

 <S>ubject Search \ Just Published



-------------------------------------------------------
      <P>revious Menu    <H>elp    <G>oodbye

Command: T
```

```
SEARCH DATABASE BY TITLE

Enter the first word(s) of the TITLE.

Omit leading 'A', 'AN','THE'. The first few letters are enough.
Only the first 20 characters will be used.

<ENTER> Previous Menu, <?> Help, <ENTER> when done : tale of two cities

# TITLE    AUTHOR                        PUB / BINDING / BK MARKS / PRICE
-----------------------------------------------------------------------------
1 A Tale of Two Cities
         Dickens, Charles              07/90 Paperback   S/O $  7.95
2 A Tale of Two Cities
         Dickens, Charles/Woodcock, George/B 06/85 Paperback   S/O $  4.95
3 A Tale of Two Cities
         Dickens, Charles              05/90 Paperback    12 $  4.99
4 Tale of Two Cities
         Dickens, Charles              08/91 Paperback     6 $  2.95

5 A Tale of Two Cities
         Dickens, Charles              12/92 Paperback    12 $  4.99
6 A Tale of Two Cities
         Dickens, Charles              09/89 Paperback     6 $  2.50
7 Tale of Two Cities (Longman Classics, Stage 2)
         Dickens, Charles              05/91 Paperback   S/O $  7.25
8 A Tale of Two Cities (World Classics)
         Dickens, Charles              11/88 Paperback   S/O $  4.95
9 A Tale of Two Cities (Courage Classics)
         Dickens, Charles              03/92 Hardcover   S/O $  5.98

<F>orward, <B>ackward, <P>revious Menu, <1-9> View Book # : 7
```

21

```
YOU HAVE SELECTED THE FOLLOWING TITLE:

Author   : Dickens, Charles

Title    : Tale of Two Cities (Longman Classics, Stage 2)


ISBN     : 0582030471
Volume   :
Subject  : General Fiction
Dewey #  :
Publisher: Addison Wesley (Longman)
Date Pub : 05/91
Binding  : Paperback
Edition  :
Bookmarks: S/O
Price    : $  7.25

How many copies would you like?, <ENTER> To Exit :
```

Again, I decide not to buy, and I back out using the P, or *previous menu,* option until I can use G to say *goodbye.*

Step 3. Summary

These are but two of hundreds of commercial services available on the Internet. One of the best places to learn about the entire range of services available is *Scott Yanoff's List of Internet Services,* available from anonymous FTP on csd4.csd.uwm.edu. If you're using fget, enter fget csd4.csd.uwm.edu:/pub/inet.services.txt.

Task 21.6: Visiting Libraries Around the World
Step 1. Description

As it turns out, I've written another book, one called *Global Software.* How about joining me as I travel through the Internet to various libraries to see what universities have my book?

Step 2. Action

1. The first library I visit is the National Library in Venezuela (Biblioteca Nacional). With gopher, the library computer is only seven steps away from the very top!

   ```
   Libraries/
     Library Catalogs via Telnet/
   ```

```
        Library Catalogs from Other Institutions/
            Catalogs Listed by Location/
                Americas/
                    Venezuela/
                        Biblioteca Nacional <TEL>
```

Once I log in as biblio, the screen looks like this:

```
                                              Catalogo Bib. Nacional
                                                        Introduccion
------------------------------------------------------------------------
                    Bienvenido al Catalogo Automatizado
                            S A I B I N

        Use los siguientes comandos:        Para buscar por:

                            A=              Autor
                            T=              Titulo
                            M=              Materia
                            K=              Palabra clave
                            C=              Cota
        Ud. puede iniciar una busqueda desde cualquier pantalla
        Para mayor informacion de busqueda en el Catalogo, presione <ENTER>.
        Para ver informacion sobre las BASES DE DATOS, escriba NOTI y
        presione <ENTER>.
        Ademas de  LUIN, ud. puede usar el comando  LUC2  donde encontrara
        ---------------------------------------------- + Pag. 1 de 4 -----------
                    INGRESE COMANDO BUSQUEDA            <F8>  AVAnza pag.
                    NOTicia


Prox. Comando:  _
```

Fortunately, my Spanish is sufficient to figure this out. I use t= to search by title (the command is T=GLOBAL SOFTWARE) for my book *Global Software*:

```
Solicitud de Busqueda: T=GLOBAL SOFTWARE              Catalogo Bib. Nacional
Resultados de Busqueda: 0 Entradas Encontradas   No existen Entradas por Titulo
------------------------------------------------------------------------
                    No se encontraron Entradas de Titulo

Las posibles razones para este mensaje son:

1.   Material no esta en la base de datos (Busque en el fichero.)
2.   Material no pertenece a la Biblioteca (Consulte al personal de referencia)
3.   Comando o termino(s)   incorrecto. (Pruebe con otro comando o cambie el
        termino de busqueda.)

        Verifique en la busqueda lo siguiente:
        --Asegurese de que estan correctamente escritos. Si no esta seguro del ti-
            tulo completo o de como se escribe acortelo al final.
```

21

```
   --Omita todos los articulos (a, en, el).
   --Elimine los signos de puntuacion.
Recuerde:  Ud. puede revisar su busqueda editandola en la linea de comandos).
------------------------------------------------- Pag. 1 de 1 -------------
COMenzar           REVisa busquedas realizadas
OTRas opciones


Prox. Comando: _
```

Ay caramba! Mi libro no está en al biblioteca nationál. Qué es la vida!

That is, there isn't a copy of my book in the library. Such is life. I can use `sali` (*leave*) to log out and return to `gopher`.

2. My next library to visit is in Australia. To get there, I need to back up a few levels in `gopher` and travel down a different path: `Asia and Pacific/` leads to `Australia/`, where I choose `Queensland University of Technology/`:

```
                                              Q U T



       L A T E S T   N E W S              L I B R A R Y


                                 EXCELLENCE IN INFORMATION SERVICES

                                 ***********************************
                                 *           OPTIONS              *
                                 ***********************************
                                 *                                *
                                 * 1.    Library Catalogue        *
                                 * 2.    Library Opening Hours    *
                                 * 3.    Logoff                   *
                                 *                                *
                                 *                                *
                                 ***********************************

                                 or press <HELP>, then <RETURN>
```

This looks likely, so I choose 1:

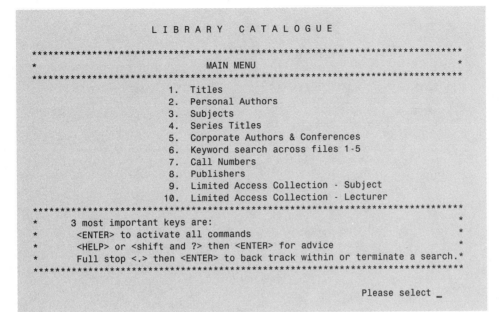

```
                    L I B R A R Y   C A T A L O G U E

*****************************************************************************
*                            MAIN MENU                                     *
*****************************************************************************
                    1.   Titles
                    2.   Personal Authors
                    3.   Subjects
                    4.   Series Titles
                    5.   Corporate Authors & Conferences
                    6.   Keyword search across files 1-5
                    7.   Call Numbers
                    8.   Publishers
                    9.   Limited Access Collection - Subject
                   10.   Limited Access Collection - Lecturer
*****************************************************************************
*    3 most important keys are:                                           *
*    <ENTER> to activate all commands                                     *
*    <HELP> or <shift and ?> then <ENTER> for advice                      *
*    Full stop <.> then <ENTER> to back track within or terminate a search.*
*****************************************************************************

                                                 Please select _
```

I want to select by title, so again I press 1:

```
                    S E A R C H   T E X T   E N T R Y
*****************************************************************************
                      TITLE ALPHABETIC BROWSING
*****************************************************************************

Please type in some text that you think may occur at the start of a title of
a work that you are attempting to find.

For example, you could type   ECONOMICS AND DEMOGRAPHY     or
                              ECONOMICS AND                or
                              ECON


And remember to use the help key if you need more information.



  Please enter your search text...
*****************************************************************************
> global software
```

I press Return to get the news:

```
B R O W S E              H E A D I N G   S E L E C T I O N

       Search text: GLOBAL SOFTWARE
Headings retrieved: 100
                                                            More pages
** TITLES ***********************************************************

  No.  Works
   1.    1    Global simulation models : a comparative study
==> GLOBAL SOFTWARE
   2.    1    Global solutions : innovative approaches to world problems :
              selections from The Futurist
   3.    1    Global sourcing strategy : R&D, manufacturing, and marketing
              interfaces
   4.    1    Global stakes : the future of high technology in America
   5.    2    Global status of mangrove ecosystems
   6.    1    Global stock market reforms
   7.    1    Global Strategic Management : Impact on New Frontiers....
   8.    1    Global strategic management perspectives
********************************************************************
Next Page           Gather Headings           Keyword Search
Previous Page       List Chosen Headings
Top of List
                                            SELECT _
```

Nope, it's not there either, but the book *Global Status of Mangrove Ecosystems* sounds quite interesting. Next time I'm on this computer system, I should look up the reference to learn more about mangrove ecosystems.

3. I'll try one more university before I give up hope! I'll check the various libraries of the University of California. Again, the process is to step back in the gopher tree, and select Americas/, United States/, California/, University of California (MELVYL) <TEL>/:

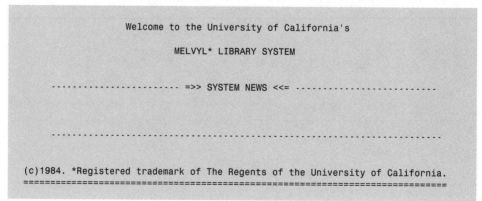

```
             Welcome to the University of California's

                      MELVYL* LIBRARY SYSTEM


   ------------------- =>> SYSTEM NEWS <<= -------------------------


   ----------------------------------------------------------------

(c)1984. *Registered trademark of The Regents of the University of California.
================================================================================
```

```
OPTIONS:  Choose an option, or type any command to enter the CATALOG database.

  HELP         - For help in getting started.

  [return]     - Press RETURN to choose a database for searching.

  START <db>   - Type START <database name> to begin searching in a database.

->  _
```

First, I can use the shortcut of entering START CAT to start with a catalog of all University of California library holdings:

```
              Welcome to the MELVYL CATALOG Database

  Contents:  As of 12/15/93, approximately 7,563,498 titles representing
             11,761,300 holdings for materials in the University of
             California libraries and the California State Library.

  Coverage:  All publication dates but incomplete for some libraries.

                    --=>> NEWS <<=--



- - - - - - - - - - - - - - - - - - - - - - - - - - - - - - - - - - - - - - - -
OPTIONS:     Type an option and press RETURN, or type any command.

  HELP       -  For help in getting started.

  E GUIDE    -  For a brief guide to using the Catalog database.

  START      -  To start over or change databases.
  END        -  To end your session.
CAT-> _
```

Did you see the number at the top of that screen? This database lists over 7.5 million different books, representing over 11 million holdings. That's quite impressive.

4. To save time again, I use the find command, specifying a title word: FIND TW GLOBAL SOFTWARE. Results in nine matches:

21

```
CAT-> f tw global software

   Search request: F TW GLOBAL SOFTWARE
   Search result:  9 records at all libraries

   Type D to display results, or type HELP.

CAT-> _
```

Entering D displays the first page of matches:

```
Search request: F TW GLOBAL SOFTWARE
Search result:  9 records at all libraries

Type HELP for other display options.

1. Clapes, Anthony Lawrence.
     Softwars : the legal battles for control of the global software industry /
   Anthony Lawrence Clapes.  Westport, Conn. : Quorum Books, 1993.
        HAST   5th Stks   K1443.C6 C56 1993
        UCB    Bus&Econ   K1443.C6 C56 1993
        UCB    Law Lib    K89 .C48
        UCI    Main Lib   K1443.C6 C56 1993
        UCLA   College    K 1443 C6 C56 1993
        UCSC   McHenry    K1443.C6C56 1993
        UCSD   Central    K1443.C6 C56 1993

2. A computer software system for the generation of global ocean tides
   including self-gravitation and crustal loading effects, by ronald h estes.
   1977.
        UCSD   Scripps    FICHE XSX 1 N77-23709 Floor 1 Microform


Press RETURN to see the next screen.
CAT->
```

I step forward a page or two:

```
Search request: F TW GLOBAL SOFTWARE
Search result:  9 records at all libraries

Type HELP for other display options.

5. Taylor, Dave, 1962-
     Global software : developing applications for the international market /
   Dave Taylor.  New York : Springer-Verlag, c1992.
        UCB    Engin      QA76.76.D47 T39 1992
        UCI    Main Lib   QA76.76.D47 T39 1992
        UCSC   Science    QA76.76.D47T39 1992
```

```
6. United States. General Accounting Office.
   Air Force Global Weather Central initiates positive action to assess
adequacy of software inventory : report to the Secretary of the Air Force /
by the U.S. General Accounting Office.  Washington, D.C. : The Office,
[1983].
    UCR    Rivera    GA 1.13:IMTEC-84-4 Govt.Pub Microfiche US
    UCSD   Central   GA 1.13:IMTEC-84-4 Documents Fiche
    CSL    Main Lib  GA 1.13:IMTEC-84-4 Govt Pubs


Press RETURN to see next screen. Type PS to see previous screen.
CAT-> _
```

Aha! You can see that there are copies of my book at the University of
California at Berkeley (UCB), at Irvine (UCI), and at Santa Cruz (UCSC).

Step 3. Summary

There are hundreds, if not thousands, of libraries connected to the Internet. If a
reference book exists, you should be able to find a reference citation.

Task 21.7: All the News That's Fit or Otherwise
Step 1. Description

No discussion of the Internet would be complete without a brief foray into the largest,
most active, and most varied discussion forum in the world—the Usenet. Imagine a
bulletin board on the wall. Imagine that as people pass it, they glance at what's there,
and if they have something to add, they stick their note up, too. Now (and here's the
big leap) imagine that there are *thousands* of bulletin boards in this building, and that
there are actually tens of thousands of buildings throughout the world, each with its
own "identical" copy of the bulletin boards. Got it? That's Usenet.

Usenet was created in 1979, when two graduate students at Duke University, Tom
Truscott and Jim Ellis, hooked their computer to another computer at the University
of North Carolina. In 1980 there were *two* sites with Usenet. Today, there are an
estimated 120,000 sites on Usenet, representing over *4.2 million* participants.

A true experiment in free speech and barely controlled anarchy, the range of
discussions, called *newsgroups*, is astonishing. Subjects covered include everything
from computer modem protocols (comp.dcom.modem) to Macintosh programming
(comp.sys.mac.programmer), topics of relevance to single men and women
(soc.singles), abortion (talk.abortion) to the wonderful TV show "Mystery
Science Theater 3000" (alt.tv.mst3k). Whatever your interest, there's a group on the
Net that talks about just what you're thinking about!

The difficulty with Usenet is that the majority of tools designed to help read the volumes of information actually do precious little to help. The first puzzle is to find the groups that you'd like to read, and although almost all Usenet sites have a succinct database of what each group discusses, little Usenet software actually knows about it. Here is a very simple C shell alias that will help out:

```
alias findgroup 'grep -i \!* /usr/local/lib/news/newsgroups'
```

At your site, this file might also be found as /usr/lib/news/newsgroups. Newsgroups are organized into seven primary hierarchies: comp groups are computer and programming related, sci groups discuss scientific issues, misc groups cover miscellaneous topics, rec are recreational, talk groups are for controversial and often heated discussion groups, soc are social groups, and news are groups containing news of the world or at least news of the network itself.

> **Comment:** For a sampling of newsgroups, see Appendix B.

One final hierarchy worth mentioning is the alt.* set of groups that are the spot for semi-disorganized anarchy on the Net. Essentially anyone can create an alt group with ease, so as you might expect, these groups are the most varied. Some examples are the excellent alt.activism for political activists and alt.books.technical for discussion of computer books (like this very book!); juvenile groups like alt.binaries.sounds-armpit.noises for, one presumes, audio files that contain sounds of armpit noises; and alt.elvis.sighting for those elusive sightings of the King. If you can't quite tear yourself away from your video game system long enough to eat, perhaps reading alt.get.a.life.nintendo.addicts will help.

One problem with the alt groups is that it's much more difficult to find out what's out there. Because there is considerably less control and organization, the convenient one-line descriptions in the newsgroups file don't contain descriptions of these alternative groups. Really the best solution is to search through your .newsrc itself for key words or abbreviations. To find alt groups that discuss Disney, for example, I could try grep disney .newsrc ¦ grep '^alt' to find alt.fan.disney.afternoon.

Once you've found a group to read, it's time to choose from among the many possible packages. Perhaps the most popular is rn, or *read news*, written by Larry Wall. Another alternative, nn, offers a more screen-oriented view from Kim Storm, and a third possibility, patterned after the elm mail program, is tin, designed and written by Iain Lea.

> **Comment:** Of the many programs available for reading netnews, I prefer
> tin, but because rn is so prevalent, I will use it in this lesson. I nonethe-
> less encourage you to use a local copy of tin if it's available. Remember
> also that you can always use archie to find a local copy.

The rn program not only has more options than you can shake a stick at, but it has
more options than even a tree full of sticks could cover! Table 21.1 lists a small number
of its particularly useful options.

Table 21.1. The most useful rn starting options.

Option	Meaning
-/	Set SAVEDIR, so that articles you save are stored in a subdirectory of ~/News named after the group, with the article name corresponding to its numeric identifier on the system.
-c	Check for news and indicate if any has arrived.
-e	Make each page of an article start at the top of the screen.
-h*hdr*	Suppress the header *hdr* in news articles.
-L	Leave information on screen as long as possible.
-M	Force mailbox format for all saved files.
-m	Use inverse video for highlighted information.
-N	Force normal, non-mailbox format for all saved files.
-r	Restart within the last newsgroup read during the previous session.
-S	Use subject search mode when possible.

> **Comment:** That's a lot of options! My alias for starting up the rn pro-
> gram is rn -L -M -m -e -S -/. Did I mention the RNINIT environment
> variable yet?

In addition to using starting options, the rn program can also read a variety of different options from environment variables. Indeed, any option that is specified at the command line can also be specified in the RNINIT variable. As a result, my RNINIT is this:

```
% echo $RNINIT
-hmessage -hreference -hdate-r -hsender -hsummary -hreply -hdistr -hlines
 -hline -hfollow -hnews -hkey -hresent -hreturn -hto -hx-original -hx-sun
-hx-note -horiginator -hnntp
```

This causes the program to suppress the display of all the specified headers in individual news articles. There are just so many options that it's overwhelming. Let's go into the program and see what it looks like!

Step 2. Action

1. First, I use the alias findgroup to identify a few newsgroups I'd like to read:

```
% findgroup mac
biz.dec.ip                IP networking on DEC machines.
vmsnet.internals          VMS internals, MACRO-32, Bliss, etc., gatewayed to
MACRO32 list.
gnu.emacs.announce        Announcements about GNU Emacs. (Moderated)
gnu.emacs.bug             GNU Emacs bug reports and suggested fixes.
(Moderated)
gnu.emacs.gnews           News reading under GNU Emacs using Weemba's Gnews.
gnu.emacs.gnus            News reading under GNU Emacs using GNUS (in English).
gnu.emacs.help            User queries and answers.
gnu.emacs.sources         ONLY (please!) C and Lisp source code for GNU Emacs.
gnu.emacs.vm.bug          Bug reports on the Emacs VM mail package.
gnu.emacs.vm.info         Information about the Emacs VM mail package.
gnu.emacs.vms             VMS port of GNU Emacs.
gnu.epoch.misc            The Epoch X11 extensions to Emacs.
comp.binaries.acorn       Binary-only postings for Acorn machines. (Moderated)
comp.binaries.mac         Encoded Macintosh programs in binary. (Moderated)
comp.emacs                EMACS editors of different flavors.
comp.lang.forth.mac       The CSI MacForth programming environment.
comp.lang.lisp.mcl        Discussing Apple's Macintosh Common Lisp.
comp.org.acm              Topics about the Association for Computing Machinery.
comp.os.mach              The MACH OS from CMU & other places.
comp.os.msdos.misc        Miscellaneous topics about MS-DOS machines.
comp.os.msdos.programmer  Programming MS-DOS machines.
comp.os.os2.programmer    Programming OS/2 machines.
comp.sources.mac          Software for the Apple Macintosh. (Moderated)
comp.sys.mac.advocacy     The Macintosh computer family compared to others.
comp.sys.mac.announce     Important notices for Macintosh users. (Moderated)
comp.sys.mac.apps         Discussions of Macintosh applications.
comp.sys.mac.comm         Discussion of Macintosh communications.
comp.sys.mac.databases    Database systems for the Apple Macintosh.
comp.sys.mac.digest       Apple Macintosh: info&uses, no programs. (Moderated)
comp.sys.mac.games        Discussions of games on the Macintosh.
comp.sys.mac.hardware     Macintosh hardware issues & discussions.
```

```
comp.sys.mac.hypercard   The Macintosh Hypercard: info & uses.
comp.sys.mac.misc        General discussions about the Apple Macintosh.
comp.sys.mac.oop.macapp3 Version 3 of the MacApp object oriented system.
comp.sys.mac.oop.misc    Object oriented programming issues on the Mac.
comp.sys.mac.programmer  Discussion by people programming the Apple Macintosh.
comp.sys.mac.system      Discussions of Macintosh system software.
comp.sys.mac.wanted      Postings of "I want XYZ for my Mac."
comp.sys.sgi.graphics    Graphics packages and issues on SGI machines.
comp.sys.sgi.misc        General discussion about Silicon Graphics's machines.
comp.text.tex            Discussion about the TeX and LaTeX systems & macros.
comp.unix.aux            The version of UNIX for Apple Macintosh II computers.
misc.forsale.computers.mac    Apple Macintosh related computer items.
rec.games.diplomacy      The conquest game Diplomacy.
sci.nanotech             Self-reproducing molecular-scale machines.  (Moder-
ated)
%
```

Remember that these are only groups that have the word mac in them. The group comp.sys.mac.announce sounds like it might be interesting. Now I'll find a few more:

```
% findgroup writing
comp.edu.composition    Writing instruction in computer-based classrooms.
misc.writing            Discussion of writing in all of its forms.
% findgroup education
k12.ed.art              Art curriculum in K-12 education.
k12.ed.business         Business education curriculum in grades K-12.
k12.ed.health-pe        Health and Physical Education curriculum in grades K-12.
k12.ed.life-skills      Home Economics and Career education in grades K-12.
k12.ed.math             Mathematics curriculum in K-12 education.
k12.ed.music            Music and Performing Arts curriculum in K-12 education.
k12.ed.science          Science curriculum in K-12 education.
k12.ed.soc-studies      Social Studies and History curriculum in K-12 education.
k12.ed.special          K-12 education for students w/ handicaps or special
needs.
k12.ed.tag              K-12 education for talented and gifted students.
k12.ed.tech             Industrial Arts and vocational education in grades K-12.
k12.lang.art            Language Arts curriculum in K-12 education.
comp.ai.edu             Applications of Artificial Intelligence to Education.
comp.edu                Computer science education.
misc.education          Discussion of the educational system.
sci.edu                 The science of education.
% findgroup movies
rec.arts.movies             Discussions of movies and movie making.
rec.arts.movies.reviews     Reviews of movies. (Moderated)
rec.arts.sf.movies          Discussing SF motion pictures.
rec.arts.startrek.current   New Star Trek shows, movies and books.
% findgroup film
rec.arts.startrek.reviews   Reviews of Star Trek books, episodes, films, &c
(Moderated)
%
```

Now I have a list of groups to check out: comp.sys.mac.announce, misc.writing, sci.edu, and rec.arts.movies.

21

2. It's time to start up the `rn` program so I can read these groups:

```
% rn

                 *** NEWS NEWS ***

Welcome to version 4.4 of rn (patch level 4).  This version corrects
many bugs of the previous version and has some enhancements you may
find useful.  Type "man rn" for more information.

If you find problems with this program, report them with trouble(1L).

This particular message comes from /usr/local/lib/rn/newsnews.  You will only
see it once.

[Type space to continue] _
```

Because I haven't used the program before, this first time out will have all
sorts of information:

```
Trying to set up a .newsrc file--running newsetup...

Creating /users/taylor/.newsrc to be used by news programs.
Done.

If you have never used the news system before, you may find the articles in
news.announce.newusers to be helpful.  There is also a manual entry for rn.

To get rid of newsgroups you aren't interested in, use the 'u' command.
Type h for help at any time while running rn.
(Revising soft pointers--be patient.)
Unread news in general                               1 article
Unread news in news.admin.misc                      88 articles
Unread news in news.admin.policy                     68 articles
Unread news in news.admin.technical                   6 articles
Unread news in news.announce.conferences             26 articles
etc.
etc.

Finding new newsgroups:

********    1 unread article in general--read now? [ynq] _
```

Don't Skip This: One of the worst aspects of rn is that by default it
subscribes you to all available newsgroups the first time you enter the
program. Fortunately the fix is easy.

3. Now that I'm a member of a few thousand groups, I want to get out of a few! The fastest way to fix the problem is to quit rn (enter q), then use vi to edit my personal Usenet database file, called .newsrc, which resides in my home directory. This file contains a list of all newsgroups, with each group followed by a special character and an indication of which articles I have already seen:

```
% head .newsrc
general: 1-699
news.admin: 1-26982
news.admin.misc: 1-6329
news.admin.policy: 1-8171
news.admin.technical: 1-445
news.announce.conferences: 1-5326
news.announce.important:
news.announce.newgroups:
news.announce.newusers:
news.answers:
%
```

To unsubscribe and have no groups included, I simply replace the colon on each line with an exclamation point. A group that isn't subscribed looks like this: news.admin! 1-26982. You can use :1,$s/:/!/ in vi to unsubscribe quickly to all groups. I suggest, however, that you make sure that you do read the group general on your system.

4. Now I start rn a second time, and here's what I see:

```
% rn
Unread news in general                                              1 article

********   1 unread article in general--read now? [ynq] _
```

Instead of answering yes or no to this question, I can go to the groups I'd previously chosen to read, using the g *groupname* command:

```
********   1 unread article in general--read now? [ynq] g
comp.sys.mac.announce
Newsgroup comp.sys.mac.announce is currently unsubscribed to--resubscribe?
[yn]
_
```

It's not surprising that I am not subscribed. I just unsubscribed from just about everything. Joining the group sounds good, so I enter y, and the screen changes:

```
********   0 unread articles in comp.sys.mac.announce--read now? [ynq] _
```

There are no articles pending in this newsgroup, as can be seen by the 0 unread message. That's good news, because I can add the other three groups by saying n here (since I do not want to read this group) then using the g command with each of the other groups specified.

The first time I choose n, however, the prompt changes to a new line:

```
******** End of newsgroups--what next? [qnp] _
```

I can enter the g *newsgroup* here just as easily.

5. Imagine it's a couple days later. I log in to my computer and again enter rn to see if there's any news. Unsurprisingly, quite a few articles have arrived since I signed up for the groups:

```
% rn
Unread news in general                                    1 article
Unread news in sci.edu                                   28 articles
Unread news in misc.writing                              81 articles


********    1 unread article in general--read now? [ynq] _
```

I start by saying n, then y when it asks about the newsgroup sci.edu. The screen changes:

```
Article 4695 (27 more) in sci.edu:
From: choy@cs.usask.ca (Henry Choy)
Subject: Re: Automation and the Need for Education
Date: 9 Dec 1993 22:00:10 GMT
Organization: University of Saskatchewan
NNTP-Posting-Host: sparkle.usask.ca
X-Newsreader: TIN [version 1.2 PL0]


Alberto Moreira (acm@kpc.com) wrote:
:        Computers can't do anything by themselves - they are raw
:        metal.  But the computer program running in a computer is
:        a transliteration of a human creator's thought processes.
:        When you play chess against a computer, you're not playing
:        against the computer; you're playing against the individuals
:        who designed Sargon, Deep Thought, or whatever chess program
:        you're battling.

In a way this is so, but the designers of these programs are working
in the way they were taught to play chess :)

Consider a chess program that is free to consider different
evaluation techniques, and other whatnot procedures and measures
concocted with some element of randomness. This program behaves
--MORE--(46%) _
```

There's a lot of information contained in the first few lines, as shown in Figure 21.1. Also, the lines that begin with a colon are *quoted text* from a previous article in the group, that one written by Alberto Moreira. All lines not beginning with a colon are the thoughts of Henry Choy, the author of this particular article.

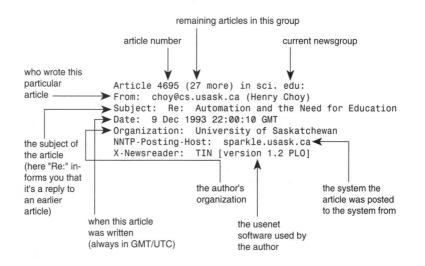

Figure 21.1. *Information on* rn *article display screen.*

6. While reading a particular article, there are a variety of different commands that I can enter to perform different actions, most notably q to quit reading this particular article, n to move to the next article, k to mark this article and all of a similar subject as read (so I don't see them), ^S (or space) to read the next article with the same subject in this group, R to reply to the author via electronic mail, and F to *follow up* this article with thoughts and reactions of my own. One particularly helpful command is =, which offers a table of contents for this group, showing all articles I have not yet read.

Shortcut: One little-known fact about rn is that you can define exactly what is shown in the = table of contents screen with the SUBJLINE environment variable. I have mine set to %t -- %s, which produces a list with both the author and subject indicated.

When I enter the equals sign (=), here's what happens:

```
  4696 office@interact.nl -- INTERACTIVE LEARNING (INTERACT 2)
  4697 yifanhan@helix.nih.gov -- Academic tenure in Australia and other
countries
  4698 cberry@tajo.edu -- Grade Point Averages: What's the point?
  4699 markline@henson.cc.wwu.edu -- Grade Point Averages: What's the point?
  4700 cravener@uhunix.uhcc.Hawaii.Edu -- Grade Point Averages: What's the
point?
  4701 jbirch@crc.sd68.nanaimo.bc.ca -- Looking for U of A - John Lind...
  4702 hrubin@snap.stat.purdue.edu -- Grade Point Averages: What's the
point?
  4703 hrubin@snap.stat.purdue.edu -- Academic tenure in Australia and other
countries
  4704 chem@uwpg02.uwinnipeg.ca -- TOSHIBA/NSTA contest info
  4705 mpriestley@vnet.IBM.COM -- Grade Point Averages: What's the point?
  4706 acm@kpc.com -- Grade Point Averages: What's the point?
  4707 acm@kpc.com -- Grade Point Averages: What's the point?
  4708 rablatch@unix.amherst.edu -- Academic tenure in Australia and other
countries
  4709 elkassas@eb.ele.tue.nl -- Q: TV use in education!
  4710 cravener@uhunix.uhcc.Hawaii.Edu -- Grade Point Averages: What's the point?
  4711 nata@aoibs.msk.su -- Subscription to Russian literature magazine in
English and in Russian!
  4712 reiser@ils.nwu.EDU -- PhD & MA Programs in Learning Sciences at
Northwestern
  4713 gaturner@npmo.pc.ingr.com -- Help needed on paper
[Type space to continue] _
```

There are more articles waiting to be read than can even fit on the screen (hence the Type space to continue at the bottom). Here I can enter q to zip back to the bottom of the article I was reading (then M to mail a response to the author, perhaps) or enter a specific article number to read that article. Article 4704, entitled TOSHIBA/NSTA contest info sounds pretty interesting, so I'll enter 4704 and move directly to that article:

```
Article 4704 (23 more) in sci.edu:
From: chem@uwpg02.uwinnipeg.ca
Subject: TOSHIBA/NSTA contest info
Date: 13 DEC 93 02:31:15 CST
Organization: University of Winnipeg
NNTP-Posting-Host: uwpg02.uwinnipeg.ca

Hi. I was wondering if anyone had sample material
regarding the NSTA/TOSHIBA explorovision contest.
SPecifically, sample storyboards and written reports.
Thanks for any info. M. Carroll U of Wpg
internet:  chem@uwpg02.uwinnipeg.ca
End of article 4704 (of 4719)--what next? [^Nnpq]_
```

At this point, again, I could use R to reply, F to post a follow-up article of my own, or any of the other commands. It seems like a good time to quit Usenet for now, so I enter q and move to the next group in the list:

```
End of article 4704 (of 4719)--what next? [^Nnpq]


********  81 unread articles in misc.writing--read now? [ynq] _
```

Another q and I'm back at my C Shell prompt.

7. Just for comparison, here's what tin looks like when I launch it on the list of newsgroups that I read on an approximately daily basis:

```
                 Group Selection (18)                      h=help

    1   396  misc.forsale.computers.mac      Apple Macintosh related comput
    2        news.announce.important         General announcements of inter
    3        news.announce.newusers          Explanatory postings for new u
    4        comp.binaries.mac               Encoded Macintosh programs in
    5    16  comp.org.sug                    Talk about/for the The Sun Use
    6        comp.org.usenix                 USENIX Association events and
    7        comp.sys.mac.announce           Important notices for Macintos
    8     2  comp.sys.sun.announce           Sun announcements and Sunergy
    9        rec.arts.movies.reviews         Reviews of movies. (Moderated)
   10    38  rec.food.recipes                Recipes for interesting food a
   11   447  alt.books.reviews               "If you want to know how it tu
   12   158  alt.education.distance          Learning over nets etc.
   13   110  alt.education.research
   14   603  alt.folklore.herbs
   15    37  misc.education                  Discussion of the educational
   16    20  misc.education.language.english

   <n>=set current to n, TAB=next unread, /=search pattern, c)atchup,
 g)oto, j=line down, k=line up, h)elp, m)ove, q)uit, r=toggle all/unread,
   s)ubscribe, S)ub pattern, u)nsubscribe, U)nsub pattern, y)ank in/out


 -
```

Many of these groups have no articles pending, but you can see (on the second number on the line) that the group misc.forsale.computers.mac has 396 new articles, comp.org.sug has 16, and so on. To read the currently highlighted group, I press Return.

```
         misc.forsale.computers.mac (318T 391A 0K 0H R)        h=help

   1  + 2  Group Purchase:  SCSI Hard Drives           David La Croix
   2  +     BernulliMD150+5(150)carts!$750NEW!          Donn Lasher
   3  +     MUST SELL:  Macintosh external AppleCD 150  Seung Jong Lee
```

```
    4  + 4   Mac Centris 650 Forsale                         M Torricelli
    5  + 2   IBM/Tandberg TDC3600/250Mb SCSI Tape Drives     asg@world.std.com
    6  +     FOR SALE: Symantec C++ 6.0.1                    FDMWINK@UCF1VM.BIT
    7  +     SCSI stuff for sale                             Victor Mark Kalyuz
    8  +     Computer Accessaries for Sale                   Qian Zhang
    9  +     DOS 6.0 FOR SALE                                Qian Zhang
   10  +     Performa 600 (Max IIVx NOT!)                    Steve Fouts
   11  + 2   WANTED: color '040 mac used.                    753mackie@gw.wmich
   12  +     Ashlar Vellum 2D and 3D for sale                robert dornbusch
   13  +     Cheap ImageWriter II for sale $95 (shipping i   Prachya Chalermwat
   14  +     PB 140                                          Jeffrey Ello
   15  +     Apple CD150 CD_ROM, new $199.00                 Victor Mark Kalyuz
   16  +     LCII 8/80 - Gotta sell soon.                    Anthony S. Kim

 <n>=set current to n, TAB=next unread, /=search pattern, ^K)ill/select,
a)uthor search, c)atchup, j=line down, k=line up, K=mark read, l)ist thread,
 |=pipe, m)ail, o=print, q)uit, r=toggle all/unread, s)ave, t)ag, w=post


 -
```

I press Return again, and I can read the specific article or use q to quit. I think I've had enough Usenet for one day, so I quit and again return to my C shell prompt.

Step 3. Summary

Usenet is a complex, wild, and almost organization-free set of thousands of newsgroups distributed to over 100,000 systems and read by millions of users throughout the world. Between Mac, PC, Amiga, UNIX, and VMS, there are at least 20 different programs available just for reading the vast volumes of information that flow past each day. If you have access to a Mac or a PC, or even a UNIX system running the X Window System, then there are some attractive programs available for reading the Net. If not, I'm a fan of tin and have also used rn for many years; both will serve you well once you learn them. Certainly, for any of these programs, start out with the included documentation or at least read through the (usually quite long) man pages.

Lesson Summary

This ends the tour of Internet navigational packages and Usenet. You have learned about archie, WAIS, The WorldWide Web, and gopher, and you have travelled with me to library computers in Australia and Venezuela, and even watched over my shoulder as I *almost* ordered a John Coltrane CD and a recent edition of *A Tale of Two Cities*. And then there's the wonderful world of the Usenet!

The Internet is an amazing resource, and it's growing dramatically each day. By the time you read this, the size of the WAIS database list, the number of archie files in that database, and the number of Usenet newsgroups will have expanded even further. If there's an Information Highway in your future, the Internet is most certainly going to be a key part of it, and you can't go wrong by spending some time learning more about it!

Workshop
Key Terms

bookmark	A saved gopher menu item through which you can easily build your own custom gopher information screens.
gopherspace	The information space that gopher travels through while you're using the program.
hypertext	A scheme for connecting information through *hypertext links*, this allows documents to reference other documents and information.
hypertext link	A pointer in a piece of information to other information (a definition of a term, a related document, a footnote, or something similar).
newsgroup	A Usenet group focused on a particular subject or topic of conversation.
quoted text	A portion of a previous article that is included in the current article to give context, particularly in disagreeing with or amplifying specific thoughts.
Request for Comment	An official UNIX design specification, also known as an RFC.
search string	The pattern specified in a search.

Questions

1. Using archie, find one or two archive sites that have a copy of the tin newsreading program.

2. What does the acronym LISP stand for? Use the WAIS system.

3. Who directed the film *Blade Runner*? What year was it released? Use the `WorldWide Web`.

4. Check in to the library at Stanford University with `gopher` and see if it has a copy of this book yet.

5. Enter the `findgroup` alias and find the groups that discuss:

   plant biology
   laser printers
   UNIX questions
   anthropology

6. Using `rn` or another news reader, check in to one of the groups you just found, and see if there are any new articles. Based on information in this lesson, how many systems do you think get this group?

Where to Go Next

This marks the end of your journey. In 21 lessons you've learned considerably more about UNIX than most people ever learn, and I hope you've had fun along the way. As with any large body of information, particularly one that evolves daily, there's still a lot more to learn. To get from here to there, I have a few suggestions.

To learn more about the Internet, I recommend the enjoyable and valuable *Navigating the Internet* by Mark Gibbs and Richard Smith. I've read it a couple times, and each time I find something new and amusing. If nothing else, you will learn what the words *aalii* and *zymurgy* mean, which is a potential boon for next time you play *Scrabble*.

To learn more about C programming, read both *Teach Yourself C in 21 Days* by Peter Aitken and Bradley Jones, and the official language definition, *The C Programming Language* by Brian Kernighan and Dennis Ritchie. Your UNIX vendor also should have supplied information on C programming tools available with your system.

If you want to become a true UNIX power user, I recommend *UNIX Unleashed*, forthcoming from SAMS Publishing. It is stuffed full of interesting and valuable information about the many UNIX commands on your system.

There are some valuable documents available on the Internet, too. Scott Yanoff has an *Internet Services List* that can be quite informative. Grab a copy at `csd4.csd.uwm.edu:/pub/inet.services.txt`. In addition to the list of Usenet newsgroups that you can access with the `findgroup` alias shown earlier, there are thousands of electronic mailing lists. You can obtain a very large listing of all groups by obtaining the file `rtfm.mit.edu:/pub/usenet/news.answers/mail/mailing-lists`. Finally, a list of some fun information servers on the Internet can be obtained as `cerebus.cor.epa.gov:/pub/bigfun`.

Finally, don't forget that your UNIX system has lots of documentation and information, and most of it's online! For any command you find yourself using frequently, the man page entry might well show you new ways to combine things, to work with starting options and files, and more. Always look for an EXAMPLES section at the end of the document, and don't forget that you can print it by using `man cmd | lpr` at the command line.

Have fun, and enjoy UNIX! It's the most powerful operating system you can work with. It's only as easy or complex as you let it be. Tame the beast, study what's in this book and other books on the subject, and you'll grow to appreciate and enjoy the system.

And don't forget to write!

21

Organizations and Magazines to Check Out

A

Though many computer-related magazines cover various aspects of UNIX, there are really surprisingly few organizations to join if you're interested in learning more about the business or technical aspects of this operating system. This appendix lists all the groups and magazines I know that cover this area, as well as contact information. Ask your UNIX expert colleagues for more ideas, too!

UNIX-Related Organizations

Interex, the International Association of HP Users
P.O. Box 3439
Sunnyvale, CA 94088
(408) 738-4848

SAGE, for System Administrators
2560 Ninth Street, #215
Berkeley, CA 94710
(510) 528-8649
`office@usenix.org`

The Sun Users Group
1330 Beacon Street, Suite 315
Brookline, MA 02146
(617) 232-0514
`office@sug.org`

The UniForum Association
2901 Tasman Drive, #201
Santa Clara, CA 95054
(800) 255-5620

The Usenix Association
2560 Ninth Street, #215
Berkeley, CA 94710
(510) 528-8649
`office@usenix.org`

UNIX-Related Publications

Advanced Systems
(formerly *SunWorld*)
IDG Communications
501 Second Street
San Francisco, CA 94107
(415) 978-3200
`mccarthy@sunworld.com`

BYTE
One Phoenix Mill Lane
Peterborough, NH 03458
(603) 924-9281

DEC Professional
Cardinal Business Media
101 Witmer Road
Horsham, PA 19044
(215) 957-4273
`detwiler@proeast.propress.com`

HP Professional
Cardinal Business Media
101 Witmer Road
Horsham, PA 19044
(215) 957-4273
`detwiler@proeast.propress.com`

InfoWorld
800 Bovet Road, Suite 800
San Mateo, CA 94402
(415) 572-7341

Open Systems Today
CMP Publications
600 Community Drive
Manhasset, NY 11030
(516) 562-5000

SunExpert
Computer Publishing Group
1330 Beacon Street
Brookline, MA 02146
(617) 739-7001
`dpryor@expert.com`

The C Users Journal
R&D Publications
1601 W. 23rd Street, #200
Lawrence, KS 66046
(913) 841-1631
`bill@rdpub.com`

The X Journal
SIGS
588 Broadway, #604
New York, NY 10012
(212) 274-0640

UNIX Review
Miller-Freeman Publications
600 Harrison Street
San Francisco, CA 94107
(415) 905-2200

UNIX World
McGraw-Hill Corp.
1900 O'Farrell Street
San Mateo, CA 94403
(415) 513-6800
`letters@uworld.com`

A Sampling of Current Usenet Groups

B

This sampling of Usenet groups is culled from a list of groups built in December 1993, but new groups are being created all the time, so check your own system for the final word (look for the file `/usr/lib/news/active-list`). Also, any group listed with *(Moderated)* means that someone serving as an editor screens all articles in the group. If you try to send an article to the group, the article instead will be mailed electronically to this person for screening. The downside of this system is that you can't instantly join a discussion, but the upside is that moderated groups are some of the best, most readable groups on the net.

Newsgroup	Topic of Discussion
`bionet.agroforestry`	Agro-forestry.
`bionet.biology.computational`	Computer and mathematical applications. (Moderated)
`bionet.biology.n2-fixation`	Research issues on biological nitrogen fixation.
`bionet.biology.tropical`	Tropical biology.
`bionet.cellbiol`	Cell biology.
`bionet.chlamydomonas`	The green alga Chlamydomonas.
`bionet.drosophila`	The biology of Drosophila.
`bionet.general`	Bioscience.
`bionet.genome.arabidopsis`	The Arabidopsis project.
`bionet.genome.chromosomes`	Mapping and sequencing of eucaryote chromosomes.
`bionet.immunology`	Research in immunology.
`bionet.info-theory`	Biological information theory.
`bionet.jobs`	Scientific job opportunities.
`bionet.metabolic-reg`	Thermodynamics of cellular processes.
`bionet.molbio.ageing`	Cellular and organismal aging.
`bionet.molbio.bio-matrix`	Computer applications to biological databases.

Newsgroup	Topic of Discussion
`bionet.molbio.embldatabank`	The EMBL nucleic acid database.
`bionet.molbio.evolution`	The evolution of genes and proteins.
`bionet.molbio.gdb`	Messages to and from the GDB database staff.
`bionet.molbio.genbank`	The GenBank nucleic acid database.
`bionet.molbio.gene-linkage`	Genetic linkage analysis.
`bionet.molbio.genome-program`	Human Genome Project issues.
`bionet.molbio.hiv`	The molecular biology of HIV.
`bionet.molbio.methds-reagnts`	Requests for information and lab reagents.
`bionet.molbio.proteins`	Research on proteins and protein databases.
`bionet.molbio.rapd`	Research on randomly amplified polymorphic DNA.
`bionet.molbio.yeast`	The biology of yeast.
`bionet.mycology`	Filamentous fungi.
`bionet.neuroscience`	Research issues in the neurosciences.
`bionet.photosynthesis`	Research on photosynthesis.
`bionet.plants`	All aspects of plant biology.
`bionet.population-bio`	Population biology.
`bionet.sci-resources`	Funding agencies. (Moderated)
`bionet.software`	Software for biology.
`bionet.software.acedb`	Discussions by users of genome DBs using ACEDB.
`bionet.software.gcg`	Using the GCG software.
`bionet.software.sources`	Sources for software relating to biology. (Moderated)
`bionet.users.addresses`	Who's who in biology.

B

Newsgroup	Topic of Discussion
`bionet.virology`	Research in virology.
`bionet.women-in-bio`	Women in biology.
`bionet.xtallography`	Protein crystallography.
`biz.comp.hardware`	Commercial hardware postings.
`biz.comp.services`	Commercial service postings.
`biz.comp.software`	Commercial software postings.
`biz.comp.telebit`	Support of the Telebit modem.
`biz.comp.telebit.netblazer`	The Telebit Netblazer.
`biz.dec`	DEC equipment and software.
`biz.dec.ip`	IP networking on DEC machines.
`biz.dec.workstations`	The DEC workstation.
`biz.jobs.offered`	Position announcements.
`biz.misc`	Miscellaneous postings of a commercial nature.
`biz.sco.announce`	SCO and related products. (Moderated)
`biz.sco.general`	SCO products.
`biz.sco.opendesktop`	ODT environment and applications tech info.
`biz.stolen`	Postings about stolen merchandise.
`comp.admin.policy`	Site administration policies.
`comp.ai`	Artificial intelligence.
`comp.ai.edu`	Applications of artificial intelligence to education.
`comp.ai.fuzzy`	Fuzzy set theory, fuzzy logic.
`comp.ai.genetic`	Genetic algorithms in computing.
`comp.ai.neural-nets`	All aspects of neural networks.

Newsgroup	Topic of Discussion
comp.ai.nlang-know-rep	Natural language and knowledge representation. (Moderated)
comp.ai.philosophy	Philosophical aspects of artificial intelligence.
comp.ai.vision	Artificial intelligence vision research. (Moderated)
comp.answers	Repository for periodic USENET articles. (Moderated)
comp.apps.spreadsheets	Spreadsheets on various platforms.
comp.arch	Computer architecture.
comp.archives	Public access archives. (Moderated)
comp.archives.admin	Computer archive administration.
comp.bbs.waffle	The Waffle BBS and USENET system on all platforms.
comp.benchmarks	Benchmarking techniques and results.
comp.binaries.acorn	Binary-only postings for Acorn machines. (Moderated)
comp.binaries.amiga	Encoded public domain programs in binary. (Moderated)
comp.binaries.apple2	Binary-only postings for the Apple II computer.
comp.binaries.atari.st	Binary-only postings for the Atari ST. (Moderated)
comp.binaries.ibm.pc	Binary-only postings for IBM PC/ MS-DOS. (Moderated)
comp.binaries.mac	Encoded Macintosh programs in binary. (Moderated)
comp.binaries.ms-windows	Binary programs for Microsoft Windows. (Moderated)

B

Newsgroup	Topic of Discussion
comp.binaries.os2	Binaries for use under the OS/2 ABI. (Moderated)
comp.bugs.4bsd	UNIX version 4BSD bugs.
comp.bugs.sys5	Reports of USG (System III, V, and so on) bugs.
comp.cad.cadence	For users of Cadence Design Systems products.
comp.client-server	Client/server technology.
comp.cog-eng	Cognitive engineering.
comp.compilers	Compiler construction, theory, and so on. (Moderated)
comp.compression.research	Data compression research.
comp.databases.informix	Informix database management software.
comp.databases.ingres	Issues related to INGRES products.
comp.databases.oracle	SQL database products of the Oracle Corporation.
comp.databases.sybase	Implementations of the SQL Server.
comp.dcom.cell-relay	Cell Relay-based products.
comp.dcom.fax	Fax hardware, software, and protocols.
comp.dcom.isdn	The Integrated Services Digital Network (ISDN).
comp.dcom.lans.ethernet	Ethernet/IEEE 802.3 protocols.
comp.dcom.lans.fddi	The FDDI protocol suite.
comp.dcom.lans.hyperchannel	Hyperchannel networks within an IP network.
comp.dcom.modems	Data communications hardware and software.

Newsgroup	Topic of Discussion
comp.dcom.servers	Selecting and operating data communications servers.
comp.dcom.sys.cisco	Cisco routers and bridges.
comp.dcom.sys.wellfleet	Wellfleet bridge and router systems hardware and software.
comp.dcom.telecom	Telecommunications digest. (Moderated)
comp.doc	Archived public-domain documentation. (Moderated)
comp.doc.techreports	Lists of technical reports. (Moderated)
comp.editors	Topics related to computerized text editing.
comp.edu	Computer science education.
comp.edu.composition	Writing instruction in computer-based classrooms.
comp.emacs	EMACS editors of different types.
comp.fonts	Typefonts—design, conversion, use, and so on.
comp.graphics	Computer graphics, art, animation, image processing.
comp.graphics.animation	Technical aspects of computer animation.
comp.graphics.avs	The Application Visualization System.
comp.graphics.explorer	The Explorer Modular Visualisation Environment (MVE).
comp.graphics.opengl	The OpenGL 3D application programming interface.
comp.graphics.research	Computer graphics. (Moderated)

B

A Sampling of Current Usenet Groups

Newsgroup	Topic of Discussion
comp.groupware	Software and hardware for shared interactive environments.
comp.human-factors	Issues related to human-computer interaction (HCI).
comp.infosystems.gis	Geographic information systems.
comp.infosystems.gopher	The gopher information service.
comp.infosystems.wais	The Z39.50-based WAIS full-text search system.
comp.internet.library	Electronic libraries. (Moderated)
comp.ivideodisc	Interactive videodiscs—uses, potential, and so on.
comp.lang.ada	Ada.
comp.lang.apl	APL.
comp.lang.c	C.
comp.lang.c++	The object-oriented C++ language.
comp.lang.clos	Lisp Object System.
comp.lang.clu	The CLU language and related topics.
comp.lang.dylan	The Dylan language.
comp.lang.eiffel	The object-oriented Eiffel language.
comp.lang.forth	Forth.
comp.lang.fortran	FORTRAN.
comp.lang.icon	Topics related to the ICON programming language.
comp.lang.lisp	LISP.
comp.lang.logo	The Logo teaching and learning language.

Newsgroup	Topic of Discussion
comp.lang.misc	Different computer languages not specifically listed.
comp.lang.modula2	Modula-2.
comp.lang.objective-c	The Objective-C language and environment.
comp.lang.pascal	Pascal.
comp.lang.perl	Larry Wall's Perl system.
comp.lang.prolog	PROLOG.
comp.lang.smalltalk	Smalltalk 80.
comp.lang.tcl	The TCL programming language and related tools.
comp.lang.vhdl	VHSIC Hardware Description Language, IEEE 1076/87.
comp.laser-printers	Laser printers, hardware, and software. (Moderated)
comp.lsi.testing	Testing of electronic circuits.
comp.mail.elm	Fixes for ELM mail system.
comp.mail.maps	Various maps, including UUCP maps. (Moderated)
comp.mail.mh	The UCI version of the Rand Message Handling system.
comp.mail.mime	Multipurpose Internet Mail Extensions of RFC 1341.
comp.mail.misc	Computer mail.
comp.mail.multi-media	Multimedia Mail.
comp.mail.mush	The mail user's shell (MUSH).
comp.mail.sendmail	Configuring and using the BSD sendmail agent.

B

Newsgroup	Topic of Discussion
`comp.mail.uucp`	Mail in the uucp network environment.
`comp.multimedia`	Interactive multimedia technologies of all kinds.
`comp.music`	Applications of computers in music research.
`comp.newprod`	New products of interest. (Moderated)
`comp.object`	Object-oriented programming and languages.
`comp.org.acm`	Topics about the Association for Computing Machinery.
`comp.org.decus`	Digital Equipment Computer Users' Society newsgroup.
`comp.org.eff.news`	News from the Electronic Frontiers Foundation. (Moderated)
`comp.org.ieee`	Issues and announcements about the IEEE and its members.
`comp.org.sug`	The Sun User's Group.
`comp.org.usenix`	USENIX Association events and announcements.
`comp.os.386bsd.announce`	The 386bsd operating system. (Moderated)
`comp.os.aos`	Topics related to Data General's AOS/VS.
`comp.os.coherent`	Discussion and support of the Coherent operating system.
`comp.os.linux`	The free UNIX-clone for the 386/486, LINUX.
`comp.os.mach`	The MACH OS from CMU and other places.

Newsgroup	Topic of Discussion
`comp.os.minix`	Tanenbaum's MINIX system.
`comp.os.misc`	General OS-oriented discussion not carried elsewhere.
`comp.os.ms-windows.announce`	Announcements relating to Windows. (Moderated)
`comp.os.ms-windows.apps`	Applications in the Windows environment.
`comp.os.msdos.apps`	Applications that run under MS-DOS.
`comp.os.msdos.misc`	Miscellaneous topics about MS-DOS machines.
`comp.os.os2.apps`	Applications under OS/2.
`comp.os.os2.misc`	Miscellaneous topics about the OS/2 system.
`comp.os.research`	Operating systems and related topics. (Moderated)
`comp.parallel`	Massively parallel hardware/software. (Moderated)
`comp.patents`	Patents of computer technology. (Moderated)
`comp.periphs.printers`	Printers.
`comp.periphs.scsi`	SCSI-based peripheral devices.
`comp.programming`	Programming issues that transcend languages and OSs.
`comp.protocols.appletalk`	Applebus hardware and software.

B

Newsgroup	Topic of Discussion
`comp.protocols.iso`	The ISO protocol stack.
`comp.protocols.kerberos`	The Kerberos authentication server.
`comp.protocols.tcp-ip`	TCP and IP network protocols.
`comp.risks`	Risks to the public from computers and users. (Moderated)
`comp.robotics`	All aspects of robots and their applications.
`comp.security.announce`	Announcements from the CERT about security. (Moderated)
`comp.simulation`	Simulation methods, problems, and uses. (Moderated)
`comp.society`	The impact of technology on society. (Moderated)
`comp.society.development`	Computer technology in developing countries.
`comp.society.privacy`	Effects of technology on privacy. (Moderated)
`comp.software-eng`	Software Engineering and related topics.
`comp.software.licensing`	Software licensing technology.
`comp.sources.acorn`	Source code-only postings for the Acorn. (Moderated)
`comp.sources.amiga`	Source code-only postings for the Amiga. (Moderated)
`comp.sources.apple2`	Source code and discussion for the Apple2. (Moderated)
`comp.sources.atari.st`	Source code-only postings for the Atari ST. (Moderated)
`comp.sources.games`	Recreational software. (Moderated)

Newsgroup	Topic of Discussion
comp.sources.hp48	Programs for the HP48 and HP28 calculators. (Moderated)
comp.sources.mac	Software for the Apple Macintosh. (Moderated)
comp.sources.misc	Posting of software. (Moderated)
comp.sources.reviewed	Source code evaluated by peer review. (Moderated)
comp.sources.sun	Software for Sun workstations. (Moderated)
comp.sources.unix	Postings of complete, UNIX-oriented sources. (Moderated)
comp.sources.wanted	Requests for software and fixes.
comp.sources.x	Software for the X windows system. (Moderated)
comp.specification	Languages and methodologies for formal specification.
comp.speech	Research and applications in speech science and technology.
comp.std.c	C language standards.
comp.std.c++	C++ language, library, and standards.
comp.std.internat	International standards.
comp.std.unix	The P1003 committee on UNIX. (Moderated)
comp.sys.acorn	Acorn and ARM-based computers.
comp.sys.amiga.announce	Announcements about the Amiga. (Moderated)
comp.sys.amiga.applications	Miscellaneous applications.
comp.sys.amiga.audio	Music, MIDI, speech synthesis, and other sounds.

B

Newsgroup	Topic of Discussion
`comp.sys.amiga.games`	Games for the Commodore Amiga.
`comp.sys.amiga.hardware`	Amiga computer hardware, Q&A, reviews, and so on.
`comp.sys.amiga.multimedia`	Amiga animations, video, and multimedia.
`comp.sys.amiga.programmer`	Amiga codes.
`comp.sys.amiga.reviews`	Reviews of Amiga software and hardware. (Moderated)
`comp.sys.apollo`	Apollo computer systems.
`comp.sys.apple2`	Apple II micros.
`comp.sys.convex`	Convex computer systems hardware and software.
`comp.sys.dec`	DEC systems.
`comp.sys.encore`	Encore's MultiMax computers.
`comp.sys.handhelds`	Handheld computers and programmable calculators.
`comp.sys.hp48`	Hewlett-Packard's HP48 and HP28 calculators.
`comp.sys.ibm.pc.games`	Games for IBM PCs and compatibles.
`comp.sys.ibm.pc.hardware`	XT/AT/EISA hardware from any vendor.
`comp.sys.ibm.pc.misc`	IBM personal computers.
`comp.sys.intel`	Intel systems and parts.
`comp.sys.laptops`	Laptop (portable) computers.
`comp.sys.mac.announce`	Important notices for Macintosh users. (Moderated)
`comp.sys.mac.apps`	Macintosh applications.

Newsgroup	Topic of Discussion
comp.sys.mac.comm	Macintosh communications.
comp.sys.mac.databases	Database systems for the Apple Macintosh.
comp.sys.mac.games	Games on the Macintosh.
comp.sys.mac.hardware	Macintosh hardware.
comp.sys.mac.hypercard	The Macintosh Hypercard: information and uses.
comp.sys.mac.oop.misc	Object-oriented programming issues on the Mac.
comp.sys.mac.programmer	Apple Macintosh programming.
comp.sys.mac.system	Macintosh system software.
comp.sys.mac.wanted	Postings of "I want XYZ for my Mac."
comp.sys.mentor	Mentor Graphics products and the Silicon Compiler System.
comp.sys.mips	Systems based on MIPS chips.
comp.sys.next.announce	Announcements related to the NeXT computer system. (Moderated)
comp.sys.next.bugs	NeXT bugs.
comp.sys.next.hardware	The physical aspects of NeXT computers.
comp.sys.next.programmer	NeXT-related programming issues.
comp.sys.next.software	Function, use, and availability of NeXT programs.
comp.sys.pyramid	Pyramid 90x computers.
comp.sys.ridge	Ridge 32 computers and ROS.
comp.sys.sequent	Sequent systems: balance and symmetry.

B

A Sampling of Current Usenet Groups

Newsgroup	Topic of Discussion
comp.sys.sgi.admin	System administration on Silicon Graphics's Irises.
comp.sys.sgi.announce	Announcements for the SGI community. (Moderated)
comp.sys.sgi.apps	Applications that run on the Iris.
comp.sys.sgi.graphics	Graphics packages and issues on SGI machines.
comp.sys.sgi.hardware	Base systems and peripherals for Iris computers.
comp.sys.sun.admin	Sun system administration issues and questions.
comp.sys.sun.announce	Sun announcements and Sunergy mailings. (Moderated)
comp.sys.sun.apps	Software applications for Sun computer systems.
comp.sys.sun.hardware	Sun Microsystems hardware.
comp.sys.super	Supercomputers.
comp.terminals	All sorts of terminals.
comp.text	Text processing issues and methods.
comp.text.frame	Desktop publishing with FrameMaker.
comp.text.interleaf	Applications and use of Interleaf software.
comp.text.sgml	ISO 8879 SGML, structured documents, and markup languages.
comp.text.tex	The TeX and LaTeX systems and macros.
comp.theory.info-retrieval	Information Retrieval topics. (Moderated)

Newsgroup	Topic of Discussion
comp.unix.admin	Administering a UNIX-based system.
comp.unix.aix	IBM's version of UNIX.
comp.unix.aux	The version of UNIX for Apple Macintosh II computers.
comp.unix.bsd	Berkeley Software Distribution UNIX.
comp.unix.internals	Hacking UNIX internals.
comp.unix.programmer	Q&A for people programming under UNIX.
comp.unix.questions	UNIX neophytes group.
comp.unix.shell	Using and programming the UNIX shell.
comp.unix.solaris	The Solaris operating system.
comp.unix.sys5.r4	System V Release 4.
comp.unix.ultrix	DEC's Ultrix.
comp.unix.wizards	Questions for only true UNIX wizards.
comp.virus	Computer viruses and security. (Moderated)
comp.windows.interviews	The InterViews object-oriented windowing system.
comp.windows.x.apps	Getting and using, not programming, applications for X.
comp.windows.x.motif	The Motif GUI for the X Window System.
comp.windows.x.pex	The PHIGS extension of the X Window System.
ddn.newsletter	The DDN Newsletter from NIC.DDN.MIL. (Moderated)

B

A Sampling of Current Usenet Groups

Newsgroup	Topic of Discussion
gnu.announce	Status and announcements from the GNU project. (Moderated)
gnu.chess	Announcements about the GNU Chess program.
gnu.emacs.announce	Announcements about GNU EMACS. (Moderated)
gnu.emacs.gnus	News reading under GNU EMACS using GNUS (in English).
gnu.emacs.help	EMACS user queries and answers.
gnu.emacs.sources	C and Lisp source code for GNU EMACS.
gnu.g++.announce	Announcements about the GNU C++ Compiler. (Moderated)
gnu.gcc.announce	The GNU C Compiler. (Moderated)
gnu.gcc.help	GNU C Compiler (gcc) user queries and answers.
gnu.misc.discuss	GNU and freed software.
ieee.rab.announce	Regional Activities Board announcements.
ieee.region1	Region 1 announcements.
ieee.tab.announce	Technical Activities Board announcements.
ieee.tcos	The TCOS newsletter. (Moderated)
ieee.usab.announce	USAB announcements.
ieee.usab.general	USAB.
k12.chat.elementary	Informal discussion among students in grades K-5.
k12.chat.junior	Informal discussion among students in grades 6-8.

Newsgroup	Topic of Discussion
k12.chat.senior	Informal discussion among high school students.
k12.chat.teacher	Informal discussion among teachers of grades K-12.
k12.ed.art	Art curriculum for K-12 education.
k12.ed.business	Business education curriculum for grades K-12.
k12.ed.comp.literacy	Teaching computer literacy in grades K-12.
k12.ed.health-pe	Health and physical education curriculum for grades K-12.
k12.ed.life-skills	Home economics and career education for K-12 education.
k12.ed.math	Mathematics curriculum for K-12 education.
k12.ed.music	Music and performing arts curriculum for K-12 education.
k12.ed.science	Science curriculum for K-12 education.
k12.ed.soc-studies	Social studies and history curriculum for K-12 education.
k12.ed.special	K-12 education for students with handicaps or special needs.
misc.answers	Periodic USENET articles. (Moderated)
misc.books.technical	Books about technical topics.
misc.consumers	Consumer interests, product reviews, and so on.
misc.education	The educational system.
misc.entrepreneurs	Operating a business.

B

Newsgroup	Topic of Discussion
`misc.fitness`	Physical fitness, exercise, and so on.
`misc.forsale`	Short, tasteful postings about items for sale.
`misc.forsale.computers.mac`	Apple Macintosh-related computer items for sale.
`misc.forsale.computers.pc-clone`	IBM PC-related computer items.
`misc.forsale.computers.workstation`	Workstation-related computer items.
`misc.handicap`	Items of interest for/about the handicapped. (Moderated)
`misc.headlines`	Current interest: drug testing, terrorism, and so on.
`misc.health.alternative`	Alternative, complementary, and holistic health care.
`misc.jobs.contract`	Contract labor.
`misc.jobs.offered`	Announcements of positions available.
`misc.jobs.resumes`	Postings of resumes and situation-wanted articles.
`misc.kids`	Children, their behavior, and their activities.
`misc.writing`	Writing.
`news.admin.policy`	Policy issues of USENET.
`news.announce.conferences`	Calls for papers and conference announcements. (Moderated)
`news.announce.important`	General announcements. (Moderated)
`news.announce.newgroups`	Calls for new groups and announcements of same. (Moderated)
`news.announce.newusers`	Explanatory postings for new users. (Moderated)

Newsgroup	Topic of Discussion
news.answers	USENET articles. (Moderated)
news.groups	Newsgroups.
news.newsites	Postings of new-site announcements.
news.newusers.questions	Q&A for users new to the Usenet.
rec.antiques	Antiques and vintage items.
rec.aquaria	Keeping fish and aquaria as a hobby.
rec.arts.animation	Various kinds of animation.
rec.arts.anime	Japanese animation.
rec.arts.bodyart	Tattoos and other body decoration.
rec.arts.books	Books of all genres and the publishing industry.
rec.arts.cinema	The art of cinema. (Moderated)
rec.arts.dance	Any aspects of dance not covered in another newsgroup.
rec.arts.disney	Disney-related subjects.
rec.arts.drwho	Dr. Who.
rec.arts.erotica	Erotic fiction and verse. (Moderated)
rec.arts.int-fiction	Interactive fiction.
rec.arts.manga	All aspects of the Japanese storytelling art form.
rec.arts.movies	Movies and moviemaking.
rec.arts.movies.reviews	Reviews of movies. (Moderated)
rec.arts.poems	Posting of poems.
rec.arts.sf.announce	Major announcements of the SF world. (Moderated)
rec.arts.sf.movies	SF motion pictures.
rec.arts.sf.reviews	Reviews of science fiction/fantasy/ horror works. (Moderated)

B

Newsgroup	Topic of Discussion
rec.arts.sf.tv	General television SF.
rec.arts.sf.written	Written science fiction and fantasy.
rec.arts.startrek.current	New Star Trek shows, movies, and books.
rec.arts.startrek.info	Information about the universe of Star Trek. (Moderated)
rec.arts.startrek.reviews	Reviews of Star Trek books, episodes, films, and so on. (Moderated)
rec.arts.startrek.tech	Star Trek's depiction of future technologies.
rec.arts.theatre	All aspects of stage work and theatre.
rec.arts.tv	Television, its history, and past and current shows.
rec.arts.tv.soaps	Postings about soap operas.
rec.audio	High-fidelity audio.
rec.autos.antique	All aspects of automobiles over 25 years old.
rec.aviation.announce	Events of interest to the aviation community. (Moderated)
rec.backcountry	Activities in the great outdoors.
rec.bicycles.marketplace	Buying, selling, and reviewing items for cycling.
rec.bicycles.racing	Bicycle racing techniques, rules, and results.
rec.birds	Bird watching.
rec.boats	Boating.
rec.climbing	Climbing techniques, competition announcements, and so on.
rec.collecting	Collecting.

Newsgroup	Topic of Discussion
rec.crafts.brewing	The art of making beers and meads.
rec.crafts.metalworking	All aspects of working with metal.
rec.crafts.textiles	Sewing, weaving, knitting, and other fiber arts.
rec.equestrian	Things equestrian.
rec.folk-dancing	Folk dances, dancers, and dancing.
rec.food.cooking	Food, cooking, cookbooks, and recipes.
rec.food.drink	Wines and spirits.
rec.food.recipes	Recipes for interesting food and drink. (Moderated)
rec.food.veg	Vegetarians.
rec.gambling	Articles on games of chance and betting.
rec.games.backgammon	Backgammon.
rec.games.board	Board games.
rec.games.bridge	Bridge.
rec.games.chess	Chess and computer chess.
rec.games.design	Game design-related issues.
rec.games.diplomacy	The conquest game Diplomacy.
rec.games.empire	Empire.
rec.games.frp.announce	Announcements of happenings in the role-playing world. (Moderated)
rec.games.frp.archives	Archivable fantasy stories and other projects. (Moderated)
rec.games.go	Go.
rec.games.mud.announce	Informational articles about multiuser dungeons. (Moderated)

B

Newsgroup	Topic of Discussion
`rec.games.mud.tiny`	Tiny muds, such as MUSH, MUSE, and MOO.
`rec.games.netrek`	The X window system game Netrek (XtrekII).
`rec.games.pinball`	Pinball-related issues.
`rec.games.programmer`	Adventure game programming.
`rec.games.trivia`	Trivia.
`rec.games.video`	Video games.
`rec.games.xtank.programmer`	Coding the Xtank game and its robots.
`rec.gardens`	Gardening methods and results.
`rec.guns`	Firearms. (Moderated)
`rec.heraldry`	Coats of arms.
`rec.humor.d`	The content of `rec.humor` articles.
`rec.humor.funny`	Jokes that are funny (in the moderator's opinion). (Moderated)
`rec.hunting`	Hunting. (Moderated)
`rec.juggling`	Juggling techniques, equipment, and events.
`rec.kites`	Kites and kiting.
`rec.martial-arts`	Martial arts forms.
`rec.models.railroad`	Model railroads of all scales.
`rec.models.rockets`	Model rockets.
`rec.motorcycles`	Motorcycles and related products and laws.
`rec.music.afro-latin`	Music with Afro-Latin, African, and Latin influences.
`rec.music.bluenote`	Discussion of jazz, blues, and related types of music.

Newsgroup	Topic of Discussion
rec.music.christian	Christian music, both contemporary and traditional.
rec.music.classical	Classical music.
rec.music.country.western	Country and Western music, performers, performances, and so on.
rec.music.dylan	Bob Dylan's works and music.
rec.music.early	Preclassical European music.
rec.music.folk	Folk music of various sorts.
rec.music.funky	Funk, rap, hip-hop, house, soul, r&b, and related music.
rec.music.gaffa	Kate Bush and other alternative musicians. (Moderated)
rec.music.gdead	The Grateful Dead.
rec.music.indian.classical	Hindustani and Carnatic Indian classical music.
rec.music.industrial	All industrial-related music styles.
rec.music.newage	New Age music.
rec.music.reggae	The melodies of the Caribbean.
rec.music.reviews	Reviews of music of all genres and media. (Moderated)
rec.music.video	Music videos and music video software.
rec.nude	Naturist/nudist activities.
rec.outdoors.fishing	All aspects of sport and commercial fishing.
rec.pets	Pets, pet care, and household animals in general.
rec.pets.birds	The culture and care of indoor birds.
rec.pets.cats	Domestic cats.

B

Newsgroup	Topic of Discussion
rec.pets.dogs	Any and all subjects relating to dogs as pets.
rec.pets.herp	Reptiles, amphibians, and other exotic vivarium pets.
rec.photo	Photography.
rec.puzzles	Puzzles, problems, and quizzes.
rec.puzzles.crosswords	Making and playing gridded word puzzles.
rec.pyrotechnics	Fireworks, rocketry, safety, and other topics.
rec.radio.amateur.packet	Packet radio setups.
rec.radio.broadcasting	Local area broadcast radio. (Moderated)
rec.radio.shortwave	Shortwave radio.
rec.railroad	Real and model trains.
rec.roller-coaster	Roller coasters and other amusement park rides.
rec.running	Running for enjoyment, sport, exercise, and so on.
rec.scouting	Scouting youth organizations worldwide.
rec.scuba	SCUBA diving.
rec.skate	Ice skating and roller skating.
rec.skiing	Snow skiing.
rec.skydiving	Skydiving.
rec.sport.baseball	Baseball.
rec.sport.basketball.college	Hoops on the collegiate level.
rec.sport.basketball.pro	Professional basketball.

SAMS
Learning
Center
Sams
SAMS
PUBLISHING

Newsgroup	Topic of Discussion
rec.sport.cricket	The sport of cricket.
rec.sport.fencing	All aspects of swordplay.
rec.sport.football.australian	Discussion of Australian (rules) football.
rec.sport.football.college	American college football.
rec.sport.football.pro	American professional football.
rec.sport.golf	All aspects of golfing.
rec.sport.hockey	Ice hockey.
rec.sport.olympics	All aspects of the Olympic Games.
rec.sport.paintball	The survival game paintball.
rec.sport.pro-wrestling	Professional wrestling.
rec.sport.rowing	Crew for competition or fitness.
rec.sport.rugby	The game of rugby.
rec.sport.soccer	Soccer (association football).
rec.sport.swimming	Training for and competing in swimming events.
rec.sport.table-tennis	Table tennis (Ping Pong).
rec.sport.tennis	Tennis.
rec.sport.triathlon	Multievent sports.
rec.sport.volleyball	Volleyball.
rec.travel	Traveling all over the world.
rec.video	Video and video components.
rec.windsurfing	Riding the waves as a hobby.
rec.woodworking	Woodworking.
sci.aeronautics	The science of aeronautics and related technology.
sci.answers	USENET articles. (Moderated)

B

Newsgroup	Topic of Discussion
sci.anthropology	All aspects of studying humankind.
sci.archaeology	Studying antiquities of the world.
sci.astro	Astronomy discussions and information.
sci.astro.fits	Issues related to the Flexible Image Transport System.
sci.astro.hubble	Processing Hubble Space Telescope data. (Moderated)
sci.bio	Biology and related sciences.
sci.bio.technology	Any topic relating to biotechnology.
sci.chem	Chemistry and related sciences.
sci.chem.organomet	Organometallic chemistry.
sci.cognitive	Perception, memory, judgment, and reasoning.
sci.comp-aided	Computers as tools in scientific research.
sci.cryonics	Theory and practice of biostasis, suspended animation.
sci.crypt	Methods of data en/decryption.
sci.econ	The science of economics.
sci.edu	The science of education.
sci.electronics	Circuits, theory, and electrons.
sci.energy	Discussions about energy, science, and technology.
sci.engr	Technical discussions about engineering tasks.
sci.engr.biomed	Biomedical engineering.
sci.engr.chem	All aspects of chemical engineering.

Newsgroup	Topic of Discussion
sci.engr.civil	Civil engineering.
sci.environment	The environment and ecology.
sci.fractals	Objects of nonintegral dimension and other chaos.
sci.geo.fluids	Geophysical fluid dynamics.
sci.geo.geology	Solid earth sciences.
sci.geo.meteorology	Meteorology and related topics.
sci.logic	Logic—math, philosophy, and computational aspects.
sci.materials	All aspects of materials engineering.
sci.math.num-analysis	Numerical analysis.
sci.math.research	Current mathematical research. (Moderated)
sci.math.stat	Statistics.
sci.math.symbolic	Symbolic algebra.
sci.med.aids	AIDS: treatment, pathology/biology of HIV, prevention. (Moderated)
sci.med.dentistry	Dental topics; all about teeth.
sci.med.nutrition	Physiological impacts of diet.
sci.med.occupational	Preventing, detecting, and treating occupational injuries.
sci.military	Discussion about science and the military. (Moderated)
sci.misc	Scientific subjects.
sci.nanotech	Self-reproducing molecular-scale machines. (Moderated)
sci.optics	The science of optics.
sci.physics.fusion	Info on fusion, especially cold fusion.

B

A Sampling of Current Usenet Groups

Newsgroup	Topic of Discussion
`sci.physics.research`	Current physics research. (Moderated)
`sci.psychology`	Topics related to psychology.
`sci.skeptic`	Pseudo-science.
`sci.space`	Space, space programs, space-related research, and so on.
`sci.space.news`	Announcements of space-related news items. (Moderated)
`sci.space.shuttle`	The space shuttle and the STS program.
`soc.bi`	Bisexuality.
`soc.college`	College, college activities, campus life, and so on.
`soc.college.gradinfo`	Information about graduate schools.
`soc.couples`	Couples (cf. `soc.singles`).
`soc.culture.afghanistan`	The Afghan society.
`soc.culture.african`	Africa and things African.
`soc.culture.african.american`	African-American issues.
`soc.culture.arabic`	Technological and cultural issues (except politics).
`soc.culture.asean`	Countries of the Association of SE Asian Nations.
`soc.culture.asian.american`	Issues about Asian-Americans.
`soc.culture.australian`	Australian culture and society.
`soc.culture.baltics`	People of the Baltic states.
`soc.culture.bangladesh`	Issues about Bangladesh.
`soc.culture.bosna-herzgvna`	The independent state of Bosnia-Herzegovina.

Newsgroup	Topic of Discussion
soc.culture.brazil	The people and country of Brazil.
soc.culture.british	Issues about Britain and those of British descent.
soc.culture.bulgaria	Bulgarian society.
soc.culture.canada	Canada and its people.
soc.culture.caribbean	Life in the Caribbean.
soc.culture.celtic	Irish, Scottish, Breton, Cornish, Manx, and Welsh culture.
soc.culture.china	China and Chinese culture.
soc.culture.croatia	The lives of people of Croatia.
soc.culture.czecho-slovak	Bohemian, Slovak, Moravian, and Silesian life.
soc.culture.europe	Discussing all aspects of all-European society.
soc.culture.filipino	The Filipino culture.
soc.culture.french	French culture and history.
soc.culture.german	German culture and history.
soc.culture.greek	Greek culture and history.
soc.culture.hongkong	Hong Kong.
soc.culture.indian	India and things Indian.
soc.culture.iranian	Discussions about Iran and things Iranian/Persian.
soc.culture.italian	The Italian people and their culture.
soc.culture.japan	Everything Japanese, except the Japanese language.
soc.culture.korean	Korea and things Korean.
soc.culture.latin-america	Topics about Latin-America.
soc.culture.lebanon	Things Lebanese.

B

Newsgroup	Topic of Discussion
`soc.culture.magyar`	The Hungarian people and their culture.
`soc.culture.malaysia`	Malaysian society.
`soc.culture.mexican`	Mexico's society.
`soc.culture.nepal`	Discussion of people and things in and from Nepal.
`soc.culture.netherlands`	People from the Netherlands and Belgium.
`soc.culture.new-zealand`	Topics related to New Zealand.
`soc.culture.nordic`	Nordic culture.
`soc.culture.pakistan`	Pakistani culture.
`soc.culture.polish`	Polish culture, Polish past, and Polish politics.
`soc.culture.portuguese`	The people of Portugal.
`soc.culture.romanian`	Romanian and Moldavian people.
`soc.culture.singapore`	The past, present, and future of Singapore.
`soc.culture.soviet`	Topics relating to Russian or Soviet culture.
`soc.culture.spain`	Spanish culture.
`soc.culture.sri-lanka`	Things and people from Sri Lanka.
`soc.culture.taiwan`	Things Taiwanese.
`soc.culture.tamil`	Tamil language, history, and culture.
`soc.culture.thai`	Thai people and their culture.
`soc.culture.turkish`	Discussion about things Turkish.
`soc.culture.usa`	The culture of the United States of America.
`soc.culture.vietnamese`	Vietnamese culture.

Newsgroup	Topic of Discussion
soc.culture.yugoslavia	Yugoslavia and its people.
soc.feminism	Feminism and feminist issues. (Moderated)
soc.men	Issues related to men, their problems, and relationships.
soc.motss	Issues pertaining to homosexuality.
soc.net-people	Announcements, requests, and so on, about people on the net.
soc.politics	Political problems, systems, solutions. (Moderated)
soc.politics.arms-d	Arms. (Moderated)
soc.singles	Single people, their activities, and so on.
soc.veterans	Social issues relating to military veterans.
soc.women	Issues related to women, their problems, and relationships.
talk.abortion	Abortion.
talk.bizarre	The unusual, bizarre, curious, and often stupid.
talk.environment	The state of the environment and what to do about it.
talk.origins	Evolution versus creationism. (This is sometimes hot!)
talk.politics.china	Discussion of political issues related to China.
talk.politics.drugs	The politics of drug issues.
talk.politics.guns	The politics of firearm ownership and (mis)use.

B

Newsgroup	Topic of Discussion
`talk.politics.medicine`	The politics and ethics involved with health care.
`talk.politics.mideast`	Middle Eastern events.
`talk.rumors`	Rumors.

Answers

C

Not every question has an easy answer, particularly the questions that require you to explore some of the organization and capabilities of your system. The answers provided here are to the questions that do have specific solutions. After all, ultimately no one has the answer to *all* questions anyway!

Chapter 1, "What Is This UNIX Stuff?"

1. The three *multi-*s are multiuser, multitasking, and multichoice.

2. UNIX is much more like a grid of streets.

3. The most important thing to remember when you're done using a multiuser system is to *log off.*

Chapter 2, "Getting onto the System and Using the Command Line"

1. If you had the same account name, the system couldn't distinguish between the two of you at login time. You can, however, share a user ID, though files created by both users will be owned by the user listed first in /etc/passwd.

2. These are good passwords: 4myMUM, Blk&Blu, 2cool., and j j kim.

3. The whoami command is different from the who command: specifying who am i has the regular who command list some information for you. Sometimes you want one, and other times the other. The most valuable on a new system is who am i because of its greater output.

4. The three are who, w, and users. The first offers a list of users and what lines they're using, the second adds what commands are in use, and the third is a succinct format that takes up a lot less space.

5. The w command also lists "uptime," which is a good way of seeing how often a system crashes. If every time you log in to the system you discover it's been rebooted that day, then beware!

7. July 4, 1997, is a Friday. July 4, 1776, was a Thursday.

Chapter 3, "Moving About in the File System"

1. The public library is usually organized in a hierarchical fashion based on the Dewey Decimal system.

2. These are hidden: `.test`, `.cshrc`, `../`, `.dot.`, and `.HiMom`.

3. The `.cshrc` is from `csh`, `.rnsoft` is from `rn`, and `.exrc` is from `ex` (and `vi`, for that matter). The `.print` could be from any of a number of programs, and so could `.letter`, `.tmp334`, and the `.excel/` directory. The `.vi-expert` is probably from the `vi` program.

4. The only absolute file name in the list is `/home/taylor/business/California`.

5. The `pwd` does not accept any command arguments: it simply tells you where you are. The other two commands, `cd` and `env`, have default actions (that is, they do something useful if you don't specify an argument), but they *do* accept arguments to change their behavior.

Chapter 4, "Listing Files and Disks"

2. There are, admittedly, many different ways to sort files. For a small number, sorting across, sorting down, and sorting by different dates can be a bit of a wash, but if you try looking at a directory with hundreds of files, you can quickly imagine a scenario where being able to list files across or down, or perhaps by modification time, could be very helpful.

4. The `du -s ..` command will generate a summary of the disk usage of all directories in the directory tree one level higher than your own. If you feed that output to `sort`, in fact, you can easily find out who uses the most disk space (try `du -s .. ¦ sort`).

Chapter 5, "Ownership and Permissions"

1. **r--rw-r--**   You want people in your group to be able to modify the contents of the file, but you don't want to touch it yourself other than for reading. (I can't think of a situation where this would be useful. Can you?)

   r--r--rw-   Similarly, this would allow you to have a file that anyone *not* in your group could modify.

   rw--w--w-   This is a common format for a log file: as the owner of the file, you would be able to see what's inside, and it's secure from other eyes, though everyone can actually add information to it.

   -w--w--w-   This is the slightly more secure version of the log file: no one can see what's inside!

   rwxr-xr-x   The most common permission for directories or executable files, this offers the owner all permissions, and everyone else read and execute permission, but no one (except the owner) can alter it.

   r-x--x--x   Finally, this is how you might set up an executable program so others can use it but cannot poke about with various UNIX utilities to learn more about it.

2.

permission	binary equivalent	numeric equivalent
r--rw-r--	100 110 100	464
r--r--rw-	100 100 110	446
rw--w--w-	110 010 010	622
-w--w--w-	010 010 010	222
rwxr-xr-x	111 101 101	755
r-x--x--x	101 001 001	511

3.

umask	default new file permissions
007	rw-rw----
077	rw-------
777	---------
111	rw-rw-rw-
222	r--r--r--
733	---r--r--
272	r-----r--
544	-w--w--w-
754	----w--w-

5. You would only be able to modify the contents of the directory `viewer`, though you'd be able to peruse the directory `shakes` also.

Chapter 6, "Creating, Moving, and Destroying"

1. The `cp` command creates a second copy of the specified file, whereas `mv` moves the existing file from one place (or one name) to another.

2. The best choice would be `cp` so that you leave the installation disk intact.

3. DOS excludes `MOVE` because, presumably, the designers realize that you can always simulate a `MOVE` by the sequence of `COPY` and `DELETE`.

5. The `rmdir` command is *much* safer because it lets you only remove empty directories and will warn if files are within the directory.

6. With the `-f` flag, `rm` is transformed from a "killer for hire" to a mass murderer: it will remove any files it can from the specified list of files, without any warning and without any messages. To add the `-r` flag for a recursive deletion is exceptionally dangerous because the program will then *silently* remove any and all files and directories below the specified point without a single message.

Chapter 7, "Looking into Files"

1. The `file` command ignores filenames because different people might prefer different notational conventions for their files (like `*.doc` or `*.txt` for text files), but by analyzing the contents of the file, the program always reports appropriate information.

3. The `file` command would probably be a bit more accurate by checking more of the file, but the problem is that the difficulty of recognizing and understanding the first ten lines, for example, of all files could be insurmountably difficult. Keeping with the desire to have a small program, the amount `file` checks is probably ideal.

4. The name `cat` comes from "concatenate."

5. The command `cat LISTS ¦ more` is functionally identical to `more LISTS`, and `more LISTS ¦ pg` is identical to `pg LISTS`.

6. Either more or pg would work fine because they both have searching capabilities, but pg would be the better choice because you could move up and down the file to find the information desired, rather than just down.

7. Again, either more or pg would work fine because they both have searching capabilities, but pg would be the better choice because you could move up and down the file to find the information desired, rather than just down, though if it's really near the top of the file, head might be the simplest alternative.

Chapter 8, "Filters and Piping"

1. | `< file wc` | This won't work: there's nothing to feed the contents of file into. |
    | `wc file <` | This also won't work: the < is in the wrong place. |
    | `wc < file` | That's the right order! |
    | `cat file ¦ wc` | That'll work too. |
    | `cat < file ¦ wc` | That's fine. |
    | `wc ¦ cat` | That will work but it won't do what you expect: the wc program is expecting input from the console because no file was specified, and the program will simply sit there, waiting for you to type in the information required. |

4. All non-numeric values are sorted according to the default sorting order, so sorting by number on a list of words actually does the right thing!

6. The eleventh file can be found with this:

        ls -1 ¦ cat -n ¦ grep "^ *11"

   The twenty-fourth file in /etc is found with this:

        ls -1 /etc ¦ cat -n ¦ grep ^24

7. | `/tmp/*` | All files in the /tmp directory. |
    | `/tmp/*w*` | All files that contain a w. |
    | `b*e*.c` | All files that start with a b, contain an e, and end with .c |
    | `test* *hi*` | All files that either start with test or contain the pattern hi. |

Chapter 9, "Power Filters and File Redirection"

1. The Big Four are these:

   < redirect input

   << create a "here" document

   > redirect output to file

   >> append output to file

2. One way would be this:

```
cat >> MEMO
```

3. The `tee` command enables you to split the flow into multiple files. With the pipe symbol you can fit multiple commands into a pipeline. With file output redirection, you can put something into the file and save it when you're done.

4. This shows the first few lines of the `passwd` file. The first colon on each line is replaced with a space, then restored to a colon through the (useless!) `sed` command.

5. The command `sed 's/^/$ /' < testme` prepends " $ " to each line of the file `testme`.

6. The two commands perform the identical function.

7. This also implements the same function!

8. The easiest command is probably this:

```
awk '{ print NF": "$0}' inputfile ¦ sort -n
```

Chapter 10, "An Introduction to the *vi* Editor"

1. It doesn't work; `vi` doesn't know what to do after it sees the `:q` command.

3. The opposite of `D` is `d0`, which will delete text from the cursor to the *beginning* of the line.

4. They're not the same: `D` and `d$` both delete to the end of the line, but `dG` deletes to the end of the *file*.

5. Badluck   Appends dluck to the end of the previous word in
                      the file.

   Window   Inserts ndow before the beginning of the next word
                      in the file.

   blad$ Adds d$ after the second letter of the previous
                      word.

6. vi +0 test   Start on line zero.
   vi +/joe/ names   Start with the first match to the pattern
                      joe in the file.
   vi +hhjjhh   Creates a new, blank file.
   vi +:q testme   Immediately quits the editor!

Your results may vary slightly due to differences in the various versions of vi. The good
news is that the commonly used flags will work fine.

Chapter 11, "Advanced *vi* Tricks, Tools, and Techniques"

1. Replaces the first occurrence of kitten with puppy on lines one through five
   in the file.

2. 15i?**ESC**h   Inserts fifteen question marks, moving the cursor
                      back one at the very end.

   i15?**ESC**h   Inserts 15? and moves the cursor back one.

   i?**ESC**15h   Inserts a question mark and moves the cursor back
                      fifteen characters.

3. The percentile indicator tries to indicate the percentage of the file above the
   current cursor point, so it can offer different information at the beginning
   and end of the same line, though this isn't true for all versions of vi.

4. The rr and Rr**ESC** both replace the next letter with the letter *r*, whereas
   cwr**ESC** replaces the next **word** with the letter *r* and Cr**ESC** replaces the rest of
   the line with the letter *r*.

6. The !}ls command pipes the current paragraph of text to the ls command
   (which doesn't read standard input, so ls discards it, instead listing the files
   in the current directory).

Chapter 12, "An Overview of the EMACS Editor"

1. Typing ^h ^h (include a space between ^h and ^h) gets you to the EMACS help system.

2. Double ESC is the equivalent of a Meta key.

3. Quit EMACS with ^x ^c.

5. Global search and replace can be easily done with the M-x query-replace command. To avoid confirming each match, simply type ! at the prompt.

Chapter 13, "Introduction to Command Shells"

1. The ksh derives from sh, and tcsh derives from csh.

2. The chsh enables you to change your login shell, and chfn enables you to change easily the full-name entry in the password file.

4. The .login file is read once upon logging in to the system, whereas the .cshrc file is read each time the shell is invoked (that is, for each subshell too).

5. The .profile file is the sh equivalent of .login.

Chapter 14, "Getting the Most out of C Shell"

1. Use set history=30; set savehist=10.

2.
!2	repeats the who command
!w	repeats the wc command
!wh	repeats the who command
echo !1	shows the first command on the list (ls)

3. Aliases of the form alias who who -a can create what are called alias loops, wherein the shell, in trying to expand this alias, finds that it ends up in a loop expanding who to who -a repeatedly, without any way of knowing when to stop. More modern UNIX systems are smarter about this and don't fall into this trap, but you can always circumvent it by specifying the full name of the command anyway: alias who '/bin/who -a'.

4.
`alias alias who`	The shell won't let you alias `alias`.
`alias ls cp`	Bound to be confusing!
`alias copy cp -i`	A helpful one that's friendly, too.
`alias logout vi`	Sure to drive you crazy!
`alias vi logout`	Also sure to be frustrating.
`alias bye logout`	The second helpful alias.

5. `set prompt="#\! - I know lots about Unix. For example:"`

Chapter 15, "Talking to Others"

All the questions in this chapter require you to explore and experiment with the programs on your own system. Your answers will differ from what I would see on my machines.

Chapter 16, "Job Control and Finding Help for Commands"

2. There are two commands on my system to accomplish this task:
```
printmail (1u)  - format mail in a readable fashion for printing
prmail (1)      - print out mail in the post office
```

6. The `jobs` command shows only programs that are running within the current shell, whereas `ps` shows you all jobs that are running on the system, notably including the login shell itself.

Chapter 17, "Printing in the UNIX Environment"

3. Use `man -k` with caution on this one. When I looked for commands related to printing, I found 47 matches, even though most of them weren't related to printing. Here's a rule of thumb: always try a couple of different words when key-word matching to ensure you see what you want.

4. These are the three:
```
lpr dickens.note
cat dickens.note | lpr
lpr < dickens.note
```

6. The two answers are these:
```
pr -h "A Tale of Two Cities" < dickens.note
pr +2 dickens.note
```

Chapter 18, "Searching for Information and Files"

1. The answers are these: `hot.*cold`, `cat[^s]`, and `[0-9]*`.

2. Use either grep `hot*cold` or grep `hot ¦ grep cold`.

3. **grep -v cabana**, **egrep -v '(jazz¦funk)'**, and, for variety: **cat << EOF ¦**
   fgrep -f - file
   jazz
   funk
   disco
   blues
   ska
   EOF

4. One is as shown in the preceding answer. The other way, one that's perhaps a bit easier, is this: egrep `'jazz|funk|disco|blues|ska'`.

5. `find . -type f -print ¦ wc -l`.

6. The first you can do with `find . -name "*abc*" -print`. The second is a bit more tricky, but I use this:
```
find . -type f -print ¦ xargs grep abc
```

Chapter 19, "Connecting with Remote UNIX Systems"

2. `louey!sheep!joe`
   `louey!ugly!aphrod!nancy`
   `huey!poodle!pookie`
   `huey!mutt!janus!twoface`

   Note that any of these can be addressed in a variety of ways. Some systems might connect more frequently than others, making some addresses *faster* than others.

3. huey!mutt!janus!remote
   huey!poodle!tor!aphrod!remote
   dewey!sheep!poodle!janus!remote
   louey!ugly!aphrod!remote

Chapter 20, "Programming in C on a UNIX System"

1. The `:tag` will move the cursor to a specific tag, and `^]` moves to the definition of the current routine, if known.

2. The `%` command matches parentheses and curly braces.

3. You want the `-c` flag to `cc`.

4. The `-g` flag to `cc` prepares the system for debugging.

5. The `Makefile` contains all the rules needed for the `make` utility to work correctly.

6. The `lint` command checks the quality and robustness of your code, `cb` improves the indenting style, and `cxref` creates a cross reference.

Chapter 21, "The Great Beyond: The Internet"

1. Both `gatekeeper.dec.com` and `novell.com` have copies of the `tin` newsreading program.

2. `LISP` stands for LISt Processor.

3. *Blade Runner* was directed by Ridley Scott and was released in 1982. It's one of my favorite films of the genre and shows a lethal Daryl Hannah, too!

5. plant biology   `bionet.plants`
   laser printers   `comp.laser-printers`
   UNIX questions   `comp.unix.questions`
   anthropology   `sci.anthropology`

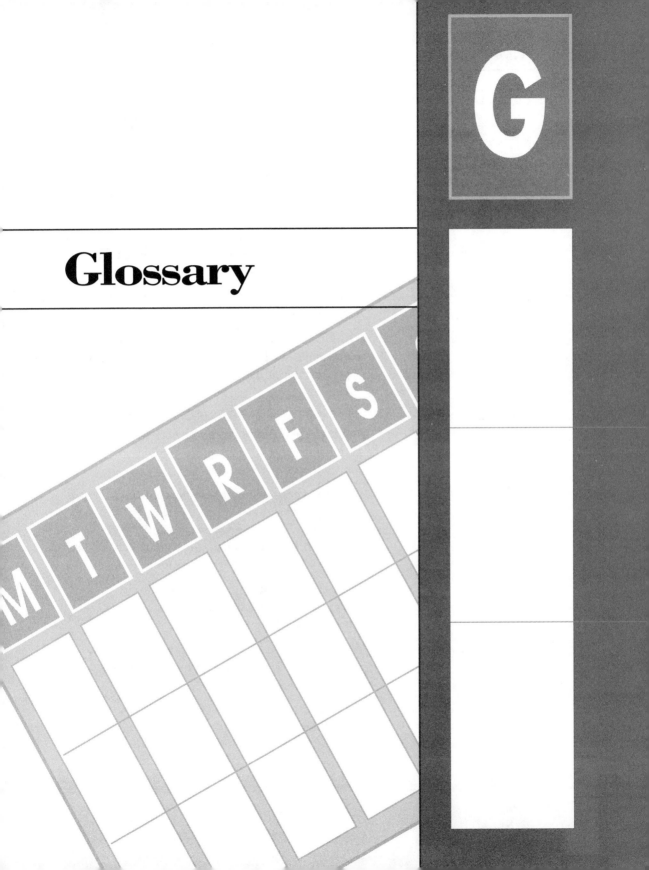

Glossary

G

absolute filename	Any filename that begins with a leading slash (/). These always uniquely describe a single file in the file system.
access permission	The set of accesses (read, write, and execute) allowed for each of the three classes of users (owner, group, and everyone else) for each file or directory on the system.
account	This is the official one-word name by which the UNIX system knows you.
account name	This is the official one-word name by which the UNIX system knows you.
addresses	Used in sed notation to specify the range over which a command should be applied. The special character . represents the current line and $ represents the last line.
addressing commands	The set of vi commands that allow you to specify what type of object you want to work with. The d commands serve as an example: dw means *delete word*, and db means *delete the previous word*.
arguments	Not any type of domestic dispute, arguments are the set of options and filenames specified to UNIX commands. When you use a command like vi test.c, all words other than the command name itself (vi) are arguments, or parameters to the program.
background job	A job that's running but not attached to the terminal or keyboard, or a running program that's not in the foreground.
binary	A file format that is intended for the computer to work with directly rather than for humans to peruse. See also *executable*.
blind carbon copy	An exact copy of a message, sent without the awareness of the original recipient.

block	At its most fundamental, a block is like a sheet of information in the virtual notebook that represents the disk. A disk is typically composed of many tens, or hundreds, of thousands of blocks of information, each 512 bytes in size. You might also read the explanation of *i-node* to learn more about how disks are structured in UNIX.
block special device	A device driver that controls block-oriented peripherals. A hard disk, for example, is a peripheral that works by reading and writing blocks of information (as distinguished from a *character special device*).
bookmark	A saved gopher menu item through which you can easily build your own custom gopher information screens.
carbon copy	An exact copy of a message sent to other people. Each recipient can see the names of all other recipients on the distribution list.
case insensitive	Something that treats upper- and lowercase letters identically, especially in searching. See *case sensitive*.
case sensitive	As you might know from working with other computer systems or typewriters, English has UPPERCASE and lowercase letters, meaning that in everyday language *CAT* and *cat* are two different words in appearance. They become the same word, however, if you're ignoring the case of each letter, which is when you're *case insensitive*. The opposite of this is *case sensitive*, when *CAT* and *cat* are considered two different words, not the same word.
character special device	A device driver that controls a character-oriented peripheral. Your keyboard and display are both character-oriented devices, sending and displaying information on a character-by-character basis.
colon commands	The vi commands that begin with a colon, usually used for file manipulation.

column-first order	When you have a list of items that are listed in columns and span multiple lines, column-first order is a sorting strategy in which items are sorted so that the items are in alphabetical order down the first column, then resume at the top of the second column, going down, then the third column, and so on. The alternative strategy is *row-first order.*
command	Each program in UNIX is also known as a command: the two words are interchangeable.
command alias	A shorthand command mapping, with which you can define new command names that are *aliases* of other commands or sequences of commands. This is helpful for renaming commands so that you can remember them or for having certain flags added by default.
command history	A mechanism for remembering what commands you have entered already and for repeating them without having to enter them again.
command mode	The default mode of vi, to which you can return by pressing ESC at any time.
command number	The unique number by which the shell indexes all commands. You can place this number in your prompt using \! and use it with the history mechanism as !command-number.
control key	The term for various combinations of the Control key with another key for commands. You hold down the Control key while you press the other key. Control-U is the same as ^u.
control key notation	A notational convention in UNIX that denotes the use of a *control key.* There are three common conventions: Ctrl-C, ^c, and C-C all denote the Control-C character, produced by pressing the Control key (labeled Control or Ctrl on your keyboard) and, while holding it down, pressing the C key.
control number	A unique number the C shell assigns to each background job for easy reference.

current job	The job that is currently attached to the terminal and keyboard (it's the program you're actually running and working within).
device driver	All peripherals attached to the computer are called *devices* in UNIX, and each has a control program always associated, called a device driver. Examples are the device drivers for the display, keyboard, mouse, and all hard disks.
directory separator character	On a hierarchical file system, there must be some way to specify which items are directories and which is the actual file name itself. This becomes particularly true when you're working with *absolute filenames*. In UNIX, the directory separator character is the slash (`/`), so a filename like `/tmp/testme` is easily interpreted as a file called `testme` in a directory called `tmp`.
domain name	UNIX systems on the Internet, or any other network, are assigned a domain within which they exist. This is typically the company (for example, `sun.com` for Sun Microsystems) or institution (for example, `lsu.edu` for Louisiana State University). The domain name is always the entire host address, except the hostname itself.
dot	A shorthand notation for the current directory.
dot dot	A shorthand notation for the directory one level higher up the hierarchical file system from the current location.
dot file	A configuration file used by one or more programs, these are called dot files because the first letter of the filename is a dot, as in `.profile` or `.login`. Because they're dot files, the `ls` command doesn't list them by default, making them also *hidden files* in UNIX.

dynamic linking	Though most UNIX systems require all necessary utilities and library routines (like the routines for reading information from the keyboard and displaying it to the screen) to be plugged into a program when it's built (known in UNIX parlance as *static linking*), some of the more sophisticated systems can delay this inclusion until you actually need to run the program. In this case, the utilities and libraries are linked when you start the program, and this is called *dynamic linking*.
e-mail	Electronically transmitted and received mail or messages.
end-of-file word	The word used with *here documents* to specify the end of the series of lines. By default, variables in a here document are expanded, but if the end-of-file word is quoted, all characters remain untouched.
escape sequence	A sequence of characters where ESC is the first character. A typical result of pressing a special or function key on most keyboards.
exclusion set	A set of characters that the pattern must not contain.
executable	A file that has been set up so that UNIX can run it as a program, this is also shorthand for a binary file. You also sometimes see the phrase *binary executable*, which is the same thing!
executable binary	A file in UNIX that is the result of a compilation process and that can be run directly.
file creation mask	When files are created in UNIX, they inherit a default set of access permissions. These defaults are under the control of the user and are known as the file creation mask.
file creator	On the Apple Macintosh, any application that creates a file (for example, a word processing document) records its own name as the file creator. This is then used by the Macintosh operating system to ascertain which program to launch if the file is opened by the user.

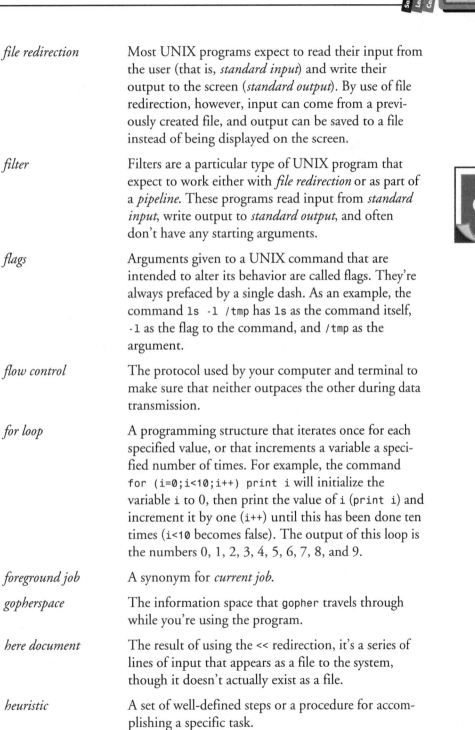

file redirection	Most UNIX programs expect to read their input from the user (that is, *standard input*) and write their output to the screen (*standard output*). By use of file redirection, however, input can come from a previously created file, and output can be saved to a file instead of being displayed on the screen.
filter	Filters are a particular type of UNIX program that expect to work either with *file redirection* or as part of a *pipeline*. These programs read input from *standard input*, write output to *standard output*, and often don't have any starting arguments.
flags	Arguments given to a UNIX command that are intended to alter its behavior are called flags. They're always prefaced by a single dash. As an example, the command ls -l /tmp has ls as the command itself, -l as the flag to the command, and /tmp as the argument.
flow control	The protocol used by your computer and terminal to make sure that neither outpaces the other during data transmission.
for loop	A programming structure that iterates once for each specified value, or that increments a variable a specified number of times. For example, the command for (i=0;i<10;i++) print i will initialize the variable i to 0, then print the value of i (print i) and increment it by one (i++) until this has been done ten times (i<10 becomes false). The output of this loop is the numbers 0, 1, 2, 3, 4, 5, 6, 7, 8, and 9.
foreground job	A synonym for *current job*.
gopherspace	The information space that gopher travels through while you're using the program.
here document	The result of using the << redirection, it's a series of lines of input that appears as a file to the system, though it doesn't actually exist as a file.
heuristic	A set of well-defined steps or a procedure for accomplishing a specific task.

hidden file	By default, the UNIX file listing command `ls` only shows files whose first letter isn't a dot (e.g., those files that aren't *dot files*). All dot files, therefore, are hidden files and you can safely ignore them without any problems.
home directory	This is your private directory and is also where you start out when you log in to the system.
hostname	UNIX computers all have unique names assigned by the local administration team. The computers I use are `limbo`, `well`, `netcom`, and `mentor`, for example. Type `hostname` to see what your system is called.
hypertext	A scheme for connecting information through *hypertext links*, this allows documents to reference other documents and information.
hypertext links	A pointer in a piece of information to other information (a definition of a term, a related document, a footnote, or something similar).
i-list	See *i-node*.
inclusion range	A range of characters that a pattern must include.
i-node	The UNIX file system is like a huge notebook full of sheets of information. Each file is like an index tab, indicating where the file starts in the notebook and how many sheets are used. The tabs are called i-nodes and the list of tabs (the index to the notebook) is the i-list.
insert mode	The `vi` mode that lets you enter text directly into a file. The `i` command starts the insert mode, and ESC exits it.
interactive program	An interactive UNIX application is one that expects the user to enter information and then responds as appropriate. The `ls` command is not interactive, but the `more` program, which displays text a screen at a time, is interactive.
job	A synonym for *process*.

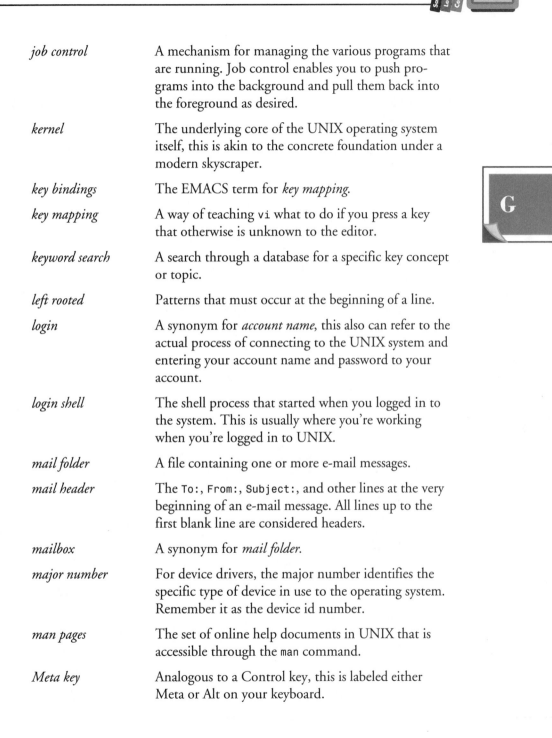
job control	A mechanism for managing the various programs that are running. Job control enables you to push programs into the background and pull them back into the foreground as desired.
kernel	The underlying core of the UNIX operating system itself, this is akin to the concrete foundation under a modern skyscraper.
key bindings	The EMACS term for *key mapping*.
key mapping	A way of teaching vi what to do if you press a key that otherwise is unknown to the editor.
keyword search	A search through a database for a specific key concept or topic.
left rooted	Patterns that must occur at the beginning of a line.
login	A synonym for *account name*, this also can refer to the actual process of connecting to the UNIX system and entering your account name and password to your account.
login shell	The shell process that started when you logged in to the system. This is usually where you're working when you're logged in to UNIX.
mail folder	A file containing one or more e-mail messages.
mail header	The To:, From:, Subject:, and other lines at the very beginning of an e-mail message. All lines up to the first blank line are considered headers.
mailbox	A synonym for *mail folder*.
major number	For device drivers, the major number identifies the specific type of device in use to the operating system. Remember it as the device id number.
man pages	The set of online help documents in UNIX that is accessible through the man command.
Meta key	Analogous to a Control key, this is labeled either Meta or Alt on your keyboard.

minor number	Once the device driver is identified to the operating system by its *major number*, the address of the device in the computer itself (that is, which card slot a peripheral card is plugged in) is indicated by its minor number.
modal	A modal program has multiple environments, or modes, that offer different capabilities. In a modal program, the Return key, for example, might do different things, depending on which mode you were in.
mode	A shorthand way of saying *permissions mode*.
modeless	A modeless program always interprets a key the same way, regardless of what the user is doing.
multitasking	A multitasking computer is one that actually can run more than one program, or task, at a time. By contrast, most personal computers lock you into a single program that you must exit before you launch another.
multiuser	Computers intended to have more than a single person working on them simultaneously are designed to support multiple users, hence "multiuser." By contrast, personal computers are almost always single-user, because someone else can't be running a program or editing a file while you are using the computer for your own work.
named EMACS command	A command in EMACS that requires you to type its name, like `query-replace`, rather than a command key or two.
newsgroup	A Usenet group focused on a particular subject or topic of conversation.
null character	Each character in UNIX has a specific value, and any character with a numeric value of zero is known as a null or null character.

password entry	For each account on the UNIX system, there is an entry in the account database known as the password file. This also contains an encrypted copy of the account password. This set of information for an individual account is known as the password entry.
pathname	UNIX is split into a variety of different directories and subdirectories, often across multiple hard disks and even multiple computers. So that the system needn't search laboriously through the entire mess each time you request a program, the set of directories you reference are stored as your search path, and the location of any specific command is known as its pathname.
permissions mode	The set of accesses (read, write, and execute) allowed for each of the three classes of users (owner, group, and everyone else) for each file or directory on the system. This is a synonym for *access permission*.
pipeline	A series of UNIX commands chained by ¦, the *pipe* symbol.
preference files	These are what *dot files* (*hidden files*) really are. They contain your individual preferences for many of the UNIX commands you use.
preserve	Ensure that a message doesn't move out of your incoming mailbox even though you've read it.
print job name	The unique name assigned to a printout by the lpr or lp command.
printer queue	The queue, or list, in which all print requests are placed for processing by the specific printer.
process	A program running within the UNIX operating system.
quoted text	A portion of a previous article that is included in the current article to give context, particularly in disagreeing with or amplifying specific thoughts.

regular expression	A convenient notation for specifying complex patterns. Notable special characters are ^ to match the beginning of the line and $ to match the end of the line.
relative filename	Any filename that does not begin with a slash (/) is a filename whose exact meaning depends on where you are in the file system. For example, test might exist in both your home directory and in the root directory: /test is an absolute filename and leaves no question which version is being used, but test could refer to either copy, depending on your current directory.
replace mode	A mode of vi in which any characters typed replace those already in the file.
Request for Comment	An official UNIX design specification, also known as an RFC.
right rooted	Patterns that must occur at the end of a line.
root directory	The directory at the very top of the file system hierarchy, also known as *slash*.
row-first order	In contrast to *column-first order*, this is when items are sorted across so that the first item of each column is in alphabetical order, then the second line contains the next set of items, and so on.
search string	The pattern specified in a search.
shell	To interact with UNIX, you type in commands to the command-line interpreter, which is known in UNIX as the shell, or command shell. It's the underlying environment within which you work with the UNIX system.
shell alias	Most UNIX shells have a convenient way for you to create abbreviations for commonly used commands or series of commands, known as shell aliases. For example, if I always found myself typing ls -CF, an alias can let me type just ls and have the shell automatically add the -CF flags each time.
shell script	A collection of shell commands in a file.

signals	Special messages that can be sent to stopped or running processes.
slash	The root directory.
standard input	UNIX programs always default to reading information from the user by reading the keyboard and watching what's typed. With *file redirection*, input can come from a file, and with *pipelines*, input can be the result of a previous UNIX command.
standard output	When processing information, UNIX programs default to displaying the output on the screen itself, also known as standard output. With *file redirection*, output can easily be saved to a file, and with *pipelines*, output can be sent to other programs.
stop a job	Stop the running program without killing it.
subshell	A shell other than the login shell.
symbolic link	A file that contains a pointer to another file rather than contents of its own. This can also be a directory that points to another directory rather than having files of its own. A useful way to have multiple names for a single program or allow multiple people to share a single copy of a file.
tags file	A file created by the `ctags` program that contains a table of contents for multifile C-source programs, and is used directly by the `vi` program.
tilde command	A command beginning with ~ in Berkeley Mail or the Elm Mail System.
transpose case	Switch uppercase letters to lowercase or lowercase to uppercase.
undelete	Restore a deleted message to its original state.
wedged process	A process that is stuck in memory and can't free up its resources, even though it's ceased running. This is rare, but annoying.

wildcards	Special characters that are interpreted by the UNIX shell or other programs to have meaning other than the letter itself. For example, * is a shell wildcard and creates a pattern that matches zero or more characters. Prefaced with a particular letter X (x*) this shell pattern will match all files beginning with x.
XON/XOFF	A particular type of *flow control*, the receiving end can send an XON (delay transmission) character until it's ready for more information, when it sends an XOFF (resume transmission).

Index

G

M

N

symbolic notation, permissions

Sams
Learning
Center

SAMS
PUBLISHING

Add to Your Sams Library Today with the Best Books for Programming, Operating Systems, and New Technologies

The easiest way to order is to pick up the phone and call

1-800-428-5331

between 9:00 a.m. and 5:00 p.m. EST.

For faster service please have your credit card available.

ISBN	Quantity	Description of Item	Unit Cost	Total Cost
0-672-22729-0		The Waite Group's UNIX Primer Plus, 2E	$29.95	
0-672-48516-8		Exploring the UNIX System, 3E	$29.95	
0-672-30402-3		UNIX Unleashed (Book/CD-ROM)	$49.95	
0-672-22810-6		UNIX System V, Release 4 Administration, 2E	$29.95	
0-672-48440-4		UNIX Networking	$29.95	
0-672-48448-X		UNIX Shell Programming, Revised Edition	$29.95	
0-672-22773-8		The Waite Group's UNIX Communications, 2E	$29.95	
0-672-22715-0		UNIX Applications Programming: Mastering the Shell	$29.95	
0-672-22562-X		The Waite Group's UNIX System V Bible	$29.95	
0-672-30194-6		The Waite Group's UNIX System V Primer, 2E	$29.95	
0-672-30448-1		Teach Yourself C in 21 Days, Bestseller Edition	$24.95	
0-672-30326-4		Absolute Beginner's Guide to Networking	$19.95	
0-672-30308-6		Tricks of the Graphics Gurus (Book/Disk)	$49.95	
0-672-30373-6		On the Cutting Edge of Technology	$22.95	
❏ 3 ½" Disk		Shipping and Handling: See information below.		
❏ 5 ¼" Disk		TOTAL		

Shipping and Handling: $4.00 for the first book, and $1.75 for each additional book. Floppy disk: add $1.75 for shipping and handling. If you need to have it NOW, we can ship product to you in 24 hours for an additional charge of approximately $18.00, and you will receive your item overnight or in two days. Overseas shipping and handling adds $2.00 per book and $8.00 for up to three disks. Prices subject to change. Call for availability and pricing information on latest editions.

201 W. 103rd Street, Indianapolis, Indiana 46290

1-800-428-5331 — Orders   1-800-835-3202 — FAX   1-800-858-7674 — Customer Service

Book ISBN 0-672-30464-3